The Journals and
Miscellaneous Notebooks
of

RALPH WALDO EMERSON

RALPH H. ORTH   *Chief Editor*

LINDA ALLARDT   RONALD A. BOSCO

HARRISON HAYFORD   DAVID W. HILL

GLEN M. JOHNSON   SUSAN SUTTON SMITH

Editors

The Journals and
Miscellaneous Notebooks

of

RALPH WALDO EMERSON

VOLUME XVI

1866–1882

EDITED BY

RONALD A. BOSCO   GLEN M. JOHNSON

THE BELKNAP PRESS
OF HARVARD UNIVERSITY PRESS

Cambridge, Massachusetts
and London, England
1 9 8 2

Library of Congress Cataloging in Publication Data (Revised)

Emerson, Ralph Waldo, 1803–1882.
    Journals and miscellaneous notebooks.

    Bibliographical footnotes.
    Vols.   accompanied by separate "Emendations and de-
partures from the manuscript," by the editors.
        CONTENTS: v. 1. 1819–1822.—v. 2. 1822–1826.—
[etc.]—v. 16. 1866–1882.
        1. Emerson, Ralph Waldo, 1803–1882—Diaries.   2. Au-
thors, American—19th century—Biography.   I. Gilman, William Henry, 1911–1976, ed.
PS1631.A3   1960   814'.3   60-11554
ISBN 0-674-48470-3 (v. 8)   AACR1
ISBN 0-674-48479-7 (v. 16)

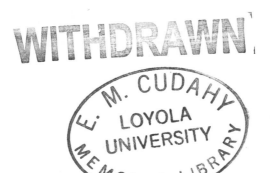

Preface

This volume has been a collaboration of Mr. Bosco and Mr. Johnson. Each editor independently established the text of each journal and notebook. Mr. Johnson has been primarily responsible for the introductory material and the notes to Journals LN and NY; Mr. Bosco has been primarily responsible for the notes to Journal ST, Notebook Books Large, and the Pocket Diaries. Each editor has contributed to and reviewed his coeditor's work, and they have prepared the text for the press together.

The editors wish to thank a number of institutions, foundations, and individuals for help of various kinds. The Ralph Waldo Emerson Memorial Association has continued to provide regular grants-in-aid which have been indispensable to the progress of the edition. The National Endowment for the Humanities provided generous support for the work of both editors and for the edition as a whole. Mr. Bosco was aided by a grant from the American Council of Learned Societies.

Among individuals who have given invaluable help in the preparation of the volume are Joel Myerson, Eleanor M. Tilton, Douglas E. Wilson, Bernadette M. Bosco, Thomas B. Byers, and Wallace E. Williams. Marian Bodian and Mary Steele Cabrera transcribed the manuscript journals and notebooks. Joseph P. McCallus assisted in preparing the index.

For other assistance and courtesies, thanks are due to Professor William H. Bond, Miss Marte Shaw, Mr. F. Thomas Noonan, and others of the staff of the Houghton Library; Mr. Edward B. Doctoroff and the staff of the Widener Library; the staffs of the Boston Athenaeum, the Boston Public Library, the Concord Free Public Library, and the Concord Antiquarian Society; and Mrs. John Dempsey of the Emerson House in Concord.

Unless otherwise noted, translations of classical quotations are from the Loeb Classical Library published by Harvard University Press.

The four illustrations are reprinted by permission of the Trustees of the Ralph Waldo Emerson Memorial Association, and by permission of the Houghton Library, Harvard University.

All the editors named on the edition title page have responsibilities of various kinds for the edition as a whole. The Chief Editor has the primary responsibility for the edition, and for certification of individual volumes.

With the present volume, this edition of Emerson's journals and notebooks, over twenty-five years in the making, comes to a close. It has published all eighty of Emerson's journals and seventy-four of his notebooks and pocket diaries. Omitted from this edition are nine notebooks containing drafts and fair copies of Emerson's poems, twenty notebooks devoted to different topics, three notebooks which were used in the preparation of lectures, several indexes, eleven account books, and a number of other manuscript volumes of various sorts (see the Editorial Title List, volume I, pp. 403–415). The editors hope to publish a significant portion of this material in the future.

R.H.O.

Contents

Illustrations

Foreword to Volume XVI

The journals printed in this volume recount Emerson's last six-teen years. That long span included for him much activity and accom-plishment, much of pleasure and importance. Growing and at last grown old, Emerson became a national eminence. His doctrines were welcome everywhere; even Harvard's Divinity School opened its pul-pit to him after a thirty-six year banishment for infidelity. He collected his works, and added to them *May-Day and Other Pieces, Society and Solitude,* and *Letters and Social Aims.* A longstanding ambition reached fruition in *Parnassus,* his collection of favorite poetry. In the decade after 1866, he traveled widely both as lecturer and as tourist. He saw Europe for the third time, and he ventured farther east—Egypt—and west—California—than ever before. He marked the centennial of American union by journeying into the South for the first time in dec-ades, speaking at the University of Virginia.

Now the associate of the famous and powerful, Emerson traveled cross-country in a private railroad car. He was received by the khedive of Egypt and the Mormon leader. President Grant was in the audience that heard his address when Concord's Minute Man statue was un-veiled in 1875; two years later, President Hayes joined in a toast to his health. At the Saturday Club Emerson regularly assembled with the most celebrated of America's intellectual and literary figures, and at Oxford he was honored by their English counterparts. But still he maintained his interest in "young America": he welcomed and en-couraged a new generation as diverse as William Torrey Harris, John Muir, Helen Hunt Jackson, and Bret Harte. He was never to be wealthy, but in his late years he achieved more security than he had known at any time. His books began to sell regularly, his lectures and "readings" were successful financially, and his business affairs prospered under the astute management of his son-in-law. Emerson had reason to be satisfied with what, during a long life, he had accomplished and was still achieving. And yet, over the whole period of sixteen years hangs the threat—and finally the fact—of "old age," Emerson's slow but relentless decline in vigor and intellectual power. The saddest thing in these journals is the extended silence with which they end.

The journals open during a time of adjustments and anxieties both spiritual and mundane. In its aftermath the Civil War remained a shadow in Emerson's mind: entries on the death of Lincoln and on the "good of evil" show him working to justify the nation's pain within his compensatory philosophy. Other problems were more strictly personal. Money was, as so often before, a preoccupation. The war had affected Emerson's income from books and lectures, his wife's property was being mismanaged by a dishonest relative, and he worried about sustaining the strenuous speaking tours that earned much of his living. William Forbes offered help in managing, and Emerson hopefully copied down his new son-in-law's "heroic" creed: "Difficulties exist to be surmounted." Yet he knew that some difficulties were less amenable to management and might, by their nature, be insurmountable. "I am always haunted," he wrote to William and Edith Forbes early in 1866, "by a dream of what might be done"; he had not relinquished faith in "the power," though it "has not come in twenty days or weeks."

"Old age" was Emerson's metaphor for the sense of uncertain powers and tasks undone, and it is a persistent topic in these journals. One response to the problem was the lofty resignation of "Terminus," probably completed in 1866. Another, equally characteristic, came in the epigraph Emerson chose for Journal LN, lines he incorrectly but revealingly labeled "Code of the Vikings." The determination "not to flinch," to "keep her full," invests the journals of his later years. Emerson was neither to rage nor to resign himself gently to his decline; he sought both to retain his equanimity and to make the best creative use of the time remaining and the powers available to him. His entries on old age seek out compensations, as when he notes that failing memory brings increasing ability to generalize. He cultivated alternate or reflex sources of inspiration. Noting that Cato learned Greek at eighty, he filled pages with translations, often choosing as subjects works of ancient inspiration like Indian puranas and the Finnish *Kalevala*. In addition, the uses of "quotation" continued to be a preoccupation in these years. The old issue of taking one's thoughts from another was not settled by Emerson's publication, in 1868, of "Quotation and Originality."

In his sixties as the nation reconstructed and embarked on expansion and the extravagances of the Gilded Age, Emerson was in ways the man of an earlier time. Contemporary photographs show him in old-fashioned dress, looking bemused or abstracted from the world of affairs. Descriptions of his lectures tended to concentrate on his presence, which seemed to be not entirely of the present. As Lowell wrote following the Phi Beta Kappa address of 1867, "It was as if a creature from some fairer world had lost his way in our fogs" (*Letters* [New York, 1894], I, 393–394). Nevertheless, Walt Whitman's complaint of 1872, that Emerson's thinking had become "quite attenuated" and had little relevance to the postwar new times (*Correspondence* [New York, 1961], I, 155), is belied by the journals. Here Emerson continued to observe and judge the public life of his century. Among other things, these pages contain what may be the first praise of baseball by an American intellectual. On a more weighty matter, the old abolitionist placed his sympathies solidly with the radicals in Reconstruction. For Andrew Johnson's "treachery" he had unusually harsh words, and he evoked the principle of "no tax without representation" to demand civil protection for freedmen. His language shows Emerson not granting blacks social or intellectual equality, but in advance of many younger people he was willing to consider possibilities for integration. Perhaps education was "the way to wash the negro white"; in any case, the unnegotiable first step was to grant him the civil rights for which he had "paid."

Emerson interested himself in other topics that would become social and political issues of the next half century, among them immigration, protective tariffs, and the dangers to democracy in the fortunes being earned during America's technological expansion. As the United States entered an era of newly international horizons and contacts with non-European cultures, Emerson labeled most forms of nationalism and political chauvinism "superstitions." He detected and deplored early stirrings of imperialism in America's covetous glances at the Hawaiian Islands. In cultural matters he remained committed to Anglo-Saxon superiority. He saw Chinese and Japanese customs as "remains of earlier & now almost extinct formations," but he welcomed signs of openness within these cultures to Western influence. In 1868 and 1872 he spoke hopefully at diplomatic gatherings for Chinese and Japanese envoys. As for the immigrants to America, now becoming a flood, Emerson had faith: "I see with joy the Irish . . . landing at Boston, at New York, & say to myself, There they go—to school."

Emerson continued to regard science as the best evidence in the nineteenth century of the potentialities of humanity. Here his age shows; though he remained committed to "newness" in all its forms, his praise of intellectual advances tends to draw its examples from the first half of the century or earlier. Emerson's chief technological fascinations were the magnetic telegraph and the railroad, inventions of earlier decades which in the 1860s were fulfilling their potentials in the Atlantic cable and transcontinental travel. The next great advance, Emerson felt, would be the balloon—though he noted his brother-in-law's opinion that air travel could become feasible only with the invention of wings. As a matter of faith, Emerson welcomed all evidences of what he called the *"Zymosis* of Science." "Natural Science *is* the point of interest now," he wrote in a letter of 1869. "These sublime & all-reconciling revelations of nature will exact of poetry a correspondent height & scope, or put an end to it."

If Emerson welcomed intellectual ferment, he also worked for it by serving his alma mater. Elected an overseer of Harvard in 1867, he devoted himself assiduously to his duties until 1879—twelve fateful years in that institution's history. During the period of Emerson's stewardship, Harvard chose Charles W. Eliot as president, revised and emphasized professional education, relaxed formal discipline, and moved toward the elective system. "Education" is one of the chief topics in the late journals, especially during the period immediately surrounding Eliot's advent in 1869. In the vigorous debates of that time, Emerson sought out a high ground above "party & passion."

The journals avoid personalities and dogmatism—but it is clear enough that Emerson allied himself with the party of reform. "The friends of Harvard," he wrote, "are possessed in greater or less degree by the idea of making it a University for men, instead of a College for boys"—and that would mean giving up some entrenched traditions. About the elective system Emerson was ambivalent. He worried that students might avoid "severer studies" in the pursuit of high marks; on the other hand, he was willing to consider that "forced" study of classical languages might be merely a "fashion" like the wearing of chignons. Emerson clearly agreed with the new president's intention to value intellectual accomplishment over genteel deportment or attendance at prayers. Many of Eliot's reforms came to fruition only after 1879, but Emerson was in at their beginnings.

Emerson perhaps found in his devotion to Harvard—in addition to overseeing, he served on academic committees and helped plan Memorial Hall—a compensation for dissatisfaction with his creative work. He published much during his last sixteen years, but any satisfaction was at least matched by frustrations. *May-Day and Other Pieces* (1867), *Society and Solitude* (1870), and *Letters and Social Aims* (1875) were major collections. Much of the material in all three volumes had been printed before, and by 1875 Emerson was reaching as far back as the *Dial* to find ready-made pieces to include in the last of them. He worked over the contents of *Society and Solitude* and experimented with their arrangement, but the volume has a more miscellaneous character than his earlier series of essays. Emerson noted with some irony that *Society and Solitude* became his best seller: "This is not for its merit, but only shows that old age is a good advertisement. Your name has been seen so often that your book must be worth buying."

Letters and Social Aims was a miscellany, though it contained an important new statement on "Poetry and Imagination." Both this volume and *Parnassus* became sources of anguish for Emerson during extended periods of preparation. Each had been conceived and contracted for years earlier, but each fell prey to external upsets and internal decline. The journals record in particular the frustrations of *Parnassus,* not so much a collection of poems as a compilation of Emerson's favorite snippets. After the volume at last appeared late in 1874, Emerson recorded complaints about its many errors, and then faced the book of essays to which he had committed himself in 1870 and which, as early as 1871, he described as weighing "heavily on my soul." By the summer of 1875 Emerson knew that he could not finish unaided, so on August 28 of that year James Elliot Cabot arrived in Concord to join Ellen Emerson in completing the book. *Letters and Social Aims,* which contains Emerson's last important creative work, appeared in December.

The financial success of his new books and collected works helped to ease the transition away from lecturing as Emerson's primary professional activity. He hoped that the long winter tour of 1867, which took him as far as Minnesota, would be his last; but he continued to make forays west and south, though shorter and less taxing ones, as late as 1871–1872. As much as possible he came to rely on private lectures or informal "readings" such as those arranged by William Forbes in 1869. He continued to welcome opportunities to speak before audiences, but he had to husband his powers and expend them on new writing primarily for special occasions or on especially congenial topics. The most sustained and eloquent writing in the late journals often draws on Emerson's personal memories. His recollections of his Aunt Mary and of the early Transcendentalists and Brook Farm, directed toward lectures which were published posthumously as "Mary Moody Emerson" and "Historic Notes of Life and Letters in New England," are examples of topics that seemed to develop easily. He tended to reserve such lectures for informal or private occasions or for audiences like the Concord Lyceum. Formal occasions were more difficult to prepare for, and there were many of these, beginning in 1867 with the second Phi Beta Kappa address. The most demanding engagement of Emerson's later years was the series "Natural History of the Intellect," which he gave as University Lecturer at Harvard in 1870 and again in 1871. The series taxed him up to, and perhaps finally beyond, his limits; after it, he was less ambitious in undertaking fresh writing for the platform. For later occasions such as the second Divinity School address (1874) and the University of Virginia lecture (1876), the journals show little or no attempt toward new formulations.

Emerson's reading continued during these years both to serve his contracted tasks and to help him work toward new inspirations, though eventually the former function preempted the latter. His chief task in the 1870s was his labor of love, *Parnassus,* and selecting poems to include there sent him back to old favorites more than it led him to seek new ones. Reviewing poets of his own century, Emerson found Wordsworth still preeminent, Tennyson compelling if less "manly" in his compass. Walt Whitman was excluded from *Parnassus,* but as these journals reveal he remained in Emerson's mind, unaccommodated but beyond dismissal. Emerson's new discoveries of promise included William Morris in England and Helen Hunt in America; both made the volume, but for the most part his Parnassus was established before he began to assemble *Parnassus.* Certainly lobbying did not help: Emma Lazarus, the New York poetaster who bombarded Emerson with poems and demands for attention, gets no mention in the regular journals or in *Parnassus.*

Among his other tasks, Emerson found particularly congenial his introduction to a new edition of *Plutarch's Morals,* perhaps his favorite work during the late years. In his miscellaneous reading he tended, as before, toward biographies of distinguished individuals. But his selections of the 1860s and 1870s emphasized the distinction of survival over that of heroic action or innovation. He was drawn to those whose productive lives were steady or prolonged rather than spectacular—most notably Varnhagen von Ense, whose "old age in Berlin" was worthy of emulation. Goethe, still fascinating, could also be tapped for lessons on making do with "leasts": "The privilege of an intelligent man," Emerson translated, "consists therein so to bear himself that his life, in so far as in him lies, shall contain the greatest possible number of reasonable, happy moments." Most others whose lives or recollections Emerson investigated were interests of long standing, such as Samuel Johnson, Mirabeau, and Humboldt. Spence's *Anecdotes* and, especially, the *Nouvelle Biographie Générale* remained favorite sources of biographical anecdotes.

Among English prose writers of his time, Emerson was still especially fond of Coleridge and Landor, reading the former's *Literary Remains* and the latter's collected *Works.* Hazlitt, Ruskin, and Arnold also attracted his interest. Among German writers, Emerson became particularly interested in Hegel, though as usual he preferred to get his philosophy at second hand—from J. H. Stirling's *Secret of Hegel* and

Albert Schwegler's *Handbook of the History of Philosophy*. Of French writers Emerson read Montesquieu, Renan, Sainte-Beuve, Taine, and, as always, Montaigne; the *Revue des Deux Mondes* was regular fare in his visits to the Boston Athenaeum. His interest in science led him to sample works on geology, paleontology, and acoustics; he read closely in Max Müller's books on philology and *The Science of Religion*. Even before the trip down the Nile became a prospect, Emerson read books on Egyptian history and culture; ancient epics and holy books of all cultures continued to attract him. His late reading included Taliesin, the *Kalevala*, Saadi's *Gûlistân*, the *Dabistan*, the *Vishnú Puráña*, Eugène Burnouf's edition of *Le Bhâgavata Purâna*, and George Small's *Handbook of Sanskrit Literature*. Closer to home, Emerson continued to value and to defend Henry Thoreau; perhaps inspired by his role in planning Harvard's Memorial Hall, he took notes on the published writings of Horatio Greenough.

During the 1870s Emerson maintained a notebook titled Books Large, devoted to comments about reading and to various lists, particularly his recommendations for libraries. While it does not constitute a summary of Emerson's lifetime reading, "Books" does outline his interests during the later years. The old favorites are there, and Emerson's suggestions characteristically emphasize books of poetry and of biography or reminiscence, with attention also to Eastern philosophy, history, moral and critical essays, and science. Very little attention goes to fiction or to the fine arts. Among Emerson's contemporaries, British writers are better represented and more perceptively chosen than American ones. In all, Books Large suggests a mind still open and inquiring, if less wide-ranging and adventurous than before.

Emerson's most adventurous explorations during his later years were not in reading but in travel. California in 1871 represented for him the future; Egypt in 1873 overpowered him with its antiquity. Writing to Lidian from California, Emerson twice suggested that, if he were young, he might stay for good: the "immense prospective advantages" of the West needed only population to realize an "assured felicity." California was for America a "new garden," and in it the future seemed guaranteed. Egypt was more ambiguous. Like the past it represented, the Nile valley seemed by turns "pandaemonic" and "full of lotus." The ancient sphinxes and temples awed Emerson, and in certain moods he saw in them "a perpetual humiliation, . . . whipping our ignorance." Later he formed a more balanced view. In a letter to William Forbes, he imagined the temples speaking: "O ye men of the Nineteenth Century here is something you cannot do, & must respect." But he added: "No creature is left in the land who gives any hint of the man who made them."

Returning from Egypt, Emerson made a progress through Italy, France, and England. All the way he was lionized and feted to the point of exhaustion. In his journal he was able to do little more than keep up a list of names. Two encounters in England were especially significant. Emerson met Carlyle for what both realized was surely the last time. As Ellen wrote, the two friends spent their final morning together "with real comfort." At Oxford, Emerson visited the chambers of John Ruskin, whose work he had greatly admired; but he was less enthusiastic when Ruskin retailed "his doleful opinions of modern society." Emerson's valedictory trip was a touching success; perhaps Moncure Conway offered the best summation of its significance: "The white-haired sage" was "beaming his last farewell, and uttering his last animating word to the class that received him as prophet at the dawn of a closing generation" (*Emerson at Home and Abroad* [Boston, 1882], p. 343).

Emerson's activities of all sorts became more sporadic and less well focused as the 1870s progressed. His serious physical and intellectual decline is conventionally dated from the fire that damaged the Emersons' Concord home in July 1872. But the decline was extended and gradual. Episodes of what Emerson forthrightly called "stupor" occurred earlier; the California trip, for example, was arranged partly out of concern for his health under the pressure of the Harvard lectures. On the other hand, he wrote directly and lucidly in many passages dating from the years after the fire. Only in the late 1870s did opacity overtake him almost completely. At that point his journalizing virtually stopped. The record of these last years appears mainly in the pocket diaries—Emerson's brief, laboriously entered reminders to himself; Ellen Emerson's painfully detailed directions for his errands into Boston; and his touching notations of births, marriages, and deaths long past.

For the most part, Emerson chose not to write in his journals when he could not write well. His notes on his Egyptian experience, for example, are disappointingly sparse, while his fuller recollections of Europe were written out of chronological order and apparently some time after the fact. Emerson recognized early what powers he was losing, and that he was losing them irrevocably. That awareness on his part lends pathos to these late journals, but it is perhaps more important as an index of his character. Crossing the Atlantic with him in 1873, Charles Eliot Norton felt that Emerson's "optimistic philosophy has hardened into a creed, with the usual effects of a creed in closing the avenues of truth. . . . To him this is the best of all possible worlds, and the best of all possible times" (*Letters* [Boston and New York, 1913], I, 503). Norton's statement contains truth but is misleading. The journals of Emerson's last years show that his optimism was a choice, the sign of his ability to accept "old age" and to work as he could within it. Copying out a sentence from Octave Gréard's book on Plutarch, Emerson transposed it into first person: "Je reprends mon bien où je le trouve."

Underlying Emerson's achieved perspective was his steady optimistic faith—his "creed" in Norton's terms. Emerson's belief in Unity and in the moral law remained solid, essentially unchanged from thirty years before: "The moral law preserves its eternal newness, & appears to each age new-born: almost abolishing memory by the splendor it lends to the passing moment." Emerson's qualifying "almost" shows something other than dogmatic hardness; but his beliefs as laid down in the late journals do lack the vibrancy of the 1830s and 1840s, when they were won out of experience rather than maintained against it. Still, Emerson's equanimity and the brightness of his outlook during his last sixteen years, evidenced in the journals printed here, were accomplishments of value. Norton's conclusion, that Emerson's "youthfulness will end only with life," is borne out in these pages.

Volume XVI includes three regular journals, LN, NY, and ST, covering the period from 1866 until Emerson ceased writing regularly in 1877; one miscellaneous notebook, Books Large, kept mostly during 1870–1877; and fifteen pocket diaries, one each for the years 1866 through 1880. The inclusive span of the volume is 1866 through

Emerson's death in 1882, although no entries can be dated later than 1880.

Editorial technique. The editorial process follows that described in volume I and the slight modifications introduced in subsequent volumes of the edition. Where erased pencil writing occurs in the journals or notebooks, every effort has been made to recover the text. Use marks in the journals and notebooks comprising volume XVI have been carefully described, transcriptions and expansions of passages have been recorded, and uses in *Society and Solitude, Letters and Social Aims,* and other published works have been noted where possible, often with help from the locations supplied by Edward W. Emerson in the manuscripts.

In the manuscripts, Emerson's topical headings are sometimes underlined, sometimes set off by a rule or by enclosing straight or wavy lines; unless he seems to have intended something more than marking to identify the matter as a heading, the various forms are interpreted by setting the heading in italics. When the text is quoted in the notes, no silent emendations are made; hence there are occasional variations between notes and text.

As in volumes XI through XV, Emerson's own cross references to his other journals can be located through the use of Appendix I, which indicates where all of the journals published in the Harvard edition appear. Because the edition carries Emerson's manuscript pagination as well as its own, the reader can easily locate any cross reference to a journal already printed.

Numbering of "Fragments on Nature and Life" and "Fragments on the Poet and the Poetic Life" follows that assigned by Edward Emerson or by George S. Hubbell, *A Concordance to the Poems of Ralph Waldo Emerson.*

A list of silent emendations has been prepared; copies are to be deposited in the Rush Rhees Library of the University of Rochester, the Library of Congress, Houghton Library, Huntington Library, and Newberry Library. The following statement describes the silent or mostly silent emendations. These range from numerous—as with punctuation of items in a series, supplying periods at the ends of sentences if the next sentence begins with a capital, or expansion of contractions—to occasional, as with supplying quotation marks, dashes, or parentheses missing from intended pairs.

Emendation of prose. A period is silently added to any declarative sentence lacking terminal punctuation but followed in the same paragraph by a sentence beginning with a capital letter. If a declarative sentence lacking a period is followed by a sentence beginning with a small letter, either a bracketed semicolon is supplied, or a bracketed period is supplied and the small letter is silently capitalized. In the second instance the reader will automatically know that the capital was originally a small letter. If a direct question lacking terminal punctuation is followed by a sentence in the same paragraph beginning with a capital, the question mark is silently added. Punctuation of items in a series, since Emerson habitually set them off, is silently inserted. Small letters at the beginning of unquestionable paragraphs or of sentences which follow a sentence ending with a period are silently capitalized. Where indispensable for clarity a silent period is added to an abbreviation. Quotation marks, dashes, and parentheses missing from intended pairs have been silently supplied; so have quotation marks at the beginning of each of a series of quotations. Apostrophes have been silently inserted or normalized in possessives and contractions. Superscripts have been lowered and double or triple underscorings have been interpreted by small or large capitals. Common Emersonian contractions like y^t for *that,* y^e for *the, wh* for *which, wd* and *shd* for *would* and *should,* and *bo't* for *bought* are silently expanded. His dates have been regularly normalized by the silent insertion of commas and periods.

Emendation of poetry. On the whole, Emerson's poetry has been left as it stands in the manuscripts; apostrophes and some commas, periods, and question marks have been supplied, in accordance with the rules for emending prose, but only where Emerson's intention was unmistakable.

Certain materials are omitted, either silently or with descriptive annotation; these will not be reported in the list of emendations. Omitted silently are slips of the pen, false starts at words, careless repetitions of a single word, and Emerson's occasional carets under insertions (assimilated into the editor's insertion marks). Underscoring to indicate intended revisions is not reproduced. Omitted, but usually with descriptive annotation, are practice penmanship, isolated words or letters, and miscellaneous markings.

CHRONOLOGY 1866–1882

1866: April 14–May 19, Emerson delivers six private lectures in the series "Philosophy for the People" at Chickering's Hall, Boston; June 27–29, with his children Ellen and Edward, he makes an excursion to Mount Monadnock in New Hampshire; July 6, he writes a letter of "high affectionate exceptional regard" to his Harvard classmate Robert Woodward Barnwell, lately a Confederate senator; July 10, his first grandchild, Ralph Emerson Forbes, is born; July 18, he receives the degree of Doctor of Laws from Harvard; November, he lectures in Lewiston, Maine, Lynn, Mass., and Hartford, Conn.; December 11, he delivers "Man of the World" before the Parker Fraternity, Boston, and repeats it December 19 in Salem, Mass.; also in December, he lectures at Harlem in New York City and in Newark, N.J.

1867: January 9–March 19, Emerson makes a lecture tour of the Midwest, speaking in Cleveland, Cincinnati, and Marietta, Ohio, in Batavia, Jamestown, and Fredonia, N.Y., in Adrian, East Saginaw, and Battle Creek, Mich., in Chicago, Lacon, Peoria, Quincy, and Bloomington, Ill., in Madison, La Crosse, Fond du Lac, Oshkosh, Ripon, and Janesville, Wis., in Winona, Faribault, St. Paul, and Minneapolis, Minn., in Washington, Independence, Cedar Falls, Keokuk, and Des Moines, Iowa, in St. Louis, in Lawrence and Kansas City, Kans., and in Pittsburgh; March, while in St. Louis he meets William T. Harris and his group of Hegelian philosophers; March 27, he lectures at Bowdoin College in Brunswick, Maine; April 10, he lectures at the Concord Lyceum; April 14, he speaks at the funeral of George L. Stearns in Cambridge; April 19, he speaks at the dedication of the Soldiers' Monument in Concord; April 26 and 29, he lectures in Malone and Champlain, N.Y.; April 29, *May-Day and Other Pieces* is published in Boston; May 12, Emerson speaks to the first meeting of the Radical Club in Boston; May 14 and 17, he lectures in Framingham, Mass., and at Vassar College in Poughkeepsie, N.Y.; May 30, he delivers remarks at the organization of the Free Religious Association in Boston; July 18, thirty years after "The American Scholar," he delivers "Progress of Culture" before the Phi Beta Kappa Society at Harvard; also in July, he is elected an Overseer of Harvard College, and serves assiduously until 1879; July 9, Abel Adams dies; July 26, Sarah Alden Ripley dies; August 15–20, Emerson visits Nantasket with Ellen; September 8 and 10, he lectures in Northampton, Florence, and Pittsfield, Mass.; September 15, he reads "Immortality" at Cyrus Bartol's church in Boston; September 16, he reads "The Preacher" at a meeting of the Radical Club in Boston; October 1–November 27, he lectures in Boston, Roxbury, and New Bedford, Mass., in New London, Conn., and in Portsmouth, N.H.; November 21, he dines with Charles Dickens at the home of James T. Fields; December, he makes a lecture tour of the Midwest, speaking in Buffalo, in Cleveland, Painesville, Steubenville, and Columbus, Ohio, in Erie, Pa., in Lincoln, Jacksonville, Mattoon, Alton, Galesburg, and Chicago, Ill., in St. Louis, in Des Moines and Davenport, Iowa, and in Adrian, Mich.

1868: January, Emerson lectures in Concord, Salem, and Cambridge, Mass.; February 11 and 14, he lectures in Stamford, Conn., and in Canandaigua, N.Y.; early March, he lectures in Leicester, Mass.; April 19, he hears Henry Ward Beecher preach at Plymouth Church, Brooklyn; April 20–25, he delivers three lectures at the Liberal Christian Union, Packer Institute, Brooklyn; May 28, he lectures at the Radical Club in Boston; July 5, he lectures in Dover, N.H.; July 6–11, he and Lidian visit Sarah Freeman Clarke in Newport, R.I.; August 11, he lectures in Middlebury, Vt., and proceeds from there to Underhill, where he climbs Mount Mansfield with Ellen and George P. Bradford; August 21, in Boston, he speaks at a banquet for the Chinese Embassy; September 13, William Emerson dies in New York with his brother at his side, and is buried in Concord September 15; October 12–November 16, Emerson delivers six private lectures at the Meionaon, Boston; November 30, he lectures in Weymouth, Mass.; December, he lectures at the Concord Lyceum and in Worcester, Andover, and Cambridgeport, Mass., and New Haven, Conn.; December 17–February 18, 1869, he delivers a series of six lectures in Providence, R.I.

1869: January 2–March 20, besides completing his lecture series in Providence, Emerson gives ten "readings" at Chickering's Hall, Boston; also in January, he lectures three times in Andover and once in Salem, Mass.; January 19–February 3, he makes a lecture tour of Buffalo, Poughkeepsie, Troy, Catskill, Albany, Syracuse, and Rochester, N.Y.; February 23, he lectures in Randolph, Mass.; March 1, he delivers "Mary Moody Emerson" before the New England Women's Club in Boston; April 4, he lectures on "Natural Religion" at the Horticultural Hall, Boston; April 6–May 11, he lectures six times in New Bedford, Mass.; April 15 and 22, he gives two readings in Providence, R.I.; May 17, he gives a reading on "Religion" at J. T. Sargent's in Boston; May 26, he speaks before the New England Woman Suffrage Association and is elected a vice president; May 28, he speaks at the second annual meeting of the Free Religious Association in Boston; September 14, in Boston, he speaks at a private evening reception marking the centenary of the birth of Alexander von Humboldt; October 27, his collected *Prose Works* is published in two volumes; November 5, he lectures in Natick, Mass.; November 18, Carlyle writes offering to bequeath to Harvard College books used in writing his histories of Cromwell and Frederick the Great; December 15 and 21, Emerson lectures before the Concord Lyceum and in Westford, Mass.

1870: February, Emerson lectures in Littleton, Marlborough, Harvard, and Salem, Mass., and in Philadelphia; late February or early March, *Society and Solitude* is published; March 8, Emerson lectures at the New England Women's Club in Boston; March 23, he lectures in Groton Junction, Mass.; April 26–June 2, he delivers, as University Lecturer at Harvard, a course of sixteen lectures on "Natural History of the Intellect"; July 14, he makes a vacation trip to Nantasket with Ellen; September 2–7, he travels to Maine and New Hampshire and ascends Mount Washington with Edward; October 6, having served on the planning committee since 1865, he attends ceremonies laying the cornerstone of Harvard's Memorial Hall; November 21–January 30, 1871, he delivers a course of six lectures in Providence, R.I.; December, his introduction to William W. Goodwin's edition of *Plutarch's Morals* is published; December 6, he lectures in Boston; December 22 and 23, he speaks at a dinner of the New England Society in the City of New York and, in Steinway Hall, delivers his Oration at the Society's Pilgrim Celebration.

1871: January, besides completing his lecture series in Providence, Emerson speaks at the Concord Lyceum and in Boston and Andover, Mass.; January 17–19, he lectures in Buffalo and Detroit; February 3, he speaks at the meeting for organizing the Boston Museum of Fine Arts; February 14–April 7, he repeats his Harvard course on "Natural History of the Intellect," seventeen lectures this time; February 15 and March 12, he lectures in Salem and Boston, Mass.; April 11–May 30, he travels to California with John Murray Forbes and family and friends; April 19, he calls on Brigham Young in Salt Lake City; April 23–May 18, he gives four lectures and a reading in San Francisco, and one lecture in Oakland, Calif.; May 9, while visiting the Yosemite Valley he meets John Muir; May 30, he arrives home, where he finds his house and family quarantined due to Edward's varioloid; June 28, his Harvard class holds its fiftieth anniversary meeting; also in June, he is elected a member of the Massachusetts Historical Society; August 15, in Boston, he speaks at the Scott centenary celebration at the Massachusetts Historical Society; October and November, he entertains Bret Harte in Concord; November 27–December 10, he lectures in Chicago, Quincy, and Springfield, Ill., and in Dubuque, Iowa.

1872: January, Emerson makes a tour south, delivering a series of four lectures at the Peabody Institute, Baltimore, and other lectures in Washington, D.C., New Brunswick, N.J., and West Point, N.Y.; January 7, he speaks at Howard University in Washington; February 7, he lectures at the Concord Lyceum; March 22, he reads "Mary Moody Emerson" at the home of Annie Adams Fields; March 23 and April 1, he lectures twice in Boston; April 15–May 20, he gives six private "Conversations" on literature at Mechanics' Hall, Boston; May 14, he lectures in Lowell, Mass.; May or June, he is elected vice-president of the Free Religious Association; July 10, he lectures in Amherst, Mass.; July 24, Emerson's house in Concord is seriously damaged by fire, and with his family he moves to the Old Manse as rebuilding begins; August 2, he makes remarks at a banquet in Boston for envoys of Japan; late August, he visits New Hampshire and Maine with Ellen; September, he vacations at Naushon Island; October 15, he speaks in New York at a dinner for J. A. Froude; October 23, on a recuperative journey, he sails with Ellen from New York for Europe;

November 3, he lands in Liverpool, and is in London on November 6, where he meets Carlyle; November 15–21, he is in Paris, where he visits the Louvre with Henry James; November 30, he arrives in Rome, having made brief stops in Marseilles, Nice, Pisa, and Florence; December 18, he journeys to Naples, where on December 21 he and Ellen sail for Egypt; December 25, he arrives in Alexandria and journeys on to Cairo, where he meets George Bancroft, visits the Museum of Egyptian Antiquities, and breakfasts with the khedive.

1873: January 7, after visiting the pyramids and the sphinx, Emerson and Ellen sail upstream from Cairo, visiting Luxor, Thebes, and the Temple of Karnak, and arriving at Assuan on January 28; January 29, Emerson visits Philae; February 13, he and Ellen return to Cairo, proceed to Alexandria and, on February 19 or 20, sail for Naples; February 25, he is in Naples, from which he travels to Rome; March 10, he proceeds to Florence, where he meets Herman Grimm and his wife Gisela von Arnim; mid-March, he arrives in Paris, where he meets Taine, Turgenev, and Renan; April 5, he moves to London for a heavy schedule of social engagements and meetings with old friends and prominent persons; April, he speaks briefly at the Working-Men's College in London; April 30–May 2, he visits Oxford, hearing lectures by Ruskin and Max Müller; May 3–15, he visits Warwick, Stratford, Durham, Edinburgh, and Alexander Ireland's home near Manchester; May 15, he and Ellen sail for America, with Charles Eliot Norton as a fellow passenger; May 27, he returns to Concord, where virtually the entire town turns out to greet him; October 1, he delivers an address at the opening of the new building of the Concord Free Public Library; December 16, he reads "Boston" at the centennial of the Tea Party, in Boston.

1874: March, Emerson serves as pallbearer for Charles Sumner; also in March, he agrees to accept nomination as Lord Rector of Glasgow University, but Disraeli is chosen; May 12, he addresses the graduating class at Harvard Divinity School, his first appearance there since his "Address" of 1838; September 19, Edward Emerson marries Annie Keyes and settles into medical practice in Concord; December 18, *Parnassus* is published.

1875: February 10, Emerson lectures at the Concord Lyceum; March 18, he lectures in Philadelphia; April 19, before President

Grant and other dignitaries, he speaks at the unveiling of Daniel Chester French's Minute Man statue in Concord; May 26, he lectures at the Radical Club in Boston; June 30 and July 1, he speaks twice at the New Hampton Institute, N.H., and with Ellen vacations in the mountains until July 6; late summer, his mental powers failing, he accepts Ellen and, soon thereafter, James Elliot Cabot as full collaborators in his literary productions; December 15, *Letters and Social Aims* is published.

1876: March 1, Emerson lectures at the Concord Lyceum; March 16 or 17, he lectures in Lexington, Mass.; April 13, he speaks to a teachers' convention in Concord; June 23 and July 1, he visits the Centennial Exposition in Philadelphia; June 28, he lectures to the Literary Societies of the University of Virginia in Charlottesville; August, Emma Lazarus visits Concord; also in 1876, *Selected Poems* and the Little Classics edition of Emerson's works are published.

1877: February 14, Emerson lectures at the Concord Lyceum; March 26, he lectures at the New England Women's Club in Boston; April 16, he lectures at the Old South Church in Boston; June 27, he attends a dinner for President Rutherford B. Hayes, in Boston, where he acknowledges a toast but declines to speak; December 17, he attends the *Atlantic Monthly*'s birthday dinner for Whittier, where he reads "Ichabod" and hears, among others, Mark Twain.

1878: January, Emerson is invited to become foreign associate in the Académie des Sciences Morales et Politiques de l'Institut de France; February 6, he lectures on "Education" at the Concord Lyceum; February 25, he reads "The Fortune of the Republic" at the Old South Church, Boston; April 7, Elizabeth Hoar dies; early April, Emerson speaks before an Educational Association meeting in Concord; April 24, he speaks on "Temperance" (i.e., "The Superlative") at the Old South Church, Boston; June 15, he lectures at Exeter Academy in New Hampshire; September, he attends with Ellen a Unitarian convention in Saratoga, N.Y., and visits Niagara Falls.

1879: March 5, Emerson lectures on "Memory" at the Concord Lyceum; March 19, he lectures in Amherst, Mass.; May 5, he reads "The Preacher" at the Divinity School Chapel at Harvard; also in 1879, his general introduction to *The Hundred Greatest Men,* prepared by Cabot and Ellen Emerson, is published in London.

1880: February 4, Emerson lectures, for the one-hundredth time, at the Concord Lyceum; also in 1880, he lectures at the Concord School of Philosophy.

1881: February 10, on the day of his friend's burial, Emerson reads "Carlyle" at the Massachusetts Historical Society; September, Walt Whitman visits Concord.

1882: March, Emerson attends Longfellow's funeral in Cambridge; April 27, Emerson dies, four weeks before his seventy-ninth birthday, and is buried April 30 in Sleepy Hollow Cemetery, Concord.

SYMBOLS AND ABBREVIATIONS

⟨ ⟩	Cancellation
↑ ↓	Insertion or addition
/ /	Variant
‖ . . . ‖	Unrecovered matter, normally unannotated. Three dots, one to five words; four dots, six to fifteen words; five dots, sixteen to thirty words. Matter lost by accidental mutilation but recovered conjecturally is inserted between the parallels.
⟨‖ . . . ‖⟩	Unrecovered canceled matter
‖msm‖	Manuscript mutilated
[ ]	Editorial insertion
[. . .]	Editorial omission
[ ]	Emerson's square brackets
⌞ ⌝	Marginal matter inserted in text
[ ]	Page numbers of original manuscript
n	See Textual Notes
∧	Emerson's symbol for intended insertion
[R.W.E.]	Editorial substitution for Emerson's symbol of original authorship. See volume I, plate VII.
*	Emerson's note
epw	Erased pencil writing
☞ ☜ 🖛	Hands pointing

ABBREVIATIONS AND SHORT TITLES IN FOOTNOTES

CEC   *The Correspondence of Emerson and Carlyle.* Edited by Joseph Slater. New York: Columbia University Press, 1964.

J   *Journals of Ralph Waldo Emerson.* Edited by Edward Waldo Emerson and Waldo Emerson Forbes. Boston and New York: Houghton Mifflin Co., 1909–1914. 10 vols.

JMN   *The Journals and Miscellaneous Notebooks of Ralph Waldo Emerson.* Ralph H. Orth, Chief Editor; Linda Allardt, Ronald A. Bosco, Harrison Hayford, David W. Hill, Glen M. Johnson, Susan Sutton Smith, Editors (volume I edited by William H. Gilman, Alfred R. Ferguson, George P. Clark, and Merrell R. Davis; volumes II–VI, William H. Gilman, Alfred R. Ferguson, Merrell R. Davis, Merton M. Sealts, Jr., Harrison Hayford; volumes VII–XI, William H. Gilman, Alfred R. Ferguson, Harrison Hayford, Ralph H. Orth, J. E. Parsons, A. W. Plumstead; volumes XII–XIII, William H. Gilman, Alfred R. Ferguson, Linda Allardt, Harrison Hayford, Ralph H. Orth, J. E. Parsons, A. W. Plumstead; volume XIV, Ralph H. Orth, Linda Allardt, Harrison Hayford, J. E. Parsons, Susan Sutton Smith; volumes XV–XVI, Ralph H. Orth, Linda Allardt, Ronald A. Bosco, Harrison Hayford, David W. Hill, Glen M. Johnson, Susan Sutton Smith). Cambridge: Harvard University Press, 1960–1982.

L   *The Letters of Ralph Waldo Emerson.* Edited by Ralph L. Rusk. New York: Columbia University Press, 1939. 6 vols.

Lectures   *The Early Lectures of Ralph Waldo Emerson.* Volume I, 1833–1836, edited by Stephen E. Whicher and Robert E. Spiller; volume II, 1836–1838, edited by Stephen E. Whicher, Robert E. Spiller, and Wallace E. Williams; volume III, 1838–1842, edited by Robert E. Spiller and Wallace E. Williams. Cambridge: Harvard University Press, 1959–1972.

Life   Ralph L. Rusk. *The Life of Ralph Waldo Emerson.* New York: Charles Scribner's Sons, 1949.

W   *The Complete Works of Ralph Waldo Emerson.* With a Biographical Introduction and Notes, by Edward Waldo Emerson. Centenary Edition. Boston and New York: Houghton Mifflin Co., 1903–1904. 12 vols. I—*Nature Addresses and Lectures;* II—*Essays, First Series;* III—*Essays, Second Series;* IV—*Representative Men;* V—*English Traits;* VI—*Conduct of Life;* VII—*Society and Solitude;* VIII—*Letters and Social Aims;* IX—*Poems;* X—*Lectures and Biographical Sketches;* XI—*Miscellanies;* XII—*Natural History of Intellect.*

PART ONE

The Journals

1866–1868

Emerson began Journal LN in March 1866, as he notes on p. [1], and used it through March 1868, when he began Journal NY. The first dated entry is March 24, 1866 (p. [3]); the last is March 29, [1868] (p. [278]). Two brief later entries, each dated August 1874, appear on pp. [1] and [133].

The covers of the copybook—marbled brown, green, red, and black paper over boards—measure 17.4 × 21.1 cm. The spine strip and the protective corners on the front and back covers are of tan leather. "LN" is written on the spine and in the upper right corner of the front cover. The dates "1866", "1867.", and "1868" appear in a vertical column centered on the front cover.

Including flyleaves (1, 2, 283, 284), there are 284 unlined pages measuring 17.5 × 20.5 cm. Four pages were misnumbered and corrected: 4⟨8⟩7, 11⟨4⟩6, 11⟨5⟩7, and ⟨1⟩229. Most of the pages are numbered in ink, but three are numbered in pencil: 116, 117, and 282. Three pages were numbered first in pencil, then in ink: 112, 114, and 115. Eleven pages are unnumbered: 1, 2, 6, 54, 56, 168, 169, 183, 207, 283, and 284. Fifteen pages are blank: 2, 6, 7, 8, 54, 55, 56, 57, 66, 90, 108, 109, 168, 169, and 170.

Laid inside the front cover are two loose sheets and two pieces of printed matter. One sheet, written in ink and measuring 11.6 × 17.9 cm, is here designated fcv_a and fcv_b. Another sheet contains a typed transcript of a letter from Philip Physick Randolph, as printed in *JMN,* XIII, 182, with Edward Emerson's notes. The printed materials are a clipping, "What the Dearborn Observatory is Doing," *Chicago Tribune,* July 20, 1871, and a four-page "Webster Centennial Number" of *Ye Granite Echo,* Rumford (Concord), New Hampshire, January 18, 1882.

3

[front cover] **LN**

1866
1867.
1868

[front cover verso] Vox immissa volat, litera scripta manet.[1]

[front cover verso$_a$][2] Common sense or law of bodies must be obeyed.
But he finds limits to this, or, itself leading to contradictions, for matter is fluent, & has no ↑solid↓ bottom; mere bubbles at last.

Then the very mathematician & materialist is ⟨led to a⟩ forced to a poetic result,—
as *metamorphosis.*
progressive or arrested devel[opmen]t.
Unity. In vain he would keep up the bars of species or genera: ⟨e⟩the pedant becomes poet against his will. ⟨in spite of himself⟩
Cuvier must approximate to Geoffroy St. Claire in spite of himself. These dreadful Okens ⟨w⟩& Goethes will be born.[3] Unity! Unity! There is this Mischievous Mind as tyrannical, ↑nay↓ more tyrannic, than the other. *Niagara currents in the mind.*

[front cover verso$_b$] The mind must think by means of Matter; find Matter or Nature the means & words of its thinking & expression. The world its school & university for Heaven or Thought.

[1] R. W. Emerson
March, 1866.

---

[1] "The spoken word flies away, the written letter remains" (Ed.). See *JMN*, VI, 116.
[2] For a physical description of pp. [fcv$_a$]–[fcv$_b$], see the bibliographical headnote to Journal LN.
[3] "Geoffroy St. Claire" is an error for Étienne Geoffroy Saint-Hilaire (1772–1844), a French naturalist who propounded a theory of organic unity holding that a single plan of structure prevails throughout the animal kingdom. Baron Georges Cuvier (1769–1832), also a French naturalist, strenuously opposed the theories of Geoffroy Saint-Hilaire. Lorenz Oken (1779–1851), a German naturalist and philosopher, sought to unify the natural sciences.

↑See query on p. 133   Aug., '74.↓[4]

LN

"When the wind bloweth strong, hoist thy sail to the top, tis joyous in storm not to flinch
Keep her full! keep her full! none but cowards strike sail, sooner
founder than take in an inch."

Code of the Vikings.[5]

[2] [blank]
[3] 1866   March 24.
I often think of uses of an Academy, though they did not rapidly appear when Sumner proposed his Bill.[6] And perhaps if it was national,
& must meet in Washington, or Philadelphia,—or even New-York
would be a far away place for me,—such benefits as I crave, [4] it
could not serve. But today I should like to confide to a proper committee to report on what are called the "sentences of Zoroaster," or
"the Chaldaic oracles;" to examine & report on those extraordinary
fragments,—so wise, deep, ⟨poetic⟩—some of them ↑poetic↓;[7]—↑&↓
such riddles, or so frivolous others,—[5] & pronounce shortly, but
advisedly, what is their true history.

Zoroaster has a line saying "that violent deaths are friendliest to
the health of the soul."[8] Attribute that among his good fortunes to
Lincoln. And in the same connection remember the death of Pindar.
Add Jones Very's washing his face to the title of Humility.[9]

---

[4] This line is loosely boxed in pencil.

[5] George Webbe Dasent, *The Story of Burnt Njal, or Life in Iceland at the End of the
Tenth Century,* 2 vols. (Edinburgh, 1861), II, 358. Emerson withdrew this volume from
the Boston Athenaeum, August 31–September 10, 1861. The quoted lines are translated
by Dasent from *Frithiof's Saga,* by the Swedish poet Esaias Tegnér (1782–1846).

[6] In 1864 Sumner had introduced in the Senate his bill to incorporate a National
Academy of Literature and Art; Emerson was specified in the proposal as a member. The
bill failed. See *L,* V, 392–393, 395–397.

[7] The first "poetic" is canceled, and the second "poetic" inserted, in pencil.

[8] Cf. "The Oracles of Zoroaster," in *The Phenix; A Collection of Old and Rare Fragments* (New York, 1835), p. 158.

[9] See p. [266] below.

Can identity be claimed for a being whose life is so often vicarious or belonging to an age or generation? ↑He is fallen in another he rises in another↓ ↑See [Notebook] M[ary] M[oody] E[merson] IV p 40 [actually 41]↓[10]

[6]–[8] [blank]
[9] Polarity. ⟨There are as many poles as natures.⟩ Every nature has its own. It was found, that, if iron ranged itself north & south, nickel or other sub⟨sanc⟩stance ranged itself east & west; ↑& Faraday expected to find that each Chemic element might yet be found to have its own determination or pole.↓ And[n] every soul has a bias or polarity of its own, & each new: Every one a magnet with a new north.

[10] Not ⟨only⟩ Niebuhr only lost his power of divination, but every poet has on the hills counted the Pleiads, & mourned his lost star. CL 59 ↑Ah the decays of memory, of fancy, of the saliency of thought! ⟨I had rather⟩ ↑Who would not rather↓ have a perfect remembrance of all I thought & felt in a certain high week, than to read any book that has been published.↓

When I read a good book, ↑say, one↓ which opens a literary question, I wish that life w⟨as⟩ere 3 000 years ⟨ye⟩long. Who would not launch into this Egyptian history, as opened by Wilkinson, Champollion, Bunsen, but for the *memento mori* which he reads on all sides.[11] [11] Who is not provoked by the temptation of the Sanscrit ↑literature↓? And, as I wrote above, the Chaldaic oracles tempt me. But so also does Algebra, and astronomy, & chemistry, & geology, & botany. Perhaps, then, we must increase the appropriation, & write 30 000 years. And, if these years have correspondent effect with the 60 years we have experienced, ⟨we shall then write 30 000 centuries⟩ some earnest scholar will move to amend by striking out the word "years," & inserting "centuries."

[10] Beginning with "Zoroaster has", the entries on p. [5] are in pencil.
[11] John Gardner Wilkinson (1797–1875) and Jean François Champollion (1790–1832) were important influences during the Egyptian revival in America; Wilkinson's *A Popular Account of the Ancient Egyptians* (London, 1854) is in Emerson's library. Emerson met Christian Bunsen (1791–1860), a German historian, in London in 1848; he withdrew volumes 3 and 4 of Bunsen's *Egypt's Place in Universal History,* trans. Charles Cottrell, 5 vols. (London, 1848–1867), from the Boston Athenaeum, January 18–February 24 and February 24–March 10, 1866.

6

[12] ↑*Reality*↓

How rarely we live, with all our reading & writing! and are coming not to deal with virtue at all, but only with its literature!

[13] ↑*Temperaments.*↓

B is a bag of wind, so is D: but ↑with a difference:↓ B is a bag of east wind, & D of southwest. But S is solid, & when one is ignorant enough to insult him, does n't mind it more than if a hen looked at him. ↑We like the wide-range temperament.↓

Country-Life, See ⟨LN⟩ 5 ↑DL 5↓ ↑?↓[12]

[14] It is plain that the War has ⟨h⟩made many things public that were once quite too private. A man searches his mind for thoughts, & finds only the old commonplaces; but, at some moment, on the old topic of the day's politics, he makes a distinction he had not made; he discerns a little inlet ⟨whe⟩not seen before. Where was a wall, is now a door. The mind goes in & out, & variously states in prose or poetry its new experience. It points [15] it out to one & another, who, of course, deny the alleged discovery.[13] But ⟨the⟩ repeated experiments & affirmations make it visible soon to others. The point of interest is here, that these gates once opened never swing back. The observers may come at their leisure, & do at last satisfy themselves of the fact.* The thought, the doctrine, the right, hitherto not affirmed, is published in set propositions, ⟨in poetry,⟩ in conversation of scholars⟨.⟩ & at last in the very chorus↑es↓ of songs.

[16] The young hear it, &, as they have never fought it, never known otherwise, they accept it, vote for it ⟨on the⟩at the polls, embody it in the laws. And this perception, thus satisfied, re-acts on the senses to clarify them, so that it becomes more indisputable. Thus it is no matter what the opposition may be of presidents or kings or majorities, but what the truth is as seen by one mind.

[17] I copy a scrap copy of ⟨a⟩ ↑my↓ letter sent to Mrs C[aro-

* See *TO* 104.

---

[12] The question mark is in pencil.

[13] A scribble in ink, possibly a canceled insertion, is located above the sentence period.

line]. [Sturgis] T[appan]., when in Europe, (⟨w⟩perhaps never sent) which I pick up today.[14] "I have let go the unreturning opportunity ⟨of⟩ ↑which↓ your visit to Germany gave ↑me↓ to acquaint you with Gisela Von Arnim, & Herman Grimm her husband, & Joachim the violinist. ⟨A⟩—and I who prize myself only on my endurance, that I am as good as new when the others are gone,—I to be slow, derelict, & dumb to you, in all your absence! I shall regret this as long as I live. How palsy creeps over us with gossamer first, & ropes afterwards! And you have the prisoner when you have once put your eye on him, as securely as after the bolts are drawn.—How strange that C[harles]. K[ing]. N[ewcomb]., whose secret you & I alone have, should come to write novels. Holmes's genius is all that is new,—nor that to you. The worst is that we can do without it. Grand behavior is better, if it rest on the axis of the world."

[18] Hegel seems to say, Look, I have sat long gazing at the all but imperceptible transitions of thought to thought, until I have seen with eyes the true boundary. I know what is this, and that. I know it, & have recorded it. It can never be seen but by a patience like mine added to a perception like mine. I know the subtile boundary, as surely as ↑the mineralogist↓ Hauy[n] ↑knows↓ the normal lines of his crystal, & where the cleavage must begin. I know that all observation will justify me, and to the future metaphysician I say, that he may measure the power of his perception by the degree of his accord with mine.[15]

[19] This is the twilight of the gods. predicted in the Scandinavian mythology.

Hegel's definition of liberty, was, *the spirit's realization of itself.*

———

Hafiz can only show a playing with magnitudes, but without ulterior aim.

———

[14] A longer version of this letter, dated May 13, 1859, appears in O. W. Holmes, *Ralph Waldo Emerson* (Boston, 1885), pp. 225–227. Gisela von Arnim and Herman Grimm had not yet married when Emerson's letter was originally written; the version printed by Holmes does not refer to them as married.
[15] Emerson had received, as a gift from its author, James Hutchison Stirling's *The Secret of Hegel*, 2 vols. (London, 1865).

8

⟨Courage.⟩ *Hafiz* fears nothing; he sees too far; he sees throughout.

Potentiality of England.

England (whether Scandinavia or Cymry ⟨m⟩poured this potent blood into her,) has Wordsworth, Coleridge, Wellington, Carlyle, Tennyson, Ruskin, Landor, Gladstone, Flaxman, Browning, Byron, John Sterling, James H. Stirling, H. H. ↑Hayman↓ Wilson, Robert Brown, ⟨Tennyson⟩ Edwin Chadwick, J[ohn]. Stuart Mill,[16]

[20]   *American Politics.*

I have the belief that of all things the work of America is to make the advanced intelligence of mankind in the sufficiency of morals practical; that, since there is on every side a breaking up of the faith in the old traditions of religion, ⟨there⟩ &, of necessity, a return to the omnipotence of the moral sentiment, that in America this conviction is to be embodied in the laws, in the jurisprudence, in international[n] [21] law, in political economy. The lawyers have always some glaring exceptions to their statements of public equity, some reserves of sovereignty, tantamount to ↑the↓ Rob Roy rule that ⟨rig⟩might makes right. America should affirm & establish that in no instance should the guns go in advance of the perfect right. You shall not make coups d'etat, & afterwards explain & pay, but shall proceed like William Penn, [22] or whatever other Christian or humane person who ⟨sh⟩ treats with the Indian or foreigner on principles of honest trade & mutual advantage. Let us wait a thousand years for the Sandwich islands before we seize them by violence.

> The ⟨poet spoke his instant thought⟩ ↑bard in corners
>   hummed his verse↓
> ⟨And⟩ Earth[n] echoed ↑with↓ his fame
> As Jove's bolt struck an inch of ground

---

[16] Persons in this list who may not be readily identifiable are: John Flaxman (1755–1826), a sculptor and illustrator; John Sterling (1806–1844), a poet; James Hutchison Stirling (1820–1909), a Scottish philosopher; Horace Hayman Wilson (1786–1860), professor of Sanskrit at Oxford; Robert Brown (1773–1858), a Scottish botanist; and Edwin Chadwick (1800–1890), a reformer and health official.

9

And lit the sky with flame
And filled the sky the flame[17]

[23] Fame is ever righting itself. In the jangle of criticism, Goethe is that which the intelligent hermit supposes him to be, & can neither be talked up nor down.

———

"He is always good when he is pleased," says the mother of her child.

———

Lidian quotes Aunt Mary as saying, "that she forgot so quick, that she never found any chance to forgive."

———

A man of no conversation should certainly smoke.
His ⟨b⟩mouth smelt like a graveyard[.]

[24] I think it would be a good subject for a competent hand to write a chapter on the Results of the War.
See *FOR* 280, & my letter to Stanley, if, as I believe, I kept a copy of it,[18] ⟨and Massachusetts, her ice burns more than others' fire.⟩ See *FOR* 258, 229, 204, ↑122↓[19]
DL 211, 207,

[25] It is peremptory for good living in houses in a cultivated age, that the beautiful should never be out of thought. It is not more important that you should provide bread for the table, than that it should be put there & used in a comely manner. You have often a right to be angry with servants, but you must carry your anger & chide without offence [26] to beauty. Else, you have quarreled with yourself, as well as with them.

———

↑June 14↓ But the surprise & dazzle of beauty is such, that I thought today, that if beauty were the rule, ↑instead of the exception,↓ men would give up business.

[17] The poem is in pencil. Later versions appear on p. [117] below and in "Fragments on the Poet and the Poetic Gift," XXXII, *W*, IX, 334.
[18] This letter, which apparently has not survived, may have been a response to Edward Lyulph Stanley's letter of December 14, 1864, expressing hope that the American government would remain committed to emancipation following the reelection of Lincoln.
[19] "122" is inserted in pencil.

[27] T. Fowell Buxton, soon after his entrance into Parliament, writes to J[ohn]. H[enry]. North;

"I do not wonder that so many distinguished men have failed in it. The speaking required is of a very peculiar kind: the House loves *good sense & joking*, & nothing else; and the object of its utter aversion is↑—↓that species of eloquence which may be called Philippian. There are not three men from whom a fine simile or a sentiment would be tolerated; [28] all attempts of this kind are punished with general laughter. An easy flow of sterling, forcible↑,↓ ⟨sense⟩plain sense is indispensable; & this combined with ⟨his⟩great powers of sarcasm gives Brougham his station. Canning is an exception to this rule. His reasoning is seldom above mediocrity; but then it is recommended by language so wonderfully happy, by a manner so exquisitely elegant, & by wit so [29] clear, so pungent, & so unpremeditated, that he contrives to beguile the House of its austerity." &c &c. *Life of Buxton* p[p]. [89–]90.[20]

In the speed of conversation L[idian]. said, "Poor God did all he could to make them so, but they steadily undid," &c. It recurs now as an example of the organic generalization. The speaker casts the apparent or hypothetical order of things into a word & names it God; but, in the instant, the mind makes the distinction or perceives the [30] eternal & ⟨disimaginable⟩ everpresent of the Perfect↑,↓[21] still whole & divine before him, & God quits the name of *God,* & fills the universe as he did the moment before.

"Euphranor comparing his own Theseus with another drawn by Parrhasius, said, that Parrhasius's Theseus eat roses, but his ↑own↓ fed on beef." *Plut[arch's]. Mor[als].* Vol. 5, p. 370[22]

[31] ↑*Bias.*↓

Seven men went through a field, one after another. One was a farmer, he saw only the grass; the next was an astronomer, he saw the horizon & the stars; the physician noticed the standing water & suspected miasm↑a↓; he was followed by a soldier, who glanced over the

[20] *Memoirs of Sir Thomas Fowell Buxton, Baronet,* ed. Charles Buxton (London, 1848), in Emerson's library.

[21] The comma is in pencil.

[22] *Plutarch's Morals: in Five Volumes, Translated from the Greek, by Several Hands,* 5th ed. (London, 1718), in Emerson's library.

ground, ↑found it easy to hold,↓ & saw in a moment how the troops could be disposed↑;↓ ⟨& found it easy to hold;⟩ then came the geologist, who noticed the boulders & the sandy loam; after him [32] came the real estate broker, who bethought him how the line of the house-lots should run, where would be the drive-way, & the stables. The poet admired the shadows cast by some trees, & still more the music of some thrushes & a meadow lark.

Here is Ralph has got a hammer, & is creeping with all his might in a bee-line for the pier-glass.[23]

[33] ↑Nash;↓   ↑*Superlative*↓   *Hyperbole*
"Every one who swears strongly fails to perform."
Welsh *Song of Adebon. Taliessin*[n] p 88[24]

"Savage from hoof to horn." [*Ibid.*, p. 88]

Another version of the first line is
"All those who are not intrepid, when exposed naked among thistles, will fail when adjured." [*Ibid.*, p. 90][25]

Urien Rheged is his ⟨p⟩Chief & Protector & "one of these poems attributed to Taliesin is not earlier than the 12th century." *Nash* [p. 118]

The poems supposed by Turner to be Taliessin in the 6th century are of later date than the 10th century   *Nash* p 119

"The truth against the world." [*Ibid.*, p. 140]

[34]   "Numbers there were incomprehensible
         Kept in a *cold*[n] hell,

[23] Ralph Emerson Forbes, Emerson's first grandchild, was born July 10, 1866.
[24] David William Nash, *Taliesin; or, The Bards and Druids of Britain, A Translation of the Remains of the Earliest Welsh Bards, and an Examination of the Bardic Mysteries* (London, 1858).
[25] A vertical line in the left margin connects this quotation to the first quoted line on p. [33].

Until the fifth age of the world;
Until Christ should release the captives," &c
⟨Talies⟨s⟩in.⟩ *Nash*[n] 147

"When I ⟨fall into⟩[26] ↑*lapse to*↓ a sinful word,
May neither you nor others hear"!

p. 151

"The brave is never cruel." [*Ibid.,* p. 160]

———

"The bee has collected it, & has not used it,
For the distilling of the luscious mead, praised be it over all
The numerous creatures the earth has produced."

p 174

———

See the poem to Ceridwen, p[p]. 187–8

———

I have transcribed part of Taliesin's "Invocation to the Wind," in *EL*
175[.]

[35] Can he make his own shoes?   ↑See *LN* 137,↓
Can he milk a cow?
Can he gr⟨om⟩oom his horse?

lunes   brackets   spandril

[36] I suspect Walt Whitman had been reading these Welsh remains when he wrote his "Leaves of Grass."
Thus Taliesin sings,
        "I am water, I am a wren;
        I am a workman, I am a star;
        I am a serpent;
        I am a cell, I am a chink;
        I am a depositary of song, I am a learned person."
                        Nash, p. 183

———

[26] These two words are canceled in pencil.

13

Singlespeech[27]

H[enry]. K[irke]. White   "[To the] Herb Rosemary"
[Robert] Pollok   "Ocean."
W[illiam]. C[ullen]. Bryant   "[To a] Waterfowl."
George Borrow, single verse in   Svend Vonved
Raleigh (if Soul's Errand is taken, nothing is left but "Pilgrimage.")

[37]   Dr J[ohn]. A Carlyle
            73 George St   Edinburg[28]

Singlespeech ↑Poets↓   ⟨Hamilton↑s↓⟩[29]

[James] Hogg only wrote   "Kilmeny"
Sam↑p↓son Reed   "Genius"
Forceythe Willson,   "Ballad of Old Sergeant"
Matthew Arnold   "Thyrsis"
S[amuel]. Ferguson   "Song of the Anchor"
[Charles] Wolfe   ⟨Dea⟩Funeral of Sir J. Moore
↑⟨Old wine old books old friends⟩↓ ↑⟨Messinger⟩↓
Ro[u]get de Lisle   Marseill⟨e⟩iaise
[Fitz-Greene] Halleck   Marco Bozzaris
[Robert Hinckley] Messenger   ⟨Me⟩Old wine, old books.
⟨T⟩H[enry]. Taylor   Philip Van Artevelde

[27] The immediate occasion for this list and the one on p. [37] is not known, but the
works cited include many of Emerson's favorites. The poems by White, Pollok, Bryant,
and Raleigh appear in *Parnassus;* Raleigh's are better known as "The Lie" and "The Passionate Man's Pilgrimage: Supposed to be Written by One at the Point of Death." For
Emerson's favorite lines from Borrow's translation of the Danish ballad "Svend Vonved,"
see *JMN,* XIII, 380.

[28] The name and address of Thomas Carlyle's brother are in pencil.

[29] Emerson included in *Parnassus* the poems by Hogg (from *The Queen's Wake,* in
Emerson's library), Arnold, Ferguson (as "Forging of the Anchor"), Wolfe (as "The
Burial of Sir John Moore at Corunna"), Messenger (as "Give Me the Old"), Wordsworth
(specifically the "Ode to Duty"), Sterling, and Lovelace (as "To Lucasta"). Emerson's
library includes two editions of Willson's "The Old Sergeant," as well as Taylor's verse
play. Emerson heard Reed's oration on genius at his graduation from Harvard in 1821;
see *JMN,* I, 293–294, and Journal NY, p. [239] below. For the Earl of Carnarvon's
speech, see *JMN,* VI, 340–341. For the "Speech of Chief Justice Crewe . . . in the Oxford Peerage case, heard in 1626," see *JMN,* VI, 336–337. The heading "⟨Hamiltons⟩"
probably refers to William Hamilton (1704–1754), whose "Braes of Yarrow" is included
in *Parnassus.*

Daniel Webster	Speech against Hayne
Lord Caernarvon	Speech on Lord Danby's
	impeachment
Chief Justice Crewe	
Wordsworth	Ode & Laodomia
Sterling	Alfred the Harper
Lovelace	Honor

[38] ⌈*Good of Evil*⌉[30]
↑Wherever there is force, it says, come & use me.↓

Gerald, Earl of Kildare, was in rebellion against Henry VII. When he was examined before the Privy Council in London, ⟨some⟩ one said, "All Ireland cannot govern this Earl."—"Then let ⟨all I⟩this Earl govern all Ireland," replied the King.

———

The New Jerusalem Magazine, in 183⟨5⟩0,[31] was the most thoughtful & valuable journal[n] of th⟨e time⟩at day. Since that time, the sect has prospered ↑externally↓ & grown numerous & rich, & the Magazine formal & worthless. When I last saw it, it was only a register of annual meetings.

[39] "Lord Russell, who had spoiled his constitution by his excesses, when he met a beggar who prayed ⟨f⟩him to give him something because he was famishing, cried out, 'Happy dog!' & envied him too much to relieve him." *Spence's* Anecdotes p 229 [actually 221][32]

Read M[ary]. M[oody]. E[merson].'s mss. yesterday—many pages. They keep for me the old attraction; though, when I sometimes have tried passages on a stranger, I find ↑something of fairy gold;—↓they need too much commentary, & are not as incisive as on me. They make the best example [40] I have known ↑⟨somewhat⟩↓[33] of the power of the religion of the Puritans in full energy, until fifty years ago, in New England. ⟨She⟩ The central theme of these endless diaries,

[30] *"Good of Evil"* is written vertically in the left margin.
[31] "5" is in pencil and is overwritten in ink with "0".
[32] Joseph Spence, *Anecdotes, Observations, and Characters, of Books and Men,* 2d ed. (London, 1858), in Emerson's library.
[33] "somewhat", in ink, is written over "Somewhat", in pencil, then canceled in ink.

is, her relation to the Divine Being; ⟨her⟩ ↑the↓ absolute submission of
her will, with the sole proviso, that she may know it is the direct
agency of God, (& not of cold laws of contingency &c) which ⟨deals
with her⟩ bereaves & humiliates her. But the religion of the diary, as of
the class it represented, [41] ⟨w⟩is biographical; it is the culture, the
poetry, the mythology, in which they personally believed themselves
dignified, inspired, judged, & dealt with, in the present & in the future. And certainly gives ↑to↓ life an earnestness, & to nature a sentiment, which lacking, our ⟨y⟩later generation appears frivolous.[34]

[42] July 2. ↑1866.↓ I went with Annie Keyes & Mr Channing
on Wednesday, 27th June, to Troy, ⟨& climbed⟩ thence to the Mountain House in wagon, &, with Edward & Tom Ward who had come
down to meet us, climbed the mountain. The party already encamped
⟨there⟩ were Story, Ward, & Edward, for the men; & Una Hawthorne, Lizzie Simmons, & Ellen E[merson]. for the maidens.[35] They
lived on the plateau just below the summit, & were just constructing
their one tent by spreading & tying India-Rubber blankets over a
frame of spruce poles[36] large enough to hold the four ladies with
sleeping space, & to cover [43] the baggage. The men must find shelter, if need is, under the rocks. The mountain at once justified the
party & their enthusiasm. It was romance enough to be there, & behold the panorama, & learn one by one all the beautiful novelties. The
country below ⟨was⟩ ↑is↓ a vast champaign,—half cleared, half forest,—with forty ponds in sight, ⟨with⟩ studded with villages & farmhouses, &, all around the horizon, closed with mountain ranges. The
[44] eye easily traces the valley followed by the Cheshire railroad, &
just beyond it the valley of the Connecticut river, then the Green
Mountain chain: in the north, the White Hills can be seen; &, on the

---

[34] Single pencil lines are drawn beside this paragraph in the left margins of pp. [39]
and [40] and in the right margin of p. [41].

[35] In addition to Ellery Channing and Emerson's son and daughter, this expedition
up Mount Monadnock in New Hampshire included Annie Keyes, future wife of Edward
Emerson; Thomas Wren Ward, son of Samuel Gray Ward; Moorfield Storey, a graduate
of Harvard in the class of 1866; Una Hawthorne, the novelist's daughter; and Elizabeth
Simmons, granddaughter of Emerson's half uncle Samuel Ripley.

[36] A sketch of a tent-shaped construction appears at this point in the text.

East, the low mountains of Watâtic & Wachusett. We had hardly wonted our eyes to the new Olympus, when the signs of a near storm set all the scattered party on the alert. The tent was to be finished & covered, & the knap-sacks piled in it. The Wanderers began to appear on the heights, & to descend, & much work in camp was done in brief time. [45] I looked about for a shelter in the rocks, & not till the rain began to fall, crept into it. I called to Channing, & afterwards to Tom Ward, who came, & we sat substantially dry, if the seat was a little cold, & the wall a little dripping, &, pretty soon, a large brook roared between the rocks, a little lower than our feet hung. Meantime, the thunder shook the mountain, & much of the time was continuous cannonade.

The storm refused to break up. One & another adventurer [46] rushed out to see the signs, & especially the sudden torrents, little Niagaras, that were ⟨r⟩pouring over the upper ledges, & descending upon our plateau. But every⟨one⟩↑body↓[n] was getting uncomfortably wet, the prospect was not good for the night, &, in spite of all remonstrance on the part of the young ladies, I insisted that they must go down with me to the "Mountain-House," for the night. All the four girls at last ⟨got⟩were ready, & descended with Stor⟨y⟩ey & me,—thus leaving the tent free [4⟨8⟩7] to be occupied by ⟨C⟩Mr Channing, Tom. W., & Edward. The storm held on most of the night, but we were slowly drying & warming in the comfortable inn. Next day, the weather slowly changed, & ↑we↓ climbed again the hill, and were repaid for all mishaps by the glory of the afternoon & evening. Edward went up with me to the summit, up all sorts of giant stairs, & showed the long spur with many descending peaks on the Dublin side. The rock-work[n] [48] is interesting & grand;—the clean cleavage, the wonderful slabs, ↑the quartz dikes,↓ the rock torrents in some parts, the uniform presence on the upper surface of the glacial lines or scratches, all in one self-same direction. Then every glance below apprises you how you are projected out into stellar space, as a sailor on a ship's [49] bowsprit out into the sea. We look down here on a hundred farms & farmhouses, but never see horse or man. For our eyes the country is depopulated, around us the arctic sparrow, *fringilla nivalis,* flies & *peeps,* the ground-robin ⟨too⟩also; but you can hear the ⟨s⟩ distant song of the wood-thrushes ascending from the green belts below. [50] I found the picture charming,[n] & more than remunerative. Later, from the plateau, ⟨I⟩ at sunset, I saw the great shadow of Monadnoc lengthen over the vast plain, until it touched the horizon. The earth & sky filled themselves with all ornaments,—haloes, rainbows, and little pendulums of ⟨r⟩cloud would hang down [51] till they touched the top of a hill, giving it the appearance of a ↑smoking↓ volcano. The wind was north, the evening cold, but the camp fire kept the party comfortable, whilst Story, ⟨s⟩with Edward for chorus,[n] sang a multitude of songs, to their great delectation. The night was forbiddingly cold;—the tent kept the girls in vital heat, but the youths could hardly keep ⟨themselves⟩ their blood [52] in circulation, the ⟨more⟩ ↑rather,↓ that they had spared too many of their blankets to the girls & to the old men. Themselves had nothing for it but to rise & cut wood, & bring it to the fire, which Mr Channing watched & fed. & this service of fetching wood was done by Tom Ward once to his great [53] peril during the night. In pitching a formless stump over ↑into↓ the ravine, he fell, ⟨himself,⟩ &, in trying to clear himself from the stump now behind him, flying & falling, got a bad contusion.

[54]–[57] [blank]
[58] I see ↑with joy↓ the Irish emigrants landing at Boston, at New York, & say to myself, There they go—to school.

Hazlitt, Lovelace's Editor, says, "Wither's song, 'Shall I, wasting in despair,' is certainly superior to the *Song to Althea.*"[37]—I will instantly seek & read it.↑—I have read it, & find that of Lovelace much the best.↓

   I find my window looking west has a certain occult way of looking east also, & has surprised me again & again ⟨of⟩ with noting arrivals or domestic incidents which I ought to know, occurring on the other side of the house. ↑Such is the trick of the spectacles.↓[38]

[37] W. Carew Hazlitt, ed., *Lucasta: The Poems of Richard Lovelace, Esq.* (London, 1864), p. xxxiv, in Emerson's library.
[38] The inserted sentence appears at the bottom of p. [59] and is joined to the paragraph on p. [58] by an ink line.

[59]   ⸻
        Young America[39]

        ⸻

William B. Wright, Goshen, N. Y.
George E. Tufts
C. J. Woodbury, Jackson, Michigan
Edward King, Springfield, Mass[achuse]tts
Tecumseh Steece, Lieut. U S. N[avy].
Forceythe Wil⟨so⟩lson
↑Henry Howard↓[40] Brownell
John Muir, San Francisco, Cal.

        ⸻

Peter Kaufmann, Canton, Ohio, 1858
        Author of *"Temple of Truth."* See *VO* 83,

        ⸻

[60][41] sudden birds
Cedar
How to pay the war-debt
The way to wash the negro white is to educate him in the white man's
useful & fine Arts, & his ethics.
honesty by temperament

[61] There is this to be said in favor of drinking, that it takes the
drunkard first out of society, then out of the world.

---

[39] Persons in the following list who have not previously been identified are: William
Bull Wright, who enlisted Emerson's help in trying to publish a long poem, *Highland
Rambles;* George E. Tufts, an aspiring writer who corresponded with Emerson as early as
1863; C. J. Woodbury, who met Emerson at Williams College in 1865 and later wrote
Talks with Ralph Waldo Emerson (1890); Edward Smith King, a young poet whom
Emerson met in Northampton in 1865; Tecumseh Steece, author of *A Republican Military System,* which Emerson read in 1864; Henry Howard Brownell, called "Our Battle
Laureate" by Holmes; John Muir, naturalist and explorer; and Peter Kaufmann, who
corresponded with Emerson and met him briefly in New York, shortly before publishing
The Temple of Truth, or the Science of Ever-Progressive Knowledge (Cincinnati and Canton, 1858).
[40] "Henry Howard" is in pencil.
[41] The entries on this page are in pencil.

The Turk is for the late centuries "the sick man", and sick, it is said, from his use of tobacco, which the great Turks of Mahomet's period did not know.

———

The scatterbrain, Tobacco.

———

Yet a man of no conversation should smoke.

———

John C↑lahan↓. told me, "he was lonesome without tobacco."⁴²

————

[62] We say as a reproach, that a man lives on Memory; but Genius on the inspiration of the moment. And it is essential mark of poetry, that it betrays in every word instant activity of mind, shown in new uses of every fact & image, in preternatural quickness or perception of relations[.]
A presence of mind that gives a miraculous command of all means of uttering the thought & feeling of the moment. The poet squanders on the hour an amount of life that ⟨would more than⟩ ↑might↓ furnish the seventy years of ⟨his⟩ [63] the man that stands next him.⁴³

In classes of men, what a figure is Charles Lamb! so much wit lodged in such a saccharine temperament.

———

At Miss Goddard's, Wright said to Alcott, A lady requests me to ask whether instinct ab⟨rog⟩negates attribute[.]⁴⁴

———

Capaneus Bent
See J 101   W[illiam] E[llery] C[hanning]
    & putting gods at vendue

⁴² The inserted "lahan" is in pencil, as is the rule below this entry. John Clahan was choreman and caretaker of the Emersons' house in Concord. With the preceding sentence about tobacco and conversation, cf. p. [23] above.
⁴³ "And it . . . him." is used in "Poetry and Imagination," *W*, VIII, 17.
⁴⁴ This sentence is used in "Historic Notes of Life and Letters in New England," *W*, X, 342. Beginning with the rule preceding this sentence, the entries on p. [63] are in pencil.

[64]   ↑Free Trade.↓   ↑Balloon.↓
The bribe of the balloon is, that the Englishman arriving with his trunk, in that conveyance, does not stop at Boston Custom-House, but alights in Concord ↑at Fairhaven Cliff↓ without paying duties. 'Tis a great economy. And the arts will one day accomplish what politics has failed to do.

[65] ↑'↓Tis[45] certain that any consideration of botany, of geology, of astronomy, administers a certain iron to the mind, adds a feeling of permanency, suggests immortality; whilst dinners, dances, & Washington-Street, have a contrary effect.

[66] [blank]
[67] Dr Channing took counsel, in 18↑40?↓,[46] with George Ripley & Mrs Ripley, to find ⟨if⟩ ↑whether↓ it were possible to bring cultivated thoughtful people socially together. He had already talked with Dr Warren on the same design, who made, ↑I have heard,↓ a party, which had its fatal termination in an oyster supper.[47] Mrs Ripley invited a large party, but I do not remember that Dr Channing came. Perhaps he did, but it is significant enough of the very moderate success, that I do not recall the fact of his presence, or indeed any particulars[n] but of some absurd toilettes.
    [68] I think there was the mistake of a general belief at that time, that there was some concert of doctrinaires to establish certain opinions, & inaugurate some movement in literature, philosophy, & religion, of which the supposed conspirators were quite innocent; for there was no concert, & only here & there, two or three men or women who read & wrote, each alone, with unusual vivacity. Perhaps they only agreed in having fallen upon Coleridge, Wordsworth, Goethe, & then upon Carlyle, with pleasure [69] & sympathy. Otherwise, their education & reading were not marked, but had the American superficialness, & their studies were solitary. I suppose all of them were surprised at this rumor of a school or sect, & certainly at

[45] The apostrophe is in pencil.
[46] "40?" is in pencil.
[47] "Dr Channing . . . supper." is used in "Historic Notes of Life and Letters in New England," *W*, X, 340–341.

the name of Transcendentalism, which nobody knows who gave, or when it was first applied. As these persons became, in the common chances of society, acquainted with each other, there resulted certainly strong ⟨& delicious⟩[48] friendships, [70] which, of course, were exclusive in proportion to their heat, & perhaps those persons who were mutually the best friends were the most private, & had no ambition of ⟨making⟩publishing their letters, diaries or conversation.[49] Such were Charles Newcomb, Sam↑l↓,[50] G. Ward, & Caroline Sturgis,—all intimate with Margaret Fuller. Margaret with her ⟨shining⟩ radiant genius & fiery heart was perhaps the real centre that drew so many & so various individuals to [71] a seeming union. Hedge, Clarke, ↑W[illiam]. H[enry].↓ Channing, W[illiam]. E[llery]. Channing, jr., ⟨George⟩ Ripley, ↑James Clarke↓[51] & many more then or since known as writers, or otherwise distinguished, were only held together as her friends. Mr ↑A↓[52] Bronson Alcott became known to all these as the pure idealist, not at all a man of letters, nor of any practical talent, & quite too cold & contemplative for the alliances of friendship, but purely intellectual, with rare simplicity & grandeur of perception, who read Plato as an equal, & inspired his companions only in proportion as they were intellectual, [72] whilst the men of talent, of course, complained of the want of point & precision in this abstract & religious thinker. Elizabeth Hoar & Sarah Clarke, though certainly never summoned to any of the meetings which were held at George Ripley's, or Dr Francis's, or Stetson's, or Bartol's or my house, were prized & sympathetic friends of Margaret & of others whom I have named, in the circle. The "Dial" was the only public or quotable result of this temporary ↑society &↓ fermentation: and yet ⟨Brook Farm⟩ the Community at Brook Farm, founded [73] by the readers of Fourier, drew also ⟨its⟩ inspirations from this circle. A little later than at our first meetings,

---

[48] "& delicious" is canceled in pencil.

[49] "I think . . . conversation.", struck through in pencil with two vertical use marks on pp. [68], [69], and [70], is used in "Historic Notes of Life and Letters in New England," *W*, X, 342–343.

[50] The inserted letter is in pencil.

[51] "James Clarke" is inserted in pencil.

[52] "A" is inserted in pencil.

Theodore Parker became an active, &, of necessity, a leading associate: And in the logic of events, the "Twenty Eig⟨th⟩hth Congregation" ↑& its "Fraternity,"↓[53] might be claimed as a robust result. I have seen Brownson & Father Taylor & ↑Charles↓ Sumner in the company.[54]   ↑See *infra* p. 115↓

↑See *infra* p. 280 notice of Brook Farm.↓

↑See some notes in *N* 2, *Y* 59↓

↑See *D* 308   on Alcott & Very↓[55]

[74] ——

↑In a warmer & more fruitful climate ⟨they⟩ ↑Alcott & his friends↓ would soon have been Buddhists.↓

An important fact in the sequel was the plantation of Mr Lane & Mr Alcott at Stillriver, "Fruitlands."[56] The labor on the place was all done by the volunteers; they used no animal food; they even for a time dressed themselves only in linen; but there were inherent difficulties: the members of the community were unused to labor, & were soon

---

[53] "& its 'Fraternity,' " is in pencil. Theodore Parker was installed in 1845 as pastor of the Twenty-Eighth Congregational Society, which met in Boston's Melodeon and included what came to be known as the "Parker Fraternity."

[54] "Charles" is inserted in pencil. Persons named in this reminiscence who may not be readily identifiable include: John Collins Warren (1778–1859), a Boston surgeon prominent in New England's cultural life; Charles King Newcomb (1820–1894), an idiosyncratic mystic; Samuel Gray Ward (1817–1907), a banker and Emerson's close friend; Caroline Sturgis, later Tappan, a friend since 1838; Frederic Henry Hedge (1805–1890), a Unitarian clergyman; James Freeman Clarke (1810–1888), a Unitarian clergyman and writer; William Henry Channing (1810–1884), nephew of William Ellery Channing and a Unitarian clergyman; Elizabeth Hoar, once engaged to Emerson's brother Charles and a close friend of the family thereafter; Sarah Freeman Clarke, sister of James Clarke and once Emerson's pupil; Convers Francis (1795–1863), a Unitarian minister and professor at Harvard Divinity School after 1842; Caleb Stetson, Emerson's Harvard classmate and a Unitarian minister; Cyrus Bartol (1813–1900), a Unitarian minister; Orestes A. Brownson (1803–1876), a clergyman, writer, and editor of the *Quarterly Review* after 1844; and Edward Taylor (1793–1871), pastor of the Seamen's Bethel in Boston.

[55] This entry and the rule above it are in pencil.

[56] Alcott brought the writer Charles Lane (1800?–1870) to America from England in 1842, and they founded Fruitlands during the summer of 1843.

very impatient of it: the hard work fell on a few, & mainly on women. The recruits whom they ⟨true⟩drew were ↑some of them↓ partly, ⟨or⟩ ↑some of them↓ quite insane. And the individuals could not divest themselves of the infirmity of holding property. When the winter came, & they had burned all the dry wood⟨,⟩ they could find, & began to burn green wood, they could not keep themselves warm, & fled to the Shakers for their warm fires.

[75] ——
What a saint is Milton!
How grateful we are to the man of the world who obeys the morale, as in humility, & in the obligation to serve mankind. True genius always has these inspirations.

Humanity always equal to itself[.] The religious understand each other under all mythologies, & say the same thing. Homer & Aeschylus in all the rubbish of fables speak out clearly ever & anon. ↑the noble sentiments of all ages.↓

Calvinism was as injurious to the justice, as Greek myths were ↑to the↓ purity of the gods. Yet noble souls carried themselves nobly, & drew what treasures of character from that grim system.

[76] We want heat to execute our plans. The good will, the knowledge, the whole armory of means are all present, but ⟨the⟩ a certain heat, that long since used not to fail, refuses its office: And all is vain, until this capricious fuel is supplied. It seems a certain ↑semi-↓ animal heat, as if tea, or wine, or sea-air, or mountains or ⟨conversation⟩ or a ⟨t⟩ new thought suggested in ⟨con⟩ book or conversation could fire the train, wake the fancy, [77] & the clear perception. Pitcoal! where to find it. 'Tis of no use that your engine is made like a watch, that you are a good workman, & know how to drive it, if there is ⟨no fire,⟩ no coal.[57] What said Bettine to Goethe, "Go to ruin with

[57] The paragraph to this point, struck through in pencil with three vertical use marks on p. [76] and p. [77], is used in "Inspiration," *W*, VIII, 276. "printed" is written in pencil in the right margin of p. [76]; "printed?" is written in pencil in the left margin of p. [77]. "⟨no fire⟩" is circled in ink.

your sentiments! Tis the senses alone that work in art, as in love, & nobody knows this better than you."[58]

I find it a great & fatal difference whether I court the Muse, or the Muse courts me: That is the ugly disparity between age & youth.

[78] July 30. ↑1866.↓ This morn came again the exhilarating news of the landing of the Atlantic telegraph cable at Heart's Content, Newfoundland, & we repeat the old wonder & delight we found on the Adirondac, in August 1858.[59] We have grown more skilful, it seems, in electric machinery, & may confide better in a lasting success. Our political ⟨statu⟩condition is better, &, though dashed by the treachery of our American President, can hardly go backward to slavery & civil war. Besides, the suggestion of an event so exceptional & astounding in the history of human [79] arts, is, that this ⟨p⟩ instant & pitiless publicity now to be given to every public act ⟨will react on⟩ must ⟨give⟩ force on the actors a new sensibility to the opinion of mankind, & restrain folly & meanness.

Old light (polarized) is much better than new. ↑The indirect & reflex ray sometimes better than the direct.[60] Quotation has its utilities.↓

On a lower stage, see the history of quotation. Leave the great wheat-countries, the Egypts, & Mississippi Valleys, & follow the harvest into the bakers' shops & pedlers' carts.

[80] Bad kings & governors help us, if only they are bad enough. Governor Seymour & the New York mob, & Wood, & Vallandigham, would have harmed us, if they had not been so mischievous.[61]

[58] Misquoted from Bettina Brentano von Arnim, *Goethe's Correspondence with a Child,* 3 vols. (London, 1839), II, 134, in Emerson's library.

[59] A pencil comma follows "Content", with an ink comma below it. For the expedition of the Adirondac Club, see *JMN,* XIII, 34–35 and 55–56.

[60] A rule, apparently drawn beneath the original entry before the insertion of two additional sentences, appears under "better" at the left margin.

[61] Governor Horatio Seymour was accused of encouraging anti-draft rioters in New York City in July 1863; Fernando Wood and Clement Laird Vallandigham were leaders of the Peace Democrats or "Copperheads."

The maiden has no guess what the youth sees in her. It is not in her, but in his eyes, which rain on her the tints & forms & grace of Eden; as the sun, deluging the landscape with his beams, makes the world he shines upon. ↑Transcribed in *L* [Camadeva] 78↓[62]

[81] Sensible men are very rare. A sensible man does not brag: avoids introducing the names of his creditable companions; drops out of his narrative every complimentary allusion to himself, omits himself as habitually as another man obtrudes himself in the discourse, and ↑is↓ content⟨s himself⟩ with putting his fact or theme simply on its own ground, & letting nature bear the expense of the conversation. ↑Printed?↓[63]

[82] *Culture*
                "What one is,
            Why may not millions be?"
                        Wordsworth   Prelude, p[p] 338–9[64]

[83] The religion of seventy years ago was a belt to the mind, giving it a concentration & force↑.↓ ⟨which is wanting now.⟩ ⟨Those people⟩[65] ↑Notable men↓ were kept respectable by the determination ⟨to the⟩ ↑of thought on the↓ Eternal world. Now men fall abroad, want polarity, & suffer in character & in intellect↑.↓ ⟨from the want.⟩ Perhaps it is the result of the temporary anarchy from the now hypocritical respect that is paid to Christianity, & [84] a sort of scientific acceptance, without Enthusiasm, of the Moral Law. We are civil to Christianity, & have not learned to abandon ourselves to the all sufficiency & beatitude of Ethics. But this is temporary, & when the awful nature & origin of the sentiment is frankly declared, it will give at once the balance & the magnanimity.

---

[62] "Transcribed in *L* 78" is in pencil.
[63] This paragraph is struck through in pencil with a diagonal use mark. "Printed?" is in pencil.
[64] *The Prelude; or, Growth of a Poet's Mind. An Autobiographical Poem* (New York and Philadelphia, 1850), in Emerson's library. The quoted lines (XIII, 88–89) are struck through in ink with two vertical use marks.
[65] "Those people" is canceled in pencil.

[85] Our thoughts ⟨a⟩ on affairs, of course, are all pitched on the measure of human life. If we had the longevity of a redwood tree, or of a stone, we should not despond under bad politics. We have made a disastrous mistake in the election of a rebel as President. But the blunder is only noxious for the time, & discloses so soon the natural checks & cures, that it would cause no anxiety in a patriot who should live to the ⟨alleged⟩[66] age of the antediluvians.

[86]   ↑*Originality & Quotation.*↓
        The thought, the literature, comes again, not because the man is servile, but because Nature is a repeater, & suggests the like truth to the new comer as to the ancient.

[87] "The early Friends had not confidence in their own convictions, & fell under the debasing influence of authority. They whom⟨o⟩ no prisons appalled, who yielded to no cruelty, were not strong enough to maintain their own simple views" against ⟨against⟩the bigoted traditions. W. L. Fisher[67]

When the Quakers settled in France, (in the early part of the French Revolution,) asked of the National Assembly to be released from military duty, Mirabeau (President) replied, "The Assembly will in its wisdom consider your requests, but, whenever I meet a Quaker, I shall say, 'My brother, [88] if thou hast a right to be free, thou hast a right to prevent any one from making thee a slave: as thou lovest thy fellow-creature, suffer not a tyrant to destroy him; it would be killing him thyself.' "[68]

"The hero of the Daityas, armed with his club, rushed against Nrisimha. But, like the insect which falls in the fire, the Asura disap-

---

[66] "alleged" is in penciled parentheses and is canceled in pencil.

[67] William Logan Fisher, *The Nature of War, together with Some Observations on the Coercive Exactions of Religious Societies* (Philadelphia, 1862), p. 39. A short line connects Fisher's name to the end of the quoted part of Emerson's entry.

[68] Fisher, *The Nature of War,* 1862, pp. 19–20. Single pencil lines are drawn beside the quoted part of this entry in the left margins of pp. [87] and [88].

peared, absorbed by the splendor of his enemy." *Bhagavat Purana*
p. 41 Vol III[69]

[89] After the destruction of Hiranyakacipu, chief of the Asuras, by
Hari, the gods go in procession before the throne, & each makes his
acknowledgement to Hari. Indra said "Ah Lord! how insignificant is
this world, which is the prey of time, for those who hear thy name! For
them, deliverance even has not much esteem. What to say then of
other goods, O Narasimha!"[70] *Bhagavat Purana* III p. 44

———

See Prahlada's reply to Nr⟨s⟩isimha, [*ibid.,*] Vol 3. p 54

———

[90] [blank]
[91] What ⟨a⟩fanatics in politics we are! There are far more important
things than free suffrage; namely, a pure will, pure & illumined.[71]

August 12. Last night in conversation with the N. Y. ladies, Alcott
appeared to great advantage, & I saw again, as often before, his singular superiority. As pure intellect, I have never seen his equal. The
people with whom he talks do not even understand him. They interrupt him with clamorous dissent, or what they think verbal endorse-
ment of what they fancy he may have been saying, or with, "Do you
know [92] Mr Alcott, I think thus & so,"—some whim or sentimentalism; & do not know that they ⟨the⟩have interrupted his large &
progressive statement, do not know that all they have in their baby
brains is spotty & incoherent, that all that he sees & says is like astronomy, lying there real & vast, & every part & fact in eternal connection with the whole. And that they ought to sit in silent gratitude,
eager only to hear more, to hear the whole, [93] & not interrupt him
with their ⟨silly⟩[72] prattle. It is because his sight is so clear, command-

———

[69] This passage, and those on pp. [89] and [95]–[107], are Emerson's translations
from *Le Bhâgavata Purâna, ou Histoire Poétique de Krichna,* trans. Eugène Burnouf, 3
vols. (Paris, 1840–1847); Emerson inscribed these books, in his library, as "the gift of
H. D. Thoreau."
[70] A pencil line is drawn in the left margin beside " 'Ah Lord! . . . Narasimha!' "
[71] This entry is in pencil.
[72] "silly" is canceled in pencil.

ing the whole ground, & ↑he↓ perfectly gifted to ⟨report⟩ state adequately what he sees, that he does not lose his temper, when his glib interlocutors bore him with their ⟨old⟩[73] dead texts & phrases. Another who sees in flashes, or only here & there a land-mark, has the like confidence in his own truth, & in the infinitude of the soul, but ⟨no conf⟩none in[n] his ⟨own⟩ competence to show it to the bores; &, if they tease him, he ⟨chides, & frets, & is⟩ ↑⟨is uneasy & present⟨s⟩ly⟩↓ silent. [94] ⟨It is⟩ Power[n] is not pettish, but want of power ↑is.↓ ⟨His⟩ ↑A[lcott].'s↓ activity of mind is shown in the perpetual invention & ⟨dexterity⟩ felicity of his language⟨.⟩↑:↓ ⟨T⟩the constitutionality of his thought, ↑apparent↓[74] in the fact, that last night's discourse only brought out with new conviction the old fundamental thoughts which he had, when I first knew him.

The moral benefit of such a mind cannot be told. The world fades: men, reputations, politics shrivel: the interests, power, future of the soul beam a new dayspring. Faith becomes sight.

[95]　　　　　　　　　　　*Maya of the Hindoos.*
Bhagavata Purana. [1840–1847,] ↑Vol II↓ ↑⟨Wil⟩ Eugene Burnouf's Translation.↓

　　Brahma, Vishnu &c　　who, partaking the qualities of Maya to produce, preserve, & destroy the Universe, put on, in each ⟨Yo⟨a⟩ga⟩ ↑Yuga↓, a distinct body. Vol II p[p]. [4–]5

Adoration to Purucha, to the Supreme Spirit, who, to make himself visible is manifested today in the figure of Richi, Him, in the bosom of whom this Universe is formed by the Maya ⟨who⟩of which he disposes, as are (it) in heaven the different figures which there appear! [II,] p. 6

In times & in places where men, (their Spirit tainted by Illusion, difficult to resist, from the god whose navel ⟨pe⟩bears a lotus,) [96][75] see false distinctions, the good man in his compassion regards them as objects of pity: but he makes no effort to punish a fault which is the work of Destiny.[n] But thou, whose spirit is not tainted with Illusion, (hard to

---

[73] "old" is canceled in pencil.
[74] "apparent" is in pencil.
[75] "*Maya*" is written at the top left of this page.

resist, with which the Supreme Spirit envelops itself,) thou who knowest all—, deign, o soverign Lord! to treat with benevolence those whose heart, hurt by this Illusion, have not thoughts except for works. [II,] p. 29

[97] ↑*Maya*↓
Dakcha says to Vishnu;
"Thou art he who, under his proper form is the Very Spirit, which is pure, delivered from (or free of) the different states of Intelligence, unique, sheltered from fear, Master of the Illusion which it arrests, & which, taking into its regard the part of man, enters into his breast, & resides there as if it were not pure,—⟨he who⟩ ↑that which↓ does not receive laws except from ⟨him⟩↑it⟨s⟩↓self" [II,] p. 32

———

Rudra says, (Vol II. p 127)
O thou, who, always unalterable, createst, conservest, & destroyest this universe, by the aid of Maya, that energy in numerous forms which, powerless when it reposes in thy bosom, makes believe that it ⟨gives⟩is distinct from thee, & gives to the world an apparent reality

[98]   *Maya*
The assistants said; In the road of birth, where is no shelter;—which great ⟨d⟩miseries make difficult; where the God of death presents himself as a f⟨ear⟩rightful reptile; where they have before the⟨m⟩↑ir↓ eyes the mirage of objects; where the opposite affections (of pleasure & pain) are precipices; where they fear the wicked as ferocious beasts; where grief is like a fire in the forest;—how should a caravan of ignorant beings, loaded with the heavy burden of the body & the soul, tormented by desire, how, o God who givest asylum! should it ever arrive at thy feet? [II,] p. 33

[99]   *Maya*
Brighu said; O thou of whom Brahma & the other beings clothed with a body, turned from the knowledge of the Spirit by the impenetrable Maya, & sleeping in the darkness, know not even today to recognize the essence, although they carry it in themselves, befriend me, thou Soul & friend of those who venerate thee!

Brahma said, No, it is not thy true form, that which man sees with his organs made to seize different objects, for thou who art the asylum of knowledge, of substance, & of quality, thou art distinct from [100][76] that product of Maya which has no real existence. [II,] p 33

The guardians of the world said: How /could/can/ we see thee, with our eyes (made only to seize that which is not reality,) thee, the internal Spectator, who seest equally the visible world. I⟨t⟩f, indeed, thou appearest as an individual being, formed of the five elements,—it is, O potent God, the product of thy Maya. [II,] p 34

The chiefs of the Yoga said, None is more dear to thee, O Lord, than he who does not distinguish himself [101] from thee, from thee who art the soul of the Universe![77]
Adoration to him who has need but of a simple act of his thought to establish[n] in himself distinctions by means of the Illusion of which he disposes,—Illusion, whose qualities divide themselves in so many ways, under the influence of Destiny, in the Phenome⟨a⟩na of ↑⟨of the⟩the↓ Creation, ⟨of⟩ the conserving, & destruction of the universe. Adoration to him, who, in order that the qualities & their trouble cease in him, has only to persist in the state which is proper to him. [II, p]p 34[-35]

[102]   Maya
⟨O⟩Druva said, O only God, it is after having created by thy proper energy, which they call Maya, & whose qualities are innumerable, this universe, which composes itself of the union of Intelligence & of ↑the↓ other principles,—⟨I⟩it is after having penetrated the qualities of Maya, which have not reality, that thou appearest multiple, as fire when it burns in fragments of distinct billets of wood. [II, p]p. 47[-48]

_____

Certainly they have the mind perverted by the Illusion with which thou envelopest thyself,—those who beholding thee, (thee who

[76] "Maya" is written at the top left of this page.
[77] A pencil line is drawn beside this sentence in the left margins of pp. [100] and [101].

dost deliver from [103][78] birth & from death, as the tree which gives all one can desire), adore thee for any thing else than for thyself; since they aspire to a sensual good made only for a carcase, & which exists even in Hell. [II,] p 48

———

↑Heaven↓—that abode so little accessible to man, the /sport/toy/ of Maya, [II,] p. 50[79]

↑Dhruva said;↓ Enveloped by the divine Maya, I see distinctions, like a man who dreams. &, in presence of another being, who has meantime no ↑real↓ existence, I suffer from grief in thinking that this being, who is my brother, is my enemy. [II,] p 51[80]

[104]   Maya

Adore, in order to escape from existence, him who can annihilate it, & whose feet are adorable; h⟨e⟩im who unites himself, whilst he remains distinct from it, to Maya, which is his energy endowed with qualities. [II,] p 63

↑Bhagavat himself said,↓ The wise, O king, & virtuous men shun in this world to do harm to creatures, because the body is not the soul. If men such as thou let themselves be misled by the divine Maya, the constant worship which they owe to the old is henceforth a useless pain. [105][81] Also the man who knows that his body is the product of ignorance, of desire, & of works, thus illumined, does not attach himself to it. Who is the ⟨wise⟩ ↑sage↓, who, once detached, would say *mine,* of his body, or the house he has built, or his children, or his goods? The Spirit which is ↑one,↓ pure, luminous by itself, independent of the qualities of which it is the asylum, which penetrates everywhere, which is absolute, which is the internal witness, & within which is no other soul, that Spirit is distinct from body.[82] [II,] p. 98

[78] *"Maya"* is written at the top left of this page.
[79] A pencil line is drawn beside this entry in the right margin.
[80] Single pencil lines are drawn in the right margin beside each of the two sentences in this entry.
[81] *"Maya"* is written at the top left of this page.
[82] A pencil line is drawn in the left margin beside "Who is . . . body."

(The whole of [Book IV,] Chap. XX, Vol. II. is of great interest[.])

[106] ——
The Veda says, "The world is born of Maya."

———

"Brahma qui n'a pas de qualités." [II, 111]

———

Cet Être exempt d'attributs et de personnalité, qui est à la fois ce qui existe et
ce qui n'existe pas [pour nos organes.]. Vol II p 111

An[83] important passage begins on p 111, Vol. II. ⟨&⟩ thus;
When once is developed in the soul a profound passion for Brahma, he
who experiences it, fulfilling the religious duties, consumes (exhaust-
ing it by the ardor of science & of detachment) ⟨the⟩his heart,—that
envelope of the life formed by the five elements, [107] as fire which in
spreading devours the wood in which it took its birth. ↑(See the whole
page 112)↓[84]

There is a maxim which those who know the Veda re⟨e⟩peat in all
places: ↑this,—↓ ⟨⟨P⟩But⟩ "⟨a⟩An action done in conformity to the law,
⟨(say they still),⟩ becomes invisible, & does not reappear." [II, 157]
↑equivalent this to Novalis's saying, "Of the wrong we are ↑always↓
conscious; of the Right never"↓[85]

"All things that man conceives in his heart, when he says, 'I, this is
mine,' are so many actions accomplished which subject him to the law
of a second birth."[86] Vol II p 157 *Bhagavata Purana*

[108]–[109] [blank]

[83] A single square bracket is drawn to the left of "An".
[84] "(See the whole page 112)" is in pencil.
[85] Emerson is incorrectly attributing to Novalis a statement from Goethe's *Wilhelm
Meister's Apprenticeship*, bk. VII, chap. 9, which Emerson apparently first encountered in
Carlyle's "Characteristics," *The Edinburgh Review*, LIV (Dec. 1831), 356. See *JMN*,
IV, 15, and VI, 220. Two subscript x's appear to the left of "are", and one to the right.
[86] A pencil line is drawn in the right margin beside this translation.

[110] ↑*Gifts*↓

The idea of sacrifice is cosmical & reappears. Hecatomb ↑is due↓ to the god; tithe to the priest; service, homage, or tax to the /king/State/; rent to the land⟨owner⟩lord; commission to the banker; ↑gleaning to the poor;↓ pasture to the cow; manure to the field: And not less in sentiment, always gifts & tokens ↑to the friend↓: seven years to Rachel:[87] our own life, if demanded, to our country.

[111] ——

William Forbes writes wisely, "Difficulties exist to be surmounted." a right heroic creed.

—— ——

↑*Gifts*↓   ↑See p 110↓

Flowers grow in the garden to be given away. Every body feels that they appeal to finer senses than his own, & looks wishfully around in hope that possibly this friend or that may be nobler furnished than he to see & read them, or at least a better naturalist. Especially they are sent to ceremonies & assemblies sacred or festal or funereal, because, on occasions of passion & sentiment, there may be higher appreciation of these delicate wonders.

[112] ↑On 31 August↓ visited[n] Agassiz by invitation with Lidian & Ellen, & spent the day at his house & on the Nahant rocks. He is a man to be thankful for, always cordial, full of facts, ⟨p⟩with unsleeping observation, & perfectly communicative. In Brazil he saw on a half mile square /172/117/[88] different kinds of excellent timber,— & not a saw mill in Brazil. A country thirsting for Yankees to open & use its wealth. In Brazil is no bread: Manioca in pellets the substitute, at the side of your plate. No society, no culture; [113] could only name three men; the Emperor, M. Coutinho, & M. Couteau. (   )[89] governor of a province, Tom Ward's friend. For the rest, immense vulgarity: and, as Longfellow said, the Emperor wished he could swap places with Agassiz, & be a professor,—which A. ex-

[87] See Gen. 29:18–30.
[88] "117" is in pencil.
[89] The parentheses are in pencil.

plained, that the Emperor said, 'Now you, when you leave your work, can always return into cultivated society, I have none.'—Agassiz says, the whole population is wretchedly immoral, ⟨wit⟩the color & features of the people showing the entire intermixing [114] of all the races. Mrs Agassiz found the women ignorant, depressed, with no employment but needle-work, with no future, negligent of their persons, shabby & sluttish at home, with their hair about their ears, only gay in the ball room: The men well dressed.

Ida A. Higginson says, the bats in Georgia are covered with bed-bugs.[90]

[115]   ↑continued from p. 73,↓

I don't remember how long the "Brook Farm" existed, I think about ⟨two⟩ ↑six or seven↓ years—⟨it⟩ ↑the society↓ then broke up, & ↑the Farm↓ was sold, &, I believe all the partners came out with loss. Some of them had spent on it the accumulations of years. I suppose they all at the moment regarded it as a failure. I do not think they ⟨would⟩ ↑can↓ so regard it at this time,[n] but probably as an important chapter in their experience, which has been of life-long value. What knowledge of themselves & of each other, what various practical wisdom, what personal power, what studies of character, what [11⟨4⟩6] accumulated culture many of the members must have owed to it![91]

[11⟨5⟩7][92] Fame—of Viasa to whom all the Indian immense Poems & Hymns & Puranas are ascribed; of Homer—⟨who⟩ ↑to↓ whom Iliad & Odyssey; of the author of the Eddas 1 & 2, of the Sagas &c[;]   of   the author of the Nibelungen Lied
of Taliesin   or of Merlin
of Walter Mapes with his Morte d'Arthure,
of the author of the Mahabarat,

---

[90] Louis Agassiz's daughter Ida was the wife of Henry Lee Higginson, a Boston banker.
    [91] This paragraph is used in "Historic Notes of Life and Letters in New England," *W*, X, 368–369.
    [92] The entries on this page are in pencil.

and ⟨&⟩of the Ramayana.

The poet spoke his instant thought
And filled the age his fame,
As ⟨lightning⟩ ↑Jove's bolt↓ struck an inch of ground
And ⟨filled⟩ ↑lit↓ the ⟨horizon⟩ ↑sky↓ the flame[93]

[118] I can find my biography in every fable that I read.

⟨Of⟩For T[homas]. W[ren]. W[ard?]. I think I find a text in Charles K[ing]. N[ewcomb]. that describes his style & manners. See *BL* 124, 121 [actually 122–123]
To be sure you must be at ease, you must look comfortable, *aliis laetus, sapiens sibi.*[94]

I hate nerves, they make such hedge hogs of people.

I find my own biography in every fable I read.

↑M[ary]. M[oody]. E[merson].↓
A robust will ↑is↓ a main convenience in the social world,—as great as false teeth. I am thinking of M M E's walk on the street with her staff[.]

[119] In the history of intellect no more important fact than the Hindoo theology, teaching that the beatitude or supreme good is to be attained ⟨is⟩ through science; namely, by the perception of the real & unreal, setting aside matter, & qualities, & affections or emotions and persons, ↑& actions,↓ as Maias or illusions, & thus arriving at the contemplation of the one eternal Life & Cause, & a perpetual approach & assimilation to Him⟨;⟩,[n] thus escaping new births or transmigration.

---

[93] A revised version of these lines, which are struck through in pencil with two diagonal use marks, appears in "Fragments on the Poet and the Poetic Gift," XXXII, *W,* IX, 334; an earlier version appears on p. [22] above.
[94] "Outwardly joyous, inwardly wise" (Ed.); see *JMN,* XIV, 292, and "Considerations by the Way," *W,* VI, 265.

[120] "As to heaven & hell, they are inventions of ⟨the⟩Maya, & are therefore both imaginary, except that the Swerga" &c *Small's Handbook of Sanskrit Literature.* p. 183   ↑in the Boston Athenaeum↓[95]

_____

Truth is the ⟨great⟩ principle,—⟨truth⟩ ↑&↓ the moral of the Hindoo theology,—truth as against the Maia which deceives Gods & Men: Truth the principle, & Retirement ⟨the⟩ and ⟨Abstinence⟩ Self denial the means of attaining it.[96] And they stop at no extreme in the statement as, (here should follow the three ⟨t⟩lines at the top of this page.)

[121] Nobility. The extreme example of the sentiment, on which the distinction of rank rests, is not to be found in Spain, Germany, or England, but in India, where poverty or crime do not interrupt or diminish the reverence for a Bramin. In India, a Bramin may be very poor, & perform daily[n] menial tasks for the English, as porters or servants, but ⟨men⟩ ↑the natives↓ still kneel to ⟨them,⟩ ↑him,↓ & show ⟨them⟩ ↑him↓ the highest respect.↑—Mr ⟨& Mrs⟩ Dall testified this fact to me on ⟨their⟩ ↑his↓ return from India.↓[97]

[122] ⟨I delight in⟩ Self respect ⟨It⟩[98] always commands. I see it here in a family little known, but each of whose members, without other gifts or advantages above the common, have that, in lieu of all: teaching that wealth, fashion, learning, talent, garden, ↑fine↓ house, servants, can be omitted, if you have quiet determination to keep your own ↑way↓ with⟨out⟩ good sense & energy. ↑The best of it is that the family ↑I speak of↓ do not suspect the fact.↓

[95] George Small, *A Handbook of Sanskrit Literature* . . . (London, 1866); Emerson withdrew this volume from the Boston Athenaeum, September 5–8, 1866. A pencil line is drawn beside the quotation in the left margin.

[96] A pencil line is drawn beside the paragraph to this point in the left margin. The inserted "&" is in pencil; "great" and "truth" are canceled in pencil and in ink.

[97] Charles Henry Appleton Dall went to Calcutta in 1855 as the first foreign missionary of the Unitarian church.

[98] "I delight in" and "It" are canceled in pencil.

Anquetil Duperron.[99]

What a counterpart to all the Bohemianism we attribute to Parisian litterateurs, is the address of Anquetil Duperron to the Indian Bramins which I have transcribed in Σ⟨!⟩ p. 90.

[123] Geometry, masonry, must make the basis of a poem also.[100]

———

Diamond will burn, but law will hold.

———

Lesley is forced to run away from the oil-men who persecute him to survey their patch.[101]

———

Louis XVI. ⟨wished to gratify⟩sent one to Anquetil Duperron with 3000 francs in a leathern bag: his friend set it down b⟨y⟩eside the chimney, & departed. As soon as he was gone, Anquetil snatched it up, ran out, & threw it at the heels of his friend, who found the bag arrived at the bottom of the staircase before him. The Society of Public Instruction, later, voted him a pension of 6000 fr. A. returned the order, saying, he had no need of it. When very near his end, he said to his physician, "I am going to set out on a voyage much more considerable than all those I have already made, but I do not know where I shall arrive." [*Nouvelle Biographie Générale,* 1855–1870, II, 734]

[124] The year 1866 has its memorabilia in the success of Atlantic Cable; in the downfall of Austria; in the checking of Napoleon, & of Maximilian;—in Agassiz's South American science; (Shall I say in the possession taken by the American Govt of the Telegraph in the postal service?) ↑(for I thought a public statement meant that.)↓

[99] The underscoring is continued so as to circle the name. Abraham Hyacinthe Anquetil-Duperron (1731–1805), a French orientalist, addressed the Brahmans about his simple, disciplined mode of living; Emerson's source is the *Nouvelle Biographie Générale* . . . , ed. Jean Chrétien Ferdinand Hoefer, 46 vols. (Paris, 1855–1870), II, 733–734, in his library.

[100] This sentence is struck through in ink with a vertical use mark.

[101] J. Peter Lesley (1819–1903), a geologist who taught at the University of Pennsylvania, had lectured at the Concord Lyceum.

[125] If ⟨I⟩one had the experience that when he sat in the boughs of a certain tree he could write his thoughts with more clearness, & not only so, but thought better— —

———

The promise of literature amazes, for ↑n↓one reads in a book in happy hour without suggestion of immensities on the right hand & on the left,—without seeing that all recorded experience is a drop of dew before the soliciting universe of thought.

———

The thought, the literature comes again not because man is servile, but because nature is a repeater, & suggests the same truth to the new comer as to the ancient one.[102]

[126] ——
⟨M⟩Thought is more ductile than gold, more expansive than hydrogen gas; nations live on one book, &, in active states, one thought, one perception, discloses endless possibilities. It is ever as the ↑attention, as the↓ activity of the mind, & not ↑as↓ the number of thoughts or sensations, that ⟨count⟩the result is.

———

A patient under the dentist's hands thinks his mouth must ⟨be⟩have ⟨been magnified⟩ ↑grown↓ ⟨to⟩to a square foot[.]

[127] ↑Egypt↓[103]
Champollion wrote his first ↑printed↓ Mémoire to demonstrate that the names of the Giants of the Bible, when traced to their Hebrew etymology, were those of natural phenomena personified & *mis en scène.*

"Know that the gods hate impudence."
inscription on the temple of Sais.
        ↑See Isis & O⟨is⟩siris   c xxxii↓[104]

———

[102] Cf. p. [86] above.

[103] "Egypt" is inserted in pencil. The following sentence is translated by Emerson from the *Nouvelle Biographie Générale,* 1855–1870, IX, 647.

[104] "See Isis . . . c xxxii" is in pencil. Emerson's source is Samuel Birch, "An Introduction to the Study of the Egyptian Hieroglyphs," in John Gardner Wilkinson, *The*

The ↑seal or die of hard stone↓ in ↑the Museum at↓ Alawic castle ⟨which⟩ is reckoned to be ↑⟨old by⟩↓ ↑more than↓ ⟨‖ . . . ‖⟩2000 years ⟨B.C.⟩ ↑older than our era,↓ ⟨has a robust antiquity.⟩ ↑See "Egyptians in time of the Pharoahs" J G Wilkinson↓ [p. 72]

[128] "Egypt was already on the decline when Troy is said to have been taken"; and "their monuments are so accurately placed north & south, that the variation of the magnet may now be ascertained from the direction of their sides;" decimal notation, division of the year into 12 mo[nth]s of 30 days, wine in glass bottles, 2400 years before our era. *Wilkinson* [pp. 2–3]

> "the Nile
> Coming all along the heaven."
> [quoted by Birch,] *Egyptian* [*ibid.*, p. 268]

A poem in praise of Rameses II, says of the tower which he built,
> "the sunlight beams in its horizon,
> And sets within it."
> [quoted by Birch, *ibid.*, p. 267]

[129] Egypt.
There is a good deal of stick in all the pictures. The masters beat the workmen.

———

↑See above p. 127,↓[105]

[130] Hafiz's poetry is marked by nothing more than his ⟨con⟩ habit of playing with all magnitudes, mocking at them. What is the moon or the sun's course or heaven, & the angels, to his darling's mole or eyebrow? Destiny is a scur⟨r⟩vy night-thief who plays him or her a bad trick. ⟨But⟩ I might & perhaps will collect presently a few examples,

---

Egyptians in the Time of the Pharaohs: Being a Companion to the Crystal Palace Egyptian Collections (London, 1857), pp. 218–219, which he withdrew from the Boston Athenaeum, September 8–15, 1866. Birch's essay is on pp. 175–282 of the volume. The Roman numeral refers to Birch's citation of his source, Plutarch's *De Iside et Osiride* (Torino, 1852).
[105] "See above p. 127," and the rule above it are in pencil.

though, as I remember, they occur *passim* in the "Divan." But I am always struck [131] with the fact that mind delights in measuring itself thus with matter,—with history. A thought, any thought, pressed, followed, opened, dwarfs ⟨matter⟩ ↑nature↓, custom, & all but itself. (Compare above, p ⟨1⟩19 *LN*)

"All the legends of the beauty of the Houris, tis only a commentary on thy beauty" &c

The fancy carries out all the sentiments into form, & makes angels in the sky & or⟨a⟩ganizes remorse into a ⟨Day of⟩ Judgment-Day, & the universe at court; And so we have painted out our heaven & hell.

[132] But I do not know but the ⟨stern⟩ ↑sad↓ realist has an equal or better content in keeping his hard nut. He sees the eternal symmetry, the world persisting to be itself, the unstooping morals of Nature, and says, I can trust it. There is no fancy in my innate uniform essential perception of Right, unique though million-formed or -faced⟨,⟩. ⟨t⟩Through all processes, through all enemies the result is Benefit, ⟨the aim⟩Beauty; the aim is the Best. I can well omit this parish propensity of casting it in small, in creeds, in punch pictures, [133] as the popular religions do, into Westminster catechisms; Athanasian creeds; Egyptian, Christian, ⟨or⟩ Mahometan⟨s⟩ or Hindoo paradises & hells. I will not be the fool of fancy, nor a child with toys. The positive degree is manly, & suits me better: the truth is stranger & grander than the gayest ⟨fiction⟩ ↑fable↓. I cling to astronomy, botany, zoology, as read by the severe Intellect, & will live & die assured that I cannot go out of the Power & Deity which rule in all my experience whether sensuous or spiritual.
↑August '7⟨3⟩4 Is all or any of these 2 pp. printed?↓[106]

[134]   Fame.
I confess there is sometimes a caprice in fame, like the unnecessary eternity given to these minute shells & antediluvian fishes, leaves, ⟨&⟩ ferns, ↑yea, ripples & rain-drops,↓ which have come safe down

---

[106] The date and query are written in pencil at the top of p. [133] and set off from the text by a long rule in pencil.

through a vast antiquity, with all its shocks, upheavals, deluges, & volcanoes, wherein everything noble in art & humanity had perished, yet these snails, ⟨&⟩ periwinkles, & worthless dead leaves, come staring & perfect into our daylight. ↑—What is Fame, if every snail or ripple or raindrop shares it?↓

[135]   ↑Perhaps printed in "Books"↓[107]
What a boon of civilization & culture is a Dictionary! For a scholar's closet, his dictionaries are the solid indispensable companions, & he can almost spare the rest of his library, or find it for his occasion ⟨in other rooms or⟩ in another house. Liddell & Scott, Spiers, ↑Grimm,↓ Flugel, & Worcester, ↑& Lemprière,↓ the American Encyclopaedia, & the Bi⟨g⟩ographie Générale, & the "Art of verifying dates," would reconcile a mature man to the sale of all his books, & to content himself with ⟨their oc⟩ ⟨borrowing them⟩ ↑consulting them at the libraries↓ as his occasion required.[108] [136] For these dictionaries are the result & condensation of the history of nations, the true history of the mind, and every word a theme for thought. Of course I must add to the above list a good Atlas, a Botany, an astronomy, &c.

[107] "Perhaps printed in 'Books' " is in pencil. The following paragraph is struck through in pencil with a wavy vertical use mark on p. [135] and a diagonal use mark on p. [136], but does not appear in "Books," *Society and Solitude,* 1870.

[108] In addition to the *Nouvelle Biographie Générale,* previously identified, Emerson's list of reference works includes: Henry George Liddell and Robert Scott, *A Greek-English Lexicon* . . . (Oxford, 1843); Alexandre Spiers and Gabriel Surenne, *Spiers and Surenne's French and English Pronouncing Dictionary* (New York, 1856); Jacob Ludwig Karl Grimm and Wilhelm Karl Grimm, *Deutsches Wörterbuch,* 15 vols. (Leipzig, 1854–   ); Johann Gottfried Flügel, *A Complete Dictionary of the English and German and German and English Languages* (London, 1830), vol. 1 of a two-volume set which includes Johann Sporschil, *Vollständiges Englisch-Deutsches und Deutsch-Englisches Wörterbuch* (London, 1830); Joseph Emerson Worcester, *A Dictionary of the English Language* (Boston, 1860); John Lemprière, *A Classical Dictionary* . . . , 6th ed. (London, 1806); the *Encyclopaedia Americana: A Popular Dictionary of Arts, Sciences, Literature, History, Politics and Biography* . . . , ed. Francis Lieber, 13 vols. (Philadelphia, 1829–1833); and Timothy Joseph Haydn, *Haydn's Dictionary of Dates and Universal Information Relating to All Ages and Nations* (London, 1841). Emerson's library includes the works by Spiers, the Grimms (vols. 1–5), Flügel, and Lemprière, as well as the *Encyclopaedia Americana;* his copy of *Haydn's Dictionary* is an American edition (New York, 1867). See Journal NY, p. [90] below.

Alcott said, "the Dictionary requires abandonment."[109]

Genius itself is glad of a dictionary, as "the King himself is served by the field."

Superlative

Rage is not a good fashion.

[137] The boast of Hippias, the Sophist, that he had made with his own hands everything he wore on his person, is found in the Dialogue, Hippias Minor. *Bohn's Plato,* Vol. IV p 270[110]

"Splendide mendax"[111] ⟨is a ‖ . . . ‖ of Horace⟩ [*Odes,* III, xi, 35]

⟨a tiptop carpenter, first rate, A no 1.⟩

> To embellish the moment, the part of woman.
> But stay ⟨a moment⟩, you Messieurs of the sword[.]
> ⟨Gentlemen⟩ of the sword.
> Are prone to be disdainful of /the/your/ word.[112]

[138] Individualism⟨,⟩ or^n Bias, ↑vs. mere practice.↓ 'Tis the difference between progress by railroad & by walking across the broken country. Immense speed, but can only go in one direction.[113]

Sept. 13. Mr Andrew Leighton brought me the volume of Poems of his brother, Robert Leighton, whose address is

---

[109] Cf. p. [180] below.

[110] *The Works of Plato: A New and Literal Version,* 6 vols. (London: Henry G. Bohn, 1848–1855), in Emerson's library; "Hippias Minor" is translated by George Burges.

[111] "Gloriously false."

[112] "But stay . . . Messieurs of the sword" is in pencil. "Gentlemen" is canceled in pencil. "your" is in pencil.

[113] "Individualism . . . practice." is loosely boxed; " 'Tis the difference . . . direction.", struck through in pencil with a vertical use mark, is used in "Natural History of Intellect," *W,* XII, 56.

Spekefield Cottages,
Edge Hill—
Liverpool[114]

See *ML* 180 some references for a good chapter on American life & culture, embodying also my last Williamstown oration.[115]

[139] Parties

I hail every step forward & godward,—every step that makes the republican party the moral party.

It were good under the head of Greatness to collect signal examples of those high steps in character by which a good greatness is dwarfed in the presence of a higher strain, & this again by another. ↑The lie of Desdemona,↓ the^n story of Rabbia; & of my monk, the paragon of humility; & Mrs Hoar's apology for her thieving client;[116] & many suggestions M[ary]. M[oody]. E[merson].'s history & letters would give. As e.g. her definition of fame, her confidence that she "would, in spite of all failures, know one [140] day what true friendship is, for the love of superior Virtue is mine own gift from God." Again "that greatest of all gifts, however small my power of receiving, the capacity, the element to love the all-perfect, without regard to personal happiness—happiness—tis itself." [Notebook] *M[ary] M[oody] E[merson]*, II. p 83

All greatness is in degree, & there's more above than below. Thus, what epic greatness in Dante's Heaven & Hell, revealing new powers in the human mind! What majestic power again in Swedenborg's

[114] The name and address are circled in pencil. Robert Leighton's *Poems* (Liverpool, 1866) is in Emerson's library.

[115] Emerson gave six lectures in his "American Life" series for the Literary Societies of Williams College, November 7–14, 1865; he may be referring here, however, to an earlier appearance before the Adelphi Union, Williams College, July 31, 1865.

[116] Emerson included in *Parnassus* James Freeman Clarke's translation of August Tholuck's inspirational poem "Rabia." The humble monk is Barcena the Jesuit (see "Greatness," *W*, VIII, 313, and p. [166] below). Mrs. Hoar has not been conclusively identified.

Heaven & Hell! What a⟨n⟩gain in the popular Calvinism of the last two centuries! each of these war against the other. Now read the Indian theory: "As to Heaven & Hell, they are inventions of Maya, & are therefore both imaginary," &c   See *supra* p. 120

[141] It costs nothing to a commander to command: & every body, the most powerful, finds himself sometime also in the hands of his commander, it may be a woman, or a child, or a favorite, but usually ⟨&⟩ it is another man organically so related to ⟨his⟩ ↑your↓ ⟨organism⟩, that he easily impresses & leads ⟨his⟩ ↑your↓ will, neutralizes ⟨his⟩ ↑your↓ superiorities;—perhaps has less general ability than his victim, but is superior where the victim is weak, & most desires to be strong. But this locally stronger man has his dragon also, who flies at his throat, & so gives the first his revenges. [142] Thus every one has his master, & no one is stronger than all the others.

The good workman never says, "There, that will do;" but, "there *that is it:* try it, & come again, it will last always." ↑printed in "Success"↓[117]

Every man has his Diminisher & his Enlarger in his set.[118] *V* 99

The ↑good↓ writer wipes out all his footsteps.

I think the habit of writing by telegraph will have a happy effect on all writing by teaching condensation.

[143] Every month of our recent politics has shown that our best friend is our enemy. ↑See↓ *LN* ↑268↓   See *XO* 117,

↑Culture. Civilization.↓
There is ↑a↓ reason to the roasting of eggs,—a best way to do every necessary or habitual act,—to dress oneself, to wash, ⟨to eat⟩ to

---

[117] "The good . . . always.' ", struck through in ink with two vertical use marks, is used in "Success," *W,* VII, 294.

[118] A pencil line is drawn beside this sentence in the left margin, and a short vertical rule is drawn in pencil to the right of "set."

sharpen a razor, to ⟨u⟩carve, to eat,—& not only so, but each of these ⟨acts⟩ is a compound act of many manipulations⟨.⟩, ↑& there is one best way of doing each of these.↓ And civilization or culture consists in having learned by ⟨wide &⟩ cumulative experience a ⟨vast⟩ sum of bests, & surpassing the result of the savage by [144] product of a thousand bests.[119]

[145] Dr Jackson said, he was at Pulpit rock, Lake Superior, when he heard ⟨the⟩ music, like rhythmical organ or vocal chanting, & believed it to come from some singers. But going on a little further, it ceased; in another direction, heard it again; & by & by perceived that it was the beating of the waves on the shore deprived of its harshness by the atmosphere.
He has never seen the subject treated scientifically, he thinks, except in a paper on sound by Dr Wollaston.[120]

———

Mr [John B.] Drake of the Tremont Hotel, Chicago, tells me, that his guests average from 250 to 260 a day through the year.

[146] Life is getting a little too somnambulic[.]
the gaudy sun, & the puffing elements—

[147]   Greatness. See above, p. 140—*LN*
M[ary]. M[oody]. E[merson]. again (in [Notebook MME,] II. p 200) has a vision of her Saint crowned, & the adorers "still ignorant that in this race could exist a capacity to find higher purer enjoyment than belonged to this martyr who was publicly crowned for his labors & motives,—that there were those in whom lived a higher aspiration, ⟨that⟩ ↑who↓ felt there might be a secret union & derivation from the Infinite, without external forms or performances. Society made only for this influx. O where is he hid? In fathomless decrees? He will pass retiring Angels & hide himself under the wing of the Absolute. [148]

[119] This paragraph is struck through on p. [143] with a vertical use mark in pencil.
[120] Charles Thomas Jackson (1805–1880), Lidian Emerson's brother, worked on a geological survey of Lake Superior during the 1840s; Emerson drew upon Jackson's experience in his poem "May-Day" (*W*, IX, 179). William Hyde Wollaston (1766–1828) was an English physicist.

Who cannot shake him off from his own gifts & emanations which Jesus revealed." &c. &c. [Notebook] *M. M. E.* II. [201-]202

[149] ——
Poetry teaches the enormous force of a few words, & in proportion to the inspiration checks loquacity.[121] The reading of a new poet frees the mind, teaches the power of the old names & symbols, & shames us again into new compression. Always to begin, to give a new glance at the fact or subject, & from the deepest centre,—is the rule, & to abhor counters, or lines, or words, to fill up.

——
It is with a book as it is with a man. We are more struck with the merits of a man who is well-mannered, ⟨&⟩ well-drest, & ⟨well-wh⟩ well-mounted, than with those of my neighbor in shoddy; and I am a little ashamed to find how much this gay [150] book in red & gold with a leaf like vellum & a ⟨type⟩ palatial page, has opened my eyes to the merits of the poet who⟨m⟩se verses I long since coldly looked over in newspapers or monthlies or in small ⟨un⟩↑cloth-↓bound ⟨collections⟩ ↑volumes↓.

——
The progress of invention is really a threat. ↑Whenever I see a railroad I look for a republic.↓

——
We must take care to ⟨abolish⟩ induct free trade & abolish custom-houses, before the ↑passenger↓ balloons begin to arrive from Europe. And I think the Railroad ⟨secretary⟩ ↑Superintendent↓ has a ⟨double⟩ second & deeper sense when he inscribes his legend over the ways,—"Look out for the Engine!"

[151] Wealth is chiefly convenient for emergenc[i]es. Day by day, every family gets well enough through its common routine, the poor as the rich. ⟨'Tis⟩[122] Only[n] now & then comes a pinch, a sudden & violent call for means; as, a marriage, or a sickness, or a visiter, or a journey, or a subscription that must be met; then it is fortunate & in-

---

[121] This sentence, struck through in pencil with a vertical use mark, is used in "Poetry and Imagination," *W*, VIII, 73.
[122] "Tis" is canceled in pencil.

dispensable to have new power. But emergenc[i]es are in [152] the contract. They will & must occur to every susceptible person. Therefore you must set your daily expense at the famine-pitch, ⟨&⟩ live within your income all the year round, to be ready with your dollars for these occasions. ↑See *VO* 297,↓

[153] Insert "Sweep Ho" in Parnassus.[123]

Oct. 12.
Dreams are mor⟨l⟩e logical sometimes than waking thought. Last night, a robust dream of an insurrection of the American St Antoine quarter. The insurgent masses filled the grand ⟨street⟩ palatial street, brought lumber, filled it with wooden ⟨building⟩ ↑barricade↓ from side to side, entered thus all the palaces, ↑by the upper windows,↓ & drove out the tenants,

[154] Every word in the language has once been used happily. The ear caught by that ↑felicity↓ retains it, & it is used again & again, as if the charm belonged to the word, & not to the life of thought which so enforced it. These profane uses of course kill it, & it is avoided. But a quick wit can, ⟨at⟩ at an⟨ly⟩y time, reinforce it, & it comes into vogue again[.] ↑printed in Quotation &c↓[124]

Originality & Quotation

Remember, in Hafiz, the original of "John Barleycorn", & "When ⟨I am⟩in death I shall calm recline."[125]

[155] Rock maples are planted for their colors.

---

[123] Ellen Sturgis Hooper's "Sweep Ho!", originally published in *The Dial*, IV (Oct. 1843), 245, appears in *Parnassus* under the title "The Chimney-Sweep."
[124] "Every word . . . again", struck through in ink with a vertical use mark, is used in "Quotation and Originality," *W*, VIII, 193.
[125] This sentence and the subject heading above it are struck through in ink with a vertical use mark; the sentence is used in "Quotation and Originality," *W*, VIII, 186. "John Barleycorn" is a poem by Robert Burns; in Notebook EF, p. [96], Emerson identifies as "Hafiz's John Barleycorn" a poem in *Der Diwan von Mohammed Schemsed-din Hafis*, trans. Joseph von Hammer, 2 vols. (Stuttgart and Tübingen, 1812–1813), I, 429. The quotation is from Thomas Moore, "The Legacy," l. 1.

[156] ↑*To writers.*↓   ↑Poetry & Criticism↓

If your subject, ⟨o writer,⟩ does not appear the flower of the world at this moment, you have not yet rightly got it. No matter what it is, grand or minute, if it has a natural prominence to you, work away until you come to the heart of it; then it will, though it were a fly or a broomstick, as fully represent the central law, & draw all tragic or comic illustration at need, as if it were the History or the Destiny of the Race.[126]

↑See on this point, *FOR* 203.↓

[157] *Dreams.* ↑Oct. 24.↓

I have often experienced, & again last night, in my dreams, the ⟨entire⟩ surprise & curiosity of a stranger or indifferent observer to the trait or the motive & information communicated. Thus some refractory youth, /of/over/ whom I had some guidance or authority, expressed very frankly his dissent & dislike, disliked my way of laughing. I was curious to understand the objection, & endeavored to penetrate & appreciate it, &, of course, with the usual misfortune, that, when I woke & attempted to recover the specification, which was remarkable, it was utterly forgotten. But the fact that I, who must be the author of both parts of the dialogue, am thus remote & inquisitive in regard to one part, is ever wonderful.

[158] ↑Oct. 25.↓

Success in your work, the finding a better method, the better understanding that insures the better performing, is hat & coat, is food & wine, is fire & horse & health & holiday. At least, I find that ⟨if⟩ any success in my work ⟨is the⟩ has the effect on my spirits of all these.[127]

Our sentiment or affection is the dark heat↑,—say blood heat,↓ with which we work out the dull logic of our few daily perceptions. But passion is the ⟨same sentiment at⟩ white heat ↑of the same,↓ shining over the whole horizon of the mind, & showing a thousand

---

[126] This paragraph, struck through in ink with a vertical use mark, is used in "Poetry and Imagination," *W*, VIII, 33-34.

[127] A pencil line is drawn beside this paragraph in the left margin.

thoughts, a thousand means & weapons all around us, which, not being seen before, were as if we had them not.

[159] What his right hand achieveth[128]

I like my neighbor T's manners, he has no deference, but a good deal of kindness, so that you see that his good offices come from no regard for you but purely from his character.[129]

———

Among classes of men do not forget to emphasize Influences.

———

I don't know but I value the name of a thing, that is, the true poet's name for it, more than the thing. If I can get the right word for the moon, or about it,—the word that suggests to me & to all men its humane & universal beauty & significance then I have what I want [160] of it, & shall not desire that a road may be made from my ⟨back door⟩ ↑garden↓ to the moon, or that the gift of this elephant be made over to me.

———

Cunning egotism. If I cannot brag of knowing something, then I brag of not knowing it. At any rate, Brag.

———

At the grave of a poor devil about whom no one ⟨th⟩could think of a single merit to mention, an old Dutchman said, "⟨W⟩Vell, he ⟨w⟩vas a goot schmoker."
↑Of him did not Wordsworth say,
"Enjoys the air he breathes."↓
["Lines Written in Early Spring," l. 12]

[161] The negro, thanks to his temperament, appears to make the greatest amount of happiness out of the smallest capital.

———

Dec. 6.
Mr J[ames]. F[reeman]. Clarke read an entertaining lecture, "What For?" founded on Aristotle's Ten Questions, which gave him a clue

———

[128] This phrase is in pencil.
[129] Edward Emerson identifies the subject of this passage as "probably Mr. Augustus Tuttle, whose farm was a half-mile below on the Turnpike" (J, X, 175n.).

for a liberal assortment of anecdotes. And I am not the person to accuse the elasticity of his association of ideas.

Mrs Grenville Temple Winthrop
  (Frances Marie Heard)
  White House, East Cowes, I[sle]. of Wight[130]

[162] Ali Ben Abu Taleb wrote
"He who has a thousand friends" &c[131]

Story of Salvani's begging, *D,* p 369
Father Taylor ⟨I⟩*B* 317
Originality & Quotation *B* 316
Newton's Club B 312
Epitaph by Bentley. *B* 312
horses B 306   Anabasis p 95
Sleep B 298 for Inspiration
C[harles] C[hauncy] E[merson]   B 296[132]

[163] Theresa made herself useful & indispensable to all her neighbors as well as inmates, by being always in possession of a match box, an awl, a measuring-tape, a mucilage pot, a corkscrew; microscope, reading-glass & operaglass;

[164] Concord voted at first for the Soldiers' Monument,

$3 000.00

[130] The name and address of Mrs. Winthrop, who wrote Emerson a letter late in 1866 or in January 1867, are in pencil.

[131] The reference is to "He who has a thousand friends, has not enough; and he who has one foe, has too many," attributed to 'Ali ibn-abi-Tālib (600?–661), son-in-law of Mohammed. Emerson's source is not known. See *JMN,* XIII, 425, and XIV, 56; cf. *W,* IX, 302.

[132] "horses . . . p 95" and "C C E   B 296" are in pencil. The reference to *Anabasis* is probably to III, ii, 17–19, but the edition to which Emerson refers by page number has not been located.

Afterwards added   1 500.00
When it was completed, called upon volunteers
for men & horses & carts to bring & fill up the
earth around the base, to the amount of say $ 50^n
Total cost $4 5⟨0⟩50.00
↑Fay says there will be a balance remaining unexpended of
$200.00↓[133]

The Acton Monument received from the Mass[achuse]tts
Legislature, $2 000.00
The additional cost estimated at $1 000.00
Total.   3 000.00
It is believed to be nearly 100 ft. high.

[165] Lessing said of the astronomers "it is easier ↑for them↓ to meet
disaster than at sea,— —& they make glorious shipw⟨er⟩reck who are
lost in seeking worlds."[134]

The treatises that are written on university reform may be acute or
not, but their chief value to the observer is the showing that a cleavage
is occurring in the hitherto firm granite of the past, and a new era is
nearly arrived.

In Prussia, still in Fred[eric]k the Great's time, "actors were also denied Xn.[Christian] burial." Say 1740 [Stahr, *Life and Works of . . .
Lessing,* 1866, I, 49]

[166]   ↑Books.↓   ↑FOLIO.↓

The advantage of the old fashioned folio, was, that it was safe from the
borrowers.

[133] "Fay says . . . $200.00" is in pencil. Addison Grant Fay, a Concord merchant,
was a member with Emerson of the committee overseeing erection of the Soldiers' Monument, dedicated April 19, 1867.
[134] Adolf Stahr, *The Life and Works of Gotthold Ephraim Lessing,* trans. E. P. Evans,
2 vols. (Boston, 1866), I, 27.

Fences. a paling, a ditch, an arbor-vitae hedge, a pair of small eyes, a pair of large eyes, & at need a whip, at more need a pistol.

———

Diderot was the best natured ⟨man⟩ writer I have read of, who, to help a poor devil who had written a book against him, wrote /a/the/ dedication ⟨of the book⟩ to a pious duke of   . He should stand in the same file of fame as the monk, my type of humility, who, when the Devil came into his cell, ↑rose &↓ gave him his only chair to sit in.[135]

[167] ———
Culture gives all the convenience of the word Jove, in poetry, rhetoric, & conversation.

———

If a man happens to have a good father, he needs less history: he quotes his father on each occasion,—his habits, manners, rules⟨,⟩. If his father is dull & unmentionable, then his ↑own↓ reading becomes more important.

———

Color. At Nantasket beach, I cannot but approve the taste which clothed the emperors in purple, when I see the ↑wet↓ porphyry pebbles.

———

Culture is partial. I know so well that frequent unhappy figure with ⟨cult⟩educated eyes, & uneducated body.[136]

[168]–[170] [blank]
     [171] 'Tis a poor play the imitating a writer's style. It deceives superficial readers, but that which took in the ⟨good writer's⟩ ↑original↓ style, ⟨was, that there⟩ was the thread of life, of fact, in every sentence. This is wanting in the imitation, which is therefore good for nothing.

---

[135] The first sentence of this paragraph is used in "Greatness," *W*, VIII, 315–316. The second sentence is used in "Greatness," *W*, VIII, 313, where the monk is identified as Barcena the Jesuit; see p. [139] above.
[136] A pencil line is drawn beside this entry in the left margin.

The good writer seems to be writing about himself, ⟨but never is,⟩ but has his eye always on that thread of the Universe which runs through himself, & all things.

[172] The word *miracle,* as it is used, only indicates the savage ignorance of the devotee, staring with wonder to see water turned into wine, & heedless of the stupendous ↑⟨wonder⟩ fact↓ of himself being there present. If the water became wine, became fire, became a chorus of angels, it would not compare with the ⟨miracle⟩ familiar fact of his own perception. Here he stands, a lonely thought, harmoniously organized into correspondence with the Universe of mind & matter.[137]

[173] [April 15, 1867.] Yesterday at the funeral of George L. Stearns. Rode to Mount Auburn in a carriage with Mr Alcott & Mr Theophilus Parsons, & had long conversation on Swedenborg. Mr P., intelligent & well-versed on Swedenborg; but his intelligence stops, as usual, at the Hebrew symbolism. Philosopher up to that limit, but there accepts the village-church as part of the sky. In a day not far off this English obstinacy of patching the ecliptic of the Universe with a small bit of tin, will come to an end.[138]

[174] Lessing wrote his father, that "one year is exactly like another" [Stahr, *Life and Works of . . . Lessing,* 1866, I, 28]

I hear the lie through all the sentences of the colonel's speech, even through all the commonplaces about virtue, just as the ear detects the jarring string through all the well-played piece on the piano. Carlyle once said to me, that "in the House of Commons, he ⟨s⟩heard, 'Whoredom, whoredom, whoredom,' in every speech."[139]

[137] "The word . . . present." and "Here he . . . matter." are used in "The Sovereignty of Ethics," *W,* X, 200.
[138] George Luther Stearns (1809–1867) was a Boston manufacturer and antislavery activist; Emerson's notice of him, which originally appeared in the *Boston Commonwealth,* April 20, 1867, is reprinted in *W,* X, 499–507. Theophilus Parsons (1797–1882), a lawyer, later published *Outlines of the Religion and Philosophy of Swedenborg* (1875). Mount Auburn Cemetery is in Cambridge, Massachusetts.
[139] On Carlyle's remark, cf. *JMN,* X, 550.

[175] ——

You comp⟨t⟩lain that the negroes are a base class. Who makes & keeps ⟨them so⟩ ↑the jew or the negro base, who↓ b⟨y⟩ut you, who exclude them from the rights which others enjoy?

Telegraph. I remember when somebody came to Mr R. G. Shaw, senior, & ⟨offered to⟩ wished his aid to a system of telegraph by which he might instantly know in his counting-room when his ships approached the coast: he replied, ⟨that⟩"My ships come soon enough for me when the captain arrives in this room. It is all I can do to attend to them then."[140]

[176] If I were rich, I should get the education I have always wished by persuading Agassiz to let me carry him to Canada; & Dr Gray to go to ⟨the⟩examine the trans-Mississippi Flora; & Wyman should find me necessary to his excavations; and Alvan Clark should make a telescope for me too, & I can easily see how to find the gift for each master that would domesticate me with him for a time. Wise were the American boys who, in Berlin, engaged ⟨th⟩Dr Waagen, the Superintendent of the Royal Gallery, to attend them on their visits to the works of art in the city, & explain them.[141] ↑See also *infra* p 278↓

[177] I thought as the train carried me so fast down the ↑east↓ bank of the Hudson River, that Nature had marked the site of New York with such rare combination of advantages, as she now & then finishes a man or woman to a perfection in all parts, & in all details, as if to show the luxuriant type of the race;—finishing in one what is attempted or only begun in a thousand individuals. [178] The length & volume of the river; the gentle beauty of the banks, the country rising immediately behind the bank on either side; the noble outlines of the Katskills; the breadth of the bays at Croton? & Tarrytown? then ⟨as⟩

[140] The subject of this anecdote is probably Robert Gould Shaw of Gouldsborough, Maine, and Boston, grandfather of the Civil War hero of the same name.

[141] Emerson's list of experts includes Asa Gray (1810–1888), a Harvard botanist; Jeffries Wyman (1814–1874), curator at Harvard's Peabody Museum; Alvan Clark (1804–1887), an American astronomer and lens maker; and Gustav Friedrich Waagen (1794–1868), a German art historian. See Journal NY, pp. [70] and [91] below.

West Point; then, as you approach N. York, the sculptured Pali-
sades;—then, at the city itself, the meeting of the waters; the river-like
Sound; & the ocean at once,—instead of the weary Chesapeake &
Delaware[n] [179] Bays.

[180] Alcott told me, that he found a dictionary fascinating: he
looked out a word, & the morning was gone; for he was led on to another word, & so on & on. It required abandonment.[142]

———

↑"than all the sermons that↓ ⟨"⟩vexed the Sabbath air"[143]

[181] Kepler's ↑three↓ laws ↑(see *BO* 31)↓ dispensed at once⟨, I
remember reading,⟩ with an immensity of special computation, and
Science dispenses always with an encyclopaedia of particulars, by a
new formula, or more universal statement; so that Thoth's [actually
Thamus's] objection to the art of writing, (in Plato,) as destructive of
memory, seems frivolous. [*Phaedrus,* 274E–275A]

Ellen reminds me that, years ago, when I had given her some
memorandum of an account or other paper important to keep, & she
had mislaid it, & could not find it when it was much wanted,—it happened that one night she dreamed where she had put it in a book, & on
waking in the morning, went directly to the place, & found it.

[182]   "⟨B⟩May day" *sent 1 May, 1867, to the following persons*[144]
         Rev. N[athaniel]. L[angdon]. Frothingham
         A[mos]. B[ronson]. Alcott

[142] Cf. p. [136] above.
[143] This entry and the rule above it are in pencil.
[144] *May-Day and Other Pieces* was published by Ticknor and Fields in April 1867.
The list on p. [182] is in three columns, indicated by breaks. The question marks preceding "⟨Mrs Child ⟩" and "C. P. Cranch" are in pencil; "Ellen T Emerson" and "Edith E.
Forbes" were fingerwiped, then restored; "Lucia Briggs" was canceled, then the cancel-
lation stroke fingerwiped. Of those who have not been previously identified or are not easily recognizable, Nathaniel Langdon Frothingham (1793–1870) was a Unitarian minister
in Boston; George Barrell Emerson was Emerson's second cousin; William Henry Furness (1802–1896) was a clergyman, reformer, and Emerson's lifelong friend; William
Emerson (1801–1868) was Emerson's brother; James Elliot Cabot, a close friend, became
the aging Emerson's literary collaborator, later his biographer and literary executor;
Edwin Percy Whipple (1819–1886) was a critic and essayist; Charles Eliot Norton

G[eorge]. B[arrell]. Emerson
W[illiam]. H[enry]. Furness
J[ames]. R[ussell]. Lowell

(1827–1908), a member of the Saturday Club, was editor of the *North American Review* and a founder of *The Nation;* Ebenezer Rockwood Hoar (1816–1895), Elizabeth Hoar's brother, was a lawyer and later Attorney General in the Grant administration; George Bancroft (1800–1891), the historian, was United States minister to Germany; George Partridge Bradford had been Emerson's friend since Divinity School; Thomas William Parsons (1819–1892), a poet, published a translation of Dante's *Inferno* in 1867; John Sullivan Dwight (1813–1893) was a music critic and a former resident of Brook Farm; Thomas Ridgeway Gould (1818–1881) was a sculptor; LeBaron Russell was a physician; Henry James (1811–1882) was a philosopher and father of William and Henry James; Charles Chauncy Shackford was a Unitarian minister; William Rounseville Alger (1822–1905) published *The Poetry of the East* (1856); Franklin Benjamin Sanborn (1831–1917) edited a Boston newspaper and later wrote biographies of Emerson, Thoreau, and Hawthorne; John Milton Cheney, Emerson's Harvard classmate, was a banker in Concord; Sarah Alden Bradford Ripley was a scholar in several languages and widow of Emerson's half uncle Samuel Ripley; Anna Cabot Jackson Lowell was the wife of James Russell Lowell's brother Charles; Paulina Tucker Nash was the sister of Emerson's first wife, Ellen; Susan Haven Emerson was the wife of William Emerson; Sarah Hammond Palfrey wrote articles and novels; Mrs. Charles Elliott Perkins, a niece of John Murray Forbes, received a visit from Emerson at her Burlington, Iowa, home early in 1867; Sarah Swain Forbes was the wife of John Murray Forbes; Susan Bridge Jackson was the wife of Charles T. Jackson; Mrs. C. Dudley was probably the wife of Elbridge Dudley, organizer of Emerson's lectures to the Parker Fraternity; Caroline Wilson was a sculptor; Margaret Forbes was a sister of John Murray Forbes; Sophia Thoreau was Henry Thoreau's sister; Annie Adams Fields (1834–1915) was a writer and the wife of James T. Fields; Sylvina Jackson was possibly the wife of William M. Jackson, a family friend of Lidian Emerson in Plymouth; Mrs. Benjamin Marston Watson had been Mary Russell, teacher of Emerson's son Waldo; Lydia Maria Child (1802–1880) was a writer and antislavery advocate; Elizabeth Ripley was the daughter of Sarah Alden Bradford Ripley; Lucia Jane Russell Briggs, mother of LeBaron Russell, was an old friend of Emerson; Elizabeth Palmer Peabody (1804–1894) was an educator who once ran a bookshop in Boston; Alice Bridge Jackson Arthur was the daughter of Charles T. Jackson; Christopher Gore Ripley (1822–1881), son of Samuel Ripley, became Chief Justice of Minnesota; Sophia Peabody Hawthorne was the novelist's widow; James Bradley Thayer (1831–1902) was a lawyer and the husband of Samuel Ripley's daughter Sophia Bradford Ripley; Abel Adams was Emerson's friend and financial advisor; Grindall Reynolds was pastor of the First Church in Concord; Horatio Woodman (1821–1879) was a lawyer and member of the Saturday Club; Christopher Pearse Cranch (1813–1892) was a clergyman, painter, and poet; Benjamin B. Wiley, a Chicago banker, had entertained Emerson there; Robert Collyer (1823–1912) was a Unitarian minister in Chicago; George Washington Greene (1811–1883) was a biographer, historian, and close friend of Longfellow; John Haven Emerson was William Emerson's son; Charles Timothy Brooks (1813–1883) was a Unitarian clergyman in Newport and translator of Richter's *Titan;* William G. Bryan was a lawyer in Batavia, New York; Samuel Storrow Higginson had graduated from Har-

W[illiam]. Emerson
O[liver]. W[endell]. Holmes
F[rederic]. H[enry]. Hedge
J[ames]. Elliot Cabot
E[dwin]. P[ercy]. Whipple
C[harles]. E[liot]. Norton
E[benezer]. R[ockwood]. Hoar
George Bancroft
George P[artridge]. Bradford
T[homas] W[illiam] Parsons
⟨J[ohn]. S[ullivan]. Dwight⟩
⟨T[homas] R[idgeway] Gould⟩
L[e] B[aron] Russell
Henry James
⟨Louis Agassiz⟩
C[yrus]. A[ugustus]. Bartol
⟨C[harles]. C[hauncy]. Shackford⟩
⟨W[illiam]. R[ounseville]. Alger⟩
F[ranklin]. B[enjamin]. Sanborn
⟨J[ohn]. M[ilton]. Cheney⟩

⟨Mrs [Sarah Alden Bradford] Ripley⟩
Elizabeth Hoar
⟨Mrs ↑A[nna]. C[abot].↓ [Jackson] Lowell⟩
Paulina [Tucker] Nash
⟨Susan [Haven] Emerson⟩
Miss Sarah [Hammond] Palfrey
⟨Mrs C[harles]. E[lliott]. Perkins⟩
Mrs S[arah]. S[wain]. Forbes
Sarah [Freeman] Clarke
Caroline [Sturgis] Tappan

---

vard in 1863; Edmund Hosmer was Emerson's Concord neighbor; Edward Atkinson (1827–1905) was a textile manufacturer and a friend of John Murray Forbes; George Bemis could be either the Boston printer who had published Concord's *Yeoman's Gazette* until 1843, or the lawyer and reformer, a former student of Samuel Ripley, who lived abroad after 1858; Bayard Taylor (1825–1878) was a poet, novelist, and travel writer; and William Willder Wheildon was Emerson's Concord neighbor.

Elizabeth Simmons
Susan [Bridge] Jackson
⟨Mrs. C. Dudley⟩
⟨Mrs [Caroline] Wilson,⟩ Cincin[nati].
Mrs G[eorge]. L Stearns
⟨Margaret Forbes⟩
Sophia Thoreau
Mrs Annie [Adams] Fields
⟨Mrs Sylvina Jackson⟩
⟨Mrs B[enjamin]. M[arston] Watson⟩
↑?↓ ⟨Mrs [Lydia Maria] Child⟩
Ellen T[ucker] Emerson
Edith E[merson]. Forbes
⟨E[dward]. W[aldo]. Emerson⟩
Elizabeth Ripley
Lucia [Jane Russell] Briggs
E[lizabeth]. P[almer]. Peabody.
⟨⟨Ell⟩Alice B[ridge]. [Jackson] Arthur.⟩
⟨C[hristopher]. Gore Ripley⟩
⟨Mrs Sophia [Peabody] Hawthorne⟩

J[ames]. B[radley]. Thayer
Abel Adams
⟨G[rindall]. Reynolds⟩
⟨Horatio Woodman⟩
↑?↓ C[hristopher]. P[earse]. Cranch
S[amuel]. G[ray]. Ward
W[illiam]. E[llery]. Channing
W[illiam]. H[enry]. Channing
⟨C[harles]. Sumner⟩
⟨B[enjamin]. B. Wiley⟩
⟨C[harles]. K[ing]. Newcomb⟩
⟨Robert Collyer⟩
⟨G[eorge]. W[ashington]. Greene⟩
[John] Haven Emerson
⟨C[harles]. T[imothy] Brooks⟩
⟨Walt Whitman⟩

59

⟨⟨‖ . . . ‖⟩W[illiam]. G. B⟨y⟩ryan⟩
⟨S[amuel]. Storrow Higginson⟩
E[dward]. W[aldo] Emerson
⟨Edmund Hosmer⟩
⟨E[dward]. Atkinson⟩
⟨Geo[rge]. Bemis.⟩
⟨E[dmund?]. Hosmer⟩
J[ohn]. G[reenleaf]. Whittier
Bayard Taylor
W[illiam]. W[illder]. Wheildon

[183]^{145} x T[homas]. Carlyle
⟨W[illiam] E[dward] Forster⟩
x ⟨C[harles]. E. Rawlins⟩
x W[illiam]. Allingham
x ⟨Coventry Patmore⟩
x ⟨Charles Bray.⟩
x ⟨Coventry Patmore.⟩
x M[oncure]. D[aniel]. Conway.
x ⟨Mrs A[rthur]. H[ugh]. Clough⟩
? ⟨ J[ohn]. J[ames]. G[arth]. Wilkinson⟩
   Alexander Ireland

[145] The list on p. [183] is in two columns, indicated by a break; the second column is in pencil, as is the question mark preceding "⟨J. J. G. Wilkinson⟩". The x beside a name probably indicates that a copy was sent. Of those who have not been previously identified or who are not easily recognizable, William Edward Forster (1818–1886) was an English Quaker manufacturer, a reformer, and a friend of Carlyle; Charles E. Rawlins, Jr., was a friend of Clough whom Emerson met in Liverpool in 1847; William Allingham (1824–1889) was an Irish poet; Coventry Patmore (1823–1896) was an English poet; Charles Bray was an English manufacturer and author; Moncure Daniel Conway (1832–1907), formerly editor of the Cincinnati *Dial,* was a clergyman in London; Mrs. Arthur Hugh Clough was the widow of the English poet; John James Garth Wilkinson (1812–1899) was a translator of Swedenborg; Alexander Ireland had organized Emerson's lecture tour of England in 1847–1848; Thomas Hornblower Gill was an English poet and writer of hymns; Arthur Helps (1813–1875) was an English historian; Herman Grimm (1828–1901) was a German art critic, historian, and novelist; Mrs. Anne Charlotte Lynch Botta (1815–1891) was hostess to literati in New York City; Richard Frederic Fuller was Margaret Fuller's younger brother; Mary Tyler Peabody Mann was the widow of Horace Mann; and Auguste Laugel was a French author who had met Emerson during an American visit in 1864.

⟨x⟩   T[homas]. H[ornblower]. Gill
⟨x⟩   Arthur Helps
x   Matthew Arnold
x   Herman Grimm.
x   Mrs [Anne Charlotte Lynch] Botta

not sent yet
R[ichard] F[rederic] Fuller
Mrs [Mary Tyler Peabody] Mann
T H Gill
Mrs Botta
⟨Bayard Taylor⟩
Matthew Arnold
[Auguste] Laugel

[184] Mr Justice Maule ⟨said to⟩ ↑requested↓ Sir Cresswell Cresswell, then at the ⟨Bar⟩bar, "to remember that his opponents were vertebrate animals," & "that his manner to them would be offensive from God Almighty to a black beetle." *Pall Mall Gazette*

[185] Aristocracy is always timid. After I had read my lecture on "Natural Aristocracy", in London, and had said, after describing the "man without duties," "who can blame the peasant if he fires his barns?" &c.—Lord Morpeth came to see me at Chapman's, & hoped I would leave out that passage, if I repeated the lecture.[146]

[186] *Song of Nature*
          ↑He lives not who can refuse me,↓
          All my force saith, come & use me.
          ⟨He⟩
          ___

          ⟨A little sun, & ↑a little↓ rain,
          And all ↑the Zone↓ is green again   *VA* 140⟩[147]

[146] Emerson's lecture was on June 17, 1848, and Lord Morpeth (George William Frederick Howard) visited him on June 28; see *JMN,* X, 285.
[147] "He lives ... again" is struck through in ink with a diagonal use mark; "the Zone" is in pencil and is circled in pencil. A revised version of these lines appears in "Fragments on Nature," XXVIII, *W,* IX, 347.

⟨A little⟩A ⟨m⟩May-day sun, a May day rain,
And all the Zone is green again. *VA* 140

[187] Why is Collins's Ode to Evening so charming? It proves nothing, it affirms nothing, it has no thought, no fable, no moral. I find it pleases only as music. It is as if one's head which was full of the sights & sounds of a summer evening—should listen to a few strains of an Aeolian Harp, & find it restoring to him those sights & sounds. 'Tis good whistling.

"—but however taste begins, we almost always see that it ends in simplicity; the glutton finishes by losing his relish for anything highly sauced, & calls for his boiled chicken," &c. Mrs [Hester Lynch] Piozzi, Anecdotes of [*the Late Samuel*] Johnson [. . . , 4th ed. (London, 1786),] p[p. 8–]9

[188] M[ary]. M[oody]. E[merson]. read Tasso in 1826. The story hurries her along, but she has "too little imagination now to relish the inventions, & all the time thinks of Homer's Iliad. Alas! how narrow the limits of human invention. Th⟨ough⟩e 'Paradise Lost' gains in the comparison, yet had *that*ⁿ never been, were it not for these. The moderns write better, but the readers are too wise to enjoy as in an unphilosophical age. A few pulsations of created beings, a few successions of acts, a few lamps held out in the firmament, enable us to talk of *time*, ⟨to⟩ make epochs, write histories,—to do more—to date the revelations of God to man. But these lamps are held to measure out some of the moments of eternity, to divide the history [189] of God's operations in the birth & death of nations,—of worlds. It is a goodly name for our notions of breathing, suffering, enjoying, acting. We personify it. We call it by every name of fleeting, dreaming, vaporing⟨,⟩ imagery. Yet it is nothing. We exist in eternity; dissolve the body, & the night is gone,—the stars are extinguished, & we measure duration by the number of our thoughts, by the activity of reason, the discovery of truths, the acquirement of virtue, the approach to God."[148]

---

[148] "& all the time . . . these." is struck through in ink with a diagonal use mark; two pencil lines are drawn in the left margin beside "—the stars . . . thoughts,".

[190] ——
    ↑Immortality↓[149]
The longest life is but a morning, but where is the Day?

———

No life of a man is an even continuous weaving of thought & will, but intermittent, occasional, spasmodic, by jumps, *staccato,* (is that the right musical phrase?)

Ju⟨ne⟩ly 2, 1867, I happen today to fall upon a line in Aeschylus, "seven gainst Thebes" which says so long ago what Dr Holmes talked of at the last Club,—the alleged standing up of the hair in terror.
    Τρὶχος δ'ορθίας πλοκαμος 'ιστάται
                                    line 563 [actually 564][150]

[191] ↑*Government of the Single Person.*↓
James Arnold said to me, Give this town of New Bedford to one man, say, an Irishman out of the street,—tell him "it is his, & he must manage it the best he can,"—and you will find he will govern it better than it is governed now by sets of men changed every year, who only want each a temporary benefit from it, but do not regard the permanent advantage.[151] See BO 35

[192]   *Writer*
The man in civil society hardly lives who can write his own inner biography for a day; ↑no,↓ but in each attempt ↑he↓ will borrow the common experiences, & pass over his own. But just in proportion to the courage & sense to cling to his own, will his record interest.

———

    In old Boston, a feature not be forgotten was John Wilson, the town crier, who rung his bell at each street corner,—"*Lost!* A child strayed this morning from 49 Marlborough Street; four years old; had on check apron, &c,
Auction! Battery-March-Square, &c &c." He cried so loud, that you could not hear what he said, if you stood ⟨too⟩ near.

[149] "Immortality" is in pencil.
[150] "My hair stands on end."
[151] James Arnold was a merchant in New Bedford.

[193] In the examples of whitewashing, as of Richelieu, Richard III., Jeffries, & Spinosa[,] I do not forget Milton, whose "Paradise Lost" was styled in his day "a ↑profane &↓ lascivious poem"[.] See *Coleridge's Lit[erary]. Remains*, III. 201 [actually 200][152]

↑*History of Liberty.*↓
—The Greeks put the figures of the gods on their coins. We put on ours the head of Liberty. And, a few years ago, when a gold piece came from our mint, without the Liberty cap, there was loud dissatisfaction in the country; as when the statues of ⟨m⟩Mercury were mutilated one night in the temples at Athens.

[194] Pindar, in the First Olympic Ode, speaks with the robust courage of a prize-fighter of his own skill in verse, & as only Kepler & Shakspeare (in the sonnets) have done among the moderns. There is the like ⟨robustness⟩ ↑stoutness↓ in his bust. Wordsworth however has shown a stout heart. ↑& Landor,↓ ↑but none compare with Kepler.↓[153]

[195] *Reading.*
↑I suppose↓ every[n] old scholar has had the experience of reading something in a book which was significant to him, but which he could never find again. Sure he is ↑that↓ he read it there; but no one else ever read it, nor can he find it again, though he buy the book, & ⟨study⟩ ↑ransack↓ every page.[154]

Classic. Mrs Barbauld's Hymns for Children are also Classics, as well as Pope & Dryden.[155]

---

[152] *The Literary Remains of Samuel Taylor Coleridge*, ed. Henry Nelson Coleridge, 4 vols. (London, 1836–1839), in Emerson's library. "Jeffries" is George Jeffreys (1644–1689), an English jurist responsible for the "Bloody Assizes" of 1685; cf. *JMN*, XIV, 364.
[153] "robustness" is canceled in pencil, with the last four letters also canceled in ink. "& Landor," and "but none . . . Kepler." are in pencil. Johannes Kepler (1571–1630), a German astronomer, formulated the three laws of planetary motion.
[154] A pencil line is drawn beside this paragraph in the left margin.
[155] Emerson's library contains Anna Letitia Barbauld's *Hymns in Prose for Children* (London, 1864), a gift to Edith Emerson from her uncle William.

[196] ↑Classes of Men↓¹⁵⁶

Difference between people is felt in this, that ⟨in⟩ whatever is said in conversation, *one* applies directly to himself, as having the quality, or not having it, in his life or in his habit, & instantly recites his adventure with whatever creditable details. He cannot help it, & does not know that he does thus. *Another* judges whether it is truly said, as it agrees or not with his experience, but with an eye to himself as man⟨.⟩, & not ⟨a⟩the private individual.

[197] ↑*The Age.*↓

⟨I have wished to say, that t⟩The good augury of our larger dedication to natural science, in this century, is not so much for the added material power which it has yielded, (though that is conspicuous, & we cannot have too much,) as for the intellectual power it evokes, &, shall I say, the sublime delight ↑with↓ which the intellect contemplates each new analogy appearing between the laws of nature & its own law & life. Newton, ⟨in the fall of the apple⟩ habitually regarding ⟨the single ⟨case⟩ ↑chance↓⟩ ↑a particular fact↓ in nature as an universal ⟨chance,⟩ ↑fact,↓—what happens in one place, at one time, happens [198] in all ⟨cases⟩ ↑places↓ at all times,—happens to see an apple fall, & says to himself, What is the moon but a ⟨big⟨ger⟩⟩ ↑bigger↓ apple ⟨What is the earth⟩ falling also to the earth? What is the earth but a ↑much↓ bigger apple falling to the sun? I see the law of all nature: Every atom falls to every atom. ⟨But⟩ ↑Then comes the farther thought↓ herein I am apprised that this universal material attraction is only ⟨one⟩ ↑a↓ particular example of a more universal law,—⟨of⟩ ↑we will call it,↓ Centrality,—which holds for mind as well as matter.¹⁵⁷

[199] Identity & Centrality, the one law for atom & sphere, ↑for↓ atom & universe, is indignantly denied by children, whether two years old or a hundred, & is ⟨clearly⟩ affirmed by those whose eyes are opened. Every breath of air is the carrier of the Universal mind. The child sees the single fact; the philosopher sees in it only the eternal identity.

¹⁵⁶ "Classes of Men" is in pencil.
¹⁵⁷ With this paragraph, struck through on p. [198] with a vertical use mark in pencil, cf. "Progress of Culture," *W*, VIII, 222.

I cannot yet say accurately what is the analogon of each cosmical or chemical law; ⟨but⟩ Swedenborg, or a possible Swedenborg, can; but I affirm with perfect security ↑that↓ such analogon for each material law observed exists in the spiritual nature, &, that, better than the satisfaction in arriving at the formula [200] of the chemic law, is the spasm ⟨of ecstasy⟩ⁿ ↑(shall I say) of pleasure↓[158] which pervades the intellect in recognizing, however dimly, the instant perception of its equal ⟨truth⟩ ↑holding↓ through heaven, as ↑well as↓ through earth. The laws below are sisters of the laws above.[159]

↑*Medical use of*ⁿ *friendship*↓

Friendship. Linnaeus cured his gout by wood-strawberries, but when Kalm returned from America, Linnaeus was ⟨s⟩laid up with severe gout. But the joy in his return, & the curiosity to see his plants, restored him instantly, & he found his old friend as good as the treatment by wood-strawberries.[160]

[201] When I see my friend, his eyes testify of much more good than his speech, for he leaves me to learn ↑from others↓ the benefits he has just conferred↑.↓ ⟨from others.⟩ ↑Great are the Silences & the Influences. See *NY* 270.↓

M[ary]. M[oody]. E[merson].[161]
A[mos]. B[ronson]. A[lcott].
C[harles]. K[ing]. N[ewcomb].
Tarbox
H[enry]. D[avid]. T[horeau].
S[arah]. M[argaret]. F[uller]
S[amuel]. G[ray]. W[ard].
W[illiam]. E[llery]. C[hanning].

---

[158] "ecstasy" is canceled in pencil; "(shall I say) of pleasure" is in pencil.

[159] This sentence is used in "Progress of Culture," *W*, VIII, 223.

[160] This paragraph, struck through in pencil with a vertical use mark, is used in "Country Life," *W*, XII, 138.

[161] As the entry above suggests, this list contains the names of some "friends" who were most influential on Emerson. "Tarbox" is probably the "Methodist laborer" whom Emerson met during the summer of 1825 in Newton, and who taught that *"men were always praying,* and that *their prayers were answered"* (see *J,* II, 98n.).

C[harles]. S[umner].
J[ames]. E[lliot]. C[abot].

[202] C[harles]. K[ing]. N[ewcomb]. has wonderful power of illustration of his refinements of sentiment by ⟨means⟩ familiar household experiences ↑e.g.
"As the youth sleeping with his brother feels how much he is not to
him."
"Bacon at home in his reflections. When intellectual, then is he himself, as a childless woman restless except when making bread, & is then
happy & singing." See what he says of Bacon further in my transcript
(B)↓[162]

A drunken man who cannot walk can run; so of those whose will is
only when in temper.[163]

[203]   ↑printed in "Quotation &c"↓
⟨The o⟩Original power in men is usually accompanied with assimilating power: and I value in Coleridge his excellent knowledge &
quotations, perhaps as much, possibly more, than his original suggestions. If you give me just distinctions, if you give me inspiring lessons,
imaginative poetry,—it is not important to me whose they are. If I
possess them, & am fired & guided by them, I know you as a benefactor, & shall return to you as long as you serve me so well. I may like
well to know what is Plato's, & what is Goethe's part, & what thought
was always dear to you: [204] but their very worth consists in their
radiancy, & equal fitness to all intelligence. They fit all my facts like a
charm. I respect myself (the more) that I know them.
   Next to the originator of a good sentence is the first quoter of it.
Many will read the book before one thinks of quoting a passage. As
soon as he has done this, that line will be quoted east & west.[164]

   [162] "e.g. . . . (B)" is in pencil. Emerson's "transcript (B)" has not been identified.
   [163] This sentence is preceded on the page by a thoroughly erased passage in pencil,
apparently the same sentence.
   [164] "Original power . . . know them." is struck through in ink with single vertical use
marks on pp. [203] and [204]; "Next to . . . west." is struck through in ink with a vertical use mark. "Original power . . . west." is used in "Quotation and Originality," *W*,
VIII, 190–191. The parentheses around "the more" are in pencil.

Warren Burton used to come to my room in College days, &
said, he did not like to read, & did not remember what he read, but
what I read or quoted to him he remembered, & never forgot.[165]

[205] ――――
We measure religions by their civilizing power. Christianity
gains & thrives against human interests. So does Buddhism, ↑& Stoi-
cism↓ & every high enthusiasm.

Read Parsons's Dante. The translation appears excellent, most
faithful, yet flowing & elegant, with remarkable felicities, as when *Per
tutti i cerchi dello* ⟨i⟩↑'↓*nferno scuri* is rendered "Thro↑ugh↓ all the
dingy circles down in hell."[166]

But Dante still appears to me, as ever, an exceptional mind, a prodigy
of imaginative function, executive rather than contemplative or wise.
Another Zerah Colburn or Blind Tom[,][167] undeniable force of a peculiar kind[,] [206] a prodigy, but not like Shakspeare, or Socrates, or
Goethe, a beneficent humanity. His fames & infamies are so capri-
c↑i↓ously distributed,—What odd reasons for putting his men in inferno! The somnambulic genius of Dante is ⟨re⟩dream strengthened to
the tenth power,—dream so fierce that it grasps all the details of the
phantom spectacle, &, in spite of itself, ⟨retains⟩ clutches & conveys
them into the waking memory, & ⟨re⟩ can recite what every other
would forget.

What pitiless minuteness of horrible details! He is a curiosity like
the mastodon, but one would not ⟨find him⟩ desire such for friends &
contemporaries. Abnormal throughout like Swedenborg. But ⟨fr⟩at a
frightful cost these obtain their fame. A man to put in a museum, but
not in your house. Indeed I never read him, nor reg⟨e⟩ret that I do not.

[165] Burton (1800–1866), a member of Emerson's Harvard class, went on to become
a Swedenborgian clergyman.
[166] *Inferno*, xxv, 13; *The First Canticle, Inferno, of the Divine Comedy of Dante Ali-
ghieri*, trans. Thomas William Parsons (Boston, 1867), p. 150, in Emerson's library.
[167] Zerah Colburn enjoyed brief celebrity during Emerson's boyhood as an arithmetical prodigy; Blind Tom has not been identified.

[207]^{168} from there p 16⟨7⟩5^n
been to conquer p 168^{169}

And two I saw there leaning back to back
Propped like a pair of dishes put to warm
                    [Dante, *Inferno,* 1867,] p 180 [xxix, 71–72]

Dante says
    " 'Living I am, & thou, if craving fame,
    Mayst count it precious,' this was my reply,
    'That I with other notes record thy name.' "
            ↑(Parsons.)↓ Inf[*erno*]. [p. 201] Cant[o]. 32 [ll. 89–91]

_____

        "For tis no task wherewith to be amused
        The bottom of the Universe to paint."
                Cant[o] 32d. l[l]. [6–]7. ↑("Parsons.")↓ [p. 197]

[208]   *"Quotation & Originality"*
subsequent to printing.

_____

Leibnitz predicted the Zoophytes. *Penhoen* Vol 1. 159^{170}
Kant the asteroids
Swedenborg, Uranus.
Goethe found the true theory of colors. Kenelm Digby stated the same
theory in 1580.
Columbus ↑nor ⟨W⟩Cabot↓ not the first discoverer of America
Sir John Franklin went to find the N W passage, & perished. The Es-
quimaux were there already, & are still thriving where he could not
live.
Linnaeus did not find the sexes in plants so soon as Van Helmont by
100 years.

    ^{168} The entries on this page are in pencil.
    ^{169} The page references in this and the preceding line are to Parsons' translation of
Dante's *Inferno;* the phrases are quoted from xxvii, 39, and xxvii, 91, respectively.
    ^{170} Auguste Theodore Hilaire Barchou de Penhoën, *Histoire de la Philosophie Alle-
mande depuis Leibnitz jusqu'a Hegel,* 2 vols. (Paris, 1836), in Emerson's library.

[209] Will not an age or a man come, when it will be thought impertinent to say of him, as soon as ↑he↓[171] is dead, *Poor Mr* A. or B. or C.?

———

There is no saying of Rochefoucauld which is ⟨as⟩ ↑so↓ bitter a satire on humanity ⟨than⟩ ↑as↓ our religious Doctor Johnson's, when some one lamented the death of a friend; "We must either outlive our friends, you know, or our friends must outlive us; and I see no man who would hesitate about the choice." See *Piozzi* [*Anecdotes of . . . Johnson,* 1786,] p. 123

⟨Q⟩Johnson, with his force of thought & skill of expression, with his [210] large learning & his true manliness, with his piety & his obstinate narrow prejudices, & withal his rude impulses, is the ideal or representative Englishman.

Note also the sharp limitations of his thought. I never can read a page of Piozzi without being reminded of Aunt Mary.

[211] Incredulity of truth is apt to be accompanied by credulity of much nonsense, as in our skeptics in religion who go blind into Mr Lister's astrology, & ⟨Mrs⟩ Mr Hume's mesmerism.[172]

Sept. 1, struggled hard last night in a dream to repeat & save a thought or sentence spoken in the dream; but it eluded me at last: only came out of the pulling, with this rag,—"his the deeper problem, But mine the better ciphered."

[212] Sept. 11, ↑1867.↓ Mr H. Lee Warner, of St John's College[,]
                    Cambridge, England.[173]

---

[171] "he" is in pencil.

[172] The Boston City Directory for 1868 lists Thomas Lister as a "professor of astrology"; "Mr Hume" may be Daniel Dunglas Home (1833–1886), a Scottish spiritualist and medium who conducted séances in America during the 1850s.

[173] The list on this page records visitors from England. For H. Lee Warner, cf. p. [226] below. John Russell and Katharine Stanley Russell, Viscount and Lady Amberley, carried a letter of introduction from John Stuart Mill. Mr. Cowper is probably William Francis Cowper, later Cowper-Temple, whom Emerson had met in 1848 in England. James Anthony Froude (1818–1894) was Carlyle's friend and later his literary executor. Anna Barker Ward was the wife of Samuel Gray Ward. Leslie Stephen (1832–1904) was

Oct.   ⟨Lor⟩Viscount & Lady Amberley
Nov. 23   Mr Cowper, Earl Morley, & Lord Cam-
                        perdown with letter from Froude
                        Hon Mr Stratt & Mr J. R. Hollond with
                        letter from Mrs Ward.

_____

                        Rev Leslie Stephen & his wife who is
                        Thackeray's daughter.

[213] Last night talked with Alcott of the clergy, & recalled the aim of my paper ⟨at⟩read at Mr⟨s⟩ Sargent's, on the 16th Sept. I wished to say to those young men, that the supposed embarrassments in the position of young clergymen exist only to feeble wills. They need never consider them. ⟨An⟩ A young man with intellectual imaginative literary turn, wishing to read & write, will still choose the clerical profession, as I did, for those large liberties. The existence of the Sunday, and the pulpit waiting for a weekly sermon, ⟨is all⟩ ↑give him the very conditions or πou στω↓ he wants. That must be filled, & he is armed to fill it. [214] Buckminster, Channing, Everett, Taylor, Beecher, Bushnell, Chapin.ⁿ It is they who are necessary, & the opinions of the floating crowd of no importance whatever. ⟨I want in my preacher a⟩A vivid thought ⟨& pow⟩ ↑⟨which⟩ brings the↓ power to paint it, and, in proportion to the depth of its source, is the ⟨power⟩ ↑force↓ of its projection. I am happy & enriched. I go away invigorated, assisted in my own work, however different from his, & shall not forget to come again for new impulses.[174]

_____

an English man of letters and father of Virginia Woolf. The other persons mentioned here have not been further identified.

[174] Emerson read "The Preacher" on September 16, 1867, at the home of John T. Sargent, a member of the Radical Club. Three segments of this paragraph are used in the published essay, "The Preacher": "the supposed embarrassments . . . consider them.", struck through in pencil with a vertical use mark, is used in *W*, X, 234; "A young man . . . fill it.", struck through in pencil with two vertical use marks from "profession" to the end of the sentence and one vertical use mark through the final two sentences, is used in *W*, X, 230; "A vivid thought . . . impulses.", which has an ink line drawn beside it in the left margin, is used in *W*, X, 234. The Greek words allude to Archimedes' boast that, given "somewhere to stand," he could move the world. The list of celebrated preachers includes Joseph Stevens Buckminster (1784–1812), William Ellery Channing (1780–1842), Edward Everett (1794–1865), Edward Taylor (1793–1871), Henry Ward

[215] At the present day, thoughtful people must be struck with the fact, that the old religious forms are outgrown; ⟨that⟩ as shown by the fact, that every intellectual man is out of the old Church: All the young men of intelligence are on ⟨the si⟩ ↑what is called the↓ radical side. ⟨Will⟩ How long will the people continue to exclude these, & invite the dull men? Beecher told me, that he did not hold one of the five points of Calvinism in a way to satisfy his father.

The good ⟨h⟩Heaven is sending every hour good minds into the world, & all of them /on opening/at maturity/,[175] discover [216] the same expansion, the impatience of the old cramps, and a bias to the new⟨,⟩ ↑interpretation.↓ ⟨i⟩If you hold them in the old ⟨ai⟩ used-up air, they suffocate. Would you in new ⟨Boston⟩ ↑Massachusetts↓ have an old Spain?

The laws of nature are simple to poverty, but their app⟨il⟩lications immense & innumerable.

[217] I wish to find in my preacher that power to illuminate & warm & purify, which I know in the fiery souls which have cheered & lifted my life, &, if possible, that power to clothe every secret & abstract thought in its corresponding material symbol.

↑Seas, &↓ mountains,[n] timber & metals, diamonds & fossils, interest the eye, but it is only with some preparatory or predicting charm; their real value comes only when I hear their meaning made plain in the spiritual truth they cover.

[218] In that Newtonian experiment we wrote of above,[176] there is the surprise & delight of finding identity, which the deep mind always anticipates. The child is perpetually amused by a new object↑,↓[177] by a chip or a wad of wool or a rope or a bed-key,—each of a hundred objects, ⟨se⟩ i⟨s⟩f before unseen, amuses him for a few moments, & he is long in learning, as the man is long in learning, that

-----

Beecher (1813–1887), Horace Bushnell (1802–1876), and Edwin Hubbell Chapin (1814–1880). "⟨I want . . . preacher⟩" is circled in pencil; "⟨which⟩" is circled in pencil.

[175] "on opening" is circled.

[176] See pp. [197]–[198] above.

[177] The comma is in pencil.

each is the old toy in a new mask; that, as Ellery said, ⟨the⟩he found in his youth in the confectioner's shop, that they had but two flavors in all the sweetmeats, [219] peppermint & checkerberry. ↑printed↓[178]

Naturel.

M. S. said on hearing the parts, at Commencement, that she did not care so much for the improvement the speakers showed, as for how much of the boy they had kept.

The beauty of the landscape is in proportion to the ⟨amount⟩ ↑quantity↓ of light,[n] from tragic to celestial.

↑Eloquence.↓

There is the eloquence of conversation,—& the eloquence of public assemblies,—not usually found in the same person[.]

[220] Bossuet said of Fenelon, "He has great talents, ↑much↓ greater than mine; ↑it↓ i⟨t⟩s his misfortune that he has brought himself into a situation in which all his talents are necessary for his defence." ap. *C[harles]. Butler Rem[iniscences].* [(New York, 1824), pp. 142–143]

I cannot recall the passage, without remembering Mrs Mary Parkman's remark to me about my friend S. W.[179]

No matter how hot may be the rivalry & animosity between nations, the love of the cultivated class will be to the most cultivated nation. We scold England, but we would not fight her. We love England, but we never [221] loved our Southern states.

History of Liberty. Pitt advocated the abolition of slavery, but permitted his cabinet to decide against it. But Fox was hardly seated in office

---

[178] "that, as Ellery . . . checkerberry." is struck through in ink with three vertical use marks on p. [218] and two diagonal use marks on p. [219]. "printed" is written in the bottom margin of p. [218].

[179] Mrs. Mary Parkman is probably the Mrs. Parkman, a "friend," who helped to plan and administer Emerson's readings at Chickering's Hall, Boston, in 1869; see *L,* VI, 43n., 53, 102.

before he abolished it. See C[*harles*]. *Butler* [*Reminiscences,* 1824,] p. 15⟨1⟩2

Butler told Fox, he had never read Smith's *'Wealth of Nations.'* "⟨Nor I either,⟩ ↑Neither have I,↓" replied Fox. "There is something in all these subjects which passes my comprehension; something so wide, that I could never embrace them myself, or find any one who did. 'Peace to the strepent horn.' " [*Ibid.,*] p. 154

⟨I cannot so excuse Mr Fox.⟩ Neither can I comprehend the West wind; but I open my hay, when it blows, or lift the anchor, & go to sea, because I know it is the right wind for fair weather.

[222] "What in respect to the orators of Rome is observed by Velleius Paterculus of Cicero, will probably be said of Lord North, that no member of either house of the British Parliament will be ranked among the orators of this country, whom Lord North did not see, or who did not see Lord North." C[*harles*]. *Butler*: Remin⟨s⟩is[*cen*]ces. [1824,] p. 121

⟨This is⟩ Another[n] example of Sterling's Zymoses ⟨as⟩↑, is↓ the dramatic ζυμωσις in Elizabethan age, & the metaphysical, in Germany, in the 19th century.[180]

[223] Napoleon said at Elba, he valued himself most on his Code Napoleon, & would be remembered by it. *Butler* [*Reminiscences,* 1824,] p. 143

⟨B⟩ The rise & fall of gold is believed to be a surer index in politics than any other expression of opinion. But that ↑judgment↓ is only true in reference to events of routine. If a new & unknown contingency occur,—disturbances from Mormonism, ↑or Antimasonry, or Spiritism,↓ or a Know Nothing Party, or a new Civil War like ours in 1861, the bankers are then on the like footing with other people, and as likely to go wrong.

---

[180] "This is" and "as" are canceled in pencil; ", is" is inserted in pencil. The Greek word is the source of the English "zymosis," fermentation.

[224] We have new parties, very powerful too, as, the railroad interest, the manufactur⟨e⟩ing, the mining, the Temperance, or Maine Law, interest,ⁿ the "Eight Hour" or "Labor" interest, concerning which we have not yet sufficient data for computing their /weight/avoirdupois/ in politics: Then the "Woman" question.

[225] the prettiness of the French éloges
Arago's incessant attempts at effect.[181]

Mem.   Philae
         Pyla   [V,] p. 372
See *Plutarch, Morals.* Vol. 5, p. 377.

Excellent page in the chapter in Plutarch, "Whether the Athenians were more warlike or learned?" V.ⁿ p[p]. 376-7 ↑in *Goodwin,* V. ⟨4⟩399↓[182]

[226]   Sept., 1867.
At Northampton, at Mr Hunt's house, Mr Aldrich called upon me, & told me, he was the husband of Mary Standish;—that she had died two years ago; & he introduced to me his son, Ralph W. Emerson Aldrich, a youth of 18 years, now an apprentice in a printing office.[183]

⟨H Warner L⟩
Mr H. Lee Warner, of St John's College, Cambridge, brought me a letter from W[illia]m H[enry]. Channing.[184]

---

[181] Emerson's reference may be to Étienne Vincent Arago (1802–1892), a French poet and playwright, or to Jacques Arago (1790–1855), a novelist and playwright. Less likely in this context is François Arago (1786–1853), a French scientist.
[182] The first three citations of Plutarch on this page are to Emerson's 1718 edition of *Plutarch's Morals;* the inserted cross-reference is to another edition, *Plutarch's Morals, Translated from the Greek by Several Hands,* corrected and revised by William W. Goodwin, 5 vols. (Boston, 1870), for which Emerson wrote an introduction.
[183] "two" is in pencil overwritten in ink. The persons mentioned in this anecdote have not been further identified.
[184] Cf. p. [212] above.

R.↑alph E[merson]. F[orbes].↓¹⁸⁵ looks as if he was afraid that all these ↑beautiful↓ things would vanish before he had time to see them[.]

[227] ——
And now for my fagots of letters!
It occurs that in my doctrine of "Classes," it cannot be forgotten how ⟨we⟩ ↑each↓ passes to ⟨each⟩ ↑every↓ person under different categories. In Boston, I pass for a scholar, but to my friend Ras, only in connexion with the cows, & my name is *Moo.*¹⁸⁶

The god of Victory is said to be one-handed, but Peace gives victory to both sides.

         Max Muller says "Wonderment"   Science of Lang[*uage*].
II Series p 384¹⁸⁷

Sansk[rit].   ⟨‖ . . . ‖⟩Sveta   white
              drapsa   drop
              star-as   stars¹⁸⁸

[228] "How much we include in the idea of God," is said to be the measure of Man. Certainly the Greek Jupiter included all the virtues & vices.

Was there not always something pathetic about those Southern judges & dignitaries coming North to Northampton or Lenox, in summer,— somewhat of superficial & under-bred men, whose early education had been neglected, & who were obliged to face it out by suave manners?

¹⁸⁵ The inserted completion of this name is in pencil.
¹⁸⁶ This entry is written over the penciled letters "A J" and a column of three figures in pencil: "120", "332", and "15".
¹⁸⁷ [Friedrich] Max Müller, *Lectures on the Science of Language,* 2d series (London, 1864); Emerson withdrew this volume from the Boston Athenaeum, October 11–November 19, 1867.
¹⁸⁸ "Sansk. . . . stars" is written, in pencil, vertically at the bottom left of this page.

[⟨1⟩229] Sensibility. It is not the value of the object, but the state of mind in which we see the object,[n] that gives importance to the poem. It is almost too plain to be stated. ⟨In⟩ At the top of my condition, I go into the sculpture gallery, & gaze at the marble Demosthenes, after reading his oration, & I come out & wonder that every visiter does not admire his form & pose, as the best figure in the Exhibition: or, ⟨I⟩in like circumstance, I am shown a cabinet of shells, & can find nothing finer in nature than [230] my selected favorites therein; or, I read Chaucer, or read Herrick, or Donne, or, as lately, Aeschylus,—& the study of that fortunate hour is memorable, & chiefest of ten thousand.

———

Oct. 31.

William F[orbes]. says, that ⟨Ra⟩little Ralph puts on his Society-face, when he sees his new born sister in the cradle, & gives her a condescending kiss.[189]

———

Of sensibility, see in [Notebook] C[harles] K[ing] N[ewcomb] p. 41

[231] *Style.*

Matthew Arnold has the true critical perception & feeling of style, & has shown more insight on that subject than any contemporary. ↑See his "Celts" & his "Homer."↓[190]

———

Earl Grey said, in the old Reform discussion, in 1832, when questioned by the tories, how far he should carry his principle, if the reformers should pull down the ⟨h⟩House of Lords, &c⟨,⟩ ↑?↓—"I shall stand by my order." Carlyle & his followers now stand as the tories did. And in their zeal to stand by the aristo⟨r⟩cratic order, one wishes to ask them,—'But, if your order stands for injustice, do you not [232] ⟨not⟩ belong to a higher order?'[191] Carlyle might well be allowed

———

[189] Edith Forbes was born October 28, 1867.

[190] Emerson withdrew Arnold's *On the Study of Celtic Literature* (London, 1867) from the Boston Athenaeum, October 26–November 1, 1867; his library contains *On Translating Homer: Last Words* (London, 1862).

[191] With the paragraph to this point, struck through in pencil on p. [231] with two vertical use marks, cf. "The Man of Letters," *W*, X, 251–252.

the liberty of genius of riding his hobby very hard,—of riding into the Inferno, if he will,—sure that ↑he↓ has the palm-branch of ⟨the⟩Poets in his hand, & the power of genius will bring him safely back. But under the attraction & prestige of his name, Tennyson, & Ruskin, & Kingsley, men of talent, but far inferior to him in character, venture ⟨to allow themselves⟩ to follow their party or *society*-proclivities also, & subscribe [233] to the infamous Eyre-fund. This is a grave misfortune to themselves, & to their society, which follows them. ⟨Well, t⟩The like wrongs are found here, and our society needs a crusade preached by our Peter Hermits, to shame the Somerset Clubs, & miserable Winthrops & Adamses, spaniels of wealth & fashion & talent, ⟨that⟩ ↑that, being tempted,↓ mislead & tempt the rest.[192]

[234] O. W. Holmes looked last night at an Englishman in the company & said, "strange that these old families, after ages of strength, can't produce any thing better than that! Why, one of us could do better at an hour's warning." Agassiz was vastly amused.

Holmes, in his Lecture to the Medical College, said, that Dr James Jackson's Preface to his "Letters to a Young Physician" compared well with the three famous prefaces, namely, Calvin's to his "Institutes," Casaubon's to ⟨(Polybi?)⟩Polybius & President De Thou's to his History.[193]

[235] 'Tis very certain that when the deluge comes in, it will not mind our garden-fences nor Boston or Portland, ↑nor New York,↓ but only

[192] The "Eyre-fund" was raised by a committee, of which Carlyle was chairman, for defense of Edward John Eyre in connection with his violent suppression, as governor of Jamaica in 1865, of a revolt by black peasants. The Somerset Club, located until 1872 at Somerset and Beacon Streets, was the most fashionable and most exclusive private club in Boston.
[193] Holmes's "Introductory Lecture Delivered before the Medical Class of Harvard University, November 6, 1867," was published as "Scholastic and Bedside Teaching"; see *Medical Essays 1842–1882*, vol. 9 of *The Writings of Oliver Wendell Holmes* (Boston, 1891), p. 310. The other works referred to in this paragraph are James Jackson, *Letters to a Young Physician Just Entering upon Practice* (1855); Isaac Casaubon, commentaries on Polybius (1609, 1617); and Jacques Auguste de Thou, *Historiarum Sui Temporis ab A.D. 1543 usque ad Annum 1607* (1608). "Polybius" is written in ink over "(Polybi?)" in pencil.

the Alleganies & the Andes, or, the lines where the pent-up fires are hottest, & the crust of the globe thinnest.

———

Words.

The vulgar politician, if he finds the honesty of a party or a speaker in his way, disposes of them cheaply as the "sentimental class."

Mr Grattan, English Consul, said at the Dickens dinner in Boston, that "the chairman's four *Vices* were as good as the four cardinal virtues of any other man." Holmes, Hillard, E. G. Loring, & T. J. Stevenson, were the vice presidents.[194]

[236] I rarely take down Horace or Martial at home, but ⟨in the Athenaeum⟩ⁿ when reading in the ⟨Boston⟩ Athenaeum, or Union Club, if I come upon a quotation from either, I resolve on the instant to read them every day. But,—at home again, homely thoughts.

———

Quotation—ye⟨t⟩s, but how differently persons quote! I am as much informed of your genius by what you select, as by what you originate. I read the quotation with your eyes, & find a new & fervent sense:[195] as my reading of Shakspeare's Richard II. has always borrowed much of its interest from Edmund Kean's rendering: though I had that play only at second hand⟨,⟩ from him, through William ↑Emerson↓, who heard him in London. When I [237] saw Kean in Boston, he played nothing so high. The reading of books is, as I daily say, according to the sensibility of the scholar, & the profoundest thought or passion sleeps as in a mine, until an equal mind or heart finds & publishes it. The passages of Shakspeare that we most prize were never quoted until ↑within↓ this century: & ⟨Burke⟩ Bacon & Milton↑'s prose,—↓&

[194] Although Dickens visited Boston in 1867, Emerson's anecdote concerns the dinner of February 1, 1842. Thomas Colley Grattan was consul at Boston, 1839–1846. George Stillman Hillard (1808–1879) was a Boston lawyer; Ellis Gray Loring (1803–1858), Emerson's classmate at Harvard, was a lawyer and later a judge. "T. J. Stevenson" is actually J. Thomas Stevenson, otherwise unidentified.
[195] The paragraph to this point is struck through in ink with a vertical use mark; "I am . . . sense:" is used in "Quotation and Originality," *W*, VIII, 194.

even Burke have their best fame within it. Every one, too, remembers his friends by their favorite poetry or other reading[196] as I recall Shakspeare's "Make mouths at the invisible event," ⟨onl⟩always from M[ary]. M[oody]. E[merson].'s ⟨mou⟩lips. & so many of Antoninus's & Milton's sentences.

[238] Max Muller, ↑Science of Language. II Series. [1864,] p 418↓[197] in one of his lectures, eliminates from the mythology of ⟨I⟩The Iliad & Odyssey, mainly the last, the expressions of eternal religion; such as; "⟨th⟩One omen is good, to fight for one's country"; "for the will of God must be done"; ⟨search thy mind⟩ ↑Mentor says to Telemachus, "Somethings thou wilt thy self perceive in thy mind, & others a divine spirit will prompt; for I do not believe thou wast born & brought up without the will of the gods."—"The gods themselves come to our cities in the garb of strangers, to watch the wanton & the orderly conduct of men." "The gods know all things." "For all men yearn after the gods." "The eye of Zeus, which sees all & knows all."↓

And something like this eclecticism might be applied with success to any narrative, or book, or conversation, of any age,[n] and as fitly to the Old Testament, [239] as to any other early record of any people. My Mr Green, ↑of New York,↓ or his friend, among the North American ⟨f⟩savages, found[198] to his surprise, that, "the Indians also had the spirit." For the intellect, if it ripen at all, will as inevitably arrive at ↑literature &↓ this perception, as at eating or fighting.

[240] The synthesis, the architecture, gives the ⟨w⟩value to all the stories. A thought contents me, but has little value to any other to

---

[196] "The reading . . . other reading", struck through in ink with a vertical use mark, is used in "Quotation and Originality," *W*, VIII, 194. The following quotation is from *Hamlet*, IV, iv, 50.
[197] The full discussion in Max Müller's *Lectures on the Science of Language*, 1864, is actually on pp. 414–419. The first two quotations given by Emerson below do not in fact appear in the passage by Max Müller; the last quotation is attributed by Max Müller to Hesiod rather than to Homer.
[198] "found" was fingerwiped, then restored. Mr. Green and his friend have not been identified.

whom I speak it. But, as soon as greater mental activity, or more scope place that thought with its right foregoers & followers, & we have a right Discourse, we have somewhat impressive & powerful, & the worth of the solitary thought vastly enhanced.

> "Many were wise, if they knew what they said."
> J[ohn]. W. Montclair.[199]

"And where then our English Hampden stood speaking for English liberty, who stands now upholding martial law as the suspension of all law?" *Goldwin Smith.* ⟨|| . . . ||⟩*Life of Pym.* [in *Three English Statesmen* . . . (New York, 1867), p. 44]

[241] Certain resemblances in nature, or unexpected repetitions of form, give keen pleasure when observed; as the figure of the oak leaf on the under shell of the tortoise; the figure of the acanthus leaf in the flame of burning wood; or, better as W[illiam]. E[llery]. C[hanning]. said, that the oak wood burning gives again the form of the oak leaf. So the vegetable form of frost on the window pane suggesting the identity of vegetation with crystallization[.]
↑So the ⟨sou⟩ piping of the hylas in the early days of April sounds at a little distance like the jingle of sleigh bells.↓
↑And Quatremere de Q[uincy]'s theory of Art is resemblance in the work to something of a different kind.↓[200]
↑And why not in the repetition in nature of her scents, as of the orange in the little Sarothra; of black birch & chequerberry,↓

[242] In this old matter of Originality & Quotation, a few points to be made distinctly.
The apparently immense amount of debt to the old. By necessity & by proclivity, & by delight, we all quote. We quote books, & arts & science, & religion, & customs, & laws↑, Yes, & houses, tables &

---

[199] "Many Things in Few Words," l. 10, in *Themes and Translations* (New York, 1867), p. 44, in Emerson's library. "John W. Montclair" was the pseudonym of John William Weidemeyer.
[200] This sentence is circled in ink. Antoine Chrysostôme Quatremère de Quincy (1755–1849), a French archaeologist and politician, wrote studies of Raphael and Michelangelo.

chairs.↓ At first view, 'tis all quotation,—all we have. But presently we make distinction. 1. By wise quotation. Vast difference in the ⟨way⟩ ↑mode↓ of quotation. One quotes so well, that the ↑person↓ quoted is a gainer. The quoter's selection honors ⟨the⟩ & celebrates the author. The quoter gives more fame than he receives aid. Thus Coleridge.[201] Quoting is often merely of a suggestion which the quoter drew ⟨from⟩ but of which the author is quite innocent.

For good quoting, then, there must be originality in the quoter,— bent, bias, delight in the truth, & only valuing the author [243] in the measure of his agreement with the truth⟨,⟩ which we see, & which he had the luck to see first.

And originality, what is that? It is being; being somebody, being your-self, & reporting accurately what you see & are.[202] If another's words describe your fact, use them as freely as you use the language & the alphabet, whose use does not impair your originality. Neither will an-other's sentiment or distinction impugn your sufficiency. Yet in pro-portion to your reality of life & perception, will be your difficulty of finding yourself expressed in others' words or deeds.

[244] And yet—and yet—I hesitate to denounce reading, as aught inferior or mean. When ⟨the⟩ visions of my books come over me, as I sit writing, when the remembrance of some poet comes, I accept it with pure joy, & quit my thinking, as sad lumbering work; & hasten to my little heaven, if it is then accessible, as angels might. For these so-cial affections ↑also↓ are part of Nature & being, ⟨also⟩and the delight in another's superiority is, as M[ary]. M[oody]. E[merson]. said, "my best gift from God." For here the moral nature is involved, which is higher than the intellectual.

————

The new knowledge is nothing but the old knowledge new vamped & painted.

The illusion of knowing. [Notebook] M[ary]. M[oody]. E[mer-son]. II, [18–]19,

————

[201] "The apparently . . . chairs.", struck through in ink with a vertical use mark, is used in "Quotation and Originality," W, VIII, 180 and 178. "At first view, . . . Coleridge." is struck through in ink with a vertical use mark.

[202] "And originality, . . . are." is struck through in ink with a vertical use mark.

[245] Montaigne	born 1533	died 1592
↑J[ulius]. C[aesar].↓ Scaliger	born 1482	died 1558
↑J[oseph]. J[ustus]. Scaliger	born 1540	died 1609↓
De Thou	born 1553	died 1617
Bacon		
Shakspeare[203]		

Quotation & Originality.

Mr Francis A. March, professor in Lafayette College, who sends me an address to the Phi Beta Kappa Society of Amherst College,—and a good discourse it is,—at the close of it, quotes from Thomas Dekker these lines;—

> "The best of men
> That e'er wore earth about him, was a sufferer;
> A soft, meek, patient, humble, ↑tranquil↓ spirit,
> The first true gentleman that ever breathed."[204]

⟨Here then is the original of that French red republican's⟩
No

[246] Dec., 1867. Chicago has 230 000 inhabitants
      St Louis   200 000
      Mattoon Ill. in eleven years 12 000
      Adrian Mich   12 000[205]

C[harles]. K[ing]. N[ewcomb]. 1183 Pine St[206]

 [247] It is not strange that everybody is not handsome, perhaps, but it is a little strange that every any body is not suited with his person, or does not look as he wishes to look. I often notice that nature

---

[203] Page [245] to this point is in pencil.

[204] Francis A. March, *The Scholar of To-day* . . . (Springfield, 1869), p. 24, originally delivered in July 1868. Dekker's lines are quoted from *The Honest Whore*, Part I, V, ii, 491–494.

[205] Emerson lectured in the four listed cities on December 23, 16, 14 and 15, and 26, 1867, respectively.

[206] The address is in Philadelphia, where Newcomb lived from 1866 to 1871; Emerson has made a slight error in copying "8" for "3" in the street number.

makes Punch pictures of her men & women[,] makes a ridiculous nose, or a mean baldness instead of a senatorial one.

——

Sometimes you must speak, if only as Aunt Mary told me, when I was a boy, & quarreled with Elisha Jones & Frank Barrett⟨, &⟩. Dr Ripley sent for them one evening to come to the house, & there made us shake hands: Aunt Mary asked me, "Well, what did you say to them"? "I did not say anything."—"Fie on you! You should have talked about your thumbs, or your toes, only to say something."

[248] The tendency of the new time is toward a religious belief compatible with the expansion of science: And each new school of metaphysics, as Hegel or Comte, is not final or universal, but only an attempt to emphasize one of the irresistible corrections which new science has made necessary.

Photograph for Wiley & E L Brown[207]

[249] The moral sentiment never held to the Hebrew, or the Ptolemaic, or the Tycho Brahe astronomy, but is of an austere mathematic fabric, as the sun & the ether are.

As gravity holds the material system, so Truth holds the intellectual universe staunch.

True genius always purifies. Genius always on the side of morals.

Elemental men, influences, not made for ball-rooms; whose silence signifies more than eloquence.

——

The levity of men is corrected by the perception of the moral destiny.

——

The moral law preserves its eternal newness, & appears to each age new-born: almost abolishing memory by the splendor it [250] lends to the passing moment.

[207] This line is in pencil. Benjamin B. Wiley was a banker in Chicago; Edwin Lee Brown of Chicago managed Emerson's western lecture tour in December 1867.

Admirable chapter of Harriet Martineau, in her "Eastern Life, Present & Past." Vol. 1. p. 230.[208] One would think it had never been read, or that the minds of the readers had been instantly dipped in Lethe. It needs instant republication, & the ↑⟨to be⟩↓ advertisement ↑to be↓ cried in the churches.

It plays into my chapter of Quotation to find this necessity of repetition. If man takes any step, exerts any volition, initiates anything, no matter what, it is law of fate that another man shall repeat it, shall simply echo it. The Egyptian legend got this tyrannical currency[,] [251] ploughed itself into the Hebrew captives.

The Henchman is possible only in the savage ↑or semi savage↓ state. Our age is not intelligent of the Jew. His religion was in ⟨every sinew of his body⟩ every drop of his blood. ⟨We⟩ ↑The↓ Americans cannot understand ⟨the Chinaman, or⟩ these Japanese, who must obey their Tycoon or whatever superior, if he commands *hari-kari:* It is in their heart & head & body to obey, & they say, their head bursts at the dismay into which they are thrown at thought of disobedience. ⟨We cannot⟩ Ourselves are our keys to find out Americans or English by; but they will not ↑quite↓ unlock ↑Chinamen or↓ Japanese. It is not our fault but theirs. They are remains of earlier & now almost extinct formations.

[252] The evidences of all the Christian doctrines, of all the Stoical doctrines, are not stone tables nor miracles, but those wonderful incarnations of Vishnu which still from time to time bring a new moral quality into nature & life-long action[.]

[253] I have no knowledge of trade & there is not the sciolist who cannot shut my mouth & my understanding by strings of facts that seem to prove the wisdom of tariffs. But my faith in freedom of trade, as the rule, returns always. If the Creator has made oranges, coffee, & pineapples in Cuba, & refused them to Massachusetts, I

---

[208] Martineau's work, 3 vols. (London, 1848), is in Emerson's library. The chapter to which Emerson refers is devoted primarily to a description of Philae and to a discussion of Osiris as "manifestation of the Supreme upon earth."

cannot see why we should put a fine on the Cubans for bringing t⟨o⟩hese to us,—a fine so heavy as to enable Mass[achuse]tts men to build costly palm-houses & glass conservatories, ⟨&⟩under which to coax these poor plants to ripen under our hard skies, & thus discourage the [254] poor planter from sending them to gladden the very cottages here. We punish the planter ↑there↓ & punish the ⟨merchant & the⟩ⁿ consumer here for adding these benefits to life.

Tax opium, ↑tax poisons,↓ tax brandy, gin, wine, hasheesh, tobacco, & whatever articles of pure luxury, but not healthy & delicious food.

[255] *Town.*
The town is attractive to families, which has a good hotel⟨, which⟩ ↑good sidewalks,↓ ↑a good town-hall,↓ good schools, a good preacher, a Lyceum, a library; which sends its surveyor, after a snowstorm, with a snow-plough through the streets, & along the sidewalks[.]

[256] Beauty unequally bestowed;—Yes, but the highest beauty is that of expression, and the same man is handsome or ugly as he gives utterance to good or base feeling. I noticed, the other day, that when a man whom I had always remarked as a handsome person, was venting democratic politics, his whole expression changed, & became mean & paltry.
↑That is, Nature distributed vulgar beauty unequally, as if she did not value it; but the most precious beauty, she put in our own hands, that of expression.

———
& the anecdote of Turner ΦB 67—↓[209]

[257] Naples without Vesuvius, or Egypt without Nile[210]

Norton read, the other night, in his lecture, the decree of the Commune of Florence for the rebuilding of the Cathedral, but wholly without effect,ⁿ from the omission, (perhaps the scorn,) of emphasis. It should be read with the cry of a herald.

[209] "That is, . . . 67—" is in pencil.
[210] This entry is in pencil.

"Each Supreme," says H[arriet]. M[artineau]. of the statues of the Egyptian gods [*Eastern Life, Present and Past*, 1848, I, 200]. And why not? & men also, as the sky is perfect & the sea; porphyry & marble & iron & bronze each is perfect & best in its place to the architect, & Roman cement under the sea, $\&^n$ wood & glass.

[258] I noticed, lately ↑ΦB 67,↓ that however highly we value all personal felicities & advantages, yet, in biography, we read with equal interest, that the man was ugly, or that he was poor, or awkward, &c. Of Cardinal De Retz, Tallemant des Réaux writes, "un petit homme noir, qui n'y voyait que de fort près, laid, et maladroit de ses mains en toutes choses." See [*Nouvelle*] *Biographie Generale* [1855–1870, XLII, 47]. ↑Cromwell's warts do him no harm with the most fastidious reader of history.↓

For an extreme case of barbarism, take the Thibetans who eat their dead. See Taine *Nouveaux Essais de Critique* [*et d'Histoire* (Paris, 1865),] p 375[211]

Taine shows the civilizing force of Bouddhism. [*Ibid.,*] p. 375

[259] A banker, Mr Manger, told me, that such is the promise of the investments of the undertakers of the Pacific Railroad, that vaster fortunes will be made in this country, than were ever amassed by private men; that men now alive will perhaps come to own a thousand millions of dollars. 'Tis well that the Constitution of the United States has forbidden entails, and the only defence of the people against this private power is from Death the Distributer.

I have lately had repeated occasion to regret the omission to ask questions,—while there was yet time,—of persons who alone could answer them; & now [260] that these are dead, there is none living who can ⟨answer them⟩give me the ⟨a⟩information. To have been so

[211] Emerson withdrew this volume from the Boston Athenaeum, March 25–May 7, 1868.

easily near the witnesses, & to have neglected ⟨the⟩an opportunity which now the whole world could not restore!

———

An advantage of the mechanical improvements, is, that it has made old age more possible, more tolerable, & more respectable. What with spectacles, artificial teeth, preservation of the hair, trusses, overshoes, drop-lights & sleeping-cars, we can hold this [261] dissolving body staunch & fit for use ten or twenty years longer than our ancestors could.

I wish the American Poet should let old times go & write on Tariff; Universal suffrage; Woman's suffrage; Science shall not be abused to make guns. The poet shall ⟨teach⟩ bring out the blazing truth, that he who kills his brother commits suicide. The gold was not hid in the Black Mountains that one man should own it all. The telegraph shall be open as ⟨lightning⟩ writing is to all men. The grape is [262] fertile, this year, that men may be genial & gentle, & make better laws, & not for their set alone. Thus shall the harvest of 1868 be memorable. The laws shall sternly hold men to their best, & fools shall not be allowed to administer what requires all the wisdom of the wisest.

"Man,—his very bones made out of the refined & purest clay," *Herder?*

[263] I read with interest this line in the II Book of Herodotus, "The Egyptians are the first of mankind who have defended the immortality of the Soul." (In my Beloe's Translation Vol. I. p. 256)[212]

———

"The book which Plutarch wrote to prove the malignity of Herodotus only proves his own." note of Beloe [*ibid.,*] Vol I p 276

———

A "⟨p⟩Piromis descended from a Piromis," read once as if ↑it↓ meant Porphyrogenet, but is now explained that Piromis only means man, [*ibid.,* I,] p 277

***

A crude opinion.
"It is my opinion that the Nile overflows in the summer season, because, in the winter, the sun driven by the storms from his usual course ascends into

[212] *Herodotus,* trans. William Beloe, 3 vols. (London, 1830).

the higher regions of the air above Libya." *Herodotus,* Book II. Beloe Vol 1, p. 177

[264] travellers in Egypt who see nothing but the bats

Miss Martineau, [*Eastern Life, Present and Past,* 1848,] Vol. 1. p 68–9 has drawn the moral of the sand,[213]

———

At Isna   "the whole of the surfaces of these temples being covered with inscriptions. The amount of labor invested here seems to shame all other human industry. It reminds one more of the labors of the coral insect than of those of men." [*Ibid.,*] Vol. 1. p. 92

[265] Extremes meet, & there is no better example than the haughtiness of humility. No aristocrat, no porphyrogenet, can begin to compare with the self-respect of the saint. M[ary]. M[oody]. E[merson]. in her vision of her place in heaven looks very coolly at her "Divine Master." "I approached no nearer the person of my Divine Master—but the Infinite must forever & ever surround me. I had too proud a spirit, too elate, too complacent from constitution, may be, ever to have that affinity to Jesus which his better holier ones have." See [Notebook] *M. M. E. 4th*; p[p], 27⟨8⟩7–8.

[266] It is simply the consciousness, however yet obscure & undefined, of resting on Deity, that destroys all other dignities, or so called divinities, & can well afford to be disgraced & degraded in their presence. "To have less than an angel" (writes M[ary] M[oody] E[merson].) "write only from benevolence, I cannot." See MME. I. 23, Jones Very, in his constant sense of the divine presence, thought it an honor to wash his own face.[214]

[213] In the passage to which Emerson refers, Martineau discusses the "appropriateness" of Egyptian architecture: "Indeed, the pyramids look like an eternal fixing down of the shifting sand-hills. . . . One way or another, the Desert has been a great benefactor to the Egyptians. . . . [I]t has taken a leading part in determining the ideas, the feelings, the worship, the occupation, the habits, and the arts of the people" (I, 69–70).
[214] This anecdote about Jones Very (1813–1880), the mystic and poet whom Emerson first met in 1838, is used in "Works and Days," *W,* VII, 177. Cf. p. [5] above.

[267] Among the men who fulfil the part of the American Gentleman, I place gladly Theodore Lyman, who went in a right spirit to the War, & who now works so faithfully & beneficently in this charge of establishing the pisciculture in Massachusetts.[215]

I understand Dr C[harles]. T. J[ackson]. in talk yesterday to say that the balloon can never be relied on as a machine for travel, since the attempt to resist the wind, & sail against it will tear the balloon to pieces: that there must be wings invented to fly against the wind; and, that gun-cotton which is so light, &, especially, which does not soil the barrel, is the [268] best force yet found. The reliance on a ⟨west⟩ permanent west wind in the upper region of the atmosphere, may hold only ⟨for⟩ over the land, & not over the sea. In the region of the trade-winds, the balloon may be applicable. The project has ceased to be presumptuous, since the ocean telegraph has become a fact.

———

What a divine beneficence attaches to Andrew Johnson! in six troubles, & in seven, he has been an angel to the Republican party, delivering them out of their distresses.
⟨Jeremy Taylor, Herbert, Pascal even, Pythagoras,⟩[216]

[269] Queenie [Lidian Emerson] has made this morning a great discovery in Science, in the application of homoeopathy to sick chicadees.

———

What could Norton mean in saying that the only great men of the American past were ⟨E⟩Franklin & Edwards? We have had Adams, & Channing, Washington, & the prophetic authors of the Federalist, Madison & Hamilton, and, if he had known it, Aunt Mary.

"The eye altering alters all."[217] The saint, with grand healthy perception, in the atheism of Byron reads the ciphers of Eternity,[n] finds in

---

[215] Theodore Lyman (1833–1897), a zoologist, became chairman of the Fisheries Commission of Massachusetts in 1866; beginning in 1868 he was a member with Emerson of the Harvard Overseers.

[216] The names here canceled appear in their proper context on p. [272] below.

[217] The quotation, from William Blake's "The Mental Traveller," l. 62, is used in "Greatness," *W*, VIII, 319.

heathen fables & mythology the veiled truths of theism. A great cosmical intellect is indifferent to the arts, may easily [270] look at them
as poor toys, as he would look at a child's picture alphabet. The saint
only ⟨as⟩ cares that the naturalist detects design ⟨everywhere⟩ in nature;
himself is quite careless of ⟨his⟩ ↑the↓ vaunted evidences. He has vision.

————

Obstructives of the present day are the Pope, with his Encyclical Letter, & his later demonstrations; Bishop of Orleans, Dupanloup; Bishop
of Oxford; the State of New Jersey; Andrew Johnson;[218]

[271]   ↑March, 1868.↓
"Boston exceeds in taxable property the whole state of Missouri by sixteen
million dollars. Ward 4 of this city is taxed for as much property as the whole
city of St Louis." B[oston]. *Daily Advertiser.* [March 5, 1868, p. 1, col. 9]

Attica was only one tenth as large as Massachusetts.

I hold it a proof of our ↑high↓ capabilities that Horatio Greenough
was born in Boston. He gave the plan of the Bunker Hill obelisk.

[272] Can any one doubt that if the noblest saint among the
Buddhists, the noblest Mahometan, the highest Stoic of Athens, the
purest & wisest Christian, Menu in India, Confucius in China, Spinoza
in Holland, could somewhere meet & converse together, they would
all find themselves of one religion, & all would find themselves de-
nounced by their own sects, & sustained by these believed adversaries
of their sects. Jeremy Taylor, George Herbert, Pascal even, Pythagoras,
If these could all converse intimately, two & two, how childish [273]
their ↑country↓ traditions would appear!

---

[218] Pope Pius IX issued in 1864 an encyclical upholding the principles of ultramon-
tanism and criticizing "progress, liberalism and modern civilization." Emerson's specific
complaints against Felix Dupanloup, French prelate and political activist, and against the
Bishop of Oxford and the state of New Jersey, have not been identified.

18 March.
Charles Newcomb said, he liked Catholics born to it, but American⟨s⟩
Catholics were disgusting. And I have never seen any such converts
who did not seem to me insane. As to the stor⟨y⟩ies told yesterday of
the vast tolerance of the New York Jesuits, &c. 'tis the mere gabble of
the auctioneer to sell his wares.   'Tis all a trade in mummy.

I suppose that what Richard Owen told me in London of Turner's
coming to him to ask him to give him the natural history of the mol-
lusk on which the whale fed, he wishing to understand it *ab ovo*
thoroughly, because he was going to paint [274] /"the Whale-
ship"/"Slave-ship"?/, was just that chance of suggestion which I
sought for my "Song of Boston" in going down the harbor, ↑to Nantasket,↓ & in my visit not yet made to Bunker-Hill Monument.[219] We
cannot ⟨have⟩ give ourselves too many advantages, & a hint to the
centre of the subject may spring from these pensive strolls around the
walls.

Turner resembled the portraits of Punch.

[275] Education. The Sunday school man who said, "his class were
already in the Swiss Robinson, & he hoped by next term to get them
into Robinson Crusoe."[220]

Somebody said to a Frenchman in Boston ⟨that⟩ who had gone to see
the "Black Crook," or somewhat of that kind;—"that only gentlemen
should see it:" he answered, "that, none but ladies should go."

Balzac & Scott had the like misery of working like giants to pay debts.

[276] "He causes the wrath of man to praise him, & the remainder of wrath he will restrain." [cf. Ps. 76:10]

[219] Richard Owen (1804–1892) was superintendent of the natural history department in the British Museum. " 'Slave-ship'?" is in pencil; the proper title of J. M. W.
Turner's painting (1840) is "The Slave Ship." For Emerson's "Boston Hymn" (1863),
see *W*, IX, 201–204.
[220] This entry is in pencil.

[277] Clytemnestra says to Agememnon; "At my request, beloved one, step forth from out this car, not planting on the bare ground thy foot, the overturner of Ilion, but on this purple tapestry."[221]

Agamemnon stipulates that some one shall ↑first↓ lo↑o↓se his sandals, lest some envy from the eyes of the gods smite him in trampling in these on vestments of purple; "for greatly do I scruple to w⟨aist⟩aste my substance by spoiling with my feet my wealth, & tissue bought with silver," &c[.]

Clytemnestra replies, "There is the sea,—& who shall drain it?—that ⟨fosters⟩ ↑supplies in abundance↓ the dye ⟨of abundance⟩ of purple, ⟨worth its weight in silver,⟩ ever fresh, the tincture of vestments, &c"————Aeschylus. Agamemnon   Jacobson. p. 163

[278] ——
    29 March. ↑(1869)?↓[222] Yesterday, at the Saturday Club, we had a little talk on the question whether it were desireable to admit no new member who might be unpleasing to any other member: And Long-fellow said, "I am sure there is no man living who could be admitted who would drive me away." Perhaps I do not quote exactly but it was to that effect.

————

I have a problem for an engineer, this,—To what height I must build a tower in my garden, that shall show me the Atlantic Ocean from its top? Where is the Coast Survey?

[279] ["You," said the Bramin Mandanis to the King, (Alexander the Great,) "are the only man whom I ever found curious in the investigation of philosophy at the head of an army." *Strabo* p. 715] *Vincent's Voyage of Nearchus* p. 15[223]

---

[221] The three quotations from *Agamemnon* on p. [277] are from *The Seven Tragedies of Aeschylus,* trans. William Jacobson, 3d ed. (Oxford, 1843), pp. 161–162, 163, and 163, in Emerson's library. The cancellations and insertions in the third quotation are Emerson's revision of Jacobson's translation.
[222] The correct date for this entry is 1868, when March 29 fell on a Sunday.
[223] William Vincent, *The Voyage of Nearchus from the Indus to the Euphrates* . . . (London, 1797); "*Strabo* p. 715" refers to Vincent's citation of his source, an edition which has not been identified.

In physical geography, the spheroidal form of the earth, it seems, plays an important part in neutralizing any disordering the poise & therefore the permanency of climate, &c to any parts of the planet from the elevation of new mountain ranges. See a *note* to p.   of Kant, *"Critique* of Pure Reason".[224]

[280] In an earlier page in this book ↑p. 67↓[225] I wrote some notes touching the so called Transcendentalists of Boston in 18⟨40⟩37. Hawthorne ⟨wro⟩ drew some sketches in his^n Blithedale Romance, but not happily, as I think: rather, I should say quite unworthy of his genius. To be sure I do not think any of his books worthy of his genius. I admired the man, who was simple, amiable, truth loving, & frank in conversation: but I never read his books with pleasure.—they are too young.

In & around Brook Farm, ⟨either⟩ whether ↑as↓ members, boarders, or visiters, were many remarkable persons, whether for character, or intellect, or accomplishments. There was Newcomb, one of the subtlest minds,—I believe I must say—the subtlest observer & diviner of character [281] I ever met,—living, reading, writing, talking there, as long, I believe, as the colony held together: Margaret Fuller, whose rich & brilliant genius no friend who really knew her could recognize under the dismal mask which, it is said, is meant for her in ⟨the⟩Hawthorne's story. C. S. too was known to them all, & I believe a frequent, ⟨&⟩ ↑certainly an↓ honored guest. G[eorge]. P. B[radford]. purest & genialest & humblest of men, with all his Culture. The Curtises,—with their elegance & worth⟨,⟩—were within the fold: Theodore Parker & the Russells were just ⟨without⟩ outside. Mrs Alvord I never knew, but she was a lady in high esteem. There were some devout persons, & many too of varied worth & talent. And, at the head, the integrity, devotion & ability of George & Sophia Ripley. Out of all this company could no better sketches be gained than that poor novel?[226]

---

[224] Immanuel Kant, *Critick of Pure Reason,* trans. Francis Haywood (London, 1838), p. 520n., in Emerson's library.

[225] "p. 67" is in pencil.

[226] Among persons mentioned in this reminiscence who have not been previously identified or may not be easily identifiable, "C. S." is probably Charles Sumner, whose brother Horace lived at Brook Farm, although it may be Caroline Sturgis; "The Curtises"

[282] *Harvard Memorial*[227]   *Class of 1821*

B[enjamin] T[yler] Reed	$ 100.	& contingent 150.
J[ohn]. B[oynton]. Hill	50.	& contingent 50.
R. W. E.	100.	
E[dward] Kent	50.	—& perhaps⟨—⟩ 50.
J[ohn]. M[ilton]. Cheney	25.	
C[harles]. W[entworth]. Upham	50.	
Cyrus Briggs	10.	
Ralph Farnsworth	50.	
Nathaniel Wood	50	
	485	

To this sum B. T. Reed
added — — — —   15.

$ 500.[n]   485

Greek Committee 1867–8[228]

R. W. Emerson
G[eorge]. F[risbie]. Hoar
E[pes]. S. Dixwell
C[harles]. K[napp]. Dillaway
J[ohn]. S. Ropes
J[ames]. C[ushing]. Merrill
F[ranklin] B Sanborn

---

are George William Curtis, later editor of *Harper's Weekly,* and his brother Burrill; "the Russells" are perhaps the family of George R. Russell, who lived in West Roxbury and held a mortgage on the Brook Farm property; "Mrs Alvord" is Anna G. Alvord, who built Brook Farm's "Cottage."

[227] Emerson had been a member since 1865 of the committee planning Harvard's Memorial Hall; at his class's meeting of 1866, he urged contributions from members, and subsequently wrote letters repeating the request (see *L,* V, 476–477). The rule below "50" in the column of figures is in pencil; the final figure "485" is in pencil.

[228] In the following list, "J. S. Ropes" is an error for John Codman Ropes, a Boston lawyer and writer on military topics. In addition to Franklin Sanborn, who has previously been identified, Emerson's colleagues on this Harvard committee included George Frisbie Hoar, a lawyer and later U. S. senator; Epes Dixwell, keeper of a private Latin school in Boston; Charles Knapp Dillaway, former Master of the Boston Latin School; and James Cushing Merrill, a Boston lawyer. William Abbot Everett and Alpheus Crosby have not been further identified.

W[illia]m. Everett
A[lpheus]. Crosby

[283]²²⁹   For Nat[ural] Hist[ory of] Phil[osophy]
copy p 143 Civilization
        141 Commander
        138 Bias
        132 Religious realist
        131 Fancy
        128 Egypt pyramids
        126 Attention
         95 Maya
         80 Good of evil
         76 Heat, Musagetes
         64 Balloon & free trade

[284] [Index material omitted]
[inside back cover] [Index material omitted]

²²⁹ The entries on p. [283] are in pencil. They probably reflect early stages of work on what became Emerson's lecture series "The Natural History of the Intellect," first given at Harvard, April 26–June 2, 1870.

1868–1870

Emerson began Journal NY in March 1868, as he notes on p. [1], and used it through late September or early October 1870, when he began Journal ST. The first dated entry is April 1868 (p. [7]); the last is September 26, [1870] (p. [275]). Three brief entries bear later dates: April 1877 (front cover verso); October 1871 (p. [37]); and 1871 (p. [248]).

The covers of the copybook—marbled brown, green, red, and black paper over boards—measure 17.4 × 21.1 cm. The spine strip and the protective corners on the front and back are of tan leather. "NY" is written in the upper right corner of the front cover. The dates "1868–9" and "1870." appear in a vertical column centered at the top of the front cover.

Including flyleaves (1, 2, 277, 278), there are 280 unlined pages measuring 17.5 × 20.6 cm. Emerson misnumbered pages 226 and 227 as 228 and 229, and repeated 228 and 229 in their proper places without correcting his earlier error. He repeated the sequence of numbers 272 and 273 and did not correct the error or adjust numbering of subsequent pages. Three pages were misnumbered and corrected: 23⟨7⟩8, 23⟨8⟩9, and 2⟨39⟩40. All page numbers are in ink, but two pages were numbered first in pencil: 30 and 31. Eleven pages are unnumbered: 1, 2, 3, 28, 29, 153, 163, 205, 224, 225, and 278. Twenty-two pages are blank: 2, 3, 13, 16, 27, 28, 29, 30, 55, 62, 85, 86, 87, 88, 98, 151, 159, 174, 176, 224, 225, and 246.

Laid inside the front cover are four loose sheets, a business card, and three clippings. One sheet, not in Emerson's hand, contains a poem, "Outward Bound," and is inscribed "M. H. Cobb" and dated October 24, 1860. Three of the loose sheets are in Emerson's hand. One contains index material, omitted here. A second sheet, measuring 17.5 × 11.5 cm, contains a fragment of poetry: "As sings the pinetree in the wind / So sings in the wind a sprig of the pine / The"; cf. "Nature in Leasts," *W*, IX, 297. A third sheet, measuring 20.5 × 20.4 cm, contains the following, substantially identical to the indicated passages in Journal IO (See *JMN*, XIII, 366–367):

" 'I know not of what use is any thing which stops there,' Goethe said. / Hayden said of the English, 'Nature puts them out.' I praise the expansive the still generalizing because it seems as if transition were the essential act of life. Nature forever aims & strives ⟨at a better⟩ at a new ↑& better↓ degree. The same nature in & out of man, the same nature in a river-drop, & in the soul of a hero. *IO* 244 / One class of minds delighting in a bounded fact, & the other class in its relations or corre-spon↑d↓ency to all other facts. *IO* 245 / Lord Elgin, *IO* 248".

97

The business card, on the back of which Emerson wrote his name and "Concord", is that of Berthold T. Steiner, Western Manager, American Literary Bureau, 378 Michigan Avenue, apparently in Chicago.

One clipping, from the *Boston Daily Advertiser*, January 6, 1869, announces a "Grand National Peace Jubilee," an "Extraordinary Musical Festival" to be held in Boston, June 15–17, 1869; a handwritten note at the top, addressed to Emerson and signed by P. F. McKeen, Andover, January 6, asks: "Sha'n't we need our 'Earthquake dresses' to wear to this?" A second clipping contains a short poem, "Coming Across," by H. H. [Helen Hunt], dated Steamship Russia, January 22, 1870. A third clipping, apparently from a Boston area paper, announces "St. Louis in Danger" from shifts in course by the Missouri River and reports a plan to cut an artificial channel.

[front cover]   NY

1868–9
1870.

[front cover verso][1]   ↑Examined, April '77↓[2]

"J'ai pris la vie par le côté poétique."   *Franz Woepke.*[3]

[1]   R W Emerson
March 1868

NY
—
1868
1869
1870

[Index material omitted]

[2]–[3] [blank]

[1] Pasted to the top left of the front cover verso is a printed slip containing the schedule of meeting places for the Concord Social Circle between October 6, 1868, and March 23, 1869. Emerson has entered several changes and additions to the schedule.
[2] "Examined, April '77" is in pencil.
[3] Quoted in Taine, *Nouveaux Essais de Critique,* 1865, p. 394n. Woepke (1826–1864) was a German mathematician and translator of Omar Khayyam.

[4] Harvard College.   Greek Committee 1867–8

R. W. Emerson
G[eorge]. F. Hoar
E[pes]. S. Dixwell
C[harles]. K Dillaway
J[ohn]. S. [actually C.] Ropes
J[ames]. C. Merrill
F[ranklin]. B. Sanborn
A[lpheus]. Crosby
W[illiam] Everett

---

[5] Revolutions.[4]

In my youth, Spinoza was a hobgoblin: now he is a saint. And Milton's "⟨p⟩Paradise Lost" was in his day styled "a profane & lascivious poem." See *LN* 193

When I see ⟨a⟩tracts of blowing sand planted with ↑pitch↓ pinetrees & held fast as if granite slabs had been laid on them, & by the annual fall of the leaves made slowly but surely into a fertile soil;* when I see the Japanese building a steam navy, & ↑their men of rank↓ sending children ⟨of their men of rank⟩ to America for their education; the Chinese, instead of stoning an ambassador if he steps out of the walls of Canton, now choosing Mr Burlingame as their Ambassador to western courts;[5] when I see a good spring of water found by a hazel-twig; and my [6] message sent from Boston to London in sixty seconds. The plough displaces the spade; the bridge displaces the ferryman; the

* ⟨then⟩ ↑when I see ⟨the⟩ farmer,↓ by draining & walling an acre of land, make a small Cuba of his garden, whilst the adjoining acre ⟨without⟩ undrained & unwalled is a small Labrador;

---

[4] "Revolutions." is in pencil.

[5] Anson Burlingame (1820–1870), previously United States minister to China, was appointed by the Chinese in 1868 to lead a delegation to make treaties with the United States and European countries. Emerson and Burlingame were among speakers at a banquet for the Chinese embassy, Boston, August 21, 1868; see *L*, VI, 30, and *W*, XI, 471–474.

press displaces the scrivener; the locomotive the coach; the telegraph the courier.

[7] Apr., 1868.
In the debate on Irish Reform in the House of Commons, 13 March, Mr Bright ⟨said⟩ is ↑thus↓ reported,—"Turning to the questions of the Irish Church & education, he characterized the Government proposition for ⟨for⟩settling them by establishing a Catholic University, as grotesque & imbecile. x x x   He recollected hearing of a man in Buckinghamshire,—he was not a Cabinet ⟨m⟩Minister, he was only a mountebank,—who set up a stall, &, in order to gull the people, offered to sell pills that were very good against an earthquake. That was about the state of things they [8] were in now. The⟨y⟩re was an earthquake in Ireland. No one could deny it. Protestant ascendancy as represented by a State Church in Ireland was inevitably doomed." &c &c[6]

[9] *Greatness.*
    The appearance of a great man draws a new circle outside of our largest orbit, & surprises & commands us. It is as if to the girl fully occupied with her paper dolls, a youth ⟨comes to⟩ ↑approaches↓ & says, 'I love you with all my heart, come to me.' Instantly she leaves all↑—dolls, dances, maids, & youths, & dedicates herself to him.↓ Or,[n] as California in 1849, or the war in 1861, electrified the young men, & abolished all their little plans & projects with a magnificent hope or terror requiring a whole new system of hopes & fears & means. ⟨Wa⟩Our little circles absorb & occupy us as fully as the heavens: we can minimise as infinitely as maximise [10] & the only way out of it is, ↑⟨(forgive the word,)⟩↓ ↑(to use a country phrase,)↓ to kick the pail over, & ⟨give us⟩ ↑accept↓ the horizon instead of the pail, with celestial attractions & influences, instead of worms & mud pies. Coleridge, Goethe, the new Naturalists in astronomy, geology, zoology, the correlations, the Social Science, the new readings of history through ↑Niebuhr, Mommsen,↓ Max Muller, Champollion, ↑Lepsius↓ astonish the mind, & detach it effectually from a hopeless routine. 'Come out of that,' they say, 'you lie sick & doting, only shifting

---

[6] The initial letters of "Cabinet" and "Minister" are underscored twice. The source of this quotation, probably a newspaper, has not been located.

from bed to bed.' And they dip the patient in this Russian bath, & he is at least well awake, & [11] capable of sane activity. The perceptions which metaphysical & natural science cast upon the religious traditions, ⟨& which⟩ are every day forcing people in conversation to take new & advanced position. We have been building on the ice, & ⟨e⟩lo! the ice has floated. And ↑t↓he ↑man↓ is reconciled to his losses, when he sees the grandeur of his gains.

[12]   Quotation & Originality.
For the notice of Antiphanes, see *Plutarch's Morals* [1718,] Vol. II. p. 454   ↑in the Greek Tauchnitz Edition, Vol. I p. 181↓[7]

See Niebuhr's letter to Savigny on the Roman *jugerum, NO* 206

See original of Luttrel's *mot* on Religion, in *NQ* 75

"Whatever I consider, I usurp." *Montaigne*[8]

"Soleo et in castra transire." *Seneca*

"Quod verum est meum est." *Seneca*[9]

M. Gréard says
       "Plutarque ne cite pas pour citer. Il s'approprie ce qu'il emprunte; il est original avec les idées d'un autre." *Gréard*, p. 421[10]

Je reprends mon bien ou je le trouve[11]

[7] *Plutarchi Chaeronensis Varia Scripta Quae Moralia Vulgo Vocantur*, 6 vols. (Leipzig: Tauchnitz, 1829–1876), in Emerson's library.
[8] "Upon Some Verses of Vergil," *The Essays of Michael Seigneur de Montaigne*, trans. Charles Cotton, 2d ed., 3 vols. (London, 1693), III, 148. Emerson owned volumes 1 and 3 of this edition of the Cotton translation; his copy of volume 2 was in the edition of 1700.
[9] The first citation of Seneca is a condensation of "soleo enim et in aliena castra transire" ("for I am wont to cross over even into the enemy's camp"), *Epistles*, II, 5. The second is "Any truth, I maintain, is my property," *Epistles*, XII, 11.
[10] Actually p. 424 of Octave Gréard, *De la Morale de Plutarque* (Paris, 1866), in Emerson's library.
[11] Cf. Gréard, *De la Morale de Plutarque*, 1866, p. 423: "Plutarque reprend volontiers son bien partout où il le trouve."

[13] [blank]

[14] ↑Henry↓ Clapp said, that "Rev. Dr Osgood was always looking about to see if there was not a vacancy in the Trinity."
He said, "that Greeley knew that he was a self-made man, & was always glorifying his maker."
He said, "that Tuckerman aimed at nothing, & always hit it exactly."[12]

Goethe's letter introducing Madame Szymanowska to Humboldt ran thus; "Since you belong to the Naturalists who hold that everything was produced by Vulcan, I send to you a female Vulcan who fully singes & burns all that still survives." [Friedrich von Müller, *Goethes Unterhaltungen* (Stuttgart, 1870), p. 78][13]

[15] "For aesthetics am I truly born; yet now (1824) too old for these, I turn ever the more to Natural Science;" said Goethe to Müller. [*Ibid.*, p. 79]

↑*Love of Life.*↓
Better bad weather than none, said Prince August von Gotha. "Es ist doch besser schlechtes Wetter als gar keines." [*Ibid.*, p. 83]

↑*Goethe.*↓
Schiller wrote to Humboldt, in 1802, "If G⟨eo⟩oethe had only a spark ⟨e⟩of faith, many things here might be improved." [*Ibid.*, p. 84]

Δυομενος γαρ ομως Ηλιος εστὶν ετι.
a pentameter falsely ascribed to Nonnus.[14] says Müller, p 84.
[*Goethes*] *Unterhaltungen*

[12] Emerson's source for these bons mots is not known. Henry Clapp (1814–1875) was a New York journalist and wit. Rev. Dr. Osgood is probably Samuel Osgood (1812–1880), pastor of the Unitarian Church of the Messiah, New York City, 1849–1869, though it may be Howard Osgood (1831–1911), pastor of Baptist churches in New York between 1857 and 1868. Clapp's other targets are Horace Greeley (1811–1872), editor of the New York *Tribune,* and Henry Theodore Tuckerman (1813–1871), author of essays, criticism, and biographies.
[13] This and the quotations on p. [15] are translated from Müller, a copy of whose book is in Emerson's library as the gift of Herman Grimm.
[14] "In its decline it remains the same" (Ed.).

[16] [blank]

[17] Res ipsa quae nunc religio Christiana nuncupatur erat apud antiquos, nec defuit ab initio generis humani quousque Christus veniret in carnem, unde vera religio quae jam erat cœpit appellari Christiana. *Augustinus. Retr*[*actions*]. *1. 13.* [3]¹⁵

ap, Max Muller "Chips" &c p XI.

Ministers should make their homes attractive. *DL* 5[16]

[18] As ⟨there⟩ I was told in Venice that there were plenty of people who ⟨were⟩ never stirred out of it to the main land, &, as my Mrs Holbrook, with whom I went from Boston to Malta, never went on deck or saw the sea;[17] so it is in sea-ports; the wharves are practically as far from the ocean as are the mountains. A boy born in Boston may often wander with boys down to the wharves[,] see the ⟨boats⟩ ships, boats, & sailors, but ⟨& is⟩his attention is occupied by the rough men & boys, very likely by the fruit ships & ↑their↓ cargoes: ↑specially the molasses casks.↓ His eye may never get beyond the islands & the light house, to the sea. He remains a cockney, &, years later, chances to visit far from his town, the shore where the ocean is not hidden by ships & the wharf population, but fills the horizon: he realizes its wonder for the first time, ↑itsⁿ chill breath comes to him a snuff of defiance↓ & now first ⟨sees⟩ beholds the maker of cities & of civilization, & may come to understand how Greece came to exist, & Tyre, & England.

[19] It takes twenty years to get a good book read. For each reader is struck with a new passage & at first only with the shining & superficial ones, & by this very attention to these the rest are slighted. But with

---

[15] Emerson's source, as he notes below, was [Friedrich] Max Müller, *Chips from a German Workshop,* 4 vols. (London, 1867–1875), I, xi; he withdrew this volume from the Boston Athenaeum, April 4–13, 1868. Max Müller translates the passage as follows: "What is now called the Christian religion, has existed among the ancients, and was not absent from the beginning of the human race, until Christ came in the flesh: from which time the true religion, which existed already, began to be called Christian."

[16] "Ministers . . . *DL* 5" is in pencil.

[17] Emerson met Mrs. Silas P. Holbrook during his voyage of 1832–1833; see *JMN,* IV, 236.

time the graver & deeper thoughts are observed & pondered. New readers come from time to time,—their attention whetted by frequent & varied allusions to the book,—until at last every passage has found its reader & commentator.

[20] ↑May 22.↓ I am delighted today in reading Schw⟨elg⟩egler's account of ⟨Aris⟩Socrates, to have intelligent justice done to Aristophanes. The rogue gets his dues.
           ↑turn to p 45↓[18]

↑July↓   ⟨|| . . . ||⟩*Seashore.*
        Here chimes no clock, no pedant ⟨cl⟩calendar,
        My waves abolish time, dwarf days to hours,
        And give my guest eternal afternoon.[19]

                                              ☞

        [21] ↑June 20.↓ M. Rouher is described by the B[*oston*]. Daily Advertiser's Correspondent "as indispensable to the Emperor as an orator, whilst his business capacity, robust health, & *intelligent initiative* render him a singularly reliable servant." [June 20, 1868, Supplement, p. 1, col. 5][20]

July 13. I have seen Sarah Clarke & her friends at Newport, with great pleasure & content,—↑at least with↓ as much as so bad a traveller & visiter as I, can find. The land & water have the unfailing charm of the sea, which abolishes time, makes it all "afternoon," or

---

[18] The inserted cross-reference is in pencil. Emerson clarified the author's name by writing "Schwegler's" above the corrected misspelling. The account of Socrates is in Albert Schwegler, *Handbook of the History of Philosophy,* trans. James Hutchison Stirling, 2d ed. (Edinburgh, 1868), pp. 39–52, in Emerson's library.

[19] These lines are written in ink over an erased pencil draft of the same poem: "⟨Here is no foolish clock⟩ ↑Here chimes no clock↓ no pedant ⟨almanac⟩ calendar / My waves abolish time, dwarf days to hours / ⟨Make for⟩ ↑⟨And⟩ And give↓ my guest eternal afternoon". "July" is in pencil, and the entire entry is circled in pencil, with one side of the circle extended onto p. [21] to touch the entry describing Emerson's impressions of Newport. The hand, also in pencil, points to the same entry on p. [21].

[20] Eugène Rouher (1814–1884) was French minister of state and chief spokesman for Napoleon III before the Corps Législatif.

vacation, & always tells us how far we are from nature, & that the first poetry is not yet written. ↑See supra, p. 18↓[21]

[22] The admirable sites for building & the combination of so many advantages point plainly to its future as the ⟨best ↑chief↓ watering-place⟩ ↑attractive, water-side↓ in the country.[22] My chief acquisition was the acquaintance of Mrs Helen Hunt, Sarah Clarke's friend, and her poetry I could heartily praise. The sonnet "Thought," & "Ariadne's Farewell," were the best, but all had the merit of originality, ↑elegance,↓ & compression.[23]

[23] Mrs Hunt wished me to admire *George Eliot*'s ↑"↓Spanish Gypsy↑"↓, but on superficial trial by hearing passages, I refused. It was manufactured↑,↓ not natural poetry. Any elegant & cultivated mind can write as well, but ↑she has↓ not ⟨an⟩ insight into nature ⟨& not⟩[n] ↑nor↓ a poetic ear↑.↓ ⟨has she.⟩ Such poetry satisfies readers & scholars too at first sight,— does not offend,— conciliates respect, & it is not easy to show the fault. But let it lie awhile, & nobody will return to it. Indeed time, as I so often feel, is an indispensable [24] element of criticism. You cannot judge of Nahant, or Newport, or of a gallery, or a poem, until you have outlived the dismay or over-powering of a new impression.[24]

I took a volume of Wordsworth in my valise, & read for the first time, I believe, carefully "The White Doe of Rylstone"; a poem on a singularly simple & temperate key, without ornament or sparkle, but tender, wise, & religious, such as only a true poet could write, honoring the poet & the reader.

[25] I transcribe this old scrap.—

[21] A line is drawn beside "charm of the sea . . . written." in the left margin; the inserted cross-reference is boxed on the top and sides.
[22] "best" is canceled in pencil; "chief" is in pencil overwritten in ink, then canceled in ink.
[23] Helen Fiske Hunt, later Helen Hunt Jackson (1830–1885), is represented (as "H. H.") in Emerson's *Parnassus* by five poems, among them the two mentioned here.
[24] In this passage, the quotation marks around "Spanish Gypsy" and the comma following "manufactured" are in pencil; two pencil lines are drawn in the left margin beside "return to it . . . indispensable" at the bottom of p. [23]. George Eliot's "Spanish Gipsy," a dramatic poem, was published in 1868.

The cable is laid, & the courage of man confirmed. No phlegm or dulness can resist that smiting hint. Who shall ever say *Impossible* again? Henceforth, if a thing is desireable, it is really practicable, & whatever you have dreamed of, go instantly & do.

↑The world owes to England↓ ⟨T⟩the two grand gifts of the Century, the Railroad Car, and ↑the↓ Ocean telegra⟨f⟩ph which have given an immense worth to human life, by enabling man⟨kin⟨g⟩d⟩ to pass a thousand miles in the time which once carried him

[26] When Henry Thoreau ⟨came⟩ in his tramp with his companion ↑came↓ to a field of good grass, & his companion hesitated about crossing it, Henry said, "You may cross it, if the farmer is not in sight: it does not hurt the grass, but only the farmer's feelings."

[27]–[30] [blank]
[31]   *Education.*

The treatises written on University Reform may be acute or not, but their chief value to the observer is the showing that a cleavage is occuring in the hitherto firm granite of the past, & a new era is nearly arrived.

See of Self education, *N* 47

In the absence of intellectual men, in the absence of many grades & ranks of power, from the lawfully educated king to the youngest page, our scholar, at his first showing of intellectual power, is hurried from the pupil's desk to the master's chair, & is thus cheated of those perfections which long training & faithful abiding in all the intermediate degrees, alone can give. [See the sequel in *Y* 100]

[32] Go into the school or the college, & see the difference of faculty: Some who lap ⟨up⟩ knowledge as a cat laps milk, & others very slow blockheads.[25]

[25] "up" is circled in pencil, then canceled in ink.

I rejoice to hear that the ball & boat clubs have the best effect on the morals of the college.

———

Cowley considered the use of a University for the cherishing of gifted persons.[26]

———

Of translations, see *DO* 86

———

[33] ↑There are critics who cannot tell a glass from a stone.↓ Write that I may know you. Style betrays you as your eyes do. We detect at once by it ↑whether the writer↓ has a firm grasp on his fact or thought,— exists ⟨in⟩at the moment for that alone,—& so has a new possession to offer us, or, whether he has one eye apologising, deprecatory, ↑turned↓ on his reader. In proportion always to ⟨the gr⟩ ↑your↓ possession of the thought is ⟨the⟩ ↑your↓ defiance of your readers. There is no choice of words for him who clearly sees the truth. That provides him with the best word.[27]

A new poet dazzles us with his lustres, the sparkle of new rhetoric, with his gay vocabulary, shop-new, & it takes some time to see him truly. But I wish to say to him ↑that↓ I like only [34] the important passages.[28] Thus if I read in a newspaper Keats's line,
        "In the large utterance of the early gods,"
                                        ["Hyperion," I, 51]
or Shakspeare's
        "Make mouths at the invisible event,"
                                        [*Hamlet*, IV, iv, 50]
or Tennyson's
        "The wrinkled sea beneath him crawls,"
                                        ["The Eagle," l. 4]

---

[26] Cf. *JMN*, XIV, 304, where Emerson gives Alcott as his source for Cowley's opinion.

[27] "Write . . . word.", struck through in pencil with a vertical use mark, is used in "Poetry and Imagination," *W*, VIII, 33.

[28] The paragraph to this point is struck through in pencil with two vertical use marks on p. [33], and in ink with a single diagonal use mark on p. [34].

or Byron's ↑Ocean,↓

> "↑Thou↓ glorious^n mirror where the Almighty's form
> Glasses itself in tempests —"
>
> [Childe Harold's Pilgrimage, IV, clxxxiii]

↑or Bailey's

> "And his five fingers made five nights in air."↓
>
> [Festus, 3d ed. (London, 1848), p. 82]

or Wordsworth's

> "⟨The⟩A light that ne⟨w⟩ver was on sea or land,"—
>
> ["Elegiac Stanzas Suggested by a Picture
of Peel Castle . . . ," l. 15]

↑or Channing's

> "If my bark sink, 'tis to another sea".↓
>
> ["A Poet's Hope," l. 36][29]

I should keep the paper, or transcribe the passage. I require that the poem should impress me so that ⟨I⟩ ↑it↓ must ⟨return to it,⟩ ↑recall me,↓ or that passages should. And inestimable is the ⟨M⟩ Criticism of Memory as a corrective. We are dazzled, I say, by the new words, & brilliancy of [35] color which occupies the fancy, & deceives the judgment. But ↑all↓ this ⟨all⟩ is easily forgotten⟨—⟩: ⟨⟨but⟩But,⟩ later, the thought, the happy image which expressed it, & which was a true experience of the poet, recurs to mind, & sends me back in search ⟨for⟩ ↑of↓ the book. ⟨Therefore I wish that t⟩The poet should foresee this habit of readers, & omit all but the important passages.[30]

> "Eyes which the beam celestial view
> That evermore makes all things new." Keble[31]

Shakspeare is made up of important passages.

[29] Emerson included in Parnassus the poems by Keats (an excerpt, "Thea"), Shakespeare (an excerpt, "Hesitation"), Tennyson, and Channing. Emerson's library contains the cited edition of Philip James Bailey's Festus: A Poem.

[30] "I require . . . passages.", struck through in pencil with a single vertical use mark on both pages, is used in "Poetry and Imagination," W, VIII, 32.

[31] John Keble, "Morning," ll. 19–20, in The Christian Year: Thoughts in Verse for the Sundays and Holidays Throughout the Year (Philadelphia and New York, 1850), in Emerson's library. See JMN, XIII, 468.

Homer said, ↑"They heal their griefs,↓ for curable are the hearts of the noble."[32]

___

And Zoroaster has three great passages.

___

Young said,
>"Tired Nature's sweet restorer, balmy sleep,
>He, like the world, his ready visit makes
>Where Fortune smiles; the wretched he forsakes,
>And lights on lids unsullied by a tear."[33]

[36]   ↑copied in *CR* 98[–99]↓
Tennyson's Sangrail

When Lycidas has been written, you shall not write an elegy on that key, unless you can do better than ⟨that⟩ ↑Lycidas↓. And so in each style of images or fables, after a best has been shown, you must come up to that, or pass it, or else abstain from ↑the↓ writing.[34] Tennyson has abundant invention, but contents himself with the just enough. He is never obscure or harsh in a new or rare word. Then he has marked virility, as if a surgeon or practical physiologist had no secrets to teach him, but he deals with these as Abraham or Moses would & with ⟨no French or English pruriency⟩ ↑out[n] prudery or pruriency↓. ↑⟨No prude & no pruriency.⟩↓ His inventions are adequate to the dignity of the fable. The gift of adequate expression is his. Bacchic phrenzy in [37] right words in right places— e.g. "is the immediate jewel of their souls".[35]

___

Maud.—A nightingale drunken with his overflowing melody. An animal heat in the verse, & its opulent continuations. The priest is astonished to find a holiness in this Knight-errant ⟨that⟩ ↑which↓ he ⟨knows

___

[32] "Shakspeare . . . passages.", struck through in pencil with one vertical and one diagonal use mark, is used in "Poetry and Imagination," *W*, VIII, 33. "Homer . . . noble.' ", struck through in pencil with a diagonal use mark, is used in "Poetry and Imagination," *W*, VIII, 33. The quotation is from the *Iliad*, XIII, 115.

[33] *Night Thoughts*, I, 1–4; Emerson included these lines in *Parnassus*, as "Sleep."

[34] "you shall not . . . writing." is set off by a faint ink parenthesis before and a faint pencil parenthesis after.

[35] This phrase has not been located in Tennyson's poetry.

never⟩ ↑himself never knew↓, & rubs his eyes. ↑The fine invention of Tennyson is in crowding into an hour the slow creations & destructions of centuries↓[.]

It suggests besides in the coming & vanishing of cities & temples what really befalls in long durations on earth. How Science of Ethnology limps after these enchantments!

↑Miracles of cities & temples made by Merlin, like thoughts.
1 Jan. 1870.↓

——————

↑The only limit to the praise of Tennyson as a lyric poet⟨ry⟩ is, that he is alive. If he ⟨should die, & be⟩ ↑were↓ an ancient, there would be none.
October, 1871.↓

[38] Fletcher said, "Let who will write the laws, if I write the songs of the people."[36] So thought the Bramins when they wrote Hindu legends, ↑e.g.↓ that Brahma was the father of all men, but not with equal rights,—the Bramins having been born from his head, the warriors from his arms, the laborers & traders from his belly, the artisans from his feet; & thus ⟨⟨was⟩were forever fixed⟩ from their origin their respective ranks⟨.⟩ were ↑for↓ever fixed.

——————

Dionysius the elder, when some one asked him if he was at leisure, replied, "May that never befall me." [*Plutarch*'s *Morals*, 1718, V, 76]

——————

[39] Self respect is the early form in which greatness appears. The man in the tavern asserts his opinion, though the whole crowd takes the other side: the porter or truckman refuses a reward for finding your money, or for pulling you out of the river.[37]

——————

" The superior man thinks of virtue, the small man thinks of comfort." Confucius[38]

---

[36] The original version of this statement appears in *An account of a conversation concerning a right regulation of governments* . . . (1704), in *The Political Works of Andrew Fletcher* . . . (Glasgow, 1749), p. 266; cf. *JMN*, VI, 55.

[37] This paragraph is used in "Greatness," *W*, VIII, 303.

[38] Cf. *JMN*, XV, 370, where Emerson locates this proverb in James Legge, *The Chinese Classics*, 5 vols. (Hong Kong and London, 1861–1872), I, 32.

What I wrote on the last leaf concerning Tennyson is due perhaps to the first reading,—to the new wine of his imagination,—& I
may not enjoy it, or rate it so highly again.   See supra, p. 36-7

[40] It chanced that a dead pine-tree blown down by the wind
fell against another dead pine, & by the friction kindled the ⟨dead⟩
↑dry↓ leaves on the ground. The wind blew the flame, & the whole
forest perished by suicide.

Calvinism is the breath of a hot village of Teutonic peasants, exalted to
the highest power,—their notions of ⟨w⟩right & wrong, their loves &
fears & hatreds, their notions of law & punishment & reward,—all
acute but narrow, ignorant & revengeful, yet devout. [41] Dr Watts's
Hymns are its exponent. I remember that Burnap in the Cambridge
Divinity School used to say, that Calvinism stood on three legs,—Dr
Watts's Psalms & Hymns, Milton's Paradise Lost, & the Westminster
Catechism. ↑—or, was there not a fourth,—⟨our Version⟩ ↑King
James's Translation↓ of the Bible.↓[39]

I should say that the opposite pole of theology was the Hindoo Buddhism, as represented in the prayers of the Bhagvata Purana, which I
have cited in *LN* 89, 95, 120.

We had a story one day of a meeting of the Atlantic Club, when the
copies of the new number ↑of the Atlantic↓ being brought in, ⟨each
man⟩ ↑every one↓ rose eagerly to get a copy, & then each sat down &
read his own article.

[42] Out of ⟨Pow⟩power a party is immensely strong; it stands
for principles, and its opponents have nothing but possession. But the
moment the radical or republican comes into place, he has then to
consider not what should be, but also what can be, which he finds a
very different & very difficult problem. ↑"Did you give Athens the

---

[39] George Washington Burnap (1802–1859) was Emerson's fellow student in the
Harvard Divinity School, and later a Unitarian clergyman in Baltimore.

best laws? 'No', replied Solon, 'but the best ⟨they⟩ ↑it↓ would re-↑c↓eive.' "↓[40]

↑*Old and New.*↓
We read the English & foreign news with relish, the American with disrelish. We read of Socrates, Antoninus, & Menu gladly; not so gladly of our hodiernal churches.

[43] When I remember how easily & ⟨superiorly⟩ ↑happily↓ I think in certain company,—as, for instance, in former years, with Alcott, ↑& Charles Newcomb,↓ earlier with ↑Peter↓ Hunt, though I must look far & wide for the persons & conditions—which yet were real,—& how unfavorable my daily habits & solitude are for this success, & consider also how essential this commerce is to fruitfulness in writing,—I see that I cannot exaggerate its importance among the resources of inspiration. Gurney seemed to me in an hour I once spent with him a fit companion. Holmes has some rare qualities. ↑Horatio↓ Greenough shone, but one only listened ↑to him.↓: So Carlyle, [44] Henry Hedge, George Ward especially, & if one could ever get over the fences, & actually on even terms, Elliot Cabot. But I should like to try George E. Tufts, my brilliant correspondent of three letters; & William B. Wright, of the "Highland Rambles." There is an advantage of being somewhat *in the Chair* of the company,—a little older & better-read,—if one is aiming at searching thought. And yet, how heartily I could sit silent,—⟨&⟩ purely listening, & receptive, beside a rich mind![41]

[45] May ⟨29⟩ 30. Heard Weiss speak ⟨in⟩on the platform of the Free Religious Society,[n] & was struck with his manhood. Use & op-

---

[40] Paraphrased from "Solon," in *Plutarch's Lives*, trans. John Langhorne and William Langhorne, 8 vols. (New York, 1822), I, 216, in Emerson's library.

[41] Of persons mentioned in this paragraph who have not previously been identified, Peter Hunt is Benjamin Peter Hunt, Emerson's pupil at Chelmsford in 1825 and later a contributor to the *Dial* and a scholar on the West Indies; Ephraim Whitman Gurney (1829–1886) was professor of Latin at Harvard, later dean, and a member of the Saturday Club; George Cabot Ward was a New York banker and the brother of Samuel Gray Ward. In the paragraph, an ink dot after "Tufts" has been clarified by a comma in pencil; the comma and dash following "silent" are in pencil; the ampersand in the last sentence is canceled in pencil; and the comma after "listening" is in pencil.

portunity with such rare talent would have made him a great orator. He ⟨has⟩makes admirable points, but ⟨does not advance fast enough, but⟩ ↑has the fault of↓ linger⟨s⟩ing around a point, & repeats it, & dulls it. But sincerity & independence & courage,—↑in short, manhood—↓ he has, which the audience heartily enjoys, & tamer speakers ⟨might⟩ learn a good lesson. He at least vindicates himself as a man, & one of great & subtle resources.[42]

[46] I thought today ⟨of⟩ in the street of a sentence I read in my youth from Aristotle in the "Collectanea Majora[,]"

O μεγαλοψυχος[,]

to the effect that this rushing to a meeting of a Committee or a society is not becoming,—is nowise[n] needful,—if your own thought is really clear & important.[43] They may well wait for it, &, when you arrive, your earnestness & weight will fully compensate the company for waiting↑.↓ ⟨for it.⟩ Besides, if you are collected, & are honestly where you are, the persons & facts on the road are not without benefit from your presence. You can [47] ask, with the philosopher, are not the gods here also? Hurry is for slaves.   o μεγαλοψυχος

Only just ⟨as⟩ ↑so↓ much effort after ⟨or ↑⟨reverence⟩↓ seeking for⟩ order ↑and elevation↓ as appears in a man's thought praises him. Any tendency in the opposite direction is destructiveness, & repels↑.↓ ⟨us.⟩

———

Mrs Sarah Alden Ripley was of so fine a nature that she could well afford to busy herself in any possible household chore. No dust nor grime could stick to the pure silver.

[48] F[rancis]. Lowell thinks we want more teachers at Cambridge on account of the increased number of students: thinks that we should not require Andrews & Stoddard's Grammar, but examine the boy in the Latin book, & see if he can read & write Latin.[44]

---

[42] John Weiss (1818–1879) was a Unitarian minister, a prominent reformer, and biographer of Theodore Parker.

[43] Emerson's library contains Andrew Dalzel, Ἀνάλεκτα Ἑλληνικὰ Μείζονα; sive, *Collectanea Graeca Majora, ad usum Academicae Juventutis Accommodata,* vol. 1 (Boston and Philadelphia, 1833); the Greek words, which also appear on p. [47] below, may be translated "great of soul."

[44] Francis Cabot Lowell was Emerson's Harvard classmate and friend.

Why money should be given to Harvard.   *J* 34

The University wants a professor of reading.
A Shakspeare chair.
The University clings to us.
How important an educator has Scott been!

↑In the Board of Overseers of the College,↓ the^n committee on honorary degrees reported unfavorably on all but the commanding names, and instantly the President ↑Hill,↓ & an Ex-President pressed the action of the Corporation, acknowledging that these men proposed for honors were not very able or distinguished persons, but it was the custom to give these degrees without insisting on eminent merit. I remember that Dr Follen, in his disgust at the Reverend & Honorable Doctors he saw in America, wished to drop the title & be called *Mister*.[45]

[49] Who listens to eloquence makes discoveries. A man who thought he was in earnest, hears, & finds out that he was not.
⟨I would⟩ ↑How we then feel that we could↓ wash the feet of the speaker for the right. *O* 214

↑C[harles]. J[ames].↓ Fox said, "⟨i⟩If he had a boy, he would make him write verses, the only way of knowing the meaning of words" Recollections of Sam[ue]l Rogers [(Boston, 1859), p. 57]   see *PY* 18⟨2⟩3

An^n alderman thinks he has made a point when he says, "I don't know Latin, but" &c[.]

[50] Saint Beuve says in reference to the German theory of plurality of authors of the Iliad, "Plus d'un érudit spirituel, en lisant les *Prolégomènes* de Wolf, se redira avec M. Boissonade cette fine parole du Comique ancien: 'Non, tu ne me persuadéras pas, non, quand

---

[45] Thomas Hill was president of Harvard, 1862–1868; Charles Follen, a German-born poet, taught at Harvard, 1825–1835.

même tu me persuadérais.' " *Portraits Contemp[orains]*. [3 vols. (Paris, 1852),] III. p. 415[46]

In like spirit, one wrote to Wolf, "Tant que je vous lis, je suis d'accord avec vous; dès que je pose le livre, tout cet assentiment s'évanouit." [*Ibid.,* III,] p. 422

[51] What Landor said of Canning is truer of Disraeli, 〈"〉that "he is an understrapper made an overstrapper."[47]

———

June 16, 1868.
In reading these fine poems of Morris, I see but one defect, but that is fatal, namely, that the credence of the reader no longer exists. 〈"King Acrisius".〉
I wrote thus last night, after reading "King Acrisius"; but, this evening, I have read〈,〉 "The Proud King," wherein the fable is excellent, & the story fits this & all times.[48]

[52] The negro should say to the government, your principle is, no tax without representation; but as long as you do not protect me at home & abroad, you do not give me the value for which I have paid. See *O* 194,

———

Each man of thought is surrounded by wiser men than he, if they cannot write as well. Cannot he & they combine? See *O* 259.

———

Beauty is in great part a moral effect. It comes to serenity, to cheerfulness, to benignity, to innocence, to settled noble purpose. It flees from the perplexed, the selfseeking, the cowardly, the mean, the despairing, 〈& t〉the frivolous, & the stupid. Self-respect how indispensable to it! a free & contented air.

———

[46] Emerson withdrew this volume from the Boston Athenaeum, May 7–June 17, 1868.
[47] Cf. *JMN,* IX, 293; Emerson's source for this witticism has not been located.
[48] Both poems are part of *The Earthly Paradise,* vol. I of which appeared in 1868. Cf. *L,* VI, 20.

[53] I believe that wherever railroads are built, ⟨there will be⟩ republics will follow.

The roots of today are in yesterday & the day & days before. Why is this girl always so unaccountably cheerful? Only because the due letter was written & posted yesterday, the valise of her brother's clothes went by the express, & he must have received them hours ago, & there is time this forenoon for all that is to be done. So with the weeks & the months. 'Tis her habit, & every day brings the gay acknowledgment of these petty fidelities, by letter or by the faces of all whom she meets.

[54] Transcend[entalis]m
The word *pay* is immoral. *LM* 53

———

⟨*Talent.*
Intelligence,—yes, but of what kind & aim? There is the intelligence of Socrates, & the intelligence of a thief or a forger.⟩

———

I do not like a foreigner better than the people do, and if it happen that his face is pitted, he is a little more foreign than before.

———

I know a man of undoubted faculty who will be the more respected, ⟨the mo⟩like Dickens, the more you do not see his person.

[55] [blank]
     [56] The ⟨boy⟩youth gets on obscurely well enough from day to day, but once he chances to meet a ⟨bo⟩young man who tells him something. He rolls it over in his mind for a day or two, & must go back to him. ⟨He⟩ ↑The friend↓ has told him his fortune; he has given him his character; he now sees somewhat he never saw, though the same things were close beside him. Every talk with that youth interests him, & all his life has a new look, whilst with him. He does not care longer for his old companions; they are tame & superficial; [57] he wants a witch, he wants a↑n↓ ⟨wise man ↑divine physician↓⟩ ↑interpreter,↓ a poet, a sympathiser; he has heard of books, and finds one at last that reminds him of his friend. This also is a dear compan⟨uon⟩ion.

116

Rulhière said, "I know not why I am called a wicked man, for I never, in the whole course of my life, committed but one act of wickedness." Talleyrand said, "But when will this act be at an end?" *Dumont* p 299[49]

See above p 54

[58] A Manilla full of pepper, & I want only a teaspoonful in a year. I admire the Dutch who burnt half the harvest.[50] 'Tis so with ontology or metaphysics. Dreary to me are the names & the numbers of volumes of Hegel & the Hegelians,—to me, who only want to know at the shortest the few steps, the two steps, or the one taken. I know what step Berkeley took, & recognise the same in the Hindoo books. Hegel took a second, & said, that there are two elements, something & nothing, & that the two are indispensable at every subsequent step, as well as at the first. Well, we have familiarised that dogma, & at least found a kind of [59] necessity in it, ↑even↓ if ⟨we⟩ ↑poor human nature↓ still feels the paradox. Now is there any third step which Germany has made of like importance & renown? It needs no Encyclopaedia of volumes to tell. I want not the metaphysics, but only the literature of them, the man who can humanise this fine science, & give me ⟨only⟩ the results. The adepts only value & rightly the pure geometry, the aerial or ideal bridge ascending from ⟨heaven⟩earth to heaven with arches & abutments of pure reason: I ⟨want only⟩ am⟨e⟩ fully contented if you tell me where are the two termini.[51]

[60]   ↑Enchantments.↓

There are inner chambers of poetry, ⟨and⟩ ↑which↓ only poets enter↑.↓ ⟨them.⟩ Thus loosely we might say, Shakspeare's sonnets are readable only by poets, and it is a test of poetic apprehension,—the value which a reader attaches to them. But also the poem,

[49] Étienne Dumont, *Recollections of Mirabeau and of the First Two Legislative Assemblies of France* (Philadelphia, 1833); Emerson withdrew this volume from the Boston Athenaeum, March 15–April 2, 1870.

[50] "A Manilla . . . harvest." is used in "Natural History of Intellect," *W*, XII, 13.

[51] "I want . . . termini.", struck through in pencil with a vertical use mark, is used in "Natural History of Intellect," *W*, XII, 13.

> "Let the bird of loudest lay
> On the sole Arabian tree," &c &c
> [Shakespeare, "The Phoenix and Turtle," ll. 1–2]

& the "Threnos" that follows it, if published for the first time today anonymously, would be hooted in all journals; and yet such a poem comes ⟨only⟩ ↑but↓ once in a century, & only from a genius.[52] I prize ↑Beaumont & Fletcher's song,↓ "Fountain heads & pathless groves," &c &c in the same way; & Collins's "Ode to Evening," (all but the last verse ↑which is Academical.↓).[53]

[61] Keats[,] ↑⟨as⟩↓ dis⟨covered⟩↑closed↓ by certain lines in his "Hyperion"[,] ↑had↓ this inward skill; & Coleridge showed at least his love & appetency for it. And Ellery Channing wrote lines, at least, of similar delicacy.

Ben Jonson's Songs, including certainly "The faery beam upon you," &c.

And Waller's "Go lovely Rose," &c

And Herbert's "Virtue" & "Easter"

This kind of poetry is not producible now, any more than a right gothic cathedral. It belonged to a time & taste that is not in the world. Perhaps to my ear, "Fountain heads & pathless groves," &c. is the best type of it I carry in my mind.[54]

[62] [blank]

[63] We think we have a key to the affair if we can find that ⟨an⟩ Italian artists were at Agra four centuries ago, & so the Taj is accounted for: Or, if Greeks were in Egypt earlier than we had found, &

---

[52] With "But also . . . genius." cf. Emerson's preface to *Parnassus* (Boston, 1874), p. vi.

[53] "I prize . . . Academical.", struck through in pencil with two vertical use marks, is used in "Poetry and Imagination," *W*, VIII, 55–56. Emerson included the three poems mentioned in this paragraph in *Parnassus*. The quotation from Beaumont and Fletcher is l. 12 of the song "Hence, all you vain delights" (called "Poet's Mood" in *Parnassus*), from *Nice Valour, or The Passionate Mad-Man*, III, i.

[54] "Keats . . . appetency for it.", struck through in pencil with two vertical use marks, is used in "Poetry and Imagination," *W*, VIII, 55; "Ben Jonson's . . . mind.", struck through in pencil with two vertical use marks, is used in "Poetry and Imagination," *W*, VIII, 55–56. Emerson included in *Parnassus* selections from "Hyperion" and the cited poems by Jonson (*The Gypsies Metamorphosed*, ll. 262 ff.), Waller, and Herbert.

ties of one race can be detected, the architectural race that built in both lands. But the wonder is the one man that built one temple; & after that, the creation of two temples or two styles or twenty is easy to accept.

[64] ↑No number of Nays will help: only one Yea.↓

We go to the Artist's studio, & see his plans. They do not satisfy this exigeant eye, which yet knows not what it wants, only knows that these drawings do not ⟨convince & capture⟩ ↑content↓ it. But any number of Nays does not help us in the smallest degree. Nothing will, but the blessed appearance from any quarter of a plan ⟨full⟩ of genius that meets all the conditions, & delights us, and we all say, *That is it.* The Cabots built the Athenaeum; Billings went into it & said, [65] this hall & staircase wants greatness, & ⟨m⟩drew his plans. The Committee & the Cabots assented at once, & Billings was added to the Cabots as one of the Architects.[55] ⟨No⟩

The Moment.   *Leasts.*
Goethe writes from Rome, 1787.
   "I have this year given heed among foreigners, & found that all efficient intelligent men, more or less finer or coarser, hereto come & remain—that the moment is ⟨all⟩everything, & that ⟨every⟩the privilege of an intelligent man consists therein so to bear himself that his life, in so far as in him lies, shall contain the greatest possible number of reasonable, happy moments." *Vol.* XXIX. p. 120[56]

[66]   1868
   16 August. Came home last night from Vermont with Ellen. Stopped at Middlebury on the 11th, Tuesday, & read my discourse on *Greatness, & the good work & influence of heroic scholars.* On Wednesday, spent the day at Essex Junction, & traversed the banks & much of

[55] Hammatt Billings submitted plans to complete the Athenaeum after the original plans proved too expensive; the story is found in Josiah Quincy, *The History of the Boston Athenaeum* (Cambridge, 1851), pp. 231–241, in Emerson's library.
[56] Emerson is translating from *Zweiter Römischer Aufenthalt, Goethe's Werke,* 55 vols. (Stuttgart and Tübingen, 1828–1833), in his library.

the bed of the Winooski River, much admiring the falls, & the noble
mountain peaks of Mansfield ⟨mountain⟩, & Camel's Hump, (which
there appears to be the highest,) & the view of the Adirondacs across
the Lake. In the evening, took the stage to Underhill Centre. And, the
next morning, in unpromising weather, strolled [67] away with Ellen
towards the ↑Mansfield↓ mountain, 4 miles off; &, the clouds gradually rising & passing from the summit, ↑we↓ decided to proceed toward the top, which we reached, (with many rests at the Half-way
House, & at broad stones on the path,) a little before ⟨1'⟩2 o'clock, &
⟨there⟩ found George Bradford at the Mountain House. We were cold
& a little wet, but found the house warm with stoves. After dinner,
Ellen was thoroughly warmed & recruited lying on a settee by the
stove, & meanwhile [68] I went up with Mr Bradford & a party to the
top of "the Chin," which is the highest land in the State,—4 ⟨3⟩400
feet. ↑I have, later, heard it stated 4 389 ft.↓ Lake Champlain lay
below us, but was a perpetual illusion, as it would appear ⟨like⟩ a piece
of yellow sky, until careful examination of the islands in it, & the
Adirondac summits beyond brought it to the earth for a moment; but,
if we looked away ⟨a moment⟩ ↑an instant↓, & then returned, it was in
the sky again. When we reached the summit, we looked down upon
the "Lake of the Clouds," & the party wh⟨o⟩ich [69] reached the
height a few minutes before us, had a tame cloud which floated by
a little below them. This summer, bears & a panther have been seen
on the mountain, & we peeped into some rocky caves which might
house them. We came, on the way, to the edge of a crag, which we
⟨had to⟩ approach↑ed↓ carefully, & lying on our bellies; & it was
easy to see how dangerous a walk this might be⟨e⟩ at night, or in
a snowstorm. The [70] White Mountains—⟨were⟩ ↑it was↓ too
misty to see; but "Owl's Head," near Lake Memphremagog, was
pointed out. Perhaps it was a half mile only from the House to the
top of "the Chin," but it was a rough & grand walk. On such occasions, I always return to my fancy that the best use of wealth would
be to carry a good professor of Geology, & another of Botany, with
you.[57]

[57] See Journal LN, p. [176] above, and p. [91] below.

In the House were perhaps twenty visiters besides ourselves, a Mr Taylor of Cincinnati,—a very intelligent gentleman,—[71] with excellent political views, republican & free-trader: George Bartlett was there with a gay company of his friends, who had come up from Stowe, where he had given a theatrical entertainment of amateurs, the night before. In the evening, they amused us mightily with charades of violent fun. The next morning a man went through the house ringing a large bell, & shouting "Sunrise," & every body dressed in haste, & went down to the piazza. Mount Washington & the [72] Franconia mountains were clearly visible, & ⟨we⟩Ellen & I climbed now the *Nose,* ↑to↓ which the ascent is made easy by means of a stout rope firmly attached near the top, & reaching down to the bottom of the hill, near the House. Twenty people are using it at once at different heights. After many sharp looks at the heavens & the earth, we descended to breakfast.

I found in this company [73] young Hacket, a classmate of William Forbes; Mr Salter of Portsmouth; Wellman, a son of Mr Wellman of ⟨Mr⟩S[amuel]. G[ray]. Ward's house; Phillips, son of the ↑late↓ ⟨G⟩M[oses]. Phillips, ⟨the late⟩ bookseller; & other agreeable people. At 9.30 A.M. Ellen & I, accompanied for some distance ⟨with⟩by George Bradford, set forth on our descent, in the loveliest of mornings, &, parting from Mr B., at one of the galleries, arrived safely at the "Half-Way House,"—there to find a troop of our fellow boarders of the "Underhill House," just mounting [74] their horses to climb the Mountain. They advised us to take a little forest path to the "Mossy Glen," before we continued our journey from this point, which we did, & found a pretty fall. Returning to the Half-Way House, which is empty, & only affords at this time a resting place for travellers, & a barn for ⟨the⟩ horses, we resumed our walk, & arrived, (without other event than a little delay ⟨to pick⟩ ↑among the↓ raspberries,) at Mr [75] Prouty's Hotel at Underhill, say at 1.30; dined↑,↓ ⟨there,⟩ re-packed our trunk, & took a wagon to Stowe, thence the Stage Coach to Essex Junction, & thence the ⟨Rutland⟩ train, which brought us to Burlington, where we spent the night; &, the next morning, the Rutland & B[urlington]. train, which brought us safely to Westminster, Mass[achuse]tts, where Ellen took a wagon for

Princeton, & I continued my railroad ride to Concord, arriving at 6.30 P.M.[58]

[76] For my Report on the Greek Committee I must not forget to insert my opinion on examinations as stated in *DL* 93[.]

———

For new lectures, as now proposed by Mr Fields, we might try as subjects,[59]

———

Art. ↑LN 257↓
Doctrine of Leasts. (once announced never read)
Superlative. Doctrine of Mosts
Criticism.   ↑including the topic of *Single speeches LI*
    120 *LN* 37↓
        ↑Shakspeare↓
Hospitality, or how to make homes attractive. ↑See *DL* 6, 5, *LN* 255,↓
NY 90
American Life & ⟨Culture⟩Letters. *ML* 180
        & last W[illia]ms.town Address   see *LN* 138, 167, 197,
        history of Transcendentalism, *LN*   Lect. *"Present Age"*
Greatness.

[77] *University.*
⟨Bias⟩ The University question divides people with some rancor, which blinds the eyes, ⟨which⟩ ↑and↓ I hope will be avoided, in consideration of the gravity of the subject. We might as well come to it after

[58] Among persons mentioned in this passage who have not previously been identified, George Bradford Bartlett was the son of Dr. Josiah Bartlett of Concord, a strolling player and director of amateur theatricals; Frank Warren Hackett was a lawyer and later Assistant Secretary of the Navy; Phillips was the son of Moses Dresser Phillips of Phillips, Sampson and Company, who died in 1859. Taylor and Wellman have not been further identified.

[59] Managed by Ticknor and Fields, Emerson delivered six private lectures at the Meionaon, Boston, October 12–November 16, 1868. The topics were: "Nature and Art," "Poetry and Criticism," "Historical Notes of American Life and Letters," "Doctrine of Leasts and Mosts," "Hospitality," and "Greatness." The insertions in the list on p. [76] are in pencil.

a late dinner in the strength of wine, as to hope to treat it wisely on the strength of party & passion.

The general uneasiness & movement in the public in regard to Education shows a certain cleavage.

Evils of the College.—
    It does not justify itself to the pupil.
    It does not open its doors to him.
    Balks him with petty delays & refusals.
    The instructers are in false relations to the student.
    Instead of an avenue, it is a barrier.
    Let him find good advice, but of a wise man, sympathetic,
[continued, p. 84]

[78] The 19th not the 15th ↑century↓ is the age of *Renaissance*. See the exordium of my Middlebury Address, Aug. 11, 1868, & add Pascal's name to the list of recovered authors. See *DL* 162.

———

Add the rewriting of Roman History by Niebuhr & Mommsen

———

Wolf's Studies of Homeric Writings

———

Romaic songs. See an important article by Madame Dora d'Istria, in *Revue des Deux Mondes. Aout. 1867.*[60]

"Cette singulière contradiction entre les lumières de son esprit & la^n timidité de son caractère" says his biographer in [*Nouvelle*] Biog[*ra-phie*]. Gen[*érale*]. [1855–1870,] of Niebuhr. [XXXVIII, 34]

[79] The Author of the Article on Sylviculture (*Rev*[*ue*]. *des deux Mondes,* Aug. 1867) says, that "the *eucalyptus* will grow everywhere & are valued on that account—plantations are made in India &

---

[60] "La Nationalité Hellénique d'Après les Chants Populaires," Aug. 1, 1867, pp. 587–627. Emerson withdrew the volume of the *Revue* containing this article from the Boston Athenaeum, August 1–November 2, 1868. "Dora d'Istria" was the pseudonym of Helene Ghica (1828–1888), a Rumanian writer.

in Algeria, with success. They have also experimented successfully in Australia with seeds of a species of *acacia,* which has the property of vegetating in the most sterile soils, with intent to try the culture in the *Sahara.* Perhaps it will succeed, ⟨"⟩but we must not conceal, that if the desart should some day be re-wooded, the result would be a serious disturbance in the climatic conditions of France & England. The heat absorbed by vegetation would not be carried by south winds to Europe, whose temperature would be sensibly lowered."[61]

[80] ⟨August 27   A note for Ellen in my Plotinus 8vo⟩

At Monadnoc, the ⟨use⟩ ↑final cause↓ of towns appears to be, to be seen from mountains.

Nature.

> Day by day for her darlings to much she added more,
> In her hundred-gated Thebes every chamber was a door,
> A door to something grander,—loftier walls, & vaster floor.[62]

[81][63] J T Williams said that he told a friend of Evarts that he considered Evarts the best candidate[n] for the U.S. Senate from N.Y. & should labor for his election. Afterwards he met Evarts, who came up to him & thanked him for the kind expressions he had used. After E. had entered the President's cabinet, ⟨he⟩ W saw him again & told him that his new action had lost him the opportunity forever. ↑He would never be ↑U.S.↓ Senator from N York.↓ Evarts said, No, he was quite mistaken, & ⟨so⟩ that he was now secure of being the man, *whichever party prevailed:* for, said he, unquestionably the democratic party will carry the next election in New York.

---

[61] Emerson is freely translating from Jules Clavé, "La Silviculture à L'Exposition Universelle," Aug. 1, 1867, pp. 692–693.

[62] This poem appears in "Fragments on Nature," XII, *W,* IX, 341.

[63] This page is written in pencil. "J T Williams" is perhaps John T. Williams, a Wall Street broker whom Emerson knew originally in Buffalo around 1854; William Maxwell Evarts was Attorney General in Andrew Johnson's cabinet, and eventually (1885) a United States senator.

[82]   "Advances
           With rapturous lyrical glances
           Singing the song of the Earth,
           Singing hymns to the gods."
                        _____

                              Is it Goethe's?
                              ask E[lizabeth]. H[oar].

[83] France is a country of method & numerical order, the palace of arithmetic: everything is centralized, &, by a necessity of their nature, the⟨y⟩ ↑French↓ have introduced the decimal system of weights & measures, & made it perfect. They measured the first degree of the meridian, Picard's. They published the first national dictionary of the language. In the revolution, they abolished the chronology of the world, & began with the year one.

_____

"On se contentait de vivre au jour le jour."
I find this phrase in ["Charles-Guillaume, baron de Humboldt," *Nouvelle*] *Bi⟨g⟩ographie Generale.* [1855–1870,] Vol 25 p. 505
_____

     Population of Paris, in 1868, ⟨2,028,736⟩ 2,150,916 Souls: whereof 2,028,736, were born in France.
_____

[84] [continued from p. 77]
a patron of the youth on entering the gates.
It gives degrees on time, on the number of dinners eaten, ↑"eat your terms"↓ not on examination.
It gives foolish diplomas of honor to every old clergyman, or successful gentleman who lives within ten miles.

⟨b⟩Ball & boat-clubs do not hurt, but help the morals of the students.[64]

If the college falls behind the culture of the people, it is instantly ridiculous,

_____

[64] See p. [32] above.

[85]–[88] [blank]

[89] The only place where I feel the joy of eminent domain is in my wood lot. My spirits rise whenever I enter it. I can spend the entire day there with hatchet or pruning-shears making paths, without a remorse of wasting time. I fancy the birds know me, & even the trees make little speeches or hint them. Then Allah does not count the time which the Arab spends in the chase.

[90] Ah what a blessing to live in a house which has on the ground-floor one room or one cabinet in which a Worcester's Unabridged; a Liddell & Scott; a↑n↓ ⟨An⟨th‖ . . .‖⟩dews Latin⟩ ↑Andrews & Stoddard↓; Lempriere's ↑Classical;↓ a *"Gradus Ad";* ⟨and⟩ a Haydn's "Dictionary of Dates"; ⟨and⟩ a "Biographie Generale;" a⟨n⟩ Spiers' French, & Flugel's German ↑Dictionary,↓ even if Grimm is not yet complete;[65]—where these & their ⟨belongings⟩ ↑equivalents, if equivalents can be,↓ are always ⟨to b⟩ at hand.—And yet I might add, as I often do,—Ah↑!↓ happier, if these or their substitutes have been in that house for two generations or for three,—for [91] Horace's Metres & Greek literature will not be thoroughly domesticated in one life: a house, I mean where the seniors ⟨can ask the juniors⟩ who are at fault about school questions, can ⟨ask⟩ ↑inquire of↓ the juniors with some security of a right answer. This is one of my dreams for the American house. Another is the use of wealth in buying for the adult the companionship, if it be only occasional, as on a journey, of the master of that science we are hungering to know. See *LN* 176

[92] *Poet.*

The distinction of the poet is ever this force of imagination which puts its objects before him with such deceptive power that he treats them as real, he talks to them as if they were ⟨really there⟩ ↑present↓, ⟨&⟩ he puts words in their mouth such as they should have spoken, & is affected by them as by Persons. As in dreams we create the persons,

---

[65] This list of reference works adds two titles to the list found in Journal LN, p. [135] above: Ethan Allen Andrews, *First Lessons in Latin; or An Introduction to Andrews and Stoddard's Latin Grammar*, 3d ed. (Boston, 1839); and [Paul Aler,] *Gradus ad Parnassum; sive Novus Synonymorum, Epithetorum, Versuum, ac Phrasium Poeticarum, Thesaurus*, . . . (Edinburgh, 1821). Both works are in Emerson's library.

then talk with them, are surprised at what they do,—we putting, of
course, the speeches into the mouths of the actors.
Vast is the difference between writing clean verses for magazines, &
creating these new persons & situations,—new language with [93]
emphasis & reality↑.↓ ⟨that surprise & delight us.⟩ The humor of Fal-
staff, the terror of Macbeth, have each their swarm of fit thoughts &
images, as if Shakspeare had known & reported the men instead of in-
venting them ⟨in⟩at his desk.[66]

[94]   Art.
        "They forget that all the elements of our civilization have been
imported." [Henry T. Tuckerman, *A Memorial of Horatio*] *Greenough*[. . . (New York, 1853), p. 61].[67] ↑*Not quite true.*↓

There is no danger from any excess of European importation of art &
learning into a country of such excessive native strength as ours.

        What ↑fabrics↓ we import from Europe, instead of making for
ourselves "owe their preference," says Greenough, "solely to design."
& the amount is immense. [*Ibid.*, p. 68]

———

        The potomac stone is friable. [*Ibid.*, p. 69]

———

        "To paint stone is like covering gold with tinfoil." *Greenough* [*ibid.*, p.
69]

"in the Rotunda, the entire masonry has been painted." [*Ibid.*, pp. 69–70]

[95] ———
        "House of Lords a gewgaw" [*ibid.*, pp. 77–78]

————

"a front which deserves to have the inverted commas of quotation affixed to
it." [*Ibid.*,] p. 78

———

        Whole chapter excellent.

[66] "The distinction . . . Persons." and "Vast is . . . desk.", each struck through in
pencil with two vertical use marks, are used in "Poetry and Imagination," *W*, VIII, 44.
        [67] This volume is in Emerson's library.

"I contend for Greek principles, not Greek things." [*Ibid.*, p. 78]

"It is incumbent on edifices, first to be strong; secondly, to look strong." [*Ibid.*, p. 80]

"In Cleopatra's needle, the base is a full diagonal of the summit of the prism." [*Ibid.*, p. 81]

[Where is Ferguson's Hand Book?][68]

"the altitude of the pyramidion, in Cleopatra's N↑eedle↓ is equal to the width of the base." [*Ibid.*, p. 81]

"Obelisk has singular aptitude to call attention to a memorable spot." [*Ibid.*, p. 82]

"It says but one word, but it speaks loud." [*Ibid.*, p. 82]

"It says 'Here!' " [*Ibid.*, p. 82]

[96] "the arithmetical sublime." [*Ibid.*, p. 83]

⟨the⟩ "a column is essentially fractional; it ⟨calls⟩ ↑cries↓ aloud for the entablature." [*Ibid.*,] p. 82

"those to whom it is indifferent whether a book be held with the right or the wrong side up." [*Ibid.*,] p[p.] 82[–83]

Temple of Minerva at Athens. [*Ibid.*,] p. 83

[Where's Ferguson again?]

[97] *Art.* keeping! keeping! It is not praise of a preacher,—is it? to say, he was as amusing as a juggler.

"I maintain that the first downward step is the introduction of the first inorganic non-functional element, whether of shape or color." [Tuckerman, *A Memorial of*] H[*oratio*]. G↑*reenough*↓. [1853,] p. 136

[68] James Fergusson, *The Illustrated Handbook of Architecture* . . . , 2 vols. (London, 1855), in Emerson's library.

Edward Cabot tells me that Greenough made a bust of his sister, Elizabeth Cabot, which is an admirable work.

Burns said, "I rhyme for fun." ["To James Smith," l. 30]

Greenough gave the design for the Bunker Hill monument.

[98] [blank]
[99] You cannot help a Shakspeare,—he does not need it,—but you can learn from him in what direction to apply your means in behalf of his young admirer. The aim of the University should be to aid the student in the direction in which the men of genius have helped themselves.[n]

[100] How we delight in Consecutiveness in a young mind! as opposed to aimless activity.

Singlespeech. Laodamia is almost entitled to that eminence in Wordsworth's literary ⟨act⟩performance. That, & the Ode on Immortality, are the best.[69] There is in several nations a prominence of one name, as we often have to say. But at this moment I think of Scandinavia & its Snorro Sturleson.[70]

I have elsewhere noted ↑(*AC* 284)↓ ⟨o⟩the organic pairs which occur in literary history:
as,   Beaumont & Fletcher
      M. Angelo & Raffaelle
      Montaigne & ⟨Boethius⟩ ↑Etienne de Boèce↓
      ↑Fox & Burke↓   ↑Goethe & Schiller↓
      ↑Webster & Everett↓ ↑Owen & Agassiz↓
      ↑Torrey & Gray↓   ↑Kirby & Spence↓[71]

[69] "Laodamia . . . best." is used in Emerson's preface to *Parnassus,* 1874, p. ix.
[70] Snorri Sturluson (1178–1241), an Icelandic historian, wrote the *Heimskringla* and the prose *Edda.*
[71] Persons in this list who have not been previously identified or who may not be easily identifiable include Étienne de la Boétie, Montaigne's friend, about whom Emerson

Shakspeare always excepted, &, as the converse of Single-Speech he has been well termed the Myriad-minded.

↑See *infra*[n] p. 103. & *LN* 37, *LI* 120,↓

[101] ↑Mediocre books↓

Library.

There are the sound stomachs & the sick: the farmer & the butcher minister to the ⟨well⟩ ↑sound↓, the physician & the confectioner to the sick. The well can look at the sun, & ⟨require⟩ ↑use↓ all his light & heat; the sick only what is reflected & shaded. It is the same in literature. Strong minds ask principles, ⟨&⟩ direct aperçus, & original forms. The sick public want ↑what is↓ secondary, conventional, & imitations of imitations. There is need of Shakspeare & Hegel, and also of Martin Tupper (if that is his name) and McCosh.[72]

[102]   *Library.*

In the perplexity in which the literary public now stands with regard to ⟨College⟩ University education, whether ⟨it⟩ ↑studies↓ shall be compulsory or elective; whether by lectures of professors, or whether by private tutors; whether the stress shall be on Latin & Greek, or on modern Sciences,—the one safe investment which all can agree to increase is the Library. ⟨It is⟩ A good book can wait for a reader hundreds of years. Once lodged in the Library, it is unexpensive & harmless whil⟨st⟩e it waits. Then it is a good of the most generous kind, not only serving [103] the ⟨students⟩ ↑undergraduates↓ of the college, but much more the Alumni, & probably much more still, the scattered community of scholars.

Advantage of the old fashioned folio, that it was safe from borrowers. So of Q[uatremère]. de Quincy's works on art.

---

read in Montaigne's works; John Torrey (1796–1873), an American botanist who collaborated with Asa Gray on volumes of *Flora of North America* (1838–1843); and William Kirby and William Spence, British authors of *An Introduction to Etymology* (1816–1826).
    [72] Martin Farquhar Tupper (1810–1889) was a successful English writer of didactic verses; James McCosh (1811–1894), president of the College of New Jersey, wrote philosophical works seeking to reconcile theism with scientific theories.

Single Speech.

———

'Tis really by a sentence or a phrase or two that many great men are remembered. Zoroaster has three or four, & Marcus Aurelius only as many.

George Tufts wrote me
"Life is a flame whose splendor hides its base."[73]

[104] *Culture.*
I was glad to learn from Ellen that Mr Dabney knew how to shoe his horse[.][74]

[105] "All these are canaille," said the Austrian Arch Duke, "the race of men does not begin till you come to a baron."

———

"by those who know the fondness of the human mind for everything foreign". *Winckelmann,* Vol. I. 203[75]

———

Ellen tells me of a man who came to the house of Wetherbee begging for something to eat. Mrs Wetherbee gave him a plate of soup, and a fork & spoon: he looked at these a little while, then pushed them aside, ⟨t⟩&, thrusting his hand into the soup, helped himself with that which was made before spoons.

[106] Boston too knows the feeling of pity: the oppressed & the suffering find help there. See *Winckelmann,* [*History of Ancient Art,* 1856,] Vol. II. 8.

The lesson of the theory of Hay⟨s⟩ on the Etruscan pottery, ⟨is⟩ namely, that the details of every ⟨vissel⟩ vase, as cover, handles, nose or

[73] For this letter, see *JMN,* XV, 392.
[74] Charles W. Dabney was a shipmate of Ellen Emerson's during a voyage to Fayal, October 1868; see *L,* VI, 63n.
[75] John Winckelmann, *The History of Ancient Art,* trans. G. Henry Lodge, 2 vols. (Boston, 1856), in Emerson's library.

spout, &c. are portions of the same ↑composite↓ ellipse which the vase itself constitutes.[76]

⟨that every⟩

————

Class of Men
Cardinal Chigi's trifler with his pen.[77]

[107] Ours is the *Zymosis* of Science, the heavens open, & the earth, & every element, & disclose their secrets. The large utterance of the gods which in every organism Nature retains, the great style, the fate or invariable adherence to its qualities & methods, & the unity of system which reigns through all ⟨immense &⟩ ↑the↓ innumerable & immense parts,—we are daily learning: & what beams of light have shone upon ⟨us⟩ ↑men↓ now first in this Century! The Genius, Nature, is ever putting conundrums to us, ⟨as⟩ & the savans, as in the girls' game of "Twenty questions", are every month [108] solving them successively by skilful exhaustive method. This success ⟨puts⟩ ↑makes↓ the student ⟨in spirits & makes him⟩ ↑cheerful and↓ confident, & his ⟨demands⟩ new illumination makes it impossible for him to acquiesce in the old barbarous routine, whether of ⟨state or⟩ politics, or religion, or commerce, or social arrangements. Nature will not ↑longer↓ be kinged, or churched, or colleged, or drawing-roomed as before.

Things oft miscalling, as the hen-
Fever raged not in fowls but men.

[109] A man never gets acquainted with himself, but is always a surprise. We get news daily of ⟨ourselves⟩ ↑the world within,↓ as well ⟨much⟩ as of the world out side, & not less of the central than of the surface facts. A new thought is awaiting him every morning.

[76] Cf. David Ramsay Hay, *The Science of Beauty, as Developed in Nature and Applied in Art* (Edinburgh and London, 1856), p. 87.

[77] See *JMN*, XIII, 372, where Cardinal de Retz is said to have regarded Cardinal Chigi, later Pope Alexander VII, as a trifler because he used the same pen for two years; Emerson's source was *Memoirs of the Cardinal de Retz*, 3 vols. (Philadelphia, 1817), III, 198.

I often think how hard it is ⟨for⟩ to say with sweetness your thought, when you know that it affronts & exasperates your audience.[78] It is even difficult to write it ↑for such readers↓ without leaving on the line some bitterness. But the French do this, & the French alone, with perfect equanimity in their excellent *Revue des Deux Mondes.*

[110] ↑*The Age.*↓
    All the babes are born infidels.

⟨in their excellent *Revue des deux Mondes.*⟩

A man grew so nervous at hearing the boys throw stones against his fence, that he emigrated to Illinois on the assurance that there was not a pebble on the prairie.

[111] He was ⟨vexed⟩ ↑disgusted↓ by a long rain storm, & packed his portmanteau, & set out to find sunshine, & never stopped till he reached Sahara. He was annoyed by the dust & went to sea.

Books—Men read so differently with purpose so unlike. I had read in Cudworth from time to time for years, & one day talked of him with Charles W. Upham, my classmate,—& found him acquainted with Cudworth's argument, & theology; & quite heedless [112] of all I read him for,—↑namely,↓ his citations from Plato & the philosophers; so that, ↑if I had not from my youth up loved the man,↓ I suppose we might have "inter-despised," as De Quincy said of Wordsworth, & (perhaps) Mackintosh.

John Hunter, ↑b⟨.⟩orn 1728, in Scotland; d⟨.⟩ied 1794,↓ was so far from resting his mind in society, that he felt real fatigue in the midst of company where the conversation *n'avait pas de suite.* [*Nou-velle*] *Biog*[*raphie*]. *Generale* [1855–1870, XXV, 574]
    ↑See above, p. 100↓

---

[78] "for" is canceled in pencil and in ink.

His Museum cost him ↑£↓70,000. The Govt. bought it for ↑£↓15 000, after long negociation. Pitt said, " 'Tis not a time to buy anatomical pieces, when I want money to buy powder." [*Ibid.*, XXV, 565]

[113] ——
"Don't ask me," he said to his pupils, "what I thought a year ago on this or that: ask me what I think today." [*Ibid.*, XXV, 567]

——

He, Hunter, first used the expression "Arrested development," which plays so important a part in modern Science.[79] [*Ibid.*, XXV, 568] paid ↑£↓500 for the body of a giant O'Bryan, & watched (by a servant) the man when he should die. [*Ibid.*, XXV, 564–565] He arrived at the conclusion of Harvey, & of Moses long before, that "the life of all flesh is the blood thereof." [*Ibid.*, XXV, 567]   See *Leviticus*, 17. 14.

[114] Adelbert de Beaumont's elevation of the Persian architecture over all western art perhaps is corrected by what was written earlier by V⟨ulor⟩iolet Le Duc, that the Roman nobles built their villas in all the East as well as west, & that the orientals have followed & kept these Roman forms of building to the present days.[80]

[115] Nov. 11. Yesterday was well occupied in accompanying W[illiam]. R[obert]. Ware to the Church he is building for the First Church Society, in Berkeley street.[81] It has a completeness & uniformity of strength, richness, & taste, perfect adaptation to its present purpose, & an antiquity in all its ornamentation that give delight. It seemed to threaten ruin to the Radical Club, retro-action in all people

---

[79] Cf. "Poetry and Imagination," *W*, VIII, 7.

[80] Adalbert de Beaumont, "Les Arts Décoratifs en Orient et en France: L'Architecture," *Revue des Deux Mondes*, Sept. 1, 1866, pp. 5–33; Emerson withdrew the volume containing this article from the Boston Athenaeum, June 29–September 19, 1867. Eugene Emmanuel Viollet-le-Duc (1814–1879) was a French architect and authority on Gothic art; Emerson withdrew his *Entretiens sur l'Architecture*, vol. 1 (Paris, 1863), from the Athenaeum, September 18–30, 1865.

[81] Ware (1832–1915) was the partner of Henry Van Brunt; in addition to the First Church, they designed Harvard's Memorial Hall and the Episcopal Theological School in Cambridge.

who shall sit down in its sumptuous twilight. I lamented for my old
friend Dr Frothingham his loss of sight, once more, [116] that he
could not enjoy this faultless temple.[82]

I looked through all the details of the drawings for the Alumni Hall at
Ware's office,[n] which conciliate the eye very fast, and the capital suggestion that the Dining Hall shall be used for daily Commons, if properly accepted & followed up, will go far to remove every ⟨ground⟩
↑point↓ of objection [117] on the old ground that this vast expense is
for three or four days only in the year.
In his Technologic Chambers, he showed one a multitude of interesting fragments of art, casts mainly, from Trajan's Column, from
English, French, & Italian Churches, a head from a statue ↑at Rheims
Cathedral↓ of the 13th Century by John ↑of Bologne?,↓[83]—which
gives, what I always seek↑,↓ when I see new sculpture,—decisive
proof of a master.
Ware believes the Romans were their own artists, & not Greeks, confirmed [118] by specimens of Etruscan art which he saw.

---

9 December 1868.

In poetry, tone. I have been reading some of Lowell's new
poems, in which he shows unexpected advance on himself, but perhaps
most in technical skill & courage. It is ⟨however⟩ in talent rather than
in poetic tone, & rather expresses his wish, his ambition, than the un-
controllable interior impulse which is the authentic mark of a new
poem, & which is unanalysable, & makes the merit of an ode of Collins, or Gray, or Wordsworth, or Herbert, or Byron,—& which is felt
in the pervading tone, rather than in brilliant parts or lines; As if the
sound of a bell, or ⟨or⟩a certain cadence expressed in a low whistle or
booming, or humming, to which the poet first timed his step, as he
looked at the sunset, or ⟨meditated a casual⟩ thought, was the incipient
form of the piece, & was regnant through the whole.[84]

[82] "Frothingham" is centered at the top of p. [116].
[83] "of Bologne?" was written in pencil, then overwritten in ink. The comma following "seek" is in pencil.
[84] "meditated a casual" is canceled in pencil.

[119]   ↑copied in *CR* 93 [actually 50]↓

Wordsworth is manly, the manliest poet of his age. His poems record the thoughts & emotions which have occupied hi⟨m⟩s mind, & which he ⟨records⟩ ↑reports↓ because of their reality.[85] He has ⟨also⟩ great skill in rendering them into simple & sometimes happiest poetic speech. Tennyson has incomparable felicity in all poetic forms, & is a brave thoughtful Englishman, ⟨but far less manly compass⟩ exceeds Wordsworth a hund↑r↓edfold in rhythmic power & variety, but far less manly compass;[n] [120] and Tennyson's main purpose is the rendering, whi↑l↓st Wordsworth's is just value of the dignity of the thought.[86]

I told Ware, that I prize Michel Angelo so much that ↑whilst I look at his figures,↓ I ⟨b⟩come to believe the grandiose is grand. Thomas Gray in poetry has relations to Michel Angelo, and the like question between the grandiose & grand is suggested in reading his odes.

[121] ↑*Conversation*↓
As I wrote lately ↑(Supra p. 44)↓ there is for your thought & expression a certain advantage in occupying the Chair in your company, or talking down. We can talk better on our own ground to intelligent young men than to our equals. Remember Pepys's description of Lord Clarendon's fine superiorities of talk. I think sometimes I could give useful lessons or hints to a class of young writers, who were yet able & sympathetic.
↑See *CD* 39, 41, use of inferiors.↓

[122] No doubt at Brook Farm there was in many a certain strength drawn from the fury of dissent. George Ripley told Theodore Parker, that "John Dwight would hoe corn all Sunday, if ⟨y⟩he would let him, b⟨on⟩ut all Massachusetts could not make him do it on Monday."[87] ↑Told me by Mr Hewins.↓

---

[85] "records" is canceled in pencil and in ink; "reports" was written in pencil, then overwritten in ink.
[86] "Tennyson has . . . variety," is used in Emerson's preface to *Parnassus,* 1874, p. x.
[87] "No doubt . . . Monday.' ", struck through in pencil with a vertical use mark, is used in "Historic Notes of Life and Letters in New England," *W,* X, 366.

The superior impression of character which the Romans make on us as compared with the Greeks.—

[123] An Englishman has firm manners. He rests secure on the reputation of his country, on his family, his education, & his expectations at home. There is in his manners a suspicion of insolence. If his belief in the Thirty nine ⟨a⟩Articles does not bind him much, his belief in the fortieth does;—namely, that he shall not find his superiors elsewhere. Hence a complaint you shall often find made against him here, that, whilst at his house he would resent as unpermissible, that a guest should come to a seven o'clock dinner in undress, [124] ↑he↓ bursts into ⟨a⟩ ↑your↑s↓↓ ⟨polite dinner-party⟩ in a shooting-jacket. Well, it is for the company to put him in the wrong by their ⟨own⟩ perfect politeness.

Greatness. In the virtues of vicious men do not forget Gerald, Earl of Kildare. See *LN* 38
Nor this ↑saying↓ of the Elder Scipio, "that he had given his enemies as much occasion to love him, as his friends." See *Montaigne, Of Vanity.* [*Essays,* 1693,] Vol. III. p. 306

Manners. "Natura, homo mundum et elegans animal est." *Seneca. Epist*[*les*]. *92*[, 12][88]

[125] When I find in people narrow religion, I find also narrow reading.[89]

In this proposition lately brought to me of a class,[90] it occurs that I could by readings show the difference between good poetry & what passes for good; that I could show how much so-called poetry is only

[88] "Man is by nature a neat and well-groomed animal."
[89] This sentence is used in "Speech at the Second Annual Meeting of the Free Religious Association," *W,* XI, 487.
[90] In November 1868, William Forbes proposed that Emerson "should have a private class of young men, . . . friends or acquaintances, for readings of poetry or prose, & conversation" (*L,* VI, 43); the proposal eventuated in a series of ten readings, held at Chickering's Hall, Boston, January 2–March 20, 1869.

eloquence; that I could vindicate the genius of Wordsworth ↑See *supra* p. 119,↓ & show his distinctive merits. I should like to call attention to the critical superiority of Arnold,[91] his excellent ear for style, & the singular poverty of his poetry, that in fact he has written but one poem, ↑"Thyrsis,"↓ & that on an inspiration borrowed from Milton.⟨—Thyrsis.⟩ I might give, too, the ⟨page⟩catalogue of the [126][92] *Poets of one Poem,* the Single-speech men.* A topic also would be this Welsh genius (& Arnold too has been attracted to that,) which I recognized today in reading this new translator, Skene.[93] And which I find, as long ago, far more suggestive, contagious, or I will say, ↑more↓ inoculating the reader with poetic madness, than any poet I now think of, except Hafiz. I can easily believe this an idiosyncrasy of mine, &, to describe it more accurately, I will add that I place these as ⟨alike⟩ ↑not equal, but *of like kind*↓ in genius & influence with the Zoroastrian sentences, & th⟨e⟩ose of the Bhagavat Geeta & the Vishnu Purana.

[127] There is always a height of land which, in a walk for pleasure or business, the party seek as the ↑natural↓ centre ↑or point of view↓; & there is in every book, whether poem, or history, or treatise of philosophy, a height which attracts more than other parts, & which is best remembered. Thus, in Morte d'Arthur, I remember nothing so well as Merlin's cry from his invisible inaccessible prison. To be sure, different readers select by natural affinity different points. In the proposed class, it would be my wish to indicate such points in literature, & thus be [128] an "old guide", like ↑⟨the old⟩↓ Stephen, who shows, after ten years ↑daily↓ ⟨|| . . .||⟩trudging through the subterranean holes, the best wonders of the Mammoth Cave.[94]

* See *LN* 37.

[91] Horizontal rules are drawn in pencil above and below "Arnold".
[92] *"Musagetes"* and *"Bards."* are inserted at the top of this page.
[93] Emerson withdrew from the Boston Athenaeum, November 20–31 [*sic*], 1868, vol. 1 of William Forbes Skene, *The Four Ancient Books of Wales, Containing the Cymric Poems Attributed to the Bards of the Sixth Century,* 2 vols. (Edinburgh, 1868).
[94] For "Stephen the guide," whom Emerson met during a trip to Mammoth Cave in 1850, see *L,* IV, 212.

[129] The gripe of Byron has not been repeated & the delightful romance which ↑came from↓ Scott ⟨threw over⟩ ↑to↓ young America has not. Tennyson has finer, more delicate beauty & variety, but does not possess men as the others did. Tennyson has a perfect ↑English↓ Culture, & its petulance.

[130] In the matter of Religion, men eagerly fasten their eyes on the differences between their own creed & yours; wh⟨en⟩ilst the charm of the study is in finding the agreements & identities in all the religions of men.

When I find in people narrow religion, I find narrow reading.[95]

[131] Remarkable families were[96]

The three Jackson brothers—Dr James, Judge Charles, & Patrick.

the three Lowell⟨s⟩ ↑brothers,↓ ⟨Rev Dr⟩John, Rev. Dr Charles, & Francis C[abot]. L[owell].

the four Lawrences, Abbott, Amos, Luther, William,

the   Cabots

The three Hunts—William, Richard, & Leavitt,   ↑Wm Hunt tells me also of his brother John, in Paris.↓

Washburns   ↑three governors, I believe.↓

James brothers

---

[95] Cf. p. [125] above.

[96] Persons listed in the following family groups include: James Jackson (1777–1867), a physician; Charles Jackson (1775–1855), a lawyer; Patrick Tracy Jackson (1780–1847), one of the founders of the textile industry in Lowell, Massachusetts; John Lowell (1769–1840), a lawyer; Charles Lowell (1782–1864), a minister and the father of James Russell Lowell; Francis Cabot Lowell (1775–1817), an industrialist for whom Lowell, Massachusetts, is named; Abbott Lawrence (1792–1855), a merchant and statesman for whom Lawrence, Massachusetts, and Lawrence Scientific School are named; Amos Lawrence (1786–1852), a merchant and philanthropist; Luther Lawrence (1778–1839), a lawyer and mayor of Lowell, Massachusetts; William Lawrence (1783–1848), a merchant; William Morris Hunt (1824–1879), a painter; Richard Morris Hunt (1827–1895), an architect; Leavitt Hunt, who received a law degree from Harvard in 1856; John Hunt, who studied medicine; Israel Washburn (1813–1883), former governor of Maine; Elihu Benjamin Washburne (1816–1887); Cadwallader Colden Washburn (1818–1882), later governor of Wisconsin; and William James and Henry James. Regarding the Washburn brothers, Emerson is incorrect about "three governors," though the three sat simultaneously in the U.S. House of Representatives during the 1850s.

[132] The *American Encyclopaedia* says that the common ciphers 1, 2, 3, &c ⟨w⟩and the decimal system were not inventions of the Arabians, but borrowed by them from the Egyptians, as is proved by Professor Seyffarth. see Article "Arabian Literature"[97]

Culture is one thing, & varnish another. There can be no high culture without pure morals. With the truly cultivated man—the maiden, the orphan, the poor man, & the hunted slave feel safe.

If only the memory were perfect, any man has seen & read & heard enough to cap any incident or experience that could be shown him.

I read today in ↑Richard↓ Owen, that he himself suggested the use of gelatine in solution to restore firmness to the crumbling bones or ivory of specimens in the British Museum, & was successful. [133] See his *"Pal[a]eontology,"* [(Edinburgh, 1860),] p[p]. 296-7

There are so many men in the world, that I can ⟨afford⟩ be spared to work a great while on one chapter;—so long, that, when at last it is finished & printed, & returns to me, I can read it without pain, & know that others can.

[134] ↑See next page*↓[98]
I have said above (see p 118) that tone, rather than lines, marks a genuine poem. Wolfe's "Not a drum was heard, nor a funeral note," is an example, so is Sterling's "Daedalus," so "Dinas Emlinn" of Scott, & Scott always has that merit, and Byron's "Incantation," & the whole of Manfred charms, in spite of its shallowness, by that unity. And Beaumont & Fletcher's "Melancholy."[99] I think the vice of the

* Many poems owe their ⟨mer⟩ fame to tone, as others to their sense.

[97] *Encyclopaedia Americana*, 1829, I, 318. Gustavus Seyffarth (1796–1885) was a German-born archaeologist who lived in the United States after 1856. A pencil line is drawn beside this entry in the left margin.
[98] Emerson's footnote is written at the bottom of p. [135].
[99] The quotation from Charles Wolfe is l. 1 of "The Burial of Sir John Moore at Corunna"; "Dinas Emlinn" is the opening of Scott's "The Dying Bard"; Byron's "In-

French, the↑ir↓ notorious incapacity of poetic power, is, the total want
of this music, which all their brilliant talent cannot supply. Voltaire
could see wholes as well as parts, & his testimony to French unpoeti-
calness is distinct. "Si le roi m'avoit donné," &c. has right tone, & that
little ⟨nothing⟩ ↑carol↓ [135] is still their best poem.
But Victor Hugo has genius in "Le Sémeur", & the *star*-piece[n] which
I have saved.[100] And, I must repeat, that, one genial thought is the
source of every true poem.
I have heard that a unity of this kind pervades Beethoven's great
pieces in music.
And why, but because tone gives unity.

[136] *Farming.*
Marshall Miles said to me, that he wants to come home to his old
farm, & thinks he shall, presently; "for it is what you get out of the
earth that is pure gain, but what we get by speculating, each on the
other, is not."[101]

A chapter on the Intellect should begin low by examples; as,
Thales & his shadow of the pyramid; or Hauy & his finding the laws of
cleavage in crystals,—& so instructing the lapidary how to cut; &
plenty of other illustrations how the laws of real nature are turned into
⟨laws⟩ ↑rules↓ of thumb; &, if I understood them, that law of the catenary (is it?) of Hooke's; & the corollaries of Chladni's central discovery of music on the steel filings, for which see Tyndal "on Sound;" &
if [137] I could understand it again, the related suggestion of the form
of the skeleton of mammals by ↑Dr↓ Wyman from the iron filings
again on the magnet.[102]

---

cantation" is from *Manfred*, I, i, 192–261; "Melancholy" is probably the poem identified
as "Fountain heads & pathless groves" on p. [60] above. The five poems mentioned to
this point in the passage are all included in *Parnassus*.
[100] Hugo's "*star*-piece" is probably "Stella," in *Châtiments* (1853).
[101] The 1860 census lists Marshall Miles as a farmer in Concord.
[102] Among the persons mentioned in this paragraph, Thales (640?–546 B.C.) was the
founder of Greek geometry; Abbé René Just Haüy (1743–1822) was a French mineralo-
gist; Robert Hooke (1635–1703) was an English experimental philosopher; Ernst Florens
Friedrich Chladni (1756–1827) was a German physicist and expert on acoustics. Emerson
withdrew from the Boston Athenaeum, September 9–October 23, 1868, John Tyndall's
Sound: A Course of Eight Lectures (London, 1867).

Mrs Sarah Alden Ripley said, "that the farmers like to be complimented with thought."

Sept. 16. Madame H. mourut aujourd'hui, et veut savoir si vous voulez lui donner des fleurs.

[138] In 1821 I heard Edward Everett preach a sermon to the Howard Benevolent Society in the Old South Church. One passage I keep in memory to this day.—"I have known a woman in this town go out to work with her own hands to pay for the wooden coffin which was to inclose the body of her only child. I prayed with her when there was none to stand up by her but he who was to bear that ⟨dust⟩body to the tomb."[103]

[139] The few ⟨sincere⟩ stout & sincere persons whom each one of us knows, recommend the country & the planet to us. 'Tis not a bad world this, as long as I know that J[ohn]. M[urray]. F[orbes].[104] & W[illiam]. H[athaway]. F[orbes]. & Judge Hoar, ⟨& General Grant,⟩ⁿ ↑& Agassiz,↓ & my three children, & twenty other shining creatures whose faces I see looming through the mist, are wa↑l↓king in it. Is it the thirty millions of America, or is it your ten or twelve ↑units↓ that encourage your heart from day to day?

[140] Of immortality, I should say, that it is at least equally & perhaps better seen in little than in large angles: I mean, that, in a calm & clear state of mind, we have no fears, no prayers, even,ⁿ that we feel all is well; we have arrived at an enjoyment so pure, as to imply & affirm its perfect accord with the Nature of things, so that it alone appears durable, & all mixed or inferior states accidental & temporary.

[141] The managers of the public conventions, political & other, understand well that they must set the fire going by ready popular speakers, like Wilson, & Russell, & Swift, who will crackle & kindle,

---

[103] See *JMN,* I, 49.

[104] John Murray Forbes (1813–1898), president of the Michigan Central and the Chicago, Burlington, & Quincy railroads, was the father of Emerson's son-in-law William Hathaway Forbes.

& afterwards they may venture to pile on the slow anthracite of argu-
mentative judges & political economists: kindlings first, & then hard
coal.[105]

↑Shakspeare.↓
    I think with all due respect to Aubrey, & Dyce, & Delia Bacon,
& Judge Holmes, that it is not by discovery of contemporary docu-
ments, but by more cunning reading of the Book itself, that we shall at
last eliminate the true biography of Shakspear.[106]

    [142] I heard Dr Channing say, in his own house, of Webster's
"Hayne" speech, "What self-subsistency!" The ⟨same quality dictated⟩
↑best example of it is↓ his famous question to the Whigs, in Faneuil
Hall, "But where shall I go?"[107]

    In many encounters with "Society," in many dinners & recep-
tions, he learns never a thought or fact, nothing but how to live with
these people.

⟨See⟩ Montaigne⟨s⟩ says, "that Socrates's virtue does not seem to have
been ever on the rack to perform its actions, but to have done them
naturally & gracefully. 'Twas a better born virtue than other
men's."[108]

[105] Henry Wilson (1812–1875) was U.S. Senator from Massachusetts and later
Vice-President. Thomas Russell is listed in the semi-centennial *Proceedings* of the Concord
Lyceum (1878); this may be the prominent Boston attorney and jurist of that name
(1825–1887). Swift is probably the same orator mentioned in *JMN*, XIV, 269, but is otherwise unidentified.
    [106] Shakespeare is the subject of one of John Aubrey's *Brief Lives*; Alexander Dyce
(1798–1869) was a Scottish scholar known primarily for his edition of Shakespeare
(1857); Delia Salter Bacon (1811–1859), whom Emerson befriended, wrote *Philosophy of
the Plays of Shakspere Unfolded*, 1857, holding for authorship of the plays by Francis
Bacon and others.
    [107] Webster delivered his "Second Speech on Foot's Resolution," part of his debate
with Robert Young Hayne of South Carolina concerning the doctrine of nullification, in
the U.S. Senate on January 26, 1830. His "famous question" probably refers to the
"Hard to Coax" speech of September 30, 1842, defending his decision to remain as secretary of state in Tyler's cabinet despite intense pressure from some Massachusetts Whigs
for his resignation in protest of Tyler's policies.
    [108] Emerson is here apparently quoting his paraphrase, in *JMN*, VI, 143, of Mon-
taigne's "Of Cruelty"; cf. Montaigne, *Essays*, 1693, pp. 146, 149–150.

143

"He is truly wise who knows he is not truly wise." Proclus[109]

[143] For my discourse for April 4 consult [Notebook] M[ary] M[oody] E[merson] IV 61, 62.[110]

In my visit to New York I saw ⟨no⟩ ↑one↓ remarkable person new to me, ⟨but⟩ Richard Hunt, the Architect. His conversation was spirited beyond any that I could easily remember, loaded with matter, & expressed with the vigor & fury of a member of the Harvard boat or ball club, relating the adventures of one of their matches; inspired, meantime, throughout, with fine theories of the possibilities of art. Yet the tone of his voice & the accent of his conversation so strongly reminded me of my rural neighbor S[amuel]. S[taples]. [144] as to be in ludicrous contrast with the Egyptian & Greek grandeurs he was hinting or portraying. I could only think of the immense advantage which a thinking soul possesses when horsed on a robust & vivacious temperament. The combination is so rare of an Irish laborer's nerve & elasticity with Winckelmann's experience & cultivation, as to fill one with immense hope of great results, when he meets it in the New York of today.[111]

[145] What shall we think of Voltaire's taste, when he writes of the tragedy of "Cato";—"M. Addison est le premier Anglais qui ait fait une tragédie raisonnable. Je le plaindrais s'il n'y avait mis que de la raison. Sa tragédie de Caton est écrite, d'un bout à l'autre, avec cette élégance mâle et energique, dont Corneille le premier donna chez nous de si beaux exemples dans son style inégal."[112]

---

[109] *The Six Books of Proclus . . . on the Theology of Plato*, trans. Thomas Taylor, 2 vols. (London, 1816), II, 477, in Emerson's library. See *JMN*, XI, 252.

[110] On April 4, 1869, Emerson delivered his lecture "Natural Religion" at Boston's Horticultural Hall.

[111] Samuel F. Staples had, as Concord's constable in July 1846, effected the famous arrest of Henry Thoreau; Johann Joachim Winckelmann (1717–1768) was a German classical archaeologist and art critic.

[112] See "De la Tragédie Anglaise," *Oeuvres Complètes de Voltaire*, 72 vols. (n.p., 1784–1801), XLVII, 278–279.

Was it in 1714, that it took Addison so long to mend his pen to write to George I. that Queen Anne was dead, & that the Crown of England waited for him?[113]

[146] Democritus the laughing, Heraclitus the weeping philosopher. *Montaigne,* ["Of Democritus and Heraclitus," *Essays,* 1693,] I. 514[-515]

Sprat said, that Cromwell's "fame, like man, will grow white as it grows old." *Johnson's Lives. Sprat.* [*Works,* 1806, X, 37]
↑Some men live from their temperament↓[.]

R[alph]. wakes from a sound sleep, has an excellent breakfast, and inquires if this is not a jolly universe?

↑no more↓ irreconcileable persons brought to annoy & confound each other in one room, than are sometimes ⟨lodged⟩actually lodged by nature in one man's skin, *GL* 22

[147] ↑*Memory.*↓
It sometimes occurs that Memory has a personality of its own, & volunteers or refuses its informations at *its* will, not at mine. I⟨t⟩ askⁿ myself, is it not some old Aunt who ⟨frequents⟩ goes in & out of the house, & occasionally recites anecdotes of old times & persons, which I recognize as having heard before,—&, ↑she↓ being gone again, I search in vain for any trace of the anecdotes?

[148]   March 29.
Alcott came, & talked Plato & Socrates[,] extolling them with gravity. I bore it long, & then said, that was a song for others, not for him. He should find what was the equivalent for these masters in our times: for surely the world was always equal to itself, & it was for him to detect what was the counter-weight & compensation to us. Was it natural science? Was it the immense dilution of the same amount of thought into nations?

---

[113] The source of this apocryphal story is Johnson's *Life of Addison, The Works of Samuel Johnson,* 12 vols. (London, 1806), X, 88, in Emerson's library.

I told him to shut his eyes, & let his thoughts run into reverie or whithersoever,—& then take an observation. He would find that the current went outward from man, not to man. Consciousness was up stream.

[149] There is no miracle so stupendous as this Health, Thought, Apprehension.

———

I suppose women feel in relation to men as geniuses ⟨a⟩feel among energetic workers, that, though overlooked & thrust aside in the press, they outsee all these noisy masters.

———

The gem adorns the picture ↑that I saw yesterday,↓ because the face in the portrait is earnest, & does not heed the gem. If it did, the face were spoiled.

———

"Man is man as far as he is triple, that is, man-woman-child." Hindoo

———

If Greece was c⟨u⟩ruel to woman, it yet gave the advantage that ⟨it punished⟩Athens punished the man who did not marry. Sparta punished also the man that married late. ↑See↓ *Cité Antique.* p. 263[114]

[150] Cardinal De Retz said he had "l'ame peutêtre la moins ecclésiastique qui fût dans l'univers."[115]

———

Pythagoras & the 47th Proposition. *Stanley* p. 389[116]

—

Nepenthe. *Stanley* p. 389

———

[151] [blank]

[114] Numa Denis Fustel de Coulanges, *La Cité Antique . . .* , 3d ed. (Paris, 1870), in Emerson's library. This entry, including the rule above, is in pencil.
[115] Jean François Paul de Gondi, Cardinal de Retz, *Mémoires du Cardinal de Retz,* 2 vols. (Paris, 1844), I, 3.
[116] Thomas Stanley, *The History of the Chaldaick Philosophy* (London, 1701), in Emerson's library.

[152] For the proposed new volume of Essays[117]

↑x↓		⟨Solitude & Society⟩	*Atlantic Monthly* Vol I. p. 225
↑x↓		⟨Books⟩	*Atlantic Monthly* Vol I p. 343
	↑+↓	Persian Poetry	*Atlantic M. Vol.* I. p. 724
	↑+↓	↑Art↓	
↑x↓		⟨Eloquence⟩	Atlantic M Vol. II. 385
		⟨American Civilization.⟩	Atlantic M. Vol. IX. 502
		The President's Proclamation.	Atlantic M Vol. X. 638
↑x↓		⟨Domestic Life.⟩	Conway's Dial
	↑+↓	Theodore Parker.	Obsequies of Rev T. Parker
	↑+↓	Henry D. Thoreau	Atlantic M

[117] Emerson had been contemplating for some time the "new volume of Essays" that would become *Society and Solitude,* 1870; the inventories of uncollected essays and lectures on pp. [152]–[155] were apparently an attempt to begin shaping the new volume. For complete information about the items listed here, see Joel Myerson, *Ralph Waldo Emerson: A Descriptive Bibliography* (Pittsburgh, 1982), and William Charvat, *Emerson's American Lecture Engagements: A Chronological List* (New York, 1961). Titles cited on pp. [152]–[154] that may not be readily identifiable include the Phi Beta Kappa oration of July 1867, published as "Aspects of Culture" in the *Atlantic Monthly* (Jan. 1868) and as "Progress of Culture" in *Letters and Social Aims* (1875); "Art" (*Dial*), actually "Thoughts on Art"; and "Literature in 1840," actually "Thoughts on Modern Literature." "Realism" and "Rhetoric" cannot be conclusively identified; "Criticism" may be one of several lectures with similar titles. The address at Tufts College was "Celebration of the Intellect," June 10, 1861; the address at Waterville, Maine, was "The Scholar," August 11, 1863; "Middletown" is probably an error for Middlebury, Vermont, where Emerson gave the address "Greatness" on August 11, 1868. Emerson made the entries in the lists on pp. [152]–[155] at various times; no attempt has been made to indicate the insertion of individual lines. The inserted x to the left of "Woman" on p. [152] is in ink; the other thirteen x marks on pp. [152]–[153] are in pencil. The eleven "+" marks on these two pages are in ink. "Theodore Parker." and "Henry D. Thoreau", on p. [152], are struck through with five vertical marks and one diagonal mark in faint ink. The first three titles on p. [153] are struck through with a diagonal mark.

	↑+↓	Phi Beta Kappa Oration.	*Atlantic*[n] M.
↑x↓		⟨Old Age⟩	Atlantic M
	↑+↓	Concord Monument Address	
		⟨Art⟩	Dial
↑x↓		Woman	
		⟨Works & Days⟩	
↑x↓		⟨Country Life⟩	
↑x↓		⟨Clubs⟩	
		⟨Courage⟩	
↑x↓	↑x↓	⟨Success⟩	
		Classes of Men	

[153]

↑x↓	↑+↓	Carlyle's Past & Present	Dial
↑x↓	↑+↓	Walter Savage Landor	Dial
↑x↓	↑+↓	Literature ↑in 1840↓　　.　　.	Dial Vol. I. p.
			137

Education

↑x↓ Social Aims

Resources

Table-Talk

Books

↑+↓ Speech at the Harvard Alumni ⟨Memorial Meeting⟩ ↑Commemoration.↓

↑+↓ Address on the Death of Abraham Lincoln. Concord.

Man of the World.

Greatness

Historic Notes of Life & Letters

Leasts & Mosts

Hospitality, & how to make homes attractive.

Poetry & Criticism.

Immortality

Realism

Rhetoric

Criticism

⟨S⟩Address at Tufts College
　　　　　at Waterville
　　　　　at Middletown

148

[154]¹¹⁸

↑approved↓	⟨Thoughts on Art.⟩	*Dial*, Vol. I. p 367
↑+↓	Literature in 1840	1841 [actually 1840] Dial Vol I p. 137
↑+↓	Landor	Dial Vol. II p 262
↑+↓	Carlyle	Dial *Vol.* IV. p 96
↑+↓	The Tragic	Dial Vol. IV. p. 515.
↑+↓	The Comic	Dial Vol. IV. p. 247
↑+↓	Persian Poetry	
↑+↓	Art	⟨Art⟩

⟨Eloquence⟩
⟨Civilization⟩
⟨Domestic Life⟩
⟨Society & Soli-
    tude⟩
⟨Domestic Life⟩
⟨Farming⟩
⟨Clubs⟩
⟨Success⟩
⟨Works & Days⟩
⟨Old Age⟩

Art
Eloquence
⟨Society & Solitude⟩
Domestic Life
↑Farming↓
Clubs
Success
Works & Days
Old Age

---

¹¹⁸ "approved" is in pencil; the significance of this word here is unclear, since in the eight-item list immediately contiguous to it, only "The Comic", "Persian Poetry", and "Art" were published in book form during Emerson's lifetime. "Carlyle" is a review of *Past and Present*. The nine-item list, "Art" through "Old Age", on the left side of the page, is in pencil and is struck through with a diagonal mark in pencil; the eleven-item list, "Art" through "Old Age", on the right side of the page, is in pencil and is boxed by a horizontal pencil line above, a vertical pencil line to its left, and the ink rule below. All the items in these two lists of nine and eleven titles eventually appeared among the twelve essays of *Society and Solitude;* only "Books" was added to the titles included here. "Landor" and "Carlyle", in the list at the bottom left of the page, are in pencil. "Lord Hervey's ... watch chain" is in pencil; Hervey's saying also appears in *JMN*, XI, 64.

⟨Art⟩
⟨Eloquence⟩   Lord   Hervey's
Tragic   saying   'Tis too
Comic   small for a house &
⟨Works & Days⟩   too large to hang to
↑Landor↓   your watch chain
↑Carlyle↓

[155] Homer has this Prerogative,[n] that he never discovers in the Iliad a preference to the Greeks over the Trojans.

It were good to contrast the hospitality of Abu Bekeur in the "Sahara" with that of Admetus in Euripides' Alcestis. That of the Arab is at once noble yet human; that of the king in the play is over-strained to absurdity.[119]

↑Characters↓[120]	Domestic Life	*Criticism*
⟨*Criticism*⟩	Clubs	Literature in 1840
⟨Lit. in 1840⟩	Social Aims	Books (Atlantic)
⟨Books⟩ (Atlantic)	Table-talk	Some good Books
Theodore Parker	Education	Persian Poetry
H. D. Thoreau	Leasts & Mosts	
Landor	Hospitality	
Carlyle	Country Life	
⟨Persian Poetry⟩	Old Age	
Abraham Lincoln	Solitude & Society	
Daniel Webster	Woman	
Edward Taylor	Resources	
Harvard Martyrs	Success	
Concord Monument		

[119] In this entry, Emerson may be recalling the discussion of Arab hospitality in Eugène Daumas, *Les Chevaux du Sahara, et les Moeurs du Désert* (Paris, 1858), pp. 366–369, which he read in 1862 (see *JMN*, XV, 245); "Abu Bekeur" may be Emerson's mistaken recollection of Abd-el-Kader. The name may also refer to the account of Bou-Bekeur in Eugène Daumas and Ausone de Chancel, *Le Grand Désert: ou Itinéraire d'une Caravane du Sahara au Pays des Nègres* (Paris, 1848), pp. 40–49. See *JMN*, XV, 5.

[120] Like those on pp. [152]–[154] above, the lists on this page are apparently an inventory of uncollected works made as an attempt to begin shaping the volume that be-

[156] Every believer holds a different Christianity, that is, all Churches are Churches of one⟨.⟩ ↑member.↓

The creeds of old Churches fast become not only untenable, but ridiculous; pass into the pages of Punch; for example, ⟨thus⟩ one of the points in the Augsburg Confession, "the declaration of damnation against all who believe not in eternal damnation." See Life of Bunsen Vol. II p. 322[121]

You cannot attempt to enter into a church communion without a sacrifice of truth & self-respect.

1870. And is there anything in the history of barbarous tribes more gross than the conclusion to which the Oecumenical Council ↑of the Roman Catholics↓ from all nations lately reached, that the Pope is infallible?

[157] Bunsen's physiognomy, as I remember him in London, suggested not a noble, but the common German scholar, with marked sentimentalism or, as we commonly say, *gushing*; And these prayers, & violent conventicle utterances to which he runs in his correspondence & diary, betray that temperament. Yet he had talent & generosity, & appears to have been highly useful.

---

came *Society and Solitude*. "Characters" is undoubtedly the essay "Character," first published in the *North American Review*, April 1866, pp. 356–373; "Carlyle" is the *Dial* review of *Past and Present*; "Criticism" could be one of several lectures with similar titles; "Literature in 1840" is the *Dial* essay "Thoughts on Modern Literature"; "Some good Books" is probably the lecture "Books" from the "American Life" series, first read in Boston on December 25, 1864, and given an alternate title here to distinguish it from "Books," first published in the *Atlantic Monthly*, Jan. 1858, pp. 343–353, and reprinted in *Society and Solitude*. No specific lectures on Daniel Webster and Edward Taylor are known. In the center list on this page, the sequence of "Domestic Life" through "Social Aims" and that of "Country Life" through "Solitude & Society" are each struck through with a vertical line. In the list at the right of the page, "Criticism" was fingerwiped, then restored; "Books" is struck through with a vertical mark.

[121] Frances Bunsen, *A Memoir of Baron Bunsen*, 2 vols. (London, 1868); Emerson withdrew volume 1 from the Boston Athenaeum, January 8–February 13, 1869.

[158] 1869   May 5, at 6 A.M. died Philip Physick Randolph, son of the late Jacob Randolph, M.D.[122]

[159] [blank]
  [160] Everything returns to its primary form. Horatio Greenough told me that (he saw?) some persons who had been starved to death, & they lay each crouched & curled up like the foetus in embryo.

———

  God had infinite time to give us; but how did he give it? in one immense tract of a lazy millennium? No, but he cut it up into neat succession of new mornings, &, with each, therefore, a new idea, new inventions, & new applications.

———

"The door of intercourse is closed between those confined & those unconfined by space," say the Ali Ilahi An. *Dabistan,* II. 452[123]

  [161] Mahomet said to Ali, "I am the town of knowledge, & ⟨thou art⟩ ↑Ali is↓ the gate to it." *Dabistan.* II 456

  The religions are the amusements of the intellect.

———

  In America, though good maps are ⟨ne⟩a necessity, like a dictionary, yet it is never quite time to buy one of the States, nor of your own State, ⟨so instant & imminent are the changes⟩ because, though ⟨the changes have been so important that⟩[124] your last map is ⟨no longer useful,⟩ ↑already old,↓ yet new changes in boundary & in roads are ⟨now⟩ so imminent, that 'tis better to wait till they are completed & recorded.

[122] Philip Randolph of Philadelphia had been Emerson's correspondent and friend since the early 1850s.
[123] *The Dabistan, or School of Manners,* trans. David Shea and Anthony Troyer, 3 vols. (Paris, 1843).
[124] In the canceled phrase, "changes have ... that" is bracketed, with another bracket extending from "changes" back to include "the".

[162]¹²⁵ Yesterday, Saturday, ⟨May⟩June 12, the committee on Scale of merit & discipline met at Dr Walker'sⁿ in Cambridge: present, Dr Walker, Prof. Runkle, Theodore Lyman & R. W. E. ⟨M⟩Rev. Mr Hale alone was absent. Dr Walker gave some details of the manner in which the scale is made up,ⁿ & stated that the Faculty were for the most part contented with it as it stands & ⟨did⟩do not wish any alteration. ⟨Mr Lyman thought tha⟩He added that there is question & inconvenience in regard to Elective studies. For ⟨Mr⟩the poor men, it is matter of grave importance that they shall have rank sufficient to obtain a scholarship, that is, an income; & when [163] elective studies are proposed, they do not choose that which they wish to learn, but that which will give the most ↑marks, that is, highest↓ rank. ⟨Mr Lyman said,⟩ ↑It was stated↓ that the idle boys would choose Botany, or some other study which cost no thought & little attention, & it was not quite fair that for such idle reading they should receive equally high marks with those who elected ↑severer studies as↓ trigonometry or metaphysics, or advanced studies in Greek.

Mr Lyman said the state of study was much superior [164] at present to that which he remembered when in College, & alluded to the performance of young Hill at the examination.

⟨It was suggested that the⟩

Some of the professors, as Mr Lowell, & Mr Pierce, senior, do not keep a daily account of merits of the students, but make up a general average,—each in a way of his own.

It was suggested that ⟨the true way would be for⟩ ↑whilst↓ each teacher ⟨to⟩ ↑should↓ keep a daily ⟨a⟩record of the quality of recitations, ⟨but by⟩ ↑he should↓ [by] no means ⟨to⟩ present that ⟨to the⟩ in his final

---

¹²⁵ The first paragraph of the following passage, through "studies in Greek." on p. [163], is struck through in ink with two diagonal marks, in the form of an X, on each page. In addition to those previously identified, persons mentioned in the passage on pp. [162]–[166] include James Walker (1794–1874), former president of Harvard; John Daniel Runkle (1822–1902), a mathematician soon to be made president of the Massachusetts Institute of Technology; Edward Everett Hale (1822–1909), minister of Boston's South Church; Henry Barker Hill (1849–1903), son of Harvard's former president Thomas Hill and a member of the class of 1869; Benjamin Peirce (1809–1880), Perkins Professor of Astronomy and Mathematics at Harvard; and George Washington Hosmer (1803–1881), a native of Concord and president of Antioch College since 1866.

report, [165] but ⟨to⟩ ↑should↓ correct it by his growing knowledge of the depth or real merit of the student, as shown to him by his proficiency & power, or his want of success as made known in decisive strokes from time to time.

⟨In regard to⟩ ↑It is the necessary result of the existing system↓ the mixing of the record of deportment with that of scholarship, & thus degrading a good scholar, if by neglect of prayers or recitations he had incurred a public admonition, or raising the rank of a dull [166] scholar if he was punctual & in deportment blameless.

↑President Hosmer of Antioch College tells me that there they do not mark for merit; &, that, for discipline, they organize the students in the Dormitory into a Society for noting & resisting all breaches of order. The students have a President & other officers, & when any disturbance ⟨is made⟩ ↑occurs,↓ they examine & vote perhaps ↑to recommend↓ the expulsion of the offenders,—which ⟨the⟩ the College Govt then considers & decides.↓[126]

———

At present, the friends of Harvard are possessed in greater or less degree ⟨w⟩by the id⟨a⟩ea of making it a University for men, instead of a⟨n⟩ College for boys.

———

One would say that this better moral record should only serve to give the casting vote in favor of good behaviour where the ⟨rank was⟩ ↑marks for scholarship were↓ equal.[127]

[167] July 1, 1869.

Judge Hoar in his speech at the Alumni dinner at Cambridge yesterday, was a perfect example of Coleridge's definition of Genius, "the carrying the feelings of youth into the powers of manhood";[128]

[126] The last four paragraphs of this entry, beginning with "Some of the professors" on p. [164], are struck through in ink with a diagonal mark on p. [164], a diagonal mark on p. [165], and two diagonal marks, in the form of an X, on p. [166].

[127] This sentence is struck through in ink with two diagonal marks in the form of an X.

[128] *The Friend,* Essay I, section II; Emerson's library contains the three-volume London, 1818, edition.

And the audience were impressed & delighted with the rare combination of the innocence of a boy with the faculty of a hero.

I think every one who has had any experience in marking a series of
recitations h⟨i⟩as found how uncertainly his 6, & 7, ⟨8⟩& 8 are given.ⁿ
↑His first attempt will be worthless except in the extreme numbers,↓
& can only be approximately trustworthy in a great number of
days.¹²⁹

[168] Sumner ⟨p⟩collects his works.¹³⁰ They will be the history
of the republic for the last 25 years, as told by a brave ⟨&⟩perfectly
honest & well-instructed man, with large social culture & relations to
all eminent persons. He is diligent & able workman, with ⟨good⟩
↑rare↓ ability, without genius, without humor, but with persevering
study, wide reading, excellent memory, & high sense of honor, dis-
daining any bribe, any compliances, [169] & incapable of falsehood.
His singular advantages of person & of manners & a statesman's conversation impress every one favorably. He has the foible of most public men, the egotism which seems almost unavoidable at Washington[.]
I sat in his room once at Washington whilst he wrote a weary succession of letters,—⟨&⟩he writing without pause as fast as if he were
copying. He outshines all his mates in historical conversation [170] &
is so public in his regards, that he cannot be relied on to push an office
seeker, so that he is no favorite with politicians; but wherever I have
met with a dear lover of the country, & its moral interests, he is sure to
be a supporter of Sumner.

1869. July 26. This morning sent my six prose volumes, revised &
corrected, to Fields & Co. for their new Edition in two volumes¹³¹

---

¹²⁹ This paragraph is struck through in ink with two diagonal marks in the form of
an X.
   ¹³⁰ Emerson's library contains his subscriber's copies of twelve volumes of Sumner's
Works, 15 vols. (Boston, 1870–1883). The observations on Sumner on pp. [168]–[170]
are struck through in pencil with a single vertical use mark on each page.
   ¹³¹ Fields, Osgood & Co. published *The Prose Works of Ralph Waldo Emerson*, 2
vols., in October 1869.

" The ennui (langeweile) of the ↑(Prussian)↓ court is so dreadful, so massive & ⟨bod⟨y⟩↑ily↓⟩ ↑corporeal↓, said a courtier, that you could cut ⟨with⟩it with knives." Varnhagen X. 71.[132]

[171] New Essays[133] Vol III.
Beware in the new book of *repetitions*[n] of favorite sentences.

_____

In society, high advantages are set down to the individual as disadvantages. *"Solitude & Society."* Atl[*antic*]. Monthly. Vol. I. [(Dec., 1857),] p. 228

_____

So on the previous page, p. 227, occurs the following; "the one event which never loses its romance is the alighting of superior persons at our gate."[134]

_____

"Is it society to sit in one of your chairs"? *Ibidem.*[n] p. 228

"No man is fit for society who has fine traits." *Ibidem,* p. 226[135]

_____

Shall restore the life of man to splendor & make his name dear to history   *Dom↑estic↓ Life*[136]

_____

[172][137] *Critical Essays.*
    Literature in 1840   Dial I ⟨36⟩137
    Landor   Dial II 262

_____

[132] Emerson is translating from Karl August Varnhagen von Ense, *Tagebücher,* 14 vols. (Leipzig [and Hamburg], 1861–1870), vol. X of which he withdrew from the Boston Athenaeum, March 7–April 23, 1870.
    [133] "New" is written over a short rule. "New Essays" became *Society and Solitude,* 1870; the work is probably called "Vol III" here because Emerson's collected *Prose Works,* soon to appear, filled two volumes.
    [134] Curved rules resembling parentheses are drawn at the beginning and end of this quotation.
    [135] This and the preceding three quotations occur in "Society and Solitude," *W,* VII, 13, 11, 14, 7.
    [136] This phrase is used in "Domestic Life," *W,* VII, 133.
    [137] Like the lists on pp. [152]–[155] above, the list on this page is an inventory of uncollected works; it apparently was made after Emerson chose the contents for *Society and Solitude,* since of the twelve titles to appear in that volume, only "Art"—possibly a different essay—is included here. "Literature in 1840" is actually "Thoughts on Modern

Carlyle	⟨C⟩Dial IV. 96
Wordsworth	
Persian Poetry	Atlantic, I. 724
x Comedy & Humor	Dial IV 247
Tragedy including To Δεινον	Dial IV ⟨247⟩ ⟨52⟩515
Art	
Some Good Books	
Quotation & Originality . . .	↑N. A.↓ Review
Phi Beta Oration	Atlantic
Concord Monument Address	

Daniel Webster
Theodore Parker
Henry D. Thoreau
Abraham Lincoln
Edward Taylor
⟨Some Good Bo⟩Thomas Taylor

[173] ——
He who sits over the fire may get a colour, but he who ⟨goes⟩ ↑keeps↓ out in⟨to⟩ the cold gets a complexion.

——

rocks which only a bird could climb

[174] [blank]
[175] Landor says, "I shall then call the times bad, when they make me so." See also in *Landor's Works* Vol. 1. p 81 the lines to Drake preserved by Camden.[138]

Landor says, "Yet a single man of genius hath never appeared in the whole extent of Austria, an extent several thousand times greater than our city (Florence;) & this very street has given birth to fifty." ["Al-

---

Literature"; "Some Good Books" is probably the lecture "Books" from the "American Life" series; the Phi Beta Kappa oration was published as "Aspects of Culture" in the *Atlantic Monthly* and eventually collected as "Progress of Culture" in *Letters and Social Aims*. No specific lectures on Daniel Webster, Edward Taylor, or Thomas Taylor are known. The Greek words may be translated as "the fearful." "Some Good Books" is circled.

[138] "Southey and Porson: Second Conversation," *Imaginary Conversations,* in *The Works of Walter Savage Landor,* 2 vols. (London, 1868), in Emerson's library.

fieri and Salomon the Florentine Jew," *Imaginary Conversations,*]
Works Vol. I. p. 191.

"Annibal Caracci said to ⟨a⟩his scholar, *What you do not understand, you must
darken.*" ["Samuel Johnson and John Horne (Tooke)," *ibid.,*] *Landor.* Vol
I. p. 168.

"He who first praises a good book becomingly, is next in merit to the author." ["Alfieri and Salomon the Florentine Jew," *ibid.,*] Vol. I. p. 193

[176] [blank]
[177] At Walden, the other day, with G[eorge]. P. B[radford]., I was
struck, as often, with expression of refinement which Nature wears
often in such places:—the bright sunshine reflected by the agreeable
forms of the water, the ⟨coast⟩ ↑shore-↓line, & the forest; the soft lap-
ping ↑sound↓ of the water.

___

At my Club, I suppose I behave very ill in securing always, if I
can, a place by a valued friend, &, though I suppose (though I have
never heard it,) that I offend by this selection, ↑sometimes too visible,↓ my reason is, that I, who see in ordinary rarely select society,
must make the best use of this opportunity, having, at the same time,
the feeling that
　　　"I could be happy with either,
　　Were the other dear charmer away."
　　　　　　[Gay, *The Beggar's Opera,* II, air XXXV]

[178] I am interested not only in my advantages, but in my
↑disadvantages, that is, in my↓ fortunes proper; that is, in watching
my fate, to notice, after each act of mine, what result? is it prosperous?
is it adverse? & thus I find a pure entertainment of the intellect, alike
in what is called good or bad.

___

In Xenophon's "Banquet," Critobulus says, "I swear by all the
gods, I would not choose the power of the Persian King in preference
to beauty."[139]

___

[139] Paraphrased from *The Minor Works of Xenophon* (London, 1813), p. 272, in
Emerson's library.

[179] ↑Washington City↓
I notice that they who drink for some time the Potomac water lose
their relish for the water of the Charles river, the Merrimack & the
Connecticut. But I think ⟨p⟩the public health requires that the Potomac water should be corrected by copious infusions of these ⟨very⟩
↑provincial↓ streams.[140] ↑Rockwood Hoar retains his relish for the
Musketaquid.↓

[180] Sumner cites Cato as ⟨c⟩saying "that Kings were carniv-
orous animals."[141]

In looking into Hesiod's "Works & Days," I am reminded how much
harm our clocks & almanacs do us by ⟨keeping⟩ withdrawing our attention from the stars, the annual winds, & rains, ↑habits of animals,↓
& whatever primary observations of Nature the ancient nations relied
on. Their year was throughout religious & imaginative.

[181] "Sit in the shade, & drink moreover dark-hued wine—— —. Pour
in three cups of water first & add the fourth of wine." *Hesiod. Bohn,* p.
107[142]

The Greek rule for marriage ⟨is in⟩for woman is in her 19th year. Mu-
lier autem pubescat quatuor annos, quinto a pubertate anno nubat.
Hesiod [ibid.,] p. 113[n.][143]

"You↑,↓ ⟨fla⟩Perses, flattered much the bribe-swallowing judges. Fools, they
know neither how much half exceeds the whole, nor how great advantage is
in mallow & asphodel." *Bohn's Hesiod.* p 76
↑dinner of herbs↓

----

[140] "I notice . . . streams.", struck through in pencil with a vertical use mark, is used
in "Boston," *W,* XII, 187.
[141] Sumner, *Works,* 1870–1883, I, 96, cites a statement to this effect from Erasmus,
Adagia, III, vii, 1.
[142] *The Works of Hesiod, Callimachus, and Theognis,* trans. J. Banks (London: Henry
G. Bohn, 1856), with omission indicated by Emerson's dashes. Emerson withdrew this
volume from the Boston Athenaeum, September 2–30, 1869.
[143] The Bohn edition translates this sentence as: "And let the woman be in her bloom
four years, and be married in the fifth."

"Sow stripped, plough stripped, & reap stripped, if thou wouldst gather the works of Ceres." [*Ibid.,*] p. 95

[182] The same periodicity—shall I say,—reigns in fable, & brings the wildest curve round to a true moral, as works in electricity, gravitation, & the crystal. ↑And this is also expressed in tone and rhythm.↓

[183] 1869   Sept.
Returning from Naushon I rode in the train with Richard L. Pease, Esq, of Edgartown, who is Indian Commissioner on the part of the State for the Gayhead Indians, & who promised to send me some arrowheads.

———

Of Görres see Robinson's Diary, II. [196–]197.[144]

———

Names. In Newport, the street in which is the graveyard is called Farewell Street.
Names of Ships. Surprise; Flying Cloud;

[184][145] Humboldt one of those wonders of the world like ⟨Shakspeare⟩ ↑Aristotle↓, like Crichton,[146] like Newton, ⟨existing now⟩ appearing now & then as if to show us the possibilities of the Genus Homo, the Powers of the eye, the range of the faculties; ⟨that the⟩ whose eyes are natural telescopes & microscopes & whose faculties are so symmetrically joined that they have perpetual presence of mind, & ⟨r⟩ can read nature by bringing instantly their insight & their momen-

———

[144] *Diary, Reminiscences, and Correspondence of Henry Crabb Robinson,* ed. Thomas Sadler, 2 vols. (Boston, 1869), in Emerson's library.

[145] Several portions of the following passage are used in "Humboldt: An Abstract of Mr. Emerson's Remarks Made at the Celebration of the Centennial Anniversary of the Birth of Alexander von Humboldt, September 14, 1869," *W*, XI, 455–459. "Humboldt one . . . faculties;" and "Our faculties . . . shoes.", each struck through in pencil with a vertical use mark, are used on p. 457. With "natural telescopes . . . presence of mind," struck through in pencil with a vertical use mark, cf. p. 457. "You could not put . . . illuminated this," partly struck through with the same mark as "Our faculties . . . shoes.", and "You could not lose . . . disappoint him." are used on p. 458.

[146] James Crichton (1560?–1582) was a Scottish prodigy of learning and athletic accomplishment.

tary observation together; whilst men ordinarily ⟨do not instanta-
neously bring their⟩ are, as it were, astonished [185] by the new object, & do not on the instant bring their knowledge to bear on it.
Other men have memory which they can ransack, but Humboldt's
memory was wide awake to assist his observation. ⟨⟨T⟩Other men⟩ Our
faculties are a committee that slowly, one at a time, give their attention
& opinion,—but his, all united by electric chain,—so that a whole
French Academy travelled on his shoes. You could not put him on any
sea or shore, but his instant recollection ⟨of⟩ of the past history of
every other sea & shore ⟨instantly⟩ illuminated ⟨it⟩ ↑this↓, & he saw in
this confirmation or ⟨explanation⟩ ↑key↓ of the old fact. You could not
lose him. He was the man of the world, if ever there was one. [186]
You could not lose him; you could not detain him[;] ↑you could not
disappoint him.↓ The tardy Spaniards were months in getting their
expedition ready & it was ↑a↓ year that he waited; but Spain or Africa
or Asia were all ⟨fields⟩ harvest fields to this armed eye, to this Lyn-
caeus who could see through the earth, & through the ocean, who
knew how mountains were built, & seas drained.

[187] Humboldt with great propriety named his sketch of the results
of Science ⟨K⟩Cosmos[.].[147]
His words are the mnemonies of science, "volcanic paps", "magnetic
storms," &c[.]

Agassiz never appeared to such advantage as in his Biographical Discourse on Humboldt, at the Music Hall in Boston, yesterday. What is
unusual for him, he read a written discourse, about two hours long; yet
all of it strong, nothing to spare, not a weak point, no rhetoric, no fal-
setto;—his personal recollections & anecdotes of their intercourse,
simple, frank & tender in the tone of voice too, no error of egotism or
of self assertion, & far enough from French sentimentalism. He is
quite [188] as good a man as his hero, & not to be duplicated, I fear. I
admire his manliness, his equality always to the occasion, to any &
every company,—never a fop, never can his manners be separated
from himself.

---

[147] This sentence, struck through in ink with three vertical use marks, is used in
"Humboldt," *W*, XI, 457.

L[ouis]. A[gassiz].   E[benezer]. ↑R[ockwood].↓ H[oar].   J[ohn].
M[urray]. F[orbes].   J[ohn]. G[reenleaf]. W[hittier].   C[harles].
K[ing]. N[ewcomb].   A[mos] B[ronson] A[lcott].   H[enry] D[avid].
T[horeau].   J[ames]. ⟨L⟩E[lliot]. C[abot].   J[ames] R[ussell].
L[owell].   O[liver]. W[endell]. H[olmes].   T[homas]. G[old].
A[ppleton].[148]

[189] "Sir Philip Sydney made the religion he professed the firm basis
of his life; for this was his judgment, as he often told me,—that our true-
heartedness to the reformed religion in the beginning brought peace, safety,
& freedom to us: concluding, that the wisest & best way was that of William,
Prince of Orange, who never divided the consideration of estate from the
cause of religion, nor gave that sound party ⟨any⟩occasion to be jealous or
distracted upon any appearance of safety whatever; prudently resolving that
to temporize with the enemies of our faith, was but (as among sea-gulls) a
strife, not to keep upright, but aloft upon the top of every billow: which
[190] false-heartedness to God & man would in the end find itself forsaken
of both; as Sir Philip conceived." (See the rest of the paragraph) *Lord Brooke
Life of Sydney* Vol. 1. p[p]. 27[–28][149]

L'extrême liberté et l'⟨l⟩extrême oppression demandaient également la dureté
Romaine   C. Martha. *Marc*[us]. *Aurelius* Re⟨w⟩vue des d[*eux*]. M[*ondes*].
Avril. [15,] 1864. [p. 885][150]

There was more iron in Rom⟨e,⟩an, more mercury in Gree⟨ce.⟩k character.

See for selections from Marcus A⟨ur⟩ntoninus ↑my↓ [Notebook]
MORALS 248

[191] I never could get beyond five steps in my enumeration of
intellectual powers, say, ⟨Perce⟩ Instinct, Perception, Memory, Imagi-

[148] "T. G. A." was written in pencil, then overwritten in ink. Thomas Gold Appleton (1812–1884) was a Boston wit.
[149] Fulke Greville, First Baron Brooke, *Lord Brook's Life of Sir Philip Sidney,* 2 vols.
(Kent, 1816).
[150] C. Martha, "L'Examen de Conscience d'un Empereur Romain"; Emerson withdrew from the Boston Athenaeum, September 17–October 27, 1870, the volume of the
Revue des Deux Mondes containing this article.

nation, (including Fancy as a subaltern,) Reasoning or Understanding[.]
↑Some of the lower divisions as ↑Genius, Talent, Logic,↓ Wit & Humor, Pathos can be dealt with more easily.↓[151]

In my Chapter on "Books," I wrote,
"A ⟨m⟩right metaphysics would do justice to the coördinate powers of Imagination, Insight, Understanding, & Will." ↑See "Solitude & Society" p. 170.↓[152]

[192] I recall today Col. Shattuck's remark to me after Dr Jackson's ↑(?)↓ lecture on the central heat of the globe,—he said "it must be sloppy there." ↑Note the power of the word.↓   ↑⟨See words, supra p⟩↓[153]

——————

The person who commands the servant successfully is the one who does not think of the manner,—solely thinking that this thing must be done. ↑Command is Constitutional.↓

——————

Count Schla⟨rben⟩berndorf denied patriotism, but allowed ⟨aristocracy⟩nationality, to the English aristocracy, who would sell the liberties of the people to the crown, but not the crown to a foreign power. See *Crabb Robinson's Diary* [1869,] Vol. 1. p. 368

↑sloppy↓[154]

[193] Oct. 19, 1869.
    Carried to Fields & Co. today the copy of the four first chapters of my so-called new book, "Society & Solitude," proposing to send the chapters in the following order;[155]

[151] "Some of . . . easily." is in pencil.
[152] The page reference is to the Little Classics edition of *Society and Solitude* (Boston, 1876). See *W*, VII, 212.
[153] Daniel Shattuck (1790–1867) was a Concord merchant and banker. "See words, supra p", in pencil, is canceled in pencil.
[154] "sloppy" is in pencil.
[155] In the following list, the figures on the right side of the page are in pencil; Emerson's footnote and the rule above it are in pencil; "⟨Greatness⟩" is in erased pencil; the first

1	Society & Solitude	10 pp	
2	Civilization	8	
3	Art.	20	
4	Eloquence.	30	
5	Domestic Life.	* 15	
6	Farming.	15	123
7	Works & Days	20	98
8	Books	20	
9	Clubs	20	
10	Courage	10	
11	Success	20	
12	Old Age	10	
	⟨Greatness⟩	198	

*The first five estimated by Mr Osgood.

[194] Copy of *Collected Prose Works* to be sent to[156]

x   T[homas]. Carlyle

x   Arthur Helps

    [John Gardner?] Wilkinson

    [Matthew] Arnold

    W[illiam]. T[orrey]. Harris

    [Francis Cabot?] Lowell

    Capt. Charles Savage

    Miss [Elizabeth Palmer] Peabody

x   John Forster

    J. G. G. [John James Garth?] Wilkinson

---

seven titles, "Society & Solitude" through "Works & Days", are struck through in pencil with a vertical mark. The twelve essays listed here, excluding "Greatness," appear in the published volume in the same order.

[156] The two-volume *Prose Works* was published on October 27, 1869. In the list below, an *x* probably indicates that a copy was sent. Persons mentioned here who have not previously been identified are William Torrey Harris (1835–1909), editor of the *Journal of Speculative Philosophy* in St. Louis; Charles Tyler Savage, part owner of a hotel in Harvard, Massachusetts; and John Forster (1812–1876), an English historian and biographer of Landor. "J. G. G. Wilkinson" is obviously an error for either J. J. G. Wilkinson or J. G. Wilkinson.

x   H[enry]. James
    Dr [Nathaniel L.] Frothingham
    James B. Thayer
    Mrs Mary Parkman
x   J[ames]. R[ussell]. Lowell
x   H[enry]. W[adsworth]. Longfellow

[195] I read a good deal of experimental poetry in the new books. The author has said to himself, '*Who knows but this may please, & bec⟨a⟩ome famous? Did not Goethe experiment? Does not this read like the ancients?*' But ⟨great⟩good poetry was not written thus, but it delighted the poet first; he said & wrote it for joy, & it pleases the reader for the same reason.

Oct. 21. I wish I could recall my singular dream of last night with its physics, metaphysics, & rapid transformations,—all impressive at the moment, that ⟨i⟩on waking at midnight I tried to rehearse them, that I might keep them till morn. I fear 'tis all vanished. I noted [196] how we magnify the inward world, & emphasize it to hypocrisy by contempt of house & land & man's condition, which we call shabby & beastly. But in a few minutes these have their revenge, for we look to their chemistry & perceive that they are miracles of combination of ethereal elements, & do point instantly to moral causes. I passed into a room where were ladies & gentlemen, some of whom I knew. I did not wish to be recognised because of some disagreeable task, I cannot remember what. One of the ladies was beautiful, and I, it seemed, had already seen [197] her, & was her lover. She looked up from her painting, & saw ⟨me⟩,[157] but did not recognize me;—which I thought wrong,—unpardonable. Later, I reflected that it was not so criminal in her, since I had never *proposed*. Presently the scene changed, & I saw a common street-boy, without any personal advantages, walking with an air of determination, and I perceived that beauty of features signified nothing,—only this clearness ⟨of⟩& strength ⟨⟨of⟩& strength⟩of purpose made any form respectable & attractive.—'Tis all vain,—I cannot restore the dream.

---

[157] "me" is canceled in pencil.

[198] ↑Concord.↓ Friday, 22 October, 1869. This morning at ⟨5 o'clock⟩ 5↑h↓. 25m. I perceived that the house was shaken by an earthquake. I think the motion was prolonged for a minute. I got out of bed, lit a match, & looked at the clock. I heard no other noise than the wave-like shaking of the house would make. At breakfast, I found that Mrs Small had also observed it, & thought it an earthquake.

[199]¹⁵⁸ *Insight.*

The man who first said, in our war, "the Southern states are a shell." Was it Sherman? was it Grant? or Lincoln?¹⁵⁹

———

John Hunter first said, "Arrested development."¹⁶⁰

———

General Wayne was the Commissioner of the Government who first saw the importance of the nook of land at the foot of Lake Michigan round which the road to the Northwest must run, & managed to ⟨include || . . .||⟩run the boundary line of Illinois in such manner as ↑to↓ include this swamp, called Chicago, within it.

———

[200]   Mem.

Write to J. A. Harwood, Littleton[,] whether I can come to their Lyceum first Tuesday of February.¹⁶¹

————————————

All shams are mean. Haydon relates, that the crown worn at his coronation by George IV. was rented of the jewellers ↑Rundle & Co↓ for £5000.¹⁶² I think the iron crown of the Lombard kings preserved at Monza has more dignity.

[201] Tides in men & children. A wave of sanity & perception comes in, & they are on a level instantly with adults,—perfectly reasonable &

¹⁵⁸ A wavy pencil line is drawn in the left margin beside the entries on p. [199].
¹⁵⁹ During his march through Georgia, Sherman was reported to have said: "Pierce the shell of the Confederacy and it's hollow."
¹⁶⁰ See p. [113] above.
¹⁶¹ "Write to . . . February." and the rule below it are in pencil. Joseph Alfred Harwood of Littleton served on the staffs of two Massachusetts governors and was later a state senator. Emerson lectured in Littleton on February 1, 1870.
¹⁶² *Life of Benjamin Robert Haydon* . . . , ed. Tom Taylor, 2d ed., 3 vols. (London, 1853), II, 261, in Emerson's library.

right; out goes the wave, & they are silly intolerable miscreants. 'Tis all the difference between the bright water with the ships & the sun thereon, & the empty bay with its mud.

M[ary]. M[oody]. E[merson] held a relation to good society not very uncommon. She was strongly drawn to it as to the reputed theatre for genius, but her eccentricity disgusted it, & she was ⟨too⟩ quite too proud ↑& impulsive↓ to sit & conform. ⟨So she⟩ ↑So she acquiesced, & made no attempt to keep place, &↓ knew it only in the narratives of a few friends like Mrs George Lee, Mrs Mary Schalkwic, Miss Searle, &c. with whom she had been early intimate [202] & who for her genius tolerated or forgave her oddities.[163] But her sympathy & delight in its existence daily appear through all her disclaimers & fine scorn.

[203] *Good Writing*

All writing should be selection in order to drop every dead word. Why do you not save out of your speech or thinking only the vital things,—the spirited *mot* which amused or warmed you when you spoke it,—because of its luck & newness. I have just been ⟨w⟩reading, in this careful book of a most intelligent & learned man, any number of flat conventional words & sentences. If a man would learn to read his ⟨man⟩own manuscript severely,—becoming really a third person, & search only for what interested him, he would blot to purpose,—& how every page would gain! [204] Then all the words will be sprightly, & every sentence a surprise.

———

Dr Hedge tells us, that the Indian asked John Eliot, "why God did not kill the devil?" One would like to know what was Eliot's answer.

———

In the heavy storm I heard the cathedral bells squeaking like pigs through the snout.

———

↑*Good Writing.*↓

I will tell you what it is to be immortal,—this namely, that I cannot

[163] Hannah F. Lee (1780–1865) was the wife of George Gardner Lee of Boston; Mary Schalkwych, who died in 1811, married first Van Schalkwych and later Judge White of Salem; Sarah Searle is mentioned in earlier journals but is otherwise unidentified.

read Plutarch without perpetual reminders of men & women whom I know.

_____

"Eternity! thou dream of stuccoed roofs," —wrote W[illiam]. E[llery]. Channing, referring, ⟨no doubt⟩ I suppose, to the immortality preached in churches.[164]

[205][165] Dec. 5. *Carlyle's Works*   I have rec[eive]d
    Sartor Resartus   1
    Schiller   1
    Miscellaneous Essays   5
    French Revolution   2 vols., the *Vol I wanting*

[206]   Dec. 8.

Scholar wants not only time but *warm time,* good anthracite or cannel coal to make ⟨every⟩ every minute in the hour avail.

_____

Adam Muller says, ↑in 1824↓ "that England has ceased to belong to Europe: it will merely be the capital of her colonies." Austria has, in his judgment, only two necessary, only two alliances to keep; her right arm must be Rome, her left arm, Prussia, (as front against Russ⟨a⟩ia); then is she impregnable." *Varnhagen Blatter* III 114 [actually 115][166]

"Harmony latent is of greater value than that which is visible."
                    Heraclitus   See Plutarch[*'s Morals,*]
                    Goodwin's [ed., 1870,] II. 358

[207] A law of life that we carry the seeds of many diseases, perhaps of every disease. Whilst there is strength in the Constitution, these seeds lie latent. When our strength decays, either of these may get the mastery.

[164] The quoted line has not been located in Channing's published poetry.

[165] The entries on this page are in pencil. Emerson is referring here to the Library edition of Carlyle's *Collected Works,* 30 vols. (London, 1869–1871), of which his library contains all but vol. 12; see p. [272₂] below.

[166] Emerson is translating from Karl August Varnhagen von Ense, *Blätter aus der preussischen Geschichte,* 5 vols. (Leipzig, 1868–1869), the third volume of which he withdrew from the Boston Athenaeum, January 29–March 7, 1870.

Calvinism

There is a certain weakness in solemnly threatening the human being with the revelations of the Judgment Day, as Mrs Stowe winds up her appeal to the executors of Lady Byron.[167] An honest man would say, why refer it? All that is true & weighty with me has ↑all↓ its force now.

[208] We meet people who seem to overlook & read us with a smile, but they do not tell us what they read.

Now & then we say things to our mates, or hear things from them, which seem to put it out of the power of the parties to be strangers again.[168] Especially if any one show me a stroke of courage, a piece of inventive wit, a trait of character, or a pure delight in character when shown by others, henceforward I must be that man's or that woman's debtor, as one who has discovered to me among perishing men somewhat more clean & incorruptible than [209] the light of these midnight stars. Indeed the only real benefit of which we are susceptible is (is it not?) to have man dignified for us.
Very fine relations are established between every clear spirit & all bystanders. ↑*Is all this printed?*↓[169]

I find myself always harping on a few strings which sound tedious to others, but, like some old tunes to common people, have an inexhaustible charm to me. We are easily tired of a popular modish tune, but never of the voice of the wind in the woods.

[210]   Society & Solitude
            to be sent to[170]
            —
        J. P[eter]. Leslie

[167] Harriet Beecher Stowe published "The True Story of Lady Byron's Life" in the *Atlantic Monthly* in 1869, and *Lady Byron Vindicated* in 1870.
[168] This sentence, struck through in ink with two vertical use marks, is used in "Social Aims," *W*, VIII, 89.
[169] "*Is all this printed?*" is in pencil.
[170] *Society and Solitude: Twelve Chapters* was published by Fields, Osgood, & Co., in

—

Phila[delphia] Phil[osophical]. Soc[iety]

—

[Cyrus] Bartol
[William Torrey] Harris
[Charles Chauncy] Shackford
J[ames]. H[utchison]. Stirling
J[ohn] Forster
H[erman]. Grimm
Paulina Nash
H[enry] James
J[ames] R[ussell] Lowell
E[benezer] R[ockwood] Hoar
E[lizabeth]. H[oar].
Caroline [Sturgis] Tappan
C[harles]. [Tyler] Savage
E[lizabeth] P[almer] Peabody

x	Charles Sumner
x	Mrs Julia W[ard]. Howe
x	Miss M[ary]. E[lizabeth]. Wyer
x	W[illiam]. H[enry] Channing
x	Edwin Arnold
	E[lizabeth]. P[almer]. Peabody
x	Mrs S[arah]. S[wain]. Forbes
x	Mr Leach
x	J[ohn]. Haven Emerson
x	Charles E[liot]. Norton

sent ⟨x E[lizabeth]. Hoar⟩ x E[dith]. E[merson].
          Forbes
     x   J[ames] R[ussell] Lowell

February or early March, 1870. The list on p. [210] is in three columns, indicated by breaks; the second column begins approximately two-thirds of the way down the page and extends to the bottom margin. "Society . . . sent to" and the entries in the first column are in pencil. Persons listed who have not previously been identified include Julia Ward Howe (1819–1910), author of "Battle Hymn of the Republic"; Mary Elizabeth Wyer, daughter of Emerson's cousin Hannah Haskins Ladd Wyer; Edwin Arnold (1832–1904), an

	x		O[liver]. W[endell]. Holmes
	x		J[ames]. B[radley]. Thayer
sent	x		W[illiam]. H[athaway]. Forbes ⟨x E[dith] E[merson] F[orbes]⟩
sent	x		⟨C[harles]. W. Dabney⟩
	x		H[erman]. Grimm
	x		Paulina Nash
	x		Henry James
sent	x		⟨E[benezer]. R[ockwood]. Hoar⟩
	x		Caroline Tappan
	x		C[harles]. K[ing]. Newcomb
⟨x⟩	x	⟨‖ . . . ‖⟩	W[illiam]. H[enry]. Furness
	x		W[illiam]. E[llery]. Channing
			H[enry]. W[adsworth]. Longfellow
	x	x	T[homas]. Carlyle
			C[yrus]. A[ugustus]. Bartol
	x		J[ames]. H[utchison]. Stirling
			G[eorge]. P[artridge]. Bradford
	x		J[ames]. E[lliot]. Cabot
	x		S[amuel] G[ray]. Ward
			Capt. C[harles]. Savage
sent	x		Concord Library
	x		F[rederic]. H[enry]. Hedge
sent	x		Dr F[rederic]. R[ichard]. Lees
	x		Mrs Botta
	x		E[dwin]. P[ercy]. Whipple
	x		L[ouis]. Agassiz
			J[ohn]. Forster
			J. P[eter]. Leslie
			W[illiam]. T[orrey]. Harris
	x		Mrs Mary Parkman
	x		C[harles]. W[entworth]. Upham
			T[homas]. W[illiam]. Parsons
	x		E[zra?]. B. Ripley

English poet and translator of Eastern works; and Frederic Richard Lees (1815–1897), an English temperance leader and writer. "E. B. Ripley" may be Ezra B. Ripley, a son of Rev. Samuel Ripley; Mr. Leach has not been identified.

x	C[harles]. T[homas]. Jackson
x	Sophia Thoreau
x	N[athaniel]. L. Frothingham
x	A[mos] B[ronson] Alcott

[211] *Memory.* A man would think twice about learning a new science or reading a new paragraph, if he believed that the magnetism was only a constant amount, & that he lost a word therefore for every word he gained. But the experience is not quite so bad. In reading a foreign language, every new word added is a lamp ⟨shi⟩lighting up related words, & so assisting the memory & the apprehension; & so is it with ↑each fact in↓ a new science.

The words are mutually explaining, & every one adds transparency to the whole mass.[171]

———

"To declare war against length of time." *Simonides.* [*Plutarch's Morals,* 1718, IV, 83]

———

Compensation of failing memory in age by the increased power & means of generalization[172]

[212] A member of the Senior Class in College asked me on Saturday, "whether, when I was in Europe, I had met with Spinosa?" I told him ↑that I did not;↓ that Spinoza must now be pretty old, since he was born in 1632.

↑*Eloquence.*↓

Whipple made us laugh with his story of the worthy man who, when Shakspeare was named, said, "Pooh! ⟨P⟩Nobody would ever have thought anything of that fellow if he had n't written those twent⟨hr⟩y three plays."

As Edward ↑B. E[merson].↓ used to say, "That's the other wag."[173]
'Twas[n] as easy to talk a thing down as up.

I asked Theodore Lyman on Saturday how it was exactly with Agas-

———

[171] "A man ... mass." is used in "Natural History of Intellect," *W*, XII, 100–101.
[172] Cf. Journal ST, p. [7] below.
[173] Emerson's younger brother Edward died in 1834.

siz's health. He said, "that no further paralysis had appeared, &
that he seemed not threatened. It was not apoplexy but a peculiarity
of his constitution, these turns of insensibility ⟨&⟩ which [213] had occurred. It was *hysteria.*" I replied, that I had often said that Agassiz
appeared [to] have two or three men rolled up into his personality,
but I had never suspected there was any woman also in his make.
Lyman insisted that he had himself seen hysteria oftener in men than
in women.

↑1870.↓ 3 February. The last ⟨She⟩proof-sheet of "Society & Solitude" comes back to me today for correction.

[214] Mr Charles Ware tells Edward, that the night before the
Cambridge Commemoration Day, he spent the night at Mr ↑Hud-
son's↓ room, in Cambridge, & woke from a dream which he could not
remember, repeating these words,—
    And what they dare to dream of, dare to d⟨o⟩ie for.
He went to the Pavilion Dinner, & there heard Mr Lowell read his
Poem, and when he came to the lines
    "Those love her best who to themselves are true
    And what— —"
⟨he⟩Ware said, now I know what's[n] coming,—but it won't rhyme, &
Mr Lowell proceeded—
    "And what they dare to dream of, dare to do."[174]

─────

We cannot easily render in English the old Schabendorf's ⟨n[?]⟩in-
scription for his tombstone, *Civis civitatem quaerendo obiit octogen-
arius.*   See *Varnhagen* [*Tagebücher,* 1861–1870,] XI. 311.[175]
The nearest translation perhaps would be,—a *republican seeking a republic, he died at eighty years.*

[215] Old age in Berlin, 1854,
    "That one in old age has the world of his own youth only as a

─────

[174] The poem is Lowell's "Ode Recited at the Harvard Commemoration, July 21,
1865," ll. 54–55. Charles Pickard Ware (1840–1921) taught at a private boys' school;
Henry Norman Hudson (1814–1886) was a Shakespearean scholar.
    [175] Emerson withdrew an unspecified volume or volumes of Varnhagen von Ense's
Tagebücher from the Boston Athenaeum, February 17–March 7, 1870.

secret, that one alone knows what no other understands, this want of communication, of sympathetic interest, is one of the heaviest burdens that is laid upon us. A sparkling fire which is steadily sprinkled with water, nearly extinguished, & still not extinguished! How often dies the word in my mouth, how often I rue the word spoken! One who in walking thinks he has an open path before him, & then, at every step, suddenly finds a block laid across the way, will soon rather give up his walk." *Varnhagen* [*ibid.,*] *XI.* 242

See also in *Varnhagen XI. p. 276,* a paragraph *"Furchtbare* ⟨re⟩*Rechnung"* &c which I desire to add at the conclusion of my ↑(alas!)↓ printed paper on "Old Age".[176]

[216] Feb. 24.
A prudent author should never reprint his occasional pieces, which, of course, must usually be based on such momentary events & feelings as certainly to conflict with his cooler habitual mundane judgments.

———

The dead live in our dreams.

———

Bettine in ⟨W⟩Varnhagen's Diary reminds me continually of M[ary]. M[oody]. E[merson]. though the first is ever helping herself with a lie, which the other abhorred. But the dwelling long with grief & with genius on your wrongs & wrong-doers, & exasperating the offender with habitual reproaches puts the parties in the worst relation & at last incapacitates [217] the complaining woman from seeing what degree of right or of necessity there is on the side of her offender, & what good reason he has to complain of her wrath & insults. This ever-increasing bias o⟨n⟩f the injured party has all the mischief of lying.

———

Feb. 27. At Club yesterday. Lowell, Longfellow, Cabot, Brimmer, Appleton, Hunt, James, Forbes, Fields; E⟨mers⟩rastus Bigelow was a guest.[177]

———

[176] Emerson translates this paragraph on pp. [219]–[220] below. "Old Age" is one of the essays in *Society and Solitude.*

[177] Martin Brimmer (1829–1896) was a Harvard overseer and first president of the Boston Museum of Fine Arts; Erastus Brigham Bigelow (1814–1879) invented power looms and wrote on the tariff.

M[ary]. M[oody]. E[merson] said to the lady who praised my mother to her for having educated her children so well, "↑Pooh!↓ they were born to be educated."

1869. *Dr Ripley*. I was educated in a certain suspicion & dislike of him from the tone in which M[ary]. M[oody]. E[merson]. spoke of him. But I now have come to believe him to have been a worthy, honorable & generous man.

[218] How dangerous is criticism. My brilliant friend cannot see any healthy power in Thoreau's thoughts. At first I suspect of course that he oversees me who admire Thoreau's power. But when I meet again fine perceptions ⟨of⟩ in Thoreau's papers, I see that there is defect in his critic that he should under-value them. Thoreau writes, in his *"Field Notes,"* "I look back for the era of this creation not into the night, but to a dawn for which no man ever rose early enough."[178]

↑a fine example of his affirmative genius.↓

March 15. My ⟨b⟩new book sells faster, it appears, than either of its foregoers. This is not for its merit, but only shows that old age is a good advertisement. Your name has been seen so often that your book must be worth buying.

[219] Plutarch, see *VA* 260

I hate protection ⟨in⟩of trade in our politics, and now I recall in what *Stillman* said of the Greek war,—that the English opposition to the independence of Greece is merely out of fear of its depriving them of the Eastern trade. ? ?[179]

"Fearful reckoning, when, in Age, one computes all which ⟨we

---

[178] Edward Emerson identifies the "brilliant friend" as "probably Lowell" (*J*, X, 311n.). The quotation from Thoreau is a journal entry for January 1853; see his *Journal*, ed. Bradford Torrey and Francis H. Allen (Boston, 1909), IV, 478.

[179] William James Stillman (1828–1901), an American painter and diplomat, was consul in Crete during an insurrection there, 1866–1868.

have⟩he has had, what ⟨we⟩he still ⟨have⟩has, and, at all events might ⟨have⟩still have! Contemporaries are mostly gone; our possessions collected; hope ⟨limited⟩ ↑shrunken↓; the approaching downfall before our eyes. We could not hold out, if we ↑lived↓ merely in our ⟨i⟨mo⟩nmost⟩ ↑own↓ personality; ⟨lived⟩ if ⟨not⟩ our sympathies with the Universal, the intellectual, the progressive, with men & humanity ⟨brought⟩ ↑did not bring↓ us rich consolations & inspirations, which far outgo the personality. And yet, it happens that th⟨ese⟩is last, in many moments, with [220] terrible counterpoise jerks all the rest into the air." *Varnhagen,* [*Tagebücher,* 1861–1870,] XI. 276.

"Every poem," said Richter, "is an occasional poem."[180]

———

France. Mirabeau said, when the National Assembly were abolishing all privileges, "This is just the ⟨temper⟩ character of our Frenchmen. They are three months disputing about syllables, & in a single night they overturn the whole venerable edifice of the monarchy." *Dumont.* Souvenirs Eng. Translation [*Recollections of Mirabeau,* 1833,] p 145

"The most leading trait in the French character is self-vanity." *Dumont.* [*Ibid.,*] p 154

↑"If a hundred persons indiscriminately were stopped in the streets of London & the same number in Paris & a proposal made to each to undertake the govt of his country, 99 wd. accept [221] the offer in Paris, & 99 would refuse it in London." *Dumont* [*ibid.,*] p 155↓[181]

⟨G⟩A gentleman, English, French, or American, is rare: I think I remember every one I have ever seen.

———

↑March 16.↓   *Musagetes.*
    After the Social Circle had broken up, last night, & only two remained with me, one said that a cigar had uses. If you found yourself in a ⟨tavern⟩hotel with writing to do,—fire just ⟨lighted⟩kindled in a

———

[180] Quoted in Sarah Austin, *Characteristics of Goethe: from the German of Falk, von Müller, etc.,* 3 vols. (London, 1833), III, 7n., in Emerson's library.
    [181] See *JMN,* XIII, 309.

cold room,— it was hard to begin; but light a cigar, & you were presently comfortable, & in condition to work. Mr Simon Brown then said, that he had never smoked, but as an editor (of the New England Farmer) he had much writing, & he often found himself taking up a little stick & whittling away on it, and, in a short time, brought [222] into tune & temper by that Yankee method.

Alvan Crocker gave me in the cars a history of his activity in the matter of the Fitchburg Railroad beginning, I think, in 1837. He is the author of the road. He was a paper manufacturer & could not get the material for making paper for less than 8 cents ↑a pound,↓ whilst in Boston & elsewhere it could be got for 2, 3, or 4 cents. He must find a way to bring Fitchburg nearer to Boston. He knew the country round him & studied the possibilities of each connection. He found he must study the nearest practicable paths to tide water. No man but he had faith in the rivers. Nashua River

[223] After studying the Hoosac Mountains well, he decided that the ↑mountain↓ must be perforated. He must see Loammi Baldwin, who was the best engineer in the state. He could not get at that busy man. He knew that his own mother's dearest friend had been the lady who was now Mr Baldwin's wife. To her he went, & told her who he was, & that he wished of all things to see Mr B. The lady said, "I loved your mother dearly, but I know nothing of you: but for her sake, I will take care that you shall see him. Come here, say, ↑next↓ Sunday after dinner, about 3 o'clock,—that is the right time, & I will see that Mr B. shall answer all your questions." He did so.[182]

[224]–[225] [blank]
[228₁][183] *Dream.*

The waking from an impressive dream is a curious example of the jealousy of the gods. There is an air as if the sender of the illusion

---

[182] Emerson has slightly mistaken the name of Alvah Crocker (1801–1874). Loammi Baldwin (1780–1838) was well known as a civil engineer. "A. Crocker" is centered at the top of p. [223].

[183] Emerson misnumbered as [228] and [229] what are actually pp. 226–227; [228] and [229] are repeated in their proper places. The editors have retained Emerson's numbers, adding subscript numbers to distinguish the two pairs.

had been heedless for a moment that the Reason had returned to its seat, & was startled into attention. Instantly, there is a rush from some quarter to break up the drama into a chaos of parts, then of particles, then of ether, like smoke dissolving in a wind: it cannot be disintegrated fast enough or fine enough. If you could give the waked watchman the smallest fragment, he could reconstruct the whole; for the moment⟨,⟩ he is sure he can & will; but his attention is so divided on the disappearing parts, that he cannot grasp the least atomy, & the last fragment or film disappears before he ↑could↓ say, I have it.

[229₁] ——
Lidian thinks that the claim made, & properly, for Christianity, is that it took away the fear of death. But, thanks to ⟨the⟩ Calvinism, it is plain that no people on earth now or heretofore were so haunted with fear of death as ↑the↓ Christians. Hell-fire for sin, hell-fire for not ⟨believing th⟩ accepting the creed of our Church, hell-fire for babes, if they ⟨did not live⟩ died before there was time to baptize them.

[228₂] ↑1870.↓ *Originality & Quotation.* I must add to the old stories, which we moderns repeat under new names, that of Epimenides of whom Plutarch says, "they say, that, having fallen asleep while he was a young man, he awakened 50 years after, & shaking off so long & close-sticking repose.—" See Plutarch Mor[*als*, 1718]. V. 58

——————

The part of each one of his class is as important & binding as that of the professor; they are like the base-ball clubs where the catcher & the pitcher are equally indispensable & the duties of each equally severe.[184] ↑printed in "Plutarch"↓

"Aimer à lire, c'est faire un échange des heures d'ennui que l'on doit avoir en sa vie, contre des heures délicieuses." *Montesquieu.* Pensées, p. 226[185]

Love of reading,—'tis to make exchange of those ⟨h⟩stupid hours which come in every life, for delightful hours.

[184] "The part . . . severe.", struck through in ink with a vertical use mark, is used in "Plutarch," *W*, X, 309.
[185] *Grandeur et Décadence des Romains . . . et Pensées* (Paris, 1846), in Emerson's library.

[229₂] ↑March, 1870.↓
Varnhagen von Ense's Tagebücher are monotonous enough with daily complaining of the meanness of the royal politics, but ever & anon with important notices of distinguished men,—very rar⟨i⟩ely of Goethe—much of Bettine von Arnim;—but it is always refreshing ⟨his⟩to meet with notices of ⟨his⟩ ↑Varnhagen's↓ reading in Pindar, Aristophanes, Terence, &c[.]
& now today, "Read in Cornelius Nepos & Julius Caesar, with boyish satisfaction."[186]

———

In "Clubs" I ought to have said that ⟨many⟩ men being each a treasure house of valuable experiences—& yet the man often shy & daunted by company into dumbness, it needs to court him, to ⟨m⟩put him at his ease, to make him laugh or weep, & so at last to get his *naturel*, his confessions, & his best experience.

[230] Varnhagen finds a sonnet in Wilhelm von Humboldt's ⟨w⟩Works, called "True Greatness,"—& inquires of Alex. Von Humboldt if it were intended against Friedrich the Great. Alex. ↑v.↓ H. does not reply. He learns from others that it meant Alexander v. H. Yet Varnhagen thinks Wilhelm could not have meant it so, & remembers Schlabrendorff's *mot*, "You have all which it belongs to a great man to have, & yet are not that;" and also that other ⟨wo⟩*mot* quoted by the same, "Il n'y a rien de véritablement grand où il n'y ait du citoyen." See *Varnhagen* [*Tagebücher*, 1861–1870,] Tom. X. [98–]99.

───────────

↑The blinded↓ *Arago's "ardent age"*—
    "Sa vieillesse est aussi remarquable que celle de M. de Humboldt, elle est même plus ardente." *Varnhagen* [*ibid.*,] X. *100*

I ought to have had Arago among my heroes in "Old Age." & Humboldt⟨.⟩↑, and Agesilaus.↓

[186] Varnhagen von Ense, *Tagebücher*, 1861–1870, X, 68; this quotation and the entries concerning Varnhagen on pp. [230]–[234] and [236] below are Emerson's translations from or summaries of passages in volume X, which he withdrew from the Boston Athenaeum, March 7–April 23, 1870.

[231] Varnhagen quotes the Nationalzeitung on the Crystal Palace at Sydenham, "Men build for the second time a tower of Babel, & this time it is finished." (in 1853) [*Ibid.*, X, 154]

1870.
23 March. On the 21st I received President Eliot's letter signifying the acceptance of Carlyle's bequest of the Cromwellian & ⟨S⟩Friedrich books by the Corporation of Harvard College, & inclosing the Vote of the Corporation. I wrote to Carlyle the same day inclosing the President's letter to me, & the Record of their Vote, & mailed it yesterday morning to him.[187]

"Although it be easy not to take praise while it is not given, yet how hard it is not to delight in the same, while it is offered!" *Van Helmont* p. 10[188]

"Study for eternity smiled on me." Van Helmont. p 10 [actually p. 12][189]

[232] Varnhagen says, "Goethe once said to me, 'How can the narrative be always right? the things themselves are not always right.' " And V. adds; "A microscopic history is not better than one seen with the natural unarmed eye;—not the rightness of the now invisible littles, but the gross impression is the main thing." Varnhagen [*Tagebücher*, 1861–1870,] Vol. X. 174

philister	cockney
eine windstille,	a calm.
hamisch	foxy[190]

Varnhagen repeats on different pages his ↑own↓ remark, that "all sensual & coarse things are the strongest appeal to nature. Thence the

---

[187] On November 18, 1869, Carlyle had written to Emerson offering to bequeath to Harvard—as a means of "testifying my gratitude to New England (New England, acting mainly through one of her Sons called Waldo Emerson)"—the books he had used in writing his histories of Cromwell and of Frederick the Great; see *CEC*, pp. 554–556 and 563–564, and *L*, VI, 104–108. The year and date at the beginning of this entry are enclosed in a circle open at the right.
[188] Jean Baptiste van Helmont, *Oriatrike or, Physick Refined* ... (London, 1662).
[189] See *JMN*, XIV, 57.
[190] "philister ... foxy" and the rules above and below are in pencil.

great force, thence the necessity of insulting & filthy words, & of coarse play with matters of sex. Every nation has its ⟨a⟩Aristophanes." [*Ibid.,*] Vol. X 177   ↑and sequel↓[191]

[233] In Varnhagen see Dr Bekse's visit to Cuba & V's blessings on America. [*Ibid.,*] Vol. X. 178.

In 55 days V. has written a stout book of 500 pages, "Life of Bulow." [*Ibid.,*] Vol. X. 179

See important biographic notice in reference to Counsellor Schul⟨z⟩tz's Life, & his correspondence with Goethe.
1853   ↑*Varnhagen*↓ [*ibid.,*] X. 179.

"Der arbeit macht den gesellen." *Goethe* [*Maximen und Reflexionen*, 71, *Werke*, 1828–1833, L, 41]

" The first Bonaparte grounded his power on the worst motives of men, money-getting & idleness, advantages of external life, & thereby destroyed all nobler foundation: he reckoned on immorality & ⟨verderbness:⟩corruption: he ⟨called out⟩ ↑appealed to↓ that. Therefore reaped he what he sowed. How did his great men, his Senate, betray him! [234] Our princes today do as he did: they hold only with the corrupt men, with idleness & ⟨vulgar⟩ base interests & frivolous toys. They also go in the same manner. Germany must be skimmed." *Varnhagen*. [*Ibid.,*] X. 219

At Wiesbaden, an Englishman ⟨delighted Varnhagen who⟩ being addressed by ⟨on⟩ another guest at the ⟨b⟩table, called the waiter, & said to him aloud, "Waiter, say to that gentleman that I won't speak with him." This delighted Varnhagen, and he adds, "Worthy of imitation. Nothing more odious than table d'hote conversation." [*Ibid.,* X, 223]

Musagetes: Goethe's fly;[192] Read not in your official professional direction too steadily,—rather less & less,[n] but where you find excite-

----

[191] "and sequel" is in pencil.

[192] Goethe's poem "Musagetes," in which an insistent fly is thanked for awakening the poet and leading him to seek the Muses in nature, is quoted in "Inspiration," *W*, VIII, 284–286.

ment, awakening. For every surface is equally near to the centre. Every one has his own experience,—but I find the contrasts most suggestive.

[235] Culture,—breeding,—yes, by all means, first of all. 'Tis ⟨a⟩the pass-word, the King's ring, not to Museums, not to the picture gallery, or the Menageri⟨ri⟩e or the Theatre, but to Society, to palaces, to the poets, the powerful men, the beautiful women, the wits, to Lady Jersey, Madame Recamier, the Granduchess Helene⟨.⟩, ↑& the rest.↓

Dumont's answer to Duchatelet who tried to sound him on the authorship of ⟨Du⟩Mirabeau's speeches.—"Nothing is more easy than imputations of this kind.⟨—⟩xxxxBut what matters it whether he lays his friends under contribution or not, provided he make them produce that which without him they could not have done. For in such case he is the real author." *Souvenirs de Mirabeau* [*Recollections of Mirabeau*, 1833], p. 222

[236] For "leasts & mosts" see paragraph on grape stones & cotton seeds, in   *EO* 85
and the anecdote of Lord Yarmouth   EO 131

Mirabeau appears to have been filled full of ⟨D⟩the Persian rule "If the poems of Dhoair Faraby fall into thy hands, steal them, though it were in the *holy* temple of Mecca itself"[193]
↑See to this point also Seneca's opinion & practice in [*Nouvelle*] *Biographie Generale*, [1855–1870,] Article *Seneque.*↓ [XLIII, 755–768]

↑*America.*↓
⟨W⟩Varnhagen says, "of politics, he does not despair.—The future[,] the whole future,—what an immeasureable kingdom! against that, what is a whole Russian Empire, though it vaunts itself to be one ninth of the ground of the ⟨e⟩Earth!" Varnh[agen, *Tagebücher*, 1861–1870,] X, 402

[193] See *JMN*, XV, 376, where this "Persian rule" is translated from Sir John Chardin, *Voyages du Chevalier Chardin, en Perse, et Autres Lieux de l'Orient . . .* , ed. L. Langlès, 10 vols. (Paris, 1811), V, 131.

↑[the following lines precede the above quotation]↓
"This temper is to me hereby possible that I expect all from the future, know that everything lies buried, & therefore is perfectly secure, happen now what will."

[237] ↑Identities. Bias.↓
The best identity is the practical one, as in the pur⟨se⟩e satisfaction felt in finding that we have long since said, written, or done, somewhat quite true & fit for ourselves.

———

Steffens relates that he went into Schelling's lecture-room at (Jena)? Schelling said, "Gentlemen, think of the wall." All the class at once took attitudes of thought; some stiffened themselves up; some shut their eyes; all concentrated themselves. After a time, he said, "Gentlemen, think of that which thought the wall." Then there was trouble in all the camp.[194]

See above *NY* 228.
↑See also *PH*↓

———

The delicate lines of character in M[ary]. M[oody]. E[merson]., Rahel, Margaret Fuller, S[arah]. A[lden]. Ripley, need good metaphysic, better than Hegel's, to read & delineate.[195]

———

[23⟨7⟩8] The scholar who abstracted himself with pain to make the analysis of Hegel is less enriched than when the beauty & depth of any thought by the wayside has commanded his mind & led to new thought & action: for this is healthy, & these thoughts light up the mind: he is made aware of the ⟨its⟩ walls, & also of the open way leading outward & upward, whilst the ↑other↓ analytic process is cold & bereaving, &,—shall I say it?—somewhat mean as spying.

[194] Emerson found this anecdote, the subject of which is actually Fichte rather than Schelling, in Heinrich Steffens, *The Story of My Career as Student at Freiberg and Jena, and as Professor at Halle, Breslau and Berlin,* trans. William Leonhard Gage (Boston, 1863), p. 39; he withdrew this volume from the Boston Athenaeum, April 25–May 14, 1870.
[195] Rahel Levin Varnhagen von Ense was the wife of Karl August Varnhagen von Ense; his *Rahel, ein Buch des Andenkens fur ihre Freunde,* 3 vols., was published in 1834.

[23⟨8⟩9] I heard on the day when I graduated at Cambridge, in 1821, Sampson Reed, who on that day took his Master's degree, deliver his oration on Genius. It was poorly spoken, as A[bel?]. Adams said, "in a meeching way," & the audience found it very dull & tiresome. John Quincy Adams who sat on the platform (his son George W⟨.⟩↑ashington↓ A. graduating on that day)¹⁹⁶ clapped ⟨th⟩ Reed's oration with emphasis, & I doubt if any one joined him. But I was much interested in it, &, at my request, my brother William, of Reed's class, borrowed afterwards the manuscript ⟨of him for me⟩, & I copied the whole of it, & kept it as a treasure. In 1826, he published "The Growth of the Mind," which I heartily prized & admired, &, in 1833, sent to Carlyle, as a⟨n American⟩ specimen of American thought. In 1830, I became much acquainted with Reed, who talked very seriously with me, both at his counting room & at my own house. In 1851,* after Webster's March [2⟨39⟩40] Speech in the U.S. Senate pronouncing for the Fugitive Slave Law, I met ↑Sampson↓ Reed in the Boston Athenaeum, & deplored to him this downfal[l] of our great man, &c. He replied, that "he thought it his best speech, & the greatest action of his life." So there were my two greatest men both down in the Pit together.¹⁹⁷

[241] ——
A drunken man who cannot walk can run; so of those whose will is only when in temper. ↑said Carlo.↓¹⁹⁸
——

Henry Thoreau was well aware of his stubborn contradictory attitude into which almost any conversation threw him, & said in the

* September.

¹⁹⁶ Two rules join the parentheses, creating a box around this phrase.
¹⁹⁷ Reed's statement about Webster is attributed to "the smoothest of Episcopal Clergymen" in Emerson's "The Fugitive Slave Law [Concord]," *W*, XI, 181. This entry contains two minor errors of fact: Emerson sent Reed's *Observations on the Growth of the Mind* to Carlyle in 1834 rather than 1833 (*CEC*, p. 100); Webster's Seventh of March Speech (as well as, apparently, Emerson's September encounter with Reed) was in 1850 rather than 1851.
¹⁹⁸ "Carlo" is probably Charles King Newcomb.

woods, "When I die,ⁿ you will find swamp oak written on my heart."
↑I got his words from Ellery Channing today.↓

From old MS. *AC* 4, 5, I copy 2 sentences
Men are a far sighted race, We can see well into the Dark Ages, &
guess bravely into the Future; but what is rolled & muffled in impenetrable folds is Today. I wrote long since,
>This shining hour is an edifice
>Which the omnipotent cannot rebuild.[199]

[242] Churches are good for nothing except when they are poor.
When the New Jerusalem Church was new in Boston they wrote an
admirable magazine. Since they have grown rich, ⟨S⟩not a thought has
come from them. ↑Churches are best in their beginnings.↓[200]

There is one other reason for dressing well than I have ever considered, namely, that dogs respect it, & will not attack you in good
clothes.

The strength of his moral convictions is the charm of the character of Fichte.

☞
Chivalry.[201]

[243] "I have never been able to comprehend why a man should take any
course but the ↑most↓ careful doing of his own work." *Steffens* [*The Story of
My Career,* 1863, p. 95]

Autograph Letters. Wise was the Turkish cadi who said, "O my
friend, my liver, the questioner is one, & the answerer is another."[202]

[199] A slightly different version of these lines appears in "Fragments on . . . Life," *W,*
IX, 350.
[200] Cf. Journal LN, p. [38] above.
[201] The hand above "Chivalry." points to the entry about Spartans at the bottom of
p. [243].
[202] Emerson is here recalling key phrases from Sir Austen Henry Layard, *Discoveries
among the Ruins of Nineveh and Babylon* . . . (New York, 1853), pp. 565–566; see *JMN,*
VI, 370–371.

"To erect a trophy in the soul against anger, is that which none but a great & victorious Puissance is able to achieve". Plutarch, Mor[als]. [1718,] I. 44.[203]

See the whole passage

_____   _____

I find ⟨him⟩ ↑Plutarch↓ a richer teacher of rhetoric than any modern.

Plutarch quotes as a true judgment, this,—"That this courteous gentle & benign disposition & behavior is not so acceptable, so obliging, & delightful to any of those with whom they converse, as it is to those who have it." *Morals* [1718,] I. 59.[204]

_____

⟨|| . . . ||⟩Custom of the Spartans always before the Fight to sacrifice to the Muses, that they might behave themselves with as much good conduct as with courage &c *Morals.* [1718,] I. 88

[244] ↑*Politics.*↓

I wish we might ⟨imitate⟩adopt in ⟨this⟩Massachusetts, & in America, the ⟨method⟩ ↑rule↓ of Sparta to *disfranchise a Citizen* who should be convicted of habitual drunkenness or other gross immorality. ↑as, for instance, failing to educate his children.↓

_____

Old Age. Here is a good text from Montesquieu;—"Les vieillards qui ont é⟨d⟩tudié dans leur jeunesse n'ont besoin que de se ressouvenir, et non d'apprendre. Cela est bien heureux." [*Grandeur et Décadence des Romains . . . et*] *Pensées.* [1845,] p. 232

[245]   9 June, 1870.

I find Philip Randolph almost if not quite on a level with my one or two Olympic friends in his insight,—as shown in /these/his/ mss. I have been reading. He made that impression on me once & again ⟨on⟩in our interviews whilst he lived, & in his paper which was promised to the N[orth]. A[merican]. Review. But in these papers on science, philosophy, poetry, painting, & Music, the supremacy of his Faith purely shines.

[203] This quotation from *Plutarch's Morals,* struck through in ink and pencil with single vertical use marks, is used in "Plutarch," *W,* X, 315.
[204] The quotation, struck through in ink with one vertical and two diagonal use marks, is used in "Plutarch," *W,* X, 316.

I have answered, on 8 June, Miss Elizabeth W. Stevenson's letter
which accompanied P[hilip]. ⟨R.⟩ ↑P↓ R[andolph].'s papers.
How much it ever pleases me that this pure spiritualist was the best
⟨p⟩chess-player in Philadelphia, &, according to Evan Randolp⟨s⟩h's account to me, had beaten the best players in Paris![205]

[246] [blank]

    [247] Plutarch rightly tells the anecdote of Alexander (badly re-
membered & misrelated usually), that he wept when he heard from
Anaxarchus that there was an infinite number of worlds; and his
friends asking if any accident had befallen him, he replied, "Don't you
think it a matter for my lamentation⟨g⟩, that, when there is such a vast
multitude of them, I have not yet conquered one?" *Plut*[*arch's*].
Morals. [1718,] I. 134

Were I professor of Rhetoric, I would urge my class to read Plutarch's
"Morals" in English, & ↑Cotton's↓ Montaigne for their English style.

    We think we do ⟨g⟩a great service to our country in publishing
this book ⟨for⟩ if we hereby force our public men to read the
"Ap⟨o⟩ophthegms[n]" of great commanders," before they make their
speeches to Caucuses & Conventions. If I could keep the secret, &
communicate it only to ⟨my⟩ [248] one or two chosen youths, I should
know that they would by this noble infiltration ⟨carry⟩ easily carry the
victory ⟨fr⟩ over all competitors. But ⟨I prefer, in the spirit⟩ ↑as it was
the desire↓ of these ⟨old⟩ ↑⟨ancient⟩↓ ↑old↓ patriots, to fill Rome or
Sparta with this majestic spirit, & not a few leaders only, we desire to
offer them to the American people. ↑printed in *Plutarch's Morals.*↓[206]

    Much is truly spoken that is untruly heard. "Theodorus, who
was called the Atheist,—for denying the existence of the gods,—was

---

[205] In the penultimate sentence of this entry, the middle initial "R." is canceled, and
the middle initial "P" inserted, in pencil. Elizabeth Stevenson has not been further identified; Emerson had met Evan Randolph during a visit to Philadelphia, and they corresponded during 1870.
    [206] The portion of this entry on p. [248] is written below "Much ... 136.", from
which it is separated by a page-wide rule and by "(continued from p. 247.)". This paragraph, struck through in pencil on p. [247] with a vertical use mark and in ink on p.
[248] with three vertical use marks, is used in "Plutarch," *W*, X, 322.

used to say, that he reached out his instructions with his right hand, but his hearers received them with their left hands." See *Plut* [*arch's*]. *Morals,* [1718,] I. 136.

———

My men.[207]

↑T[homas]. Carlyle↓
Louis Agassiz
E[benezer]. R[ockwood]. Hoar
J[ames]. E[lliot]. Cabot
J[ohn]. M[urray]. Forbes
C[harles] ⟨N⟩K[ing]. Newcomb
P[hilip]. P[hysick]. Randolph
R[ichard]. [Morris] Hunt
Alvah Crocker
W[illiam]. B[utler]. Ogden

S[amuel]. G[ray]. Ward
J[ames]. R[ussell]. Lowell
S[ampson]. Reed
H[enry]. D[avid]. Thoreau
A[mos]. B[ronson]. Alcott
Horatio Greenough
O[liver]. W[endell]. Holmes
John Muir.
J[ames] Elliot Cabot

↑*Written in 1871*↓

[249] Poetry is a free⟨e⟩ manner of speaking ⟨of⟩ ↑by↓ one in a larger horizon ⟨of⟩ than ⟨he⟩ ↑is↓ his wont, free, therefore, to help himself with many more symbols ⟨of⟩ ↑for↓ his thoughts, & consciously playing this game, delighting in this liberty & whim to magnify & dwarf things alternately, by ⟨sa⟩ using many symbols never before so used.

---

[207] The list of names on p. [248] is in two columns, indicated by a break. *"Written in 1871"* is in pencil and is written diagonally from the bottom left corner of the page. All of the men mentioned here have been identified previously except William Butler Ogden (1805–1877), the former mayor of Chicago and first president of the Union Pacific Railroad. Emerson originally wrote "Alvan" Crocker, then added a stroke to change the "n" to "h".

⟨t⟩There must be no forcing ⟨them⟩ ↑of types↓; ↑each↓ unusual, but accurately painting the thought he would convey. Any forcing at once
convicts of affectation, & repels.

[250] M[ary]. M[oody]. E[merson].
When somebody praised to her my mother's good education of her
children, ⟨she⟩ ↑Aunt Mary↓ replied, "they were born to be educated."[208]

[251] The reason of a new philosophy or philosopher is ever that
a man of thought finds that he cannot read in the old books. I can't
read Hegel, or Schelling, or ⟨understand⟩ find interest in what is told
me from them, so I persist in my own idle & easy way, & write down
my thoughts, & find presently that ⟨some people⟩ ↑there are congenial
persons who↓ like them, so I persist, ⟨perhaps,⟩ until ⟨a⟩ ↑some↓ sort of
outline or system grows. 'Tis the common course: Ever a new bias. It
happened to each of these, Heraclitus, or Hegel, or whosoever.

The part of each one of the class is as important & binding as that
of the professor: they are like the baseball players where the catcher &
the bat & the pitcher are equally important. ↑*Bis*, see above p. 228↓[209]

[252]   ↑Pendleton King↓[210]
            Pen. King
            Oak Ridge
June. 30, '70.   N. C.

[253] It characterizes a man for me that he hates Charles
Sumner: for it shows that he cannot distinguish between a foible & a
vice. Sumner's moral instinct & character are so exceptionally pure,
that he must have perpetual magnetism for honest men; his ability &

[208] Cf. p. [217] above.
[209] "The part . . . important.", struck through in ink with a vertical use mark, is used
in "Plutarch," *W*, X, 309. As Emerson here indicates, this sentence also appears above,
on the page the editors have designated [228₂].
[210] The inserted name is in pencil and is set off by a curved pencil rule to the left and
below. The entry on this page probably records a visit; on April 26, 1876, "Pen" King
wrote to Emerson from Philadelphia, and recalled visiting him in Concord in 1870.

working energy such that every good friend of the Republic must vote for him. Those who come near him & are offended by his ⟨vanity⟩ egotism, ⟨&⟩ ↑or↓ his foible of classic quotations ⟨&⟩ ↑or↓ other bad taste, easily forgive them if themselves are good, or magnify^n [254] them into disgust, if they are themselves incapable of his Virtue.[211]

I cannot but please myself with the recoil when Plutarch tells me, that, "the Athenians had ⟨so utter⟩ ↑such↓ an abhorrence of those who accused Socrates, that they would neither lend them fire, nor answer them any question, nor wash with them in the same water, but commanded the servants to pour it out as polluted, till these sycophants, no longer able to bear ↑up↓ under the pressure of this hatred, put an end to their own lives." *Plut*[*arch's*]. *Mor*[*als*]. [1718,] II. ⟨120⟩ 96.

[255] ↑*Inspiration*↓
Evenus said, "Fire makes the best sauce." (It was well said, but who is Evenus?)[212]   And George Sand spoke to the same purpose.

In "Leasts & Mosts," I ought to have insisted on the mass of experiences which we all have of delicate observations & inferences from faces & manners & tones, which go to imprint the character of our fellow men on our mind, ⟨&⟩ ↑yet↓ are utterly unreportable in themselves: & so, the nameless yet potent influences of ↑external↓ Nature.

[256]   *Voting.*
I read in Plutarch, *Morals,* [1718,] V. 419 that Epaminondas left his army, when fighting against the Spartans, to go to Thebes to be present at a public Election of Magistrates,

I find *Nouvelle Biographie Generale* a perpetual benefactor,—almost sure ⟨in⟩on every consultation to answer promptly & well. Long live ⟨le⟩M. le Docteur Hoefer! Just now he has answered fully on Plutarch, Suetonius, Amyot, but I dared not believe he would know Dr Phile-

[211] With this paragraph, cf. *JMN*, XV, 478–479.
[212] Evenus, a poet and sophist of Paros, 5th century B.C., is quoted in *Plutarch's Morals,* 1718, V, 409.

mon Holland,—yet he answered at once joyfully concerning him: &
even cites the epigram upon him;

> "Philemon with translations will so fill us
> He cannot let Suetonius be Tranquillus."[213]

[257] Remember that *Exercitus* means drill.

July 14, 1870.

Here at Nantasket Beach, with Ellen, I wonder that so few men
do ⟨not⟩penetrate what seems the sec⟨c⟩ret of the inn-keeper. He runs
along the coast, & perceives, that b⟨u⟩y buying a few acres ⟨of⟩ well-
chosen ⟨on⟩of ⟨sh⟩ sea-shore, which cost no more or not so much as
good land elsewhere, & building a good house, he shifts upon nature
the whole duty of filling it with guests, the sun, the moon, the stars,
the rainbow, [258] the sea, the islands, the whole horizon,—not elsewhere seen,—ships of all nations⟨,⟩↑.↓ ⟨all⟩ ↑All↓ of these, (& all un-
paid,) take on themselves the whole charge of entertaining his guests,
& filling & delighting their senses with ⟨their⟩ shows; and it were long
to tell in detail the attractions which ⟨they⟩ ↑these↓ furnish. Every
thing here is picturesque;—the long beach is every day renewed with
pleasing & magical shows, with variety of color, [259] with the
↑varied↓ music of the rising & falling water, with the multitudes of
fishes & the birds & men that prey on them; with the strange forms of
the radiates sprawling on the beach; with shells; with the beautiful variety of ↑sea-↓rolled pebbles,— ⟨of⟩ quartz, porphyry, sienite, mica, &
⟨marble⟩ limestone. The man buys a few acres, but he has all the good
& all the glory of ⟨many⟩ ↑a hundred↓ square miles, by the cunning
choice of [260] the place; for the storm is one of the grand entertain-
ers of his company; so is the sun, & the moon, & all the stars of
heaven, since they who see them here, in all their beauty, & in the
grand area or amphitheatre which they need for their right exhibition,
feel that they have never rightly seen them before. The men &
women who come to the house, & swarm or scatter in [261] groups
along the spacious beach, ↑or in yachts, or boats, or in carriages, or as

---

[213] The epigram on Holland (1552–1637), an English classical scholar, is found in
the *Nouvelle Biographie Générale,* 1855–1870, XXIV, 943n. Jean Chrétien Ferdinand
Hoefer was its chief editor.

bathers,↓ never appeared before so gracious & inoffensive. In these wide stretches, the largest company do not jostle one another. Then to help him, even the poor Indians from Maine & Canada creep on to the outskirts of the hotel to pitch their tents, & make baskets & bows ↑& arrows↓ to add a picturesque feature. [262] ⟨m⟩Multitudes of children decorate the piazza, ⟨well,⟩ⁿ & the grounds in front, with their babble & games; and in this broad area every individual from least to largest is inoffensive & ⟨a⟩ ↑an entertaining↓ variety↑.↓ ⟨in the picture⟩ To make the day complete, I saw ⟨in⟩from the deck of our boat ⟨in⟩ this morning, ⟨in coming down hither⟩ ↑coming out of the bay↓ the ⟨s⟩English steamer ⟨coming out of the bay⟩ which lately made the perilous jump on Minot's Ledge, [263] ⟨⟨on which it was nearly wrecked,⟩⟩ & this afternoon saw the ⟨monitor⟩ turret ⟨g⟩monitor, *Miantonomok,* sailing into Boston.

The ↑parlors,↓ chambers, & the table of the Rockland House were all good, but the ↑supreme↓ relish of these conveniences was this superb panorama which the ↑wise↓ choice of the place ⟨afforded⟩, on which the house was built⟨.⟩↑, afforded.↓ This selection of the site ⟨of⟩ [264] gives this house the ⟨t⟩like advantage over other houses that an astronomical observatory has over other towers,—namely,—that ⟨in⟩ this particular tower leads you to the heavens, & searches depths of space before inconceivable.

[265] ↑July 21.↓

   I am filling my house with books which I am bound to read, & wondering whether the new heavens which await the soul, (after the fatal hour,) will allow the consultation of these?

What good things I read in Plutarch today, "Whether an aged man ought to meddle in state affairs?"[214]

↑FAME.↓

"that, in a ruler, ⟨the⟩ ↑his↓ good obeying as well as good ruling ⟨adds⟩ is an honorable monument, & adds to death the glory accruing

[214] This phrase is the title of a section of *Plutarch's Morals,* 1718, V, 56–87.

from life. For this thing, as Simonides said, goes last under ground." Thucydides said, that not the desire of honor only never grows old, but much less also the inclinations to Society & affection to the State, which continues ↑even↓ in ants & bees to the very last. ↑printed in my Preface to *Plutarch's Morals*↓[215]

[266] Xenophon ⟨has written of⟩ ↑says of↓ *Agesilaus,* ⟨these words,⟩ "What youth was ever so gallant, but that *his* ↑old↓ age surpassed it?" See all this in *Plut*[arch's]. *Mor*[als]. [1718,] V. 58–60.[216] ↑I saw too that Agesilaus, & ↑Arago, & Humboldt,↓ should have been remembered by me in my old men.↓

———

A snuffs his lamp very well, but there's a plentiful lack of oil.

———

Aimless activity,—no sequence.

_____

↑*Bis.*↓
⟨"What man's youth was ever so gallant but Agesilaus's old age surpassed it?" *Plutarch*⟩

———

Eugene Benson, Louisville (Commercial) Journal   Louisville, Ky[217]

Pairs.[n] Brutus & Cassius. Kirby & Spence. Darwin & Wallace. Beaumont & Fletcher

[267] ———
What's in a name? Why, much. 'Tis hardly respectful to say of a ⟨man⟩worthy gentleman that he died of the *grippe*.

[215] " 'that, in a ruler . . . last." is quoted from *Plutarch's Morals,* 1718, V, 57–58; the second sentence, struck through in pencil with one vertical use mark and in ink with four, is used in "Plutarch," *W,* X, 310. Emerson's "Plutarch" was originally the introduction to the edition of the *Morals* edited by William W. Goodwin (1870).
[216] The quotation from Xenophon is paraphrased from V, 60. Emerson's mention of "my old men" in the sentence below refers to "Old Age," recently printed in *Society and Solitude.*
[217] The *Commercial* was Louisville's Republican newspaper. Benson, whose name and address also appear in Journal ST, p. [149] below, has not been identified.

↑There are more insane men than are counted in the census as such.↓

We cannot treat quite cheerfully the fact of a bad temperament. The man ⟨|| . . . ||⟩ T[homas]. [Wren] W[ard?]. I can never trust. He has too many enemies in himself. He struggles hard to throw himself into line & position. But the strange current from within is against him. He cannot be true. Where is the hospital, who the physician that can heal him?

———

[268] I honor the author of the "Battle Hymn," and of "The Flag." She was born in the city of New-York. I could well wish she were a native of Massachusetts. We have had no such poetess in New England.[218]

[269] ↑1870.↓ This morning (August 7) I think no subject so fit for poetry as Home, the Massachusetts or the American Home.

[270] I find my readings of M[ary]. M[oody]. E[merson]. ever monitory & healthful as of old, & for the reason that they are moral inspirations. All ⟨my⟩ ↑the↓ men & women whose talents challenge my admiration from time to time lack this depth of source, & are therefore comparatively shallow; they amuse; they may be inimitable; I ⟨say⟩am proud of them as countrymen & contemporaries; but it is as music or pictures,—& other music & pictures would have served me as well; ⟨but⟩ they do not take rank hold of me as consolers, uplifters, & hinder⟨ing me⟩↑ers↓ from sleep. But the moral Muse is eternal, & wakes us to eternity,— [271] pervades the whole man; Socrates is not distant; Sparta is nearer than New York; Marcus Antoninus is of no age; Plotinus & Porphyry, Confucius & Menu had a deeper civilization than Paris or London; and the deeply religious men & women in or out of our churches are really the Salt of our civilization, & constitute the nerve & tension of our[219] politics in Germany, England & America. The men of talent see the power of principle, & the necessity of respecting it, but they deal with its phenomena, & not with the

[218] The subject of this encomium is Julia Ward Howe.
[219] "our" is circled in pencil.

source. It is learned & wielded as an accomplishment & a weapon. [272₁]²²⁰ As I have before written, ↑that↓ no number of *Nays* will help;—only one *Yea,* and this is moral.²²¹

Strength enters according to the presence of the moral element. There are no bounds to this power. If it have limits, we have not found them. It domesticates. They are not our friends who are of our household, but they who think & see with us. But it is ever wonderful where the moral element comes from.

———

The Christian doctrine not only modifies the individual character, but the individual character modifies the Christian doctrine in Luther, in Augustine, in Fenelon, in Milton.—↑⟨&⟩Something like this I read in Lèvéque ⟨i⟩on Antoninus.↓²²²

[273₁] ↑1870.↓ September 2d. With Edward took the 7.30 A.M. train from Boston to Portland, thence to South Paris, where we took a carriage & reached Waterford, Mr Houghton's inn, at 5 P.M.

Thence at 2 P.M. the next day ↑Sept. 3d↓ to S. Paris carried by Mr Wilkins, & took the ⟨r⟩train for G⟨ur⟩orham, & thence immediately the stage to the Glen House, Mt. Washington, where we arrived near 9 o'clock P.M., spent Sunday ↑Sept. 4,↓ & on Monday ↑Sept. 5↓ at 8 ↓o'c.↓ ⟨took⟩ascended the mountain in open carriage; descended at 3 ↑o'c.↓, in the railway coach, at 3 P.M. & reached the Crawford House at 5. P.M. ⟨n⟩Next morning, Sept. 6, took stage to Whitefield arriving to dine, thence ↑by↓ railway to Plymouth, arriving at 9 P.M. Next morning, Sept. 7, took ⟨coac⟩railroad at 5. ↑o'c.↓ & arrived in Boston at 11.30 & home in an hour.

[272₂] The avatar or second appearance of the Rosetta Stone is one year older than I am, as it was discovered in 1802.

²²⁰ Page numbers [272] and [273] are duplicated; the editors have added subscript numbers to distinguish the two pairs.

²²¹ See p. [64] above.

²²² Emerson may here be confusing two articles in the *Revue des Deux Mondes:* Charles Lévêque, "Un Médecin de l'Ame Chez les Paiens," Oct. 1, 1867, pp. 724–754, the subject of which is Plutarch; and C. Martha, "L'Examen de Conscience d'un Empereur Romain," April 15, 1864, quoted on p. [190] above. Lévêque's article contains a reference to Martha's essay (p. 732n.).

Tonight, September 14th, have come to me from Carlyle ten volumes of the Library Edition of his works,[223] namely,

1	Life of Sterling	1
2	Latter-Day Pamphlets	1
3	Heroes & Hero-Worship	1
4	Past & Present	1
5	Cromwell's Letters & Speeches	Vol. I
⟨6⟩	⟨do⟩	⟨Vol. II⟩ ↑none↓
7	do	Vol. III
8	do	Vol IV
9	do	
10	2 ⟨vols⟩copies of ⟨Vol⟩	Vol. V.

I have thus the

↑See *ST* 57 for later additions↓[224]

[273₂] I ha⟨ve⟩d already
   1 Sartor Resartus   2 copies
   1 Life of Schiller
   5 Miscellaneous Essays
   2 French Revolution   Vols II & III
       (Vol 1. not received)

now 18 volumes in all.[225]

The order of the Library Edition is
   Vol I   Sartor Resartus
   II., III, IV.   Fr[*ench*]. Revolution
   V   Life of Schiller
   VI VII VIII IX X   Miscellaneous Essays
   XI

[223] See p. [205] above.
[224] This notation is in pencil.
[225] "now . . . all." is set off by a curved rule above, to the right, and below.

XII	Heroes & Hero Worship
XIII	Past & Present
XIV ⟨Oliver⟩XV XVI XVII XVIII	Oliver Cromwell
XIX	
XX	Life of John Sterling[226]

I have two copies of Sartor Resartus
  and two of *Cromwell Vol V*
  and lack Vol. I. of French Rev[*olutio*]n & II. of Cromwell.
⌊Since, Carlyle has made his gift complete by sending the remainder
of his Works; in all 32, 8*vo* Volumes.⌋[227]

[274] Very much afflicted in these days with stupor:—acute at-
tacks whenever a visit is proposed. ↑or made.↓

———

Montesquieu's prediction is fulfilled, "La France se perdra par
les gens de guerre." [*Grandeur et Décadence des Romains . . . et*]
Pensées [1845,] ↑p.↓ 227

———

I know not when Carlyle found his phrase of "swallowing for-
mulas," but he could have found a good text in this sentence of Montesquieu; "L'héroisme que la morale avoue ne touche que peu de gens:
C'est l'héroisme qui détruit la morale, qui nous frappe, et cause notre
admiration." *Pensées.* ↑p.↓ 233

[275] 1870.
On Saturday, 2⟨5⟩4 September, at the Club, present Sumner, Longfellow, Lowell, Hoar, James, Brimmer, Fields, ↑E[stes].↓ Howe,
Holmes, ↑R. W. E,↓ and, as guests, Mr Catacazy the Russian Minister, Hon Samuel Hooper, & Henry Lee, Esq.[228]

———

[226] "The order . . . Sterling" is in pencil except for "XV".
[227] "Since, Carlyle . . . Volumes" is written vertically, from bottom to top, in the
right margin of this page. "32, 8*vo* Volumes" was written in pencil, then overwritten in
ink.
[228] Dr. Estes Howe had been associated with the Club at least since the Adirondac
expedition of August 1858; Samuel Hooper (1808–1875), a Boston merchant, was a

26 Sept.

Chivalry, I fancied, this afternoon, would serve as a good title for many topics & some good readings which I might offer to the Fraternity on 6 December.[229]

George Ticknor, Hallam, & Renan (in his paper on the Paris Exposition) have ⟨f⟩each given me good texts: Fauriel has others; and the wonderful mythology & poetry of Wales, of Brittany, of Germany (in the Nibelungen Lied) & Scott, & Joinville, & Froissart, can add their stores.

It might be called "Imagination" as well, & what we call chivalry be only a ri⟨c⟩ch illustration. Every reading boy has marched to school & on his errands, to fragments of this music, & ↑swinging↓ a cut stick for his broadsword, brandishing it, & plunging it into the swarm [276] ↑of↓ airy enemies whom his fancy ⟨marshalled⟩ ↑arrayed↓ on his right & left.

The life of the topic, of course, would be the impatience in every man of his limits; the inextinguishableness of the imagination. We cannot crouch in our hovels or our experience. We have an immense elasticity. Every reader takes part with the king, or the angel, or the God, in the novel or po⟨m⟩em he reads, & not with dwarfs & cockneys. That healthy surprise which a sunset sky gives to a man coming out on it alone, & from his day's work;—or which the stars unexpectedly seen give.

E[dward] W E[merson]   62 W Cedar St[230]

---

member of the U.S. House of Representatives; Henry Lee is probably the 1836 Harvard graduate who later became a founder of the American Bell Telephone Company.

[229] Emerson actually read "Immortality" before the Parker Fraternity on December 6, 1870. Authors mentioned in the following paragraph include George Ticknor (1791–1871), author of *History of Spanish Literature* (1849); Henry Hallam (1777–1859), an English historian who wrote on the Middle Ages; Ernest Renan (1823–1892), a French historian whose *Essais de Morale et de Critique*, 2d ed. (Paris, 1860), containing on pp. 353–374 "La Poésie de l'Exposition," Emerson withdrew from the Boston Athenaeum, January 9–February 25, 1869; Claude Charles Fauriel (1772–1844), author of *Histoire de la Poésie Provençale* (3 vols., 1847); Jean de Joinville (1224?–1317), chronicler of the Sixth Crusade; and Jean Froissart (1333?–1400?), author of *Chronique de France, d'Angleterre, d'Écosse et d'Espagne*.

[230] The address is in the Beacon Hill section of Boston, where Edward Emerson lived while studying medicine. The initials and address are in pencil.

[277]   Notes for Solitude & Society
Beware of repetition
     In Atl[*antic*]. Monthly   I [(Dec. 1857),] p. 228   read "In so-
ciety high advantages are set down ⟨as d⟩ to the individual as disadvantages"
     The same sentence is in Essays II p. 124[231]

J. W. Holman   Toledo   14   16   18

———

Thomas Loomis   Secy. Buffalo
     offers Jan. ⟨3d   17th   24, 31.⟩   ↑Yes, 17th Jan.↓

———

G[eorge]. W[ashington] Atherton   N[ew]. Brunswick—N. J.
asks some day in January

———

Toledo, O.   Rev Mr Mellen

———

Parker Fraternity, John C Haynes   ⟨Nov. 22⟩ ↑Dec. 6↓   ↑not then
but later↓   ↑Chivalry↓

———

Clarke Association, Boston, T. Dana, 2d   ⟨⟨2⟩ Jan. 2, or 9th⟩ ↑Jan.
(say) 23 ⟨or 30⟩ Jan.↓   ↑ART↓

———

⟨New Bruns⟩⟨Washington⟩
Salem   25 January
⟨Offered Mr Weeden Wednesday 16 Nov.⟩
Andover   13 January proposed[232]

---

[231] "Character," *Essays: Second Series* (Boston, 1844); see *W*, III, 114. This sentence
also appears on p. [171] above. The entry to this point is in pencil.
     [232] In the schedule of proposed or requested lecture dates above, two short vertical
rules follow "Jan. ⟨3d . . . 31.⟩"; "⟨Nov 22⟩" is circled; "Chivalry" is written in the right
margin of p. [276] and enclosed in a square bracket extending onto p. [277] to indicate
placement with the "Parker Fraternity" entry; "⟨⟨2⟩ Jan 2, or 9th⟩" is circled; "ART" is
written in the right margin of p. [276], with a rule below which extends onto p. [277] to
indicate placement with the "Clarke Association" entry. William Babcock Weeden was
often Emerson's host when he lectured in Providence, Rhode Island.

[278] [Index material omitted]
Is p. 209 printed?[233]

[inside back cover] [Index material omitted]

[233] This question is in pencil and is circled in pencil.

$\mathcal{ST}$

1870–1877

The last of Emerson's regular journals, Journal ST was begun late in 1870 and used until 1877. Emerson apparently carried the journal with him during his journeys to the western states in 1871 and to Europe and Egypt in 1872–1873. The earliest dated entry is October 2, 1870 (p. [3]); the last is January 1877 (p. [254]).

The covers of the copybook—brown, green, red, black, and yellow marbled paper over boards—measure 17.8 × 21.1 cm. The spine strip and the protective corners of the front and back covers are of tan leather. "ST" is written on the spine, and portions of a worn "ST" are visible in the upper right corner of the front cover. "1870", "1871", "1872", "1873", "1874", and "1875" are written in columnar fashion in the upper middle part of the front cover.

Including flyleaves (1–2, 279–280), there are 280 unlined pages measuring 17.5 × 20.5 cm. In his pagination, Emerson misnumbered and then corrected the numbering of twenty pages: 1⟨0⟩1, 2⟨0⟩2, 2⟨1⟩3, 2⟨2⟩4, 2⟨3⟩5, ⟨24⟩26, 2⟨ 5⟩7, 2⟨6⟩8, 2⟨7⟩9, ⟨28⟩30, ⟨29⟩31, 3⟨0⟩2, 3⟨1⟩3, 3⟨2⟩4, 3⟨3⟩5, 3⟨4⟩6, 3⟨5⟩7, 3⟨6⟩8, 3⟨7⟩9, and 24⟨2⟩4. Most of the pages are numbered in ink, but fourteen are numbered in pencil: 47, 54, 130, 131, 149, 154, 155, 242, 243, 248, 252, 254, 256, and 258. Thirteen pages were numbered first in pencil, then in ink: 50, 51, 52, 53, 127, 132, 150, 170, 171, 244, 245, 246, and 250. Eighteen pages are unnumbered: 1, 55, 135, 203, 207, 217, 259, 262, 265, 271, 272, 273, 274, 275, 276, 277, 279, and 280. Twenty-nine pages are blank: 6, 28, 40, 63, 77, 86, 100, 108, 109, 110, 112, 156, 194, 201, 203, 217, 225, 248, 251, 252, 262, 265, 271, 272, 273, 274, 275, 276, and 277. Additionally, two leaves have been pasted into ST. The first, a piece of white paper measuring 12.9 × 20.5 cm, is pasted to the bottom of p. [137] and has been numbered pp. [136ₐ] and [136♭] by the editors. The second, a piece of white paper measuring 12.6 × 20.3 cm, was at one time pasted to the top of p. [152] but is now loose. The editors have numbered this leaf pp. [152ₐ] and [152♭]. Pages [136♭] and [152ₐ] are blank; pp. [136ₐ] and [152♭] bear writing in Emerson's hand which has been incorporated into the text by the editors.

Inside the front cover a number of materials are laid. Of these, seven are in Emerson's hand:

(1) a sheet of white paper, originally intended to be used for a letter accepting an invitation, measuring 22.8 × 17 cm, which has been folded in half lengthwise to produce four writing sides on which is written (first side) "Francis Cabot Lowell." in ink, and in pencil "My friend had inherited from his father chemical Mills, but from what-

ever causes the property had sadly depreciated. He was advised to sell them at any price. But he undertook the charge of them himself,—studied chemistry with direct reference to the work done in the mills, made himself master of all the profo⟨ciars⟩↑esses↓ [processes?] required and ⟨against⟩ corrected the mistakes [second side] and against all advice stayed there until its depreciated shares came up to par then sold his shares & retired"; (third side) in ink, "Concord June 26, 77 / Mr R. Waldo Emerson accepts with great pleasure the"; (fourth side) blank.

(2) a printed invitation, measuring 12.4 × 19.8 cm, to attend the Harvard College Board of Overseers meeting on commencement day, June 28, 1872, on the address side of which Emerson made the following two entries, the first in ink, the second in pencil: "The distinction of the poet that his images are new, whilst the rhymer's ⟨use⟩ ↑are↓ the conventional. Take any ⟨cop⟩ newspaper & you will find &c &c ST 224"; "Poets who take things, & poets who give things".

(3) a piece of white paper, measuring 15.4 × 10.3 cm, inscribed in ink on both sides. The entries read (first side) "Life. 'We do not ⟨bring⟩take into account what life is in the concrete,—the agre⟨a⟩eable habit of working & doing, as Goethe names it,—the stead⟨y⟩ily engaging, incessant in-streaming of sensations in↑to↓ the bodily comfortableness.' Hegel. ap. Varnhagen [Tagebücher, 1861–1870] IX 297   Copied in PH 168"; (second side) "Defective verbs   forego   quoth".

(4) a piece of paper, measuring 12.8 × 10.7 cm, torn from an announcement of "Dividend Number Twenty" from the Chicago, Burlington and Quincy Railroad Co., August 3, 1870. On the reverse is written: "Charles Lévèque in his paper, Un Médecin de l'Ame cites his études de M. Martha sur Lucrèce, Perse, et Marc Aurèle, dans la Revue des ↑Deux Mondes↓ (8) Mars, 1863? 15 Septembre 1863, & 15 Avril 1864." Beneath this entry another is begun, but only the tops of unrecovered letters remain above the line of the tear.

(5) a piece of lined white paper, measuring 19.5 × 12.6 cm, on which the following lines are written lengthwise on one side:

"All inborn power that could
Consist with homage to the good
Flowed from his martial eye;
Fronting foes of God & man,
Frowning down the evil doer,
Battling for the weak & poor.
His from Youth the leader's look
Gave the law which others took,
And never poor beseeching glance
Shamed that sculptured Countenance."

(6) a piece of white paper, measuring 12.6 × 13.9 cm, on which the following is written lengthwise on one side:

"Chronology

Egypt. Manetho↑⟨o⟩lo Empire↓	5004 B.C.	
Middle Europe	2200 BC	
Latin Empire	1520 BC	
Greek Rule	332 BC	
Roman Rule	30 BC	
Theodosius & Xy ⟨38⟩		381 A.D.
Taliessin AD 10th century"		

(7) a piece of lined white paper, measuring 13.4 × 9.1 cm, on which the following list of potential topics appears:

"For Williamstown

> Social Aims
> Resources
> Tabletalk   clubs
> Poetry   Culture
> Success
> American ⟨Life⟩ Character"

In addition to the materials in Emerson's hand, the following items are also present: two post-office receipts, the first dated March 21, 1874, showing the receipt of a letter from Emerson to "Serson Jennings   Jacobs Forks, Catawba Cy N.C.", and the second dated April 1877, showing receipt of Emerson's post-office box rent ($.15).

Seven newspaper clippings are also laid inside the front cover: (1) an announcement of the contents of *The Atlantic Monthly* for June 1860, from an unidentified source; (2) a poem entitled "DION", inscribed to Lyman R. Goodman, attributed to Charles Warren Stoddard, advertised "For the Californian," from an unidentified source; (3) a poem entitled "NITILLA GRACILIS", advertised "For the Transcript," attributed to "H. S."; (4) a report of a lecture given before the Literary Institute Course by John Muir on "The Glaciers of California," from the Sacramento *Daily Record* for Wednesday, January 26, 1876; (5) an extract of a poem with no author or title cited, from an unidentified source; (6) an article dealing with uncomplimentary obituaries of James Fish, Jr., from the New York *Times* and the New York *Tribune*, apparently from a Baltimore, Maryland, paper; (7) a report entitled "Alcott and Wolcott: The Past and Present of a Connecticut Township" in which notice is taken of the centennial observances at Wolcott, Connecticut, and Bronson Alcott's participation in them, from an unidentified source.

Finally, laid inside the front cover is a statement on glossy paper attributed to Henry Wadsworth Longfellow from an unidentified source; it reads: "Last night I dreamed of Emerson. He said 'The Spring will come again, but shall we live to see it, or only the Eternal Spring up there?', lifting both his hands on high."

[front cover]   1870
                                    1871
                                    1872
                                    1873
                                    1874
                                    1875

[front cover verso]
Additions to *"Parnassus,"* see p. 147 in this book.
                                    258
                                    263

203

[Index material omitted]
Epicharnian[1]

[1]   R. W. Emerson.
                                                      Concord, Mass.

                        1870.
                        1871.
                        1872.
                        1873
                        1874
                        1875.

[2]   Poetry & Criticism
             Originality
             Inspiration
             Homes
             Waterville Address
             Leasts
             Greatness

[3] October 2, 1870.
La portée, the range of a thought, of a fact observed, & thence of the
word by which we denote it, makes its value. Only whilst it has new
values, does it ⟨excite⟩ warm ⟨us⟩ & invite & enable to write. And this
range or ulterior out-look appears to be rare in men:—a slight primi-
tive difference, but essential to the ⟨writer⟩ ↑work↓. For this
/poet/possesser/ has the necessity to write,—'tis easy & delightful to
him;—the other, finding no continuity,—must begin again up-hill
⟨with⟩ ↑at↓ every step. Now Plutarch is not a deep man, & might well
not be personally impressive to his contemporaries; but, having this
⟨facility [4] of⟩ ↑facile↓ association in his thought,—a wide horizon to
every fact or maxim or character which engaged him,—every new
topic re-animated all his experience or memory, ⟨of⟩ & he was impelled
with joy to begin a new chapter. Then there is no such ⟨string⟩ ↑cord↓
in nature for fagoting thoughts as well as actions, as *religion,* which

---

[1] "Epicharnian" is written diagonally across the lower left corner in pencil.

means *fagoting*.[2] He had a commanding moral sentiment, which indeed is common to all men, but in very unlike degree, so that in multitudes it appears secondary, as if aped only from eminent characters, [5] & not native. But in Plutarch was his genius. This clear *morale* is the foundation of Genius in Milton, in Burke, in Herbert, ↑in↓ Socrates, ↑in↓ Wordsworth, Michel Angelo, and, I think, also in many men who like to mask or disguise it^n in the variety of their powers,—as Shakspeare & Goethe. Indeed, we are sure to feel the discord & limitation in men of rare talent in whom this sentiment has not its healthy or normal superiority; as, Byron, Voltaire, Daniel Webster.

↑The writer is an explorer. Every step is an advance into new land.↓

[6] [blank]
[7] *Memory.* The compensation of failing memory is,—the assistance of increased & increasing generalization.

———

Not the chemist, but the trees reveal the secret of the soil. ⟨Put⟩ ↑Drop↓ the pine seed in yonder hopeless sand; the tree knows the alliance of the air with the earth, & what with sand, & what with air, a forest of huge trunks & broad branches springs out of the desart.

———

Old age stands not in years, but in directed activity.

———

Memory. Among my Mnemonics I record that I went ↑in↓to France just three hundred years after Montaigne did. He was born 1533; I visited it in 1833.

———

[8] "les langues d'oil, d'oc, et de si, c'est-a-dire, la francaise, la romane, et l'italienne." [*Nouvelle*] *Biog*[*raphie*]. *Gen*[*érale,* 1855–1870, XIII, 44]. article *Dante*

Subjects   American Society
            Resources   Inspiration
            Memory
            Books

———

[2] "cord" is written in pencil.

America
Relation of Intellect to Morals
Comic   & Gulistan
Woman
Chivalry[3]

Providence[4]
Social Culture
Memory
Resources & Inspiration
Wit ⟨or⟩& Humor
Relations of Intellect ⟨to⟩& Morals
National Character

[9] October 6. Last night ⟨to⟩heard Mrs Dallas Glyn read or act Antony & Cleopatra. A woman of great personal advantages & talent,—great variety ⟨& pe⟩of style, & perfect self possession: in dialogue between Antony & Cleopatra, the manly voice & the woman adequately rendered: and the dialogue between ⟨the⟩ the queen & the boy with the asp was perfect. The great passages in which I have always delighted were not du⟨l⟩ely felt by her, & ⟨some of the⟩had therefore no eminence: Some of them quite omitted. She ought [10] to go on to the stage, where the interruption by the other actors would give her the proper relief, & enhance her ⟨perfor⟩ own part. Her cries & violence were all right,—⟨&⟩ never vulgar. Her audience was not worthy of her reading, impertinently read newspapers & had a trick of going out. I am afraid they would have done the like to [Sarah Kemble] Siddons herself, until they had been told it was Siddons, & so had been afraid of being found out.[5]

---

[3] With the exception of "Woman", these nine lines are in pencil.
[4] *"Providence"* has been three-fourths encircled in ink by extending the underscore rule up and over the word.
[5] "Mrs Dallas Glyn" is Isabella Glyn (Gearns) Dallas, who was recommended to Emerson by letter by Tom Taylor, the playwright (*L*, VI, 135). Billed as the "Greatest Living English Actress," Miss Glyn began a series of Shakespearean readings at the Tremont Temple on October 5, 1870.

[1⟨0⟩1] 1870.

6 October. Today at the laying of the cornerstone of the "Memorial Hall," at Cambridge. All was well & wisely done. The storm ceased for us, the company was large,—the best men & the best women all there, or all but a few;—⟨and⟩ the arrangements simple & excellent, and every speaker successful. Henry Lee, with his uniform sense & courage, the Manager; ⟨Rev⟩the Chaplain, Rev. ⟨⟨Phil⟩Brooks⟩ Phillips ↑Brooks,↓ ⟨ma⟩offered a prayer, in which not a word was superfluous, & every right thing was said.

Henry Rogers, William Gray, Doctor Palfrey, made [12] each his proper Report. Luther's Hymn ↑in Dr Hedge's translation↓ was sung by a great choir, the cornerstone was laid, & ↑the⟨reafter⟩n↓ Rockwood Hoar read a discourse of perfect sense, taste, & feeling,— full of virtue & of tenderness. After this, an original song by Wendell Holmes was given ⟨us⟩ by the choir. Every part in all these performances was in such true feeling, that people praised them with broken voices, & we all proudly wept. ⟨The⟩ Our Harvard soldiers of [13] the war were in their uniforms, & heard their ↑own↓ praises, & the tender allusions to their dead comrades. General Mead[e] was present, & "adopted by the College," as Judge Hoar said, & Governor Claflin sat by President Eliot. Our English guests, Hughes, Rawlins, Dicey, & Bryce, sat & listened.[6]

"I bear no ill will to my contemporaries," said Cumberland. "After you, Maame, is manners," said Swett.[7] The only point in

[6] Those persons present at the Memorial Hall ceremony who have not been previously identified or are not easily recognizable include Rev. Phillips Brooks (1835–1893), American Episcopal Bishop, pastor of Trinity Church, Boston, 1869–1891; Henry B. Rogers, chairman of the Harvard College Building Committee, cochairman of the Committee of 50; William Gray, president of the Harvard College Association of the Alumni; John Gorham Palfrey (1796–1881), American Unitarian clergyman, proprietor and editor of the *North American Review* 1835–1844, and cochairman of the Committee of 50; George Gordon Meade, American army commander; Thomas Hughes (1822–1896), English jurist, reformer and writer, author of *Tom Brown's School Days* (1857); Charles E. Rawlins, Jr., who had a part in early stages of Emerson's friendship with Arthur Hugh Clough; Edward James Stephen Dicey (1832–1911), English journalist, author, and editor of the London *Observer* 1870–1889; James Bryce, Viscount Bryce (1838–1922), English jurist, historian, and diplomat.

[7] "Swett" may be John Sweet (1830–1913), a New Hampshire–born writer and educator who moved to California in 1862 and became a close friend of John Muir.

which I regret priority of departure is that I, as every one, keep many
stories of which the etiquette of contemporariness forbids the airing, &
which burn uncomfortably being untold. I positively resolve not to kill
A. nor C. nor N.—but I could a tale unfold like Hamlet's father. Now
a private class gives just this liberty which in book or public lecture
were unparliamentary, & of course [14] because here at least one is
safe from the unamiable presence of reporters. Another point. I set
great value in Culture on f⟨re⟩oreign literature—the farther off the
better—much on French, on Italian, on German or Welsh,—more on
Persian or Hindu, because if one read ⟨or⟩& write only English, he
soon slides into narrow conventions, & believes there is no other way
to write poetry than as Pope or as Milton. But a quite foreign mind
born & grown in different latitude & longitude,—nearer to the pole or
to the equator,—a child of Mount Heckla, like Sturluson, or of the
Sahara, like Averroes, astonishes us with a new nature, gives a fillip to
our indolence & we promptly learn that we have faculties which we
have never used.

[15] How right is Couture's rule of looking three times at the
object, for one at your drawing,—of looking at nature, & not at your
whim. & ↑Wm.↓ Hunt's emphasis, after him, on the mass, instead of
the details! & how perfectly, (as I wrote upon Couture long ago,) the
same rule applies in rhetoric or writing![8] Wendell Holmes hits right in
every affectionate poem he scribbles, by his instinct at obeying a just
perception of what *is* important, instead of ⟨minding⟩feeling about how
he shall write some verses touching the subject; and eminently this is
true in Rockwood Hoar's mind,—his tendency to the integrity of the
thing!

[16] What a lesson on culture is drawn from every day's intercourse with men & women. The rude youth or maid comes as a visiter
to a house, ⟨in⟩& at the table cannot understand half the conversation
that passes ↑in↓ so many allusions to books, to anecdotes, to persons,—hints of a song, or a fashion of the ↑War, or the↓ College, or

---

[8] Thomas Couture (1815–1879) was a French painter; Emerson's written statement
on him has not been located. William Morris Hunt (1824–1879), an American painter,
maintained a studio in Boston after 1864.

the boatmen, ⟨when a⟩or a single french or latin word to suggest a line
or sentence familiar to ⟨all the rest,⟩ ↑inmates,↓ unknown to the
stranger,—so that practically ⟨the family speak one language the
stranger a⟩ 'tis as if the family spoke another language than the guest.
Well, there is ⟨the⟩ an equal difference, ⟨in all their⟩ if their culture is
better, in all their [17] ways, & the like abbreviation by ⟨shorter or⟩
better methods, and ⟨time &⟩ⁿ only ⟨the⟩ long acquaintance, that is,
slow education, step by step, in their arts & knowledge can breed ⟨an⟩
↑a practical↓ equality. The like difference ↑of course must↓ appear⟨s⟩
in the father, the son, the grandson, & the great grandson, if ⟨as⟩ better
opportunities of education are provided to each successor, than his parent enjoyed.

[18] The reindeer was as useful to the Laplander, as the palm to
the Arab. "His flesh furnished food; his skin, clothing; his sinews,
threads; his horns were fashioned into harpoons, javelins, & sockets—
for the reception of spearheads & hatchets."   J. W. Foster, ⟨Whit-
neys⟩ *Recent Advances in* Geology   *Naturalist*[9]

⟨A man⟩A scholar says as proudly, "I have not read that book," as he
says, "Yes, I have read it⟨.⟩," ↑when you name another.↓[10]

[19] The progress of religion is steadily to its identity with
morals. The ⟨m⟩ancient & the modern religions were ↑immoral,—↓
full of selfishness. God belonged only to the *gen⟨s⟩tes,* & in no wise to
the *plebs.* ⟨⟨And⟩They⟩ ⟨They⟩ ↑These↓ were out of relation to the
altar, *the foyer,* & therefore had no marriage, no rights, might be killed
with impunity. It was so in ↑India,↓ Athens, & Rome; and the "heathen", in the middle ages, had no more rights than the brute.[11] The
Catholic & the English Episcopal Church & the Calvinistic Church

---

[9] John Wells Foster (1815–1873) was an American geologist and paleontologist;
"Whitneys" probably refers to Josiah Dwight Whitney (1819–1896), American scientist
and geologist, and professor at the Lawrence Scientific School, Harvard College
1875–1896. Though Foster and Whitney each wrote extensively on scientific subjects,
the source of this entry has not been located.

[10] The comma following "it" is in pencil over an ink period; "when . . . another." is
in pencil.

[11] The commas following " 'heathen' " and "ages" are in pencil.

are still deeply tainted with this barbarism. The fathers of [20] New England shared it still.

[21] *Greatness*
    "They deride thee, O Diogenes!" He replied, "But I am not derided." *Plutarch's Morals* [1718, I, 51].

[2⟨0⟩2] When there was question about the ⟨Count & Countess⟩ ↑Marchese & Marchesa↓ d'Ossoli coming to America, (alas that day!) a young lawyer↑, G.R.,↓ remarked, "I suppose that title is about equivalent to *Selectman* here." Well it appears that the *Kings* of Homer & later Greeks di⟨id⟩d not really possess more authority, they were simply the heads of the families, *gentes.* But, *memo.* I must procure a Greek Grammar. O for my old Gloucester again![12]

A passage in the *Convito* of Dante testifies that he knew Greek too ⟨in⟩imperfectly to read Homer in the original. [*Nouvelle*] *Biog[raphie]. Gen[érale*, 1855–1870, XIII, 43].

[2⟨1⟩3]   *Objection to Metaphysics.*
    The poet sees wholes, & avoids analysis. W[illiam]. E[llery]. C[hanning]. said to me, he would not know the botanical name of the flower, for fear he should never see the flower again. ⟨So t⟩The metaphysician dealing as it were with the mathematics of the mind, puts himself out of the way of the Inspiration, loses that which is the miracle, & ↑which↓ creates the worship.

[2⟨2⟩4] The writer is an explorer.[n] Every step is an advance into new land.

[2⟨3⟩5] Memo. in N. Y. Weale's Series of Mechanics at *Virtue & Yorston's* 10 & 12 Dey Street

The[13]

[12] Emerson is likely referring to *The Gloucester Greek Grammar,* which appeared in many editions.
    [13] "The" and the rule above it are in pencil.

America.

We get rid in this ⟨co⟩republic of a great deal of nonsense which disgusts us in European biography. There a superior mind, a Hegel, sincerely & scientifically exploring the laws of thought, is suddenly called by a necessity of pleasing some King, or conciliating some Catholics, to give a twist to his universal propositions to fit these absurd people, & not satisfying them even by these sacrifices of truth & ⟨honor⟩ manhood, another great genius, Schelling, is called in, when Hegel dies, to come to Berlin, & bend ⟨his mind to the same base accommodations of⟩ truth to [⟨24⟩26] the crotchets of the king & rabble. Not so here. The paucity of population, the vast extent of territory, the ⟨multitude⟩ solitude of each family & each man, allow⟨s⟩ some approximation to the result that every citizen has a religion of his own,—is a church by himself,—& worships & speculates in a new quite independent fashion.

Count Rumford

Look up Palfrey's History of New England[14]

The American Mind is not written in books, but on the land, & in the institutions & inventions.[15]

[2⟨5⟩7] ⟨A scholar forgives everything for⟩ *Good of evil.* King Henry VIII.'s urgency for his divorce secured the Protestantism of England. The leanings of Elizabeth to the old form, & ⟨the hatred of⟩ Abp. Whitgift's hatred of nonconformists, drove these last to expatriate themselves.[16]

[14] John Gorham Palfrey, *History of New England,* 5 vols. (Boston, 1858–1890).
[15] "The American . . . inventions." is in pencil.
[16] The comma following "nonconformists" is in pencil. John Whitgift (1530?–1604), archbishop of Canterbury 1583–1604, carried out Queen Elizabeth's policy of enforcing religious uniformity, and in 1593 forced the passage of a law making Puritanism an offense to the Crown.

Darius. "By difficulties he grew wiser than himself."[17]

Plutarch treats every subject except Art. ↑He is ingenious to draw medical virtue from every poison, to detect the good that may be made of evil↓[.]↓[18]

An admirable passage concerning Plato's expression ↑"↓that God geometrizes,↑"↓ in Plutarch's *Symposiacs.*[19] See especially in the Old Edition, [*Plutarch's Morals,* 1718,] Vol. III p. 434.

[2⟨6⟩8] [blank]
[2⟨7⟩9] Stanley, in his life of Arcesilaus, separates one sentence, "He was very good, & much excited hope in his auditors."   *Stanley* p. 218[20]

The delicate lines of character in M[ary]. M[oody]. E[merson]., Rahel Von Ense, Margaret Fuller, and S[arah]. A Ripley, need good metaphysic, better than Hegel's, to read.[21]

In the History of ⟨religion⟩ ↑opinion↓, the pinch of)alsehood shews itself not first in argument & formal protest↑,↓ but in insincerity, indifference & abandonment of the Church, or the scientific or political or economic institution for other better or worse forms. Then good heads feeling or observing [⟨28⟩30] this loss, formulate the fact in protest & argument, & suggest the correction & superior form. Rabelais, Voltaire, Heine, are earlier reformers than Huss, & Luther, & Strauss, & Parker, though less solemn & to less solemn readers.[22]

[17] Cf. an anecdote relating to Darius III, King of Persia (336–330 B.C.), in *Plutarch's Morals,* 1718, I, 466.
[18] "He is . . . evil" is in pencil.
[19] In " 'that . . . geometrizes' " the *t*'s in " 'that" are crossed and the quotation marks are inserted in pencil. See *JMN,* IX, 261.
[20] Thomas Stanley, *The History of Philosophy Containing the Lives, Opinions, Actions and Discourses of Philosophers of Every Sect,* 3rd. ed. (London, 1701). This volume is in Emerson's library.
[21] See Journal NY, p. [237] above.
[22] In the first sentence of this entry, the *t* in "argument" is crossed and the comma following "protest" is inserted in pencil. Persons mentioned here who have not been previously identified or are not easily recognizable include Heinrich Heine (1797–1856), German lyric poet and literary critic; John Huss (1369?–1415), Bohemian religious reformer and author of the influential *De Ecclesia;* David Friedrich Strauss (1808–1874), German theologian and philosopher, and author of the controversial *Das Leben Jesu, Kritisch Bearbeitet* (1835–1836).

↑Voltaire's Spinosa

"Je soupçonne, entre nous, que vous n'existez pas."

Satires. Les Systèmes.↓

_____

The Shah of Persia drank champagne for the first time in Russia & drank too much. One said "It appears the Shah is fond of French wine." Lord Russell replied, *C'est bien naturel: dans la nuit tous les chats sont gris.*[23]

_____

[⟨29⟩31] Huxley (Lay Sermons) cites *"Essays on a Liberal Education."* What? & Whose?[24]

_____

It really appears that the Latin & Greek continue to be ⟨taught⟩ ↑forced↓ in Education just as chignons ⟨hol⟩ must be worn, in spite of the disgust against both, for fashion.

If a wise traveller should visit England to study the causes of her power, it is not the Universities in which he would find them; but Mr Owen, Mr Armstrong, Mr Airy, Mr Stephenson, Sir J[ohn]. Lubbock, Mr Huxley, Mr Scott Russell, Bolton, Watt, Faraday, Tyndal, Darwin,[25]

[3⟨0⟩2] If any of these[n] ⟨are⟩were college men, 'tis only the good luck

[23] This anecdote of Lord Russell, 1st Earl Russell of Kingston Russell (1792–1878), British statesman and author, may have been entered here after Emerson visited Lord Russell in London, April 11, 1873. See Pocket Diary 23, p. [18] below.

[24] Thomas Henry Huxley, *Lay Sermons, Addresses, and Reviews* (London, 1870). Emerson borrowed this volume from the Boston Athenaeum October 22–29, 1870; however, the author of the *Essays* is not identified there or in modern editions of Huxley's work.

[25] Of those prominent Englishmen mentioned here who have not been previously identified or are not easily recognizable, William George Armstrong, Baron Armstrong of Cragside (1810–1900), invented a hydroelectric machine that produced frictional electricity, the hydraulic crane, and various types of modern artillery; Sir George Biddell Airy (1801–1892) was an astronomer; Sir John William Lubbock (1803–1865) was an astronomer, mathematician, and banker; John Scott Russell (1808–1882) was a naval architect; Charles Watt along with Hugh Burgess invented the soda process for making paper from wood pulp (1851–1854); John Tyndall (1820–1893) was a physicist, explorer, and popularizer of science. "Mr Stephenson" likely refers to George Stephenson (1781–1848), inventor of the miner's safety lamp and founder of several railways, or to Robert Stephenson (1803–1859), his son, railroad construction engineer and bridge builder, or to George Robert Stephenson (1819–1905), the senior Stephenson's nephew, civil engineer and builder of railways and bridges in England and abroad. Bolton is unidentified.

of the Universities, & not the⟨se⟩ir normal fruit. What the⟨y⟩se ↑men↓ have done, they did not learn there,

[3⟨1⟩3]↑*Plutarch.*↓

"Plato says that Time had its original from an intelligence." *Plut*[*arch's*] *Mor*[*als*, 1718,] *III.* 158

⟨On⟩The Greek text is, Πλατων δε γεννητον Κατ' εχινοιαν, and Goodwin prints,

"Plato,—that time had only an ideal beginning." G[oodwin, *Plutarch's Morals*, 1870]. Vol III. p. 128[26]

↑Dionysius Elder, being asked if he was at leisure, replied, 'May that never befall me.'↓ [*Plutarch's Morals*, 1718, V, 76]

"*Pythagoras* first called the World χόσμος, from the order & beauty of it." G[oodwin] III. 132 *Plut*[*arch's*]. *Mor*[*als*, 1870].[27]

μισέω μνάμονα σημπόταν, G[oodwin] ↑Plut[*arch's*]. Mor[*als*, 1870].↓ III 197

I remember that Mr Tom Lee complained of Margaret Fuller, that she remembered things.[n]
↑[And "the ancients used to consecrate ⟨f⟩↑F↓orgetfulness, with a ferula ↑in hand,↓ to Bacchus, thereby intimating that we should either not remember any irregularity committed in mirth & company, or should apply a gentle & childish correction to the faults."] *Ibidem*↓ [Goodwin, *Plutarch's Morals*, 1870, III, 197]

[26] "The Greek text . . . p. 128" is in ink over pencil. The ink and pencil versions are identical; however, the pencil under "The Greek . . . Plato,—" is not erased while the pencil under "that time . . . 128" is erased but readable; the comma following "prints" is in pencil only; and the bibliographic entry, with "G." circled in ink as it is for all succeeding abbreviations for Goodwin, is written to the right of the erased bibliographic entry. From this entry on, Emerson refers variously to two editions of *Plutarch's Morals*: the previously cited 1718 edition, sometimes called "Old Edition" (see p. [27] above), and *Plutarch's Morals*, ed. William G. Goodwin, 5 vols. (Boston, 1870), for which Emerson wrote the preface.
[27] " '*Pythagoras*" is underscored in pencil.

[3⟨2⟩4] A scholar ⟨c⟩forgives everything to him whose fault gives him a new insight, a new fact.

———

Let a scholar ↑begin↓ to read something to a few strangers ↑in a parlor,↓ & he may find his voice disobedient, & he reads badly. Let him go to ⟨an intelligent⟩ an assembly of intelligent people in a public hall, & his voice will behave beautifully, & he is another person, & contented.

[3⟨3⟩5] Superstitions

———

Effect of ash-bough on a viper.

———

Remora; Echeneis, ship-stopper,

———

the sight of a ram stops an e⟨r⟩nraged elephant.

———

amber
&
loadstone   Plut[*arch's*]. Mor[*als*, 1870].
                                            G[oodwin] III. 252²⁸

———

↑If the jaundiced look upon the bird Charadios, they are cured. P[*lutarch's*]. M[*orals*, 1718]. III 358↓

———

The conqueror at the Isthmian Games was crowned with a garland of pine, afterwards parsley.

——————

"The eye being very vigorous & active sends forth a strange fiery power, so that by it men act & suffer very much. — — —
the lover, when he looks upon his fair, flows out↑,↓ ⟨&⟩ as it were, & seems to mix with her." [condensed from] *Plut*[*arch's*]. *Mor*↑als↓ [1718,] III 357
"There is such a communication such a flame raised by one glance, that those must be altogether unacquainted [3⟨4⟩6] with love, who wonder ⟨that⟩at the

———

²⁸ According to legend, a viper will remain stock-still if touched with an ash-bough or beechen leaf; the remora, a fish with a sucking disk on top of its head, will stop ships to which it has attached itself; amber will draw all light-colored objects to it; loadstone will not draw a piece of iron that is rubbed with garlic.

Median naphtha ⟨that⟩ ↑which↓ takes fire at a distance from the flame." [*Plutarch's Morals*, 1718,] III. 357[-358]

Plutarch's style picturesque with his active, objective eyes, seeing every thing that moves, shines, or threatens, in nature, art, or thought, or dreams,[n] superstitions ↑& ghosts↓; believes in the evil eye, ⟨&⟩ ↑but↓ prefers, if you please, to talk ⟨in the morning⟩ of these things in the morning.[29]
He loves apples like ↑our↓ Thoreau, & well praises them   P[*lutarch's*]. M[*orals,* 1718]. III. 362

Why old men read at a long distance. G[oodwin, *Plutarch's Morals,* 1870,] III 222[-224]

⟨his⟩ ↑Plutarch's↓ picturesque & realistic style

Appleton's horse chestnuts with retroactive power.[30]

[3⟨5⟩7] *Art*   Imitation preferred to the reality.
Palmer the actor acting the part (was it of King Richard?,) when he should die on the stage, fell down really dead, & the audience hissed until they learned the fact.[31]
And Plutarch tells us of Parmen↑i↓o that he imitated the ⟨d⟩grunting of a pig so well, that, when a rival carried a pig under his cloak, & the audience heard the very pig, they still continued, "This is nothing comparable to Parmenio's sow," and the actor threw his pig among them. See *Plut*[*arch's*]. *Mor*[*als,* 1718]. III 344

↑Shall we drive nails in ⟨o⟩the plum tree to keep off the curculio, & carry horse chestnuts in our pockets to hinder rheumatism↓

[29] "Plutarch's style . . . in the morning.", which is struck through in ink and pencil with single vertical use marks and has a vertical line in pencil drawn in the left margin beside it, is used in "Plutarch," *W*, X, 300–301.
[30] Cf. Notebook OP Gulistan, p. [111], where Thomas Gold Appleton is reported to have said that horse chestnuts both cure and prevent rheumatism.
[31] John Palmer (1742?–1798), English actor, despondent over the death of his wife and a favorite son, died on stage on August 2, 1798, during the fourth act of *The Stranger*. See *JMN*, VI, 121, 233.

His excessive & fanciful humanity reminds one of Charles Lamb, whilst it much exceeds him.

"he would leave one lamp burning, only as a sign of the respect he bore to fires; for nothing so resembles an animal as fire. It is moved & nourished by itself, & by its brightness, like the soul, discovers & makes everything apparent [3⟨6⟩8] and in its quenching shows some power that seems to proceed from a vital principle; for it makes a noise & resists, like an animal dying or violently slaughtered. ⟨he wishes⟩ The ancients did nothing absurd when they highly reverenced an oak. The Athenians forbade any one to cut down an olive. Such observances do not make men superstitious, but persuade us to think of others, by being accustomed to pay this respect to inanimate creatures. And the Romans, dealing well with lamps, did not take away the nourishment they had given, but permitted them to live & shine by it." G[oodwin] Plut[arch's]. Mor[als, 1870]. III. [372-]373-4,[32]

[3⟨7⟩9] "It would be generous to lend our ears & ⟨y⟩eyes, nay, if possible, our reason & fortitude, to others whilst we are idle or asleep." G[oodwin, *Plutarch's Morals,* 1870,] III. 374[33]

There is no such safe bank ⟨in⟩wherein to deposit money as in paying a debt.

The result of the long conversation appeared to be, that men have precious little intellect, & women, if possible, less.

Inspiration
Seneca says, "the thought of my father who could not have sustained such a blow as my death, restrained me: I commanded myself to

---

[32] "His excessive . . . violently slaughtered." is struck through in pencil with two vertical use marks and in ink with one, and has a vertical line in pencil drawn in the left margin of the portion on p. [37], while the portion on p. [38] is struck through in pencil with two vertical use marks and in ink with one. " 'And the Romans . . . shine by it.' " is struck through in pencil with one vertical use mark and in ink with three. "His excessive . . . shine by it.' " is used in "Plutarch," *W*, X, 316. "His" and "He" in the opening lines refer to Florus, who loved the ancient customs. *"Plutarch"* is inserted at the top of p. [38].
[33] " 'It would be . . . asleep.' " is struck through in pencil with a vertical use mark and in ink with a vertical use mark.

live." See [*Nouvelle*] *Biog*[*raphie*]. *Generale* [1855–1870, XLIII, 756.] *Seneca*.

———

Goethe says, "I work more easily when the barometer is high than when it is low: Since I know this, I endeavor when the barometer is low, to counteract the injurious effect by great exertion,—& my attempt is successful." *Eckermann*. II. 272[34]

[40] [blank]

[41] 'Tis so hard not to believe your eyes. Every one goes thro' life assured that sunshine puts out fire.

[42] Peter Oliver, in the "Puritan Commonwealth," insists like a lawyer on the duty ⟨of⟩ the Pilgrims owed to their Charter, & the presumed spirit & intent in which it was given. He overlooks the irresistible instruction which the ↑actual↓ arrival in the new continent gave. That was a greater King than Charles, & insisted on making the law for those who would live in it. They ⟨were⟩ could not shut their eyes on the ⟨danger⟩ terms on which alone they could live in it. The savages, the sands, the snow, ⟨&⟩ the mutineers, & the French were antagonists who must be dealt with on the instant, ⟨or⟩ and there was no clause [43] in the Charter that could ⟨save⟩ deal with these. ⟨It was⟩ No^n lawyer ⟨who⟩ could help them to read the pitiless alternative which Plymouth rock offered them,—Self help or ruin. Come up to the real conditions, or die.[35]

———

names of Streets

———

101 *Benefit St.* Providence—
   Farewell St.   Newport, in which is ↑the↓ Burial Ground

[34] "Seneca says . . . *Seneca.*" and "Goethe says . . . II. 272", struck through in pencil with a common diagonal use mark, are used in "Inspiration," *W*, VIII, 283. *Conversations of Goethe with Eckermann and Soret,* trans. John Oxenford, 2 vols. (London, 1850), is in Emerson's library.

[35] Peter Oliver, *The Puritan Commonwealth: An Historical Review of the Puritan Government in Massachusetts* (Boston, 1856). Emerson withdrew this volume from the Boston Athenaeum November 18, 1870–January 13, 1871. The deleted "or" on p. [42] is struck through once in pencil.

[44] November 13, 1870. Received by mail from Thomas Carlyle, Life of Friedrich Vol. V. ⟨&⟩³⁶

Voting,
    Epaminodas   Plutarch, Morals G[oodwin, V, 458]³⁷
"Sir Richard Saltonstall was fined four bushels of malt for ab-
senting himself from the meeting of the Third Court." Sept. 26,
1630. Palfrey [*History of New England,* 1858–1890,] Vol. I, p. 320

R. W. E.³⁸

↑Every election in this country is a revolution. Morton chosen Govr of
Masstts, in 1839, by one vote↓

↑Nov. 20.↓³⁹ [1870]
Recd from Carlyle by hands of Fields & Co   Life of Sterling &
Friedrich   Vol I

Judge Wilbur of Rhode Island was not a great man & resented
some slight ⟨of⟩ ↑he received from↓ Tristram Burgess at the Bar, by
asking him if he knew before whom he was speaking, who replied,
"Yes, your honor; before the inferior court of the inferior ⟨b⟩Bench of
the inferior State of Rhode Island."

[45] Mr Weeden told me, that his old Aunt said of ⟨p⟩the people
whom she knew in her youth, that, "they had to hold on hard to the
huckleberry bushes to hinder themselves from being translated."

America has been called an "England under a magnifying glass."⁴⁰

At a certain stage, a crop of poets is inevitable as a crop of violets.

---

³⁶ This volume and those mentioned below under the entry for November 20 were
part of Carlyle's *Collected Works,* 1869–1871. See the note to Journal NY, p. [205]
above.
  ³⁷ See Journal NY, p. [256] above.
  ³⁸ The inserted entry that follows is written around "R. W. E."
  ³⁹ "Nov." is written through the full page rule preceding it; "20." is written atop the
rule.
  ⁴⁰ The quotation marks around this entry are in pencil.

Our politics a magnified whim. *RS,* 97

A country governed in bar-rooms [*RS* 97]

See sentences under *Politics,* in *Index Major.*

Formless America *CD* 29. 43

"Your overcoming yourself hath overcome me," wrote Dudley to Winthrop. Palfrey [*History of New England,* 1858–1890] I. 374[41]

[46] I delight ever in having to do with the drastic class, the men who can do things, as Dr C[harles]. T. Jackson; & Jim Bartlett; & Boynton.[42] Such was Thoreau. Once out of doors, the poets ⟨&⟩paled like ghosts before them. I met Boynton in Rochester, ↑N. Y.↓ & was cold enough to a popular unscientific lecturer on Geology. ↑But I↓ talked to him of the notice I had read of repulsion of incandescent bodies, & new experiments. "O," he said, "nothing is plainer: I have tried it;" &, on my way to Mr Ward's, he led me into a forge, where a stream of melted iron was running out of a furnace, & ↑he↓ passed his finger through the streamlet again & again, & invited me to do the same. I said, Do you not wet your finger? "No," he said, "the hand sweats a little & that suffices."

[47] Parnassus
So words must sparks be of those fires they strike   Lord Brooke[43]

---

[41] "'Your . . . I. 374" is in pencil.

[42] Jim Bartlett may be James W. Bartlett, mechanical superintendent of the locomotive works, whom Emerson met in Detroit in 1866; see *L,* V, 457. Boynton may be Samuel Boynton, who wrote to Emerson in 1863, possibly after Emerson's lecture visit to Rochester, New York, in January of that year; see *L,* VI, 375.

[43] "Parnassus . . . Brooke" is in pencil. Emerson used two editions of Lord Brooke's writings: *Certaine Learned and Elegant Workes* . . . (London, 1633), withdrawn from the Boston Athenaeum February 4–March 11, 1871, and *The Works in Verse and Prose Complete,* ed. Alexander B. Grosart, 4 vols. ([Blackburn,] 1870), withdrawn from the Boston Athenaeum February 4–14, 1871. "So words . . . they strike" is from Lord Brooke's *A Treatise of Humane Learning,* l. 660, and, misquoted, is used as the motto for the "Oracles and Counsels" section in *Parnassus.*

Shelley was shining sand. *J* 96[44]

Caroline Sturgis.	*Lines on a Picture.* Dial
Wilkinson	*Lines on Turner's Pictures* ↑x↓
Miss Palfrey's	*Sir Pavon & St Pavon* ↑x↓
	Licoo ↑x↓
	Leigh Hunt's *Song to Ceres* ↑x↓
Jamieson's Ballads,	*Stroude's Song* ↑x↓
	True Thomas, IT 2,
Lord Brooke's lines	L See *IT* 1,
Ben Jonson Vol III. 164	Epitaph on a child
↑x↓ Donne's "Extasy," p.	S. P. in ⟨E⟩Q. Elizabeth's
	Chapel. ↑x↓
Drowned Lovers— —	Child's Ballads

↑x↓ Cruel Sister	In the ⟨Moray⟩Moravian
	Hymn, ↑x↓
Gay Goss Hawk	for "important" read transcendant
Glen logie	or — transcending
Lizzie Lindsay	or — majestic
	or ↑decisive↓

This Hymn, "O draw me Father after thee," to be inserted in "Parnassus." ↑x↓

Griselda   28 pages
↑x↓   *To a mouse.* Burns
↑x↓   Lady Geraldine's Courtship
 ?   Norris[45]

---

[44] This statement is attributed to Elizabeth Hoar, who meant by it, according to Emerson, that Shelley's poetry "always looks attractive & valuable but try never so many times you cannot get anything good." See *JMN,* VIII, 178.

[45] In the list on p. [47] all inserted *x*'s are in pencil; "Drowned Lovers", "Cruel Sister", "Gay Goss Hawk", "Glen logie", "Lizzie Lindsay", and "decisive" are in pencil; in the right-hand column, a vertical line in ink is drawn to the left of *"Lines on a Picture . . . Licoo"* and *"True Thomas, . . . Chapel.";* single vertical lines in ink are drawn to the left of

[48] *Parnassus*
Carlyle is of Montaigne's opinion concerning poetry. See *Montaigne* [*Essays* . . . , 1693,] Vol. 1 261, 263–4

Nature is nothing but a skin, &c *RO* 104

"Child's Ballads", "In the ⟨Moray . . . decisive", and "This Hymn . . . Parnassus.' " in such a way that the lines form brackets with the rules they intersect; the *x* following "Hymn," is written above "important"; and the *x* following " 'Parnassus.' " is written through the rule preceding the entry. This list and several that appear later in this volume contain Emerson's preliminary jottings of authors and titles that he wished to include in *Parnassus;* however, not all authors and titles were finally included there. Caroline Sturgis's "Art and Artist" appeared in *The Dial,* I (Oct. 1840), 232; James John Garth Wilkinson's *Improvisations from the Spirit* (London, 1857), in Emerson's library, contains two poems on Turner, of which "Turner: Painter. His Art," ll. 21–24, 29–38, 45–50, is the source of "Turner" in *Parnassus.* Sara Hammond Palfrey's *Sir Pavon and St. Pavon* (Boston, 1867), written under the pseudonym E. Foxton and in Emerson's library, appears in *Parnassus* as "Sir Pavon and St. Pavon." "The banquet song of the Tonga Islanders," anonymous, which begins "Come to Licöo . . ." and was copied by Emerson in its entirety into Notebook Universe 7 (see *JMN,* I, 385), appears abridged in *Parnassus* as "Song of the Tonga-Islanders." Leigh Hunt's "Song to Ceres" appears in *Parnassus.* Robert Jamieson's *Popular Ballads and Songs from Tradition, Manuscripts, and Scarce Editions* . . . , 2 vols. (Edinburgh, 1806), which Emerson withdrew from the Boston Athenaeum March 16–April 1, 1872, is the source of William Stroude (or Strode), "On Music," which appears in *Parnassus* as "Music," and of the anonymous "True Thomas," which does not appear in *Parnassus.* Ben Jonson's *"An Epitaph on* S. P. *a Child of Queen* Elizabeth's Chapel" in *The Works of Ben. Johnson* [*sic*], 6 vols. (London, 1716), III, 164, in Emerson's library, does not appear in *Parnassus.* John Donne's "The Ecstasie" in *Poems on Several Occasions. Written by the Reverend John Donne . . . with Elegies on the Author's Death* (London, 1719), pp. 36–38, in Emerson's library, appears in *Parnassus* as "The Ecstasy." Francis James Child's *English and Scottish Ballads,* 8 vols. (Boston, 1857), in Emerson's library, is the source of the anonymous poems "The Drowned Lovers" and "The Cruel Sister"; "The Drowned Lovers" appears in *Parnassus. Minstrelsy of the Scottish Border: Consisting of Historical and Romantic Ballads,* ed. Sir Walter Scott, 3 vols., 4th ed. (Edinburgh, 1810), is cited as the source of the anonymous "The Gay Goss-Hawk" that appears in *Parnassus.* R. A. Smith's *The Scottish Minstrel, A Selection from the Melodies of Scotland, Ancient and Modern,* 6 vols., 2nd ed. (Edinburgh, n.d.), is cited as the source of the anonymous "Glenlogie" that appears in *Parnassus.* "Lizie Lindsay," a ballad preserved in Jamieson, *Popular Ballads and Songs* . . . , 1806, II, 149–153, does not appear in *Parnassus.* John Wesley's hymn, which begins "O Draw me, Father, after thee . . . ," appears in *Parnassus* as "Moravian Hymn" with "transcendent" inserted for "important" in l. 16. "Griselda" refers to "Griselda. The Clerkes Tale" in *Parnassus,* which is derived from Chaucer's "The Clerkes Tale" (ll. 57–1212), in *The Canterbury Tales,* which Emerson owned in two editions. Burns's "To a Mouse" and Elizabeth Barrett Browning's "Lady Geraldine's Courtship" both appear in *Parnassus.* Norris has not been identified.

For an old list of selections from Ben Jonson, see *AZ* 268,
Poetry is always affirmative.

———

Nothing can be done but by it. *CO* 89[46]

———

Gives us the eminent experiences only; a god stepping from peak to
peak, nor planting his foot but on a mountain.

———

The instinct is resistless, & knows the way, & is melodious, & at all
points a god.[47]

———

1873.[48] ↑x↓   Is *Cowper's*ⁿ *Ice palace* included?
        ↑Rejected↓   and A[lexander]. Selkirk—"I am out of hu-
manity's reach"

———

Clare, *K* 24
↑x↓   Motherwell
↑x↓   Macdonald   ↑The king & the skipper↓

[46] Referring to inspiration, "Nothing . . . it." is used in "Inspiration," *W*, VIII, 271.
[47] Cf. "Inspiration," *W*, VIII, 274, and *JMN*, XI, 394.
[48] In the entries that follow to the end of p. [48], all *x*'s are in pencil; a rule above
"Motherwell" has been struck through with one short diagonal line, perhaps to represent
an *x*; the *x* preceding "Logan" has been written over a rule above it; "Rejected" is inserted in pencil. The entries all relate to selections intended for inclusion in *Parnassus*.
William Cowper's "The Ice Palace" appears in *Parnassus*, but his "Verses Supposed to be
Written by Alexander Selkirk" does not. John Clare's "Address to Plenty, Winter," ll.
35–40, 49–54, appears in *Parnassus* as "The Laborer." *The Poetical Works of William
Motherwell*, 4th ed. (Boston, 1859), in Emerson's library, may have been the source of
"Jeanie Morrison" from which Emerson extracted stanzas 2, 3–5, 7, 8, and 12 to form
the poem that appears in *Parnassus* under the same title. "The Yerl O'Waterydeck," a
ballad by George Macdonald (1824–1905), appears in *Parnassus* as "The Earl O'Quarter-
deck. A New Old Ballad." Herbert Knowles's "Stanzas Written in the Churchyard of
Richmond, Yorkshire," of which "If thou . . . Moses appear" are ll. 2–3 misquoted, appears in *Parnassus*. "Murdered Traveller," "The Death of the Flowers" (probably the
work alluded to by "Autumn" in the list above), "To a Waterfowl," "The Rivulet"
(probably the work alluded to by "Brook" in the list above), and "To the Fringed Gentian" appear with alterations in *Parnassus*; *Poems by William Cullen Bryant* (New York,
1832), from which these works may have been taken, is in Emerson's library. Thirty-two
excerpted lines of "The Braes of Yarrow," a ballad by John Logan (1748–1788) of which
"They sought him east . . ." is l. 29, appear in *Parnassus*.

↑x↓   Herbert Knowles
         "⟨T⟩If thou wilt, let us build, but to whom?"
         "Nor Elias nor Moses appear," &c &c

↑x↓   Bryant—"Murdered Traveller," "Autumn," "Waterfowl,"
"Brook," "Gentian"

↑x↓   Logan—"They sought him east," &c

[49] One reason for Parnassus is that I wish a volume on my
own table that shall hold ⟨all my Poets⟩ the best poems of all my Poets:
and ⟨a⟩shall have nothing that is not poetry.

———————

From Shakspeare, insert from *Troilus & Cressida* III Act, III Scene,
[116–123, misquoted]
         "⟨For no⟩No man is the lord of anything
         Till he communicate his parts to others,
         Nor doth he of himself know them for aught
         Till he behold them formed in the applause
         Where they are extended, which, like an arch, reverberates
         The voice again: or like a gate of steel
         Fronting the sun, receives & renders back
         His figure & his heat."[49]

[50]   Chivalry

———————

         Condé, *AZ* 156
         John Adams, *CO* 113 [112–116]
         Columbus, *BO* 74   30   103   162
         Algernon Sidney's Letter, *T* ⟨v⟩5
Lecture on Aristocracy
When I count puddings, I shall die. *Luther*[50]
Vasari's account of L⟨i⟩eonardo da Vinci. *Bohn*, II 390[51]

———————

[49] Attributed to Shakespeare, these lines appear in *Parnassus* under the title "Fore-
sight."
[50] See *JMN*, VI, 349, quoting *Colloquia Mensalia; or, Dr. Martin Luther's Divine
Discourses at His Table*, 1652. See also *JMN*, X, 98; *L*, III, 412–413.
[51] Giorgio Vasari, *Lives of the Most Eminent Painters, Sculptors, and Architects*, trans.
Mrs. Jonathan Foster, 5 vols. (London, 1850–1852). This edition, published by Henry G.
Bohn, is in Emerson's library.

Murat, from Byron.[52]

↑An advantage of the old times (of chivalry) over ours; see *J* 20.↓

[51] *Home*   The wind murmurs & now howls in the walls of the
house. The Lars & lemurs are angry & threaten me.

———

Plutarch   of philosophy. See spec[i]ally *Plut*[*arch's*] *Mor*[*als*, 1718,]
I 448–9[53]

  Good Thoreau in Goodwin's Plutarch[*'s Morals*, 1870], Vol. V.
419–20[54]

  || epw || Plutarch   III   5
    God's mills   P[*lutarch's*]. M[*orals*, 1718]. IV 148[–149]
    ↑Good↓ sentence of Leonidas   G[oodwin, *Plutarch's Morals*,
1870,] I. 418
    Good mathematics   P[*lutarch's*]. M[*orals*, 1718]. III [433–]434

L'Étude sur Horace et Virgile de M. Patin, en tête de la traduction
d'Horace ⟨b⟩publié⟨d⟩e par ⟨M⟩ Garnier   p 19

———

  M. Egger[55]

———

[52] Emerson is likely referring to Lord Byron's "Ode from the French" (1816) in
which Joachim Murat (1767?–1815), one of Napoleon's cavalry commanders, is memori-
alized for his valor.
[53] "Plutarch . . . 448–9" and the rule preceding it are in pencil. The edition of *Plutarch's Morals* to which Emerson refers here has not been established. In *Plutarch's Morals*,
1718, "The Fortune or Vertue of Alexander the Great" is discussed on these pages, while
in *Plutarch's Morals*, ed. Goodwin, 1870, "Caution about [the] Admiration" of others is
the topic under discussion.
[54] "Good Thoreau . . . 419–20" is written over a pencil entry that reads "Good
Thoreau in G↑oodwin↓ V 419–20". On these pages Plutarch deals with the problem of
having to work to satisfy the interest owed after one has borrowed to satisfy his wants.
The "Good Thoreau" is summarized thus: ". . . if we would be content with such things
as are necessary for human life, usurers would be no less rare in the world than Centaurs
and Gorgons. But luxury and excess, as it has produced goldsmiths, silversmiths, per-
fumers, and dyers of curious colors, so has it brought forth usurers."
[55] "God's mills . . . M. Egger" is in pencil. Émile Egger (1813–1885), French phi-
lologist and Hellenist, was the author of the influential *Essai sur l'histoire de la critique chez
les Grecs suivi de la poétique d'Aristote et d'extraits de ses problèmes avec traduction française
et commentaire* (Paris, 1849). Emerson's reference to "L'Étude sur . . . Garnier   p 19"
has not been clarified.

[52] Plutarch says "In the early times friends went in pairs" G↑oodwin↓ [*Plutarch's Morals*, 1870,] I. 465 [misquoted]

They always do; that's what friends are
Pairs   G↑oodwin↓ [*Ibid.*] V. 450

Demosthenes   action   G↑oodwin↓ [*Ibid.*] V. 45[56]

———

υποηρισισ should be rendered *acting*, as the *acting* of a tragedy.
υποηρινεσθαι to act, as a player. See G[oodwin]'s Plutarch[*'s Morals*, 1870]. Vol. V. 45

[53] Dec. 26, [1870.]

I saw that no pressman could lay his sheets so deftly but that ⟨a⟩under every one a second sheet was inadvertently laid; & no book-binder could bind so carefully, but that ⟨each⟩ second sheet was bound in the book; then I saw, that if the writer was skilful, every word he wrote sank ⟨deeply⟩ into the inner sheet, & there remained indelible; & if he was not skilfu⟨ll⟩l, it did not penetrate, & the ink faded, & the writing was effaced.

———

Quot que aderant vates rebar adesse Deos. *Ovid.*[57]

———

[54]   ⟨Verses for Reading⟩Readings.   Parnassus[58]

———

Spenser's ⟨sonnet⟩ "Mother Hubbard"
      "Full little knowest thou who hast not tried"

———

[56] "Plutarch says . . . V. 45" is in pencil. "Demosthenes   action" refers to the time when, after being hissed for an oration during which memory failed him, Demosthenes stated that the first, second, and third parts of oratory are "Action."

[57] "Whatever prophets were present, I believed gods were present" (Ed.). This statement is used as the motto for the section "Intellectual" in *Parnassus*.

[58] "⟨Verses . . . Parnassus" is in pencil. Of Emerson's readings for *Parnassus* in the list that follows, these works have been identified: Edmund Spenser's "Prosopopoia: or Mother Hubberds Tale," ll. 895–906, in *Works* (London, 1844) and in *The Works of Edmund Spenser* . . . , ed. Rev. Henry John Todd (London and New York, 1872), both of which are in Emerson's library, which appears in *Parnassus* as "Spenser at Court"; Sir Richard Owen, *Odontology; or, A Treatise on the Comparative Anatomy of the Teeth* . . . , 2 vols. (London, 1840–45). The reprint concerning William Drummond of Hawthornden

Olympus & Kissavos   in [Notebook] Σ
_____

And passages from Asser's Life of Alfred
_____

And that *introuvable*[n] citation from Lord Kaimes.
_____

And another *introuvable*[n] from R. Owen's Odontology.
_____

Drummond of Hawthorneden in the ↑Camden (?)↓ Collection, re-print;
_____

And conversations with C[harles]. J. Fox, in S⟨.⟩↑amuel↓ Rogers's Life.
_____

Courage of Sir Jerome Bowles, in [Notebook] *Morals* & the Engl⟨y⟩ish Ship of War that went down in battle
_____

the story of Fra Cristoforo.
_____

Bolingbroke, in Spence.

[55]   *Readings.*[59]
Henry D. Thoreau's "Inspiration." *HT* 51,
                "Hound, Horse, & Turtledove," *HT* 4, 5,

(1585–1648), Scottish poet, to which Emerson refers may be *Auctarium bibliothecae Edinburgenae, sive Catalogus Librorum quos Guilielmus Drummondus ab Hawthornden bibliothecae* . . . (Edinburgi, 1627; reprinted Edinburgh, 1815). "Rogers's Life" most likely refers to Samuel Rogers, *Recollections*, 2nd ed. (Boston, 1859), which Emerson withdrew from the Boston Athenaeum December 21, 1860–February 19, 1861, and in which pp. 5–78 deal with Charles James Fox. The "story of Fra Cristoforo" is from Alessandro Manzoni's novel, *I Promessi Sposi*, 3 vols. (Torino, 1827), in Emerson's library. "Spence" most likely refers to Joseph Spence, *Anecdotes, Observations, and Characters, of Books and Men* . . . , 2nd ed., 1858.

[59] Some of the readings in the list that follows were undertaken as part of Emerson's consideration of works for inclusion in *Parnassus*. Henry David Thoreau's "Inspiration" appears in *Parnassus*, and its first three stanzas introduce "Inspiration," *W*, VIII, 268; "Hound . . . Turtledove," is an allusion to Thoreau's claim in *Walden; or, Life in the Woods* (Boston, 1854), p. 20, in Emerson's library, that he has lost these items but is "still on their trail." In Notebook ΦB, p. [227], Emerson writes of sleep, "It is neither mortal

Sleep, ΦB 225 [actually 227], from Alexis.
Shakspeare's "If the bird of loudest lay" *PY* 290, 278
From Demosthenes' Oration
Portia, Uxor Bruti.
Conclusion of the Mahabarat
Saint Anthony's address to the fishes
Gibbon's Autobiography,
Lord Clarendon's portraits.
Synesius's Osiris & Typhen
Saadi at Kuarem
Thomas Taylor's naivetés
Ben Jonson's masques & songs.
Romaic Poems.
In Thomas Taylor, the Sphynx.
                    the Dance of Plotinus

———

Lines. Death of Abraham Lincoln. in *"Punch," Apr. 1866*

———

nor immortal, & of so strange a nature that it lives neither after man's way, nor after God's way, but is always steadily new-born, changeable to the end"; "This," he states, "is Goethe's version of the riddle of Alexis." Shakespeare's "The Phoenix and the Turtle," of which "If the . . . lay" is l. 1 misquoted, appears in *Parnassus* as "Phoenix and Turtle Dove." The "Conclusion . . . Mahabarat" probably refers to William Rounseville Alger, *The Poetry of the East* (Boston, 1856), pp. 37–45; see *JMN*, XIV, 321. "Saint Anthony's address . . ." probably refers to St. Anthony's "Discourse to an Assembly of Fish," in Joseph Addison, *Remarks on Several Parts of Italy, &c., In the Years 1701, 1702, 1703* (London, 1705), pp. 62–74; cf. *JMN*, XI, 127–128. "Lord Clarendon's portraits" most likely refers to Edward Hyde, 1st Earl of Clarendon, whose *The Beauties of Clarendon* . . . , ed. Alfred Howard (London, n.d.) is in Emerson's library. "Synesius's Osiris & Typhon" is found in "Extracts from the Treatise of Synesius on Providence," in *Select Works of Plotinus, the Great Restorer of the Philosophy of Plato* . . . , trans. and ed. Thomas Taylor (London, 1817), pp. 508–559, in Emerson's library. Ben Jonson's "masques & songs" were probably read in the previously cited *Works*, 1716. Entries in *Select Works of Plotinus* . . . , 1817, pp. 53–59, 84, refer to "the Sphynx" and "the Dance of Plotinus". In *Punch, Or the London Charivari*, May 6, 1865, 182, 185, appear the unsigned verses on Lincoln that appear in *Parnassus* as "Abraham Lincoln" and are attributed there to Tom Taylor (1817–1880), English dramatist. For "Song of the Tonga Islanders," see the note to p. [47] above. The John Brown references are allusions to "How Old Brown Took Harper's Ferry," in *The Poetical Works of Edmund Clarence Stedman* (Boston, 1873), pp. 64–70, in Emerson's library; the lines appear in *Parnassus* as "John Brown of Osawatomie." Not cited in Notebook XO, Robinson's defense of Wordsworth is found in John Forster, *Walter Savage Landor, a Biography*, 2 vols. (London, 1869), II, 316, in Emerson's library.

⟨Co⟩Song of the Tonga Islanders.

———

John Brown of Ossawatomie
& John Brown's Knapsack, &c.
Dalto [actually Datto], the porter, *IO* 34
Crabbe Robinson's defence of Wordsworth, *XO* 96

[56]   *Readings.*
For the high morals we must give words of the Trismegisti
Lao⟨med⟩damia[60]

———

James Naylor's dying words[61]

———

Address of the Parliament Soldier to the Army. (in Coleridge's
"Friend")[62]

———

Sampson Reed's oration.

———

Van Helmont, p. 34   story of poor woman good specimen of the
nobile volgare eloquenza.[63]
Pan   Plutarch's Morals [1870] (G[oodwin]) Vol. 4, p 23
Articles. Geoffroy Saint Hilaire in *Biographie Generale,* & in *Ecker-mann*[64]

---

[60] See *Select Works of Plotinus* . . . , 1817, where on the inside back cover Emerson refers to the Trismegisti in a handwritten index and cites pp. 55, 3; the intention of this reference has not been determined. Wordsworth's "Laodamia" appears in *Parnassus.*

[61] This may be a reference to James Nayler (1617?-1660), a persecuted English Quaker, who during his last confinement wrote the often reprinted *Milk for Babes; and Meat for Strong Men* . . . (London, 1661).

[62] See Samuel Taylor Coleridge, *The Friend: A Series of Essays . . . to Aid in the Formation of Fixed Principles in Politics, Morals, and Religion* . . . , 3 vols. (London, 1818), III, 71–77. This work is in Emerson's library. See *JMN,* VI, 320.

[63] "Van Helmont . . . *eloquenza.*" is struck through in pencil with six diagonal use marks. The story appears in Van Helmont's *Oriatrike* . . . , 1662, p. 34. See *JMN,* XI, 267.

[64] See *Nouvelle Biographie Générale,* 1855–1870, XX, 40–48, and *Conversations of Goethe with Eckermann* . . . , trans. John Oxenford, 1850, II, 291–292.

↑I have translated the story of the evacuation of Acre,—See my *"Waterville Address."*↓[65]

[57] 1870, Dec. 25.   Christmas Day
I have received, this morning, from Thomas Carlyle, through Chapman & Hall, his booksellers, as a gift, five volumes of the Library Edition of his works; namely, *"Miscellaneous Essays"* Vol. I. & Vol. VI.
     French Revolution Vol. I
     Life & Letters of Cromwell Vol. II
     Life of Friedrich of Prussia. Vol. III.[66]

[58] S[amuel]. G[ray]. W[ard]. said, nothing is so mean as the man that has a million, unless it be the man who has two.

[59] *Rhetoric.*
All conversation & writing is rhetoric, and the great secret is, to know thoroughly, & not to be affected ↑& to have a steel spring↓.

———

For *History of Liberty.* There was a great deal of Whig poetry written ↑in Charles' & Cromwell's time↓: not a line of it has survived.[67]

[60] Gifts.
The pleasing humiliation of gifts.

———

     California is teaching in its history & its poetry the good of evil, & confirming my thought one day in Five Points in New York, twenty years ago, that the ruffians & Amazons in that district were only superficially such, but carried underneath this bronze about the same morals as their civil & well dressed neighbors.

———

[65] This story does not appear in the printed version of this address, which was originally delivered before the literary societies of Dartmouth and Waterville Colleges in 1863. See "The Man of Letters," *W,* X, 241-258.
[66] These volumes were part of Carlyle's *Collected Works,* 1869-1871. Emerson wrote to Carlyle on January 19, 1872, to say that his set was completed (*CEC,* pp. 586-587).
[67] "in . . . time" is inserted in pencil.

Gifts. The saying is attributed to Sir Isaac Newton, that "they who give ⟨only after⟩ ↑nothing before↓ their death, never in fact give at all."[68]

[61]   *Class-Day*
⟨T⟩See of Turnbull, *LO* 47

[62] ⟨o⟩Of Gravitation, ↑John↓ Mill said to Carlyle, "A force can act but where it is." "With all my heart," replied Carlyle, "but where is it?"

[63] [blank]
[64] *Old Age.* "Man is oldest when he is born, & is younger & youn-ger continually." Taliessin. *Skene,* [*The Four Ancient Books of Wales* . . . , 1868,] Vol. I. 544
↑Swedenborg says the same↓[69]

[65]   ↑*Moment.*↓

"A good hour is worth more than all fame." *Varnhagen.*
↑"↓And what fame stands fast that is not ↑angetastet?"↓   ↑assailed, questioned↓[70]

V⟨.⟩↑arnhagen↓ reports all his dreams, as well as his readings; keeps an eye ever on England, & a most friendly one ever on the United States.

———
Of Bettine, see Varnhagen, [*Tagebücher,* 1861–1870]
↑Vol.↓ XI 101, 105
XI 104
↑245   Jesus↓
↑247   final causes↓[71]
Old Age.
"Why is old age commonly so dumpish & dejected? Because from all

[68] Cf. "Spiritual Laws," *W,* II, 160.
[69] "Swedenborg . . . same" is inserted in pencil.
[70] The quotation marks enclosing this question and "angetastet?" are in pencil.
[71] "245 . . . causes" is inserted in pencil.

life so much of lustre which was its ornament decays: also the /proper/*private*/ ↑lustre↓ which accompanies us, & without which existence, which is the main thing,—is less intelligible & represent-able. In this view old age, to which else the greatest satisfactions are assured, remains unsatisfactory to most men." *Varnhagen,* [*Tage-bücher,* 1861–1870,] XI. 104[–105]

[66] February 10, ↑187[1]↓.[72]
    I do not know that I should feel threatened or insulted if a chem-ist ↑should↓ take his protoplasm or mix his hydrogen, oxygen & car-bon, & make an animalcule incontestably swimming & jumping before my eyes. I should ↑only feel↓ that it indicated that the day had arrived when the human race might be trusted with a new degree of power, & its immense responsibility; for these steps are not solitary or local, but only a hint of an advanced frontier supported by an advancing ⟨nation⟩ ↑race↓ behind it.
            ↑[Read in Lecture I. 1871]↓[73]
    ↑⟨See⟩ ↑Count↓ the multitude of inventions of the ⟨9⟩nineteenth[n] century.↓[74]

[67] ————————
Note the "fascination which facts superficially considered the very strongholds of materialism are beginning to exert on the minds which have the least sympathy with a low materialism."
                            P[hilip]. R⟨a⟩↑andolph↓
                                ↑Read 1871↓[75]

————————

What at first scares the Spiritualist in the experiments of ↑natural↓ Science,—⟨al⟩as if thought were only finer chyle, fine to aroma,—now redounds to the credit of matter, which, it appears, is impregnated

[72] "187" is inserted in pencil.
[73] "[Read . . . 1871]" is inserted in pencil. "Lecture I." most likely refers to the lec-ture of February 14, 1871, the first of seventeen lectures on "Natural History of the In-tellect" that Emerson gave at Boylston Hall, Harvard College, February 14–April 7, 1871.
[74] See pp. [91]–[92] below, where Emerson outlines the "splendors of this age".
[75] "Read 1871" is inserted in pencil. For the quotations from Philip Randolph on pp. [67]–[68], see Journal NY, p. [245] above, where Emerson notes that he has Ran-dolph's manuscripts in his possession.

with thought & heaven, & is really of God, & not of the Devil, as he had too hastily believed. All is resolved into Unity again. My chemistry, he will say, was ↑blind &↓ barbarous, ⟨& blind,⟩ b⟨y⟩ut my ⟨pe⟩ intuition is, was, & will be true.

[68] I believe that every man belongs to his time, if our Newtons & philosophers belong also to the next age which they help to form.

"Our progress appears great, only because the future of science is hidden from us," P[hilip] R[andolph]

How to draw medical virtue from every companion, & to detect the good that may be made of evil.

Βαξω, φασηω, βασηαινω,   fascinate

Mediums—spiritualists,—are Vampyres.

Souls are naturally endued with prediction. *Plutarch,* [*Plutarch's Morals,* 1718, IV, 71] *E 7, NO* 173

[69]   *Divination*
The soul contains in itself the event that shall presently befall it, for the event is only the actualization of its thoughts or state.[76] *C* 135
Dreams the key to metaphysics. *HO* 107

"Souls are naturally endued with prediction." *Plutarch*—[*Plutarch's Morals,* 1718, IV, 71]

[70] Edinburgh held in 1⟨8⟩9th Century
↑[↓ Robert Burns ↑born 1759   died 1796]↓[77]

[76] "The soul . . . state." is used in "Demonology," *W*, X, 8–9.
[77] "[Robert Burns . . . 1796]" is enclosed in a rectangle drawn by connecting the corners of brackets with rules. Persons in the Edinburgh list who have not been previously identified or are not easily recognizable include Sir James Mackintosh (1765–1832), philosopher and professor of law at Haileybury College; Dugald Stewart (1753–1828), philosopher and professor of moral philosophy at Edinburgh; John Wilson, pseudonym Christopher North (1785–1854), poet, essayist, and professor of moral philosophy at

Sir James Mackintosh
Dugald Stewart ↑till 1828↓
Walter Scott ↑till 1832↓
John Wilson from 1815
Sir J[ohn]. Leslie professor Ed[inburgh] 1819
[John] Playfair professor in 1803 d 1819
James Hogg till 1835
 [Thomas] De Quincy 1828
↑Lord↓ Jeffrey b 1773 d. 1850
 ⟨Lockhart⟩ ⟨till 1825⟩
 [Thomas] Chalmers professor in Edinh. 1828
Allan Cunningham
Sir William Hamilton till
 [John Gibson] Lockhart 1794 to 1825
 [Henry Peter] Brougham till 1807
 Robert Knox
 [William] Blackwood
 Lord Cockburn b. 1779 d. 1854 d till 1854

In 1871 J⟨ohn⟩ames Hutchinson Stirling

[71] In ↑March↓ 1802, Sydney Smith, Brougham, & Jeffrey decided to start the Edin[*burgh*]. Review[.]

[72] 5 March 1871.
Dr E. B. Pusey of Oxford surprises me two or three days ago with sending me "with greetings" a book, "Lectures on Daniel &

Edinburgh; Sir John Leslie (1766–1832), mathematician and physicist; John Playfair (1748–1819), mathematician and geologist, professor of mathematics and natural philosophy at Edinburgh; James Hogg (1770–1835), poet, friend of Scott, Byron, and Wordsworth; Francis Jeffrey, Lord Jeffrey (1773–1850), critic and jurist; Thomas Chalmers (1780–1847), theologian and preacher, professor of moral philosophy at St. Andrews and of theology at Edinburgh; Allan Cunningham (1784–1842), poet and man of letters, friend of Hogg and Scott; Sir William Hamilton (1788–1856), philosopher, professor of civil history and later of logic and metaphysics at Edinburgh; John Gibson Lockhart (1794–1854), editor and novelist, biographer of Scott and Burns; Henry Peter Brougham, Baron Brougham and Vaux (1778–1868), jurist, reformer, and political leader; Robert Knox (1791–1862), anatomist; William Blackwood (1776–1834), publisher; Henry Thomas Cockburn, known as Lord Cockburn (1779–1854), jurist.

the Prophets," with the following inscription written on the blank leaf;[78]

———

> To the Unwise & wise
> A debtor I.
> Tis strange if true.
> And yet the old
> Is often new.

———

⟨I⟩When, in England, I did not meet him, but I remember that, in Oxford, Froude one day ↑walking with me↓ pointed to his window, & said, "There is where all our light came from."
↑I ought also to have ⟨w⟩recorded that Max Muller, on ↑last↓ Christmas Day, surprised me with the gift of a book.↓[79]

[73] Coleridge says, "The Greeks, except perhaps ↑in↓ Homer, seem to have had no way of making their women interesting, but by unsexing them, as in the instances of the tragic ⟨m⟩Medea, Electra, &c. Contrast such characters with Spenser's Una, who exhibits no prominent feature, has no particularization, but produces the same feeling that a statue does, when contemplated at a distance.'"

> "From her fair head her fillet she undight,
> And laid her stole aside: her angel's face
> As the great eye of Heaven shined bright,
> And made a sunshine in a shady place;
> Did never mortal eye behold such heavenly grace."
>   *Literary Remains* [1836–1839]. Vol I. 95.

[74] See date of conversation with Sampson Reed in 1859 [actually 1850]. *CO* 27 [actually 25]

[75] *Greatness.*
    Chateaubriand says, that ↑President↓ Washington granted him an audience in Philadelphia, and adds, "Happy am I that the looks of

———

[78] Edward Bouverie Pusey, *Daniel the Prophet: Nine Lectures Delivered in the Divinity School of the University of Oxford,* 3rd ed. (Oxford, 1869), in Emerson's library.
    [79] Friederich Max Müller, *Introduction to the Science of Religion; Four Lectures . . .* (London, 1870), in Emerson's library, is the gift recorded here.

Washington fell on me. I felt myself warmed by them for the rest of my life"—Calvert gives the anecdote.[80]

———

None is so great but finds one who apprehends him, and no historical person begins to content us; And this is our pledge of a higher height than he has reached. And when we have arrived at the question, the answer is already near.

———

[76][81] Carlyle   Poetry & Imagination
        Landor   Inspiration
        Wordsworth   Originality
        Persian Poetry   Wit & Humor
        Wit & Humor   Persian Poetry
        Books again.   Wordsworth
        Henry ⟨T⟩D. Thoreau   ⟨Carlyle⟩↑⟨Burns⟩↓
        Theodore Parker   Milton
        Abraham Lincoln   Michel Angelo
        Concord Monument   Landor
        ⟨Harvard Alumni ⟨M⟩Commemoration.⟩   ↑Harvard Martyrs↓
        Burns' Centennial Anniversary.   Shakspeare
        Daniel Webster   Carlyle
        Father Taylor   Burns.
        Michel Angelo   Goethe
        Milton   Wit & Humor
                                         Father Taylor

[77] [blank]
[78] California notes.[82]   Cape Horn

———

[80] George Henry Calvert (1803–1889), poet and essayist, Harvard 1823, who spent a number of years abroad in the 1820s, 1840s, and 1850s, is likely the source of this anecdote.

[81] A vertical line in ink is drawn to the left of the right column of the following list. "Commemoration." is written through the line and into the right column. See earlier lists of Emerson's uncollected essays and lectures in Journal NY, pp [152]–[154], [155], and [172] above.

[82] The notations that follow on pp. [78]–[80] combine Emerson's jottings from Titus Fey Cronise's *The Natural Wealth of California* . . . (San Francisco, 1868), which is in Emerson's library and is cited on p. [78]; John Shertzer Hittell, *The Resources of Cali-*

irrigation

tea   impossible culture where labor is dear
    as in America

Silk

Wine ⟨cannot⟩is not adulterated because
    grapes at 1 cent a pound are cheaper
    than any substitute.

Cape Donner

↑Lake Tahoe   cornelians, black sand,
    trout,↓

↑Golden Gate: named of old from its flow-
    ers.↓

Asia at your doors & S. America

↑Inflamed↓ expectation^n haunting men.

Henry Pierce's opinion of the need of
    check, calamity, punishment, to teach
    Economy.   nickel ⟨s⟩cents.

Early ripe boys. "Happy to make your
    acquaintance, Sir."

Mission Dolores.

Brigham Young

Flora

The altered year   See *Hittel*

John Muir

---

fornia . . . , 2nd ed. (San Francisco and New York, 1866), which Emerson withdrew from the Boston Athenaeum April 8–June 24, 1871, and which is cited on p. [78]; and his own observations during his stay in California April 21–May 2, 1871. The notations are repeated in part in Pocket Diary 22, pp. [fcv]–[i] below. Contemporary records of Emerson's western journey were kept by Emerson's traveling companions and by persons he met. See, for instance, James B. Thayer, *A Western Journey with Mr. Emerson* (Boston, 1884); John Murray Forbes, *Letters and Recollections of John Murray Forbes,* ed. Sarah Forbes Hughes (Boston and New York, 1899); and William Frederic Badè, *The Life and Letters of John Muir,* 2 vols. (Boston and New York, 1923). Of the persons mentioned here who have not been previously identified, Henry Augustus Peirce was born in Dorchester, Massachusetts, in 1808 and became a California pioneer, and General Edwin Vose Sumner (1797–1863), American army officer, was once governor of New Mexico (1852) and commander at Fort Leavenworth, Kansas, during the freesoil and slavery struggle. Thayer, in *A Western Journey* . . . , 1884, pp. 100–102, reports that Muir introduced Emerson's party to the trees of California by their names, so that "we grew learned," which may account for Emerson's extensive notes on trees and their names here and in Pocket Diary 22.

General Sumner
antelopes, prairie dogs, elk horns, wolves
　　　buffalo 〈eagles〉
　　　eagles, vultures, prairie hen, owls
Cave
Sequoias generally have marks of fire: hav-
　　　ing lived 〈so〉1300 years, must have
　　　met that danger, & every other, in
　　　turn. Yet they possess great power of
　　　resistance to fire.
　　　　　　　　　　See *Cronise,* p 507–8

[79] Pinus Lambertiana, (Sugar pine) reaches sometimes a height of
300 feet, & diameter of ten or fifteen feet. Cones—Sometimes 18
inches long.

———

Sarcodes Sanguinea   snow-plant   growing in the snow
　　　a parasite from decayed wood.   monotropa
Caeanothus   wild lilac
Madrona———Arbutus Menziesii
Manzenita   〈Acrostophy〈u〉los〉 ↑〈Acrstaphylos〉↓ ↑Acrostaphylos↓
Glaucus
　　　Black sand at Lake Tahoe & Cornelians

———

Mono Lake. Glaciers. Clarence King.

———

Volcanic mountains, cones. Enneo county.

————

Mirage very frequent: the appearance 〈of〉as of lakes in the horizon,
which disappeared as we approached them.

———

The attraction & superiority of California are in its days. It has better
days, & more of them, than any other country.

————

　　　[80] Mount Shasta   14,440 feet high in Sis〈ik〉kiyou
County, N. E. corner of the State.

————

Mount Whitney. 15,000 ft. in Tulare County.

___

In Yosemite, Grandeur of these mountains perhaps unmatched ⟨i⟩on the Globe; for here they strip themselves like Athletes for exhibition, & stand perpendicular granite walls, ⟨exposing⟩ showing their entire height, & wearing a liberty cap of snow on their head.
Sequoia Gigantea
Pinus Lambertiana, Sugar pine, 10 ft. diam., 300 ft. height, cones 18 inches.
Pinus Ponderosa, Yellow pine
Pinus Albicaulis
Dry season from 1 May till November

[81] Life insurance
Best market, cheap hotels yet good.

At the request of Galen Clark, our host at Mariposa, & who is by State appointment the Protector of the trees, & who went with us to the Mammoth Groves, I selected a Sequoia Gigantea, near Galen's Hospice, in the presence of our party, & named it *Samoset,* in memory of the first Indian ally of the Plymouth Colony, and I gave Mr Clark directions to p⟨u⟩rocure a tin plate, & have the inscription painted thereon in the usual form of the named trees;

Samoset—
12 May.
1871.

& paid him its cost. The tree was a strong healthy one, girth at 2½ feet from the ground, 50 feet.[83]

[82] What they once told me at St Louis is truer ⟨at⟩in California, that there is no difference between a boy & a man: As soon as a boy is "that high," (high as the table,) he contradicts his father. When

[83] Contemporary accounts of this episode are preserved by John Muir, in Badè, *The Life and Letters of John Muir,* 1923, I, 256, and by Thayer, *A Western Journey* ..., 1884, p. 108. Thayer reports that Emerson first considered the name "Logan" for the sequoia. The three-line inscription is centered on the page, circled in ink, with "named trees ... The tree" written above it.

introduced to ⟨a⟩the stranger, he says, "I am happy to make your acquaintance," and shakes hands like a senior.

[83] Mr Walcott tells me that Ephraim Bull, whose right arm was shot off ⟨the oth⟩on the Fourth of July, whilst loading the cannon, came to himself today, & complained that he could not open the fingers of his hand. His brother John went to the   where his ⟨hand⟩arm was buried, to⟨k⟩ok it out, & opened the fingers of the hand; ⟨after⟩ &, on returning, he found that his brother was relieved of the supposed difficulty! Mr W[alcott]. said, ⟨he⟩ he had heard of such cases three or four times before.[84]

[84] We are sometimes startled by coincidences so friendly as to suggest a guardian angel: And sometimes, when they would be so fit, & every way desireable, nothing but *dis*-incidences occur. 'Tis perhaps ↑thus;↓ the coincidence is probably[n] the rule, & if we could retain our early innocence, we might trust our feet ↑uncommanded↓ to take the right path to our friend ↑in the woods.↓: But we have interfered too often, & the feet have lost, by our distrust, their proper virtue, & we take the wrong path, & miss him. ↑'Tis the barbarian (Instinct) within us, which Culture deadens.↓[85]

Inscription for Mrs S[arah]. S[wain]. Forbes's Memorial Fountain.
   Fall, Stream! to bless. Return to Heaven as well;
      So did our ⟨braves,⟩ ↑sons,↓ Heaven met them as they fell.

[85] What was the name of the nymph "whom young Apollo courted for her hair"? That fable renews itself every day in the street⟨,⟩ & in the drawing-room. Nothing in nature is more ideal than the hair. Analyse it by taking a single hair, & it is characterless & worthless; but in ⟨th⟩its mass it is recipient of such variety ↑of form,↓ & momentary

[84] Henry J. Walcott, Emerson's college classmate, became cashier of the Concord National Bank in 1869; Ephraim Wales Bull (1806–1895), American horticulturist and developer of the Concord grape, was Emerson's neighbor.
[85] A vertical line in pencil is drawn in the left margin beside "if we could retain . . . which Culture deadens.", which is struck through in pencil with three vertical use marks and is used in "Powers and Laws of Thought," *W*, XII, 37.

change from form to form, that it vies in expression with the eye & the countenance. The wind & the sun play with it & inhance it, & its coils & its mass are a perpetual mystery & attraction to the young poet. But the doleful imposture of buying it at the shops is suicidal, & disgusts.

[86] [blank]
   [87] Nature lays the ground-plan of each creature,—accurately, sternly fit for all his functions,—then veils it.

[88]   ↑See *supra p. 70*↓
   Scott.   Edinburgh, in 1848, held Jeffrey, Wilson, De Quincy, Sir W[illiam]. Hamilton,

---

In 18   ⟨M⟩Dugald Stewart, Playfair, Mackintosh, Lesley, Hogg, Knox, Mackenzie[86]

---

[89][87]   William Clerk, Esq.   Aug. 1827
              General Gourgand

Scott said to Mr Cheney, "Superstition is very picturesque & I make it at times stand me in great stead; but I never allow it to interfere with interest or conscience"   Loc[k]hart [vol.] 7, [p. 2]81.[88]

I think he spoke honestly & well, but his superstit⟨o⟩ion was dearer to him⟨.⟩
(Scott died 21 September 1832)
& more comprehensive than he well knew: I mean that it made ⟨a⟩him a sterner royalist, churchman and Conservative than his intellect should allow.

---

[86] With the exception of Henry Mackenzie (1745–1831), Scottish novelist, "Lesley", a variation on Sir John Leslie's name, and the other persons listed here are identified in the note to p. [70] above.
   [87] The entries on this page are written in ink over a partially erased pencil version of substantially the same material. Neither William Clerk nor General Gourgand has been identified.
   [88] John Gibson Lockhart, *Memoirs of the Life of Sir Walter Scott, Bart.*, 7 vols. (Boston, 1837–1838), in Emerson's library.

[90]⁸⁹ Correlation of forces is an irrepressible hint which must compel the widest application of it. It gives ⟨new⟩ ↑unforseen↓ force to the old word of Cicero's, ⟨to the old ↑word↓ of Cicero's⟩ *aliquid commune Vinculum,* & we realise the correlation of sciences. But poetry correlates men, and genius, and every fine talent, & men the most diverse; & men that are enemies hug each other when they hear from that once hated neighbor the synonym of their own cherished belief.

[91] The splendors of this age outshine all other recorded ages. In my lifetime, ⟨I⟩ have been ⟨done⟩ ↑wrought↓ ⟨four⟩five miracles, namely, ↑1. the Steamboat,↓ ↑2.↓ the railroad; ↑3.↓ the Electric telegraph; ↑4.↓ the application of the Spectroscope to astronomy; ↑5.↓ the photograph; ↑five miracles↓ which have altered the relations of nations to each other. Add ⟨the⟩ cheap Postage; and the Sewing machine; &, in agriculture, the Mowing machine & the horse-rake.⁹⁰ A corresponding power has been given to manufactures by the machine for pegging shoes, & the power-loom↑;↓ ⟨in the factories,⟩ & the power-press of the printers. And in dentistry & in surgery Dr Jackson's discovery of Anaesthesis. It only needs to add the power which up to this hour eludes [92] ⟨all⟩all human ingenuity, namely a rudder to the balloon, to give us the dominion of the air, as well as of the sea & the land. But the account is not complete until we add the discovery of Oersted, of the identity of Electricity & Magnetism, & the generalization of that conversion by its application to light, heat, & gravitation. The geologist has found the correspondence of the age of stratified remains to the ascending scale of structure in animal⟨s⟩ life.

↑Add now, the daily predictions of the weather for the next 24 hours for North America, by the Observatory at Washington.↓

[93]⁹¹ Poetry. "The newness." Every day must be a new morn. ⟨Fit⟩

⁸⁹ The entries on this page are written in ink over a partially erased pencil version of substantially the same material.
⁹⁰ In the second sentence, "five miracles" is inserted in pencil; in the third sentence, "the" is struck through once in pencil.
⁹¹ Down to the full-page rule, entries on p. [93] are written in ink over erased pencil. "Clothe" appears only in the ink version; the second paragraph ended after "meaning." in the pencil version.

↑Clothe↓ the new object with a coat that fits it alone of all things in the world. I can see in many poems that the coat is second-hand.

Emphasis betrays poverty of thought, as if the man did not know that all things are full of meaning⟨.⟩↑, and not his trumpery thing only.↓

↑'Tis one of the mysteries of our condition, that↓ ⟨T⟩the poet seems sometimes to have a mere talent,—a chamber in his ⟨head⟩ ↑brain↓ into which an angel flies with ↑divine↓ messages, but the man, apart from this privilege, common-place. Wordsworth is an example; (& Channing's poetry is apart from the man.) ⟨'Tis certain that t⟩Those who know & meet him day by day cannot reconcile the verses with their man. ⟨Poetry is thus sometimes a life apart. 'Tis one of the mysteries of our condition.⟩[92]

↑Ah not to me these /dreams/heights/ belong↓
A better voice sings through my song.

[94] *Beauty.*
What a privilege is beauty! Here comes into ⟨a⟩the room a lady ⟨into the room⟩who has only to take off her bonnet, to draw the eyes & delight the heart of every person in the house, and the joy follows her wherever she goes.

⟨⟨t⟩Transferred to *LO* 54⟩[93]

[95] I read today good notes in Ross's "Account of the Life & Works of Saadi," in Fields' Edition, Taj of Agra ↑Fields' Saadi p. 78↓, Hunter ↑Saadi, p. 75↓, &c &c[;] but Mr. Ross is sadly clumsy with his Latin & with his quotations from Byron & Beattie &c[.][94]

---

[92] "⟨'Tis certain . . . condition.⟩" is struck through in ink with two diagonal use marks. For "Ah not . . . song.", below, see "Fragments on the Poet and the Poetic Gift," XXX, in *W,* IX, 333.
[93] "What a privilege . . . she goes." is struck through with three diagonal use marks. "⟨⟨t⟩Transferred . . . 54)" is encircled by rules drawn to join the parentheses.
[94] Musli uddin Saadi, *The Gulistan; or, Rose Garden. With an Essay on Saadi's Life and Genius by James Ross, and a Preface by R. W. Emerson* (Boston, 1865), in Emerson's library.

Philip Randolph had one eminent advantage in his studies, that he not only saw clearly the supremacy of the moral element in art, in intellect, in ⟨N⟩history, & Nature, but he also dearly loved it.

The vice of Wordsworth is that he is a lame poet: he can ⟨sc⟩ rarely finish worthily a stanza begun well. He suffers from asthma⟨.⟩ ↑of the mind.↓
↑Aug. '73   See what is said of the Poet, *BO* 185↓[95]

↑1876, December 20. In reading the above lines on Wordsworth, ⟨I must⟩ which were probably written five years ago, I must add that in my new 8vo. Edition of his works, I find great improvement of the Sonnets which he must have made in ↑his↓ later days.↓[96]

[96] A telegram came to me today from Mr Oliver, ↑(↓in New York ↑I believe)↓, which ran thus,
      "Persuaded Ward to sail in the Calbria with us on the 15 September."
Now I believe that Mr Saml G. Ward does sail on the 15th Septr⟨.⟩; Yet I did not hesitate to make my version of the message, & send it to E[dward]. W. E[merson], at Naushon, in this form; *"Persuade Edward to sail with us in the Cambria on the 15th Septr"*[97]

[97] Is the Club exclusive? 'Tis made close to give value to your election. There are men who can afford to wait. Be wealthy, & buy Kings.
      ↑Quotque aderant vates, rebar adesse deos.↓ [Ovid]

↑*Affirmative.*↓
Men of today cannot be organized in a more advanced age, any more than the saurians on the granite of Massachusetts.

---

[95] "The vice ... *BO* 185" and the rule that precedes the entry are in pencil.

[96] William Wordsworth, *Poems,* new ed. (London, 1851), is in Emerson's library.

[97] Edward Waldo Emerson was listed as a passenger aboard the *Malta,* which left Boston for Liverpool on September 5, 1871; see p. [107] below. As it happens, Emerson's only recorded letter to Edward at Naushon Island during the period of this journal is cited as likely written in 1873; see *L,* VI, 173n, 253.

The English write better ↑than we↓," but I fancy we read more out of their books than they do. *EA* 97, 104. Potentiality against power" ↑is ours.↓[98]

"The heart makes the memory," said Napoleon. And Goethe, "Wo der Antheil ↑sympathy↓ sich verliert, verliert sich auch das Ge-dächtniss." *Sprüche* p 53   ↑*Loesser* [actually Loeper]↓[99]

In ⟨active⟩ ↑certain ⟨states⟩↓ minds   thought /obliterates/expels/ memory. I have this example,—that, eager as I am to fix & record each experience, the interest of a new thought is sometimes such that I do not think of pen & paper at all, and the next day I puzzle myself in [98] a vain attempt to recall the new perception that had so captivated me.

Lecture on *Art* should not omit Ruskin's & Wiseman's high lessons. Into *Home* transplant
    A good house, *Art,* p. 3 or 5
It may admit also the topic of Travel & American ⟨national⟩ & natural & political advantages from *EA*[100]

[99]   *Available Lectures*[101]
⟨Social Aims⟩
Wit & Humor
Hospitality
⟨Poetry⟩
Doctrine of Leasts
Art

---

[98] "is ours." is inserted in pencil. For Ovid, see p. [53] above.

[99] Johann Wolfgang von Goethe, *Sprüche in Prosa. Zum ersten Mal erlautert und auf ihre Quellen Zurückgefuhrt von G. von Loeper* (Berlin, 1870), in Emerson's library. *"Loesser"* is inserted in pencil.

[100] During the period of this journal Emerson lectured on "Nature and Art" on November 27, 1871, in Chicago, and on "Art and Nature" on December 1, 1871, in Quincy, Illinois, and on January 11, 1872, in Baltimore. "Lecture on *Art* . . . from *EA*" is in pencil.

[101] In the list that follows, "Social Aims", "Poetry", and "Immortality" are each struck through with one vertical use mark, perhaps to indicate that the lecture was read; the column beginning "4   Inspiration" and ending "3   Imagination" is struck through in pencil with one vertical use mark; "An . . . Lecture" is in pencil, as is "English . . . *ED*".

⟨Inspiration⟩
⟨Greatness⟩ ↑printed one chapter; one or two still remain unprinted.↓
Chivalry.
Books
Memory
⟨Immortality⟩
Rule of Life
⟨Resources⟩
An Third Cambridge Lecture
English Experience & Anecdotes   in *ED*

4	Inspiration	1.	Analogy
2.	Memory		Memory
1.	Analogy		Imagination
3	Imagination		Inspiration
			Humor

[100] [blank]
[101] Channing's poetry does not regard the reader. It is written to himself; is his strict experience, the record of his moods, of his fancies, of his observations & studies, & will ⟨be⟩ interest good readers as such. He does not flatter the reader by any attempt to ⟨enter into his⟩ meet his expectation, or to polish his record that he may gratify him, as readers expect to be gratified. He confides entirely in his own bent or bias for meditation & writing. ⟨But⟩ He will write as he has ever written, whether he has readers or not. But ⟨I value⟩ his poems have to me & to others [102] an exceptional value for this reason. We have not been considered in their composition, but either defied or forgotten, and therefore read them securely as original pictures which add something to our knowledge, & with a fair chance to be surprised & refreshed by novel experience[.][102]

[103] I am not sure that I have recorded Mr Samuel Hoar's remark to me of his friend William Prescott Esq of the Boston bar, "that

---

[102] On p. [101], "He will . . . not." is struck through with two vertical use marks. On p. [102], "an exceptional value . . . by novel experience" is struck through with one irregular vertical use mark.

he repeated his statement of his case once more for every one of the twelve jurors."

[104] George Bradford said, that Mr Alcott ↑once↓ said to him ⟨⟨long ago⟩ of memory,⟩ "that ⟨the⟩as the child loses, as ⟨he grows ⟨in⟩up, the world⟩ ↑he comes into the world,↓ his angelic memory, so the ⟨old⟩ man↑,↓ ⟨loses⟩ as he grows old, loses his memory of this world."⟨—or somewhat to that purpose.⟩

Oct. 18, [1871.]   ↑Bret Harte's visit.↓[103]
Bret Harte referred to my Essay on Civilization, that the piano comes so quickly into the shanty, &c. & said, "do you know that on the contrary it is vice that brings them in. It is the gamblers who bring in the music to California. It is the prostitute who brings in the New York fashions of dress there, & so throughout." I told him that I spoke ⟨also⟩ from Pilgrim experience, & knew on good grounds the resistless culture that religion effects.

———

Culture. Nothing better can be said of it than Goethe's sentence about his own, in the "Characteristics" translated by Mrs Austin. D [295][104]

Oct. 21 '71. Miss Christine Kipp. Stockbridge. Mass.

[105] ———
'Tis a good definition, "Faith is the substance of things hoped for, the evidence of things not seen." [Heb. 11:1]

———

Ruskin is a surprise to me. This old book ⟨⟨vol⟩ of Modern painters⟩ ↑"Two Paths,"↓ is ⟨new⟩ ↑original,↓ acute, thoroughly informed, & religious.[105]

[103] "Bret Harte's visit." is inserted in pencil. Bret Harte visited Emerson in October and November, 1871; details of his two visits and the uneven reception given him by Emerson's Concord friends are related in Rusk, *Life,* pp. 448–449.
[104] See *JMN,* VII, 199.
[105] John Ruskin, *The Two Paths: Being Lectures on Art, and Its Application to Decoration and Manufacture, Delivered in 1858–59* (New York, 1859), in Emerson's library. Emerson withdrew the London, 1859, edition of this work from the Boston Athenaeum September 15, 1871–April 9, 1872. The lines of verse that follow have not been identified.

"Wie der Fischer aus dem Meer
Fische zieht die niemand sah."

As the fisher from the sea
Pulls the fish that no man saw.

[106] "Every great idea which comes into the world as a gospel
is to the stockish pedantic people an offence, & to the variously-, but
half-cultivated, a folly." *Goethe.* Spruche [*in Prosa,* 1870] (Loeper) p
120

"Every such idea comes into appearance as a strange guest, &, ⟨as⟩
↑when↓ it begins to realize itself, is hardly to be distinguished from (a
fancy &) the fantastic." *Ibidem* p 120[106]

"People can recognize the usefulness of an idea, & yet not rightly understand how to use it perfectly." *Ibidem* [p. 120]

———

Paper at Carter   Milk Street
          Mac Adam   Spring Lane[107]

———

[107] Edward sailed. 5 September↑, 1871.↓[108]
↑A[rthur]. H[elps].'s letter dated 25 Sept.↓

———

Arthur Helps's address. Council office
                    Downing street   London[109]

———

Dr William Mac Cormac, 13 Harley St. Cavendish Sq.[110]
———

[106] The parentheses around "a fancy &" are in pencil.
[107] The rules that set off this entry are in pencil.
[108] ", 1871." is inserted in pencil. Regarding Edward's voyage, see p. [96] above.
[109] Sir Arthur Helps (1813–1875), historian, entertained Emerson in England in
1848, and later the two maintained a casual correspondence.
[110] Young Dr. William MacCormac, son of Emerson's Belfast correspondent Dr.
Henry MacCormac, was recommended by Sir Arthur Helps as a European friend for Edward. See *L,* VI, 213.

Edward arrived in London   Sept.
    left London, in Antwerp Steamer, Sept. 28
       at Cologne   Sunday Oct. 1
       at Cassel   Oct. 2

His address; Care of Frau Alma Budnitz née von Wurmb, 17 Ober Carl Strasse, Cassel, Hesse Cassel. Germany.

---

[108]–[110] [blank]
    [111] Names should be of good omen, of agreeable sound, commending the person in advance, &, if possible, keeping the old belief of the Greeks, "that the name borne by each man & woman has some connection with their part in the drama of life." The name then should look before & after.

[112] [blank]
    [113]¹¹¹ We have two or three facts of natural education   1. First the commonsense or merciless dealing of matter with us, punishing us instantly for any mistake about fire, water, iron, food, & poison: 2. & this world perfectly symmetrical, ↑so that its laws can be reduced to one law.—↓ 3. Then we have the world of thought, & its laws, like Niagara currents.¹¹² 4   Then the astonishing relation between these two.

       1. Common sense or true dealing with matter, which will not stand any nonsense
       2. The world of Thought & its laws
       This reacts directly on the other[.]

    [114]¹¹³ The necessity of the mind is poetic, the hardest chemist[,] the ⟨sternest⟩ ↑severest↓ analyser ⟨& man⟩ scornful of all but pro-

---

¹¹¹ Entries on p. [113] are in pencil; however, "natural" in the first line is written over in ink.
¹¹² A vertical line in pencil is drawn in the left-hand margin beside "3. Then . . . currents."
¹¹³ Entries on pp. [114]–[116] are in pencil.

saic fact, is forced to keep the poetic curve of nature, & his result is like a myth of ⟨Orpheus or⟩ Theocritus. Thus see the result of anatomy & osteology, nat[ural] ⟨&⟩ history,—one animal, arrested or progressive development, as in botany, one ⟨globule⟩ ↑cell↓ which becomes according to ⟨its sepal⟩ the need, ⟨sepal, cellule,⟩ leaf, anther, sepal, petal, stamen, bark, fruit, root, seed, one little cell holds all the future[,] all the /capabilities/possibilities/ of the plant ⟨or animal⟩.[114] We can trace the formation of minerals as well; show how carbon made the diamond; & granite & chalk & slate the mountain, & how gases made ⟨these⟩ the water & the land. It is plain that Kepler, Hunter, Bonner, Buffon, Geoffroy Saint-Hilaire, Linnaeus, Hauy, Oken, Goethe, & Faraday were poets in science as compared with Cuvier[.][115]

[115] ——
But a town that hears ⟨⟨fr⟩ daily⟩ ↑every day↓ from Europe ↑& Asia↓ what happened a minute ago, is a livelier place to live in, than the most charming wilderness.[116]

The physicists in general repel me. I have no wish to read them, & thus do not know their names. But the anecdotes of these men of ideas wake curiosity & delight. Thus Hooke's catenary problem, & Hauy's crystals, & Goethe's & Oken's theory of the Skull as a metamorphosed vertebra; & Hunter's "arrested development;" & Oersted's "correlation of forces"; & Hay's theory of the form of vases; & Garbett's & Ruskin's architectural theories; & Vitruvius's relation between the human form & the temple; & Pierce's showing that the orbits of comets (parabolic) make the forms of flowers; & Kepler's relation of planetary laws to music: & our Dr Wyman's hint from the

---

[114] Single vertical lines in pencil are drawn in the left-hand margin beside "The necessity . . . Theocritus." and "Thus see the . . . animal⟩."; the first is also struck through in pencil with three vertical use marks. Both are used in "Poetry and Imagination," *W*, VIII, 7–8.

[115] The scientists mentioned here who have not been previously identified or are not easily recognizable include Charles Bonnet (1720–1793), Swiss naturalist, philosopher, and expert on aphids; Comte Georges Louis Leclerc de Buffon (1707–1788), French naturalist, director of Jardin du Roi and of the royal museum (1739); Carolus Linnaeus (1707–1778), Swedish botanist, a father of modern systematic botany; Michael Faraday (1791–1867), English chemist and physicist.

[116] A vertical line in pencil is drawn in the left-hand margin beside this entry.

action of the magnet on steel filings to the form of the mammal skeleton; and Tyndall's experiment of the effect of sounds on different gases; & Franklin's kite;[117]

[116] All science must be penetrated by poetry. I do not wish to know that my shell is a strombus, or my moth a vanessa, but I wish to unite the shell ⟨or⟩& the moth to my being: to understand my own pleasure in them; to reach the secret of their charm for me.

Reality ⟨too⟩ ↑however↓ has a sliding floor.

[117] Look sharply after your thoughts. They come unlooked for, like a new bird seen on your trees, &, if you turn to your usual task, disappear; & you shall never find ⟨it⟩ ↑that perception↓ again; never, I say,—but perhaps years, ages, & ↑I know not↓ what events & worlds ⟨!⟩ may lie between you & its return! In the novel, the hero meets with a person who astonishes him with a perfect knowledge of his history & character, & ⟨who⟩ draws from him a promise that whenever & wherever he shall next find him, the youth shall instantly follow & obey him. So is it with ⟨the⟩you, & ⟨your⟩ ↑the new↓ thought,[118]

"⟨I⟩For deathless powers to verse belong
And they like demigods are strong
On whom the Muses smile."

"There can be no true valor in a bad cause."   Ancient Gleaman[119]

Rhyme, D 326–7
Poet or Maker   3 steps   G 109
                 several steps   N 11, 133, 134, 135
                 ‖epw‖ H 17   86   E 342, 343[120]

---

[117] The scientists mentioned here who have not been previously identified or are not easily recognizable include Hans Christian Oersted (1777–1857), Danish physicist, who founded the science of electromagnetism; Edward Lacy Garbett, author of *Rudimentary Treatise of the Principles of Design in Architecture*, 1850; and Marcus Vitruvius Pollio, Roman architect and engineer of the first century B.C.

[118] The remainder of p. [117] is written in pencil.

[119] Cf. Shakespeare, *Much Ado About Nothing*, V, i, 120: "In a false quarrel there is no true valor." See *JMN*, VI, 319.

[120] "H 17 . . . 343" is erased pencil writing.

[118] In Twistleton's "Handwriting of Junius," I find the quotation from Johnso⟨o⟩n, of Bacon's remark, "Testimony is like an arrow shot from a ⟨cross⟩long bow; the force of it depends on the strength of the hand that draws it. Argument is like an arrow from a cross-bow, which has equal force ⟨by⟩though shot by a child."

Twistleton.[n] p. xiv.[121]

Tibullus (on Sulpicia, IV. 2. 7) says of Venus,
   Illam, quidquid agit, quoquo vestigia vertit,
   Componit furtim, subsequiturque decor.[122]

Then Twistleton's motto from Epicharmus is good
"Νοῦς ὁρῇ καὶ νοῦς ἀκούει τἆλλα κωφὰ καὶ τυφλά."[123]

Cuvier et Geoffroy Saint-Hilaire.

"Jamais controverse plus vive ne d⟨e⟩ivisa deux adversaires plus resolus, plus fermes, munis de plus de ressources pour un combat depuis longtemps prévu, et, si je puis ainsi dire, *plus savamment préparés à ne pas s'entendre." Flourens* [*Nouvelle Biographie Générale,* 1855–1870, XX, 48].

[119] The multiplication of ⟨kings⟩ ↑monarchs↓ known by telegraph & daily news from all countries to the daily papers, & the effect of freer institutions in England & America, has ⟨transferred the⟩ robbed the title of ↑King of↓ all its romance, ⟨&⟩ as that of our commercial *Consuls* as compared with the ancient Roman. It is rich men, in America, who are now considered as the more stable & the more enviable of the two notabilities. ↑We shall ⟨have⟩ ↑come↓ to ⟨put⟩ ↑add↓ "Kings" in the "Contents" of the Directory, as we do "Physicians", "Brokers," &c.↓

Geoffroy-Saint-Hilaire is a true hero. Read his behavior, in August 1792, when his masters Lhomonde & Hauy, professors in his

---

[121] Charles Chabot, *The Handwriting of Junius Professionally Investigated, With a Preface and Collateral Evidence, by Edward Twistleton* (London, 1871), in Emerson's library.

[122] "Whate'er she does, where'er she turns her step, / Grace is her tire-woman, and her follower." The rule below this entry is in pencil.

[123] "Mind sees and mind hears, other things are blind and deaf" (Ed.). This motto appears on the title page of Chabot, *The Handwriting of Junius* . . . , 1871.

College of Cardinal-Lemoine, ⟨were⟩ ↑& all the rest of↓ the professors were arrested & sent to the prison of Saint Firmin as priests, near ⟨‖ . . . ‖⟩his own residence. In disguise ⟨he⟩of a commissary of prisons, he ⟨obtained⟩ ↑got↓ access to them, & tried to persuade some of them of means of escape. "No," replied Abbé Keranin, "we will not quit our brothers; our escape would decide their fate." Then Geoffroy at night came with a ladder, & waited 8 hours until one of them appeared; then saved 12 of them.[124]

[120] G[eoffroy]. ⟨C⟩Saint Hilaire was very ill in consequence of these exertions. Hauy wrote to him. "Leave your problems of crystals, rhomboids & dod⟨è⟩écaèdres; stick to plants which are full of beauty; a course of botany is pure hygiène." He went with Bonaparte to Egypt, & saved the scientific results, by a brilliant stroke of heroism when Alexandria was taken[n][.][125]

General Hutchinson ↑&c—excellent story↓[126]

———

I have translated the whole passage about the capitulation of Alexandria—in my *Waterville Address;* which manuscript see.[127]

[121] *Indians.* The Indian inquires of the spider whether the fox has been in his hole today. See too of the Woodsman. *WA* 93

la Séance du 19 Juillet
In the debate in the Académie des Sciences, in 18⟨2⟩30(?) the contest between Cuvier & G. Saint Hilaire broke out: see *supra* p. 118 & ⟨resembled⟩ reminded of the old sects of philosophers who shook the

---

[124] The preceding paragraph is Emerson's translation of passages in the *Nouvelle Biographie Générale,* 1855–1870, XX, 41–42.
[125] A vertical line in pencil is drawn in the left-hand margin beside "stick to . . . hygiène." "G. Saint Hilaire . . . hygiène." is Emerson's translation of passages in the *Nouvelle Biographie Générale,* 1855–1870, XX, 42. In "He went . . . taken", the comma preceding "by", the dots above the *i*'s in "scientific" and "brilliant", and the cross for the *t* in "scientific" are in pencil; for this line, see *Nouvelle Biographie Générale,* 1855–1870, XX, 44.
[126] "&c . . . story" is in pencil above unrecovered erased pencil writing. For the story of General Hutchinson, English commander in charge during the French surrender of Egypt, see *Nouvelle Biographie Générale,* 1855–1870, XX, 44.
[127] See p. [56] above.

world with their contests. The austere & regulated thinkers, men of severe science took part with Cuvier; the bold mind↑s↓ ranged themselves with Geoffroy. ⟨Great⟩ ↑What↓ changes have come into the contests of Churches! The debates of the Oecumenical Council are only interesting to the Catholics & a few ⟨in⟩ abnormal⟨; as the few⟩ⁿ readers, interested as the billiard ↑⟨c⟩players↓ in the contests of the billiard Champions[.]

[122] Oct. 31.   I recall today, after 50 years, a couplet of W[illiam]. H. Furness, in college verses, which ran,
> "O there are minds whose giant thoughts devise
> Deeds whose fulfilment asks eternities."
I doubt if I have recalled it in all the interval.

"A man who does not understand French is like a beast invited to dine with the birds: Every moment they fly up & leave him alone." *Varnhagen* [*Tagebücher,* 1861–1870] See *FOR* 46

Algernon Coolidge, aged ↑(6 or 7)↓ years, was shown a picture of a Centaur.[128] He looked at it a good while, & then asked, "↑Aunt Nina,↓ whenⁿ that Centaur goes to sleep, does he go to a bed, or to a stable?"—which speech I think an unanswerable criticism on Greek art.

Journals,—	"Spiritual Philosophy"	6	B. Daily Advertiser
	"Atlantic Monthly"	1	Commonwealth
	"Old & New"	1	N. Y. Nation
	"Naturalist"	1	Weekly Tribune
		1	Golden Age
		1	Independent
		1	Liberal Christian
		1	Standard
		1	Woman's Journal
		1	Dumb animals
		15	newspapers

[128] "(6 or 7)" is inserted in pencil.

254

[123] ↑*Culture*↓

The ⟨general⟩ ↑wide↓ diffusion of ⟨c⟩taste for poetry is a new fact. We receive twelve newspapers in this house every week, & eleven of them contain a ↑new↓ poem or poems,—all of these respectable, ↑—perhaps↓ one or two fit to clip from the paper, & put into your anthology.[129] Many of these poems are quite as good as many of the pieces in Aikin's or Anderson's standard Collections↑.↓ ⟨of English poetry⟩[130] and re⟨m⟩call ⟨Mo⟩ Walter Scott's reply ⟨to Moore⟩ ⟨said⟩when ↑T[homas].↓ Moore said,*[131] "See how good this poetry is of so many young writers, & the public takes no note of them." Scott replied, "Egad, man, we were in the luck of time." Verses of conversation are now written in a hundred houses or "picnics," or "private theatricals," which would have made reputation a century ago, but are now unknown out of ⟨the⟩some family circle. Webster wrote excellent lines in an album; Macaulay did the same. his "Cod": then ↑(↓somebody's↑)↓ ↑Byron's↓ Riddle of the letter *H*.
⌊Yet poetry is as rare as ever.⌋

[124] ↑*Homes.*↓ George Bartlett's wit & luck in the privatest "game parties" are charming. Yet the public never heard ⟨of him⟩ his name. ↑Arthur Gilman too.↓ In England, in France, appear the Freres, Tom Taylors, Luttrels, Hendersons (⟨M⟩Newton's Cotes too, of whom but for Newton's one remark we should have never heard,)[132]

*Now, Scott, it seems to me that these young fellows write better poetry than we did, & nobody reads it.

---

[129] "—perhaps" is inserted in pencil.

[130] Emerson is likely referring to *Select Works of the British Poets; with Biographical and Critical Prefaces by Dr. [John] Aiken* (London, [1820]); the "Anderson" collection has not been identified.

[131] Emerson's footnote appears in pencil above the list of journals and newspapers on p. [122].

[132] "In England . . . heard,)" is struck through in pencil with a diagonal use mark. Persons in this list who have not been previously identified or are not easily recognizable include Arthur Gilman (1837–1909), American educator; "the Freres," a family of French painters that included Charles Théodore Frère (1814–1888), Pierre Édouard Frère (1819–1886), and Pierre Édouard's son, Charles Édouard (1837–1894); and Tom Taylor, the dramatist. The identity of Luttrel, Henderson, and Cote has not been established.

Beware of the minor key.

What a benediction of heaven is this cheerfulness which I observe with delight,—⟨that⟩which no wrath & no fretting & no disaster can disturb, but keeps its perfect key & heals insanity in all companies & crises.

[125] An Englishman in Parliament House is a narrow partisan, but in his castle he is a cultivated European gentleman.[133]

[126] How vain to praise our literature, when its really superior minds are quite omitted, & utterly unknown to the public. Sampson Reed is known only to his sect, which does not estimate him. And Newcomb ⟨wr⟩ is a subtiller thinker than is any other American. And Philip Randolph a deep & admirable writer, utterly unknown,—died unknown. Thoreau quite unappreciated, though his books have been opened & superficially read. Alcott, the scholars do not know how to approach, or how to discriminate his tentative & sometimes tiresome talking, from his insights. Horatio Greenough has no rightful fame: ↑his genius surpassed all the artists of his time.↓[134]

[127] Like Bacon, who said, "I bequeath my books to my countrymen, when some little time has past;" or Kepler;—
"I can well wait a hundred years for a reader, since God Almighty has been content to wait 6 000 years for an observer like myself."[135]
Kepler, born 1571, died 1630.   Aet. 59 years

[128] Dull people are at the mercy of their feelings, fears, & gossip; but "Imagination is the sympathy with Beauty, which is the

---

[133] This entry is in pencil.

[134] The colon following "fame" in the last sentence was made by an alteration of the original end-of-sentence period.

[135] Bacon's statement, "I bequeath . . . past", appears to be a paraphrase of a passage in "The Last Will of Francis Bacon, Viscount St. Alban," in which Bacon left two "register books" to the Bishop of Lincoln and the Chancellor of Lancaster, who were to exercise discretion in their final disposition, for "they touch upon business of state." See Francis Bacon, *Works,* 10 vols. (London, 1824), IV, 411–412; this work is in Emerson's library. Kepler's statement, which Emerson may have taken from the popular work by Sir David Brewster, *The Martyrs of Science* (New York, 1843), p. 217, is used in "The Scholar," *W,* X, 270.

melody of truth, & so secures reality & accuracy, as sympathy between friends secures humanity in each." C[harles] K[ing] N[ewcomb]

[129] Dreams are jealous of being remembered: they dissipate
instantly & angrily if you try to hold them.

[130] ↑"Little boys should be seen not heard": Very well, but↓ poets^n
are not to be seen. Look at the foolish portrait↑s↓ of Herrick & Gray,
one a but⟨h⟩cher, & the other silly. ⟨Poets⟩ The Greek form answered
to the Greek character, but Poets are divided from their forms,—live
an official life. Intellect is impersonal.[136]

Blackwood's Magazine   "Byron secured the suffrages of the poeti-
cally minded by his genius:—he secured the common by his triumphant
commonplace." See ["A Century of Great Poets; From 1750 Downwards,"
in] "Littell['s Living Age,]" [No. 1471 (August 17, 1872),] p. 389

Poetry. Things not seen by reason, but by the flower of the mind. Z

    "Thoughts that voluntary move
    Harmonious numbers"

    "Wanton heed, & giddy cunning,
    The melting voice thro' mazes running;"

"Poets are standing transporters whose employment consists in producing
apparent imitations of unapparent natures." *Zoroaster*[137]

[131] "Things not seen by reason, but by the flower of the mind."[138]

[136] This entry is in pencil.
[137] With " 'Things not seen . . . mind.' ", cf. "God who cannot be apprehended otherwise than by the flower of the mind . . ." in Ralph Cudworth, *The True Intellectual
System of the Universe,* ed. Thomas Birch, 4 vols. (London, 1820), bk. I, chap. IV, sec.
XVI, in Emerson's library; see *JMN,* VI, 179. " 'Thoughts . . . numbers' " is from Milton, *Paradise Lost,* III, 37–38; see *JMN,* VI, 173. " 'Poets are . . . natures.' " is quoted by
Thomas Taylor in "Collection of the Chaldaean Oracles," *Monthly Magazine and British
Register,* III (1797), 520; see *JMN,* IX, 81.
[138] For " 'Things not . . . mind.' ", see p. [130] above. The remainder of p. [131] is
written in ink over an erased pencil version of substantially the same material.

257

The father cannot control the child from defect of sympathy. The man with a longer scale of sympathy, the man who feels the boy's sense & piety & imagination, and also his rough play & impatience & revolt, who knows the whole gamut in himself,—knows also a way out of the one into the other, & can play on the boy as on a harp, & ⟨l⟩easily lead him up from the scamp to the angel.

[132] *America.*

⟨'Tis easy to see how⟩ Oxford, working steadily now for a thousand years,—or the Sorbonne in France,—and a ↑royal↓ court steadily drawing ⟨from generation to generation⟩ ↑for centuries↓ men & women of talent & grace throughout the kingdom ↑to the capital city,↓ must give an impulse & sequence to learning & genius. And ⟨'tis easy to see that⟩ the history of this country has been far less friendly to a rich & polished literature than England & France. ⟨When we⟩ Count[n] our literary men, & they are few, & their works not commanding. But if the question be not of books, but of men,—question of intellect, not of literature, there would be no steep inferiority. For every one knows men of wit & special or general power↑, whom↓ to compare with citizens of any nation.[139] Edward Taylor lavished more wit & imagination on his motley congregation of sailors & caulkers, than you [133] might find in all France. The coarsest experiences he melted & purified, like Shakspeare, into eloquence. Wendell Phillips[n] is a Pericles whilst you hear him speaking. Beecher, I am sure, is a master in addressing an assembly though I have never heard ⟨him to advantage.⟩ ↑such good speeches of his as I have read.↓[140] Webster was majestic in his best days: And the better audience these men had, the higher would be the appreciation. Neither of them could write as well as ⟨they⟩ ↑he↓ spoke. Appleton's wit is quite as good as ↑Frere's or↓ Selby's or Luttrel's, who shine in the biographies. And England has no Occasional ⟨p⟩Poet to surpass Holmes.[141] Dr Channing, I must believe, had no equal as a preacher in the world of his time. Then we have men of affairs, who would rule ⟨in any country as they rule here⟩

---

[139] ", whom", inserted in pencil, was later traced in ink.

[140] The line that cancels "him ... advantage." is in pencil; "such ... read." is inserted in ink over pencil.

[141] The "O" and "P" of "Occasional Poet" are each underlined twice.

wherever there were men,—masters in commerce, in law, in politics, in society. Every civil country has such, but I doubt if any has more or better than we↑.↓ ⟨have.⟩ Add, that the Adamses have shown hereditary skill in public affairs, & Judge Hoar is as good [134] a lawyer, a statesman, & an influence in public & in private, as any city could hope to find.

I pass over my own list of thinkers & friends, as I have counted some of them a few pages back, and only add, that I believe ⟨that⟩ our soil yields as good women, too, as England or France, though we have not a book from them to compare with [Madame de Staël's] "Allemagne." Yet M[ary]. M[oody]. E[merson].'s journals shine with genius, & Margaret Fuller's Conversation did.

———

"Shleiermacher knew how much iron there was in their ⟨minds,⟩blood"

[135]¹⁴² 15 Nov. '71. Rec[eive]d of J R Osgood & Co
   6   copies of Wanderer   bound
       copies   unbound

———

   1   copy b[oun]d   RWE
   1   d[itt]o   Mrs ⟨G⟩E T
   1   d[itt]o   Anna Keyes

———

Unbound
   1 copy to E[dward] W E[merson]

[136] For "*Historic notices,*" see *N* 2, 6, 127, 134, 136
C[harles]. Lane, *N* 36
Fourier, *K* [25–]27, 60[–61],

[136ₐ] Show of fruits
     Pears & au mous(?)
        Dr Madden
   Caros
   Masstts   little

———

¹⁴² All entries on p. [135] are in pencil. William Ellery Channing's *The Wanderer, A Colloquial Poem* (Boston, 1871), is in Emerson's library.

Chicago opinion
Ch[ica]go now bigger
Illinois
    once doleful prairie

California
    Central Pacific
    in car through wolves, bison, grizzly, Shoshone   Pyut
    Echo   Weber Canons
    Devil-slide   cape-Horn
What are these attractions of Cal⟨i⟩afornia?
    Climate
    Grand position
    Port

[136ᵦ] [blank]
[137] Dec. 14 '71
Home again from Chicago, Quincy, Springfield, & Dubuque, which I
had not believed I should see again, yet found it easier to visit than before, & the kindest reception in each city. Must note here that I am
bound to send South⟨maid's⟩↑worth's↓ ↑large↓ photograph to Rev.
Laird Collier, & to B[enjamin]. W. Wiley: & a copy of *Concord Historical Oration* to Mrs L. Collier's friend, ↑(Shorey?)↓ whose name I
have lost, but who removed to Chicago from Bedford, Masstts & is a
prized writer for the Chicago Magazines. What shall I send to Mrs
Anna B. Bull, of Quincy (care of C. H. Bull,)? & to Mrs Austin
Adams, of Dubuque? Ah me! I have never yet replied to Mrs James
Dana of Detroit, nor to Mrs Neal, of Columbus! nor to John Muir,
nor to Mrs Grenville Winthrop, nor to more English correspondents
than I dare recall. Remember also Mr Clark of Troy N. Y.[143]

[138] Abbott of Toledo asks me to write for his "Index."ⁿ If I
do, I must remember to give him Sir Philip Sydney's counsel, which I
have copied in *NY* 189[-190].

[143] Between November 27 and December 10, 1871, Emerson presented lectures in
Chicago (Nov. 27), Quincy, Illinois (Dec. 1, 2, and 3), Springfield, Illinois (Dec. 5), and
Dubuque, Iowa (Dec. 8, 9, 10). Evidently persons mentioned on p. [137] were either
met on that tour or, as some entries make clear, were owed letters from Emerson.

Also ⟨see⟩ of the bad working of Calvinism, see *NY* 229, & the absolute reliance on moral constitution, ΦB 24⟨3⟩5, *DL* 200[–202]

———

See of the theologies. *J* 145

———

Advantages of American society for religious freedom over German, or Spanish, or Italian. *ST* 25–26

———

Bible, *N* 10

———

Religion has failed, &c *N* 28   Calvinism, *N* 101

———

It is becoming to the Americans to dare in religion to be simple, as
they have been in government, in trade, & in social life. See *KL*
195–6–7–8–9–

———

"We cannot speak rightly of the gods, without the gods." *Iamblichus.*

↑Like can only be known by like. Heraclitus.↓[144]

———

As the Greeks from time to time refined their ideal Apollo, so
each century has done with Christ. *IL* 113,

———

'Tis becoming in the Americans to dare ↑in religion↓ to be simple, as
they have been in government, in trade, in social life. ↑Bis↓[145]

———

Paper on the Catholics. Also *FOR* 73, 78

———

Religion, *ST* 19, 29, ↑*LN* 39, *ST* 209.↓

[144] *Iamblichus on the Mysteries of the Egyptians, Chaldeans, Assyrians, Translated from
the Greek by Thomas Taylor* (Chiswick, 1821), p. 164. This volume is in Emerson's library. See *JMN*, XIV, 131. The exact wording of "Like can . . . like." appears in Samuel
Taylor Coleridge's *Statesman's Manual*, Appendix B, in *The Complete Works of Samuel
Taylor Coleridge*, ed. W. G. T. Shedd, 7 vols. (New York, 1853), III, 203, but not attributed to Heraclitus.

[145] " 'Tis becoming . . . social life." is struck through in pencil with four diagonal use
marks. "Bis" is inserted in pencil.

[139] Christianity is pure Deism.

"Hunger & thirst after righteousness." [Matt. 5:6]

"The kingdom of God cometh not by observation." [Luke 17:20]

" is received as a little child." [Matt. 18:3]

"God considers integrity, not munificence." *Socrates*

⟨"Like can only be known by like."⟩ *Heraclitus.*[146]

"nec sentire deum, nisi qui pars ipse deorum est."[147]

——

The argument for Xy[Christianity] fails with percipient men. *FOR* 107, 127[-128],

——

Power belongeth unto God, but his secret is with them that fear him. [cf. Ps. 62:11 and 25:14]

——

Sch⟨e⟩lei⟨a⟩ermacher said, "the human soul is by nature a Christian".

——

Goethe speaks of Roth, *ML* 158

——

One thing is certain: the religions are obsolete when the reforms do not proceed from them. *AC* 79

——

↑You say,↓ the^n Church is an institution of God.[148] Yes, but ⟨is⟩ ↑are↓ not wit, & wise men, & good judgment whether a thing be so or no,—also institutions of God, & older than the other?

——

[140] Concord Lyceum. See the promise of the Concord Reading Room, in 1842↑,↓ recorded, *J* 142[149] ↑See also a note about school-yard in *ML* 6,↓

——

[146] For Socrates, see *JMN*, VI, 93, 179; for Heraclitus, see p. [138] above.

[147] "Only if man be himself the infinite, can the infinite be known by him." Quoted and so translated (but not identified) by William Hamilton in his review of Victor Cousin's *Cours de Philosophie*, in *Edinburgh Review*, L (Oct. 1829), 208. See *JMN*, VI, 144.

[148] "You say," is inserted in pencil.

[149] The comma after "1842" is inserted in pencil.

At Judge Gray's, Lowell told a good story of ⟨the⟩ ⟨Duke of⟩ ↑Égalité↓ Orleans on ⟨the⟩his way to the guillotine desiring wine; they brought him Chateau something, now called Orleans wine, which having tasted, he said, "Lead on!"

———

Concord Lyceum. For that local lecture which I ⟨p⟩still propose to read at our Town Hall concerning the hanging of private pictures, each for one month, in the Library, &c &c

Remember that a Scholar wishes that every book, chart, & plate, belonging to him should draw interest every moment by circulation: for

> "No man is the lord of anything
> Till he communicate his part to others,
> Nor doth⟨e⟩ he of himself know them for aught
> Till he behold them formed in the applause
> Where they're extended; Where, like an arch, ⟨extended⟩reverber-
>   ates
> The voice again, or, like a gate of steel
> Fronting the sun, receives & renders back
> The figure & its heat."
> [Shakespeare,] *Troilus & Cressida* [III, iii, 116–123, misquoted]

[141] When a boy I used to go to the wharves, & pick up shells out of the sand⟨,⟩ which vessels had brought ⟨to the⟩ as ballast, & also plenty of stones, gypsum, which, I discovered would be luminous when I rubbed two bits together in a dark closet, to my great won-der,—& I do not know why luminous, to this day. That, & the mag-netising my penknife, till it would hold a needle; & the fact that blue & gambooge would make green in my pictures of mountains; & the charm of ⟨s⟩ drawing vases by scrawling with ⟨ink⟩ ↑ink↓ heavy random lines, & then doubling the paper, so as to make another side symmetri-cal,—what was chaos, becoming symmetrical; then hallooing to an echo at the pond, & getting wonderful replies.

[142] Still earlier, what silent wonder is waked in the boy by blowing bubbles from so⟨p⟩ap & water with a pipe.

1872

March 31.   Judge French restored to me today my lost wallet which
Mr F. D. Ely, Esq. of Dedham, Masstts had brought to him & which
had been found by ⟨Ellen⟩ ↑Hannah↓ Ryan, of Dedham.[150] It contained $113.05 & a bank cheque for $5.00 more. The young woman
came to Mr Ely with it & said she had found it at the corner of Tremont & Winter streets. He looked for an advertisement, & found that
which I had sent to the Herald, & so brought it to Judge French who
paid the reward of 20.00, as I had requested him; & I hope to make
the acquaintance of ⟨Ellen⟩ ↑Hannah↓ Ryan.

[143][151] We spend a great deal of time in waiting.

"The last ten years of his (Palmerston's) life, during which he did nothing
will weigh more with posterity than the whole threescore & ten during a
great part of which he was so active." *"Littell's Living Age."* Oct. 15. '71.
from Fortnightly Review⟨,⟩

> "No more I seek, the prize is found
> I furl my sail, the voyage is o'er."

─────────

Whose lines?
↑Mine I believe, part of translation of some Latin lines for Mrs
Drury↓[152]

───

> "And to be wroth with one we love
> Doth work like madness in the brain."
> [Coleridge, "Christabel," ll. 412–413]

───

Boucher de Perthes at Abbeville, 1841.

1841	"the apparition of man on the globe contemporary with the
1842	mastodon, the elephas prim⟨o⟩igenius, Rhinoceros tickor-
1853	hinus, & in general of species of the quaternary fauna."

[150] Judge Henry Flagg French was the father of Daniel Chester French, the sculptor.
[151] Entries after "Fortnightly Review" on this page are in pencil.
[152] Emily Mervine Drury, of Canandaigua, New York, first met Emerson on a Mississippi steamboat in 1850, and later the two maintained a friendly correspondence.

In the cave of La Madeline, a leaf of ivory, on which is engraved the mammoth with his long mane—(presented, in 1865, to the Academy of Sciences.)[153]

[144][154] The good writer is sure of his influence, because, as he is always copying not from his fancy, but from real ⟨observation of⟩ facts,—when his reader afterwards ⟨meets &⟩ comes to ⟨his own experiences⟩ ↑⟨as deep⟩ ↑like↓ experiences of his own↓, he is always reminded of ⟨him⟩ ↑the writer↓.

Nor do I much care for the question whether the Zendavesta or the Desatir are genuine antiques, or modern counterfeits, as I am only concerned with the good sentences; & it is indifferent ⟨to me⟩ how old a truth is, whether ⟨a truth is⟩ an hour or ⟨a⟩ ↑five↓ centur⟨y⟩↑ies↓, ⟨old⟩. ↑The advantage of a San⟨c⟩scrit sentence over as good a sentence from the "Boston Radical," is that it comes without any taint of ↑an↓ existing party statement↓ whether it first shot into the mind of Adam, or ⟨the mind of me.⟩ ↑your own.↓ If it be truth it is certainly much older than both of us.

[145][155] *Queries*
    Who first said "Correlation of Forces"?
answer. Cicero: "aliquid commune vinculum."

---

[153] Jacques Boucher de Crèvecoeur de Perthes (1788–1868) was a French archaeologist and writer of tragedies and fiction. Appointed *douane* at Abbeville in 1825, he wrote there his monumental work, *Antiquités celtiques et antédiluviennes,* 3 vols. (n.p., 1847, 1857, 1864), in which he established the existence of man in the Pleistocene period. The exact source of Emerson's entries has not been identified.

[154] Entries on p. [144] are in pencil. The inserted statement "The advantage . . . statement" in the second entry is written in pencil on the bottom of p. [145] and circled in pencil; its intended position on p. [144] is indicated by two pencil lines connecting the circle with "old".

[155] Entries on p. [145] are written in pen over a pencil version of substantially the same material. The differences between versions are these: there is no pencil "Queries"; "Grant" and "Sherman" are underlined in the pencil; in the pencil "arrested . . . *Hunter.*" reads " 'Arrested development?' ↑Answer.↓ *John Hunter.*"; in the pencil "animals . . . *Agassiz.*" reads "animals ⟨?⟩ in the strata? Answer. *Agassiz.*" The first three of these queries were mentioned earlier in this volume; for "Correlation of Forces" see p. [90] above; for "The South . . . shell" see Journal NY, p. [199] above; for "arrested development" see Journal NY, p. [113] above. The expression "arrested and progressive development" is

Who first said, "The South is a shell"?[n] Was it Grant? or was it Sherman?

Who said arrested development? *John Hunter.*

Who showed that the foetal development determined the order or succession of fossil animals in the strata? *Agassiz.*

[146][156]   *Parallax.*
The eye of the intellect has to ⟨make⟩ allow for parallax as well as the other[.]
The mind's eye⟨s⟩ as well as the body's eye must allow for parallax of ⟨the⟩ ↑its↓ object. We correct our estimate of distance of Shakspeare from other poets by successive comparisons or more knowledge of them, as we find the height of the fixed star by its unaltered position at the two extremes of the earth's orbit.

Parallax. The merit of a poem is decided by long experience. *N* 80,

For "Parnassus." Mem. Ask Bartol for the address of young Willson.[157]

[147][158] Notes for *Parnassus.*

---

used in "Poetry and Imagination," *W*, VIII, 7, and attributed there to Hunter; the expression "Hunterian law of arrested development" is used in "Inspiration," *W*, VIII, 270. However, in *JMN*, IX, 233, Emerson credits Robert Chambers, *Vestiges of the Natural History of Creation* (New York, 1845), as the source of the expression "arrested development."

[156] *"Parallax. . . . earth's orbit."* is in pencil, but *"Parallax."* is written in ink over pencil "Parallax". "The eye . . . the other" is struck through in pencil with two diagonal use marks.

[157] Unknown to Emerson, young Forceythe Willson, the poet, whose work Emerson respected and whose poem "In State" is included in *Parnassus*, had died in Alfred Center, New York, in 1867. See p. [214] below.

[158] Of the fifteen short rules on p. [147], the first through fourth, the sixth, ninth, tenth, and fourteenth are struck through with a short diagonal pencil line each, probably to indicate that the material following them was read. The *x* inserted above the eleventh

Read Milnes's *"Lay of the Humble"*

↑x↓　See Critical Notice of Bryant in the N. Y. Nation [XIV] Feby. 15, '72 [p. 107].

↑x↓　"John Brown of Osawotomie," ⟨attributed to Whittier.⟩ ↑Steadman↓

↑x↓　Walter Scott's songs of the Spirit in "The Abbot"
　　　"Forms that men spy
　　　With the half shut eye
　　　In the beams of the setting sun, am I."

↑x↓　In *Thomson's Seasons*　the snow-storm.

---

rule and "Mui⟨u⟩potmos of Spenser" are in pencil. "Read . . . *Humble'* ", "From Cra-shaw, . . . p. 148", "Insert . . . thee.' ", and "Mrs Julia Dorr's . . . 'Outgrown'." are each struck through with one diagonal use mark; the passages " 'John Brown . . . ↑Steadman↓", "Walter Scott's . . . am I.' ", and "In *Thomson's* . . . snow-storm." are struck through with one common diagonal use mark. Of the items listed here for the apparent purpose of deciding on their inclusion in *Parnassus*, those that have not been previously identified or are not easily recognizable include Richard Monckton Milnes's "The Lay of the Humble," ll. 33–40 of which appear in *Parnassus* as "Humility"; a portion of the song of the White Lady of Avenel in Sir Walter Scott's *The Abbot*; James Thomson's *The Seasons*, from which ll. 276–321 of "Winter" appear in *Parnassus* as "Lost in the Snow"; Edmund Waller's "An *Apology* for having Lov'd before," which in a modernized version appears in *Parnassus*; Richard Crashaw's *Sospetto d'Herode*, "Libro Primo," stanzas 5, 13, 20, 21, 22, 23, from *Specimens of the Earlier English Poets* (London, 1824), in Emerson's library, which appear in *Parnassus* as "Satan"; Bishop George Berkeley's "On the Prospect of Planting Arts and Learning in America," from which ll. 21–25 appear in *Parnassus* untitled; Caroline Sturgis Tappan's lines "The Poet," which appear in *Parnassus*; Julia Caroline Ripley Dorr's "Outgrown," from *Poems* (Philadelphia, 1872), in Emerson's library, which appears in *Parnassus*; "Let such . . . sacred floor." which is l. 13 misquoted of Alexander Pope's "VERSES *on a* GROTTO *by the River* Thames *at* Twickenham, *composed of Marbles, Spars, and Minerals*; "Ah God! . . . hand," from Tennyson's *Maud*, X, 60; and Edmund Spenser's "Muiopotmos: or, the Fate of the Butterflie." From John Ruskin's *Sesame and Lilies. Two Lectures Delivered at Manchester in 1864* (New York, 1872), in Emerson's library, thirty excerpted lines of Wordsworth's "Lucy" poem that begins "Three years she grew in sun and shower . . ." are borrowed and appear in *Parnassus* as "Lucy," while Coventry Patmore's "The Queen," of which only ll. 9–16 are printed by Ruskin, appears in its entirety in *Parnassus* under the same title. The critical notice of Bryant consists of an unsigned review of his *Poems* (New York, 1871).

Waller's "Apology for having loved before." *L* 22

↑x↓   The lines from Troilus & Cressida, copied *supra* p. 140

From Crashaw, insert verses from the Sospetto d'Herode in *Specimens of Earlier Poets.* p. 148

Insert B[isho]p. Berkley's Lines. *Spence* p 191

↑x↓   Insert Wesley's Hymn, "O draw me Father after thee."

↑x↓   Insert lines from Wordsworth cited in Ruskin's "Sesame" p. 93
↑x↓   and lines from Patmore Coventry in Ruskin   p. 88

Lines written by C[aroline]. S[turgis]. ⟨or by E[llen]. S[turgis].⟩ to the Poet.

Mrs Julia Dorr's poem, "Outgrown".ⁿ   (?)

Let such only tread this sacred floor. *Pope's Grotto*

↑x↓   Tennyson's lines,
          "Ah God↑!↓ for a man with heart, head, hand,"

& *vide* [Notebook] *PY* 170
↑Mui⟨u⟩potmos of Spenser↓

[148]¹⁵⁹ *Parnassus.*

Milnes' Lay of the Humble.

¹⁵⁹ Of the sixteen short rules on p. [148], the fifth through twelfth, the fifteenth, and the sixteenth are struck through with one short diagonal pencil line each, probably to indicate the material following them was read or considered for inclusion in *Parnassus.* The *x* that precedes "Ben Jonson, Epistle . . ." and the passage "He has . . . behemoth," are in pencil. "Wordsworth's Skating." is struck through in pencil with two diagonal use marks; "Ben Jonson's . . . *Restored.*" is struck through in pencil with three diagonal use marks. Of the items listed here, those that have not been previously identified or are not easily recognizable include William Ellery Channing's *The Wanderer* . . . , 1871, from which several segments of section IV, "Henry Camp" (pp. 61, 40, 41, 42–43), appear in *Parnassus* as "The Mountain" and a segment of section III, "The Mountain," appears in

Two Extracts from Channing's *"Wanderer."*

In Ben Jonson, the Countess of Bedford. *Works* [1716]. III. p. 141

"The Cronach's cried on Bennachie," &c

↑x↓   Channing W[illiam]. E. Lines to A[nna]. B[arker]. W[ard].

↑x↓   Mrs Barbauld's poem, "Life."

↑x↓   For Crashaw & Sospetta d'Herode, see "Retrospective Review [*and Historical and Antiquarian Magazine*]," *Vol.* 1. 1820 [pp. 241–243]

↑x↓   Shakspeare's lines in ↑Troilus & Cressida↓.

↑x↓   Wordsworth's Skating.

↑x↓   Ben Jonson's *Manes.*
      "See yonder souls set far within the shade."
                                        Golden Age Restored.

Parnassus as "The Hillside Cot"; Ben Jonson's piece "*On Lucy, Countess of* Bedford," which appears in *Parnassus* under the same title; Anna Laetitia Barbauld's "Life," from *The Works of Anna Laetitia Barbauld* . . . , 2 vols. (Boston, 1826), in Emerson's library, which appears in *Parnassus* under the same title; a selection from William Wordsworth's *The Prelude; or, Growth of a Poet's Mind* . . . , 1850, I, 425–463, which appears in *Parnassus* as "Skating"; Ben Jonson's "See yonder . . . the shade." from *The Golden Age Restored. In a MASQUE at Court, 1615,* in *Works,* 1716, III, 483, l. 189, which appears in *Parnassus* as the motto for the section on "Heroic" poetry; John Fletcher's "Upon an Honest Man's Fortune," which appears in *Parnassus* as "An Honest Man's Fortune." The "good lines of Keats's . . . ↑Hyperion.↓" that appear in *Parnassus* include "As Heaven and Earth are fairer, fairer far . . ." from *Hyperion,* II, 206–215, which appears as "From Hyperion"; "So Saturn, as he walked into the midst . . ." from *Hyperion,* II, 105–109, which appears as "Saturn"; "Leaving with parted lips, some words she spake . . ." from *Hyperion,* I, 47–51, which appears as "Thea." Another of Keats's lines, "Northward he turneth through a little door . . ." from "The Eve of St. Agnes," III, 19–21, appears in *Parnassus* as "Music" and is mistakenly indexed there as "Hyperion (Music)." The last eighteen lines of Sir William Jones's translation of "A Hymn to Náráyena," from *The Works of Sir William Jones,* 6 vols. (London, 1799), VI, 367–373, appear in *Parnassus* as "Narayana, Spirit of God." " 'The Cronach's . . . &c" and "Channing . . . to A. B. W." are unidentified.

↑x↓   "For no man is the lord of anything
       Till he communicates his part to others,"
       &c &c [Shakespeare,] *Troilus & Cressida* [III, iii, 116–117]

↑x↓ Be sure to insert the good lines of Keats's ⟨Endymion⟩ ↑Hyperion.↓

See *PY* pp. 168, 171, 175, 180, 186,

One line poems, *PY* 205, 206, 257,

↑x↓ Sir Wm Jones's translation of the Hindu poem to Narayena[n] *Works* Vol. 5, or 6,

↑x↓ Fletcher's Epilogue to Honest Man's Fortune, *LI* 58,
↑x↓ "Ben Jonson, Epistle to Wroth & others, Penshurst & a Masque (in [*Works,* 1716] Vol III [470–478]) of Nature & Prometheus." *C* 179

He has an eagle's eye, the speed of a horse, the mastiff's courage, can swim like a dolphin, endurance of behemoth,

[149] ⎯⎯⎯⎯
      ↑*Mem.* the address of↓
Eugene Benson, Louisville, Kentucky, writing for the "Commercial" newspaper. 1870.

    "Anything that obliges a man or a woman to think of something different from themselves tends to make them better." [Auguste Laugel,] *Nation,* [XIV] March 7, '72. Article, *French Stage* [pp. 151–152].

    In the "Nation" of 7 March '72, see notice of Uberweg's Hist. of Philosophy; & of "Golden Treasury"; & of Jones Very.[160]

⎯⎯⎯⎯⎯⎯

[160] For notices of Palgrave's "Golden Treasury," a collection of poems, and of Jones Very, see the review of John Earle, *The History of the Philology of the English Tongue* (Oxford, 1871), in *The Nation,* XIV (March 7, 1872), pp. 154–155. "Uberweg's Hist. of Philosophy" is not mentioned there.

↑See what work we play with History.↓ A man surprises us with some unexpected wisdom or magnanimity, & instantly we carry out our picture of him to a symmetry with this trait,—sink his foibles: If brave, we make him Achilles; if generous, Hatem Tai; if   & the epithets we add, & exaggerations, presently become history, & thus the ⟨gods⟩ ↑heroes↓ of nations grew to be gods. We play the same game with their faults[.]¹⁶¹

[150]   *Nineteenth Century.*
    Our life is sad prose, ↑& hurtful,↓ if read literally. If read mystically, it is edifying ⟨&⟩ fruitful ↑& poetic↓. Our superstitions today, are, ⟨1⟩ fear of Roman Catholicism, pauperism, excessive immigration (as of paupers, convicts, Chinese, &c.), ⟨Manufacturing interests,⟩ ↑Mischievous "rings⟨,⟩" in politics & in trade;↓ⁿ radicalism; & democracy. Our faith is in steam & chemistry.

——

Catholics. See "*Spen⟨s⟩ce's Anecdotes*[, *Observations, and Characters* . . . , 1858]," ↑p. 38,↓ for Pope Clement X↑I.↓'s opinion.

[151] Parallax↑, as you know,↓ is the apparent displacement of an object from two points of view;—less & less of the heavenly bodies, because of their remoteness,—& of the fixed stars, none at all. Well, it is thus that we have found Shakspeare to be a ↑fixed↓ star. Because all sorts of men have in three centuries found him still unapproachable.

Our first view is only a guess: We feel that here is somewhat that we had not seen before; ⟨&⟩ our attention is won, & presently riveted, so that we carry away a deeper impression than ordinary. Still it is a wild guess,—wide of the mark. But the impression of somewhat superior remains, & works in the memory, so that when we meet the man or his work again, we give the greater heed.

    [152] I wrote in 1853 (*HO* 165) that the Revival of letters by telling in the Hebrew & the Greek mind on the Gothic brain, produced the English inspiration, which culminated in Shakspeare, & England was for two centuries religious & poetic; then it lost imagination & Unity, profoundness & connection, & a transcendental mind,

¹⁶¹ "See what . . . faults" is in pencil.

271

like Coleridge, Wordsworth, or Swedenborg, is not only ungenial but unintelligible. Shakspeare's transcendences are only pardoned for his perfect objectiveness. &c &c. ↑See↓ *HO* 166 [actually 165][162]

[152ₐ] [blank]

[152ᵦ][163] x ⟨Books⟩

         x   Poetry & Imagination

            Poetry

            Culture

            ⟨T⟩ Friendship

                Beauty

                Love

            Wit & Humor

            Heroism

            Ethics

            France

            Criticism

                Writing

                Compression

[153] April 16, [1872][164]
First Reading. "Books."

[162] With "Revival of letters . . . his perfect objectiveness.", cf. "Literature," *W*, V, 234–235.

[163] Emerson's list on this sheet may be relevant to the Boston "conversations" described in the note to p. [153] below.

[164] Apparently Emerson had two purposes for the list that follows on pp. [153]–[154]. First, the dates and topics generally correspond to the outline of six private "conversations" on literature that Emerson gave at Mechanics' Hall, Boston, April 15–May 20, 1872; see William Charvat, *Emerson's American Lecture Engagements: A Chronological List* (New York, 1961), p. 47, where, given the evidence presented on p. [153], Charvat's dates "Apr 22?" and "Apr 29?" should be corrected to "Apr 23" and "Apr 30". Second, given Emerson's comment "All these marked are now inserted in Parnassus", the poems that were read after the conversations may have been selected for the occasion in order to test them for use in *Parnassus*. "After the Essay, . . . Strode's 'Music,' " and "Lewis's . . . Ode to Himself." are each struck through in ink with one vertical use mark; " 'Schill' ", " 'Island' ", "Dinas", and "Egremont;" are each struck through in ink with one vertical use mark; "Timrod's poem;" is struck through in ink with two vertical use marks. Persons in this list whose poems in fact appear in *Parnassus* include Thoreau, Helen Hunt, David Lewis, Sir Walter Scott, Ben Jonson, Wordsworth, Henry Timrod, and Byron. For "lines . . . Licoo", see p. [47] above.

After the Essay, read Thoreau's "Inspiration"

H. Hunt's	"Thought,"
	"Joy,"
Strode's	"Music,"
Ballad	"Thomas the Rhymer"
Lewis's	Lines to Alexander Pope
Scott's	Look not thou on Beauty's
	Charming
Ben Jonson's	Ode to Himself.

Apr. 23   "Poetry & Imagination" as far as t⟨t⟩hrough "Creation."
          & read Wordsworth's "Schill"

Byron's	"Soul"
lines from	"Island"
	Licoo

⟨Single⟩One line poems

Apr. ⟨29⟩30 "Poetry & Imagination" concluded & read.
          Taliessin
          Dinas Emlyn
          Saadi, from "West Ostlichen Divan"
          Arab ballad,   d[itt]o.

May 6.   Criticism (Montreal)
          & read   Klephtic Lochinvar; Timrod's poem; ⟨Boy of⟩
          Egremont; ⟨Lir's lonely daughter⟩; ⟨Murat⟩
          ↑All these marked are now inserted in Parnassus↓

[154] May 13. *Culture.* Goethe, Pascal, Pope, Bolingbroke, Lionardo
              Da Vinci, Varnhagen, &c
          Manners, Beauty, Love,

May 20. Morals   Religion

For Lecture V
⟨Consult [Notebook] M[ary] M[oody] E[merson] on Manners of Miss
T⟩ ↑not read.↓
⟨Caesar   Σ 49⟩ ↑not read↓
Bolingbroke   ZO 147[165]

---

[165] "For Lecture ... 147" is in pencil.

[155]¹⁶⁶ J. S. Reed, 210 N Eutaw St   Baltimore

Note for Lecture VI
    ⟨passage in *ML* 152⟩ ↑not read↓
    ⟨Schleiermacher ML 157⟩ ↑not read↓
        156 Barclay
    No hope so brilliant but is the beginning of its own fulfilment
&c   p 176   [*ML*]

Charles K Newcomb   Glendower Hotel
    Market Place, Great Portland street
           London
1872 May 2⟨6⟩0

[156] [blank]
[157] 1872, May 2⟨5⟩6. Yesterday, my sixty ninth birthday, I found
myself on my round of errands in Summer street, &, though close on
the spot where I was born, was looking into a street with some bewilderment and read on the sign *Kingston street,* with surpr↑i↓se, finding
in the granite blocks no hint of Nathaniel Goddard's ⟨long wooden
fe⟩pasture & long wooden fence, & so of my nearness to my native
corner of Chauncy Place. It occurred to me that few living persons
ought to know so much of the families of this fast growing city, for the
reason, that Aunt Mary, whose MSS. I had been reading to Hedge &
Bartol, ⟨the⟩on Friday Evening, had such a keen perception of character, & ⟨a⟩ taste for aristocracy, & I heard in my youth & manhood
every name she knew. It is now nearly a hundred [158] years since
she was born, & the founders of ⟨all⟩the oldest families that are still no-
table were known to her as retail-merchants, milliners, tailors, distill-
ers, as well as the ministers, lawyers, & doctors, of the time. She was a
realist, & knew a great man or "a whale hearted woman,"—as she
called one of her pets,—from a successful money maker.

[159] If I should live another year, I think I shall cite still the last
stanza of my own poem, "The World-Soul."

    ¹⁶⁶ Entries on p. [155] are in pencil. Notes for "Lecture VI" most likely refer to the
last conversation of the series outlined on pp. [153]–[154] above.

[160] Walk in the city for an hour, and you shall see the whole history of female beauty. ⟨h⟩Here are the school girls in the first profusion of their hair covering them to the waist, ⟨then⟩ & now & then one maiden of 18 or 19 years, in the moment of her perfect beauty. Look quick & sharply,—this is her one ⟨day o⟩meridian day. To find the like again, you must meet, on your next visit, one who is ↑a month↓ younger today. Then troops of pleasing well dres⟨t⟩sed ladies, sufficiently good looking & graceful, but without claims to the prize of the goddess of Discord.

[161] "no sign that our mighty rocks had ever tingled with earthquake." John Muir

———

"I lodged in a crease of the bark of a Sequoia"   J[ohn]. M[uir].

John Muir said he slept in a wrinkle ⟨of the bark⟩ of the bark of a Sequoia, on the night after we left him[.][167]

[162] June 12. Sarah Clarke gratified us with her visit of twenty six hours, ever the same peaceful, wise, just, & benevolent spirit, open, gentle, skilful, without a word of self assertion. I regret that I did not recall & testify to her my oft recollection of her noble & oft-needed & repeated sisterly aid to Margaret Fuller, in old times, in her cruel head-aches. We talked of many friends of both of us, but of Charles K. N[ewcomb]. it seems she knew nothing. Of Greenough, she did not know much. I was glad, in describing his last visit to me, ↑to add↓ that he was one who to his varied perception added the rare one of the To δεινον.

We would all be public men if we could afford it. I am wholly private: such is the poverty of my constitution. Heaven "betrayed me

———

[167] " 'no sign ... J. M." is in pencil. After meeting Emerson during his western journey, Muir initiated an extensive correspondence that was not consistently maintained by Emerson. On March 26, 1872, Muir wrote to Emerson, inviting him to Yosemite again and describing an earthquake then in progress (*L*, VI, 204). Thayer reports that ten months earlier, when Emerson and Muir had last met, Emerson and his party "left Muir standing in the forest alone ... to pass the night there in solitude" (*A Western Journey* ... , 1884, pp. 108–109). Muir's letter to Emerson has not apparently survived.

to a book, & wrapt me in a gown".[n] I have no social talent, no wealth of nature, nothing but a sullen will, & a steady appetite for insights in any or all directions, to balance my manifold imbecilities.

[163] ————

Men of genius in their rare moments, say things quite beyond their ordinary calibre, or perhaps adopt such sayings of their wisest compan⟨o⟩ions. Thus Mahomet writes in the Koran, "Paradise is under the shadow of swords"; and then, with ma↑t↓chless all-atoning generosity, "Paradise,—⟨⟨w⟩b⟩whose breadth equals the Heaven & the earth."[168]

Goethe.

What proof of Goethe's wealth of mind like the *Sprüche* [*in Prosa*, 1870]? which, no doubt, could he have lived twice eighty years, he would have orderly ⟨written⟩ ↑expanded↓ into consecutive chapters & volumes, but, in despair at his shortening days & multiplying aperçus, was forced to string into a magazine [164] of proverbs.

Goethe's statement on ⟨King⟩ Royalty & Popular govt   *West-Östli-chen Divans*   p. 94[169]

↑Printed?↓   Waagen said that Greek sculpture was born, & was ever kept, in a subserviency ⟨as⟩to architecture, & hence its severe /moderation/tenue/. That may be true ↑law↓ of sculpture, but not of poetry, which will never be a simple means, as when history or philosophy is rhymed, or laureate odes on state occasions are used: Poetry must be the end to which it is written, or it is nothing. See Spenser's delight in his art for his own skill's sake, in the Muiopotmos. ↑Printed probably   In "Letters & Social Aims"↓[170]

[168] " 'Paradise . . . swords' " is used in "Heroism," *W*, II, 243. See *JMN*, VII, 401.
[169] Johann Wolfgang von Goethe, *West-Easterly Divan*, trans. John Weiss (Boston, 1877), is in Emerson's library; however, this reference has not been found in that volume or in contemporary editions of the same work.
[170] "Printed?" is written in pencil diagonally between "Waagen" and "said". "Printed . . . Aims' " is in pencil. "of poetry, which . . . Muiopotmos.", struck through in pencil with a diagonal use mark, is used in "Poetry and Imagination," *W*, VIII, 54.

[165] Note for "Poetry & Imagination."

———

The sentence of Moore about "prose poets" must not be omitted.[171]

———

☞ so likewise the paragraph on the opposite page.[172]

———

Read once more the Muiopotmos [of Spenser].

———

See also the notes in my pocket Diary ⟨from⟩ from "Aids to Contentment," selected by John Morris, London, Deighton, Bell, & Co., 1870[173]

———

[166] 11 July, '72. Yesterday read my paper on Character or Greatness to the "Social ⟨Institute⟩ ↑Union↓," comprising the four Classes at Amherst College. Stayed with Ellen at President Stearns's house, there finding H[enry]. W[ard]. Beecher, Judge Lord, & other gentlemen, with Miss Gleason, Miss Good/win/man/, of Lenox, Miss ↑Annie Lee↓ of ⟨Boston⟩ ↑Charlestown,↓ & the daughters of the President S[tearns].[174]

Visited the Boltwoods, & with Professor C[harles]. U[pham]. Shepard, went through his rich collection of minerals in the Walker Hall. Learned this morning, in our call at the house, that Mr Boltwood Sen[io]r died ⟨dur⟩last night of paralysis, aged 80 years.

———

I prefer the photograph to any other copy of the living head: the light is the best painter, & makes no mistakes. ↑Truth evermore.↓

———

[167] 'Tis easy to write the technics of poetry, to discriminate Imagination & Fancy, &c. but the office & ⟨&⟩power which that word

———

[171] "The sentence . . . omitted." is struck through in pencil with seven diagonal use marks. See "Poetry and Imagination," *W*, VIII, 50.

[172] The "☞" points to the paragraph beginning "Waagen said . . ." on p. [164].

[173] See Pocket Diary 23, p. [194] below.

[174] "man", "Annie Lee", and "Charlestown," are inserted in pencil in the preceding paragraph; "Boston" is deleted in pencil.

Poetry[n] covers & suggests are not so easily reached & defined. What heaven & earth & sea & the forms of men & women are speaking or hinting to us in our healthiest & most impressionable hours,—What fresh perceptions a new day will give us of the old problems of our own being & its hidden source↑;↓ what is this Sky of Law↑,↓ & what the Future hides[175]

House burned, Wednesday, 24 July [1872].

[168] Norway, Maine.

August 20, '72.[176]   Forgot, in leaving home, twenty necessities—forgot to put Horace, or Martial, or Cicero's Letters, ↑"Le Cité Antique,"↓ or Taine's England, in my ⟨po⟩wallet: forgot even the sacred chocolate Satchel itself, to hold them or their like.[177] Well, at the dear Vale, 11 miles off yet, I may recall or invoke things as good. Yet I should there remember that letters are due to Ellen Gurney, & Pauline Shaw, & M⟨rs⟩iss Dorr, & Mrs Edwards, & Alice Hooper, & Dr Hooper. I shall not forget the dear names of Caroline T[appan]. & her children, Ellen & Mary; Perhaps I will venture on a letter of proposals of a voyage to J. Elliot Cabot, & a letter to the kindly Alexander Ireland is more than due. ⟨A letter also instantly due in reply to G[eorge]. B. E[merson]., who happily knows nothing of fire. And Mrs Niel's letter must be found & sent.⟩[178]

[175] The semicolon following "source" and the comma following "Law" are in pencil.

[176] "Norway, Maine." and "August 20, '72." are separated from the paragraph by an angled line. The period following "Maine" is outside the configuration. In the days following the fire in Emerson's house, Emerson's family and friends became alarmed at the decline in his health. For that reason it was decided that the house was to be rebuilt without Emerson's direct involvement and that Annie Keyes, who had become engaged to Edward at this time, would superintend the rebuilding. In addition to living at the Old Manse, Emerson was encouraged to go away on short visits to New Hampshire, Maine, and Naushon Island. In time it was decided that Emerson and Ellen would voyage to Europe. See *L*, VI, 213–221; *Life*, pp. 452–457.

[177] " 'Le Cité Antique' " is Numa Denis Fustel de Coulanges, *La Cité Antique; Étude sur le Culte, le Droit, les Institutions de Grèce et de Rome*, 3rd ed. (Paris, 1870); "Taine's England" is Hippolyte Adolphe Taine, *Essais de Critique et d'Histoire* (Paris, 1858).

[178] "A letter also . . . sent." is struck through in pencil with a vertical line. Of the persons mentioned here, those who have not been previously identified or are not easily recognizable include Ellen Gurney, the daughter of Ellen Sturgis Hooper and Dr. Robert

Remember to write to W. B. Wright, Buffalo, to ask for tidings of George Tufts.

———

[169]^{179} ⟨Waterford, 22⟩ August. 13, 1872

Mrs Caroline Tappan	Thomas G. Appleton
Miss Ellen S. Tappan	Francis George Shaw
Miss Mary A. Tappan	E. R[ockwood]. Hoar
Mrs Ann S. Hooper	George C. Ward
Miss Alice Hooper	William Gray
Mrs George R. Russell	Edward Wigglesworth
Mrs Abel Adams	H. P. Kidder
Mrs George Faulkner	James B. Thayer
Mrs Anna C. Lodge	H. H. Hunnewell
Mrs M. F. Sayles	William Whiting
Misses Wigglesworth	R[obert]. W. Hooper
Mrs Henry Edwards	T. Jefferson Coolidge
Miss S. E. Dorr	J. J. Bowditch
Mrs Lucia J. Briggs	James H. Beal

W. Hooper and the wife of Ephraim Whitman Gurney; Pauline (or Paulina) Shaw, a close friend of Emerson's daughter Edith; Alice Hooper, the daughter of Anna Sturgis Hooper and Samuel Hooper; and possibly Anna M. Neil, mentioned in Emerson's April 27, 1871, letter to Lidian (*L*, VI, 153). A Miss S. E. Dorr and Mrs. Henry Edwards are mentioned on p. [169] below.

^{179} The list on p. [169] probably represents people to whom Emerson owed letters, perhaps in order to acknowledge their generosity and concern after the fire in his house. Of the persons mentioned here, those who have not been previously identified or are not easily recognizable include Mrs. George R. Russell, whose husband was listed as a member of the Town and Country Club in *JMN*, XI, 237; Mrs. Abby Adams, the widow of Abel Adams, Emerson's financial adviser; Mrs. George Faulkner, Abby Larkin Adams, the adopted daughter of Abel and Abby Adams; the Misses Wigglesworth, related perhaps to Edward Wigglesworth listed below; Francis George Shaw, whose home was at New Brighton, Staten Island; Edward Wigglesworth (1804–1876), Boston lawyer, editor, and businessman; William Whiting, a native of Concord, who became a solicitor of the War Department in 1862; T. Jefferson Coolidge, who served with Emerson on the Committee to Visit Academical Departments at Harvard College; J. J. Bowditch, probably J. Ingersoll Bowditch, the executor of Abel Adams's will; and Frederick Beck, a Concord resident. Mrs. Anna C. Lodge, Mrs. M. F. Sayles, Mrs. Henry Edwards, Miss S. E. Dorr, H. P. Kidder, H. H. Hunnewell, R. W. Hooper, James H. Beal, James A. Dupee, and John E. Williams are unidentified.

James A. Dupee
J[ames]. R. Osgood, & Co
John E. Williams
John M. Forbes
Frederick Beck
Le Baron Russell
Samuel G. Ward
George Bancroft

[170]¹⁸⁰   August 1, 1872.

Mrs Pauline Shaw,	500.	
Ellen Gurney,	100.	
Henry Lee,	500.	
H. L. Higginson,	500.	
In memory of C[harles]. R[ussell].		
Lowell and Stephen Perkins,	100.	
⟨S⟩J. ⟨S⟩J. Higginson,	⟨250.⟩	300.
G. H Jr. &		
Mary L Blake,	500.	
F. L. Higginson,	500.	
George Higginson,	500.	
Mr & Mrs Bangs,	500.	
⟨Nina⟩Francis C. Lowell		
and		
Nina Lowell:	1000.	

¹⁸⁰ After the fire at Emerson's house, friends and acquaintances were quick to respond with financial aid. Rusk reports that Francis Cabot Lowell, Emerson's classmate at Harvard and his friend, one day visited and "... left a letter which, he said, was to be given to Emerson later. When ... opened, it proved to contain a check for $5000, the gift of several friends" (*Life*, p. 453). The list on p. [170] provides the names of those friends and the sums of their individual donations. Persons who have not been previously identified or are not easily recognizable include Henry Lee Higginson, soldier, banker, and husband of Ida Agassiz; Charles Russell Lowell, the brother of James Russell Lowell; Francis Lee Higginson, a member of the Harvard class of 1863; Mr. and Mrs. Bangs, possibly Edward Bangs, the young Harvard graduate and lawyer mentioned in *JMN*, XIV, 37, and his wife; and Nina (or Georgina) Lowell, Francis Cabot Lowell's daughter. J. J. Higginson, Stephen Perkins, Mary L. Blake, and George Higginson are unidentified. Emerson records the deep impression Francis Cabot Lowell's generosity made at this time in the long entry on the occasion of Lowell's death; see pp. [236]–[241] below.

[171]   M[ary] M[oody] E[merson]
    "These artists in dancing & music &c beguile, delight, & we feel that
sculpture & painting give the idea of immortality. ['Tis because ⟨we are⟩ ↑the
spectator is↓ so poo⟨o⟩r, that the arts ⟨are⟩ ↑appear so↓ rich.] But were the
spirit able to contemplate, to be conscious of the Divinity, how mean wd all
the mediums of the senses become! As these amusements ↑prevent↓ licen-
tiousness, they are all worthy for the mass. Yet it does seem that no true philanthropist would use his money to encourage them, when misery asks such
redress as it does through out the earth. One sacrifice to alms gives a rapture
to soul unknown to art. In early youth I said, it was for the rich that the poor
trembled with cold & hunger; not because their creator was unkind. Ah, the
joys of opening mind long since fled! & cold inability surrounds Age."

    [172] Naushon, 31 Augt. '72. I thought today, in these rare
seaside woods, that if absolute leisure were offered me, I should run to
the College or the Scientific school which offered best lectures on
Geology, chemistry, Minerals, Botany, & seek to make the alphabets
of those sciences clear to me. How could leisure or labor be better em-
ployed. 'Tis never late to learn them, and every secret opened goes to
authorize our aesthetics. Cato learned Greek at eighty years, but these
are older bibles & oracles than Greek. Certainly this were a good *pis
aller* if J[ames]. E[lliot]. C[abot]. & Athens & Egypt should prove an
abortive dream.

    I think one must go to the tropics to find any match to this en-
chanting isle of Prospero. It needs & ought to find its Shakspeare.
What dells! what lakelets! what groves! what ⟨g⟩clumps of historic
trees of unknown age, [173] hinting ⟨histories⟩ ↑annals↓ of white men
& Indians, histories of fire & of storm & of peaceful ages of social
growth! Nature shows her secret wonders, & seems to have impressed
her fortunate landlords with instant & constant respect for her soli-
tudes & centennial growths. ⟨No w⟩Where else do such oaks &
beeches & vines grow, which the winds & storms seem ↑rather↓ to
adorn ⟨rather⟩ than ⟨injure⟩ ↑spoil↓ by their hurts & devastations,
touching them as with Fate, & not wanton interference? And the sea
binds the Paradise with its grand belt of blue, with its margin of beautiful pebbles, with its watching herons & hawks & eagles, & its endless
fleet of barques↑,↓ ⟨&⟩ steamers, yachts, & fishers' boats. ↑(See *infra,*
p. 177)↓

281

[174]¹⁸¹ ↑Raffaelle   born 1483   died 1520↓
Vasari's introduction of Life of Raffaelle.

"How liberal & good Heaven sometimes shows itself, when it heaps up the infinite wealth of its treasures & rarest gifts in a single person, which, ⟨otherwise⟩ ↑commonly↓ it is wont to distribute ⟨during⟩ ↑over↓ a long time ⟨in⟩among many individuals,—⟨may⟩ we ↑may↓ clearly see in the not less distinguished than lovely Raffaelle d'Urbino. This person was ⟨gifted⟩ ↑endowed↓ by Nature with all the modesty & goodness which are wont to be seen in those who↑m↓, more than in others, ↑⟨the lordly ornament of ⟩↓ with a certain humanity growing out of a noble nature, the lordly ornament of a lovely friendliness binds, which ⟨itself in⟩ ↑shows itself amiable & complying↓ to every kind of people & in all relations ⟨steadily shows itself amiable & complying⟩. Of him nature made a gift to the world, when, conquered by art ⟨in⟩ ↑through↓ the hand of Michel Angelo, she wished in Raffaelle to be conquered by art & by manners also. And truly since the greater number of artists until [175] his time⟨s⟩↑,↓ had received from nature a certain dowry of madness & savageness? which, seeing that it made them crazy, strange people, also drew thereon the fault that in them the human infirmity came to sight, rather than the fame & lustre of free Art, which makes men immortal: so it befel as a natural ⟨res⟩ compensation that, in Raffaelle, she made clearly to shine all the rarest virtues of the mind, accompanied by such grace, study, beauty, modesty, & best manners as might suffice ⟨never so great fault⟩ ↑to overcome what faults soever↓ of his nature, ⟨never so great stain of his being. to overcome⟩ ↑what stains soever of his life.↓ It can be safely said, therefore, that ⟨such as⟩ ↑they who↓ are possessed of such rare gifts as we behold in Raffaelle, ⟨no⟩are not mere men, but, if we may so speak, mortal gods; & that those who in the Roll of Fame   leave ↑behind them,↓ through their works among us in the earth, [176] ⟨leave behind them⟩ an honorable name, may also cherish the hope to find in Heaven a corresponding recompense of their labors & merits." *Vasari*

---

¹⁸¹ The long entry on pp. [174]–[176] is in pencil, except for "Raffaelle . . . 1520" on p. [174], inserted in ink to the left of " 'How liberal . . .'" and separated from the text by an irregular vertical ink line. The entry is Emerson's translation of Herman Friedrich Grimm, *Das Leben Raphaels, von Urbino: Italiënischer Text von Vasari* (Berlin, 1872), I, 1–2. This volume is in Emerson's library.

[177] The island compel⟨ls⟩s them—glad to be compelled—to be skilful sailors, yachtsmen, fishermen, & swimmers, thus adding all the charm of the sea to their abode, & adds ⟨all⟩ the surprise & romance of hunting.

[178] Continued from p. 173, *Supra*

There is an order in his mind which disposes the thoughts & facts which he finds; ⟨but⟩ the order or its source is unfathomable, unaccountable,—but its ⟨do⟩arrangements, its doings are sure & right. He relies on ⟨the⟩ it absolutely & it has never deceived him.

[179] In St Peter's Church, ⟨Tilton⟩ showed me the tomb of ⟨U⟩Pope Urban, & on it the bees & the dark hints of the betrayal of the sister of Bernini.[182]

[180] Admirable page in Herman Grimm's Life of Raphael (p. 166) whom he contrasts with Michel Angelo & Lionardo Da Vinci, who put ⟨themselves into their⟩ ↑each his↓ own portrait⟨s⟩ into "the dead Christ in the arms of his mother,"—Or into "The Last Supper", at Milan;—⟨& with⟩ "but of Raphael,—not a ponderous weight of individuality, but an uplifting ⟨feeling⟩ ⟨sense⟩ ↑absence↓ of all personal peculiarity is his distinction. He seems not to belong to those who surpass the average character of their nation, but he stands there as the personification of this average character itself;—holds the ⟨measure⟩ ↑scale↓ by which the great Mass is to be measured; stands near to every one, is every one's friend & brother. No one feels himself ⟨smaller⟩ ↑dwarfed↓ beside him, but each rather feels himself related to him, & so elevated by him to the like height. Ra⟨ff⟩phael is a child with children, a man with men, and there are only two artists who stand [181] with him on the same level, Shakspeare & Mozart." &c.   Grimm, [*Das*] *Leben Raphael's* [1872, I], p. 166[-167]

---

papyrus is of more importance to history than cotton

———

Invicta quidquid condidit manus, coelum est. Martial. Lib[*er*]. IX Epig[*ram*]. 2. [actually I]

[182] J. R. Tilton, otherwise unidentified, lived in Palazzo Barberini, Rome, at the time of Emerson's visit in 1872. See Pocket Diary 23, p. [179] below.

"And born in Boston needs no second birth." *Saxe.*[183]

[182] Shepard's Hotel, Cairo Egypt   30 December, '72.

"Egyptian bride of Anastasius adds 250 false plaits to the 150 which grew from her head, & in forming the joint mass into an edifice so ponderous that a second head merely for use would have been very acceptable." Vol II [actually VI]. pp. 59, 62   See Conder, Vol. 1 [actually V], p 174[–175][184]

Kohl or surmeh ↑& henna↓[185]

"Indeed I have never seen any women who have displayed so much easiness of manner, or so fine a carriage, being superior in this respect even to the women of Circassia.⟨"⟩ Probably the elegance & dignity of their gait may arise from the habit of carrying every thing on their heads. They are taller in general than our European Women". Quoted in *Conder*, [*The Modern Traveller* . . . , 1830, V,] p. 175

Nothing has struck me more in the streets here than the erect carriage & walking of the Copts (I suppose them), better & nobler in figure & movement than any ⟨figures⟩passengers in our cities at home.

[183][186] Oriental system gives the succession to the oldest member of the reigning family,—to the brother of the last King, & not the son. Every son is by a different mother.

Mimosa lebbek[187]

---

[183] All entries below the full-page rule on p. [181] are in pencil. Martial's statement is translated, "Whatever an unconquered arm has founded, that is of heaven." Edward Waldo Emerson notes that Emerson once used Saxe's statement when he delivered "Aristocracy" in Boston; see *W*, XII, 454. John Godfrey Saxe (1816–1887), American poet, was proprietor-editor of the Burlington (Vt.) *Sentinel* 1850–1856.

[184] Josiah Condor, *The Modern Traveller. A Description, Geographical, Historical, and Topographical of the Various Countries of the Globe*, 30 vols. (London, 1830).

[185] Condor, *The Modern Traveller* . . . , 1830, V, 174, defines "Kohl": "an almost unpalpable black powder used to tinge eyelids under the idea that it improves sight." See Emerson's comment on Egyptian eyes, p. [185] below.

[186] A newspaper clipping of unknown origin describing the evolution of Egypt's independence from Turkey during the period 1811–1866 is pasted onto the bottom of p. [183].

[187] "Mimosa lebbek" is in pencil.

Egypt very poor in trees: We have seen hardly an orange tree. Palms are the chief tree along the banks of the river, from Cairo to Assuan. Acacia↑s,↓ ⟨&⟩ the fig,

In Cairo, we had a banian with ↑its↓ boughs planting themselves around it under my window. ↑at Shepard's Hotel.↓

Egypt is the Nile & its shores. The cultivated land is a me⟨e⟩re ⟨riband⟩ ↑green↓ ribbon on either shore of the river. You can see, as you sail, its quick boundary in rocky mountains or desert sands. Day after day & week after week of unbroken sunshine & though you may see clouds in the sky, they are merely for ornament, & never rain.

———

The Prophet says of the Egyptians, "It is their strength to sit still.'" ↑In the 3d century, it was proverbially impossible to extort a secret from an Egyptian by torture. [copied from my Manuscript of 1823.]↓ [See *JMN,* II, 362.]

[184] All this journey is a perpetual humiliation, satirizing & whipping our ignorance. The people despise us because we are helpless babies who cannot speak or understand a word they say; ⟨the Obelisks⟩[188] the Sphinxes scorn dunces; the obelisks, the temple-walls defy us with their histories which we cannot spell. Every new object only makes new questions which each ↑traveller↓ asks of the other, & none of us can answer, & each sinks lower in the opinion of his companion. The people whether in the boat, or out of it, are a perpetual stu⟨t⟩dy for the excellence & grace of their forms & motion. No people walk so well, so upright as they are, & strong & flexible; and for studying the nude, our artists should come here & not to Paris. Every group of the country people on the shores as seen from our dearbeah, look like ⟨a company of⟩ ↑the↓ ⟨p⟩ ancient philosophers going to the School of Athens. The women too are as straight as arrows from their habit of carrying every thing on their heads. In swimming, the⟨y⟩ ↑Arabs↓ show great strength & speed, ⟨with⟩ all using what at Cambridge we

[188] The "O" of "Obelisks" is underlined once, probably to indicate a long vowel sound.

used to call the "southern stroke," alternating the right arm [185] & the left.

All the boys & all the babes ⟨we see⟩ have flies roosting about their eyes, which they do not disturb, ↑n↓or seem to know their presence. 'Tis said that the ophthalmia, which is so common here, is thus conveyed from one to another. 'Tis said that it is rare to find sound eyes among them. Blind beggars appear at every landing led about by their children.

From the time of ⟨landin⟩our arrival at Cairo to our return thither, ↑six↓ weeks, we have had no rain;—unclouded summer on the Nile to Assuan & back, & have required the awning to be spread over us on the deck from 10 A. M. till late in the afternoon.

———

On Tuesday, 7 January [1873], we sailed from Cairo ↑for Philae,↓ in the Darbeeah Aurora, with Mahmoud Bedowa, Dragoman; a Reis or Captain, & his mate; ten oarsmen, 2 cooks, a *factotum* boy, a head waiter named Marzook, & 2d waiter Hassan,—in all 18; ⟨O⟩The company in the cabin were Mr & Mrs ↑⟨W. S. ⟩↓ Whitwell, Miss [Bessie] Whitwell & Miss [May] Whitwell. Miss Farquahr; Ellen & I, the seven passengers.[189]
We ⟨re⟩arrived at Thebes   19th January   Esne, 24th, and at Assuan, 28 ⟨Febr⟩↑Jan↓uary; visited Philae, on Wednesday 29th ⟨Feby⟩Jan., arrived in Cairo Thursday, 13 February, making 38 days for our expediti⟨n⟩on & return.

[186] The magnet is the mystery which I would fain have explained to me, though I doubt if there be any teachers. It is the wonder of the child & not less of the philosopher. Goethe says, "The magnet is a primary phenomenon, which we must only express in order to have it explained. Thereby is it then also a symbol for all besides for which we use to speak no ⟨name⟩ word or name."

[189] In a letter dated San Francisco, May 5, 1881, Edward Waldo Emerson tells of seeing Dr. William Whitwell, his old medical school classmate, whose parents sailed with Emerson up the Nile. See *L*, VI, 230n. Miss Farquahr has been identified only as "a Scottish lady." See *Life*, pp. 464, 466, 470.

↑See Plutarch Morals [1718,] Vol I [p]p. [155–]156, Old copy↓[190]

[187] Tuesday, 28 ⟨February⟩ ↑January↓, Met Mr George L. Owen at Assuan↑;↓[191] our party & his exchanging visits. I found him a very intelligent & agreeable companion. ↑In↓ ⟨T⟩the darbeah in which we found him on the Nile, he shared the cabin with only one companion, Mr ⟨C⟩Ralph Elliot.

In the Hotel de Lorraine, Rue de Beaune, Paris, where Ellen & I took rooms ↑for some weeks↓ during both our visits to Paris, we lived with James R. Lowell & his wife, & John Holmes, to our great satisfaction. There also I received, one evening, a long & happy visit from Mr ↑James Cotter↓ Morison, who is writing the Life of Comte. At the house of Mr Laugel, I was introduced to Ernest Renan; to Henri Taine; to ⟨A⟩E⟨mile⟩lie de Beaumont; & to some other noted gentlemen. M. Taine sent me, the next day, his "Litterature Anglaise," in 5 volumes.[192]

[188] 1873.[193]   In London, I saw Ferguson the Architect; Browning

---

[190] "See . . . copy" is inserted in pencil.

[191] "January" is inserted above "February", struck through with a pencil line, in a hand that may be Edward Waldo Emerson's. In a letter to William Hathaway Forbes dated Alexandria, January 19, 1873, Emerson describes George L. Owen as an Englishman "who made two or three days kindlier to me." Ralph Elliot is unidentified.

[192] "lie" is written in pencil. Unlike their stay in Paris in November, when most of the Paris society they wished to see was out of the city, Emerson's and Ellen's visit in March 1873 was a great success. The persons mentioned here who have not been previously identified or are not easily recognizable include James Augustus Cotter Morison (1832–1888), English positivist; Auguste Laugel, author of *Science et philosophie*, 1863, who visited America in 1864 and described Emerson as "a sort of Montaigne" (*L*, VI, 228n) and who with his wife Élizabeth entertained the Emersons in Paris; Hippolyte Adolphe Taine (1828–1893), philosopher and critic, who through Élizabeth Laugel gave Emerson his *Histoire de la littérature anglaise*, 5 vols., 2d. ed. rev. et aug. (Paris, 1866–1869), which is in Emerson's library; and Élie de Beaumont (1798–1874), geologist and professor at the Collège de France.

[193] Emerson and Ellen returned to London on April 5, 1873. During their stay, which lasted until May 15, when they sailed for home aboard the Cunarder *Olympus,* they made some new acquaintances, but mostly they enjoyed the company of Emerson's friends and correspondents of earlier days. Those persons mentioned on pp. [188]–[190] who have not been previously identified or are not easily recognizable include James Ferguson (1808–1886), Scottish industrialist and student of architecture; Sir Henry Holland,

the Poet; John ↑S.↓ Mill; Sir Henry Holland; Huxley; Tyndall; Lord Houghton; Mr Gladstone; Dean Stanley; Lecky; ⟨Ar⟩Froude; Thomas Hughes; Lyon Playfair; Sir Arthur Helps; the Duke of Argyle; the Duke of Cleveland; the Duke of Bedford; Sir Frederic Pollok; Charles Read; Mr Dasent;—With the Amberleys ⟨we⟩I paid a visit to Lord Russell at his house, & lunched there. I failed to see Garth Wilkinson, though I called on him twice, & he left his card twice at my door↑, in my absence↓. Mr ⟨Hughes⟩Tyndall procured for me the freedom of the Athenaeum Club. W[illiam]. H. Channing was, as always, the kindest of friends. Monc⟨a⟩ure Conway was incessant in his attentions, and William Allingham gave us excellent aid. ⟨Charles⟩ ↑George↓ Howard, who will one day, I hope, be Earl of Carlisle, was the most attentive & generous of friends.

[189] At Oxford, I was the guest of Professor Max Muller, & was introduced to Jowett & to Ruskin & to Mr Dodson, author of "Alice in Wonderland," & to many of the University dignitaries. Prince Leopold was a student, & came home ⟨with us⟩ from Max Muller's lecture to lunch with us, & then invited Ellen & me to go to his house, & there showed us his pictures & his Album⟨.⟩ ↑and there we ⟨and⟩ drank tea↓.ⁿ The next day I heard Ruskin's lecture, & we then went home with ⟨him⟩ ↑Ruskin↓ to his chambers, where he showed us his pictures, & told us his doleful opinions of modern so-

---

whose company Ellen once described as "perfect bliss" (see *Life,* p. 476); Richard Monckton Milnes, 1st Baron Houghton (1809–1885), poet; Arthur Penrhyn Stanley (1815–1881), canon of Canterbury, 1851, and Dean of Westminster, 1864–1881; William Edward Hartpole Lecky (1838–1903), Irish historian and essayist; James Anthony Froude (1818–1894), historian and Thomas Carlyle's literary executor and biographer; Lyon Playfair, 1st Baron Playfair (1818–1898), chemist, who helped to lay the foundations of modern sanitation; John Douglas Sutherland, 9th Duke of Argyll (1845–1914), governor general of Canada (1878–1883); the Duke of Cleveland, whose acquaintance Emerson made in 1848 (*L,* IV, 15–16); Sir Frederick Pollock (1845–1937), jurist, professor of jurisprudence at University College, London, 1882, and at Oxford, 1883–1903; Charles Reade (1814–1884), novelist and dramatist; George Webbe Dasent (1817–1896), English Scandinavian scholar, assistant editor of the London *Times,* 1845–1870; Lord Russell, probably Lord John Russell, 1st Earl Russell of Kingston (1792–1878), statesman, biographer, and historian; George James Howard, 9th Earl of Carlisle (1843–1911), trustee of the National Gallery and connoisseur of art; Benjamin Jowett (1817–1893), Greek scholar; Henry George Liddell (1811–1898), classical scholar; William Wetmore Story (1818–1895), American sculptor and man of letters; and Edward Fordham Flower, whom Emerson met in 1848 and who visited the Emersons in Concord. Prince Leopold is unidentified.

ciety. ↑In the evening we dined ↑with↓ the ↑vice↓ Chancellor Liddell & a large Company↓[.]

[190] Mr Thomas Hughes introduced me to the Cosmopolitan Club, which meets every Sunday & Wednesday night at 10'o'clock, and there I saw on two evenings very agreeable gentlemen, ↑Sir Fred[eric]k Pollock; Ferguson,↓ Lord Houghton, William Story, & others. ⟨Ho⟩Professor Tyndall procured me the privileges of the Athenaeum, which is ↑still↓ the best of the great London Clubs; and also of the Royal Institution, in Albermarle street, where he presides since the death of Faraday.

Visited John Forster at his own house *Palace Gate House*   Kensington West
Stayed 3 days with Mr E[dward]. F[ordham]. Flower at Stratford on Avon
Breakfasted with Sir Henry Holland on our return to London.

[191] In Florence, I hoped to find Herman Grimm, who, as I had heard, was residing there to complete his Life of Raffaelle. Immediately on my arrival, I sent Curnex to the German bookstores to inquire his address. Neither of these knew of his presence in the city. In the street, I met Mr Bigelow, our American Minister at Paris, & asked him for news of Grimm. He did not know that he was here. On my return to the *Hotel du Nord,* I found Mr Bigelow's Card saying that immediately after leaving me, he had met Grimm in the street, & learned his address which he had written out for me on his card: And Grimm had also called & left his own. I went at once to Grimm, & was ⟨at once⟩ received & introduced to Gisela his wife, & invited them to ⟨come⟩dine with us that evening, which they did, to the great satisfaction of Ellen & me. He speaks English very well, & Gisela, who does not, talked [192] with Ellen in German.[194]

[193] In Egypt, the sandstone or limestone instructs ⟨them⟩ ↑men↓ how to build,—stands in square blocks, & they have only to make a square door for tombs, & the shore is a pair or a series of steps

[194] John Bigelow (1817–1911), writer and diplomat, was U.S. consul at Paris 1861–1865 and U.S. minister to France 1865–1866. Curnex was the Emersons' traveling servant.

or stairs. ⟨S⟩The lateen sail is the shadow of a pyramid: and the pyramid is the simplest ⟨w⟩ copy of a mountain, or of the form ↑which↓ a pile of sand or earth takes when dropped from a cart.↑—I saw a crocodile in the Nile at a distance.↓

Heeren's observation on Culture of Egyptians, *D* [80–]81[195]

---

[194] [blank]

[195]   ↑*Kalevala of the Fins.*↓

"Cease to flow, o ↑warm↓ blood! Cease to gush out on me & inundate my breast. Stay firm as a wall, immoveable as the wall of a field, as a sword in the sea, immoveable as the seaweed in the marsh, as the millstone on the road, as the rock in the midst of the roaring cataract.

But if thine instinct urge thee to flow, to precipitate thee with violence, flow at least within the flesh,—bound across the ⟨t⟩bones. It is better for thee to redden the flesh, to boil in the veins, to bedew the bones, than to flow on the ground, & prostitute thyself among the ordures. Yes, it i⟨t⟩s unworthy of thee, o innocent blood, to soil thyself in the dust,—unworthy of thee, o beauty of man, o treasure of heroes, to lose thyself in the grass of the prairies or on the hillsides. Thy place is in the heart, thy seat is ⟨in⟩ ↑under↓ the lungs, ⟨thy seat is under the lungs   Art thou⟩ Hasten to return thither. Art thou a river to roll thus thy waves? a lake to overflow with such impetuosity? a source of marshes to leap with such noise? a bark pierced to pour water in every part? Check by degrees thy flowing, O ⟨c⟩precious blood! rather stay at once. Already ⟨the⟩ the cataract of Tyra checks ⟨instantly⟩ gradually its fall, the river of Tuonela stops instantly, the sea dries up, the heaven ceases to rain during the great drought, during the days of fire.

[196] If thou refuse to obey me, I will have recourse to other means. I will demand of Hiisi his gr⟨a⟩eat cauldron, that wherein they cook the blood,—wherein they make the red blood boil, without a single drop falling on the earth, & lo⟨sng⟩sing itself in the dust. And if the man is not in me, if the hero is not in the son of the ancient sire,—the

---

[195] Arnold H. L. Heeren, *Historical Researches into the Politics, Intercourse, and Trade of the Carthaginians, Ethiopians, and Egyptians,* trans. D. A. Talboys, 2 vols. (Oxford, 1832).

man, the hero who can find a dike for this river, this torrent of the veins, I shall invoke the Celestial father; the great Jumala who dwells above the clouds, the potent among all⟨,⟩ men, the ⟨puissance⟩ skilful among all heroes, and he will shut the mouth of the blood, will chain that which rushes forth.

O ⟨u⟩Ukko! highest Creator, Celestial Jumala, come hither, for we have need of thy succor. Hither! they call thee! Staunch with thy vast hand, with thy strong thumb, this gaping hole, ↑this↓ ghastly wound↑.↓ ⟨this⟩ Spread a *[196] ⟨leaf⟩ nenuphar leaf, a lily of gold, across this path of blood, that it may cease to spout on my beard, & pour over my garments.⟨"⟩   Then the old man shut himself the bloody mouth,—he chained the red torrent; then he sent his son to the forge to prepare a balm, a balm made [197] with the seed of the turf, with the stems of a thousand plants saturated with honey. The young man set out for the forge: he met an oak, & said to it, 'Hast thou ⟨n⟩honey on thy branches, honey under thy bark?'

The oak replied with wisdom, 'Yesterday the honey flowed on my branches, it inundated my crown,—a honey fallen from the height of heaven, from the height of the liquified clouds.' The old man's son cut the branches of the oak, the boughs of the fragile tree. ⟨He inundated my crown⟩ He took then the seed of the turf: he took the stems of a thousand plants"[197]

[198] July, 1873.

My friend's address, as well as I can read it on his card, runs thus
James Hutchison Stirling, L.L.D.   F.R.S. Edin.
4 Laverock
Bank Road, Trinity.[198]

*on p. 196 *Nenuphar*—water lily, The same name to the plant occurs in Von Hammer's translation of Persian p. 142

[196] The note keyed to this asterisk appears at the bottom of p. [197], where it is separated from the rest of the page by a full-page rule. Joseph von Hammer-Purgstall, *Geschichte der schönen Redekünste Persiens, mit einer Blüthenlese aus zweyhundert persischen Dichtern* (Vienna, 1818), in Emerson's library.
[197] The foregoing is Emerson's translation from the French of *La Kalévala, épopée nationale de la Finlande*, trans. L. Léouyon le Duc (Paris, 1867), pp. 73–75. This volume is in Emerson's library.
[198] "James . . . Trinity." is encircled in ink.

Baron Richard Von Hoffmann,
Villa Celimontana.
Roma

[199] The enjoyment of travel is ⟨the⟩ in the arrival at a new city, as Paris, or Florence, or Rome,—the feeling ↑of↓ free adventure, you have no duties,—nobody knows you, nobody has claims, you are like a boy on his first visit to the Common on Election Day. Old Civilization offers to you alone this huge city, all its wonders, architecture, gardens, ornaments, Galleries, ↑which had never cost you so much as a thought↓. For the first time for many years you wake master of the bright day, in a bright world without a claim on you;—only ⟨but⟩ leave to enjoy. This dropping for the first time the doleful bundle of Duty creates, day after day, a health as of ⟨a⟩ new youth. ↑Then the cities know the value of travellers as purchasers in their ⟨shops &⟩ factories & shops, & receive them gladly.↓

[200] In Paris, your mere passport admits you to the vast & costly ↑public↓ galleries on days on which the natives of the city ⟨are⟩ ↑can↓ not ⟨permitted to⟩ pass the doors. ⟨Your⟩ Household[n] cares you have none: ⟨can⟩You take your dinner, lunch, or supper where ↑& when↓ you will: ⟨horses⟩ ↑cheap cabs↓ wait for you at every corner,—guides at every door, ⟨and endless⟩ magazines of sumptuous goods & attractive fairings, unknown hitherto, solicit your eyes. Your health mends every day. Every ⟨spee⟩ word spoken to you is a wonderful & agreeable riddle which it is a pleasure to solve,—a pleasure & a pride.[n] Every experience of the day is important, & furnishes conversation to you who were so silent at home.

[201] [blank]
    [202] Concord Library should contain

———

Jowett's translation of Plato.

———

Stendhal⟨l⟩

———

Autobiography of Edward, Lord Herbert of Cherbury.

Daniel Kirkwood of Indiana University's book on Comets & Meteors.

———

Huxley's Lay Sermons.[199]

———

[203] [blank]
      [204] June 23, 1873.[200]
Charles Ryan, [⟨5 York Buildings⟩ ↑1 Westbourne Place,↓ Weymouth, England,] sends me a beautiful watercolor painting drawn after Ruskin's rule of exact copying of nature: And Mr Walter Smith, who brings it to me, gives me another sketch painted by *J. A. Benwell,* "whose eastern subjects are becoming so famous in England."
Mr Walter Smith's address is, "Board of Education, State House, Library. Boston," or, Walter Smith, State Director of Art Education, City Point, South Boston, Mass.

———

↑1873.↓ ———
July 15. Mr B. B. Titcomb ↑of Watertown↓ brings me today a very pretty silver trinket sent by his hand from *Mr Christopher James of Gold Hill, Nevada,* where he works in the Comstock Lode. Mr Titcomb tells me that Mr James is a Welshman by birth, about 23 or 24 years old, & interests himself in my books: and is a *Comtist.*

[205] We all know the rule of umbrellas,—if you take your umbrella, it will not rain; if you leave it, it will↑.↓ ⟨rain.⟩

———

[199] Items in this list that have not been previously identified include Plato, *Dialogues,* trans. B[enjamin]. Jowett, 5 vols., 3rd ed. rev. (Oxford, 1875), in Emerson's library; Edward Herbert, 1st Baron Herbert of Cherbury, *Life of Edward Lord Herbert, of Cherbury, Written by Himself* (London, 1828), withdrawn by Emerson from the Boston Athenaeum May 25–June 9, 1863, January 14–February 18, 1868, and August 10–October 11, 1871; and Daniel Kirkwood, *Comets and Meteors: Their Phenomena in All Ages; Their Mutual Relations; and the Theory of Their Origin* (Philadelphia, 1873).
[200] The date of this entry has been called into question by Rusk. External evidence indicates that this episode may have taken place as early as June 1872 or as late as June 1875. See *L,* VI, 278. Apart from the information on them contained in this entry, persons mentioned on p. [204] are unidentified.

Egypt.

Mrs Helen ⟨Choate⟩Bell, it seems, was asked "What do you think the Sphinx said to Mr Emerson?" "Why," ⟨said⟩ ↑replied↓ Mrs ⟨Choate⟩Bell, "the Sphinx probably said to him, 'You're another.' "[201]

Miss Ware, 108 Concord St. Boston

Memo. Abraham B Morrison, alleging himself to be a brother in law of   Billings of Boston, borrowed £75 sterling of H. A. Babbitt in Cairo, Egypt, Vice Consul general, promising to refund by Jan. 10, '73, & has not done so. Feb. 18, 1873.   H. A. B[abbitt].[202]

[206] Sam. G. Ward writes me from Siout, Egypt, Dec. 20, 1872,

"Indeed what we have already seen   Cairo & the Pyramids, Beni Hassan, & the Nile, amply repays the voyage to Egypt — — — I find two things in Egypt   or rather two men,—First, Aladdin & his lamp, and the Fisherman & ⟨his⟩the Genie & the Forty Thieves; at every turn you meet men ⟨who⟩that have all ↑of↓ them in their look, however ragged. The grace with which they wear their turbans, & fold their rags about them, never fails.

The eye never wearies in following & making pictures of them with their background of mosques & palms & camels & donkeys: & their eye for color, which makes ⟨all⟩ [207] them all dress as for a *tableau vivant*. Second: the Old Egyptian whom you build up again by the aid of the Pyramids & the rock-caves⟨,⟩ filled with pictures. They seem to have solved better than most the problem of getting their best men to govern them according to such lights as they had. Their antiquity is like the distances of the fixed stars. They are so old that you have no measure for it, and give it up, & feel that they

---

[201] This anecdote almost certainly refers to Helen Choate Bell, wife of Joseph Bell, a person whose "genius" Emerson once saluted in a letter to Lydia Cabot Parker (*L,* V, 268–269). Following this entry is pasted a note measuring 11.9 × 2.2 cm, the exposed side of which reads: "An acknowledgment of the recept. of this vol. will oblige. Address the author, Jersey, Channel Islands, England." The note is not in Emerson's hand; however, following "England.", the name "John Lewis Peyton" is inserted in Emerson's hand, and on the reverse side of the note Emerson writes "Memoir of Wm Madison Peyton of Roanoke. Lond. 1873". Beneath the note, "Miss Ware, . . . Boston" is written in pencil.

[202] As the details provided here and in Pocket Diary 24, p. [100], and Pocket Diary 25, p. [36], below suggest, Emerson was asked by Babbitt to look into the matter of his missing £75 upon his return to America. This Emerson agreed to do, but apparently the search for Abraham B. Morrison and the money was unsuccessful.

lived only yesterday. The pictures in Beni Hassan are said to be ⟨one⟩4 ↑four↓ hundred years older than Sinai—a thousand years older than Homer. My mind tries to sieze it

[208] But Homer & Moses remain obstinately my standard of antiquity, & the Egyptians as modern as the English.↑"↓ ⟨We⟩

[209] I find on a stray ↑MS.↓ sheet the following scrap which perhaps I have already printed, perhaps not.

[Yet now & then we say things to our mates, or hear things from them, which seem to put it out of the power of the parties to be strangers again.]

For the writers on Religion,—none should speak on this matter polemically: it is the *Gai Science* & only to be chanted by troubadours.

[210] Professor Max Muller has dedicated his new book to me, & sent me a copy. I have read it, & though I am too dull a scholar to judge of the correctness of his courageous deductions from resembling names, or to relish this⟨,⟩ ⟨book⟩ as I did his earlier books, I respect & thank his erudition & its results.[203]

[211] It is interesting that Gascony in France, [which comprised the departments now known as *Hautes Pyr⟨a⟩énées, Gers, & Landes,* & portions of the country now included in the departments of *Basses Pyr⟨a⟩énées, Haute Garonne⟩ & Lot et Garonne,*] was the birthplace of Montaigne ↑born 1533↓,[n] Montluc ↑born 1503↓, Montesquieu ↑born 1689↓, Murat, & Lannes.[204]

---

[203] Friedrich Max Müller, *Introduction to the Science of Religion; Four Lectures Delivered at the Royal Institution, with Two Essays on False Analogies and Philosophy of Mythology* (London, 1873). This book, with an inscription dated May 25, 1873, is in Emerson's library.

[204] Persons mentioned here who have not been previously identified or are not easily recognizable include Blaise de Lasseran-Massencome, Seigneur de Montluc (1501?–1577), professional soldier, who served in the armies of Francis I, Henry II, Charles IX, and Henry III; Joachim Murat (1767?–1815), cavalry commander, who under Napoleon Bonaparte served variously as governor of Paris, marshal of France, prince and high admiral, and king of Naples; and Jean Lannes, Duc de Montebello, Prince de Siévers (1769–1809), soldier in the Revolutionary and Napoleonic armies, created marshal of France (1804).

[212] Be a little careful about your Library. Do you ⟨know⟩ foresee what you will do with it? Very little to be sure. But ⟨do you⟩ the real question is, What it will do with you? You will come here & get books that will open your eyes, & your ears, & your curiosity, & turn you inside out ↑or outside in↓.ⁿ You will find a book here that will tell you such ⟨an account⟩ ↑news↓ of what has been seen lately at the observatories ⟨that you⟩ in the sun & the other stars, that you will not rest until you find a telescope to see the eclipse with your own eyes. 'Tis only the other day that they found out what the stars are made of: what chemical elements ⟨that ⟨our⟩⟩ ↑identical with those that↓²⁰⁵ are in our planet, are found in Saturn: what in the sun. & that human life could not exist in the moon.

[213] They have just learned that Italy had people before the Romans, before the Etruscans, who made just such arrowheads as we find in Concord, & all their tools were stone: ↑Mr [George Perkins] Marsh told me he picked them up in Africa: as in Vermont.↓ & they find these all over the world,—& the world, instead of being six thousand years old, ↑has↓ had men on it a hundred thousand years.
All the new facts of science are not only interesting for themselves, but their best value is the rare effect on the mind, the electric shock; each new law of nature speaks to a related fact in our thought; for every law of Chemistry has /some/its/ analogon in the soul, ⟨and though the student⟩ & however skilful the chemist may be, & how much soever he may push & multiply his researches, he is a superificial trifler in the presence of the student who sees the strict analogy of [214] ↑the↓ experiment to the laws of thought & of morals.

I add from my old MSS. the following,—
⟨Equality of⟩ Aⁿ ↑reader of↓ profound apprehension ↑has an equality↓ to the greatest poet. The creative seems mere knack. The reader of Shakspeare must be for a time a Shakspeare, or find no joy in the page.

²⁰⁵ The initial "that" is canceled, and "identical . . . that" inserted, in pencil.

9 Oct. '74.

Lowell writes that Byron Forceythe Willson was born at Little Gene-
see, Western New York, 10th April, 1837: Died at Alfred Centre,
N. Y. 2d February, 1867.

[215] *Books*
        Their costliest service that they set us free from themselves also.
We read a line, a word, that lifts us; we rise into a succession of
thoughts that is better than the book.
The old saying of Montluc, that, "⟨a⟩one man is worth a hundred, and
a hundred are not worth one," is quite as true of books.[206]

Our reading sometimes seems guided. I open a book which happens to
be near me,—⟨which⟩ ↑a book↓ I had not thought of before,—and,
seeing the name of a known writer, I sit down to read the chapter,
which presently fixes my attention as if it were an important message
directly sent to me.

[216]   *Duties*
To Wm Allingham. See Osgood & Co. in reference to an Edition of
Allingham's Selected Works.

Write to Mr Beaver, whom, I fear, my letter acknowledging his gift
never reached.

See President Eliot on Oscar Jackson's Scholarship; and Gurney.

To write to [Charles Eliot] Norton

[206] Cf. *The Commentaries of Messire Blaize de Montluc, Mareschal of France,* trans.
Charles Cotton (London, 1694), pp. 160, 186, 259, 398, where this sentiment is expressed in several ways. Emerson withdrew this volume from the Boston Athenaeum May
25–June 9, 1863. See Notebook Books Large, pp. [61], [63], and [66] below.

Virginia Vaughan, & send her letter of R. H. Horne and a letter for Allingham[207]

—————————————

[217] [blank]
    [218] 'Tis notable how recent are most of our important arts & inventions—more I think in our nineteenth century than in any other. ↑See *VS* 93↓[208]   ↑See a list of them in ΦB 99, 172,↓

Darwin's "Origin of Species" was published in 1859, but Stallo, in 1849, writes,
"Animals are but foetal forms of man," &c. See *AZ* 53,
———

A new article by Stallo, it is announced, is in the ⟨Magazine⟩ "Scientific Monthly."

Stallo quotes Liebig as saying, "The secret of all those who make discoveries is, that they regard nothing as impossible."
"the lines of our ancestry run into all the phenomena of the material world." *Stallo.*[209]

[219] *Scholar and Times.* If I have occasion to address Scholars, turn to *VO* 110[-111]

    [220] The sun is the fuel, the day the flame. See *GL* 55,

---

[207] "Virginia . . . Allingham" and the rules that set it off are in pencil. Of the duties and persons mentioned on p. [216], nothing is known of Emerson's effort on Allingham's behalf; Oscar Roland Jackson, son of Dr. Charles T. Jackson, was Emerson's nephew; and Virginia Vaughan lectured on "Poetry of the Future" at Sargent's in Boston in April 1872. Mr. Beaver is unidentified.
    [208] "See *VS* 93" is inserted in pencil.
    [209] Double pencil lines are drawn in the left and right hand margins beside "A new article . . . Monthly.' " The "new article" has not been located in contemporary issues of *Scientific Monthly.* For the three statements by Stallo, see John Bernhard Stallo, *General Principles of the Philosophy of Nature* (Boston, 1848), pp. 304, 15, and 165. This volume is in Emerson's library.

"Distance in thought has a greater power than distance of time." *Outlines of German Literature*. By Joseph Gostwick and Robert Harrison. p. 14[210]

[221] ——————
　　To R. W. E.

　　　　Blest of the highest gods are they who die
　　　　Ere youth is fled. For them their mother Fate,
　　　　Clasping from happy earth to happier sky,
　　　　Frees life, & joy, & love from dread of date.

　　　　But thee, revered of men, the gods have blest
　　　　With fruitful years. And yet for thee in sooth,
　　　　They have reserved of all their gifts the best;—
　　　　And thou, though full of days, shall die in youth.
　　　　——————

　　May 25, 1873.   C[harles]. E[liot]. Norton

[222]   *Theologic Mysteries.*
　　Our theology ignores the identity of the worshipper: he has fallen in another, he rises in another. Can identity be claimed for a being whose life is so often vicarious, or belonging to an age or generation? See [Notebook] *M*[ary]. *M*[oody]. ⟨I⟩*E*[merson] IV. p. 40[-41]

[223] Harvard College.
My ⟨term⟩new term as overseer begun at the close of Commencement Day, 1873, & ends at the close of Commencement Day 1879.

[224] See for Poetry & Criticism, article *Imagination,* in my *Index Major, p. 163*[n]

———————————————————————————

　　The distinction of the poet—that his images are new,—whilst the rhymer's are the conventional. There are poets who take things, and poets who give things.

[210] Joseph Gostwick and Robert Harrison, *Outlines of German Literature* (London, 1873), in Emerson's library.

[225] [blank]

[226]   *Readings.*[211]

Sterling's "Alfred, the Harper."

Mrs Clark's ↑"The↓ ⟨"⟩Trust" & "The Remittance"

Ben Jonson's "Gipsy Song," "The Faery beam upon you"

Beaumont & Fletcher's B⟨eau⟩oadicea

―――

Dr Lowell's Speech

―――

[227] For Sumner's merit, go back to the dark times of 1850 & see the position of Boston & its eminent men. ↑See *BO* [201–]204, 210[–211], 259,↓[212]

[228]   *Subjects. Studies.*

Bias, Individual genius, proclivity, subjectiveness. See *ZO* 118[–119], 3,   *IL* 112[–113], 115[–118], [199–]200, 1–3–   272, 122

[229]   *Proposed Readings.*

Alexis's (died A.C. 290) Lines on Sleep.[213]

―――

Paganini, in *MS. The Poet.* p. 8

―――

Plotinus's Dance, ⟨s⟩See *BL* 40

    [230] January 5, 1876.

    Committee of University of Virginia
The Washington & The Jefferson Societies
                            W. C. Perry
                            W Rice Kenney
                            Alfred P. Thorn [actually Thom][214]

――――――――――

[211] Among the previously unidentified items on p. [226], both John Sterling's "Alfred, the Harper" and "Bonduca" by Beaumont and Fletcher appear in *Parnassus*.
   [212] "See ... 259," is written in ink over an identical erased pencil version.
   [213] See p. [55] above.
   [214] Acting in the name of the University of Virginia, Perry, Kenney, and Thom wrote to Emerson on November 25, 1875, informing him that he had been selected ora-

[⟨3⟩231] I ought to have many notes ⟨f⟩of my pleasant memories of Abel Adams one of the best of my friends whose hospitable house was always open to me by day or by night for so many years in Boston, Lynn, or West Roxbury. His experiences as a merchant were always interesting to me. I think I must have somewhere recorded the fact which I recall today that he told me that he & two or three merchants had been counting up, in the Globe Bank, out of a hundred ↑Boston↓ merchants how many had ↑not↓ once failed, and they could only count three.

———

Abel Adams was the benefactor of Edward W. E[merson]. in College, & of all of us in his last will.

[232] *Titus Munson Coan,* [*325 W. 27th St. N. Y.*] sends me an article called "The tree of life," in "Galaxy" of April '74, which is excellently written,—& in which he quotes, ⟨the follow⟩without naming the author, the following lines;

> "Of heaven or hell I have no power to sing;
> I cannot ease the burden of your fears,
> Nor make quick-coming death a little thing,
> Nor for my words shall you forget your tears."[215]

———

Giulio Monteverde, Rome, Sculptor
His address to be found at Maquay & Hooker's
He is the sculptor of *The Young Columbus,* in the Boston Athenaeum[216]

---

tor for the joint celebration of Virginia's two literary societies scheduled for June 28, 1876. On December 21, 1875, Emerson gave a conditional promise to come, and details were arranged through correspondence over the next several months. Emerson visited Virginia on June 28 and 29, as the guest of George Frederick Holmes, professor of history and general literature, and a Professor Southall, professor of international law, and he read his address "The Natural and Permanent Functions of the Scholar." Although the reception that Emerson and Ellen received was generally friendly, Emerson's audience, which had difficulty hearing the lecture, and the Charlottesville press were not very kind on the occasion. See *L,* VI, 287, 291, 294–295; *Life,* pp. 496–498; Hubert H. Hoeltje, "Emerson in Virginia," *The New England Quarterly,* V (Oct. 1932).

[215] Titus Munson Coan is the author of "The Tree of Life," in *The Galaxy,* XVII, no. 4 (April 1874), 526–535; the lines cited above appear on p. 535 but are unidentified.

[216] "*Giulio* . . . Athenaeum" and the rules above and below it are in pencil.

Augustus P[orter]. Chamberlain[217]

[233] The boy grew to man and never asked a question, for every problem quickly developed its law

"The arch is the parent of the vault, the vault is the parent of the cupola." *Edw. A. Freeman*[218]

Monday night   Nov.   Parker House
The secret of poetry is never explained,—is always new. We have not got farther than mere wonder at the delicacy of the touch, & the eternity it inherits ⟨achieves⟩. In every house a child that in mere play utters oracles, & knows not that they are such, 'Tis as easy as breath. 'Tis like this gravity, which holds the Universe together, & none knows what it is.

[234] "All this world is but the transmutation of oblations." *Hindoo*[219]

[235] September 1, '74. Mr H[ubert]. H[owe]. Bancroft, & Mr Wallace Smith Bliss came to me with proposals to p⟨r⟩ublish a book concerning Central America. The wife of Mr Smith is the daughter of General Taylor, late President of U.S.[220]

[236] The death of Francis C[abot]. Lowell is a great loss to me. Now for fifty seven years since we entered college together, we have

---

[217] Augustus Porter Chamberlain, member of the Harvard class of 1847, donated books to the Concord Library in 1873 and through Emerson apparently offered to buy books for the Concord and Harvard College libraries in 1878. See *L*, VI, 248.

[218] "The boy grew ... *Freeman*" is in pencil. Edward Augustus Freeman (1823–1892) was an English historian and student of architecture.

[219] This entry is in pencil. *The Vishñu Puráña, a System of Hindu Mythology and Tradition* (London, 1840), p. 100. This work, in Emerson's library, was a bequest from Thoreau. See *JMN*, IX, 303, 352.

[220] Hubert Howe Bancroft eventually published four major works on Central America: *The History of New Mexico, 1516–1887*, 4 vols. (San Francisco, 1883–1886); *The History of North Mexican States*, 2 vols. (San Francisco, 1884–1889); *A Popular History of the Mexican People* (San Francisco, 1887); and *The Resources and Development of Mexico* (San Francisco, 1893). For details of Bancroft's visit to Emerson in Concord, see *L*, VI, 264.

been friends, ⟨and⟩ meeting sometimes rarely, sometimes ⟨seldom⟩often; ⟨even⟩ seldom living in the same town, we have always met gladly on the ⟨same⟩ ↑old↓ simple terms. He was a conservative, I always of a speculative habit; ⟨But⟩ and often in the wayward politics of former years, ↑we↓ had to compare our different opinions. ⟨But⟩ He[n] was ⟨thoroughly true, &⟩ a native gentleman, ↑thoroughly true,↓ & ⟨though⟩ of decided opinions, always frank, ⟨&⟩ considerate, & kind. On all questions his opinions were his own, & ⟨appeared to have be⟩ ⟨considerately⟩ ↑deliberately↓ formed. ⟨On some points, he wrote them out, &⟩ One[n] day came to [237] Concord to read to me ⟨from paper⟩ some ⟨considered⟩ opinions he had written out in regard to the education ↑now↓ given at Cambridge. ⟨He always commanded respect & love. His thoughts were his own, &⟩ ↑⟨I regret that⟩ He did not leave the paper with me & I regret that I cannot recall its substance↓[.] However[n] you might differ from him, he always inspired respect & love. I have never known a man of more simplicity and truth. ⟨Of course⟩ I heard gladly, long since, from Doctor Hobbs of Waltham, what I had never heard from himself,—the story of ⟨↑Mr↓ Lowell's⟩ ↑⟨his⟩↓ ↑Lowell's↓ relation to the Chemical Mills in Waltham. ⟨Mr⟩His father, Mr Frank Lowell, Senior, had founded them, and his son inherited in them an important interest ↑⟨in them;⟩↓. ⟨But f⟩From whatever causes, the property had ↑sadly↓ depreciated. [238] But Mr Lowell undertook the charge of them himself, studied chemistry with direct reference to the work done in this mill, made himself master of all the processes required,[n] ⟨therein & against⟩ ↑⟨reformed the⟩ corrected the mistakes, and against↓ all advice stayed therein until its ↑depreciated↓ shares came up to par, then he sold ⟨the⟩ ↑his shares in the↓ property & retired. A man of a quiet inward life, silent & grave, but with ⟨fixed⟩ opinions & purposes which he ↑quietly↓ held ⟨firmly,⟩ & frankly stated, when his opinion was asked:—⟨a quiet man⟩ ↑gentle,↓ but with a strong ⟨& last⟩ will, & a persever⟨ing⟩ance which at last carried his point. ⟨Mr ↑Henry↓ Higginson⟩ told me how scrupulously honest he was, how slow to avail himself of the right to take up ⟨a⟩ mortgages, the terms of which had not been kept. Mr H[igginson]. ⟨did not⟩ thought him romantically honest: And his truth was of the like strain. ⟨He was speaking at⟩ He said to me, at his house, that when his club [239] had lately met there, several gentlemen expressed to him their satisfaction at being ⟨there⟩ ↑his guests↓; & ⟨he added⟩ ↑this led him to say↓ that he did not believe he had ever expressed to any man more regard for the person than he really felt. Exact & literal in affairs & in intercourse, he was the most affectionate parent, and ⟨the⟩ ↑his↓ children's children filled the house with their joy. His generosity was quiet, but sure & effective. Very strict in its direction, but ample in amount. He was the friend in need, ⟨and⟩ silent ⟨and⟩ but sure, and the character of the giver added ⟨immense⟩ ↑rare↓ value to the gift, as if ⟨ange⟩ ⟨gold were brought you by⟩ an angel brought you gold. I may well say this, when I recall the fact that ⟨when my⟩ ↑on the next day after my↓ house was burned, ⟨he came[n] to see⟩ ⟨surprised me⟩ ↑⟨he came⟩↓ ⟨on the next day⟩ he came to Concord to ⟨see me &⟩ express his sympathy in my misfortune, & a few days afterward surprised me with a munificent donation from himself & his children which went far to rebuild it.

[240] ⟨I⟩We were classmates in college, and I w⟨i⟩ell remember the ⟨simple appearance⟩ ↑innocence↓ of the youth when we first met↑;—↓ & ⟨his⟩ ↑the↓ perfect simplicity of his manners he never lost. Yet ↑Long years afterward↓ I well remember that when we stood together to witness a marriage in the ⟨s⟩Stone Chapel, my wife inquired who was the gentleman who stood by me, and who looked ↑so↓ like a king; I was delighted by the perception.

When in College he joined the Harvard Military Company, ↑t↓he orderly sergeant placed him in the fourth section, but observing that he was taller than those next to him ⟨c.⟩ changed his place by three or four men, then ↑removed him↓ into the third section; still he was a little taller, and ↑the↓ removed him into the second; still he was a little taller, & was ordered into the first, then he found he was still a little taller, & at last carried him to the head of the company.   ↑See note in ⟨W⟩ *AC* 174↓[221]

[241] ⟨Since⟩ ⟨He was, with Upham & Reed, le⟩ ⟨On⟩ ⟨he was the Standing Committee of⟩ On leaving college ↑in 1821↓ Upham, Lowell, & Reed, were appointed the standing Committee of our class,

---

[221] "See . . . 174" is inserted in pencil.

& they called the class together from year to year till our Fiftieth Anniversary, ↑⟨& the usage of⟩↓ when our diminished numbers ⟨permitted⟩ ↑and the usage of the College justified↓ them ⟨to⟩in announc⟨e⟩ing that they should no longer summon the meetings.

I dearly prize the photograph taken from Rowse's drawing of his head, which is an admirable likeness, my gift from his daughter, Georgina Lowell.

His daughter tells me, that he thought he did not interest his acquaintances. I believe that he always had their entire respect, & a friendship akin to love.

His death is the loss of a pure ⟨life⟩man to the community in which he ⟨has⟩ spent his long & honored life. Fortunate in his birth & education, accustomed always to a connexion of excellent society, he was never ⟨f⟩confounded with others by the facility of interest & neighborhood, but remained ↑as↓ independent in his thought as if he had lived alone.

[242] [Jan. 6, 1875.]
            "*Parnassus*" published December 1874[222]
I have sent a copy of the book to

Edith E. Forbes	George Bancroft
Concord Library	S[amuel]. G[ray]. Ward.
Elizabeth Hoar	W[illiam]. E[llery]. Channing

---

[222] The publication of *Parnassus,* a long-planned-for and long-awaited event as the entries in this and earlier journals show, was a great relief to Emerson, who had rescued the growing manuscript of the volume from his burning house in 1872. In the list that follows on p. [242], "Elizabeth B. Ripley" and "44" are inserted in pencil. Of the persons mentioned here, those who have not been previously identified or are not easily recognizable include John Shepard Keyes, who with his wife founded Sleepy Hollow Cemetery, Concord, and whose daughter Annie married Edward Waldo Emerson; Mrs. Corinne Frazar Chamberlain, wife of the aforementioned Augustus Porter Chamberlain; Mrs. George Ware Briggs, wife of the pastor of the First Congregational Church, Plymouth, Massachusetts; Dr. Alexander Milton Ross, who corresponded irregularly with Emerson from 1864 to 1879; W. Robertson Herkless, president of the University Independent Club of Glasgow University; Baron Richard von Hoffmann, husband of Lily Ward, Samuel Gray Ward's daughter; Dr. William Benjamin Carpenter (1813–1885), English physiologist, who first met Emerson in 1848; George Washburn Smalley (1833–1916), foreign correspondent for the *New York Tribune* and other papers; and Robert Traill Spence Lowell (1816–1891), American Episcopal clergyman and author.

E. R[ockwood]. Hoar
↑Elizabeth B. Ripley↓
Georgina Lowell
Mrs A. Coolidge
George P. Bradford
George Higginson
Henry Lee
Le Baron Russell
Caroline S. Tappan

J. Elliot Cabot
Edward Bangs
J[ames]. R. Lowell

O. W. Holmes
George B. Emerson
Paulina T. Nash

Ellen H. Gurney   ↑44↓
J[ohn]. S[hepard]. Keyes
Mrs C[orinne]. Chamberlaine
Miss Sara Palfrey
↑F.↓ Henry Hedge
C[harles]. E. Norton
H. L. Longfellow
Mrs G[eorge] W[are] Briggs
27   J. Haven Emerson

Mrs Abel Adams
Dr A. ⟨R⟩M. Ross, To-
   ronto, Canada
T[homas]. Carlyle
Dr J[ames]. H. Stirling
W. Robertson Herkless
William H. Channing
Herman Grimm
Baron Richd von Hoff-
   mann
George Howard, Esq.
Dr W[illiam]. B. Carpenter
G[eorge]. W[ashburn].
   Smalley
Moncure D. Conway
Mrs Edward F Flower
   35 Hyde Park Gardens

Miss Sophia Thoreau
Robert Lowell
Prof Max Muller

[243]²²³ Edward W. Emerson
Edith ↑E.↓ Forbes ⟨jr⟩

²²³ On p. [243], the "E." is written in ink over pencil and "jr" is struck through in pencil in "Edith . . . jr"; "Ralph E. Forbes" is written in ink over pencil; "Herman Grimm . . . in 1876" is circled once in pencil and struck through with two diagonal ink and two diagonal pencil lines, probably to indicate that the noticed book was sent; "To these . . . in 1876" is in pencil; in "Unsent 6 January", "Unsent 6 J" is written in ink over blue pencil; "Miss Thoreau" is in blue pencil, lined through with one ink line and struck through with one diagonal ink line; "Charles Emerson" is in blue pencil; "Dr Furness" through the second "sent" is in blue pencil; "Mr Alcott" is written in ink over pencil.

Ralph E. Forbes
Lidian Emerson
⟨L⟩Robert Lowell
Herman Grimm, 5 Matthai Kirch Strasse, Berlin
Barone Richard Von Hoffmann   Villa Collimontana   Roma
Bayard Taylor
      ↑To these three sent "[*Letters and*] Social Aims" in 1876↓

Unsent   6 January [1876.]
⟨Miss Thoreau⟩
↑x↓   Charles Emerson ↑sent↓
↑x↓   Dr Furness   ? ⟨perhaps sent⟩sent
⟨Rev. Robert Lowell,⟩ Nassau Hall, sent by Osgood
↑x↓   Mr Alcott

[24⟨2⟩4][224]   Mrs Hastings
                              San Francisco
———

Why are gypsies more attractive to us than bishops? Because we like those who affect vices which they have not, & we hate the claim of sanctity.   X 64   Y 232

[245] ??? Synesius descended in the ⟨fifth⟩ generation from Hercules. See Gibbon, "Decline & Fall," Vol. III p. 296
↑Stanley showed me capital mistake in my reference to the book↓[.][225]

"Eic↑h↓horn would have the order of studies ⟨& the⟩ & the establishment of rigor therein in our universities increased. Others agreed. Then Schleiermacher quite simply said, 'he did not see how each must prescribe the way by which he came to his knowledge: the ↑routine↓ was in our ways of study so demolished, ⟨that⟩ the rules of all kinds so heaped, that to him nothing seemed better to do than to pull down all the universities.' 'And what to put in their place?' they asked; 'That

[224] On p. [244], "Mrs Hastings" is in erased pencil writing; "San Francisco" is in pencil; "X 64" and "Y 232" are each written in ink over pencil.
    [225] "Stanley . . . book" is inserted in pencil. Edward Gibbon's *History of the Decline and Fall of the Roman Empire*, 12 vols., new ed. (London, 1821), is in Emerson's library.

would it ⟨do⟩ ↑find↓ of itself ↑at once↓, & quite rightly,' answered Schleiermacher."[226] ⟨Von⟩ ⟨H⟩Varnhagen Von Ense Blatter aus der preussischen Geschichte, [1868–1869,] Vol. V. p. 144

[246] ↑The very air & the soil felt the anger of the people.↓
In 1775, the patriotism in Massachusetts, was so hot that it melted the snow, & the rye waved on the 19 April. Our farmers have never seen it so early, ⟨probably because they have not reached the same heat of⟩ GL 121.[227]

It occurs that the short limit of human life is set in relation to the instruction man can draw of Nature. No one has lived long enough to exhaust its laws.

[247] December 4, 1875, Thomas Carlyle's 80th birth-day.
↑1876↓
↑1877↓
↑1878↓[228]

[248] [blank]
[249] The delicacy of the touch & the eternity it inherits.
In every house a child that in mere play utters oracles, & knows not that they are such: 'tis as easy as breath⟨.⟩ing. 'Tis like gravity which holds the universe together, and none knows what it is.

[250] ↑1876.↓ ⟨I⟩On Saturday, 5 February, received through the Post Office a pacquet containing a silver medal, on one face bearing the profile of Carlyle, with the name *"Thomas Carlyle"* inscribed; on the other face

---

[226] In "that the rules," "that" is canceled in pencil; in "do . . . at once", "do" is canceled in pencil; "find" and "at once" are written in ink over pencil.
[227] "The very air . . . heat of" is struck through in pencil with five diagonal use marks.
[228] The three added years are in pencil. The entry on p. [249] also occurs on p. [233] above.

"In Commemoration
1875
December 4."[229]

A card enclosed reads "To R W Emerson   from Alex. Macmillan.   The Elms. Streatham Lane.   Upper Tooting, S. W.   Surrey, England" for which welcome & precious gift I wish to write immediately my thanks to the kind sender.
Sunday, 6 Feb. 1876.

[251]–[252] [blank]
[253][230]   *Queries.*
"Vestiges of Creation," who is the author?[231]

    [254] 1877, January.
All writing should be affirmative.

[255][232] "If this great world of joy & pain
              Revolve in one sure track"
                        ["If this great world of joy and pain," ll. 1–2]
                            ↑Wordsworth [*Poems,* 1851,] p 381↓

Mottoes
        "Thoughts the voluntary move
        Harmonious numbers."
                            [Milton, *Paradise Lost,* III, 37–38]

"Things not seen by reason, but by the flower of the mind."

---

[229] " 'In . . . 4.' " is circled. The medal that Emerson describes here was struck to commemorate Carlyle's eightieth birthday. Andrew Macmillan, the publisher, was introduced to Emerson by letter from Matthew Arnold in 1867 (see *L,* VI, 293n).

[230] A copy of William Allingham's "Poesis Humana" is pasted in the left-hand margin of p. [253]. Some emendations are made on the copy in ink, and in the lower right corner "W. Allingham" appears in Emerson's hand.

[231] Robert Chambers's *Vestiges of the Natural History of Creation* (New York, 1845) is in Emerson's library.

[232] On p. [255], "Wordsworth p 381" is inserted in pencil. In the citations of Wordsworth's poetry that follow on p. [255] and after, Emerson is quoting from two editions, both in his library: the aforementioned "new edition" of *Poems,* 1851, and *Poetical Works,* 4 vols. (Boston, 1824). For "Things not . . . mind.", see p. [130] above.

⟨Touching as now in thy humility⟩
⟨The mountain borders of this scene of care⟩
                    [*Yarrow Revisited,* Sonnet XVII, ll. 11–12]
                    ⟨Wordsworth [*Poems,* 1851] 8vo Ed. p. 340⟩

[256] ——

"Like thoughts whose very sweetness yieldeth proof
That they were born for immortality."
                    [*Ecclesiastical Sonnets,* Sonnet XLIII, ll. 13–14]
                    Wordsworth [*Poems,* 1851,] XLII[I] p 333

——

"By pain of heart, now checked, & now impelled,
The ⟨I⟩intellectual power through words & things
Went sounding on, a dim & perilous way!"
                    [*The Excursion,* III, ll. 699–701]
                    Wordsworth. [*Poems,* 1851,] p. 472[233]

——

"Farewell, farewell! the Heart that lives alone
Housed in a dream, at distance from the kind."
                    ["Elegiac Stanzas, Suggested by a Picture of Peele
                    Castle, in a Storm, by Sir George Beaumont," ll. 53–54]
                    Wordsworth [*Poetical Works,* 1824,] III 215

——

"For Gods are to each other not unknown."
                    Homer Odyss⟨ey⟩y V. 79

——

"In the breast feeding, eyeless, rapid Love." *Orpheus*

——

"Touching as now in thy humility
The mountain borders in this scene of care,"
                    [*Yarrow Revisited,* Sonnet XVII, ll. 11–12]
                    Wordsworth [*Poems,* 1851,] 8vo Edit. p. 340, XVII.

——

The unimaginable touch of Time.
                    [*Ecclesiastical Sketches,* Sonnet XVI, l. 14]
                    12 mo. Wordsworth [*Poetical Works,* 1824,] Vol III, 297.

——

[233] These lines are used as the motto for the section entitled "Intellectual" in *Parnassus.*

From her unworthy seat, the cloudy stall
Of Time, breaks forth triumphant Memory.
            [*The River Duddon,* Sonnet XXI, ll. 9–10]
        12 mo. Wordsworth, [*Poetical Works,* 1824,] III. 42

May never the love of the powers above
Cast on me a glance that none can elude!
            Aeschylus, Prometheus [*Bound,* ll. 936–937]

[257]²³⁴   *Mottoes.*

"For words must sparks be of those fires they strike." *Lord Brooke.*

"Quot que aderant vates, rebar adesse Deos." [Ovid]

"For fragments of the lofty strain
Float down the tide of years,
As buoyant on the stormy main
A parted wreck appears."   *Scott*

"Quotque aderant vates, rebar adesse Deos." *Ovid*

"Saadi wrote a line of poetry that met the approbation of God Almighty."

---

²³⁴ Entries from p. [257] through the first half of p. [258] apparently deal with last-minute details concerning *Parnassus.* For the lines of Lord Brooke and Ovid see pp. [47] and [53] above. Scott's unidentified lines " 'For fragments . . . appears.' " are used as the motto for "Narrative Poems and Ballads" in *Parnassus.* Not used in *Parnassus,* " 'Saadi wrote . . . Almighty.' " is used in "Poetry and Imagination," *W,* VIII, 64. John Gower's lines " 'The privates . . . winds were.' " from *Confessio Amantis,* I, ll. 2806–2808, are used as the motto for poems of "Human Life" in *Parnassus,* and they also appear in "Ethics," *Lectures,* II, 150, and in "Poetry and Imagination," *W,* VIII, 9; see *JMN,* XII, 68. Not used in *Parnassus,* the lines of Nicholas Grimoald (or Grimald) are from an extract of *The Death of Zoroas, an Egyptian Astronomer . . .* , in *Specimens of the Early English Poets,* ed. George Ellis, 3 vols. (London, 1803), II, 74–77. John Keble's lines, from "Morning," ll. 19–20, are used as the motto for poems "Contemplative.—Moral. Religious" in *Parnassus* and occur in *Lyra Innocentium . . .* (Oxford, 1867), in Emerson's library; see *JMN,* XIII, 468.

"The privates of man's heart—
They speken and sound in his ear
As tho' they loud winds were."

[John] *Gower.*

"O how fair fruit may you to mortal men
From wisdom's garden give! How many may
By you the wiser & the better prove!"

Nicholas Grimoald
1519–1562

"Eyes which the beam celestial view
Which evermore makes all things new."

[John] *Keble.*

"From her unworthy seat, the cloudy stall
Of Time, breaks forth triumphant Memory."
[*The River Duddon*, Sonnet XXI, ll. 9–10]
Wordsworth [*Poetical Works*, 1824,] III. Vol. p 42.

[258]²³⁵ *Parnassus*

"Burial of Moses." *Who is Mrs Alexander*

²³⁵ Entries on the first half of p. [258] continue matters introduced on p. [257], while those on the second half of p. [258] through p. [260] and on pp. [263]–[264] deal with questions about and revisions for an intended second edition of *Parnassus*, which in fact appeared in 1875. Mrs. Cecil Frances (Humphreys) Alexander's "The Burial of Moses," from *The Sunday Book of Poetry* (London and Cambridge, 1865), p. 75, appears in *Parnassus* under the same title. Elizabeth Stuart Phelps's "That Never was on Sea or Land," from the *Atlantic Monthly*, XXXIV, (Oct. 1874), 410–412, does not appear in *Parnassus*. Eight lines of Arthur Bourchier's broadside verse *A worthy mirrour, wherein you may marke, an excellent discourse of a breeding larke* (London, 1589) appear in *Parnassus* as "Breeding Lark" and are credited to Arthur Boar. The four poems of Ellen Sturgis Hooper that appear in *Parnassus* (credited to "E.S.H.") were probably taken from a bound, unsigned volume of her works that was in circulation among her friends and is now preserved in the Houghton Library. From Philip James Bailey's *Festus, A Poem*, 3rd ed. (London, 1848), p. 16, in Emerson's library, four lines appear in *Parnassus* as "Forecast"; see *JMN*, XI, 413. No parts of Sir Henry Taylor's *Philip Van Artevelde*, 2 vols. (Cambridge, 1835), in Emerson's library, appear in *Parnassus*. Eight lines from Edward Young's "Night IX," including those quoted here, appear in *Parnassus* as "Penitence"; the lines " 'Forgive his . . . the right.' " are also used in "Holiness," *Lectures*, II, 352, and

Miss Phelps's poem *"That never was on sea or land"*

Arthur Boar or Bourcher

Miss Lowell's collection of *Ellen Hooper's Poems.*
Bailey's Festus
H[enry]. Taylor   Van Arteveldt

"Forgive his crimes, forgive his virtues, too,
Those small faults, half converts to the right."
                    Young. [*Night Thoughts,* "Night IX," ll. 2316–2317]

↑1874↓
Dec. 15,
"Parnassus" being printed, I propose to insert here additions or corrections for any second Edition.

Under "Terror," from "Julius Caesar," Shakspeare
    "Between the acting of a dreadful thing,
    And the first motion,"—&c   7 lines.

In *AZ* 268, Select poems of Ben Jonson   compare with the selection in our book.

    Is a passage from Sprague's poem inserted beginning (of the Indians)
        "Alas for them, their day is o'er," &c
                                            See *L* 61

"Circles," *W,* II, 317; see *JMN,* VI, 157, 230–231. Shakespeare's *Julius Caesar,* II, i, 63–69, of which " 'Between the acting . . . motion,' " are ll. 63–64, appears in *Parnassus* as "Crime"; see *JMN,* XII, 78. Strophe XIX from Charles Sprague's *An Ode, Pronounced before the Inhabitants of Boston, September the Seventeenth, 1830, at the Centennial Celebration . . .* (Boston, 1830), which is in Emerson's library, appears in *Parnassus* as "Indians"; the first seven lines of strophe XIX are used in "Historical Discourse," *W,* XI, 62; see *JMN,* XII, 21. The eight lines of Sir Walter Scott's *Lady of the Lake,* I, xxxiii, appear in *Parnassus* as "Dreams"; see *JMN,* VI, 46. Matthew Arnold's "The Gypsy Scholar" does not appear in *Parnassus.*

Is Scott's "Dreams" in?
The "Gypsy Scholar," of Arnold?

[259]²³⁶ ————

⟨⟩There is a pleasing poem by "Almira," which I have cut from a newspaper, ⟨&⟩addressed to T. F. Marshall, then in Congress, which I have pasted in My Manuscript Σ p. 15, Same paper holds notice of George Sand on the other side.

———

Errata in Parnassus
l. 5, p. 509—for [chooses] read [chaoses]
l 238, 2d col, l. 18 insert (is) (in his hair,!)
l 425, 1st col. l 11 for (came) read (come)

I wished to omit all the clo⟨s⟩sing verses in Gray's "Eton College" poem—the doleful ones. But they are inserted, alas!

———

⟨w⟩Who wrote "⟨t⟩*The Loyal woman's NO*" in the Atlantic?   ↑Lucy Larcom↓

———

Who wrote "Southwells" poem? *"Christmas Day."*

———

Consult Fox on a writer in the "Transcript" who finds errors in B[isho]p. Berk↑e↓ley's lines to America

———

²³⁶ A 4.8 × 2.3 cm cardboard tab (possibly a bookmark) is pasted in the top right corner of p. [259]. The errata in *Parnassus* that are noted on this page are corrected in the second edition. Of the items mentioned here, those that have not been previously identified or are not easily recognizable include the "pleasing poem" by " 'Almira' ", the clipping of which in Notebook Σ apparently has been lost; Robert Southwell's "The burning Babe," a poem of Christmas day, which appears in *Parnassus* as "The Burning Babe"; the lines "I'll Never Love Thee More," by James Grahame, Marquis of Montrose (1612–1650), which appear in *Parnassus* but are not in any of the aforementioned ballad collections used by Emerson in the preparation of *Parnassus;* and Lucy Larcom's "A Loyal Woman's No!", from *Poems* (Boston, 1869), in Emerson's library, which in the first edition of *Parnassus* is cited "from Atlantic Monthly", where it has not been found, and in the second edition is attributed to the author. For George Stillman Hillard's letter, see *L,* VI, 469.

See Campbell's corrections of "Hohen Linden" as cited by Mr Hillard. See his letter.

Then compare Marquis of Montrose's lines as printed in Evans's Ballads, (1810) with the lines in Parnassus.

p. 373 1st Col. l. 9, for (Ma'am) read (Madam)

add Wordsworth's "Picture at Peel Castle."

⟨Read Arnold's "Gipsey Scholar."⟩

Add to "Parnassus," Wordsworth's poem on Beaumont's picture of Peel Castle, in 8vo. Wordsworth p. 434,

p. 159 (Mrs E. H.) is to ⟨be⟩read (E[llen]. S. Hooper)
   159 Col. 2, line 8th for (ear,) read (ear:)

p. 246 "A Loyal Woman's No" was written by Lucy Larcom
                                        continued infra, p. 263

[260] I confess that I have inserted some poems for ↑the sake of↓ one ⟨single⟩ verse; nay, possibly for a single happiest word. Tennyson's "the *stammering* thunder"; Shakspeare's "How many a glorious morning have I seen *Flatter* the mountain tops with sovereign eye;" Herrick's "tempestuous petticoat" &
Chaucer's language is often as wonderful. I know not in poetry a more pathetic stroke than the plea of Griselda to her husband,
   "Let me not like a worm go by the way."
It can only be /compared/paralleled/with his own Ariadne's to Th⟨i⟩eseus,
   "Meker than thee, ⟨I⟩ find ↑I↓ the beastès wild."
It was said of Rogers↑'s↓ poem of "Memory," that there was but one good line in it, "All other pleasures are not worth its pains." and one in Scott's "Helvellyn," addressed to the dead traveller's dog, "When the wind waved his garments, how oft ⟨thou⟩didst thou start!"

[261] Wordsworth has secured his fame not only against his critics but against himself, a prey long time to the critics in his puerile poems, I may say infantile, & the self conceit which he could not exclude from his loftier strains[.] All this he outgrew at the last ⟨& ⟨in a⟩ many noble sonnets &⟩ in the Ode on Immortality, in the poems of Laodamia, Dion, The Happy Warrior, and in some noble sonnets has established his claim to the highest thought in England in his time.

[262]²³⁷ [blank]
[263]²³⁸ *Parnassus*

p   133   Col. 1 l. 2   for (isle) read (aisle)
          Col 1 l. 5, for (Whole) read (Whose)
p. 145   Col 1 l. 4   for (Ryme) read (Rhime)
          Col 2 l. 10 for (Churches) read (Churche↑'↓s("))   ?
p. 191   Col. 2 5 lines from bottom for (Respects) read
                          (Respect)
p. 148   Strike out 3 stanzas
          ———
          Strike out Mrs Sage's line from the
          ———
p. 496   Col. 1. line 17, for (our fiddle;) read (one fiddle;)
          ———
p. xxii   ⟨For thou hast passed all change of human life⟩
          ⟨And not again to thee shall beauty die.⟩   dele[te]
          ———

²³⁷ Two newspaper clippings are pasted onto p. [262]: one, entitled "Mr. Emerson's Monday Conversations. The Literary Seances at Mechanics' Hall," deals with Emerson's "conversations" of April 15–May 20, 1872; and another, entitled "Poetical Misprints," from the *Boston Evening Transcript* of Tuesday, December 22, 1874, deals with errors in the first edition of *Parnassus*.
²³⁸ On p. [263], in "(Churche↑'↓s(")) ?" the apostrophe is added and quotation marks deleted in pencil, and a vertical line is drawn between the end parenthesis and the question mark; a double-pointed pencil arrow to their left connects "Strike out" and "And not"; "Geo. H. . . . inserted" is in pencil. Except for "Churche's", which appears as "Churches' " in the second edition of *Parnassus*, corrections to *Parnassus* as indicated here are made in the second edition; otherwise, except for the following, most pertinent items mentioned here have been previously identified. Sir Henry Wotton's "The Character of a Happy Life," from *Reliquiae Wottonianae. Or A Collection of Lives, Letters, Poems; with Characters of Sundry Personages* . . . , 4th ed. (London, 1685), in Emerson's library, appears in *Parnassus* as "The Happy Life." Neither " 'Short is . . . thy mind.' ", from John Dryden, *Absalom and Achitophel*, ll. 847–849, nor " 'Tis virtue . . . can fit.' ", from Ben Jonson, *Cynthia's Revels*, V, xi, 117–118, appears in *Parnassus*.

↑Geo H. Vibbert, who noted the above errata, asks to have Whittier's "Eternal Goodness" inserted↓

---

p. 146   Compare Sir H[enry]. Wotton's poems with the version in "Parnassus"

---

p. 192   For ⟨thou⟩ read ⟨Thou⟩

---

p 230   In 2d verse of Maryland, (Hark to   wandering son's appeal)??

"Burial of Moses", to be inserted among "Pictures."

Dr J. F. Clarke wrongly accredited with two poems, "Thekla's Song" and "America"

---

p. 225,[n]   Correct Bishop Berkeley's lines on America.

I fear I have omitted the fine passages from Dryden, which I once collected. as,

"Short is the date of all immoderate fame;—
It looks as ⟨if⟩Heaven our ruin had designed,
And dared not trust thy fortune & thy mind."

In Ben Jonson's "Cynthia's Revels," occur the lines
"Tis Virtue which they want, & wanting it,
Honor no garment to their backs can fit."

See that they are put in the Fragments, if not yet inserted.

[264] I do not find in Parnassus[n] ↑the following lines.↓ ⟨Should⟩ ↑Can↓ they ⟨not⟩ have dropped from the ballad "Fair Annie"?
"And when she was trimly attired in the same,
Her beauty shined most bright
For staining every other brave & comely dame
That did appear in sight."[239]

---

[239] Cited as "Scott's version," "Fair Annie" appears in *Parnassus* under the same title. The source of this poem is probably Child, *English and Scottish Ballads*, 1857, III,

317

See if Burns's lines are contained

"To snow that falls upon a river,
A moment white then gone forever."[240]

[265] [blank]
[266] March, 1875.

In the new volume which I hope to publish, with *"Poetry & Criticism"* I ⟨hope⟩ ↑wish↓ to insert a chapter called *"Influences"*; and *"Greatness;"* and *"Inspiration"*; and, probably, *"Social Aims"*; and perhaps *"Immortality."* There remain *"Originality & Quotation,"* already printed in the "North American Review"; *"Character"* printed in the same; *"Saadi"* in the "Atlantic""[n], & ⟨the⟩ ↑my↓ *Preface* to Ticknor & Fields' Edition of The Gulistan,[n] which is another chapter on *Saadi*, though it may borrow some paragraph from ⟨the⟩ ↑my↓ *Atlantic* paper.   There remain *"Table Talk"*; *"Homes & Hospitality;"* ⟨*Influences,*⟩ and the later Lecture on *"Eloquence,"* ↑two articles in "The Dial," *"Landor,"* and *"Carlyle"*;↓ and my *"Cambridge Lectures on Philosophy"*, fourteen, I believe, in number, from which I should rather select the best pages, than [267] ⟨pr⟩attempt to print any entire discourses. The Lecture called *"Perpetual Forces,"* I believe, I reckoned good when it was first written, but have never read it twice in public, nor in private. One called *"Demonology,"* interested Henry James [Sr.], I remember.

There is also my *Preface to Plutarch's Morals,* printed in Little & Brown's Edition of Plutarch[241]

Steffens says of the first performance of Schiller's Wallenstein at Weimar, in the presence of Schiller & Goethe,—

192–197, where it is paired with a version by William Motherwell (on pp. 198–204). However, the lines " 'And when . . . in sight.' " do not appear in either version.

[240] Robert Burns's "Tam o'Shanter. A Tale," of which " 'To snow . . . forever.' " are ll. 61–62 misquoted, appears in *Parnassus*.

[241] The volume that Emerson outlines here was published in 1876 as *Letters and Social Aims*. The titles finally included in that volume are "Poetry and Imagination," "Social Aims," "Eloquence," "Resources," "The Comic," "Quotation and Originality," "Progress of Culture," "Persian Poetry," "Inspiration," "Greatness," and "Immortality."

"Goethe was himself chief manager; & his eminence gave him an influence over the whole theatre corps which was hardly ever ↑equalled elsewhere↓. *The performers did not so much fear him for his greatness as they respected him for his skill.*" [Steffens, *The Story of My Career* ..., 1863, p. 48.]

[268]   December, '76.
For the next volume we have the following possibilities
> Influences
> Perpetual Forces
> Demonology
> The Virginia Oration
> Plutarch's Morals
> Homes & Hospitality[242]

[269][243] *possibili⟨es⟩ties for N. American*
Egypt
Demonology
Memory

France
> M de Sartine, *HO* 238

[270] Mr Buttrick, father of ↑Steadman B.,↓ said to me that he saw Captain Davis on the 19 April, 1875 [actually 1775], in the morning, and he looked very much worried: "his face was red as a beet." Afterwards, describing the same fact, he said, "his face was as red as a piece of cloth."

[271]–[277] [blank]
[278] *Names of Grace.*[244]
↑March 31, 1872.↓ Hannah Ryan of Dedham.
↑1873, June 24, I have now a new benefactor of this name. Mr C. Ryan.↓

---

[242] "Influences ... Hospitality" is in pencil.
[243] Entries on p. [269] are in pencil.
[244] Persons named in the list that follows are identified elsewhere in this volume by their various kindnesses toward Emerson.

Mr B. S. Holt of Belmont, Mass[achuse]tts

———

Dr Wm. MacCormac, 13 Harley St, Cavendish Square, W. London.

———

Dr Henry Mc Cormac, Belfast, Ireland,
C[harles]. K. Newcomb, Glendower Hotel, Market Place, Great Portland St. London

———

William B. Wright, 63 ↑East↓ Eagle street, Buffalo, N. Y.

———

⟨Cristop⟩

———

Christopher James, of Gold Hill, Nevada, working in the Comstock Lode, a miner, a Welshman by birth, a Comtist in his politics, and about 23 or 24 years old—a good friend of mine, though I have never seen him.
↑His ⟨let⟩token brought me by B B Titcomb of Watertown, Mass.↓

———

[279] 1870[245]
Dec.	1	Friday	J Jan.	1	Monday	
	2	Sat Dubuque		2	Tues	Baltimore
	3	Sun		3	Wed	
	4	Mon Chicago		4	Thurs	Balt[imore]
	5	Tu. Quincy		5	Fri	
	6	Wed. Quin[cy]		6	Sat	
	7	Thursday ("Jacksonville")		7	Sun	
	8	Frid		8	Mon	
	9	Sat		9	Tues	Balt[imore]
	10	Sun		10	Wed	
	11	Mon		11	Thurs	"
	12	Tu		12	Fri	New Brunswick
	13	Wed		13	Sat	W[est]. Point

[245] All entries on p. [279] are in pencil. The lists appear to be a preliminary outline of Emerson's lecture engagements for December 1871 and January 1872, when he lectured in Illinois, Iowa, Maryland, West Point (New York), and New Brunswick (New Jersey).

14	Thurs		14	Sunday
15	Frid		15	Mon
16	Sat		16	Tu
17	Sun		17	Wed
18	Mon		18	Thurs.
19	Tu		19	Friday
20	Wed		20	Saturday
21	Thurs		21	Sunday
22	Fri		22	Mon
23	Sat		23	Tuesday
24	Sun		24	Wed
25	Mon		25	Thursd
26	Tues		26	Friday
27	Wed		27	Sat
28	Thurs		28	Sun
29	Fri		29	Mon
30	Sat		30	⟨W⟩Tues
31	Sun		⟨2⟩31	Wed

[280] [Index material omitted]
[inside back cover] [Index material omitted]

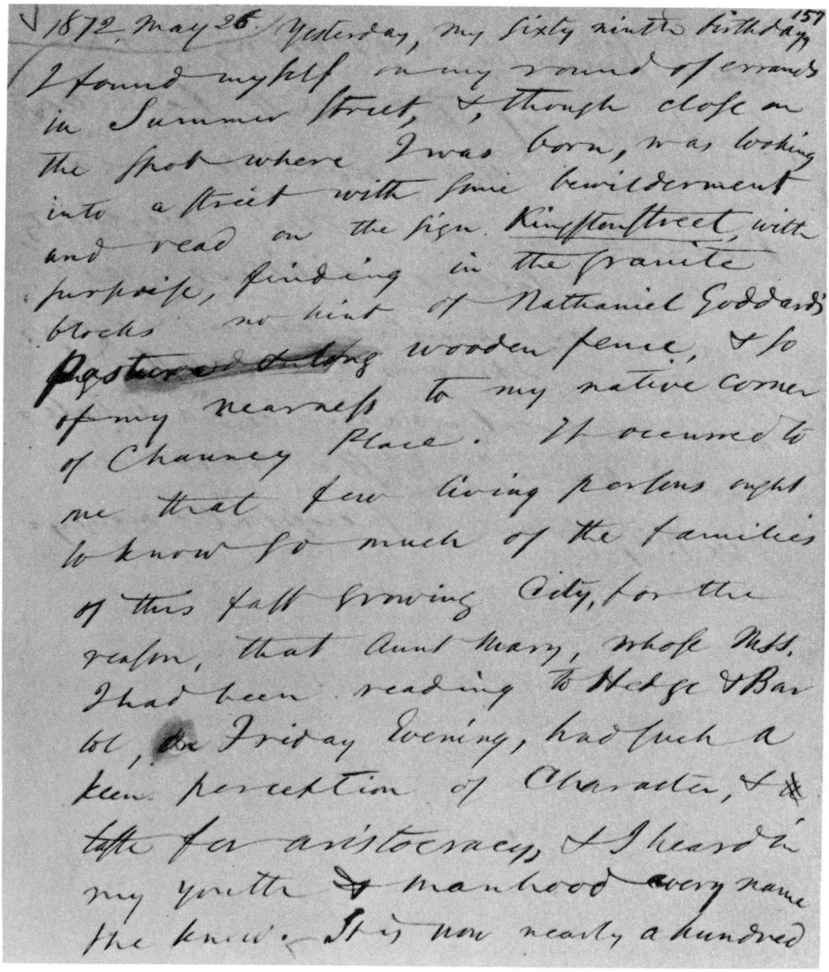

1872. May 26. Yesterday, my sixty ninth birthday
I found myself in my round of errands
in Summer Street, &, though close on
the spot where I was born, was looking
into a street with some bewilderment
and read on the sign Kingston Street, with
purpose, finding in the granite
blocks no hint of Nathaniel Goddard's
~~pastured along~~ wooden fence, & so
of my nearness to my native corner
of Chauncy Place. It occurred to
me that few living persons ought
to know so much of the families
of this fast growing City, for the
reason, that Aunt Mary, whose MSS.
I had been reading to Hedge & Bartol, on Friday Evening, had such a
keen perception of Character, & a
taste for aristocracy, & I heard in
my youth & manhood ~~every~~ name
she knew. It is now nearly a hundred

Plate I   Journal ST, page 157   Text, page 274
Yesterday, my sixty ninth birthday

280 In an earlier page in this book I wrote some notes touching the so called Transcendentalists of Boston in 1857. Hawthorne drew some sketches in his Blithedale Romance; but not happily, as I think: rather, I should say quite unworthy of his genius. To be sure I do not think any of his books worthy of his genius. I admired the man, who was simple, amiable, truth loving, & frank in conversation: but I never read his books with pleasure. — They are too young. In & around Brook Farm, whether as members, boarders, or visiters, were many remarkable persons, whether for character, or intellect, or accomplishments. There was Newcomb one of the subtlest minds, — I believe I must say — the subtlest observer & diviner of character

Plate II   Journal LN, page 280   Text, page 94
Notes on Nathaniel Hawthorne and
the Transcendentalists of Boston

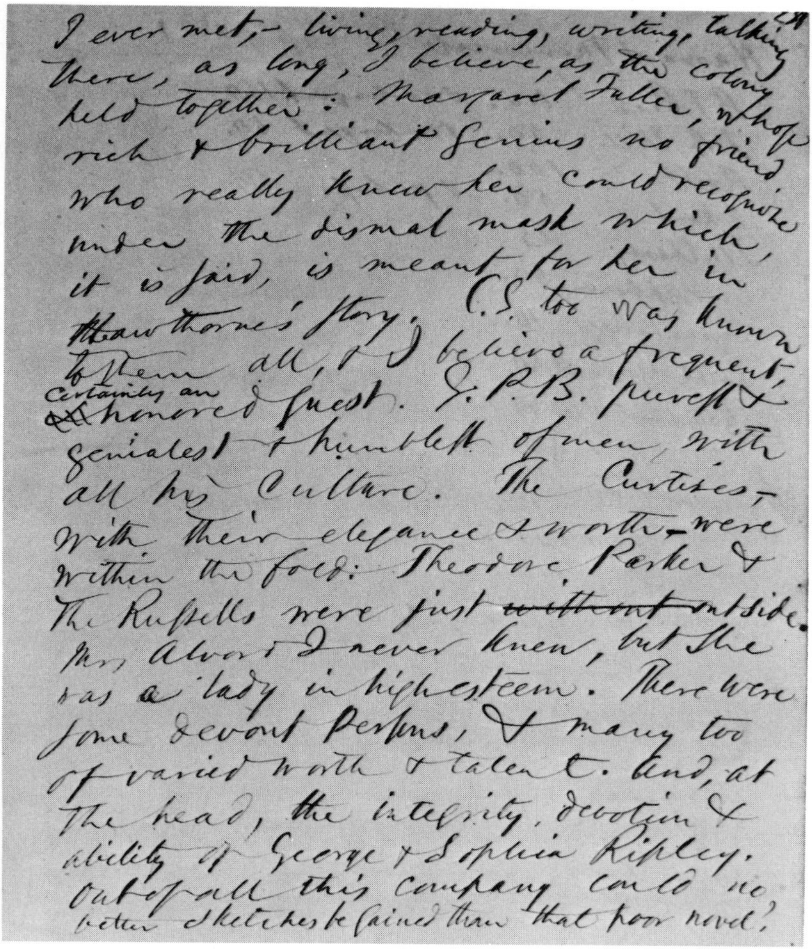

I ever met,— living, reading, writing, talking there, as long, I believe, as the colony held together: Margaret Fuller, whose rich & brilliant genius no friend who really knew her could recognize under the dismal mask which, it is said, is meant for her in Hawthorne's story. C.S. too was known to them all, & I believe a frequent, certainly an & honored guest. S.P.B. purest & genialest & humblest of men, with all his culture. The Curtises, with their elegance & worth—were within the fold: Theodore Parker & the Russells were just without outside. Mrs Alcott I never knew, but she was a lady in high esteem. There were some devout persons, & many too of varied worth & talent. And, at the head, the integrity, devotion & ability of George & Sophia Ripley. Out of all this company could no better sketches be gained than that poor novel?

Plate III   Journal LN, page 281   Text, page 94
Margaret Fuller, Theodore Parker, and others remembered

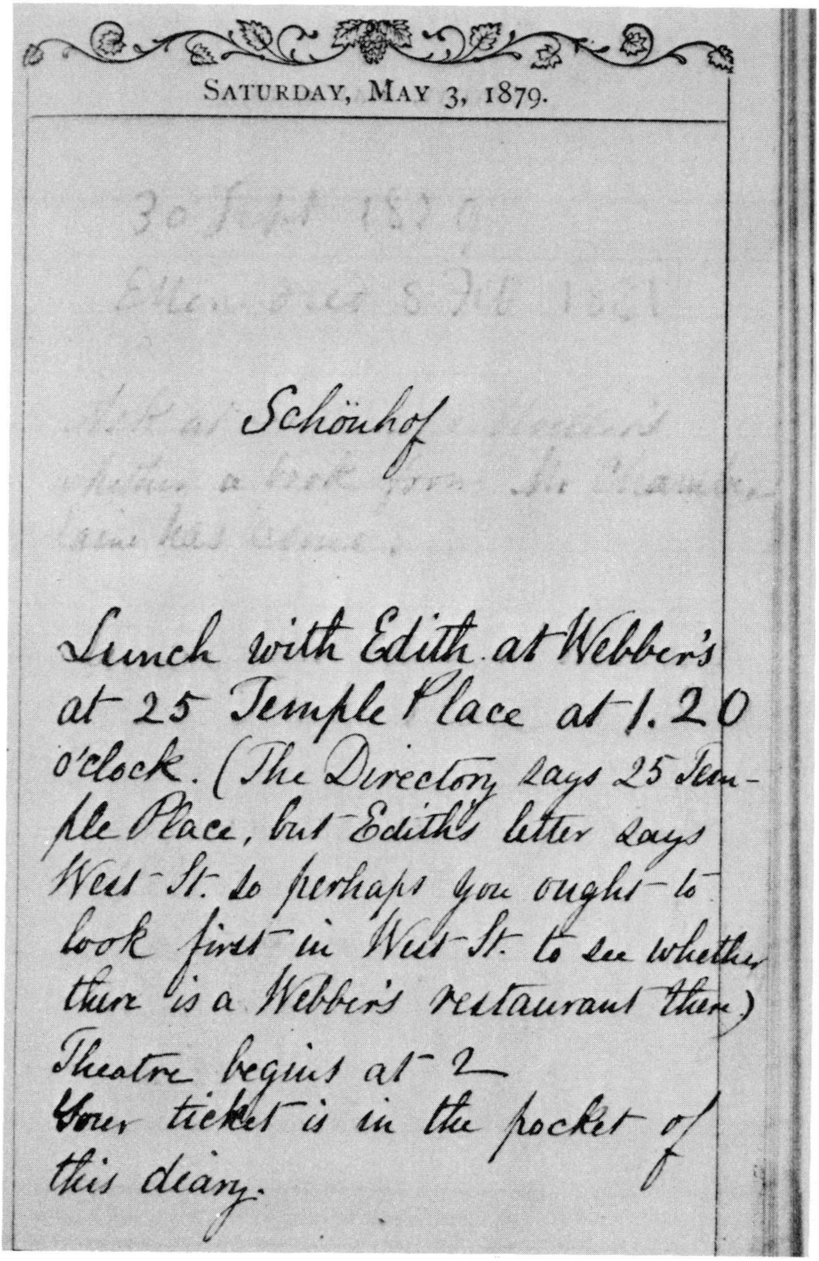

SATURDAY, MAY 3, 1879.

30 Sept 1879

Ellen died 8 Feb 1831

Schönhof

Lunch with Edith at Webber's
at 25 Temple Place at 1.20
o'clock. (The Directory says 25 Temple Place, but Edith's letter says
West St. so perhaps you ought to
look first in West St. to see whether
there is a Webber's restaurant there)
Theatre begins at 2
Your ticket is in the pocket of
this diary.

Plate IV   Pocket Diary 30, page 155   Text, page 525
                    Ellen died 8 Feb 1831

PART TWO
Miscellaneous Notebooks

Books Large

1870–1877

The notebook Emerson called "Books" has been designated Books Large by the editors. In its dual nature as a notebook for notes on Emerson's reading and on books and as a notebook for lists of books appropriate for libraries in which Emerson was interested, Books Large complements Journal Books Small [Sequence I] and Notebook Books Small [Sequence II] (see *JMN*, VIII, 442–479, 550–576).

Books Large was an old prayer copybook kept by Emerson's father, Rev. William Emerson, in the years 1809–1810, as indicated by crossed-out entries on the inside front cover that record the elder Emerson's use of the book in the preparation of two prayers and by three dates evenly spaced apart in stubs remaining in the book: January 22, 1809; November 1809; and April 2, 1810.

Emerson tore or cut out the first forty-four leaves and one-third of the forty-fifth leaf, which contained entries by his father. The stubs of most torn or cut-out leaves bear a letter or two of writing in the verso margins, and the dates noted above are written in top verso margins. Although this matter is clearly not in Emerson's hand, on the verso side of the thirty-third leaf two partial words are visible in the margin that appear to be in Emerson's writing; these are the only instances of Emerson's use of the portion of the copybook originally used by his father. After he removed the leaves on which his father had written, Emerson turned the book upside down and began to use it for Books Large.

Emerson may have begun to use the notebook in the 1860s, as indicated by the entry dated March 8, 1864, on page [7], which may have been copied from another book, and the list dated January 1860 on the inserted page [68ₐ]. More likely, he used the notebook only in the 1870s, particularly the period from 1870 to 1877, when he was keeping Journal ST. Internal evidence for dating indicates that he used the book in 1870, 1872, 1873, 1876, and 1877. The earliest dated entry is August 1870 (p. [26]) and the last is December 1876 (p. [30]), although page [31] bears a reference to an issue of a periodical dated September 29, 1877.

All book entries in Books Large not identified in the notes are identified in Appendix II of this volume.

The covers of the copybook, black paper over boards worn through to the boards in many places, measure 16.8 × 20.5 cm. The spine strip is of black leather that is also worn. "BOOKS" is printed in ink on a strip of white paper measuring 5.9 × 1.5 cm that is pasted onto the middle of the spine. Additionally, *"BOOKS."* is printed on a strip of white paper measuring 10.7 × 4.3 cm that is pasted onto the middle of the front cover.

Including front flyleaves (i, ii)—back flyleaves are torn out—there are 96 unlined pages measuring 16.5 × 19.9 cm, but the bottom third of the leaf bearing pages 93 and 94 is torn out. In his pagination, Emerson misnumbered and then corrected the numbering of three pages: $5\langle 0\rangle 1$, $5\langle 1\rangle 2$, and $5\langle 2\rangle 3$. Most of the pages are numbered in ink, but four are numbered in pencil: 9, 11, 13, and 15. Twenty-three pages are unnumbered: i, ii, 10, 12, 14, 34, 36, 38, 42, 44, 46, 71, 73, 75, 77, 81, 83, 87, 90, 91, 92, 93, and 94. Forty-six pages are blank: ii, 10, 12, 13, 20, 21, 24, 28, 32, 33, 34, 35, 36, 37, 38, 40, 41, 42, 43, 44, 45, 46, 47, 48, 50, 70, 71, 72, 73, 74, 75, 76, 77, 78, 79, 80, 81, 82, 83, 85, 86, 87, 88, 92, 93, and 94. Additionally, three inserts have been placed in the copybook. The first, a piece of white lined paper measuring 19.4 × 24.6 cm, is folded to form four writing sides and is ticked into the fold between pages [2] and [3]. The editors have numbered this insert [2$_a$], [2$_b$], [2$_c$], and [2$_d$]. The second, a piece of white lined paper measuring 25.4 × 20.2 cm, is folded to form four writing sides and is laid in between pages [68] and [69]. The editors have numbered this insert [68$_a$], [68$_b$], [68$_c$], and [68$_d$]. The third insert, a piece of white paper measuring 12.2 × 14 cm and bearing an impression of the seal of the Union Club, is laid in between pages [84] and [85]. The editors have numbered this insert [84$_a$] and [84$_b$]. Pages [2$_c$], [2$_d$], [68$_c$], and [84$_b$] are blank; pages [2$_a$], [2$_b$], [68$_a$], [68$_b$], [68$_d$], and [84$_a$] bear writing in Emerson's hand which has been incorporated into the text by the editors.

Inside the back cover is laid a clipping from the New York *Weekly Tribune* for Saturday, September 14, 1861, which describes a walking and boating tour of the region around Saranac Lake, New York.

[front cover] *BOOKS.*

[front cover verso] [Index material omitted]

[i]   R. W. Emerson
                              Books

[ii] [blank]
[1] Laws of Alfred, in Thorpe's admirable edition, *"Ancient Laws & Institutes of England." London. 1840.*

"Lectures on the History of Rome" By B. G. Niebuhr. Edited by Dr Leonhard Schmitz. Second Edit. III Vols. London, 1849.

Lectures on the elements of Comparative Anatomy. By Thos. H. Huxley. London 1864.

Read Plato's "Sophist" & "Parmenides." See *S* p 142

[2] Robert Brown's Botanical Writings   Esenbeck's Collection.[1]

[2ₐ]   *Concord Library*
    Browning's Poems
    Channing's Poems
    Aurora Leigh
    Piozzi

    Mather's Magnalia

    Sir R. Wilson

    Allingham's Poems

    Ockley's History of the Saracens

    Spence's Anecdotes
    Selden's Table Talk[2]

[2ᵦ] Luther's Table Talk

[2𝒸]–[2𝒹] [blank]
[3]   ↑For *Concord Library*↓ⁿ
    Ritson

---

[1] "Robert Brown's . . . Collection." is half-encircled twice in ink.
[2] "Selden's . . . Talk" is struck through in ink with three diagonal lines, and "Ockley's . . . Saracens", above, is struck through in ink with three vertical lines.

Clough's Bothie of Toper-na-Fuosich

Luther's Table Talk.
Grimm: Memoires
Lord Hervey's History of England
Hobbes's Works
Chesterfield's Letters
↑Duc de↓ Saint Simon. 20 Vols

Wilkinson's Egypt   2 vols

Social Essays from Saturday Review

Koran

Social Condition of England
Cinq Mars

Renan's Relig. History & Criticism   Translation of O B Frothingham

[4] Ure's Chemical Dictionary, *word* Saltpetre.

Saussure's ascent of the Alps

Arago

Life of General Sir Wm Napier, K.C.B. Edited by H.A. Bruce,
M.P. (Murray,)

Lew⟨i⟩es's Life of Goethe, 2d Edition.

Joshua Giddings.

Lieber's Reminiscences of Niebuhr.

328

Trench's "Past & Present of the English Language," & "On the study of Words"

[5] There are some books, to have r⟨a⟩ead which is a rare distinction; as Ste Beuve says of Biot, "Il était du petit nombre de ceux qui ont lu la *Mécanique Céleste* de Laplace."[3]
In some degree, this power attaches to the readers of Montesquieu, of Adam Smith. So of Spinosa, so of Kant.

Books & mss which are written only for the best. See *BL* 114[–116]

[6] ————
The book of Swedenborg which Henry James values is "Angelic Wisdom Concerning the Divine Providence"

Tyndall's *Lecture on Sound.* now printing by Longmans & Co Dec. 1866

[7] 1864 March 8.
Concord Library, now that the Agricultural Library is added, contains 4600 volumes

Gilchrist's Life of Blake 2 vols 8vo. London.   Mr Norton says it can be had for 8.00

Herschel's Familiar Lectures on Scientific Subjects

Landor's Works.

Max Muller's

Ruskin's Ethics of the Dust. ↑also, one Volume of Stones of Venice↓

---

[3] For this statement on Jean-Baptiste Biot, see Charles-Augustin Sainte-Beuve, *Nouveaux Lundis,* 13 vols., 3rd ed. (Paris, 1870), II, 94.

William Blake's Poems
Boswell's Johnson (?)

[8] Put one good book into a public library, say, *Lord Brooke's Life of Sir Philip Sidney,* or Aubrey, or *Wood's Athenae Oxonienses,* & the library instantly obtains & keeps an affectionate interest in the mind of all scholars in the town.
 Pepys's Diary
 Cavendish's Life of Wolsey

[9] 1876   White's Natural & Antiquities of Selborne ⟨b⟩By *Gilbert White.* London Macmillan & Co. 1875 8vo pp. 591, $12.00

[10] [blank]
[11] Frere's Aristophanes
Life of Lessing
New America, Dixon

———

Sh⟨e⟩leiermacher's Essay on Σιρōνεὶα

———

Max Muller's article ⟨i⟩on "Comparative Mythology," in the *Oxford Review* 1856.
And his late book called "Science of Language."

————

Small's "Hand-book of Sanscrit Literature". *See my ms. LN* 120

———

[12]–[13] [blank]
[14] Wm. F. Poole, Librarian   Athenaeum[4]

[15]   *Boston Athenaeum*

———

Fraser's Magazine, 1864, *Nala & Damayanti*

———

Memoires de Duclos.

———

[4] A blue paper insert, measuring 10.9 × 9.3 cm and bearing writing not in Emerson's hand, is loose between pp. [14] and [15].

330

"Cultur der Renaissance in Italien" by Burkhardt ("a very satisfactory treatise on that Epoch, omitting art, which he promises in another volume." J[ames]. E[lliot]. C[abot].)

———

Landor's Complete Works

———

E[rnest]. Renan makes reference to "le beau Memoire de M. Naudet dans les Memoires de l'Academie des Inscriptions et Belles Lettres, T[ome]. XIII. nouvelle série,"—for slaves of Crassus[5]

[16] Coppet et Ferney, See S[ainte-]Beuve   Portraits de femmes p. 141

[17] 1876   *Concord Library.*
     Life of Lessing
     Landor's Works
     Hazlitt's Translation of Montaigne
     Plutarch's Morals
     Miss Martineau's Egypt   3 vols
     ⟨Montaigne's Essays   Hazlitt's⟩
     Chaucer
     George Herbert's Poems
     Life of Lord Herbert of Cherbury
     Emerson's Forest Trees
     King Arthur & Knights of the Round Table
     Tennyson
     Knox on Races.
     Luther's Table Talk
     ↑Ruskin↓

Harriet Martineau's Autobiography
I Promessi Sposi

[5] Although the precise source of Emerson's reference is unknown, comparable comment on Joseph Naudet (1786–1878) appears in *Nouvelle Biographie Générale,* 1855–1870, XXXVII, 521. Naudet's *Sur les Secours Publics chez les Romains* was published in Paris in 1838 as volume XIII of *Recueil de l'Académie des Inscriptions et Belles-Lettres.*

Faustina   see *V* 65,
Edwd L. Pie⟨e⟩rce's *Memoir* & *Letters of Sumner*
↑Edwd↓ Dowden's ⟨Sch⟩Shakspe⟨a⟩re

[18]   *Oriental Books.*
    Akhlak-y-Jalaly.   Mahometanism
    Vedas. Rig Veda Sanhita. Wilson
    Bhagavat Geeta. Charles Wilkins
    Vishnu Purana.
    Bhagavata Purana.
    Upanishads: Translated by Dr. E. Roer
    Institutes of Menu. Sir W. Jones
    Lotus de la Bonne Loi. Burnouf
    Bibliotheca Indica, Vol. XV, containing *Mandukya Upanishads,*[n]
    &c   Translated by Dr. E. Roer. Calcutta, 1853.

[19]   *Oriental.*
Antar or *Andar,* Arabian Prince in the 6th Century, describes in his
Moullaka his warlike deeds, & his love for Alba.
⟨Translated⟩ ↑described↓ by Sir William Jones. T. Hamilton translated
it. London, 1819. 4. vols.

———

See article *Antar* in the American Encyclopaedia.

———

[20]–[21] [blank]
[22] *Michelet, Renaissance.*[n] p 168[–169][6]
"M Vitet proved in his *Cathedrale de Noyon,* that the Gothic works,
which we had believed anonymous, were built by known people, by
free-masons, laie & married.
In 1846, L'Académie des beaux-arts, by the organ⟨e⟩ of Raoul Ra-
chette, launched a manifesto against the Gothic.
M. Violet Leduc, man of sense as well as distinguished artist, found a
word to save the situation,—the word *national,* "Tis the national architecture they are attacking."

    [6] Emerson withdrew Jules Michelet's *Renaissance,* which is vol. VII of his *Histoire de
France,* 17 vols. (Paris, 1833–1866), from the Boston Athenaeum May 13–June 8 and
June 30–September 4, 1865.

[23] M. Laviron, *"Revue Nouvelle"* 1846–7, threw himself into the contest between the Greeks & the Goths. *Assez d'imitations. Essayez d'inventer.*

Then M. Jules Quichersat proves that *Gothic did not calculate* till 15th Century. Thirty years after Brunelleschi, they raised the Spire of Strasburg, (1439), falsely ascribed to Erwin. And if these Gothic churches still stand, 'tis because they are perpetually repaired. Every part is changed and renewed, & ↑on↓ the prized antiquities he reads recent dates; 1730 on the great rose of Notre Dame.

[24] [blank]
[25] Hogg's Life of Shelley. *A*[rthur] *H*[ugh] *C*[lough]

———

In 1858 A. H. Clough writes "The Frenchman who translated the Canterbury Tales has found at Paris the original of the Squiers Tale, in 30 000 lines. I wonder if it is like Spenser's in any respect."

———

Barth's Africa   Clough's Remains. p. 289[7]

———

Sir Philip Sidney's Life, By Mrs Davis. Ticknor & Fields   1 vol
$1.00.

———

   [26] Tom Ward tells me his father's great value of "La cité antique"   par   Fustel de Coulanges.
      Aug., 1870.
[27][8] *May, 1872.*[n]
Spencer F Baird's Annual Record of Science & Industry for 1871. (Harper & Bros.)
↑Book Library folios   *NY* 102↓

   [7] For Clough's statement, see his letter of April 10, 1858, to Professor Francis J. Child in *Letters and Remains of Arthur Hugh Clough* ... (London, 1865), p. 284. This volume is in Emerson's library. On pp. 288–290 of the same volume is a letter of October 1, 1858, to Charles Eliot Norton, which contains a reference to "Barth's 'Africa,' " that is, Heinrich Barth, *Reisen und Entdeckungen in Nord-und-Central-Afrika in den Jahren 1849 bis 1855* ... , 4 vols. (Gotha, 1857–1858).
   [8] The entries on p. [27] are in pencil, except for "Book ... NY 102". A slip of paper, measuring 2.7 × 9.9 cm, is pasted to the top right corner of p. [28], where it was probably used as a marker.

Le Coque aux cheveax d'or

[28] [blank]
[29] 1873   *Concord Library*
    Dr Legge. Life of Confucius
Novr. 15. Books which should be in Concord Library

————

Jowett's Translation of Plato.

————

↑W. S.↓ Landor's Works—

————

Luther's Table Talk

————

⟨B⟩Plutarch's Morals

————

Eckermann's Conversations of Goethe.

————

Timrod's Poems

————

Professor Gray's Darwiniana

[30] '76 Dec.
    In the Levant. By C. D. Warner

————

Darwiniana. By Asa Gray.

————

The Ottoman Power in Europe   By Edward A. Freeman, 1877

————

Biographical Magazine. *Trubner & Co.* June 1877   first number   containing lives of T Carlyle ↑22 pages↓, & George Sand

————

[31] ——— 1877.
    Literature Primers. Shakspere. ⟨b⟩By Edward Dowden. LL.D.
↑London: Macmillan & Co. 1877↓
↑See *"The Academy"* of Sept. 29, 1877↓

Exploration of the Colorado River   by F. W. Rudler
↑Washington, Gov. Printing Office 1875↓

[32]–[38] [blank]
[39]   Welsh Books

[40]–[48] [blank]
[49]   Carlyle's List.

[50]–[5⟨o⟩1] [blank]
[5⟨1⟩2][9] See on Books some good notes in *LI* 94, 116, 117,
[118–119]

[5⟨2⟩3]   *Books.*
     John Newton said, "The best way to prevent a bushel being filled
with chaff, is to fill it with wheat."

Proverbs are the poetry & literature of unreading nations. Books the
immense advantage of the civilized.
———
There are nations subsisting on one Book, *NO* 272, *E* 192,
———
We want a Library just as much as we want a shoe-shop, or a bakery,
or a blacksmith. *S* 208,
———
Painting & Sculpture decay; Poetry & eloquence & science & history
are perennial through Books, *S* 51,
———
We must read between the lines, *LN* 195,
———
Asylums of the Mind. *D* 202

[54] Books written for one reader. ⟨*VA* 206⟩ *BL* [114–]115[–116]

---

[9] A cardboard strip, measuring 2.2 × 9.2 cm, is pasted to the top right corner of
p. [52], where it was probably used as a marker.

"The poet wounded writes a satire, & it remains to the day of the resurrection." *Firdousi.*

A well-read man can always find the originality of a new writer in an old book. 'Tis only a new crater of an old volcano. *FOR* 238

Cherish printing: it is your lot in the urn;—said Galiani to the French.[10]

———

Love of reading,—What is that? It is to exchange those stupid hours which come in every life, for delightful hours.
Many times the reading of a book has made the fortune of the reader,—has decided his way of life.

[55] ———
↑Bis↓ ⟨We must read between the lines. *LN* 195⟩

———

Best value of books, that they suggest more thoughts than they record,↑—↓that the reader, once warmed, thinks faster & better than the author.

———

⟨What with⟩ ↑Vain is the↓ reading that ends in reading? *CD* 50 [actually 49]

———

Best of literature is perhaps the feeling of immortality it awakens.[11]

———

When you find narrow religion, you find narrow reading.

———

What is the most certain mark of character? To know the man, I shall not read the lines on his hand, but ⟨see⟩ ↑⟨observe⟩↓ ↑inquire↓ what books he reads.

———

[10] The statement by Fernando Galiani is quoted in Charles-Augustin Sainte-Beuve, *Causeries du Lundi,* 15 vols. (Paris, 1851–1862), II, 339, and the statement by Firdousi, above, is quoted in the same work on I, 339. See *JMN,* XIII, 271, 278.
[11] Cf. "Books," *W,* VII, 190.

Best value of books,—that they suggest more thoughts than they record,—that the reader thinks faster & better than his author.

[56] ——
Books written for one reader, & even for the writer only. *ST* 126

——

'Tis with thought as with the thunderbolt; which strikes but an inch of ground, but the light of it fills the horizon. *KL* 173.

——

Plenty of books, but they require good readers; the meadow is full of milk, but it needs a cow to extract it. &

——

"study of Eternity smiled on me." *Van Helmont.*[12]

——

⟨The⟩ ↑Schools, Churches, Galleries, Acquaintances, yes all good,— but the↓ friend, the true Power that abode with us, is, the book,— which made night better than the day;—that may well be counted.

——

[57] The ⟨value⟩ essential ground of a new book is a new spirit.

——

Reading that ends in reading. *CD* 50 [actually 49]

——

I expect to find a great man a good reader, or, in proportion to the spontaneous power, should be the assimilating power. *N* 17—[13]

——

Loftiest ben⟨i⟩efit of books is that they set us free from themselves also. *LI* 117.

——

We all know something of the Omniscience of Music,—so absolutely impersonal,—yet every sufferer feels his secret sorrow reached. ⟨Yet⟩ ↑But↓ to a scholar there comes no hour or vexation, which, on a

[12] Jan Baptista van Helmont, *Oriatrike or, Physick Refined* ..., 1662, p. 12, misquoted. The quotation is used in "The Celebration of Intellect," *W*, XII, 131. See *JMN*, XIV, 57.
[13] "I expect ... power." is used in "Culture," *W*, VI, 142; "Quotation and Originality," *W*, VIII, 178; and "Address at the Opening of the Concord Free Library," *W*, XI, 504. See *JMN*, VIII, 254.

little reflection will not find diversion & relief in the library. His companions are few; at the moment, ↑he has none, but↓ year by year, these silent friends supply their place.

[58] ——

↑*Bis*↓ ⟨Love of reading, what is that? It is to exchange those stupid hours which come in every life for delightful hours.⟩[14]

——

"Victurus genium debet habere liber" *Martial* [*Epigrams,* VI, 61].[15]

——

"Quotq⟨a⟩ue Aderant Vates, rebar adesse deos." *Ovid.*[16]

——

> "All Peggy /read/heard/ she deemed extremely good,
> But chiefly praised the parts she understood."
>
> *Jane Taylor*[17]

'Tis sad to see people reading again their old books merely because they don't know what new books they want. *Y* 231

——

Note the composition of the Bibles & Epics of the nations,—the inception & growth of the Fable, or mysteries, or mythologies, till the ⟨g⟩Genius arrives. When this work is admirably done, all the contributors & hodmen ⟨perish⟩ ↑disappear,↓ & the memory of them, & the Master stands alone & ⟨a⟩unaccountable.

[59] ⟨I once interpreted t⟩The law of Adrastia, "that he who had any truth should be safe from harm until another period," I once interpreted as pronounced of originators. But I have discovered that the profound satisfactions,—which I take to be the sentence of Adrastia itself,—belong to the truth received from another soul,—come to us in reading, as well as in thinking.[18]

---

[14] "Love of . . . hours." is struck through in pencil with two diagonal use marks.
[15] "A book, to live, must have a genius." See *JMN,* XIII, 389.
[16] See Journal ST, p. [55] above.
[17] Jane Taylor, "Philip. A Fragment," *Memoirs, Correspondence, and Poetical Remains of Jane Taylor,* ed. Isaac Taylor (Boston, 1832), p. 281; this volume is in Emerson's library. See *JMN,* XIII, 378.
[18] The quotation is used in "Experience," *W,* III, 84. See *JMN,* XIII, 302–303.

Witchcraft. Experience of not finding in a book what you remember to have read there. *LN* 195

The inserted sheet at the printe⟨r⟩r↑'↓s.

It makes a tie between men to have read the same book.

[60] What have we to do with reading that ends in reading? *NO* 264   *CD* 50 [actually 49]

The virtue of books is to be readable.

[In my college days it used to be ⟨was⟩ a proverb for impossibilities, "You might as well try to read Neal's History of the Puritans."][19]

Samuel Rogers said, "that whenever he heard of a new book, he read an old one."

Duclos remarks, that few distinguished works have been produced by any but authors by profession. *A.W. Schlegel.*

[61] "He that borrows the aid of an equal understanding, doubles his own: he that uses that of a superior, elevates his own to the stature of that he contemplates." *Burke.*[20]

All books fabulous, or only approximate statements. *N* 94[-95]

Each will read only what he already knows,—on all the rest his eyes will shut. *VO* 202[-203].

[19] "Neal's" is in ink over pencil; the top of Emerson's first bracket and the bottom of his second are each elongated to form the rules that set off this entry.
[20] This statement is paraphrased from "Substance of the Speech in the Debate on the Army Estimates in the House of Commons, on Tuesday, February 9, 1790." See *The Works of the Right Honorable Edmund Burke*, 12 vols. (Boston, 1865–1867), III, 219, and *JMN*, XIII, 403.

The old saying of Montluc, that "one man is worth a hundred, & a hundred are not worth one," is quite as true of books.[21]

Some minds are viviparous like Shakspeare,—every word is a poem. *TU* 216[22]

---

[62] "Books are the money of Literature, but only the counters of Science." *Hobbes.*[23]

The Bible will not be ended until the Creation is.

The virtue of books is to be readable.[24]

What a signal convenience is fame! Do we read all authors to grope our way to the best? No, but the world selects for us the best, and we select from these our best. *W.* 67

"Learn how to produce eternal children." *Demophilus.*[25]

---

[63] Louis XV remarked, "The claps of thunder would have been better than all this scratching of pens".[26]

---

[21] "The old saying . . . books." is struck through in pencil with a vertical use mark. See Journal ST, p. [215] above, and pp. [63] and [66] below.
[22] "Some minds . . . *TU* 216" is struck through in pencil with a vertical use mark. Cf. "Powers and Laws of Thought," *W*, XII, 18. See *JMN*, XI, 160.
[23] This statement is adapted from "For words are wise mens counters, they do but reckon them: but they are the mony of fooles, that value them by the authority of an *Aristotle*, a *Cicero*, or a *Thomas*, or any other *Doctor* whatsoever, if but a man." See Thomas Hobbes, *Leviathan, or The Matter, Forme, & Power of a Common-Wealth Ecclesiastical and Civil* (London, 1651; reprinted Oxford, 1909), p. 29.
[24] See p. [60] above.
[25] See "The Pythagoric Sentences of Demophilus," trans. Thomas Taylor, in William Bridgman, *Translations from the Greek* (London, 1804), pp. 133–134: "Learn how to produce eternal children, not such as may supply the wants of the body in old age, but such as may nourish the soul with perpetual food."
[26] This quotation is taken from Arsene Houssaye, *Men and Women of the Eighteenth Century*, 2 vols. (New York, 1852), I, 356–357. See *JMN*, XIII, 124.

Tout ce qui s'est fait de bien et de mal dans cette revolution est dû à des écrits. *André Chenier.*[27]

———

See Lord Mansfield's prophecy, *HO* 13 which I have printed in "English Traits."[28]

———

⟨What Montluc said of soldiers, "that one man is worth a hundred, and a hundred & a hundred are not worth one," is quite as true of books.⟩ ↑repeated from p. 61↓[29]

———

"What is bravely done is of one age; what is written for the world's good, of all ages." *Vegetius.* See *E* 74[30]

[64] ———
"We mark the aim (animus), and are untuned," said Goethe, that is, if the book was written for the irresistible beauty or force ⟨or⟩ of the story or of the thought in the writer's mind, we freely read, but if we detect that Miss Martineau wrote the story to bolster up some dogma of political economy, & thus the book is nothing but a paid opinion, we drop the book, *GL* 128

[65] ———
Gauss, I believe it is, who writes books that nobody but himself can understand, & himself only in his best hours. And Pierce & Gould & others in Cambridge are piqued with the like ambition. But I fancy more the wit of Defoe, & Cervantes, & Montaigne, who make deep & abstruse things popular. I like the spirit of Kean, who said, "the boxes, say you↑?↓ a fig for the boxes;—the Pit rose to me:" and of Mrs Stowe, who had three audiences for "Uncle Tom,"—the parlor, the kitchen, and the Nursery.[31]

---

[27] Quoted in Charles-Augustin Sainte-Beuve, *Causeries du Lundi* . . . , 1851–1862, IV, 117. See *JMN,* XIII, 269.

[28] For the use of Lord Mansfield's prophecy, see "The Times," *W,* V, 261–262.

[29] "What Montluc . . . books." is struck through in ink with a diagonal use mark.

[30] This quotation is Emerson's translation of "Unius aetatis sunt quae fortiter fiunt, quae, vero, pro utilitate reipublicae scribuntur, aeterna" as quoted by Robert Burton in *The Anatomy of Melancholy,* 2 vols. (London, 1804), I, 93, which is in Emerson's library.

[31] Karl Friedrich Gauss (1777–1855), German mathematician and astronomer, was director of the Göttingen observatory from 1807; Benjamin Peirce (1809–1880), Ameri-

[66] ⟨The old saying of ↑Marshal↓ Montluc that "one man is worth a hundred, and a hundred are not worth one" is quite as true of books.⟩ ↑Repeated again from p[p]. 61 & 63↓[32]

The Shaker at Harvard told me, ⟨that⟩ "he took up a sound cross in not reading."[33]

As long as you feel the voracity of reading, ↑read,↓ in God's name. *R* 105

A good head cannot read amiss. *IO* 190

↑Law of Adrastia. *IO* 24↓
Andre Chenier. *HO* 22.
        Vegetius, *E* 74
Nations fed on one book   *NO* 272
Literature inevitable. *TO* 30[–31]
Novels, *E* 259
Raft principle, *KL* 32
Criticism   VA 281
Florian   VA 59   Montesquieu   *VA* 62,
Latimer   VA 45

---

[67] But of one thing I am well aware, that it is comparatively of little importance that I praise books to you. You will not read them the more that I should, nor the less if I held my peace. A better orator than I pleads for them with some of you, & to some of you a stronger dissuasion than I or any man could attempt,⟨—d⟩debars you from their

---

can mathematician and astronomer, was professor at Harvard College 1833–1880; Benjamin Apthorp Gould (1824–1896), American astronomer, was founder and editor of the *Astronomical Journal.* The Kean anecdote appears in a review of Brian Waller Proctor's *Life of Edmund Kean* (London, 1835) in the *Quarterly Review,* 54 (July 1835), 115; see *JMN,* XI, 185. For the comment concerning *Uncle Tom's Cabin,* cf. "Success," *W,* VII, 286, and see *JMN,* XIV, 166.

[32] "The old . . . books." is struck through in ink with four diagonal use marks.

[33] During his several visits to the Shaker community in Harvard, Massachusetts, Emerson became acquainted with Joseph Myrick, who may be the source of this statement. See *JMN,* XIII, 90.

use. I mean that some men are born to read, & must & will read at whatever cost, & others are born to work & executive skills, that take tyrannical possession of the man, & so absorb [68] him that he has no ears or eyes for those pursuits which constitute the chief happiness of other souls. Books only put him to sleep. I surrender such willingly to the Fates,—I hope, in each case, noble ones,—that wait for them at the door.

———

English judges in the old times used to recommend prisoners to mercy, because they could read and write.

———

Transubstanti⟨u⟩ation of poetry. *FOR* 220[–221]

———

[68$_a$]^{34} Jan., 1860
    "Professor": Holmes
    Biglow Papers
    Self Help
    ↑Philosophy of sin lo. Hamilton↓
    ⟨Darwin⟩ Selden T[able] T[alk]
    Luther Table Talk
    Goethe   Eckermann
    Hazlitt T[able] T[alk]
    Spence's Anecdotes
    ⟨Dr Rom⟩ Coleridge T[able] T[alk]
    ↑Piozzi Anecdotes↓
    Helper   Impending Crisis
    John Brown
    Darwin on Species
    Starr King
    Nott   Types of Mankind
    Arnold's Roman History
    (Appleton) Two Volumes

[68$_b$] Niebuhr   Letters by Miss Winkworth

---

^{34} The entries on p. [68$_a$] are in pencil, except for the parentheses around "Appleton", which are in ink over pencil.

[68$_c$] [blank]
[68$_d$][35] ——
    Hodsdon's Memoirs
    ——

↑x↓ Starr King's Mountain book
    ——

↑x↓ John Brown

    De Vacca's De Soto Narrative ↑x↓
        pubd in Washington↑——↓
    ——

    Ballantyne's Residence in N.W. America
    ——

    Nott & Glidden. Types of Mankind ↑x↓
    Landor's Works ↑x↓
    ——

    Last Sticks ↑x↓
    ——

    New fagoted ↑x↓
    ——

Hazlitt ↑Table Talk↓
Asrayh ↑Lectures↓ ↑x↓

[69] Every sentence a cube. *VA* 87 [actually 88]
⟨Nations fed on one book⟩
Brave /actions/deeds/ of one time, but what is written for the use of
the state, of all time. *Vegetius E* 74
Classic & Romantic, *GL* 140, *FOR* 124
Mommsen on Poetry. *VA* 52
    ——

Of grand style, *RT* [133,] 154, 167,
    ——

See Selden's *Table Talk* p. 224
    ——

Of Rousseau's Émile, *Index M⟨i⟩ajor*, p. 300

[35] The insertions on p. [68$_d$] are in pencil; the rule following "Washington" is encircled with eight short pencil dashes.

[70]–[83] [blank]
[84] *Desireable Books*   Jan., 1875.
Cave Hunting, By W. ⟨D⟩B. Dawkins, Macmillan & Co 1874

[84ₐ] Genuine Poems of Ossian, Translated by Patrick McGregor, under patronage of Highland Society of London, 1. Vol. 12mo 1807.
        ↑Robt. McTavlane↓³⁶

[84ᵦ]–[88] [blank]
[89] ↑H.D.↓ Thoreau writes to D. Ricketson, Oct. 1, 1854, "By the way, let me mention here, for this is my thunder lately,—William Gil-pin's long series of books on the Picturesque, with their illustrations. If it chances that you have not met with them, I cannot just now frame a better wish than that you may one day derive as much pleasure from the inspection of them as I have."³⁷

[90]   *Books ⟨o⟩for a Lyceum Library.*
        Arago's Biographies
        Ferguson's· Architecture
        Life of Lessing
        Chronicle of the Cid
        Wright edition of Morte d'Arthure
        Plutarch's Morals
        Max Muller's
        Bhagvad Geeta   Wilkins' Translation
        Thoreau's Works
        ↑M.↓ Arnold's Essays.
        Coleridge's Literary Biography
        Lacy Garbett's Architecture

    ³⁶ "Robt. McTavlane" is in pencil. Beneath this insertion and upside down is written "Mr. R. W. Emerson", not in Emerson's hand.
    ³⁷ Henry David Thoreau, *Letters to Various Persons,* ed. Ralph Waldo Emerson (Boston, 1865), pp. 111–112, misquoted.

[91] Pepys's Diary
   Life & Works of Lessing. By Stahr, Translated by Evans
   Luther's Table-Talk.
   Eckermann's Goethe
   Selden
   Knox on Races
   Hodsdon's Memoirs
   Landor's Works
   Niebuhr's Letters, Translated by E. Winkworth
   Huc's Travels

[92]-[94] [blank]
[95]-[182] [leaves torn out]
[inside back cover] [Index material omitted]

Pocket Diary 17

1866

Pocket Diary 17 is devoted primarily to recording Emerson's lecture engagements for 1866. It also contains miscellaneous expenses, addresses, quotations, and memoranda. A few entries may have been made late in 1865 or early in 1867.

The notebook, bound in black stamped leather, is a commercially published diary entitled "POCKET / DIARY / 1866.", published by Wm. H. Hill, Jr., Boston. The covers measure 7.6 × 12.5 cm. The back cover extends into a tongue that, when the book is closed, fits into a loop on the front cover; the back cover also contains an expandable inside pocket. "DIARY / 1866" is stamped in gold on the top of the tongue. A paper label fastened to the spine is inscribed "1866. x".

The white, unnumbered pages, whose edges are marbled, measure 7.4 × 12.2 cm; pages 25–184 are lined. The book consists of a front flyleaf (i, ii); a title page (page 1); rates of postage (page 3); eclipses in 1866 (page 4); the phases of the moon and tide tables for 1866 (pages 5–17); an account, "MEMORABLE EVENTS / in the / Secession Rebellion, / Together with the / Fluctuations in Gold." (pages 18–24); daily appointments for 1866, three to a page (pages 25–146); pages for memoranda (pages 147–153); pages for cash accounts (pages 154–178); additional pages for memoranda (pages 179–184); and a back flyleaf (pages 185–186).

Entries by Emerson occur on forty-five pages. Printed matter in Pocket Diary 17 is reproduced here only in the sections on daily appointments, cash accounts, and memoranda. Dates are supplied where relevant. Otherwise, pages are designated as blank if they bear no inscription by Emerson; the presence or absence of printed matter is not specified.

[front cover verso] [blank]

[i]¹

R.W. Emerson
Concord, Masstts

¹ "50", in pencil, in the upper right-hand corner of p. [i] may be a stationer's mark.

[ii]–[24] [blank]
[25]² [Tues., Jan. 2] Boston ?
[Wed., Jan. 3] ⟨Concord⟩Salem   "Resources."

[26] [Thurs., Jan. 4] Concord.   "Social Aims". as read at Salem
[Sat., Jan. 6] Library Committee

[27] [Tues., Jan. 9] ⟨Hudson   A.S. Peet⟩

[28]³ [Thurs., Jan. 11] Erie   ⟨Res[ources]⟩A[ndrew] H Caughey
60 "Resources"
[Fri., Jan. 12] Oberlin   People's Books
     "Social Aims"   Salem Edition   50

[29] [Sun., Jan. 14] At house of Charles Paine
[Mon., Jan. 15] Laporte, Ind.   T[able] T[alk]   "Social Aims"   65

[30] [Tues., Jan. 16] Aurora, Ill.   S[ocial] A[ims]   50
     Rev. Dr. Forester   "Social Aims"
[Wed., Jan. 17] Princeton, Ill.   S[ocial] A[ims]   75
     Social Aims
[Thurs., Jan. 18] Rock Island   S[ocial] A[ims]   65
     Social Aims

[31] [Fri., Jan. 19]   75
     Davenport   ⟨Social Aims⟩   Res[ources].   50
               Remitted to the Lyceum   25.   Bennett
_____

20 Jan
Sent E⟨TE⟩llen a draft from the Nat[ional]. B[an]k. of Davenport, on
the Nat[ional]. Exchange B[an]k Boston, for $220.00

[Sat., Jan. 20] ⟨DeWitt⟩   ↑⟨DeWitt⟩↓

----

² On p. [25], "Boston ?" is in pencil; "Concord", in pencil, is overwritten by
"Salem" in ink to cancel.
³ On p. [28], "Res", in pencil, is overwritten by "A H Caughey" in ink to cancel;
"People's Books" is in pencil.

[32]⁴ [Mon., Jan. 22] Lyons   S[ocial] A[ims]   ↑75↓
[Tues., Jan. 23] ⟨DeWitt⟩ ?   DeWitt   Res[ources].   ↑50↓
[Wed., Jan. 24] Dubuque   T[able] T[alk]   75
    Social Aims   with T[able] T[alk] & Clubs

[33] [Thurs., Jan. 25] Freeport ⟨?⟩
[Fri., Jan. 26] Janesville   S[ocial] A[ims]   75
[Sat., Jan. 27] Delavan Wis.   Res[ources]

[34]⁵ [Mon., Jan. 29] ⟨Beloit ?⟩   T. Dwight
[Tues., Jan. 30] Kalamazoo   ⟨P[eople's] B[ooks]⟩
    ⟨[Soc[ial] Cir[cle].]⟩   ↑Res[ources]↓   75

[35] [Wed., Jan. 31] Battle Creek   T[able] T[alk]   50
[Thurs., Feb. 1] Jackson   ⟨Res[ources]⟩   ↑S[ocial] A[ims]   75↓⁶
[Fri., Feb. 2] Ann Arbor   S[ocial] A[ims]   75

[36] [Sat., Feb. 3] Detroit   S[ocial] A[ims]   75
[Mon., Feb. 5] Toledo   ⟨T[able] T[alk] 75⟩   ↑S[ocial]. A[ims].↓

[37] [Tues., Feb. 6] Cleveland   Res[ources]   75
[Wed., Feb. 7] Buffalo   S[ocial] A[ims]
ˣdeposited $200. with a banker. Ask *Wm Dorsheimer* Esq⁷
[Thurs., Feb. 8] Dunkirk ⟨?⟩   ⟨Batavia ?⟩   S[ocial]. A[ims]. 50

[38]⁸ [Fri., Feb. 9] ⟨Ashtabula? E[dward] H Fitch⟩   Batavia   Social
Aims
[Sat., Feb. 10] Ashtabula?   E[dward]. H. Fitch

[39]⁹ [Mon., Feb. 12] Ashtabula?   Richmond Ind
    Isaac Kinley   Social Aims

---

⁴ On p. [32], the inserted "75" and "50" are in pencil.
    ⁵ On p. [34], "Beloit ?" and "PB" are each struck through in pencil with a diagonal
line; "Res" is in pencil.
    ⁶ "Res" is struck through in pencil with a diagonal line; "S A   75" is in pencil.
    ⁷ "ˣdeposited . . . Esq" is in pencil.
    ⁸ On p. [38], "Ashtabula? E H Fitch" is struck through in ink with a diagonal line;
"Ashtabula? E. H. Fitch" is in pencil.
    ⁹ On p. [39], "Ashtabula? . . . Ind", "Indianapolis", and "Cincinnati" are in pencil.

[Tues., Feb. 13] Indianapolis   B D Jones   Social Aims
[Wed., Feb. 14] ⟨Cincinnati⟩   ↑Wm. F. Phillips   Cinn. Ohio↓
⟨Al⟩Mansfield?   O H Booth
New Albany?   E[dward] S Crosier   Social Aims

[40]¹⁰ [Thurs., Feb. 15] ⟨Mansfield   O.H. Booth⟩
    ⟨Harrisburg ?   ↑Bata[via]↓⟩
⟨A[lfred] T Goodman   Box 330   Care Hon W[illiam] H Miller⟩
⟨Terre Haute ?   ⟨J⟩E[dward] Saxton⟩
[Fri., Jan. 16] Trenton ?   ⟨Antioch ?⟩

[41]–[42] [blank]
[43] Wordsworth said of Blake There is something in the madness of
this man that interests me more than the sanity of Lord Byron &
Walter Scott.¹¹

[44] [Tues., Feb. 27] Hudson.   C. Macy.   Social Aims   ↑60↓

[45] [blank]
[46] [Tues., Mar. 6] ⟨Lewiston⟩¹²
[Wed., Mar. 7] ⟨Lewiston⟩

[47] [Thurs., Mar. 8] ⟨Lewiston⟩
[Fri., Mar. 9] ⟨Lewiston⟩

[48] [Tues., Mar. 13] ⟨Lewiston⟩

[49] [Wed., Mar. 14] ⟨Lewiston⟩
[Thurs., Mar. 15] ⟨Lewiston⟩

¹⁰ On p. [40], "Mansfield   O.H. Booth", in pencil, is struck through in ink and
pencil with single diagonal lines; "Harrisburg . . . Saxton" is struck through in ink with a
diagonal line; "Harrisburg ?" and "Trenton ?" are in pencil.
¹¹ "Wordsworth . . . Scott.", in pencil, is used in "Poetry and Imagination," *W*,
VIII, 27.
¹² This entry for "Lewiston" and the six "Lewiston" entries that follow it are in
pencil; the first entry is struck through in pencil with a zigzag line, while each of the remaining entries is struck through in ink with a single diagonal line.

[50]–[53] [blank]
[54] [Fri., Mar. 30] At 2 o'clock to examine Miss Coe as teacher for Nine Acre Corner.

[55]–[127] [blank]
[128][13] [Tues., Nov. 6] ⟨Lynn ?⟩
[Thurs., Nov. 8] ⟨Lynn 8⟩Auburn Me   Social Aims

[129] [Fri., Nov. 9] Lewiston, Me.   Resources

[130] [Tues., Nov. 13] ⟨Lynn ?⟩Lynn[14]   Resources

[131]–[132] [blank]
[133][15] [Wed., Nov. 21] Hartford Conn   Alfred Hall
     Y[oung]. M[en's]. I[nstitute].   Resources
[Thurs., Nov. 22] ⟨Norwalk ?⟩
[Fri., Nov. 23] ⟨Harlem ?⟩

[134]–[138] [blank]
[139] [Tues., Dec. 11] Fraternity Lecture   Boston

[140]–[141] [blank]
[142] [Wed., Dec. 19] Salem   "Man of the World"
[Thurs., Dec. 20] Harlem.
     Dr T. F[ranklin]. Smith   128 Street between 4 & 5 Avenues
     Baptist Church corner of 5th Avenue & 127th street
          "Resources."

[143] Mrs [Anne Charlotte Lynch] Botta, 31 W. 37th st N.Y.
Miss Hannah W. Jackson   Care of John P. Jackson   Newark N.J.

---

[13] On p. [128], "Lynn ?" and "Lynn 8", both in pencil, are struck through in pencil by single diagonal lines; the latter is overwritten by "Auburn Me" in ink to cancel.
[14] "Lynn ?", in pencil, is overwritten by "Lynn" in ink to cancel.
[15] On p. [133], "Norwalk ?", in pencil, is struck through in ink with two diagonal lines; "Harlem ?" is in pencil.

351

[144] [Mon., Dec. 24] Newark, N.J.   Newark[16]   "Social Aims."
At Mrs Jackson's   Miss Hannah ↑W.↓ Jackson
[Wed., Dec. 26] ⟨Paterson.⟩Salem[17]   "Man of the World"

[145]–[152] [blank]
[153][18] Charles Ellet built in 1847 the Suspension Bridge at Wheeling, Va. 1000 ft span
&, in the same year, the temporary bridge over Niagara River, afterwards replaced by Mr Roebling's.

[154] From Chicago	200
Davenport	220
Chicago	300
Detroit	300
Buffalo	200
Indianapolis	165

[155]	Erie	⟨50⟩60
	Oberlin	⟨75⟩50
	LaPorte	65
	Aurora	50
	Princeton	75
	Rock [Island]	⟨50⟩65
	Davenport	⟨75⟩50
	Lyons	75
	Dewitt	50
	Dubuque	75
	Freeport	50

[156] *Athenaeum*[19]
———

Hogg's Life of Shelley

[16] "Newark" is in pencil.
[17] "Salem" is in pencil.
[18] The entry on p. [153] is in pencil.
[19] The works listed on pp. [156], [157], and [158] include Thomas Jefferson
Hogg, *The Life of Percy Bysshe Shelley*, 4 vols. (London, 1858); Sir James Gardner Wilkinson, *The Egyptians in the Time of the Pharaohs* (London, 1857); Thomas H. Huxley,

———

Wilkinson's Egypt

———

T.H. Huxley. Lectures on the elements of Comparative Anatomy

———

Robert Brown's Botanical Writings. Esenbeck's Collation

———

Chesterfield's Letters

———

Saussure: Ascent of the Alps.

———

[157] Trench   Past & Present of the Eng[lish]. Language

———

Thorpe. Laws of Alfred   Ancient Laws & Institutes of England.

———

Cultur de Renaissance in Italien. By Burkhardt.

———

Linnaeus, *Prolepsis*

———

Mahabarat

———

Michelet. Historie de France
[158] Wilkinson's Herodotus

———

[159]–[177] [blank]

Lectures on the Elements of Comparative Anatomy . . . (London, 1864); Robert Brown, *Prodromus florae Novae Hollandiae et Insulae Van-Diemen* . . . (Norimbergae, 1827); Philip Dormer Stanhope, 4th Earl of Chesterfield, *Letters,* ed. Lord Mahon, 5 vols. (London, 1845–1853); Horace Benedict de Saussure, *Voyage dans les Alpes* . . . (edition unknown); Richard Chenevix Trench, *On the English Language, Past and Present* (edition unknown); "Laws of Alfred," in *Ancient Laws and Institutes of England* . . . , ed. Benjamin Thorpe, 2 vols. (London, 1840); Jakob Christoph Burckhardt, *Die Cultur der Renaissance in Italien* (edition unknown); C. Linnaeus, *Prolepsi Plantarium* (Upsaliae, 1736); Jules Michelet, *Histoire de France,* 16 vols. (Paris, 1833–1866); and Sir James Gardner Wilkinson, *The History of Herodotus,* 4 vols. (London, 1858–1860). From the Boston Athenaeum Emerson withdrew Wilkinson's *The Egyptians* . . . , September 8–15, 1866, and his *The History of Herodotus* (vol. 1), December 1, 1866–January 5, 1867; and Michelet's *Histoire* . . . (vol. 10), April 4–May 22, 1866, and (vol. 2) September 15–November 7, 1866.

[178]²⁰ Leasts & mosts
power in the⟨?⟩ least form
  in the purity, in the nothing too much & of speech espe[c]ially poverty of words prodigality of meaning.

  _____

  & in architecture the law is, to economize material by
skilful arrangement;
[179] by thought

[180]–[181] [blank]
[182]²¹ T. & F. Lowell
      Post
      83 state street
      Bates

[183]²² Palgrave   Essays in Art.
F[rancis].P[hilip] Nash   96 E 19 ↑& 53 Exch[ange] Pla[ce]↓
J H Haven   34 W 23

[184] [inscription by Ellen Emerson]²³

[185]²⁴ Ber⟨ar⟩nard Roelker   49 W[illia]m St   N.Y.
Forster
$7. gold

Dr A V Lewis   14 Montgomery Place
H H Whitten   Box 4088   N.Y.

_____

Smyth & Emerson   Box 1956 P.O.   New York

²⁰ The entries on pp. [178] and [179] are in pencil.
²¹ The entry on p. [182] is in pencil.
²² The entries on p. [183] are in pencil, except for "F.P. Nash . . . E 19". Emerson
withdrew Francis Turner Palgrave, *Essays on Art* (London and Cambridge, 1866) from
the Boston Athenaeum April 8–17, 1867.
²³ Here and in all pocket diaries that follow, inscriptions by Ellen Emerson will be
noted in the text in this manner; the content of her inscriptions will not be specified.
²⁴ The entries on p. [185] are in pencil, except for "H H Whitten . . . New York".

[186] W[illia]m. T[orrey]. Harris, Corner Salisbury & Tenth streets, St Louis, Mo.
J.C. Thompson, P.O. Box 112. Nashville Tenn
J.E[dward]. Saxton, Esq. Terre Haute
Dr E[dward]. ⟨J⟩S. Crosier   New Albany

Lexington & W[est] Camb[ridge].

[railroad schedule omitted]

Feb 28

[inside back cover]²⁵ Dec 5   33   9.90
Hillsdale   w of Wells
Chicago Av & Dearbor[n]
S.G. Ward, 89 Madison Avenue

2 Jan   8¼ lb   2.75
17   10½   3.50
17 ⟨Feb⟩   7½   2.50

Picture
2 ft. 11, by 3 ft. 10

²⁵ "Lexington & W Camb." and "Feb 28", above, are in pencil; the entries on the inside back cover are in pencil, except for "S.G. Ward . . . Avenue" and "Picture . . . 3 ft. 10".

Pocket Diary 18

1867

Pocket Diary 18 is devoted primarily to recording Emerson's lecture engagements for 1867. It also contains miscellaneous expenses, addresses, quotations, and memoranda. A few entries may have been made late in 1866 or early in 1868.

The notebook, bound in black stamped leather, is a commercially published diary entitled "ILLUMINATED / DIARY / for / 1867. / Published for the Trade". The covers measure 7.5 × 12.5 cm. The back cover extends into a tongue that, when the book is closed, fits into a loop on the front cover; the back cover also contains an expandable inside pocket. "DIARY / 1867" is stamped in gold on the tongue. A paper label fastened to the space between the back cover and the tongue is inscribed "1867. x".

The white, unnumbered, gilt-edged pages measure 7.4 × 12.1 cm; pages 23–182 are lined. The book consists of two front flyleaves (i–iv); a title page (page 1); a calendar for 1867 (page 3); rates of postage (page 4); a table of stamp duties (pages 5–9); eclipses in 1867 (page 10); the phases of the moon and tide tables for 1867 (pages 11–22); daily appointments for 1867, three to a page (pages 23–144); pages for memoranda (pages 145–151); pages for cash accounts (pages 152–176); additional pages for memoranda (pages 177–182); and a back flyleaf (pages 183–184).

Entries by Emerson occur on seventy-nine pages. Printed matter in Pocket Diary 18 is reproduced only in the sections on daily appointments, cash accounts, and memoranda where relevant. Otherwise, pages are designated as blank if they bear no inscription by Emerson; the presence or absence of printed matter is not specified.

Laid in the notebook are the following enclosures: between pages 70 and 71, an unidentified newspaper clipping on Swedenborgianism; between pages 78 and 79, a folded pencil list, measuring 9.8 × 13.4 cm, concerning payment for apples; between pages 100 and 101, a folded pencil list, measuring 10.1 × 12 cm, concerning payment for apples; and between pages 144 and 145, a folded piece of paper, measuring 12.6 × 10.6 cm, bearing, not in Emerson's hand, the names of three Mexican scientists. In the back cover is a newspaper clipping of the obituary of Forceythe Willson (1837–1867) by Oliver Wendell Holmes.

[front cover verso][1] Dacier, Doctrines de Platon. Vol 1. p. 79

[i]   R.W. Emerson
                                                       Concord, Mass.

West[minster] Rev[iew]   1850 Oct   Hindu Drama   )C
1850 April   Persian Cuneiform   )C
⟨Oct⟩1848, Oct   Hindu Poetry   )C
Jan 1851   Makamat   )C
Anecdotes of Al Hariri   Spanish Lit[erature]   )[2]

[ii] [blank]
[iii] F.G. Wheeler, Stamford, Ct.
E.D. Sabine   Windsor Vt
J.T. Platt   New Haven
J.E Tristram, 54 Rutger st. N.Y.
S.H Emery   Quincy Ill
Darwin C. Carey. Rome, N.Y.
H. Catlin   Erie, Pa. Whittier Lit[erary] Assoc[iation]
J.N. Dickinson, Westfield Mass
C.S. Aldrich, Canandaigua, N.Y.
R McCurdy, Youngstown, O.
J.C. Paulison   Paterson N.J.
H.D. Preston, Fulton N.Y.

[iv]–[22] [blank]
[23] [Thurs., Jan. 3] Lowell,[n] Mass.   "Social Aims."   50

[24] [blank]
[25] [Tues., Jan. 8] ⟨Batavia   W C Walron.   E Taggart⟩
   ⟨⟨Clevelan[d]⟩Resources.[3]   ⟨75⟩   50⟩

---

[1] "35" and ".65", in pencil, in the upper left corner of the front cover verso may be stationer's marks.

[2] "West Rev . . . Spanish Lit   )", in pencil, is upside down. Each item in this list appeared in the *Westminster Review:* "Hindu Drama," 54 (Oct. 1850): 1–37; "Persian Cuneiform Inscriptions and Persian Ballads," 53 (April 1850): 38–57; "Indian Epic Poetry," 50 (Oct. 1848): 34–62; "Makamat" [anecdotes of Al Hariri], 54 (Jan. 1851): 323–335. Only the first three items are signed "C".

[3] "Batavia . . . Resources." is struck through in ink with a zigzag line.

[Wed., Jan. 9] ⟨Cleveland O.   Amos Townsend.⟩
Batavia   Resources   ⟨75⟩   50

[26] [Thurs., Jan. 10] Cleveland   Amos Townsend
    ⟨M[an]. o[f]. t[he]. w[orld].⟩Man of the world⁴   75
[Fri., Jan. 11] Jamestown N.Y.   C E Bishop.   Social Aims   75

[27] [Mon., Jan. 14] Fredonia N.Y.   A.H. Judson
    Resources   ⟨75.⟩   50

[28] [Wed., Jan. 16] Adrian, Mich.   S.   ⟨H[enry].C. Northrop⟩
    Social Aims   Mr [Samuel L.] Tait   ⟨75.⟩   50.
[Thurs., Jan. 17] ⟨Cleveland⟩
[Fri., Jan. 18] ⟨East Saginaw,ⁿ Mich.   Irving M. Smith⟩   75.⁵

[29]⁶ [Mon., Jan. 21] ⟨Pontiac Mich   Students' Lect[ure]. Assoc[ia-
tion]⟩
    ⟨Charles Hurd⟩   E[ast] Saginaw   ⟨75⟩

[30] [Tues., Jan. 22] At Detroit
[Wed., Jan. 23] ⟨Battle Creek Mich   P.H. Emerson⟩⁷   50.
[Thurs., Jan. 24] Chicago   Man of the World   75.

[31] [Fri., Jan. 25] ⟨Madison Wis   Social Aims⟩⁸
[Fri., Jan. 26] Madison Wis   Social Aims   75

[32] [Mon., Jan. 28] ⟨LaCrosse Wis   Social Aims   100⟩
[Tues., Jan. 29] LaCrosse, Wis.   Social Aims.   100   Hugh Ca-
meron
[Wed., Jan. 30] Winona Minn.   100   Man of the World   100

⁴ "M. . . . w.", in pencil, is overwritten by "Man . . . world" in ink to cancel.
⁵ "East . . . Smith" is struck through in ink with one vertical and four diagonal lines.
⁶ On p. [29], "Pontiac . . . Assoc" is struck through in ink with one vertical and two
diagonal lines; "Charles Hurd" is struck through in ink with a diagonal line.
⁷ "Battle . . . Emerson" is struck through in ink with three diagonal lines.
⁸ "Madison . . . Aims" is struck through in ink with four diagonal lines.

[33] [Thurs., Jan. 31] Faribault, Minn   J.W. Griggs ↑of Dike & Co↓

Social Aims   75
[Fri., Feb. 1] St Paul, Minn   Man of the World   100
[Sat., Feb. 2] Minneapolis   Man of the World
    W[illiam]. D[rew]. Washburn   ⟨75⟩   100

[34] [Mon., Feb. 4] From Minneapolis all day to LaCrosse, with Hole-in-the-Day in the car & in the ⟨om⟩stage, to Lacrosse.
[Tues., Feb. 5] $160 draft on 9th National Bank N.Y. from Thompson Brothers, 1st National B[an]k Minnesota for $160.
    St Paul, 2 Feb.

[35] [Wed., Feb. 6] Fond du Lac, Wis   Dr E.L. Griffin
    ⟨Man of the World⟩   Social Aims   75
[Thurs., Feb. 7] Oshkosh Wis   Man of the World   75.
[Fri., Feb. 8) Ripon

[36] [Sat., Feb. 9] Janesville Wis   Man of the World   50
[Sun., Feb. 10] Read at Mr   Church   "Immortality"
[Mon., Feb. 11] Lacon Ill.   Man of the World   75

[37] [Tues., Feb. 12] Peoria   ⟨M⟩Social Aims   75
Mr Coy was to send E[llen] T[ucker] E[merson] a draft
[Thurs., Feb. 14] Washington, Iowa   Man of the World

[38] [Fri., Feb. 15] ⟨⟨Rock Island⟩⟩
[Sun., Feb. 17] ⟨⟨Port Byron⟩⟩[9]

[39] [Mon., Feb. 18] ⟨⟨Freeport⟩⟩[10]   Nullers
[Tues., Feb. 19] Independence Iowa   Resources   75
Washapinnicon River
[Wed., Feb. 20] Cedar Falls   Man of the World

[9] "⟨Rock Island⟩" and "⟨Port Byron⟩" are each struck through in ink with a diagonal line.
[10] "⟨Freeport⟩" is struck through in ink with a diagonal line.

[40] [Fri., Feb. 22] Battle Creek   P.H. Emerson
Man of the World   55.

————

[J.G.] Lodge
[William F.] Neal[e]
[Henry] Willis

[Sat., Feb. 23] Draft of $240 from Merchants Savings Loan & Trust
Co., Chicago, on National Hide & Leather Bank, Boston, signed by
Charles Henrotin, Cash[ie]r

[41]¹¹ [Mon., Feb. 25] A. McCoy, Chicago
[Tues., Feb. 26] Quincy   J.M. Bishop   Mr Emery
Man of the World   75

[42] [Wed., Feb. 27] On the Mississipp⟨e⟩i River in steamboat to
Keokuk
[Thurs., Feb. 28] Keokuk, Iowa   ⟨Mr Emery   7⟩¹²
[Fri., Mar. 1] Des Moines

[43] [Sat., Mar. 2] ⟨Chicago⟩
[Mon., Mar. 4] Chicago   Eloquence 75
Draft by B B Wiley $100. sent to Ellen.

[44] [Tues., Mar. 5] ↑Dr Dunn   Rev J[onathan]. B[axter] Harri-
son↓
        Bloomington Ill   Mrs H Everly   Man of the World   50
[Wed., Mar. 6] St Louis   Social Aims   J J Bailey¹³
    Sent Ellen T[ucker]. E[merson]. draft from Chicago, $100.
[Thurs., Mar. 7] Bought a draft on First Nat[ional] Bank Boston for
100 of the Fourth Nat[ional]. B[an]k St Louis to my own order.¹⁴

[45] [Fri., Mar. 8] Kansas City   Crawford James
Man of the World

---

¹¹ The entries on p. [41] are in pencil, except for "Quincy   J.M. Bishop".
¹² "Mr Emery   7" is in pencil.
¹³ "Social Aims" is in pencil; "Aims" is overwritten by "J J" in ink.
¹⁴ "Bought a . . . order." is in pencil.

[Sat., Mar. 9] Lawrence   W M Johnson   Man of the World.
[Sun., Mar. 10] At Mr Tenney's Church   read "Immortality"

[46] [Tues., Mar. 12] ↑Sent letter & draft of 100 to Ellen↓
    St Louis   Phil[osophical] Society.   Inspiration
Bought a draft for 100 to my order from the Fourth Nat[ional]. Bank
of St Louis on First Nat[ional]. B[an]k. Boston
[Wed., Mar. 13] ⟨Springfield⟩

[47] [Thurs., Mar. 14] Cincinnati   W.F. Phillips
    Social Aims   100
[Fri., Mar. 15] Marietta   Ad.H. Siegfried   Social Aims   50
[Sat., Mar. 16] Marietta   "Man of the World"   50

[48] [Sun., Mar. 17] Read at the Unitarian Ch[urch].
    "Immortality"
[Mon., Mar. 18] (Cincinnati)[15]
[Tues., Mar. 19] Pittsburgh,   J.B. Scott   Man of the World
    J Morgan

[49][16] [Wed., Mar. 20] (Marietta)
[Fri., Mar. 22] Pittsburgh

[50] [blank]
[51] [Wed., Mar. 27] Brunswick, Maine   Man of the World. $50.
    Mr Cutts
    Mr Newman
    Mrs Coburn

[52]–[56] [blank]
[57] [Sun., Apr. 14] "Radical" Lecture in Boston   S.H. Morse

[58]–[60] [blank]
[61] [Fri., Apr. 26] Malone N.Y.   Cantwell   W.P. Cantwell

[15] "(Cincinnati)" is in pencil.
[16] The entries on p. [49] are in pencil.

[62] [Mon., Apr. 29] ⟨Champlain⟩Champlain, N.Y.[17]   C.A. Foote

[63]–[64] [blank]
[65] [Tues., May 7] Framingham   C C Esty[18]

[66] [Sun., May 12] Radical Lecture   "Rule of Life"

[67] [Tues., May 14] ⟨Framingham?⟩Framingham.[19]   C.C. Esty

[68] [Fri., May 17] Poughkeepsie   Vassar College   Man of the World

[69]–[71] [blank]
[72] [Thurs., May 30] Unitarian Meeting

[73]–[94] [blank]
[95] [Wed., Aug. 7] [John] W[eiss] & [David Atwood] Wasson?

[96] [Thurs., Aug. 8] [John] W[eiss] & [David Atwood] Wasson?

[97] [Sun., Aug. 11] Northampton ?

[98]–[105] [blank]
[106][20] [Sun., Sep. 8] ⟨Northampton?⟩Northampton & Florence—
   "Truth" and "Success"
⟨[Mon., Sep. 9]⟩ Tuesday 10   Pittsfield
   Medical Association   Man of the World

[107] [Tues., Sep. 10] ⟨Radical Club at J[ohn].T. Sargeant's⟩[21]

[108]–[124] [blank]
[125] [Tues., Nov. 5] ⟨Portsmouth   B[enjamin]. Norton⟩

[17] "Champlain", in pencil, is overwritten by "Champlain, N.Y." in ink to cancel.
[18] "Framingham . . . Esty" is in pencil.
[19] "Framingham?", in pencil, is overwritten by "Framingham." in ink to cancel.
[20] On p. [106], "Northampton?", in pencil, is overwritten by "Northampton" in ink to cancel; "Pittsfield", in pencil, is overwritten by the same in ink.
[21] "Radical . . . Sargeant's", in ink, is struck through in pencil with a zigzag line.

[126] [Wed., Nov. 6] ↑Munroe↓   ⟨Roxbury⟩Roxbury,[22] Mech[an-ics]. Instit[ute].
        ↑⟨(Munroe)⟩↓   "Man of the World"

[127]–[130] [blank]
[131] [Thurs., Nov. 21] J[ames].T. Fields
[Fri., Nov. 22] Wendell Phillips's Lecture at Concord

[132] [Mon., Nov. 25] New London,   ⟨Q⟩G.F. Tinker
        "Man of the World"
[Tues., Nov. 26] ⟨New Bedford ?⟩New Bedford[23]   "Eloquence"

[133] [Wed., Nov. 27] ⟨New London 27 ?⟩Portsmouth N.H.[24]
        B[enjamin]. Norton.   "Man of the World"
[Thurs., Nov. 28] ⟨⟨‖ . . . ‖ 28 ?⟩J[ames] T Fields⟩Thanksgiving Day[25]

[134] [Sat., Nov. 30] Saturday Club

[135][26] [Tues., Dec. 3] Buffalo   H[oward] H Baker   Eloquence
[Wed., Dec. 4] Cleveland   W[illiam].N. Hudson   Eloquence
[Thurs., Dec. 5] I offered Erie   Eloquence

[136] [Fri., Dec. 6] Painesville, O.   M.L. Saunders
        "Social Aims"

[137] [Mon., Dec. 9] ⟨Manchester Iowa   Jas. P. Rule⟩
[Wed., Dec. 11] ⟨Mendota Ill   J N Battin⟩[27]

---

[22] "Roxbury", in pencil, is overwritten by "Roxbury," in ink to cancel.

[23] "New Bedford ?", in pencil, is overwritten by "New Bedford" in ink to cancel.

[24] "New London 27 ?", in pencil, is overwritten by "Portsmouth N.H." in ink to cancel.

[25] " ‖ . . . ‖ . . . Fields", in pencil, is overwritten by "Thanksgiving Day" in ink to cancel.

[26] The entries on p. [135] are in pencil, except for the three occurrences of "Elo-quence".

[27] "Manchester . . . Rule" and "Mendota . . . Battin" are each struck through in ink with an X.

[138] [Thurs., Dec. 12] Lincoln, Ill.   R.W. Beard   "Social Aims"
[Fri., Dec. 13] Jacksonville, Ill.   J[ohn]. A[llen]. Ayers
    ↑[Charles Moseley] Eames   [George W.] Williams↓
    "Social Aims" $90.
[Sat., Dec. 14] Mattoon, Ill.   W.B. Dunlap   ↑⟨Eames   Williams⟩↓
    "Success."

[139] [Sun., Dec. 15] Mattoon   "Immortality"
    ↑Dr Noyes   Mr Lane   Dr Wilcox   Rev Mr Drouthet↓
[Mon., Dec. 16] St Louis   J.J. Baily   "Success"
[Tues., Dec. 17] Alton, Ill.   R.W. Atwood   "Social Aims"

[140] [Wed., Dec. 18] Crossed the Missisippi⟨e i⟩on a skiff
[Thurs., Dec. 19] Des Moines, Iowa   Seward Smith
    "Success"   Desm[oines]   ⟨|| . . . ||⟩[Young] M[en's] L[ecture?]
    A[ssociation]
[Fri., Dec. 20] Davenport, Iowa   H.W. Bennett   "Success"

[141] [Sat., Dec. 21] Galesburg Ill   T J Hale, Briggs, Walbridge
    "Social Aims"
Mr Briggs will send me a draft of 100, to my address in Concord

Chicago, Dec 23 Draft of C Follansbee & Son on National Park Bank
of N.Y. for $300. B B Wiley to R W E

[Mon., Dec. 23] Chicago   E[dwin]. L[ee]. Brown   "Country Life"
    Safford   D. Gilman   J. Robson   Emily G.
    Rev. Mr Cushman, Cambridge

[142] [Tues., Dec. 24] ⟨Niles, Michigan   C B Thomas.⟩
    ⟨Y[oung] M[en's] L[ecture?] A[ssociation]⟩[28]
[Thurs., Dec. 26] Rev E.P. Powell   Adrian Mich   N.H.A.
    "Success"

---

[28] "Niles . . . YMLA" is struck through in ink with three vertical lines.

[143] [Fri., Dec. 27] ⟨Columbus, Ohio   E.L. Taylor
"Social Aims"⟩[29]
[Sat., Dec. 28] Steubenville Ohio   J. Buchanan   "Social Aims"
    Mr Reid

[144] [Mon., Dec. 30] Columbus, Ohio   "Social Aims."
E.L. Taylor

[145] *aufheben,* set aside
daseyend, extant
Gehalt

[146] Erie, Pa. Sent home a draft by Mr [Andrew H.] Caughey for
$250.

[147] St Louis Dec 17
Sent ↑home↓ a draft of Allen, Copp, & Nisbet, on Vila & Co. Boston,
for $300.

———

Send E[dwin]. L[ee]. Brown, my photograph

———

Send B.B. Wiley, my photograph, & 19 April Speech.

———

pd. Ely for 2 shirts, $9.00
    Nos. 3 & 4 Washington st. Chicago

[148] Marietta Ohio
send to ↑Col.↓ R[ufus].R. Dawes, a drawing of the Soldiers' Monument in Concord & of Acton Monument.
send Charles [Hazeltine] Goddard a carte du visite of Carlyle's head.

——— ———

    Sent it.

———

"Next time he will hit you harder."

[29] "Columbus . . . Aims' " is struck through in ink with two vertical lines.

Nature has a little taste for making Punch figures of aging men. If he is blonde & struts a little, she⟨g⟩ gives a baldness that is ridiculous; not the senatorial, but the shopkeeper kind; or knocks out a front tooth.

[149]³⁰ Out of hate of H[orace]. G[reeley]. they buy the Times. That is the capital of this paper[.]

Lake birds have a wild difference of taste from ours in this cold blue day. In old biography it is just as well & interesting that the man was awkward as graceful but ⟨very not⟩ by no means as well to him living. The seafowl sees the mournfull race of men[.]

[150]³¹ to remove grease use benzole or naphthaline   4010
to remove pitch, spirits of turpentine   alcohol
for paint benzine   camphene

      50
      35
    2.25
    2.50
    ————
    5 60

[151]³² ⟨50⟩   ·⟨6.75⟩5.60   at Boston
        ⟨35⟩   12.75   ticket to Buffalo
        ⟨2.25⟩   15.50   — to Chicago
        ⟨2.50   5.   at Buffalo
        ————   1.25

[152]   Nullus argento color est avaris
         Abdito terris inimice lamnae
         Crispe Sallusti, nisi temperato
         Splendeat usu.
                        Hor[ace]. Carm. 1, Lib. II [*Odes,* II, ii, 1–4]³³

³⁰ The entries on p. [149] are in pencil.
³¹ On p. [150], "4010" and the column "50 . . . 5 60" are in pencil.
³² The entries on p. [151] are in pencil.
³³ "Gold hath no lustre of its own; / It shines by temperate use alone, / And when in earth it hoarded lies, / My Sallust can its mass despise."

[153]   ——Non si male nunc et olim
        Sic erit.

                        Carm II. 2. [Horace, *Odes,* II, x, 16–17][34]

[154] Jan   B[oston] & P[rovidence]
              Plymouth
              Mich[igan]. Central
      Feb.   Mad River
              Barrett
      Mar.   C[hicago] B[urlington] & Q[uincy]
      Apr   Atlantic
              B[urlington] & M[issouri]
              Plymouth
              Boston
      May   Barrett
      June   V[ermont] & C[anada]
      July   B[oston] & P[rovidence]
              Mich[igan]. Cen[tral].
              Plymouth
      Aug.   Mad River & Barrett
      Sept   ⟨Barrett⟩ C[hicago]. B[urlington]. & Q[uincy].
      Oct   B[urlington] & M[issouri]
              Atlantic
[155] Nov.   ⟨Nov⟩Barrett

[156]–[175] [blank]
[176] Peter Bulkeley
      Edw[ard] Bulkeley
      Joseph Emerson   Men[don]
      Joseph Emerson
      ⟨T⟩Sam[uel] Moody

           E
           Sam[uel]. Moody
           Joseph E[merson]   Malden

[34] "Full oft the darkest day may be / Of morrows bright the sire. . . ."

W[illiam] Emerson
W[illiam] Emerson

[177] [blank]
[178] Among the negatives should be set down the name of the king
(& who was the coxcomb?) who when offered by a sophist to teach him
the art of memory replied he would give him ⟨more⟩ a greater reward
to teach him to forget.

[179] Chicago   Drake   Turner

    Miss Waterman   147 E Munroe St.
———

    Edward Ely, 3 & 4 Washington St   Chicago
———

    G[eorge].S. Phillips, Thornton, Ill.

[180]		
Jamestown	170	
Detroit	100	
Faribault	280	
St Paul, mailed at Fon⟨t⟩ du Lac.	60	
Chicago	300	1010[35]
Peoria	75.	

[181] W[illiam] B[ull] Wright, Goshen NY
    Walter F. Chester, Buffalo

    S L Blakeley   Poug[h]keepsie

    Stephen M Newman   Brunswick Me[36]

[182][37] Rev Henry W Brown   Augusta
    Providence R I
    Care of Stephen K Rathbone

---

[35] "Chicago . . . 1010" is in pencil.
[36] "S L Blakeley . . . Brunswick Me" is in pencil.
[37] The entries on p. [182] are in pencil.

Cleveland & Burlington

[183] S[amuel] G[ray] Ward   89 Madison Avenue
     F[rancis]. P[hilip]. Nash   96 E. 19th st   53 Exch[ange] Place
     J Haven Emerson   ⟨34⟩ ↑27↓ W 23[38]
     Mrs A[nne] C[harlotte] L[ynch] Botta   31 W 37
     C. Emerson, 50 Broad St   Box 1956 PO

[184][39] J[ames]. Ingersoll Wyer Jr   Northfield Minn

Rev L.F. Waldo—Quincy, Ill.
Judge N. Holmes   223 Chestnut st.   between 2d & 3d
C.C. Gage, Lacrosse Wis
List of Books for C[harles] H[azeltine] Goddard

[inside back cover] Corn in Illinois   50 bushels to the acre is well
plenty of good land at $5. per acre $5.

Lawrence   3 days   1550

[38] "27" is in pencil.
[39] The entries on p. [184] and the inside back cover are in pencil, except for
"Lawrence . . . 1550".

Pocket Diary 19

1868

Pocket Diary 19 is devoted primarily to recording Emerson's lecture engagements for 1868. It also contains miscellaneous expenses, addresses, quotations, and memoranda. A few entries may have been made late in 1867; as noted in the text, a few entries were made early in 1869.

The notebook, bound in black stamped leather, is a commercially published diary entitled "ILLUMINATED / DIARY / for 1868. / Published / for the Trade". The covers measure 7.5 × 12.4 cm. The back cover extends into a tongue that, when the book is closed, fits into a loop on the front cover; the back cover also contains an expandable inside pocket. "DIARY / 1868" is stamped in gold on the tongue. A paper label fastened to the spine is inscribed "1841.—1868. x".

The white, unnumbered, gilt-edged pages measure 7.3 × 12.2 cm; pages 25–184 are faintly lined. The book consists of a front flyleaf (i, ii) that has been torn out; a title page (page 1); a calendar for 1868 (page 3); a table of time differences relative to Boston and New York (pages 4–5); rates of postage (page 6); a table of stamp duties (pages 7–11); eclipses in 1868 (page 12); the phases of the moon and tide tables for 1868 (pages 13–24); daily appointments for 1868 and January 1–January 18, 1869, three to a page (pages 25–152); a page for memoranda (page 153); pages for cash accounts (pages 154–178); additional pages for memoranda (pages 179–184); and a back flyleaf (pages 185–186).

Entries by Emerson occur on fifty-seven pages. Printed matter in Pocket Diary 19 is reproduced only in the sections on daily appointments, cash accounts, and memoranda where relevant. Otherwise, pages are designated as blank if they bear no inscription by Emerson; the presence or absence of printed matter is not specified.

[front cover verso] 36
           hmo
           ho[1]

[1] "36 . . . ho" is in pencil.

Council of Library
_____

Rev. Dr [James] Walker
Prof H W Torrey
 S[amuel]. Eliot, Esq
 F[rancis]. E[dward]. Parker Esq
Prof Wolcott Gibbs
Prof F[rancis]. J[ames]. Child

[i]–[ii] [leaf torn out]
[1]–[24] [blank]
[25]² Sanscrit
Hima   cold   Hiems Himalaya Imaus
Cniz   snow   nix niege
Gal   cold   gelu (gel Fr.)   kald   cold
Arna   arnava   river   hence Arno Erne R⟨i⟩hin
Taranta, torrent
Marmaru, rock   marmor marbre

[26]–[33] [blank]
[34] [Wed., Jan. 29] Salem Lyceum   "Eloquence,"
[Thurs., Jan. 30] Cambridge   Lecture on Immortality

[35]–[37] [blank]
[38] [Tues., Feb. 11] Stamford   Social Aims³

[39]⁴ [Wed., Feb. 12] ⟨⟨Can[andaigua]⟩⟩Rome   Charles Tuttle⟩
 ⟨Miss Emma Lazarus   36 W. 14th st⟩
[Thurs., Feb. 13] ⟨Rome⟩   Thursday   ⟨Canan[daigua]⟩   D[arwin] C
Carey
 "Social Aims"
[Fri., Feb. 14] Canandaigua   "Social Aims"

---

² The entries on p. [25] are in pencil.
³ "Stamford . . . Aims" is in pencil.
⁴ On p. [39], "⟨Can⟩Rome . . . D C Carey" is in pencil; "Canandaigua", in pencil, is overwritten by the same in ink.

[40]-[46] [blank]
[47] [Sat., Mar. 7] Leicester   "Society in America"
    Mr Everett Finley   Mrs E.H. Flint.
[Sun., Mar. 8] "Immortality"

[48]-[57] [blank]
[58] [Thurs., Apr. 9] ⟨Dickens at Union Club⟩

[59]-[60] [blank]
[61] [Mon., Apr. 20] Brooklyn N.Y.   "Eloquence"

[62] [Wed., Apr. 22] ⟨M⟩Brooklyn, N.Y.   "Man of the World."

[63] [Sat., Apr. 25] Brooklyn, N.Y.
    "Relation of Intellect to Morals."
[Sun., Apr. 26] Brooklyn   "Rule of Life"

[64]-[70] [blank]
[71] [Mon., May 18] F[ree]. R[eligious]. Club at 13 Chestnut st
[Wed., May 20] Oriental Society

[72] [blank]
[73] [Mon., May 25] Edith Forbes[5]

[74] [Thurs., May 28] Mr J[ohn].T. Sargent
    Read a paper on "Greatness" to the Religious Club.

[75] [blank]
[76] [Wed., June 3] Mrs A[dams] & Abby L[arkin] A[dams] sail
from N.Y.[6]

[77] [Sun., June 7] Lincoln

[78]-[79] [blank]
[80][7] [Tues., June 16] Senior Greek Examination
    9 to 11   No 23 University H[all]

[5] "Edith Forbes" is in pencil.
[6] "Mrs A & . . . N.Y." is in pencil.
[7] The entries on pp. [80] and [81] are in pencil.

[81] [Thurs., June 18] Overseers' Meeting[8]
at No 6 University Hall 11 o'clock, a m
Davis
Humphreys
Williams
Winlock
Tuttle
McCosh

[82]–[83] [blank]
[84] [Sat., June 27] Club[9]

[85][10] [Mon., June 29] Freshmen Greek Exam   8 to 11.   Harvard
Hall
      Overseers at 11. o'c
[Tues., June 30] Sophomore Greek Ex[am]
      8 to 11   in 12 Univ[ersity]. Hall

[86] [blank]
[87] [Sun., July 5] Dover, N.H.   F.E. Abbott
[Mon., July 6] 12 Washington st on the point.   Miss S[arah]. [Free-
man] Clarke
[Tues., July 7] Senior Greek Exam
      8 to 11 o'c.   in 12 Univ[ersity]. H[all].[11]

[88] [blank]

[89][12]   Columbus at Barcelona
              And on his far resounding path
              Sink crucifix & crown

---

[8] Emerson was a member of the Harvard University Overseers from 1867 to 1879.
Serving with him were Henry Lee, 1867–1879; Ebenezer Rockwood Hoar, 1868–1880;
Theodore Lyman, 1868–1880; John Codman Ropes, 1868–1876; and Martin Brimmer,
1870–1877.
   [9] "Club" is in pencil.
   [10] The entries on p. [85] are in pencil.
   [11] "Senior . . . Univ. H." is in pencil.
   [12] The entries on pp. [89], [90], and [91] are in pencil.

And from high tower & balcony
The light of Spain looks down
For Beautys dark dark virgin eyes
Gleam ceaseless round him now
As stars from still upheaving skies
Would newborn from the waves arise
On his advancing prow

G[renville] Mellen[13]

[90]   Now deeper roll the maddening drums
The mingling host, like Ocean heaves
While from the midst a horrid wailing comes
"And, high above the fight, ⟨the lonely bugle grieves⟩
    The lonely bugle grieves"

(Ode at celebration of the Bunker Hill fight 1825)
By G[renville] Mellen[14]

[91] [Brook Farm] West Roxbury,
April, 1841 opened
G[eorge] P[artridge] B[radford] 2½ years
    200 acres
        W[illiam]. Allen
        [Nathaniel] Hawthorne
        [Charles King] Newcomb
        [Warren] Burton
        Bancrofts, Blisses
    (Amelia ⟨Mah[?]⟩ Russell)
    3 new houses built
    1 old enlarged
        80 or 90

[92]–[97] [blank]
[98] [Fri., Aug. 7] Library Committee   Cambridge   10 o'clock

---

[13] Grenville Mellen's "Columbus," stanza IV, from *The Martyr's Triumph; Buried Valley; and Other Poems* (Boston, 1833), appears in *Parnassus* as "Entrance of Columbus into Barcelona."

[14] Grenville Mellen's "ODE. On the Celebration of the Battle of Bunker Hill, June 17, 1825," ll. 97–100, from *The Martyr's Triumph* ..., 1833, appears in *Parnassus* as "Bunker Hill."

374

[99] [Tues., Aug. 11] Middlebury ?[15]

[100]–[123] [blank]
[124] [Mon., Oct. 26] Boston Lecture

[125] [Tues., Oct. 27] ↑H[arvard]. C[ollege].↓ Overseers' Meeting

[126]–[130] [blank]
[131] [Sat., Nov. 14] ⟨New Haven   E. Marble⟩[16]
[Mon., Nov. 16] Meionaon   Greatness

[132]–[134] [blank]
[135] [Thurs., Nov. 26] Thanksgiving

[136] [Mon., Nov. 30] Weymouth   Leasts & Mosts[17]

[137] [Wed., Dec. 2] Concord   Historic Notes[18]

[138] [Mon., Dec. 7] Worcester   Leasts & Mosts

[139] [blank]
[140] [Fri., Dec. 11] Andover   "Art."[n]

[141] [Mon., Dec. 14] New Haven   E. Marble   "Greatness"
[Tues., Dec. 15] Dowse Institute   "Art"

[142] [Thurs., Dec. 17] Providence   87 Benefit Street
    W.B. Weeden
[Fri., Dec. 18] Andover

[143] [Mon., Dec. 21] Andover

[144]–[145] [blank]
[146] Morte d'Arthur   Vol 1. p. ⟨47⟩ xlvii

[15] "Middlebury ?" is in pencil.
[16] "New ... Marble" is struck through in ink with two diagonal lines.
[17] "Leasts & Mosts" is in pencil.
[18] "Historic Notes" is in pencil.

[147] [Sat., Jan. 2, 1869] Readings at Chickering Hall.

[148] [Tues., Jan. 5, 1869] Andover

[149] [Thurs., Jan. 7, 1869] Providence

[150] [Mon., Jan. 1, 1869] Andover

[151] [Wed., Jan. 13, 1869] Salem   "Hospitality."
[Thurs., Jan. 14, 1869] Providence
[Fri., Jan. 15, 1869] Andover

[152] [blank]
[153][19] 18   Rochester ?
           19   Tuesday
                 Buffalo
        20 W   Cortland ?
⟨Th⟩ 21 Th   Clinton
        22 F   Poughkeepsie
           23
           24
           25   New Haven
           26   Troy
           27   Catskill
           28   Albany
           29   Syracuse
           30   ⟨Syracuse⟩
           31   Syracuse

[154]–[169] [blank]
[170] Ernst Perabo   15 Hayward Place   [Not Mondays][20]

[171][21] Les Reformes de l'Enseignement;
      ⟨a⟩by ⟨Vacherot⟩ ↑Gaston Boissi⟨reau⟩er↓

[19] The entries on p. [153] are Emerson's tentative lecture schedule for January 18–31, 1869. He does not appear to have spoken in Cortland or Clinton, New York, or in New Haven, Connecticut.
[20] "Ernst . . . Mondays]" is in pencil.
[21] The entries on p. [171] are in pencil.

Rev[ue] des Deux Mondes   June 15, 1868   [pp. 863–884]

[172]–[173] [blank]
[174] Mr Dean   Dowse Institute[22]
↑Miss↓ J[uliette] H Dana   146 W 14 st

[175][23] T[icknor] & F[ields]
Qu of paying full cost of stereotype plates

ask Longfellow & Lowell
      Holmes of percentage insurance

[176] Mrs Kate Cobb   57 London Terrace   W. 23 Street ?

[177][24] photograph head for
⟨Mrs A.C.L. Botta,⟩
Mr E.L. Brown
⟨Mr S. Phillips Day⟩
  ↑B.B. Wiley↓

Mar. 19 Mr Trego
⟨L. Eaton⟩
T[icknor]. & F[ields].'s contract
H. Grimm books
Torbert
⟨Boardman⟩
Radical $3. & $20
Brooklyn
Professor Goodwin

[178] [blank]
[179] [*Memoirs of the Cardinal*] De Retz, [1817,] Vol. II p 120   *HO*
159

[22] "Mr Dean ... Institute" is in pencil.
[23] The entries on p. [175] are in pencil.
[24] On p. [177], "Mrs A.C.L. Botta,", "Mr ... Day", "L. Eaton", and "Board-man" are canceled in pencil; "B.B. Wiley" is in pencil.

[André] Dacier ⟨Platon⟩ Doctrines de Platon Vol. I. p. 79
———
   turn over the leaf[25]

[180] Aussi Antiphane, un des amis de Platon comparoit en riant ses écrits a une ville on les paroles le geloient en l'air des qu'elles estoient prononcées, et l'esté suivant, quand elles venoient à êstre echauffées et fondues par les rayons du soleil, les habitans entendoient ce qui avoit esté dit l'hiver, car les discours de Platon pour êstre entendus doivent estre echauffés et comme fondus par [181] les rayons d'une intelligence bien exercée.
   read Athenaeus as far 389[26]

[182] Athenaeum
[*Memoirs of the*] Cardinal De Retz, [1817,] II, 120

[183] Mrs Drury ⎫
   E L B[rown] ⎪
   B.B. W[iley]. ⎬ phot[ographs]
   S P Day ⎭
_____

Grimm, [*Deutsches*] *Worterbuch*
   1   Bande ⎫
   2   ⎬ perfect
   3   ⎭
   4, ⟨2⟩ ↑1st & 2d↓ lieferungs only
   5, seven lieferungs

[184] Mr Lazarus 36 W 14th st
Miss J[uliette].H. Dana 146 W 14th st

[185] [blank]
[186][27] Dalrymple Ld Kaimes's word of Alfred

---

[25] "turn . . . leaf" is in pencil. The work by Dacier has not been located.
[26] "Aussi Antiphane, . . . as far 389" is in pencil. The source of the entry on pp. [181]–[182] has not been located.
[27] The entries on p. [186] and the inside back cover are in pencil.

"I have left English as free as thoughts"
cited by Guizot "Etudes" sur Alfred et les Anglo-Saxons et in Article
de M. Ed. Thierry dans le Moniteur ⟨du⟩See 26 Aout 1656

See "L'Esprit dans l'Histoire" par [Édouard] Fournier, p 394

[inside back cover] Wm Everett
            G F Hoar
            E S Doe
            C K Dillaway
            J.S. Ropes
            J C Merrill
            F B Sanborn
            A Crosby

Mrs Sampson 57 N. Allen st

D.R. Sheridan Purchase st

J.O. Spear Ticknor & Fields

Ernst Perabo

Pocket Diary 20

1869

Pocket Diary 20 is devoted primarily to recording Emerson's lecture engagements for 1869. It also contains miscellaneous expenses, addresses, quotations, and memoranda. A few entries may have been made late in 1868 or early in 1870.

The notebook, bound in black stamped leather, is a commercially published diary entitled "ILLUMINATED / DIARY / for / 1869. / Published / For the Trade". The covers measure 7.6 × 12.4 cm. The back cover extends into a tongue that, when the book is closed, fits into a loop on the front cover; the back cover also contains an expandable inside pocket. "DIARY / 1869" is stamped in gold on the tongue.

The white, unnumbered, gilt-edged pages measure 7.5 × 12.1 cm; pages 25–184 are faintly lined. The book consists of a front flyleaf (i, ii); a title page (page 1); a calendar for 1869 (page 3); a table of time differences relative to Boston and New York (pages 4–5); rates of postage (page 6); a table of stamp duties (pages 7–11); eclipses in 1869 (page 12); the phases of the moon and tide tables for 1869 (pages 13–24); daily appointments for 1869, three to a page (pages 25–146); pages for memoranda (pages 147–153); pages for cash accounts (pages 154–178); additional pages for memoranda (pages 179–184), from which the bottom of pages 179–180 has been torn out; and a back flyleaf (pages 185–186).

Entries by Emerson occur on sixty-six pages. Printed matter in Pocket Diary 20 is reproduced here only in the sections on daily appointments, cash accounts, and memoranda where relevant. Otherwise, pages are designated as blank if they bear no inscription by Emerson; the presence or absence of printed matter is not specified.

Laid in between page 186 and the inside back cover is a library call slip measuring 12.8 × 6.6 cm and bearing book titles inscribed in Emerson's hand; the editors have numbered it pp. [186$_a$]–[186$_b$].

[front cover verso]¹ Art
                    Poetry & Criticism
                    Historic Notes
                    Hospitality
                    Leasts & Mosts
                    Greatness

[i] F. Bowen   Follen st
Bennett H. Nash   Instructor Italian & Spanish
Louis C. Lewis   Tutor in Mod[ern]. Lan[guages]   C. 29
Thos S. Perry   Tutor in Mod[ern]. Lan[guages]   S. 7

[ii] 1868
   Dec   1
           2   Concord
           3
           4
           5
           6
           7 M   Worcester
           8
           9
          10
          11 F.   Andover
          12
          13
          14 M   N[ew]. Haven
          15   Cambridgeport
          16
          17
          18 F   Andover
          19
          20
          21   Andover
          22

¹ The entries on the front cover verso and p. [i] are in pencil.

23
24
25
26
27
28
29
30   ⟨Andover⟩
31

[1]–[24] [blank]
[25] [Fri., Jan. 1] Milton
[Sat., Jan. 2] First Reading at Chickering Hall.

[26] [Tues., Jan. 5] Andover   "Leasts & Mosts"   Professor Phelps

[27] [Thurs., Jan. 7] ↑II↓   Providence   "Poetry & Criticism"[2]
    At Mr W.B. Weeden's

[28] [Mon., Jan. 11] Andover   "Hospitality."   Mrs A[nnie].
S[awyer]. Downs
[Tues., Jan. 12] Agassiz at Concord Lyceum

[29] [Wed., Jan. 13] Salem   Historic Notes
[Thurs., Jan. 14] ↑III↓   Providence   "Brook Farm" &c[3]
    "Historic Notes"
[Fri., Jan. 15] Andover   Greatness

[30] [blank]
[31] [Tues., Jan. 19] Buffalo   "Greatness"   Mr Wardwell
[Wed., Jan. 20] Bishop Coxe[4]
[Thurs., Jan. 21] ⟨Clinton⟩

[32] [Fri., Jan. 22] Poughkeepsie   Hospitality[5]

---

[2] "II" is in pencil.
[3] "III" is in pencil.
[4] "Bishop Coxe" is in pencil.
[5] "Hospitality" is in pencil.

[Sat., Jan. 23] ↑Mem.↓   New York   W[illiam]. B[ull]. Wright
      3⟨1⟩54 ⟨E⟩ W. 14th St[6]
from Walter T. Chester, Buffalo
Miss C.M Scholefield. Whitesboro.

[33] [Mon., Jan. 25] ⟨New Haven⟩
[Tues., Jan. 26] Troy   E.H.G. Clark   "Hospitality."
[Wed., Jan. 27] Catskill   C Moor   "Hospitality"[7]

[34] [Thurs., Jan. 28] Albany   Hospitality
[Fri., Jan. 29] Syracuse   C.D.B. Mills[8]   Hospitality

[35] [Sun., Jan. 31] ⟨Syracuse ?⟩

[36] [Wed., Feb. 3] Rochester   T. Dransfield   "Hospitality &c" 80

_____

      Rev. Clay McCaulay.
[Thurs., Feb. 4] ↑IV↓   Providence   "Hospitality &c"[9]

_____

Mrs H.C. Weston   Care of Wm Hilton & Co.   Boston   Tickets

[37] [Sat., Feb. 6] IV.   Readings,   Boston

[38] [Thurs., Feb. 11] ↑V.↓   Providence   Leasts & Mosts

[39] [Sat., Feb. 13] V.   Readings   Chickering's Hall

[40] [blank]
[41] [Thurs., Feb. 18] VI   Providence   "Greatness."[10]
[Sat., Feb. 20] VI.   Readings   Chickering's Hall

[42] [Mon., Feb. 22] ⟨Club at Union Club. House⟩
      ⟨Francis Philip Nash⟩

[6] "New York . . . 14th St" is in pencil.
[7] "C Moor" is in pencil.
[8] "C.D.B. Mills" is in pencil.
[9] "IV" is in pencil.
[10] "Providence", in pencil, is overwritten by the same in ink.

[Tues., Feb. 23] ⟨Randolph ?⟩Randolph
    W.E. Jewell[11]
leave Old Colony Depot 5.40 P.M.
At Mrs J[ohn] M[urray] Forbes to meet Perabo

{43} [Thurs., Feb. 25] ⟨Providence⟩[12] Overseers' Meeting

{44} [Sat., Feb. 27] VII   Readings.   Chickering's Hall   Club
[Mon., Mar. 1] Women's Club   M[ary]. M[oody]. E[merson].

{45} [Tues., Mar. 2] ⟨Randolph⟩   Plymouth[13]

{46} [Sat., Mar. 6] VIII.   Readings   Chickering's Hall

{47} [Tues., Mar. 9] Social Circle.[14]

{48} [Fri., Mar. 12] E[dwin]. P[ercy]. Whipple[15]
[Sat., Mar. 13] IX   Readings   Chickering's Hall

{49} [blank]
{50} [Thurs., Mar. 18] Music Hall   3.30 pm
    Triple Concerto of Beetho[ve]n Opus 56[16]

{51} [Sat., Mar. 20] X.   Readings   Chickering's Hall

{52} [blank]
{53} [Sun., Mar. 28] ⟨Horticultural Hall⟩[17]

{54}–{55} [blank]
{56} [Sun., Apr. 4] Discourse at Horticultural Hall.
[Tues., Apr. 6] New Bedford   "Art & Nature"

---

[11] "Randolph ?", in pencil, is overwritten by "Randolph" in ink to cancel; "W.E. Jewell", in pencil, is overwritten by the same in ink.
[12] "Providence" is canceled in pencil.
[13] "Randolph   Plymouth" is in pencil; "Randolph" is canceled in pencil.
[14] "Social Circle." is in pencil.
[15] "E.P. Whipple" is in pencil.
[16] "Music . . . Opus 56" is in pencil.
[17] "Horticultural Hall", in pencil, is struck through in pencil with a zigzag line.

[57] [Thurs., Apr. 8] Providence.   Reading

[58] [Sat., Apr. 10] ↑Concord↓ Library Meeting
[Mon., Apr. 12] Mr Gurney

[59] [Tues., Apr. 13] New Bedford   Poetry & Criticism
[Thurs., Apr. 15] Providence.   2d Reading.

[60] [blank]
[61] [Tues., Apr. 20] New Bedford   Historic Notes

[62] [blank]
[63] [Tues., Apr. 27] New Bedford   Leasts & Mosts

[64]–[65] [blank]
[66] [Tues., May 4] New Bedford

[67] [blank]
[68] [Tues., May 11] New Bedford   Greatness

[69] [blank]
[70] [Mon., May 17] Sargent's

[71] [Wed., May 19] Oriental Society.   Academy Room.   10 o'c
A.M.

[72] [blank]
[73][18] [Wed., May 26] Weiss at Mrs Sargent's   12 o'clock
Horticultural Hall   Women's Suffrage   11 o'c

[74] [Fri., May 28] Horticultural Hall   Free Religious
       10 o'clock

[75]–[78] [blank]
[79] [Sat., June 12] Committee at Dr Walker's house
⟨11⟩3½ o'clock ⟨A⟩P.M.   Sparks st

[18] The entries on pp. [73] and [74] are in pencil.

[80]–[82] [blank]
[83] [Sat., June 26] Club.
C[hicago]. B[urlington]. & Q[uincy].
Book for Mr Clarke, ⟨&⟩ F[ields]. O[sgood]. & Co.
Pratt, Lowell, Quincy, Reed.
Antislavery Journal
Tolman

[84] [Tues., June 29] Overseers at 9.30 at Librarian's Room

[85]–[109] [blank]
[110]¹⁹ [Wed., Sep. 15] ↑Borrowed books at Pub[lic]. Lib[rar]y
    Boston↓

Gertrude O'Gorman   59 Rutland Squar[e]   Boston

Edith O'Gorman

[111]²⁰ [Sat., Sep. 18] General Committee at Cambridge
⟨11 o' A.M.⟩   3½ o'clock at 6 Univ[ersity]. Hall

[112]–[115] [blank]
[116]²¹ [Sat., Oct. 2] 332.56   B[urlington] & M[issouri]

[117]–[124] [blank]
[125] [Sat., Oct. 30] Club.

[126] [Mon., Nov. 1] Examiner Club at Parker's   6 o'clock P.M.
    Prof. Atkinson reads on "Schools"

[127] [Thurs., Nov. 4] Overseers H[arvard]. C[ollege]. at Boston
    11 o'clock.
[Fri., Nov. 5] Natick   G.D. Tower   Subject   *"Social Aims"*²²

---

¹⁹ The entries on p. [110] are in pencil.
²⁰ The entries on p. [111] are in pencil, except for "General ... A.M."; "11 o'
A.M." is canceled in pencil.
²¹ The entry on p. [116] is in pencil.
²² " *'Social Aims'* " is in pencil.

[128]–[130] [blank]
[131]²³ 5th Henry IV. Chap 4
'It shall be felonie to use the craft of multiplicatio[n] of Gold & Silver'

[132]–[137] [blank]
[138] [Mon., Dec. 6] Attended *Examiner Club—*
& heard E[dward]. Atkinson's paper on Claims of Free Trade.

[139]–[140] [blank]
[141] [Wed., Dec. 15] Concord Lyceum.   Leasts & Mosts.

[142] [blank]
[143] [Tues., Dec. 21] Westford   "Success."

[144]–[146] [blank]
[147] Committee of Mod[ern]. Languages Rhetoric & Education
    S[amuel]. Eliot
    R[alph]. W[aldo]. E[merson].
    E[dward] E[verett] Hale
        I do not know whether Mr Eliot or R.W.E. is chairman

_____

A committee also on Scale of Merit & Methods of Discipline
R[alph]. W[aldo]. E[merson]
E[dward]. E[verett]. Hale
J[ames]. Walker
J.D. Rundle [actually Runkle]

[148]²⁴ ⟨S C⟩G[iles B.] Stebbins

[149] J E Cabot	1840
W A Richardson	1843
E E Hale	1839
W G Russell	1840

²³ The entry on p. [131] is in pencil. See John Reeves, *History of the English Law, from the Time of the Saxons, to the End of the Reign of Philip and Mary,* 4 vols., 2nd ed. (London, 1787), III, 237–238, for an explanation of the occasion and terms of this law as enacted by statute during the fifth year of the reign of Henry IV.
²⁴ The entries on pp. [148] and [149] are in pencil.

W Higginson
G O Shattuck

[150] [Memoranda.] *for 1870*
↑1 Feb Littleton↓
3 Feb ⟨Littl⟩Marlborough
7 Feb. Philadelphia
offered Tyngsboro 13 or 20 Jan.
        Harvard 19 Jan.

[151]–[153] [blank]
[154]²⁵   W[illiam] H[athaway] F[orbes]   600
                                               260
                                               140
                                              ─────
                                              1000

	[CASH ACCOUNT. JANUARY.]	
[Date.]	[Received.]	[Paid.]
19	100	12 50
22	60	1 50
26	100	75
27	60	37
28	100	10 75
29	75	1 65
		1 ⟨00⟩25
		9 5⟨5⟩0
		1 00
		80
		3 75
		⟨5⟩60
29		8 50
		8
		3

²⁵ The entries on p. [154] are in pencil. "53" is written below "1000".

388

[155]   [CASH ACCOUNT.   JANUARY.]
       [Date.]
       Jan 28 ⟨Draft of T. Squ⟨a⟩ire's of Albany N.Y (Squire's Banking
              Office) on Trevor & Colgate 47 Wall st N.Y. for two
              hundred & forty dollars pd .60 cts & made it payable to
              E[dward]. W[aldo]. Emerson⟩

                         ―――――
                         Pd.[26]
                         ―――――

[156]–[171] [blank]
[172][27]   [CASH ACCOUNT.   OCTOBER.]
                                   [Received.]   [Paid.]
                                   332 ⟨3⟩50   104
                                   140   1⟨6⟩7 50
                                                          8

              Commonwealth
              Radical

[173]–[181] [blank]
[182][28] think on such grounds as have been shown them that the appointment is premature ↑had better lie over for the present↓

              Nympha pudica Deum videt et erubuit
                              Richard Crashaw 1634[29]

[183] [Robert] Jamieson's [*Popular*] Ballads [1806,] Vol II p.
295[–296]
       To Music. By *Wm Stroude*

―――――――――――――――――――――――――――

[26] "Pd." and the rules that precede and follow it are in pencil. "Draft . . . Emerson",
in ink, is struck through in pencil with an X and a vertical line.
   [27] The entries on p. [172] are in pencil.
   [28] The entries on p. [182] are in pencil.
   [29] Richard Crashaw, "Joann. 2. Aquae in vinum versae," from *Epigrammatum Sa-*
corum Liber (Cantabrigiae, 1634). In Pocket Diary 22, p. [83] below, Emerson translates
this line "The modest water saw its God & blushed".

1688 | Burnet's History I. 822
1689 | Lord's^n Journals

$$\begin{array}{r} 141 \\ 3 \\ \hline 423 \\ \langle 7 \rangle 70 \\ \hline 493 \end{array}$$

[184]^{30} *Monday March 1*
Woodman
F[rancis Philip]. Nash
A. Jackson
Dr C[harles]. T[homas]. J[ackson].

[185] 1. filling the year
       2 excluding undergraduates

[186] Dibdin's Bibliographic Decameron, Vol III pp 62 117^{31}
£2260

1858   Bib[liothèque] Imp[eriale]. held
        858 000 p books
        8⟨8⟩6 000 mss
     average increase per ann. 12,000

[186$_a$] Puckler-Muskau   Mehemet Ali

[186$_b$] Bibliog[raphical] Tour in France & Germany   1829

Bibliomania   1811

---

^{30} The entries on pp. [184], [185], [186], [186$_a$], and [186$_b$] are in pencil, as is the column of figures on p. [183].

^{31} Thomas Frognall Dibdin, *The Bibliographical Decameron; or, Ten Days Pleasant Discourse upon Illuminated Manuscripts* . . . , 3 vols. (London, 1817). Emerson withdrew this work from the Boston Athenaeum December 6–7, 1869.

Bibliophobia   1832

Library Companion   1825

Rare & Valuable Editions   1827
Reminiscences   1836
Andrews' Dictionary[32]

[inside back cover][33]
   knife
   s⟨pectro⟩tereoscope
   compass
   Andrews
   German
   shovel   R [alph] E[merson] F[orbes]
                E[dith] F[orbes]
   purse   E[dith] E[merson] F[orbes]
   stereoscope W[illiam] H[athaway] F[orbes]
   Travelling Bag
   Turner's France

[32] Emerson's references in this list are to Thomas Frognall Dibdin, *A Bibliographical, Antiquarian and Picturesque Tour in France and Germany*, 3 vols., 2nd ed. (London, 1829); *Bibliomania; or Book-madness: A Bibliographical Romance*, 2 vols. (London, 1811); *Bibliophobia. Remarks on the Present Languid and Depressed State of Literature* . . . (London, 1832); *The Library Companion; or, The Young Man's Guide, and the Old Man's Comfort, in the Choice of a Library*, 2nd ed. (London, 1825); *An Introduction to . . . Rare and Valuable Editions* . . . , 2 vols. (London, 1827); *Reminiscences of a Literary Life*, 2 vols. (London, 1836); and to Ethan Allen Andrews, *A Copious and Critical Latin-English Lexicon* . . . , edition unknown.

[33] The entries on the inside back cover are in pencil.

Pocket Diary 21

1870

Pocket Diary 21 is devoted primarily to recording Emerson's lecture engagements for 1870. It also contains miscellaneous financial transactions, addresses, quotations, and memoranda. A few entries may have been made late in 1869 or early in 1871.

The notebook, bound in black stamped leather, is a commercially published diary entitled "ILLUMINATED / DIARY / for / 1870.", published by Nichols & Hall, Boston. The covers measure 7.5 × 12.5 cm. The back cover extends into a tongue that, when the book is closed, fits into a loop on the front cover; the back cover also contains an expandable inside pocket. "DIARY / 1870" is stamped in gold on the tongue. A paper label fastened to the spine is inscribed "1870–1871. x".

The white, unnumbered, gilt-edged pages measure 7.4 × 12.1 cm; pages 25–184 are faintly lined. The book consists of a front flyleaf (i, ii); a title page (page 1); a calendar for 1870 (page 3); a table of time differences relative to Boston time (pages 4–5); rates of postage (page 6); a table of stamp duties (pages 7–11); eclipses in 1870 (page 12); the phases of the moon and tide tables for 1870 (pages 13–24); daily appointments for 1870, three to a page (pages 25–146); pages for memoranda (pages 147–153); pages for cash accounts (pages 154–178), from which pages 169–170 have been torn out; additional pages for memoranda (pages 179–184); and a back flyleaf (pages 185–186).

Entries by Emerson occur on fifty-one pages. Printed matter in Pocket Diary 21 is reproduced here only in the sections on daily appointments, cash accounts, and memoranda where relevant. Otherwise, pages are designated as blank if they bear no inscription by Emerson; the presence or absence of printed matter is not specified.

In the expandable pocket in the back cover is an unused three-cent stamp.

[front cover verso]   R.W. Emerson
                                              Concord, Mass.

[i]–[33][1] [blank]
[34] [Fri., Jan. 28] ⟨Club   Committee of Fifty⟩
[Sat., Jan. 29] Club   Committee of Fifty

[35] [Tues., Feb. 1] Littleton   "Courage"

[36] [Thurs., Feb. 3] Marlborough   Calvin Stebbins
at Mr Swift's house Main St   "Courage"[2]

[37] [Mon., Feb. 7] Philadelphia   T[homas] B Pugh   2212 Post
Office Box
        American Society   Evan Randolph, 2002 Arch St

[38] [Fri., Feb. 11] Harvard.   (S.G. Clarke)   "Courage"
—————
At Captain Charles Savage's house

[39] [blank]
[40] [Wed., Feb. 16] Salem ?   G.L. Streeter   "Courage."

[41]–[45] [blank]
[46] [Mon., Mar. 7] Examiner Club   J[osiah] P[hillips] Q[uincy?]
assessment 5. pd.

[47] [Tues., Mar. 8] "Women's Club," Tremont Place
        Classes of Men

[48] [blank]
[49] [Tues., Mar. 15] Social Circle, Character of John M. Cheney.

[50] [blank]
[51] [Tues., Mar. 22] W[illiam]. B[utler]. Ogden at Lowell Institute

---

[1] "42", in pencil, in the upper right-hand corner of p. [i] may be a stationer's mark.
[2] "at Mr Swift's . . . St" is in pencil.

[52]³ [Wed., Mar. 23] Groton Luncheon ?   P.C. Lathrop
Classes of Men. Rev Mr   of Andover

[53] [Sat., Mar. 26] Club   Mr J McCarthy
⟨tone⟩
⟨Reed's "Growth of the Mind"⟩⁴

[54]–[55] [blank]
[56] [Wed., Apr. 6] T[homas]. C[arlyle].'s letter

[57] [Thurs., Apr. 7] Fast   At Mr E[phraim]. W[hitman]. Gurney's
[Fri., Apr. 8] Wrote to Carlyle that his letter with corporation vote
was sent to London 14 March⁵

[58]–[62] [blank]
[63] [Tues., Apr. 26] Cambridge   Lecture I⁶

[64] [Thurs., Apr. 28] Cambridge   Lecture II
[Fri., Apr. 29] Cambridge   Lecture III

[65] [Mon., May 2] Overseers   11 o'clock   State st⁷
[Tues., May 3] Cambridge   Lecture IV

[66] [Thurs., May 5] Cambridge   Lecture V
[Fri., May 6] Cambridge   Lecture VI

[67] [blank]
[68] [Tues., May 10] Cambridge   Lecture VII
[Thurs., May 12] Cambridge   Lecture VIII

[69] [Fri., May 13] Cambridge   Lecture IX

³ The entries on p. [52] are in pencil, except for "Classes of Men."
⁴ "tone . . . Mind' ", in pencil, is struck through in pencil with a diagonal line.
⁵ See Journal NY, p. [231] above.
⁶ Between April 26 and June 2, 1870, Emerson gave sixteen lectures at Harvard
College on "Natural History of the Intellect."
⁷ "Overseers . . . st" is in pencil.

[70] [Tues., May 17] Cambridge   Lecture X

[71] [Thurs., May 19] Cambridge   Lecture XI
[Fri., May 20] Cambridge   Lecture XII

[72] [Tues., May 24] Cambridge   Lecture XIII

[73] [Thurs., May 26] Cambridge   Lecture XIV
        Cond[uct] of Int[ellect]
[Fri., May 27] ⟨Cambridge   Lecture XV⟩   Morals[8]

[74] [blank]
[75] [Tues., May 31] Cambridge   Lecture ⟨XVI⟩ XV.   ART
[Thurs., June 2] Cambridge   Lecture ⟨XVII⟩ XVI
        Intellect   Lit[erature].[9]

[76] [Fri., June 3] ⟨Cambridge   Lecture XVIII⟩
[Sun., June 5] *Memo.*   Answer J. ↑H↓ Holman, Chairman of Toledo,
Lib[rar]y Assoc[iatio]n & J.F Williams Sec[retar]y St Paul Minnesota
Historical Soc[iety] concerning a Lecture this summer

[77]–[78] [blank]
[79] [Mon., June 13] Watchkey[10]

[80]–[83] [blank]
[84] [Tues., June 28] Commencement Day.

[85]–[119] [blank]
[120] [Fri., Oct. 14] Mrs Boon, 47 ⟨Tilden⟩ ↑Kildare↓ st.
Dublin writes 1st October to Mrs E[merson] announcing the death of
C[harles]. Brown o↑n↓ 23d May last.[11]

---

[8] "Cond of Int" and "Morals" are in pencil.
[9] "ART" and "Intellect   Lit." are in pencil.
[10] "Watchkey" is in pencil.
[11] Charles Brown, husband of Lucy Jackson Brown, Lidian's sister, deserted his wife
and moved to Dublin, Ireland, where at the time of his death he was reported to be a
merchant tailor living in one of the best parts of Dublin; see *L,* VI, 144.

[121]–[128] [blank]
[129] [Fri., Nov. 11] Sent "Plutarch" to Little & Brown[12]

[130] [blank]
[131] [Tues., Nov. 15] ⟨Woburn⟩ Westford   C.O. Whitman
   Social Aims

[132] [blank]
[133] [Mon., Nov. 21] Providence   Social Aims[13]

[134] [Thurs., Nov. 24] Thanksgiving

[135] [Mon., Nov. 28] Providence   "Memory"[14]

[136]–[137] [blank]
[138] [Tues., Dec. 6] Fraternity   "Immortality"

[139]–[141] [blank]
[142] [Mon., Dec. 19] Memoranda for N.Y.
"Society & Solitude" for ⟨Miss⟩Mrs Parsons

———

Couture for S. Ward

———

Garbett, *Weales Builder Series*[15]

———

Pay subscription to N Y Nation

[143] [Wed., Dec. 21] New York   Pilgrim Society
[Thurs., Dec. 22] New York

[12] "Sent . . . Brown" is in pencil. In 1870 Little, Brown and Company published the edition of *Plutarch's Morals* by William W. Goodwin for which Emerson wrote an introduction.
[13] "Providence" is in pencil.
[14] "Providence 'Memory' " is in pencil.
[15] For Couture see Journal ST, p. [15] above. Edward Lacy Garbett, *Rudimentary Treatise on the Principles of Design in Architecture* . . . (London, 1850). This volume appeared in John Weale's "Series of Rudimentary Works," vols. 18–19. Emerson withdrew this work from the Boston Athenaeum December 15, 1868–January 18, 1869, and April 6–10, 1869.

[144] [Mon., Dec. 26] ⟨Rutgers College New Brunswick N Jersey⟩
⟨G[eorge] W[ashington] Atherton⟩

[145] [Tues., Dec. 27] Providence   "Resources."
    Party at [W. B.] Weeden's   101 Benefit Street

[146] Sunday, 1 Jan. 1871[16]
            M   2
            Tu   3
            W   4
            Th.   5
            F   6
            Sat   7
            Sun   8
            M.   9
            Tu   10
            W   11
            Th   12
            F   13
            Sat   14
            Su   15
            M   16
        Tuesday   17   Buffalo

[147] Jan 20   Pay W[illiam] H[athaway] F[orbes]
                                            4.00

Charge W[illiam]. H[athaway]. Forbes for cash
                paid by me to Dr Bartlett   3.00

        2 Mond
        9
        16
        23

[148] Committee of visiting the Academical Department

_____

[16] The entries on pp. [146] and [147] are Emerson's tentative lecture schedule for
January 1871.

397

Sub-Committee on Modern Languages Rhetoric & Elocution
R[alph] W[aldo] E[merson] Chairman
⟨R H Dana⟩Rev J[ames]. F[reeman] Clarke
C[harles]. C[allahan]. Perkins, Esq.

SubCommittee on Philosophy.
    C[harles]. F[rancis]. Adams
    R[ichard]. H[enry]. Dana [Jr.]
    R[alph]. W[aldo]. E[merson]
Second Term begins 17 Feb[ruar]y

[149]   [MEMORANDA.] 1871
Jan 1 Sunday
    2 M
    3 Tu
    4 W
    5 Th
    6 F
    7 Sat
    8 Sun
    9 M
  10 Tu
  11 W
  12 Th
  13 F   Andover? 5 P.M.
  14 Sat
  15 Sun
  16 M
  17 ↑Tu.↓ Buffalo
  18 Wed.
  19
  20
  21
  22
  23 Church of Disciples T Dana 2d
  24

25   ⟨Salem?⟩Salem[17]
26
27
28
29
30
31

[150]–[165] [blank]
[166][18] old mortar
      for peach trees
      air slacked lime

---

lead incased
block tin
      54 Broad st   Corner of Milk st   Boston Lead Co

[167]–[179] [blank]
[180] Thos. Ainsworth
      J.R. Leeson   66 Milk st[19]

[181][20] Ask Lowell of the London Society for making the Dictionary.

---

      also of Mr Cutler

      Dryden born ↑1631↓ died ↑1700↓
      Bacon   born ↑1561↓ died ↑1626↓
      Shakspeare   ↑1564↓   ↑1616↓
      Phil[emon] Holland's translation ↑Morals↓ ↑1603↓
          Dryden's ↑Lives↓   ↑1683↓
          Morris   1718

[17] "Salem?", in pencil, is overwritten by "Salem" in ink to cancel.
[18] The entries on p. [166] are in pencil.
[19] "Thos. Ainsworth" and "J.R. ... Milk st" are each circled in ink.
[20] All inserted material on p. [181] is in pencil. In the list on p. [181], Philemon Holland, John Dryden, and John and William Langhorne each translated Plutarch into English; Thomas North translated Plutarch into English from the French of James Amyot; and John Florio and Charles Cotton each translated Montaigne into English.

399

↑↑Amyot↓North ↑*Lives*↓   1579↓
        ↑Langhorne ↑*Lives*↓   1770↓
    ↑↑Montaigne↓ Florio   1603↓
            ↑Cotton   1693↓

[182]²¹   7.90   to Portlan[d]
          2.90   to Paris
          2 00   to W[aterford]
          2   at W[aterford]
          3   to Paris
          3.80   to Gorham
          3   to Glen H[ouse]
         17.90   Glen House
          5.00
          1.   for trunk
    ?   12.   to Crawford
          6.50   Crawford
         18.90   ↑Cr[awford]. to↓ Nashua
          2.00   Whitefie[l]d

[183]²² 195

Hutchinson   I. 312
——

Nationale Bulgare et chants populaires   Dora d'Istria
    Revue de[s] D[eux] M[ondes] Vol 76 319²³

———

Boissier   Pompéi et la vie de province.
    Rev[ue]. d[es]. Deux Mondes Avril 1866²⁴

———

²¹ The entries on p. [182] are in pencil.
²² On p. [183], "195" is in pencil. *Memoirs of the Life of Colonel Hutchinson, . . . Written by His Widow Lucy,* 2 vols., 4th ed. (London, 1822); this work is in Emerson's library.
²³ Dora d'Istria, "La Nationalité Bulgare D'Après Les Chants Populaires," *Revue des Deux Mondes,* 76 (July 15, 1868): 319–354.
²⁴ Gaston Boissier, "Pompéi, La Vie De Province Dans L'Empire Romaine," *Revue des Deux Mondes,* 62 (April 1, 1866): 559–589.

[184] Revue des Deux Mondes
        1 March,   1863
        15 September, 1863
        15 April,   1864
⟨t⟩les études de M. Martha, sur Lucrece, Perse, et Marc Aurèle[25]

"De la Morale de Plutarque," par M. Octave Gréard
    1 Vol. 8vo. [Paris,] 1867

"La Cité Antique" par M. Fustel de Coulanges

---

[185] Plutarch born, say in latter years of Emperor Claudius (AD
48–53) at Chaeronaea, Boe⟨t⟩otia. His nephew Sextus taught Greek
language to Marcus Antoninus.
d. probably 5th year of Hadrian aet. 70

    ↑Plutarque↓   Vol 71 Revue [*des Deux Mondes*] 1867[26]

[186] Annual Meeting   2 Thursday of July[27]

[George] Small's Handbook of Sanskrit Lit[*erature,* 1866,] p 183

For the law passed by the Mass[achuse]tts legislature for the division
of Estates see ST 1870 c 257

Plutarch
See Montesquieu Esprit des Lois. livre I. chap. 1. et *Defense de l'Esprit
des lois.* Conf *Pensees.*

---

[25] The articles in *Revue des Deux Mondes* by M. C. Martha that are alluded to here
are, in chronological order, "Le Poète Lucrèce," 44 (March 1, 1863): 187–215; "Un
Poète Stoicien: A Rome et les Satires de Perse," 47 (September 15, 1863): 291–325;
"Marc-Aurèle et L'Examen de Conscience d'un Empereur Romaine," 50 (April 15,
1864): 870–893.
[26] The entry on p. [185] is in pencil. Charles Lévêque, "Un Médecin de l'Ame chez
les Grecs—Plutarque, Sa Vie et Sa Morale à propos d'un Ouvrage Récent," *Revue des
Deux Mondes,* 71 (October 1, 1867): 725–754.
[27] "Annual . . . July" is in pencil.

401

Edin[*burgh*]. Review. June [actually July], 1850, Goethe by Rogers.[28]

[inside back cover] Dr J[ames] F[reeman] C[larke] 3 & 4 o'c in his church[29]
Phila[delphia]
S. Bradford, 1628 Walnut
    Lesley
R. Randolph
B.P. Hunt
Miss E.R. Fisher
W[illiam]. H[enry]. F[urness].
C.K. Newcomb
Mrs Harding Davis

———

1871
Course at Cambridge
2 lectures a week from Feb. 11 to June 17[30]

---

[28] Herman Merivale, "Göthe's Festival," *Edinburgh Review,* 92 (July 1850): 188–220.

[29] "Dr J F C . . . church" is in pencil.

[30] This entry refers to the seventeen lectures on "Natural History of the Intellect" that Emerson gave at Harvard College February 14–April 7, 1871.

Pocket Diary 22

1871

Pocket Diary 22 is devoted primarily to recording Emerson's lecture engagements for 1871 and memoranda inscribed during his tour of the western states during April and May, 1871. It also contains miscellaneous financial transactions, addresses, quotations, and memoranda. A few entries may have been made late in 1870 or early in 1872.

The notebook, bound in black stamped leather, is a commercially published diary entitled "Pocket / DIARY / 1871", published by the New England News Co., Boston. The covers measure 7.4 × 12.4 cm. The back cover extends into a tongue that, when the book is closed, fits into a loop on the front cover; the back cover also contains an expandable inside pocket. "DIARY" is stamped in gold on the tongue. A paper label fastened to the spine is inscribed "1871. x".

The white, unnumbered pages, whose edges are marbled, measure 7.3 × 12.1 cm; pages 33–192 are lined. The book consists of a front flyleaf (i, ii); a title page (page 1); a calendar for 1871 (page 3); a table of time differences relative to Boston and New York time (pages 4–5); an account, "COMMENCEMENT OF THE YEAR." (page 6); an account, "DIVISIONS OF TIME." (page 7); a table of stamp duties (pages 8–12); eclipses in 1871 (page 13); the phases of the moon and tide tables for 1871 (pages 14–25); a Chicago almanac (pages 26–31); rates of postage (page 32); daily appointments for 1870, three to a page (pages 33–154); pages for memoranda (pages 155–161); pages for cash accounts (pages 162–186); additional pages for memoranda (pages 187–192); and a back flyleaf (pages 193–194).

Entries by Emerson occur on eighty-seven pages. Printed matter in Pocket Diary 22 is reproduced here only in the sections on daily appointments, cash accounts, and memoranda where relevant. Otherwise, pages are designated as blank if they bear no inscription by Emerson; the presence or absence of printed matter is not specified.

[front cover verso]¹
Hemlock Spruce   175 ft by 4 ft
Pinus Albicantis   highest liver
Picea amabilis   silver fir
Pinus contorta   Tamaric
Juniperno Occidentalis

[i]   R W Emerson
                                                                          Concord

Glaciers   Mono Lake
Volcanic mts.   cones.   Enneo Co.

1540 ft above level valley
La Casa Nevada
5600 ft above sea

3100 ft   Liberty Cap

Pinus Lambertiana   ↑10 ft by 300 ft↓
sugar pine   great cone

Pinus Ponderosa
Yellow pine

Sabine Pine
Pinus Fremontiana

[ii] Wm Stroude 1656
        Jamieson's Ballads   Vol II p 295
Edwin the Fair²

[1] [blank]

---

¹ The entries on the front cover verso and p. [i] are in pencil. "1540 . . . Nevada"
and "5600 ft above sea" on p. [i] are enclosed in rectangles in pencil.
² Sir Henry Taylor, *Edwin the Fair, an Historical Drama* (London, 1842). Emerson
withdrew this volume from the Boston Athenaeum June 26–July 12, 1871.

[2] July 19   *Desideranda.*
Song to Music by Wm Stroude, in [Robert] Jamieson's [*Popular*] Ballads, [1806] Vol II p 295[−296]
> "O lull me, lull me, charming air!
> My senses rock with wonder sweet;
> Like snow on wool thy fallings are,
> Soft like a spirit's, are thy feet."

———
Licoo
———
Glenlogie
———
The Drowned Lovers
———

The consent of Mr R[obert T. S.] Lowell & of Miss [Sara Ham-
mond] Palfrey, to the insertion of their poems [in *Parnassus.*][3]

[3]–[32] [blank]
[33][4] [Sun., Jan. 1] At Milton
[Tues., Jan. 3] Providence, R.I.   ↑at Rev. Diman's↓   "Wit &
Humor"

[34] [Wed., Jan. 4] Concord.   Lecture on ⟨"Leasts & Mosts."⟩
[Thurs., Jan. 5] ⟨F.C. Lowell⟩At F[rancis]. C[abot]. Lowell's,[5] 5th &
6th

[35] [Sun., Jan. 8] At Milton Sat night to Monday P.M.
[Mon., Jan. 9] Providence   "Immortality"[6]

[36] [blank]
[37] [Fri., Jan. 13] Andover.   Mr [Roderick] Terry   5 PM train
   "Immortality."

---

[3] The entries on p. [2] relate to material under consideration for inclusion in *Par-nassus*. For "Licoo", "Glenlogie", and "The Drowned Lovers" see Journal ST, p. [47] above.
[4] On p. [33], "At Milton" and "at Rev. Diman's" are in pencil.
[5] "F.C. Lowell", in pencil, is overwritten by "At ... Lowell's," in ink to cancel.
[6] "Providence" is in pencil.

[38] [Tues., Jan. 17] Buffalo   Home & Hospitality   Mr L.T. Ives
[Wed., Jan. 18] Detroit   Readings   At Mr Bagley's

[39] [Thurs., Jan. 19] Detroit, L.T. Ives   "Books."[7]

[40] [Mon., Jan. 23] Dr [James Freeman] Clark↑e,↓ Church of Disciples
    Tho[ma]s Dana, 2d.   "Chivalry."

[41] [Wed., Jan. 25] Salem

[42] [Mon., Jan. 30] Providence   American Nationality
    Fortune of the Republic

[43] [blank]
[44] [Fri., Feb. 3] Meeting of the Art Committee
A little speech reported from my ⟨mss.⟩ ↑notes↓ in the "Daily Advertiser"[8]

[45]–[46] [blank]
[47] [Tues., Feb. 14] ↑1↓   Cambridge.   4 P.M.
    ↑⟨Introduction⟩↓[9]
Course on Philosophy in Dr Wyman's Room
West lecture room in Boylston H[all].

[48] [Wed., Feb. 15] Salem   *Home & Hospitality*
[Fri., Feb. 17] 2   Cambridge   3 P.M   ↑Transcendency of Physics↓[10]
Mr Gray's at 6 P.M.

[49] [blank]
[50] [Tues., Feb. 21] 3   Cambridge

---

[7] "Detroit, . . . Ives" is in pencil.
[8] The speech reported is for the organization of the Museum of Fine Arts.
[9] "1" and "Introduction" are in pencil. This is a reference to the first of seventeen lectures on "Natural History of the Intellect" that Emerson gave at Harvard College February 14–April 7, 1871.
[10] "2 . . . Physics" is in pencil.

[51] [Fri., Feb. 24] 4.   Cambridge   Memory   No I[11]
Mr Jefferson Coolidge

[52][12] [Tues., Feb. 28] 5   Cambridge   ↑Imagination↓

[53] [Fri., Mar. 3] 6.   Cambridge   Memory   no II

[54] Yt[?] sen[?]
Mariposa Grove
[Galen] Clark & Decker measur[e] a sequoia prostrate 228 ft
The great lying tree 268 we first saw.

[Tues., Mar. 7] 7   Cambridge   Inspiration

[55] *Forest giant* a burned stump. [Galen] Clark found it 34 ft in diameter when he first measured it; now 26.6 inches

[Fri., Mar. 10] 8   Cambridge   Common Sense

[56][13] [Sun., Mar. 12] Horticultural Hall   "Rule of Life."

[57] [Tues., Mar. 14] 9.   Cambridge   Wit & Humor

[58] [Fri., Mar. 17] 10   Cambridge   *Genius.*

[59] [Tues., Mar. 21] Cambridge   11.   Demonology

[60] [Fri., Mar. 24] Cambridge   12   Poetry
[Sat., Mar. 25] Mrs Nash   Heywood
                    Jackson
                    Froude
                    Apothecary

[11] "3   Cambridge" and "4.   Cambridge . . . No I" are in pencil.
[12] The entries on pp. [52]–[55] are in pencil.
[13] "Horticultural Hall" on p. [56] and all of the entries on pp. [57]–[65] are in pencil.

[61] [Tues., Mar. 28] Cambridge   13   Metres

[62] [Fri., Mar. 31] Cambridge   14.   Metres

[63] [Mon., Apr. 3] 15   Cambridge   Will & Conduct of Intellect

[64] [Tues., Apr. 4] ⟨Cambridge⟩
[Wed., Apr. 5] 16   Cambridge   Conduct of Intellect

[65] [Fri., Apr. 7] 17   Cambridge   Relation of Int[ellect] &
Morals.

[66] [Tues., Apr. 11] ⟨Cambridge⟩[14]
Remain in Atl[antic]. Bank 205
Left Boston for California at 3 P.M.
[Wed., Apr. 12] PM at Suspension Bridge

[67] [Thurs., Apr. 13] Morning arrived at Chicago
[Fri., Apr. 14] x ⟨Cambridge⟩[15]

[68][16] [Tues., Apr. 18] Echo & Weber canons
     Night   Salt Lake City

[69] [Wed., Apr. 19] Called on B[righam]. Young
     ⟨Night⟩   Salt Lake City   Tabernacle   Left Ogden
[Fri., Apr. 21] Cape Horn   ↑Sacramen[to]↓   San Francisco

[70] [Sat., Apr. 22] Cliff   Golden Gate   Sealions
A drive with Dr Horatio Stebbins, Edith, & Mr J[ames]. B[radley].
Thayer
[Sun., Apr. 23] "Immortality"   San Francisco[17]

---

[14] "Cambridge", in pencil, is struck through in pencil with two diagonal lines.
[15] "x" is in pencil; "Cambridge", in pencil, is stuck through in pencil with one vertical and four diagonal lines.
[16] The entries on pp. [68] and [69] are in pencil.
[17] "Cliff . . . Sealions" is in pencil; " 'Immortality' " and "San Francisco", in pencil,
are overwritten by the same in ink.

[71] [Wed., Apr. 26] San Francisco   Lecture on "Society in America"

[72] [Sat., Apr. 29] San Francisco   "Resources"

[73][18] [Mon., May 1] ⟨Character or Greatness⟩San Francisco "Greatness"
pd
pd eyeglass 1.50
pd Occid[ental] House 34
[Tues., May 2] Left the Occidental Hotel for Modesto & Yo Semite ⟨Robert's⟩Robert's Hotel
[Wed., May 3] Coulterville

[74][19] [Thurs., May 4] ↑Caves↓   ⟨Cave⟩Hazle Green   took horses ⟨Crane's Flat⟩Slept at Crane's Flat
[Fri., May 5] ⟨Yo Semite⟩at the Yo Semite Valley
    at Leidig's Hotel
[Sat., May 6] ↑Yo Semite↓   To the Crystal Lake   ↑Mirror Lake↓
Wilkie James & I measured a prostrate Sugar Pine lying near the Leidig Hotel, & adding 6 ft. sawed off at the butt, & 2 ft. standing of the burned stump, made 210 ft for the living tree.

[75][20] [Sun., May 7] To Nevada Fall & Casa Nevada
a day of wonders   stripped mountains   our best day yet.
rainbows our companions   mountains our geologists
cedars = arbor vitae   hemlock major, spruce
⟨[Tues., May 9]⟩ Today to Mirror Lake again   again imperfect.
Then to the Yo Semite Fall across 2 bridges   Then to Hutchings'

[18] On p. [73], "Character or Greatness", in pencil, is overwritten by "San Francisco 'Greatness'" in ink to cancel; "pd" and "pd eyeglass . . . 34" are in pencil; "Left the Occidental . . . Semite" and "Coulterville", in pencil, are overwritten by the same in ink; "Robert's", in pencil, is overwritten by "Robert's Hotel" in ink to cancel.
[19] On p. [74], "Cave", in pencil, is overwritten by "Hazle Green" in ink to cancel; "Crane's Flat", in pencil, is overwritten by "Slept . . . Flat" in ink to cancel; "Yo Semite", in pencil, is overwritten by "at the . . . Valley" in ink to cancel; "To the Crystal Lake" is in pencil.
[20] The entries on p. [75] are in pencil.

House. Saw him   he gave me Sequoia cone. Mr Roche gave me 6 photographs. Bought 2 of Reilly

[76]²¹ [Wed., May 10] ⟨Grizly 29 & 31 diam⟩Grizly Giant, 29 & 31 ft in diameter
⟨99⟩ 91
[Thurs., May 11] ⟨Clark says these sequo[ia] reach 27⟨0⟩2 ft⟩Galen Clark says the Sequoias reach 272 ft. in height.
⟨Whitney found 327 ft in Calaver[as]⟩Whitney found 372 ft in one in Calaveras.
[Fri., May 12] ⟨Friday night at White & Hatch⟩Spent the night at White & Hatch's Hotel
Crossed the Merced   Snellings

[77]²² [Sat., May 13] Dined at Hornitos
⟨Evening Roberts' Ferry on Tuolumne River⟩Spent the night at Roberts' on the Tuolumne River.
[Sun., May 14] ⟨Stockton Grand Hotel⟩reached Stockton & the "Grand Hotel"
[Mon., May 15] ⟨San Francisco⟩Monday noon reached San Francisco Occidental Hotel.

[78] [Tues., May 16] ⟨"Chivalry"⟩
[Wed., May 17] Lecture on Chivalry   San Francisco
[Thurs., May 18] Lecture on Hospitality.   Oaklands
In the morning, drive with Mr Henry Pierce & Dr Stebbins to Thorpe's Tavern 12 miles out

[79] [Fri., May 19] Left [San] Francisco   reached Truckee

²¹ On p. [76], "Grizly . . . diam", in pencil, is overwritten by "Grizly . . . diameter" in ink to cancel; "Clark says . . . ft", in pencil, is overwritten by "Galen Clark . . . height." in ink to cancel; "Whitney found . . . Calaver", in pencil, is overwritten by "Whitney found . . . Calaveras." in ink to cancel; "Friday . . . Hatch", in pencil, is overwritten by "Spent . . . Hotel" in ink to cancel; "99   91" and "Crossed . . . Snellings" are in pencil.
²² On p. [77], "Dined at Hornitos" is in pencil; "Evening . . . River", in pencil, is overwritten by "Spent . . . River." in ink to cancel; "Stockton . . . Hotel", in pencil, is overwritten by "reached . . . Hotel' " in ink to cancel; "San Francisco", in pencil, is overwritten by "Monday . . . Hotel." in ink to cancel.

[Sat., May 20] In carriages to Lake Tahoe
[Sun., May 21] Lake Tahoe

[80] [Mon., May 22] Left Lake Tahoe for Truckee
    Walked to Lake Donner.

Left Truckee at 11 P.M. for Ogden &c

[81] [Fri., May 26] Omaha
Switched off at 3 A.M. Sat., ⟨the⟩at Ottumwa, the ⟨car⟩sleeping car
containing Mr & Mrs J.M. Forbes & Alice.
[Sat., May 27] Arrived at Burlington, at 6 a.m.
    Left here Wilkie James, & G[eorge]. [Ward] Holdre[d]ge.

[82] [Sun., May 28] Arrived at Cataract House, Niagara. Mr Peabody in the train told his story of Dick Pratt, the hunter, in Arkansas,
& of his buffalo hunting with Gov Crawford, & some thirty others

Niagara was never so great to my eyes as today. I rode on the engine
20½ miles in 21 minutes

[Mon., May 29] Happy at Niagara till 2 o'clock P.M.
Then took the train for Albany & Boston. ⟨Arrived in Boston at 1⟩
[Tues., May 30] Arrived in Boston at 11 o'clock A.M. & at Concord
at 3.45 P.M.
Slept at the Manse the guest of Elizabeth Ripley

[83]   Nympha pudica Deum videt et erubuit
       The modest water saw its God & blushed[23]

[Fri., June 2] At Milton

[84] Parnassus   The boatie rows   Jamieson[24]

[23] See Pocket Diary 20, p. [182] above.
[24] "Parnassus . . . Jamieson" is in pencil. "The Boatie Rows," an anonymous ballad
from Robert Jamieson, *Popular Ballads,* 1806, appears in *Parnassus.*

[85] [Wed., June 7] Mem   E. Stone Esq   Maynard Mass
Deputy Collector of Internal Revenue

[86]–[87] [blank]
[88] [Sat., June 17] Atlantic Monthly 12 vols already bound to 1863
inclusive
Now remain to be bound

	Vols 13 for the year ⟨1864⟩
14	186⟨5⟩4
$\overline{15}$	⟨66⟩
16	186⟨7⟩5
$\overline{17}$	68
18	186⟨9⟩6

[89]   Vol $\overline{19}$ ⎫
     & 20 ⎭   18⟨70⟩67

[Sun., June 18] Paint
[Mon., June 19] Reading at Bartol's 11 A.M.

[90]–[91] [blank]
[92] [Wed., June 28] Commencement Day.
Meeting of Class of 1821   Seventeen members present.

[93] [blank]
[94] [Tues., July 4] Miss E[lizabeth] B Ripley departed for Europe.
    Letters sent to Carlyle & Mrs [Josephine Shaw] Lowell[25]

[95]–[96] [blank]
[97] [Wed., July 12] Overseers' Meeting at 11, o,c

[98] [blank]
[99] ↑W. Stroud in↓ [Robert] Jamieson [*Popular*] Ballads [1806,] II
295

---

[25] The letter to Carlyle is preserved in *CEC*, pp. 581–583; the letter to Mrs. Lowell
is preserved in *L*, VI, 168.

Miss [Sara Hammond] Palfrey. ↑Revd↓ R[obert]. [T.S.] Lowell
J[ames]. B[radley]. Thayer
⟨R⟩Dr [Nathan C.] Keep
Athenaeum & City Lib[rary].

[100]–[105] [blank]
[106] [Thurs., Aug. 10] Overseers

[107] [blank]
[108] [Tues., Aug. 15] Scott

[109]–[110] [blank]
[111]²⁶ Sara[h Freeman] Clarke   Care Geo. Hill
        Florence Sewing Machines   19 Montgomery St

[112]–[113] [blank]
[114] [Sat., Sept. 2] Books for Atlanta University. ↑Georgia↓
Care of Thos. N. C⟨a⟩hase   to be left at Post Office Concord

[115]–[137] [blank]
[138] [Tues., Nov. 14] Academical Committee
      11 o'c at 13 Pemberton Square

[139]–[142] [blank]
[143] [Mon., Nov. 27] Chicago Star Course   "Art & Nature"

[144] [Thurs., Nov. 30] Chicago. Thanksgiving. at house of
Robert Laird Collier.   Indiana Avenue.

———

B.B. Wiley, 854 Prairie Avenue.

———

Mrs Charles Davis, 1246 Prairie Av.
[Fri., Dec. 1] ⟨A⟩Quincy, Ill.   *"Art & Nature"*
At house of C.H. Bull   Mrs Anna Bull
Alice; Fanny; Edith⟨,⟩ B[ull]

²⁶ The entries on pp. [111] and [114] are in pencil.

413

[Sat., Dec. 2] ⟨"⟩*Friends in Council.* A M
      Readings   P.M.

[145] [Sun., Dec. 3] Quincy   "Immortality."
[Mon., Dec. 4] ⟨Chicago   Star Lecture Course   C.M. Brelsford⟩
⟨B W Williams, 119 Washington St. Boston⟩[27]
      ⟨Nat⟩
[Tues., Dec. 5] Springfield   "Greatness."
At ⟨M⟩Rev ⟨Mr⟩ ↑J.K↓ McL⟨ane⟩ean's Church.

[146] [Fri., Dec. 8] Dubuque, Ia.   G.L. Torbett, Esq.
      A↑ustin↓. Adams Esq.   Mr Shiras, Esq
↑"Greatness"   "Immortality."   "Inspiration" & *Readings.*↓

[147]–[153] [blank]
[154][28] M 1
      Tu 2
      W
      Th 4

[155] *April*   Letter to T[homas]. C[arlyle].
——

      See Fields for Landor
      Tolman — Duster
                  eye-glass
                  penknife
                  truss
      Atl[antic]. Bank
——

      ⟨Mrs Wistar⟩
——

      ⟨Mr S. Eliot⟩
——

      F[rancis]. C[abot]. Lowell
            Upham's Letter

---

[27] "Chicago . . . Boston" is struck through in ink with a vertical and a diagonal line.
[28] The entries on pp. [154] and [155] are in pencil.

John A. Lowell, Esq.

My book for J[ames]. R[ussell] Lowell

Doherty
Gourdin

[156]–[161] [blank]
[162]   [CASH ACCOUNT.   JANUARY.]
    [Date.]   [Received.]   [Paid.]
      1   Edw[ard Emerson] $5.
          E[llen] T E[merson] 2.50   ⟨5⟩7.50
          Foster   39[29]

[163]   [CASH ACCOUNT.   JANUARY.]
    [Date.]   [Received.]   [Paid.]
      1   Rec[eive]d B[urlington] & M[issouri] in Neb[raska]
          by W[illiam] H[athaway] F[orbes]   140
                    in Iowa   39
          N[ew]. E[ngland]. Society   100

[164]–[168] [blank]
[169][30] Bridal Veil
          El Ca⟨i⟩pitano
          Half dome
          Valley
          B Brothers
          Mt Watkins

[170] 300   gold bill
      1⟨5⟩60   gold
       50   gold
       25   currency
       20   d[itt]o

---

[29] "Foster" and "39" are in pencil.
[30] The entries on pp. [169] and [170] are in pencil.

455		Edw[ard].	5.
86		Ellen	20.
———			61
369			———
150	Concord B[an]k		86
———			
219			
34			
———			
185			
5			
———			
190			
33			
———			
223			
89			
———			
312			

[171]–[173] [blank]
[174]³¹ Concord Library
John Woolman's Journal
Masson's Life of Milton
    2 vols ready; 1 to come
Memoir of Charles Young
Hughes' Life of Alfred
Tyndall Fragments of Science

[175]³² Pinus Lambert   Sugar Pine   16 or 13 inches cone

---

³¹ On p. [174], "166" in pencil is written over "100" in pencil with an addition line in pencil below them under "Hughes' . . . Science". The list of books includes *A Journal of the Life, Gospel Labours, and Christian Experiences of . . . John Woolman* (Warrington, 1840), in Emerson's library; David Masson, *The Life of John Milton . . .* , 7 vols. (London and New York, 1859–1894); Thomas Hughes, *Alfred the Great* (Boston, 1871); and John Tyndall, *Fragments of Science; A Series of Detached Essays, Addresses, and Reviews*, in many editions.
³² The entries on pp. [175] and [176] are in pencil.

Quercus Sonomiensis   Acorn edible

[176] Named a Sequoia near Galen's Hospice
              Samoset   12 May 1871
girth at 2½ ft from ground   50 ft
in presence of Galen Clark & J[ames] B[radley] Thayer

[177]–[178] [blank]
[179] Quircus Hindsii   or   California White Oak, or long acorned
oak, 60 ft high, & branching 125 ft from side to side
      acorns edible, & chief f⟨r⟩ood of the Indians

Quercus Agrifolia   California Live Oak

[180]   [CASH ACCOUNT.   OCTOBER.]
     [Date.]   [Received.]   [Paid.]
          From H[arvard] College   340
          From S Low & Co
             by Osgood & Co   166 20

[181]–[184] [blank]
[185]³³ 29 March   23.
       10 Apr   42.
       11 Apr   100.

[186] [blank]
[187] At Niagara
      A certain ⟨gro⟩crazing influence of increasing force at moments
to jump into a stream which cannot hurt much, action is so swift
Then ⟨th⟩ⁿ in the ↑Cataract↓ Hotel life you go from the drawing
rooms to piazza overlooking the Rapids & find Nature a second conscience to purify & uplift
the low morning rainbows too are delightful

³³ The entries on pp. [185] and [187] are in pencil.

417

[188] Richd D. Webb Esq   ⟨Great Brunswick St⟩
     Abbey Street   Dublin
W.F. Littledale   Solicitor   Dublin[34]

measureably

[189] [blank]
[190][35] Ballads
     Chaucer
     Phil[ip] Sydney
     Cov[entry]. Patmore
     Clough   2 things only

     ↑Rev↓ C.G. Ames   San Jose

     120   S. Forbes   121
     107   A. Anthony   111

[191] Richard D. Webb   177 Great Brunswick St.   Dublin

M.D. Brown.   Waltham

     Tube-well

↑May 25↓

     ↑141↓   RWE   weight Apr 17 1871   lb 140½
     ↑142↓   J[ames] B[radley] Thayer   ⟨same weight⟩   140½
     ↑166½↓   W[ilkie] James   159
     ↑158↓   [George Ward] Holdredge   153
     ↑156½↓   A[lice H.] Forbes   157
     ↑170½↓   W[illiam] H[athaway] F[orbes]   174[36]

[34] "Richd . . . Solicitor   Dublin" is in pencil. Webb was to secure an attorney in Dublin to settle the affairs of Charles Brown, Lidian's brother-in-law. See *L*, VI, 144, and Pocket Diary 21, p. [120] above.
[35] The entries on p. [190] are in pencil. The first list may have been intended as a reminder of items pertinent to *Parnassus*.
[36] "May 25 . . . 174" is in pencil, as are the entries on p. [192].

[192] Georgiana Bruce [Kirby]

California   Mrs R C Kirby   Santa Cruz
_____

C[harles].A. Murdock   San Francisco

[193] Grandeur of the↑se↓ mountains I suppose unmatched in the
globe for here they strip themselves like athletes for exhibition, &
stand perpendicular granite walls, ⟨for⟩ showing their entire height, &
wearing a liberty-cap on their head[37]

[194][38] Sherry. 5.00 per doz[en]
                    1.75 per gall[on]
_____

White wine
   3.50
   1.50   pr. case in N.Y.
   ___

   5.00
Champaigne
   13.00
   1.50   N.Y.
   ___

Claret
Zinfandel   Landsberge[r]
   ___

   4.00
   1.50
   ___

   5.50

[inside back cover]   Dr J H.
        Mrs Hastings   1215 Sutton St   [San] Francis[c]o

[37] "Grandeur of . . . their head" is in pencil. Emerson is referring here to the prospect afforded by the Yosemite Valley; see Journal ST, p. [80] above.
[38] The entries on p. [194] and the inside back cover are in pencil.

San F[rancisco] Cooperative Land Co   300 Montgomery St

John F Hastings
H.B Congdon Sec[retar]y Cooperative Land Co

Mission Grape
  3.50
  1.50

  5.00   N.Y

Port Wine   Landsberger
  5.00
  1.50

  6.50   N Y

Pocket Diary 23

1872

Pocket Diary 23 is devoted primarily to recording Emerson's lecture engagements and memoranda for his travels in England, France, and Italy during 1872. It also contains miscellaneous financial transactions, addresses, and quotations, of which some of the last are early selections for *Parnassus*. A few entries may have been made late in 1871 or early in 1873.

The notebook, bound in dark blue stamped leather, is a commercially published diary entitled "POCKET / DIARY / 1872", published by the New England News Company, Boston. The covers measure 7.5 × 12.3 cm. The back cover extends into a tongue that, when the book is closed, fits into a loop on the front cover; the back cover also contains an expandable inside pocket. "DIARY" is stamped in gold on the tongue. A paper label fastened to the spine has been torn away.

The white, unnumbered, gilt-edged pages measure 7.3 × 12.1 cm; pages 31–190 are faintly lined. The book consists of a front flyleaf (i, ii); a title page (page 1); a table of time differences relative to New York time (page 3); a catalogue of "THINGS WORTH KNOWING" (page 4); an account, "DIVISIONS OF TIME." (page 5); a table of stamp duties (pages 6–10); eclipses in 1872 (page 11); the phases of the moon and tide tables for 1872 (pages 12–23); a Chicago almanac (pages 24–29); rates of postage (page 30); daily appointments for 1872, three to a page (pages 31–152); pages for memoranda (pages 153–159), from which pages 153–154 have been torn out; pages for cash accounts (pages 160–184); additional pages for memoranda (pages 185–190); a back flyleaf (pages 191–192); and four pasted-in pages (pages 193–196).

Entries by Emerson occur on ninety-two pages. Printed matter in Pocket Diary 23 is reproduced here only in the sections on daily appointments, cash accounts, and memoranda where relevant. Otherwise, pages are designated as blank if they bear no inscription by Emerson; the presence or absence of printed matter is not specified.

The following items are enclosed in the expandable pocket in the back cover: two calling cards, one measuring 8.4 × 5 cm, the other 9.2 × 6.1 cm, both signed by Emerson; a portion of an unidentified newspaper clipping praising the language of Oliver Wendell Holmes, Nathaniel Hawthorne, and Emerson; an unidentified newspaper clipping about "Consul Dabney" signed "T.W.H."; and a list of titles and arithmetic in Emerson's hand. The editors have numbered the last item p. [197].

[front cover verso]¹ Care of Baring, Brothers, & Co   London

---

146 Lawrence St
F.S. Reed   210 Eutaw St
G.B. Coate.
C.J.M. Eaton   52 Mt Vernon

---

69 W. Cedar st   corner house   perhaps ↑Mr.↓ *Hale*

↑158↓ Charles St   Miss Gilley   probably

[Charles Eliot] Norton   Cleveland Sq. W. 33

[i]²   ⟨20⟩R.W. Emerson
                                            Concord, Mass.

Giro ↑best↓   Giraud ↑or Goodwin↓
German
    Louis Herman   Jobuse   Mrs Ad

Neal   Scots
            Beebe

C[harles]. K[ing]. Newcomb, Glendower Hotel,
Market Place, Great Portland St.   London

[ii] fastest train in Eng[lan]d at 11.45 ↑o'clock↓ every day from Pad-
dington, does 78 miles in 87 minutes & reaches Plymouth in 6 hours³

T[homas]. Hughes   80 Park St. Grosven[o]r Sq.

N. Hawthor[n]e   8 Woodfield Terrace
    Harrow Road, Paddington   London W

¹ On the front cover verso, "146 Lawrence . . . Vernon" is in red pencil, and "69
W. Cedar . . . Sq. W. 33" is in pencil.
² On p. [i], "20" and "Giro ↑best↓ . . . Beebe" are in pencil.
³ "fastest train . . . hours" is in pencil.

W.J. Stillman, 8 Attenbury Gardens   Clapham Co⟨u⟩mmon
    Best Station is Clapham Junction

C[harles]. E[liot]. Norton, 33 Cleveland Sq. W.

[1] [blank]
[2]⁴   G B B 1
    J[ames] B[radley] T[hayer] 2
↑Miss↓ E[lizabeth] R[ipley]. 1
    Mrs ⟨W F⟩J[ohn] M[urray] F[orbes] 3
      Miss V[irginia]. V[aughan]. 1
    Dr C[harles] T[homas] J[ackson] 3

    Atl[antic] B[an]k   Sept 12   325.29
    Concord B[an]k Sept 12   1202.41

[3]–[30] [blank]
[31] [Mon., Jan. 1] Tiffany   74 Decker, Biddle & John
Rev Edw C. Guild
A. Leo Knott, Esq.
Mr Waters
N[athaniel]. H Morison
[Tues., Jan. 2] Baltimore   Peabody Institute
    ⟨Imagina⟩Imagination & Poetry⁵

[32] [Thurs., Jan. 4] Peabody Institut[e]
↑Resource &↓ Inspiration⁶
F.S. Reed, 210 N Eutaw St   Baltimore
[Fri., Jan. 5] At Washington, at Charles Sumner's
Professor Spencer F. Baird   Smithsonian Ins.
    Hon S[amuel]. Hooper

---

⁴ The entries on p. [2] are in pencil.
⁵ "Tiffany . . . N.H Morison" is in pencil; "Imagina", in ink, is overwritten by "Imagination & Poetry" in pencil to cancel.
⁶ "Resources & Inspiration" is in pencil.

[33] [Sun., Jan. 7] Howard Institute.   Talk about Books
[Mon., Jan. 8] At the Senate House   Returned to Baltimore
[Tues., Jan. 9] Peabody Institute
⟨Homes & Hospitality⟩"Homes & Hospitality"[7]

[34] [Wed., Jan. 10] Mrs Morison at 1. o'c
Called on Miss Sophia Howard
[Thurs., Jan. 11] Peabody Institute
⟨Art & Nature⟩"Art & Nature"
[Fri., Jan. 12] ⟨New Brunswick N.J.   Homes & Hospitality⟩
J.H. Van Cleef[8]

[35] [Sat., Jan. 13] West Point
O[swald].H. Ernst   Capt of Engineers USA
Gen Emory Upton
Col Thos. H. Ruger, Commandant
Prof. H.E. Kendrick
[Sun., Jan. 14] ⟨West Point⟩West Point.   Cozzens Hotel
⟨"Immortality"⟩"Immortality."
Rev Dr Forsyth[9]
Dined with Col. Ruger   Commandant of the Military Academy.
[Mon., Jan. 15] New Brunswick, N.J.
J.H. Van Cleef, Esq.
James Neilson Esq
   Leave N.Y. at 3 P.M.
"Homes & Hospitality."

[36] [Tues., Jan. 16] Washington D C   Jas. T. Smith
"Homes & Hospitality."
[Wed., Jan. 17] Reached Concord at 6.30 PM

---

[7] "Homes & Hospitality", in pencil, is overwritten by " 'Homes & Hospitality' " in ink to cancel.

[8] "Art & Nature", in pencil, is overwritten by " 'Art & Nature' " in ink to cancel; "New Brunswick . . . Hospitality" is struck through in ink with a diagonal line; "Homes & Hospitality" is in pencil; "J.H. Van Cleef" is in red pencil.

[9] "O.H. Ernst . . . H.E. Kendrick" and "Rev Dr Forsyth" are in pencil; "West Point", in pencil, is overwritten by "West Point." in ink to cancel; " 'Immortality' ", in pencil, is overwritten by " 'Immortality.' " in ink to cancel.

[Thurs., Jan. 18] Memo.
 "Great Artists & great Anatomists"   By Robert Knox
                              ⟨Vol. 1 p 60⟩
 Goodsir's Anatomical Memoirs   Vol. I. p. 60,
Milne Edwards' Manual of Zoology. Translated by Knox.[10]

[37] [blank]
[38] [Mon., Jan. 22] W[illiam]. H. F[orbes]. & Edith, with their family departed for N.Y. & England.
[Tues., Jan. 23] ⟨⟨Concord Lyceum   Immortality⟩Concord
   Lyceum   "Immortality."⟩[11]

[39][12] [Thurs., Jan. 25] Pd J. Malcolm Forbes $10. to be added to
E[dward]. W. E[merson].'s $40 to buy me share of Nebraska stock

[40] [Tues., Jan. 30] Social Circle.

[41] [Wed., Jan. 31] Concord Lyceum

[42] [blank]
[43] [Wed., Feb. 7] Concord Lyceum.   "Immortality."

[44] [blank]
[45] [Tues., Feb. 13] Mrs [Mary Ward] Dorr

[46]–[47] [blank]
[48][13]   ↑Iron Boat if possible↓
↑1↓   How many can go in a boat↑?↓   ↑6 to 14↓
↑2↓   Are there staterooms with berths, & how many berths to a
room?   ↑one person in each↓

---

[10] Robert Knox, *Great Artists and Great Anatomists; a Biographical and Philosophical
Study* (London, 1852); *The Anatomical Memoirs of John Goodsir,* ed. William Turner, 2
vols. (Edinburgh, 1868); Milne Edwards' "Manual of Zoology" is unidentified.
  [11] "Concord Lyceum   Immortality", in pencil, is overwritten by "Concord Lyceum   'Immortality.' " in ink to cancel; the second entry was then fingerwiped to cancel.
  [12] The entries on pp. [39], [40], and [41] are in pencil, as is "Mrs Dorr" on p.
[45].
  [13] The entries on pp. [48] and [49] are in pencil.

↑3↓   Is Brindisi or Naples the cheapest way.

Naples is 275 francs & the boat sails on Saturdays. What day from Brindisi?

[49] 4   Where does one find the dragoman, & how does ⟨he⟩one go to work to find him?   ↑At Cairo   Shepherd's Hotel↓

5   Is French or English gold the right money

6   Lice?   ↑none↓

7   How does one go from Alexandria to Cairo.   ↑By Rail↓

8   Is there any greater trouble about much baggag[e] than elsewhere

[50] Price at

90   Piastres in silver for a pound

140   ″   ″   ″   ″ ″   ″

At Cairo change all into copper.

Shepherd's H[otel]. Cairo

Landlord or Sec Thomas finds the dragoman.[14]

[Thurs., Feb. 29] Judge Gray 4 Mt. Vernon Place

[51]–[55] [blank]

[56]   οὐ γάρ πω τέθνηκεν επὶ χθονὶ δῖος 'Οδυσσεὺς,

        ἀλλ' ετι που ζωὸς κατερύκεται ευρέι πόντω,

        νήσω εν ἀμφιρύτη, χαλεποὶδέ μιν ανδρες εχουσιν,[15]

                                    [Homer, *Odyssey*, I, 196–198]

Inscription on snuff box sent to Lord Holland by Napoleon from St Helena

———

Inscription suggested by J.H Frere

[57] [blank]

[58][16] [Fri., Mar. 22] ⟨Mrs Fields' "At home"⟩Mrs J[ames].T Fields' "At home"

[14] "Price at . . . the dragoman." is in pencil.

[15] "Yet hath not Odysseus the godlike from the earth departed yet; / Alive he is and hoarded, it seems, amidst of the deep, / In an isle by the sea begirdled. . . ." This entry is in pencil.

[16] On p. [58], "Mrs Fields' 'At home' ", in pencil, is overwritten by "Mrs J.T. Fields' 'At home' " in ink to cancel; "10 A.M." is in pencil; "Beacon Hill Place", in pencil, is overwritten by the same in ink.

Read "M[ary] M[oody] E[merson]."
[Sat., Mar. 23] Reading at house of Miss [Katherine] Loring. ↑10
A.M.↓
    Beacon Hill Place   Read "Social Aims."

[59] [Tues., Mar. 26] Virginia Vaughan

[60] [blank]
[61] [Sun., Mar. 31] *Ellen Ryan* of *Dedham* Masstts sent me today
through F.D. Ely Esq of Dedham & through Judge [Henry Flagg]
French my lost wallet which contained $115.05.[17]
[Mon., Apr. 1] Lecture to the Woman's Club.
    Mrs Maria S. Porter Secy.   "Inspiration."

[62]–[65] [blank]
[66] [Mon., Apr. 15] Mechanics Hall   3 o'clock P.M.   "Books"[18]

[67] [blank]
[68] [Mon., Apr. 22] ↑*II Reading*↓   Mechanics Hall
    "Poetry & Imagination"

[69] [blank]
[70] [Mon., Apr. 29] Mechanics Hall
    ↑III Reading↓   "Poetry & Imagination."   Concluded

[71]–[72] [blank]
[73] [Mon., May 6] Mechanics Hall   ↑(Montreal)↓   "Criticism"
Lochinvar, Timrod, Murat, Force of Prayer.
Lir's lonely daughter.

[74] [blank]
[75] [Mon., May 13] Mechanics Hall   Culture   Egremont[19]
[Tues., May 14] Lowell, Mass.   Channing Society
    ⟨Culture⟩"Inspiration"   Rev H. Blanchard

    [17] See Journal ST, p. [142] above.
    [18] For details of Emerson's Mechanics' Hall lectures and poetry readings see Journal
ST, pp. [153]–[155] above.
    [19] "Egremont" is in pencil.

427

[76] [blank]
[77] [Mon., May 20] Mechanics' Hall   Morals.   Religion

[78] [Tues., May 21] ⟨Lowell   Channing Club   Rev. Henry Blan-
chard⟩[20]

[79]–[85] [blank]
[86] [Sat., June 15] Athenaeum Gallery[21]

[87] [Mon., June 17] Need Radical Club
[Wed., June 19] Overseers

[88] [Thurs., June 20] ⟨Φ.B.K.⟩
[Sat., June 22] ⟨Club⟩

[89] [blank]
[90] [Fri., June 28] Charles Jackson

———

C[harles].D.B Mills, Syracuse

———

Alfred Stebbins   San Francisco

———

    Merc[antile]. Lib[rar]y Association

———

James B Thayer, Esq.

[91]–[93] [blank]
[94] [Wed., July 10] Amherst College   W.M. White   Hodgman
    "Greatness."

[95][22] How much the single man has accomplished, as Livingston
Nations banded had not found the secret of the Nile

———

[20] "Lowell . . . Blanchard" is struck through in ink with a diagonal line and in pencil
with a zigzag line.
    [21] "Athenaeum Gallery" is in red pencil, as is "Overseers" on p. [87].
    [22] The entries on p. [95] are in pencil. The source of the Samuel(?) Sharpe citations
has not been identified.

As long as Jerusalem stood, the Jew was sure. With its downfall, Christianity became possible to nations

Blemmyes having no heads[,] eyes & mouth on the breast
    Sharpe, II. 130

"St Jerome (in Psalm. 81) remarks that miracles prove nothing either for or against the truth of a religion."
    S. Sharpe II 137

God did not create death. See Wisdom of Solomon
                                        III. 14. I. 13

[96]–[98] [blank]
[99]²³ [Wed., July 24] Our house burned

pd Mrs Hare 2.00	
Cash to Ellen for Fayal	20.00
d[itt]o for d[itt]o	3.51
↑Saturday↓ pd washerwoman	3.00
Aug 3 paid Jordan & Marsh	59.
3. pd Costello for 6 ⟨d⟩½ days	14.00
pd Parker House Club	5.20
pd Boardman, wine.	11.00
pd Walcott & Holden	86.09

[100] Aug. 5.   Pd Rogers for boots & shoes to first August, full am[oun]t of bill

shaving brush	1.25
⟨d⟩Drugs at Melvin's	2.25
pd Concord Bank	300.00
pd Bicknell	3.00

²³ On p. [99], "Our house burned", in pencil, is overwritten by the same in ink; "pd Mrs Hare . . . 3.00" is in pencil.

Aug 3. pd Reynolds & Derby   35.
    6. pd Buttrick & Pratt   23.
      pd Eaton   7.
      pd Walcott & Holden in full

[101]–[106] [blank]
[107] [Sat., Aug. 17] Ocean House   Rye Beach
Wm Y. DeFord   Baltimore
Mrs   Saratoga
Dr   Washington
Dr   Eliot   St Louis
[Sun., Aug. 18] Rye Beach

[108] [Mon., Aug. 19] Portland   Preble House
[Tues., Aug. 20] Norway, Maine
    Waterford.
  Houghton's Bear-Mountain-House
    Mr Barker
    Mr (T.H.)? Mead wished to be remembered to his schoolfellow
Longfellow

[109] [Fri., Aug. 23] By boat by Sebago Lake, &c. to Portland. By
rail to Boston
Mr Mead, schoolmate of Longfellow
[Sat., Aug. 24] Concord

[110] [blank]
[111] [Wed., Aug. 28] From Boston to Naushon[24]

[112] [blank]
[113] [Tues., Sep. 3] Drew cheques on Concord & Atlantic B[an]ks
13000

        "North, south, in rings & amulets,
        Throughout the crowded world 'tis borne,

[24] "From . . . Naushon" is in pencil, as is "Drew . . . 13000" on p. [113].

Which, as a fashion long outworn,
Its ancient mind forgets."
            [William] *Allingham*. ["The Touchstone," ll. 29–32][25]

for (*avail*) read (*prevail*).

[114] [blank]
[115][26] [Wed., Sep. 11] To Boston from Nausho[n]

[116] [Thurs., Sep. 12] Paid ↑B.↓ Williams   25.00
[Fri., Sep. 13] Concord Bank   Deposit 1202.41

[117]–119] [blank]
[120] [Tues., Sep. 24] B.G. Niebuhr, Letters, Vol III 196[27]
[Wed., Sep. 25] Drew on the Atl[antic]. B[an]k $40.00
[Thurs., Sep. 26] ↑Remember Conway's Letter   Welch & Bigelow↓
Dr White.   Dr Bartlett.
Harper's Weekly for Sat. 28
Banks.   Sands & Furber.
        At Concord, Welsh Bards
                John Clahan

ED.   Geoffroy St. Hilaire   / Anthology / Chivalry
                        Judge Hoar

[121][28] [Fri., Sep. 27] Johnathon Amory   16 Pemberton Sq
        Passports for self & Ellen

Bigelow & Welch

[Sat., Sep. 28] J[ames]. E[lliot]. Cabot
                Dr [Jeffries] Wyman

[25] These lines are omitted from "The Touchstone" as it appears in *Parnassus*.
[26] The entries on pp. [115] and [116] are in pencil.
[27] Barthold Georg Niebuhr, *The Life and Letters of Barthold George Niebuhr; with Essays on His Character and Influence by Bunsen, Brandis, and Loebell,* 3 vols. (London, 1852). "B.G. Niebuhr . . . 196" and "Drew . . . $40.00" directly below it are in pencil.
[28] On p. [121], "Johnathon Amory . . . Ellen" and "J T. Fields" are in red pencil.

Dr [Estes] Howe
Henry James
C[harles C.]. Perkins
Dr [Oliver Wendell] Holmes
↑J[ames] T. Fields↓

[122] [Mon., Sep. 30] *Memo.*
   Tax due in Concord 1 November $307.08

[123] [blank]
[124]²⁹ Concord Bank

↑⟨Oct⟩ Sept 13↓	1202.41	Sept 12	1000
		Sept 12	202
		↑Sept 28↓	⟨4⟩50
			152

↑Oct. 19↓	$1966.49	Atlantic
pd	546.67	S.G. Ward & Co
	1419.82	
	100	
	1319.82	20

Recd from Abraham Jackson from Court St rent
   ⟨3⟨66⟩79.49⟩   379.74

[125] [Wed., Oct. 9] Concord Bank   137.68
_____

pd my only note at Concord Bank.   100.00   by cheque on the
Atl[antic]. B[an]k.
_____

[126] [blank]
[127] [Tues., Oct. 15] Banquet to Froude

---

²⁹ The entries on pp. [124]–[127] are in pencil, except for "Concord Bank
137.68" on p. [125] and "Banquet to Froude" on p. [127].

[Wed., Oct. 16]   1686
                    50
Atl[antic]. B[an]k   1636.77
                     379.74
                    2016.51
                    1966

[128] [blank]
[129] [Mon., Oct. 21] Cary & Co.   90 Pine st   N. York
[Wed., Oct. 23] Wyoming Sails.

[130]³⁰ [Thurs., Oct. 24] 12 o'c.   247 miles
———

Length of Steamer W⟨omi⟩yoming from stem to stern, 400 ft.
———

[Fri., Oct. 25] 260 miles   / 507
[Sat., Oct. 26] 12 o'c 270   / ⟨4⟩777

[131] [Sun., Oct. 27] 280 miles   / ⟨55⟩777
[Mon., Oct. 28] 284 miles
[Tues., Oct. 29] 268 miles

[132] [Wed., Oct. 30] M[i]l[e]s 288   / 1897
                                         290
[Thurs., Oct. 31] 290   ⟨19⟩2187
[Fri., Nov. 1] 242   2⟨3⟩429
                                       251
                                      2680

[133]³¹ [Sat., Nov. 2] 251   2680
        George Langtry, Belfast ↑Ireland↓
[Sun., Nov. 3] Arrived at the Docks.   Liverpool
[Mon., Nov. 4] Chester.   Called on Bishop [William] Jacobson
     ↖↑found Edward.↓

---

[30] The entries on pp. [130]–[132] are in pencil, as is "Cary & Co. . . . N. York" on
p. [129].
[31] On p. [133], "251", "2680", and "Liverpool" are in pencil.

[134] [Tues., Nov. 5] Breakfasted with Bishop [William] Jacobson
Lunched at Dean Hanson's
Attended Archaeologic Architectural & Historic Society's Meeting
Mr Ewen read a paper on Tapestry
Visited the Cathedral
Saw Mr Clough & daughter
Mr Thomas Hughes, Hon. Secy / East Gate Row.
[Wed., Nov. 6] Left Chester at 1.55   Arrived in London
At Mrs Bennet's, Down St. 8.30 PM   ⟨St⟩
[Thurs., Nov. 7] Visited Carlyle
Received A[lexander]. Ireland, Esq[32]

[135] [Fri., Nov. 8] At the Barings' office
                              Russell Sturgis
                              Mr Hodgson
                              Mr Baring
                              Kensington Museum
[Sat., Nov. 9] Dined at the Inner Temple with Thomas Hughes M.P.
———

       [William] Allingham
       [William] M[a]cCormac
       [Thomas] Carlyle
[Sun., Nov. 10] Service at the Temple.
———

       Mr Wm MacCormac   13 Harley St, Cavendish Square
       Charles [Eliot] Norton
       Miss Jane Norton
       Mr Henry Lee

[136] [Mon., Nov. 11] Sir Frederick Pollack   59 Montagu Sq.
Mrs Arthur Clough   39. D. Onslow Sq.
[Arthur Penrhyn Stanley, the] Dean of Westminster & Lady Augusta
       [Stanley]

---

[32] Except for Thomas Hughes, bookseller, antiquarian, and secretary of the Chester
Archeological, Architecture, and Historical Society, identifiable persons met by Emerson
during his visit to Europe and Egypt in 1872–1873 are noted in Journal ST, pp. [179],
[185], [187]–[192] above.

Miss Mary C. Aitken
Rev W.H. Channing   15 Hornton St   Kensington
Sir Henry Holland
Charles K. Newcombe
Mr Wm MacCormac
Mr Edwin Arnold, & Mrs A[rnold].
Thomas Hughes, Esq.

[137]³³ [Fri., Nov. 15] ↑arrived at Paris↓   Paris
    ⟨Night   Rue de Baune⟩7 Rue de Baune.
        Hotel de Lorraine
            Madame Garrier
Found there J[ames].R[ussell]. Lowell & wife   & John Holmes

[138]³⁴ [Sun., Nov. 17] Chapelle Evangélique de l'Etoile, Pasteur
Bersier
[Tues., Nov. 19] ↑At↓ Louvre with Henry James
Charles & T⟨erch⟩herchie Emerson dined with us³⁵

[139] [Wed., Nov. 20] Dined with [Auguste] Laugel
[Thurs., Nov. 21] Left Paris   Rue de Baune   Madame Garrier

———

    Isabella in the cars
[Fri., Nov. 22] Marseilles

[140] [Sat., Nov. 23] Marseilles   Drew on ⟨L⟩Rabaud ⟨500⟩200
francs

———

    heather abounding on hills.

———

[Sun., Nov. 24] Nice   Hotel   ⟨P⟩Date trees   pepper trees³⁶

———

    ³³ On p. [137], the inserted "Paris" is in pencil; "Night   Rue de Baune", in pencil,
is overwritten by "7 Rue de Baune." in ink to cancel; "Hotel de Lorraine" and "Madame
Garrier", in pencil, are overwritten by the same in ink.
    ³⁴ The entries on pp. [138] and [139] are in pencil.
    ³⁵ Charles Emerson, Emerson's nephew, married Therchi Kaveschi in Switzerland in
1871, and they eventually settled in Concord.
    ³⁶ "Marseilles   Drew . . . pepper trees" is in pencil; "500" is overwritten by "200"
in ink to cancel.

[Mon., Nov. 25] Steamer from ⟨R⟩Nice to ⟨Leghorn⟩ Genoa
and thence all night in steamer to Leghorn

[141] [Tues., Nov. 26] ⟨|| epw || ⟩³⁷ ⟨By⟩ By rail from Leghorn to
Pisa.   Duomo   Baptistery   Leaning Tower   Campo Santo   Echo
From Pisa to Florence by rail & took chambers in the Hotel du Nord.
[Wed., Nov. 27] ⟨|| epw ||⟩Uffizi Gallery
[Thurs., Nov. 28] Birth Place of Dante   Palazzo Buonaroti
Michel Angelo's MSS   Bargelo   Drive to the new

[142] [Sat., Nov. 30? Sun., Dec. 1?] Arrived at Rome.
Piazz⟨d⟩a d'Espagna no. 151, Pension de Mme Tellenbach

[143] [blank]
[144] [Sat., Dec. 7] ⟨Course of Lectures for Young Women⟩
⟨J[ames].T. Fields, Secy⟩³⁸

[145] [blank]
[146]³⁹ [Fri., Dec. 13] Diocletian   Pantheon   Villa Pamfile Doria
pd Curnex 50 lire

[147]–[152] [blank]
[153]–[154] [leaf torn out]
[155] The bells
     Turn again Huntington
———
Arabia Felix

---

³⁷ Of three erased pencil lines here, only "Leghorn" on line 1 and "Charles &
Thercie Emerson" on line 2 are able to be read.
³⁸ "Course . . . Fields, Secy" is struck through in ink with two diagonal lines.
³⁹ The entries on pp. [146], [155], and [156] are in pencil.

[156] Trubner & Co.   Paternoster Row

$\langle 4\rangle 777$
  280
——
1057
  284
——
1341
2$\langle 56\rangle$68
——
1609
  288
——
1897

[157]–[159] [blank]
[160]   [CASH ACCOUNT.   JANUARY.]
   [Date.]   [Received.]
   Nov. 8   20 or 30 pounds[40]
        13   Fifty pounds
        20   one thousand francs   1015 francks
             Marseilles.   Rabaud
             200 francs   200 ——
   2$\langle 5\rangle$7   Fenzie & Co   400 ——
        29   Fenzie & Co   39$\langle$0$\rangle$2 franks Fr

[161]–[173] [blank]
[174] J. Dunn Smith
   2 Park Villa, Myddleton Road, Hornsey, Middlesex.
Pamphlet on "First Principles of Religion"

[175][41] ↑Mr [John Rollin] Tilton's contract↓
Badowi Muhammed Dragoman
   2 months, paying all charges
   boat, board, backsheesh, &c
   £130. sterling.
   from Cairo up & back to Cairo, Nov 1870

———

[40] "20 or 30 pounds" is in pencil.
[41] The entries on pp. [175]–[177] are in pencil.

437

[176]   Dal ciel discese ecol mortal suo poi
          In viste ebbe

[177] Stowell & Eldon both misers
How much vin he could drink at a sitting   any given quantity
Answered Bozwell's ? for definition of taste
That faculty of the mind which leads a Scot to prefer England to his
own country[42]

[178] [blank]
[179]   Addresses
Nov 12 Barone R. ↑Von↓ Hoffman   Villa Celimontana   Roma
———

Mrs [Arthur Hugh] Clough   39 D. Onslow Square
———

W[illiam]. Allingham, 18 Neville St. Onslow Gardens S.W.
———

Hon. Mr [George Perkins] Marsh, 8 Via San Bazillio Barberina
———

Miss S[arah Freeman] Clarke, Via Quattrofontane, 26
———

Mr ↑J[ohn].R[ollin]↓ Tilton   Piazza Barberini
———

Hon Geo P. Marsh, 8 San Ba⟨z⟩silio
———

Gu[i]seppe Artoni   472 Corso
J B Gould ↑MD↓   107 Via del Barberini[43]
Mr [John Rollin] Tilton   Palazzo Barberini
———

Madame Laura Minghetti   4 Piazza Paganica
———

Mr & Mrs Terry, Palazzo Odescalchi

———

[42] James Boswell, *The Life of Samuel Johnson,* May 16, 1763. Emerson's source is
probably the one-volume London, 1827, edition in his library. William Scott, Baron
Stowell (1745–1836), English jurist, was an intimate of Dr. Johnson; his brother, John
Scott, 1st Earl of Eldon (1751–1838), was lord high chancellor of England almost con-
tinuously from 1801 to 1827.
[43] "Guseppe Artoni . . . Barberini" is in pencil.

[180] Je suis riche des biens dont je sais me passer. Vigee.

A better voice sings through our song[44]

[181] [blank]

[182] Goethe's Italian Journey is chiefly important to his biography: what a self inquisition! Shakspeare how vastly superior, who never worried us with this weary egotism. One can hardly predict the greatness that Goethe attained, from this very unpromising early exhibition. Yet I want the egotism for its value to the portrait, whilst I regret it as diminution.

[183] Rainbow at morning
   Sailors take warning
   Rainbows at night
   Sailors delight

[184] 1872. 11 Nov. Memoranda
   Hotten
   Stillman
   Newcomb
   John Chapman
   Mr Forsyth
   Mrs Clough
   C.E. Norton

     Cook, Entrepeneur.
   Osgood & Co.
   Mr Hughes's "Nation"

[185][45] Osgood
   Higginson
  x brushes

---

[44] "A better . . . song" is in pencil. "Vigee" is either Louis Vigée (1727–1767), painter, or his son, Louis-Jean-Baptiste-Étienne Vigée (1758–1820), writer, or his daughter, Marie-Louise-Élizabeth Vigée LeBrun (1755–1842), painter.

[45] The entries on p. [185] are in pencil.

    A Jackson
    Dr White
  x Rogers   not send to Beverly
    Ask Mr Thayer
  x Ladies Club

    Sands & Furber
    Franklin Insurance Co.

[186]⁴⁶   Tickets. April 1872
          Mrs P. Cobb   Van Runsaeller⟨A⟩   3
        x Miss Webster   3   3
          Judge French
          Hannah Ryan, Dedh[am]
        x Anna Keyes   2
        x Mrs Cheney
        x Mrs Dudley   2
        x Edith Davidson
        x Abby Faulkner   2
        x J.M. Forbes   3
        x G.P Bradford   1
        x V Vaughan   1
        x C.T. Jackson   ⟨3⟩   3
        x C.A. Bartol   ⟨2⟩   2
        x J.B. Thayer   2
        x Dr Hedge   1

[187] *Athenaeum*
        Sir Wm Jones's ["A] Hymn [to Náráyena"]⁴⁷

[188]⁴⁸ Cult[ure?]. Minor key

---

⁴⁶ The first *x* in the list that follows is in pencil. This is a list of persons who received complimentary tickets to Emerson's six private conversations in Boston April 15–May 20, 1872.
   ⁴⁷ See Journal ST, p. [148] above.
   ⁴⁸ The entries on p. [188] are in pencil.

3000	93	2187
2429	20	242
571	1860	2429
	8	
	14880	
	2	
	296	

[189] Cyclamen Capuccino

Les Auteurs Grecs avec traductions Francaises
    Eschefe Par M. Malerne
    Paris   L Hachette & Co   Boulevard St Germaine no 77

[190] L'Etude sur Horace et Virgile de M. Patin en tête de la traduction d'Horace publié par M. Garnier[49]

Voltaire's Spinosa   Satires.   *Les Systèmes.*

[191][50] ⟨Copy of N[orth]. A[merican]. Review⟩
        ⟨Michel Angelo⟩
        ⟨John Milton⟩

        Feller to be bound
        Copyright law
        Osgood & Co   Copyright twice
        Miss Whitney   Sculpto[r]
↑Barber↓ Mr Keith
        ⟨Mr Gould⟩
        ⟨Pay N.Y. "Nation."⟩   Barbour

[192][51]   Ware
            ⟨Russell⟩   30.00

---

[49] "L'Etude . . . Garnier" is in pencil; see Journal ST, p. [51] above.

[50] The entries on p. [191] are in pencil. "N. A. Review . . . John Milton" is struck
through in pencil with a vertical line; "Mr Gould . . . 'Nation.' " is struck through in pencil with three vertical lines.

[51] The entries on p. [192] are in pencil. "Russell", "Foster", "Tichnor.", "Dick-
son", "Mr Brooks", and "Mills" are each struck through in pencil with a diagonal line.

441

```
              ⟨Foster⟩    14
      3000    ⟨Tichnor.⟩   3.30
      2680    ⟨Dickson⟩    4.30
       320    Dr Russell
              ⟨Mr Brooks⟩
                  ⟨Mills⟩  5.30
              ⟨Muller⟩
         x    A Jackson
         x    ⟨Atl[antic] B[an]k    195⟩
              Lee                          2429
              ⟨L.B. Russell⟩                251
              Thaxter                      2680
              Milruse
              Whipple photograph
         x    ⟨Ward⟩
              Thayer
```

[193] W[illiam].H[enry]. Fur↑n↓ess, 1426 Pine St   Phila[delphia].

———

M[oncure].D. Conway, 51 Notting Hill Sq.   Bayswater. W.   London

———

20 Oct. [1872.]
  Atlantic B[an]k.   1249
  Concord B[an]k.   137

———

Drew on Atl[antic] B[an]k.   say 149
leaving 1100
Drew on the Concord B[an]k 137[52]

———

   Hotten

[194][53]   Parnassus

---

[52] "20 Oct. . . . Concord Bk 137" is in pencil.

[53] The entries on p. [194] are part of Emerson's collection of materials for possible inclusion in *Parnassus*. William Byrd's "My Mind to Me a Kingdom is" appears in *Parnassus*; "Happy the man . . ." is from Alexander Pope's "Ode on Solitude," l. 1; for John

Byrd.   Psalms, Sonnets, &c.   1588
See Aids to Contentment   Selected by John Morris
London. Deighton, Bell, & Co. 1870.

Pope's Happy Man
    "Happy the man whose wish & care" &c.

"He that is down needs fear no fall." *Bunyan* Pilgrim's Progress

---

"Welcome pure thoughts welcome ye silent groves." Sir H. Wotton

---

"How happy is he born & taught," &c Wotton

> "My wishes are but few
> All easy to fulfil
> I make the limits of my power
> The bounds unto my will."
>   *Southwell*

> Then pass the dark brown hours of night
> No more in dreaming how you may
> But load your chests, &c
>   *Chartier*

[195] Allingham's "Poesis Humana"[54]

[196][55] 72.54

[inside back cover] [Co]rner of 9th & D street
    Lincoln Hall
    Metropolitan RR

Bunyan's line see the song of the shepherd boy in *The Pilgrim's Progress from This World to That Which Is to Come* (see also *JMN*, V, 434); Sir Henry Wotton's "How happy . . ." is from "The Character of a Happy Life," l. 1, in *Reliquiae Wottonianae*, 1685. Wotton's "Welcome pure thoughts . . ." and the lines by William Southwell and by Alain Chartier are unidentified.

[54] This entry is in pencil.

[55] The entries on p. [196], the inside back cover, and p. [197] are in pencil.

Summer 8th st
G[eorge] B[arrell] Emerson
Atl[antic Bank]   June 25   145.45

[197] ↑Wm↓ Strode DD
      Floating Island a tragicomedy   Lond[on] 1665
    Concerning   Strode   see   [Anthony   à   Wood,]   Athen[*ae*].
      Oxon[*iensis*] ↑(Bliss)↓   Vol III p 151
    [George] Ellis's Specimens [*of Early English Poets,* 1803,] Vol
      III. p. 173
    Gent. Mag. Vol. xciii, part 2. p 7[56]

    200
    200
    150
     60   40
    610   20

[56] Emerson copied the information on Strode and Ellis from "Fly Leaves, No. XIII," in *The Gentleman's Magazine,* 93, part 2 (July 1823), p. 7. The material that follows on p. [197] is upside down.

Pocket Diary 24

1873

Pocket Diary 24 is devoted primarily to recording Emerson's memoranda of his travels in Egypt and Europe during early 1873. It also contains numerous addresses, notations of social engagements, and miscellaneous financial transactions. A few entries may have been made late in 1872 or early in 1874.

The notebook, bound in black stamped leather, is a commercially published diary entitled "THE / ILLUSTRATED UNIVERSAL / POCKET DIARY / AND ALMANACK / 1873", published by N. J. Powell & Co., London. The covers measure 6.9 × 10.7 cm. The front cover extends into a tongue that, when the book is closed, fits into a loop on the back cover; the front cover also contains an expandable inside pocket. A paper label fastened to the spine is inscribed "1873".

The white, unnumbered, gilt-edged pages measure 6.7 × 10.3 cm; pages 4–69 are lined. The book consists of two front flyleaves (i–iv); a title page (page 1); a second title page (page 3); daily appointments for 1873, seven to a page (pages 4–56); pages for cash accounts (pages 57–69); eclipses in 1873 and a table of fixed and moveable feasts (page 70); historical monthly calendars for 1873 (pages 71–82); a table of high water times at London Bridge for 1873 (pages 83–85); a list of European sovereigns (page 86); a list of English public holidays (page 87); an inventory of the English royal family (page 88); rates of postage and postal schedules (pages 89–90); miscellaneous charts and tables that include the names of army, navy, and emigration agents, interest and annuity accounts, and tax tables (pages 91–98); and a back flyleaf (pages 99–100).

Entries by Emerson occur on forty pages. Printed matter in Pocket Diary 24 is reproduced here only in the sections on daily appointments and cash accounts where relevant. Otherwise, pages are designated as blank if they bear no inscription by Emerson; the presence or absence of printed matter is not specified.

In the expandable pocket in the front cover is a Fitchburg Railroad timetable.

[front cover verso]¹ ⟨£250⟩

⎡Dahabééh⎤
Dragoman
Reis
mate
10 oarsmen
1 cook
factotum boy
Marzook, head waiter
Hassan assistant

_____

17 men

_____

Marzook Hanzar   Table servant
Mohammed Abd Ennabi   Cook

$$38305$$
$$\underline{25}$$
$$357$$

[i]   R.W. Emerson.

[ii]–[1] [blank]
[2] [inscription by Ellen Emerson]
[3] [blank]
[4] [Mon., Dec. 30, 1872] Breakfast with the Khedive²
[Tues., Dec. 31, 1872] Shepard's Hotel. Cairo, Egypt.
[Sat., Jan. 4] Visit to the Pyramids & the Sphynx.

For Mission Dolore[s] see Francis Javier-Claviero, in Junipero Serro³

¹ The entries on the front cover verso are in pencil; "38305 . . . 357" is upside down.
² "Breakfast . . . Khedive" is in pencil.
³ "For Mission . . . Serro" is in pencil. Francisco Javier Clavijero (1731–1787), Mexican historian, lived among the Indians as a missionary until the expulsion of the Jesuits from Mexico in 1767; Junípero Serra (1713–1784), Spanish Franciscan missionary in America, established missions throughout California.

446

[5]⁴ [Tues., Jan. 7] Sailed from Cairo in the Aurora

[6] [blank]
[7] [Sun., Jan. 19] eye-glass for Mustapha Aga, Eng[lish].
Consul Luxor
[Mon., Jan. 20] ⟨Eng⟩ ↑Am[erican].↓ Consul ↑Medinet Abou↓
    Ali Effendi Moorad   Luxor
[Tues., Jan. 21] Karnak   pd 20 pounds
    Miss Farquah[a]r   ⟨6⟩paid also 6£
[Wed., Jan. 22] Tombs of the Kings   17, 9, 11
[Thurs., Jan. 23] Karnak   Sailed
[Fri., Jan. 24] Sailed   Esne   w. bank

[8] ↑January↓
[Tues., Jan. 28] Assuan   Mr G[eorge].L. Owen
[Wed., Jan. 29] Philae   at night sailed for Cairo
[Thurs., Jan. 30] Ombos
[Fri., Jan. 31] Edfou, / Apollopolis
[Sat., Feb. 1] Thebes

[9] [Sun., Feb. 2] Memnonium   Medinet Abou
[Mon., Feb. 3] It blew. Elliot & Owen's party
[Tues., Feb. 4] Left Thebes
[Wed., Feb. 5] Dendara
[Thurs., Feb. 6] Abydos   Tablet of the Kings

[10]⁵ [Mon., Feb. 10] Siout. Tombs & Bazaar
[Tues., Feb. 11] Rhoda
[Wed., Feb. 12] ⟨Rhoda⟩ Benesouaf
[Thurs., Feb. 13] ⟨Evening   Cairo⟩Cairo
Drew £105. on Tod, Rathbone, & Co. & deposited £80. with them
for Mr Whitwell
[Fri., Feb. 14] Met Mr J.T. Emmerson, of Peover, Knutsford   &
Mr

---

⁴ The entries on pp. [5] and [7]–[9] are in pencil, except for "January" on p. [8].
⁵ On p. [10], "Siout. . . . Benesouaf" is in pencil; "Evening   Cairo", in pencil, is
overwritten by "Cairo" in ink to cancel.

[Sat., Feb. 15] At Alexandria

[11]–[12] [blank]
[13] [Sat., Mar. 8] at Baron [Richard] Von Hoffman's

[14] [Sun., Mar. 9] At Mr [William Wetmore] Story's
[Mon., Mar. 10] Left Rome 9 A.M   Arrived in Florence 7. PM

[15]–[16] [blank]
[17] [Sat., Apr. 5] 16 Donn St   2d floor

[18] [Sun., Apr. 6] 8 o'clock   ↑Mr Grenfell   Max Muller↓
     15 St James Place
[Mon., Apr. 7] ⟨730⟩
     ↑Dowager↓ Lady Stanley[6]
[Tues., Apr. 8] 67 Cadogan Place   Mr Edward Dicey
[Wed., Apr. 9] [inscription by Ellen Emerson]
[Thurs., Apr. 10] ⟨Lady Amberley⟩Lord Amberley[7]
     30 Weymouth St.   Portland Place
[Fri., Apr. 11] Visit to Earl Russell
     Called on Mr Owen & Sir Henry Taylor
[Sat., Apr. 12] ⟨⟨Mr. C⟩   1 Queens Gate⟩   ↑B⟨e⟩reakfast 9¾↓
     ↑Notting Hill Square↓   5.20[8]

[19][9] [Sun., Apr. 13] Mrs Paulet   ⟨Miss⟩Cathcart Road
     Boltons, Brompton S.W.   ⌈after church⌉
[Mon., Apr. 14] Dean [Arthur Penrhyn] Stanley at 7.30 pm
[Tues., Apr. 15] Lady Amberley at 11 P.M.
     10 o'c Blue Coats mansion.   Bank
[Wed., Apr. 16] Breakfast at 10 o'clock with Duchess of Argyll.
[Thurs., Apr. 17] Mr [Charles Eliot] Norton   33 Cleveland S⟨t⟩quare
W

[6] "730" is in pencil; "Lady Stanley", in pencil, is overwritten by the same in ink.
[7] "Lady Amberley", in pencil, is overwritten by "Lord Amberley" in ink to cancel.
[8] "Mr. C", "Notting Hill Square", and "5.20" are in pencil.
[9] On p. [19], "Dean ... 7.30 pm", "10 o'c ... Bank", "Breakfast ... Argyll.",
"Mr Norton", "Geo Howard ... Road", and "W. Allingham" are in pencil.

[Fri., Apr. 18] Mrs Smalley   9.30 A.M.
    Geo Howard   1 Palace Green   Kensington W
    ↑Palace Garden Road↓
[Sat., Apr. 19] W[illiam]. Allingham   18 Neville St, Onslow Gardens S.W.

[20]¹⁰ [Sun., Apr. 20] 2 o'clock   Dr [William Benjamin] Carpenter   St Paul's
    Evening Service at the Abbey.
[Mon., Apr. 21] Sadlers   Miss Jewsbury   House of Commons
    Working Men's College   8 o'clock
[Tues., Apr. 22] Breakfast Sir H[enry]. Holland   9.15
    Mr Hughes   7.⟨3⟩oo   Windsor
[Wed., Apr 23] 12   Mr Allingham   ⟨Mr.⟩Mr. Field   10 A.M.
    Lady Airlie   8 o'clock   Airlie Lodge   Camden Hill
[Thurs., Apr. 24] ⟨Ironmongers⟩Mr Gladstone
    Sir [William] F[rederick]. Pollock.   dinner 7.30
    Dr Quaine will come between 5 & 6
[Fri., Apr. 25] Mr [Moncure D.] Conway at 6   Mrs Arnold 1.30
[Sat., Apr. 26] ⟨Royal Society⟩1 Queen's Gate   Breakfast 9.¾ o'clock
    Mr Lyon Playfair. 4 Queensbury Place, S Kensington

[21]¹¹ [Sun., Apr. 27] Start for Wales
[Mon., Apr. 28] Ravenscroft
[Wed., Apr. 30] Oxford   [Benjamin] Jowett
[Thurs., May 1] ⟨Mr E[dward]. F[ordham]. Flower   The Hill Stratford⟩
    ⟨Jow⟩   Oxford
[Fri., May 2] ⟨Stratford⟩Oxford   [John] Ruskin
[Sat., May 3] Stra⟨d⟩tford

¹⁰ On p. [20], "Evening . . . Abbey.", "Saddlers", "Working Men's . . . o'clock", "Mr Hughes   7.⟨3⟩oo", "Lady Airlie . . . Hill", and "Mrs Arnold 1.30" are in pencil; "Ironmongers", in pencil, is overwritten by "Mr Gladstone" in ink to cancel; "Royal Society", in pencil, is overwritten by "I Queen's Gate" in ink to cancel.
¹¹ The entries on pp. [21]–[23] and [26] are in pencil, except for "Ravenscroft" on p. [21].

[22] [Sun., May 4] Stratford
[Mon., May 5] ⟨York pm⟩Stratford
[Tues., May 6] ⟨York⟩Durham
[Wed., May 7] Durham
[Thurs., May 8] Edinburg

[23] [Wed., May 14] Mrs Williams   153 Duke St

[24]–[25] [blank]
[26] [Wed., June 4] Thos MacManus

$$\frac{46.65}{7.00}$$
39.65

[27]–[28] [blank]
[29] [Wed., June 25] Commencement.   Overseers.

[30] [Wed., July 2] Boston Schools   3.45 o'clock Winter st[12]

[31] [Sun., July 6] Mrs Henry Adams   At Mr Gaskell's.   Park Lane London
    sent to Sands & Furber 2396 boxes o⟨r⟩f ⟨2 crates⟩ strawberries. Charge Ballou with 56 boxes or 2 crates[13]

[Wed., July 9] Overseers   H[arvard]. C[ollege].
    11 o'clock. Boston.
[Thurs., July 10] Historical Soc[iet]y   11 o'clock
[Fri., July 11] Library Committee   Gore Hall, 11 o'c.

[32] [Sun., July 13] A. Hamilton Lepper. Cambridgeport

[33]–[48] [blank]
[49] [Fri., Nov. 14] The Frenchman who translated the Canterbury Tales has found at Paris the original of the Squire's Tale in 30,000

[12] "Boston Schools" is in pencil.
[13] "Mrs Henry Adams . . . 2 crates" is in pencil.

lines. I wonder if it is like ⟨Spenser⟩ in any respect.   A[rthur]. H[ugh]. C[lough].

[50]–[53] [blank]
[54]   Emenda
        Corkscrew
        Photograph
            Pocket book
            Fez[14]

[Tues., Dec. 16] Athenaeum
Ups & Downs
Off the Skelliggs
[Wed., Dec. 17] Billings
                [H.A.] Babbitt

[55] [Tues., Dec. 23]   Envelopes
        Mrs [Henry] Adams   91 Marlboro St
        Mrs Emerson   Joy St
            ⟨S⟩Mason   54 Beacon St
[Thurs., Dec. 25] Mr Forbes
[Sat., Dec. 27] Mrs Sargent

[56] ⟨Mrs Lombard   11 Rue Bienfaisance⟩[15]
        ⟨Mrs Jewett   116 Rue de Grenelle   St Germain   Paris⟩
        ⟨Mr Morrison   75 Rue Vaugirard⟩

[Mon., Dec. 29] ⟨Overseers⟩
[Tues., Dec. 30] Overseers   10½
[Wed., Dec. 31] Governor at Mr Forbes   10 o'c
        ⟨Charles G Leland⟩   Mrs Sargent, 3 o'clock
[Thurs., Jan. 1, 1874?] Milton

---

[14] "Emenda . . . Fez" is in pencil.
[15] "Mrs Lombard . . . Bienfaisance" is struck through in ink with three diagonal lines.

Fools they did not know that the half was better than the whole cig[ar]¹⁶

[57]¹⁷   ⟨£   s⟩
    ⟨Marsala   1.   4⟩
    ⟨Medoc   36 & 24 shilling⟩
    ⟨St Julian   ⟨£⟩ 18.   6⟩
    ⟨Sherry   3⟩
    ⟨Beer   1⟩

↑W. Wood. New Eng[lan]d Prospect↓

Athenaeum

Vaughan
St James

———

Humphrey, Bromfield st.

———

Mr Forbes' Letter for Sanborn.

———

See Mrs Jackson about sale of rights.

———

Athenaeum

[58] Mission Dolores
General C[harles].P. Stone referred me to Fran. Savier Claviero
    sub. Junipero Serre¹⁸

———

    R[ichard]. Beardsley, Consul Gen[era]l, Cairo.
    H.A. Babbitt, V[ice]. Consul Gen[era]l Alexandria

———

¹⁶ See p. [66] below.
¹⁷ On p. [57], the list of wines and prices is in pencil. William Wood's *New England Prospect*, one of the best early descriptions of Massachusetts Bay, was first printed in 1634.
¹⁸ See p. [4] above.

[59] For G[eorge] P[artridge] B[radford]
Libraire Hachette over the Seine in Latin Quarter
Traductions lineaires

———

Latin Horace, *Odes & Satires* & no more
Greek *Sophocles*   Electra   Oedipe Roi
      Oedipe à Colone, Philoctete,
Eschylus Suppliants   Eumenides   Persae

[60] *Paris*

———

Photographs & Engravings at a corner shop not far from Place Palais
Royale

———

Cretés   Optician   11 Rue d'Ecole de Médécine
      for opera glasses, &c

[61]^{19} W Higginson   Hotel de France et de Bath   239 Rue St
Honore

———

Mrs Lombard   11 Rue de la Bienfaisance

———

Mrs C.C. Jewett   116 Rue de Grenelle   St Germaine
      A la Mairie

[62]–[63] [blank]
[64]^{20} G[eorge].L. Owen   United University Clu[b]   London
Ralph Elliot   Chester Sq.
Mr C Berkeley   Ida
J.T. Emmerson, Peover Knutsford
      Reed
      Morison   75 Rue Vaugirard
Mrs C[harles]. C[offin]. Jewett   116 Rue de Grenelle   St Ger-
maine   Paris
Chez Mme Felliat

---

[19] The entries on p. [61] are in pencil.
[20] The entries on pp. [64] and [65] are in pencil, except for "J.T. Emmerson ...
Felliat" on p. [64].

453

[65] pyramid
      lateen sail
      & shadow
      minaret
      all picturesque
      hovels are arches cut into the mountain walls
      & their clothing—all go into pictures well as ours does not.

[66] half better than the whole cigar *Hesiod.*[21]

flies roost in the eyes of all the Arab children[22]

Mission Dolores
   Fran Savier Claviero
   Sub. Junipero Sarro

------

      as noted by Gen[era]l Charles B. Stone, Cairo Egypt[23]

Divinity School   any day but Friday.

[67][24] John Rollin Tilton

      Charles P Stone
      Richard Von Hoffmann

         Morison
      75 Rue de Vaugirard

For James B Thayer, Esq
Edition of Virgil
of P. Masvicius, 2 vols. 4to.
Leauvarden, 1727.
not to be bought if it cost more than $10 or $12 gold.

[21] Cf. Hesiod, *Works and Days,* l. 40: "How much more the half is than the whole."
Quoted by Abraham Cowley, "Of Agriculture." See *The Essays and Other Prose Writings,*
ed. A. B. Gough (Oxford, 1915), p. 150. See *JMN,* VI, 138; cf. p. [56] above.
[22] "flies . . . children" is in pencil.
[23] See pp. [4] and [56] above.
[24] On p. [67], "Morison . . . Vaugirard" and "pd Hachette . . . 12 francs" are in
pencil.

pd Hachette for Horace & Sophocles   ⟨$⟩ 12 francs

[68] Dec. 29.

Thoreau's greyhound
—Morison[25]

Decr. 29.
Duties to W[illiam]. H[athaway]. F[orbes]
        E. A.
        ————

    Engineer in Canada who has named the town Emerson
    ————

[69] Mr Geo. Howard   1 Palace Green, Kensington
_____

Mrs Paulet   2 Cathcart Road   Boltons. Brompton S.W
_____

[70]–[98] [blank]
[99][26] dreams   jealous of being remember[e]d, dissipated instantly &
angrily if you try,
could the glass hold all it has shown me, for you, you need not come
yourself to Egypt
The sandstone or limestone instructs them how to build—stands in
square blocks & they have only to make a square door for tombs & the
shore is a pair or a series of ⟨steps⟩ or stairs.   ↑Shadow at pyramid.   lateen sail↓
The whole nation has one dear word "Backsheesh Howatjee" whether
it mean Virtue, or Wisdom, or Contemplation or Contempt of
Wealth.

[100] Florence
Whitwell's eyeglass

    [25] "Thoreau's ... Morison" is in pencil. For Thoreau, cf. Journal ST, p. [55]
above.
    [26] The entries on p. [99] are in pencil. For "The sandstone ... sail", see Journal
ST, p. [193] above.

455

Mustapha Aga's eyeglasses
   Hat
   kidgloves[27]

Memoranda. June 1873.
   Write to W.S. Whitwell

       Thos. R. Gould, Boston.
       56 Studio Building.

   Call on Mr Billings with Mr Babbit's errand[28]

Write to E.J. Broadfield, Examiner & Times office, Manchester,
England.

Mr Thayer

C. De la Prynne   86 Glocester Place   Portman Square   London
  ↑Reform Club↓

Thos. Fall   55 Baker st. Portman Square

[inside back cover] Square's Mount   Hampstead   Mrs Field

⟨Adams Sherman Hill⟩*Billings*[29]
   St James Hotel. Miss V[irginia]. Vaughan.
Hotel Pelham, Mrs Anna Parsons.
Mrs [Henry] Adams, 91 Marlboro St.
Mrs [Sidney] Mason, 54 Beacon st.

   [27] "Florence . . . kidgloves" is in pencil.
   [28] See Journal ST, p. [205] above, and Pocket Diary 25, p. [36] below.
   [29] "Adams Sherman Hill", in pencil, is overwritten by *"Billings"* in ink to cancel.

Pocket Diary 25

1874

Pocket Diary 25 is devoted primarily to recording Emerson's notes, quotations, and selections for *Parnassus,* which was published in December 1874. It also contains miscellaneous financial transactions, addresses, and memoranda. A few entries may have been made late in 1873 or early in 1875.

The notebook, bound in faded blue stamped leather, is a commercially published diary entitled "POCKET / DIARY / 1874 / PUBLISHED / FOR / THE TRADE." The covers measure 7.5 × 12.5 cm. The back cover extends into a tongue that, when the book is closed, fits into a loop on the front cover; the back cover also contains an expandable inside pocket. "DIARY" is stamped in gold on the tongue. A paper label fastened to the spine is inscribed "1874–1875. x".

The white, unnumbered pages, whose edges are marbled, measure 7.4 × 12.1 cm; pages 33–192 are faintly lined. The book consists of a front flyleaf (i, ii); a title page (page 1); a calendar for 1874 (page 3); a table of time differences relative to Boston time (page 4); interest rate tables (pages 5–6); a chart of foreign gold and silver values (pages 7–10); rates of postage (page 11); eclipses in 1874 (page 12); star and daylight tables (pages 13–14); phases of the moon and tide tables for 1874 (pages 15–26); a Chicago almanac (pages 27–32); daily appointments for 1874, three to a page (pages 33–154); pages for memoranda (pages 155–161); pages for cash accounts (pages 162–186); additional pages for memoranda (pages 187–192); and a back flyleaf (pages 193–194).

Entries by Emerson occur on fifty pages. Printed matter in Pocket Diary 25 is reproduced here only in the sections on daily appointments, cash accounts, and memoranda where relevant. Otherwise, pages are designated as blank if they bear no inscription by Emerson; the presence or absence of printed matter is not specified.

A canceled two-cent stamp is pasted to page 47. Laid in between pages 60 and 61 is a calendar for 1875. In the expandable pocket in the back cover is an unidentified newspaper clipping on "Fruit Printing," that is, the writing of messages on fruit.

[front cover verso][1] *Parnassus*   1874.

In *AZ 268* compare Select Poems of Ben Jonson with those in Parnassus

---

Arnold's "Gypsy Scho⟨al⟩lar"

Wordsworth's Peel Castle, 8vo. p 434

For Marquis of Montrose's lines, compare Evans's Ballads with Parnassus.

Fox can tell me of the errors in B[isho]p Berkeley's lines to America

---

Who wrote *"The Loyal Woman's No."*? [Lucy Larcom]

⟨Davies' or Daniel's⟩
⟨Love is a sickness full of woes⟩

Under "Terror" insert Caesar's lines in Shaksp[eare].,

"Between the acting of a dreadful thing"
                                   [Shakespeare, *Julius Caesar,* II, i, 63]

[i][2]   R.W. Emerson
                                             Concord, Masstt⟨.⟩s

---

p. ⟨509⟩
  238   2d col. l. 18, insert is
  425   1st col. l. 11,[n] for (came) read (come)

Berkeley's lines on America

---

[1] On the front cover verso, "Davies' . . . full of woes", in pencil, is overwritten by "Under 'Terror' . . . dreadful thing' " in ink to cancel. Except for "Love is a sickness full of woes", the first line of Samuel Daniel's "Song of the First Chorus," from *Hymens Triumph,* I, v, 446–461, other items in this *Parnassus* list have been previously identified.
[2] "TS/42", in pencil, in the upper right-hand corner of p. [i] may be a stationer's mark. All of the *Parnassus* items on p. [i] have been identified previously.

Peel Castle of Wordsworth

Van Arteveldt

Mr [Charles?] Sprague's death?

[ii]   *"A loyal woman's No."* Lucy Larcom

Burns' Scotland. p 125, 1 Ms.
"I mind it well"   longer?[3]

P. xxii ↑For↓ Thou hast past all change of human life

[1][4] S[amuel] G[ray] W[ard]
Cha[rle]s. Emerson
Rob[er]t. [T.S.] Lowell
Miss [Sophia] Thoreau
[Edmund Clarence] Stedman
Dr A M Ross

[2][5] Chaucer
Ariadne
Destiny
Duchess Blanche

---

[3] In *Parnassus*, "I mind it well . . .", the first line of Robert Burns's "Epistle to Mrs. Scott, Gudewife of Wauchope-House, Roxburghshire," is the first of sixteen excerpted lines from that poem that appear as "Scotland." "For Thou . . . life" below is unidentified.

[4] The list on p. [1] is written over the printed matter on the page.

[5] On p. [2], "Chaucer . . . The Poet" is in pencil. Except for "Allingham's . . . breakers.", which is unidentified, the items in this list refer to Chaucer pieces used in *Parnassus*, where *The Legend of Good Women*, ll. 2181–2225, appears as "Ariadne"; "The Knightes Tale," ll. 1663–1672, appears as "Destiny"; *The Book of the Duchesse*, ll. 805–1010 with omissions, appears as "Duchess Blanche"; *The Hous of Fame*, I, ll. 43–52, appears as "Forecast"; "The Nonnes Preestes Tale," ll. 554–581, appears as "Fox and Cock"; "The Clerkes Tale," ll. 57–1212, appears as "Griselda. The Clerkes Tale"; *The Hous of Fame*, III, ll. 1091–1109, appears as "Prayer to Apollo"; *The Hous of Fame*, II, ll. 935–956, appears as "The Milky Way"; *The Hous of Fame*, II, ll. 643–659, appears as "The Poet." "The Cuckow and The Nightingale," incorrectly attributed to Chaucer in the editions of Chaucer's poetry that Emerson owned, appears in *Parnassus*.

459

Forecast
Fox & Cock
Griselda
Prayer to Apollo
Cuckoo & Nightingale
Milky Way
The Poet
Allingham's line about breakers.

[3]–[32] [blank]
[33] [Fri., Jan. 2] Miss Virginia Vaughan
Care of Charles Edward Rawlins, ⟨Li⟩Esq, Liverpool, Engd

[34] [Sun., Jan. 4] Letters to be written to
     Christopher James, Gold Hill   Comstock Lode   Nevada.

Wm Munroe, Esq.
W[illiam] H[enry] Furness
Mrs Parsons

↑Mrs↓ [Henry] Adams   91 Marlboro
↑Mrs↓ [Caroline Sturgis] Tappan   407 or 9 Beacon st
[Mrs. S.] Mason   54 Beacon[6]

[35] Moses G. Farmer   15 Congress St   Room 15
     Torpedo Machines   out from 1 to 2
          Dennett (Nation)
     T.S Perry 11 Park Sq
H Furness   Phil Pa
Wendell Holmes Jr
          Sanborn
George Lathrop   20 Wendell St   Cambridge

[36] [Sat., Jan. 10] Abraham B. Morrison borrowed £75 sterling of
H.A. Babbitt, promising to refund by Jan 10, ⟨7⟩1873, & has not done
so Feb. 1873. H.A.B[abbitt].[7]

---

[6] "Mrs Adams . . . Beacon" is in pencil, as are the entries on p. [35].
[7] See Journal ST, p. [205] above.

Copy of Vice-Consul Babbitt's memorandum

Thomas Maguire   Provinc[e] House   16⟨0⟩3 Washington st   Boston

[37] [blank]
[38]⁸ Parnassus
W[illiam]. Habington "th[e] sweetest & purest of amorous poets"

Cowper's poem on his Mother

Burns

Barnes
As passing here thro' evening dew
    Title?

[39]–[46] [blank]
[47] [Fri., Feb. 13] Agassiz Memorial
    Wesley Hall   Bromfield st   11 o'clock

[48]–[72] [blank]
[73]⁹ [Fri., May 1] In May promised a Lecture to the Students in the Divinity School Cambridge. I am to fix the time & communicate with J[ohn].G[raham]. Brooks. Divinity Hall any day but Friday

[74] "The Grammar of Painting" by Charles Blanc is said to be a translation of a part of another & more valuable book by the same author. If the latter in French could be had at the Athaneum some a⟨a⟩mateurs would be glad.

---

⁸ The entries on p. [38] are in pencil. Excerpts from William Cowper's "On the Receipt of My Mother's Picture Out of Norfolk" appear in *Parnassus* as "My Mother's Picture"; the source of William Barnes's "As passing . . . dew", which appears in *Parnassus* as the first line of "The Peasant's Return," is unidentified.

⁹ The entries on pp. [73], [74], [77], and [84] are in pencil. On p. [74], Emerson's reference is to Auguste Alexandre Philippe Charles Blanc, *The Grammar of Painting and Engraving*, trans. Kate Newell Doggett (New York, 1874), which is based on Blanc's *Grammaire des Arts du Dessin, Architecture, Sculpture, Peinture* (Paris, 1867).

461

[75]–[76] [blank]
[77] [Wed., May 13] 3 o'c. P.M.   Woman's Club Rooms

[78]–[83] [blank]
[84] [Thurs., June 4] Mr Alcott's Club   Read "Inspiration"

[85]–[95] [blank]
[96] Public Lib[rar]y *Book of Poetry* Mr Whitney's *Fields'* Forceythe Wil[l]son[10]

[97][11]   *Memoranda*
My Foss Photograph from W. Hunt for godchild
     & Mrs Chamberlaine
———

Write to Mrs [John Peter] Leslie
          Miss [Sophia] Thoreau
     of Weiss poem & the trunks
———

     to Sir Frazier
———

     to Conway
———

     Alex. Ireland, Manchester
———

[98] ⟨Write to Mr Frederick Beck to thank him for Landor's book⟩
———

to Mrs [Richard Henry] Dana [Jr.] with remainder of Report
———

     Return themes to H[arvard]. C[ollege].
———

     Write to Mrs [Mary Peabody] Mann
          Miss Viall

———

[10] This entry is in pencil. *"Book of Poetry* Mr Whitney's" is unidentified. Forceythe Willson's *The Old Sergeant, and Other Poems* (Boston, 1867) was published by Ticknor and Fields.
     [11] The entries on pp. [97] and [98] are in pencil. On p. [98], "Write to . . . book" is struck through in pencil with a vertical line.

———

Mr Gideon Nye, Jr.   Canton China

———

Miss Thoreau accounting for the deposit of Henry's trunks.

———

[99]¹² ⟨Photographs at Foss's⟩

———

Chris[topher]. Cranch

———

Return C[aroline] S[turgis] T[appan]'s Mandsley

———

⟨Mrs Lesley⟩
Mrs Wells, 155 Boylston St.

———

Note-paper at Rice & Co

———

Life of Theodore Parker

———

[100] *Books.* Magnetism.
              English Year-Book
              Darwin

[101] Mem⟨.⟩o. To send book to Mrs Newton, mother of Mrs Trow-
bridge   at Arlington, Masstts

Books
      [Theodore] Parker's Life by O[ctavius] B[rooks] F[rothingham]

[102] [Anna Laetitia] Barbauld
              Man is the nobler fruit our realms supply
              And souls are ripened in our northern sky

———

              Let India boast her palms nor envy we¹³

¹² The entries on p. [99] are in pencil; "Photographs at Foss's" is struck through in
pencil with two diagonal lines. The last reference is to Octavius Brooks Frothingham,
Theodore Parker: a Biography (Boston, 1874).
¹³ "Let India . . . envy we" is from Alexander Pope's *Windsor Forest,* l. 29.

[103]–[105] [blank]
[106] Albert M. Smith   Elocutionist
     to be found at Christian Union,
     W.H. Baldwin, Esq. 300 Washington Street

[107]–[109] [blank]
[110] Susan Ida Dudley
        Christine H.L. Dudley
        10 Concord Square   Boston

[111]¹⁴ ? ⟨Hallowed Ground⟩
                    ⟨Campbell⟩
              ⟨Gertrude of Wyoming⟩
              ⟨Kosciusk⟨i⟩o fell⟩

_____

        Glenlogie   Child's Ballads
        Heir of Lyn⟨de⟩ne

_____

        Throwing of Excalibar   Tennyson

_____

        ⟨Palmer, *Marmion*⟩
        ⟨J Q Adams   historical⟩

[112]¹⁵ ⟨Pope   "Dying Christian to Soul."⟩

¹⁴ The entries on p. [111] are in pencil. "Hallowed . . . fell" and "J Q Adams   historical" are each struck through in pencil with single diagonal lines. Apparently pp. [111]–[114] constitute another list of materials for possible inclusion in *Parnassus;* items on p. [111] not previously identified include Thomas Campbell's "Hallowed Ground" and *Gertrude of Wyoming; a Pennslyvania Tale* (1809); Samuel Taylor Coleridge's sonnet VII: "O what a Loud and Fearful Shriek was There," a poem on the death of Kosciusko; and the ballad "The Heir of Lynne," which appears in *Parnassus.* "Throwing of Excalibar" is an allusion to Tennyson's "The Coming of Arthur," from *Idylls of the King,* ll. 242–324, which appears in *Parnassus* as "The Crowning of Arthur." References to Palmer and J. Q. Adams have not been clarified.

¹⁵ The entries on p. [112] are in pencil. Items on p. [112] not previously identified include Alexander Pope's "The Dying Christian to his Soul, Ode", his *Fragment of a* SATIRE," ll. 43–66, which appears in *Parnassus* as "Portrait of Addison," and his Epistle III, "To Allen Lord Bathurst," ll. 249–286, which appears in *Parnassus* as "The Man of Ross"; "Vital spark", an allusion to Pope's "The Dying Christian to his Soul, Ode," which begins "Vital spark of heav'nly flame!"; Matthew Arnold's "Indifference"; "Love

──────

⟨"Addison"⟩

──────

⟨Man of Ross⟩

──────

⟨Vital spark⟩
Happy the man

──────

Arnold   "Indifference"   Dana p. 321
Love is   Ayton
⟨Barnes⟩
⟨Brooks⟩
Arabian Ballad

[113]^{16} Akenside
       "Each passing hour sheds tribute from her wings"

──────

Forsaken Merman of M. Arnold.

──────

Motto for Heroic & Historical

──────

⟨What for Ariadne   ?⟩

──────

is", an unidentified allusion to, perhaps, a work of Sir Robert Ayton (1570–1638); and "Arabian Ballad", an allusion to Thomas Moore's *Llalla Rookh,* new ed. (Boston, 1828), in Emerson's library, from which pp. 222–224 appear in *Parnassus* as "Araby's Daughter." For "Happy the man" see Pocket Diary 23, p. [194] above.

   [16] The entries on p. [113] are in pencil. "Willis's Mother ... Queen's Wake" is struck through in pencil with two diagonal lines. Items on p. [113] not previously identified include John Logan's ode "To the Cuckoo"; Hannah Reba Hudson's "April" from *Poems* (Boston, 1874), in Emerson's library; and James Hogg's "Eighth Bard's Song" from "Night I" of *The Queen's Wake; a Legendary Poem* (Boston, 1815), in Emerson's library, which appears in *Parnassus* as "The Witch of Fife." Excerpts from Mark Akenside's *The Pleasures of Imagination, a Poem, in Three Books* (Boston, 1816), in Emerson's library, appear in *Parnassus* as "Pleasures of Imagination"; " 'Each passing ... her wings' " is from Book III, l. 591. For "Motto ... Historical" see Journal ST, p. [148] above; for "Ariadne" see pp. [2]–[3] above. Nathaniel Parker Willis's "Mother" probably refers to "Lines on Leaving Europe," in which Willis expresses assurance of a safe return to America because of his mother's love; it is quoted in "Swedenborg; or, the Mystic," *W,* IV, 145. The lines attributed to Byron have not been located.

Logan's Cuckoo   ?

〈Byron   For who the fool that doth not know〉
〈How bloom & beauty come & go〉

H. Hudson's April

〈Willis's Mother〉

〈Witch of Fife〉

〈Queen's Wake〉

[114]¹⁷ Wilkinson's Diamond
"And loves (?) his life out to his flock"

Channing   Poet's Hope

Coventry Patmore   Tithonus

Put on the muckle *pot*. Mickle
〈son〉
There's no luck about the house

Love is a sickness full of woes
Davies? or Daniel?

---

[115]–[135] [blank]
[136] *Rhetoric Committee*
George B. Chase   Kilby St
T[homas]. W[entworth]. Higginson, Newport

¹⁷ The entries on p. [114] are in pencil. Items on p. [114] not previously identified include " 'And loves . . . his flock' ", l. 10 of James John Garth Wilkinson's "The Diamond," from *Improvisations from the Spirit*, 1857, excerpts of which appear in *Parnassus;* William Ellery Channing's "A Poet's Hope," ll. 37–78 of which appear in *Parnassus;* William Julius Mickle's "There's Nae Luck about the House," which appears in *Parnassus* in an abridged form. For Samuel Daniel's line see the front cover verso above. The reference to Coventry Patmore is unidentified.

Rev H[enry] W Foote
    W[illiam] J. Rolfe, Cambridgeport
    [Christopher Pearse] Cranch

[137]–[140] [blank]
[141]¹⁸   Death
        Endymion

Mrs Estes Howe owns Maria White Lowell's poems
    Africa

Mr Adams   57 Mt. Vernon St
Henry Adams   91 Marlboro St

[142] *Duties*   Mr Foster & Co
          Mr Bowditch's letter
          Haynes' Lecture
          Gannett, Lecture
          Longfellow "1775"
          St Louis lecture
          Hon W.E. Forster

    F.O. Balch   39 Court St

    Mrs Hastings

[143]¹⁹ Hearts of Eternity
        W[illiam] E[llery] C[hanning]
        Greek fire ↑to↓ E[lizabeth]. H[oar].
        Author of dreaming
        Earning a living   W T

---

[18] The entries on p. [141] are in pencil. The poems of Maria White Lowell (1821–1853) were collected by James Russell Lowell, her husband, after her death and were published as *The Poems of Maria Lowell* by the Riverside Press in 1855 for distribution to family and friends; "Africa" appears on pp. 12–18 of that volume.

[19] The entries on p. [143] are in pencil. William Ellery Channing's "Dreaming. To ———" appeared in *Poems,* 1843.

Bret Harte
Dickens

[144]–[155] [blank]
[156] Arthur Bourch[i]er   Breeding Lark   printed 1589[20]

[157][21]   O What is Heaven but the fellowship
            Of minds that each can stand against the world
            By its own meek but incorruptible will

————

            Within the ocheate depths of the fine air

————

                        Ellery

[158] Letter to Sterling
          to Conway
          to Westford   W.E Frost
          to Mrs Wells
          to Miss Derby 166 Charles St
          to Ansley Gray, Sec[retar]y
    Law Class of State University
    Madison, Wisconsin, next June
    Joseph F. Fowler   Nashville, Tenn.

———————————————————————————

Ch: Elkin Mathews; The Poplars
Bibliomaniac   Codford St   Wilts England

———————————————————————————

Harvard College

[159]–[161] [blank]
[162] 7 ft l[o]ng   4 by 5 ft   8 tons[22]

[163]–[164] [blank]
[165] 9 February 1875   Westford

[20] "Arthur . . . 1589" is in pencil.
[21] The entries on p. [157] are in pencil. For "O what is . . . will", see *W*, IX, 395.
[22] "7 ft . . . tons" is in pencil.

[166]–[182] [blank]
[183]²³ Mr H[ubert] H[owe] Bancroft of San Francisco
     letter to Mr Bryant
         & to Dr

[184] Miss Nina Lowell   22 W. Cedar St

[185] Dr J Hutchison Stirling,
     4 Laverock Bank Road, Edinburgh.

---

[186] *Harvard Hall*
     Dining Hall   165 long
                  60 wide
               50 to 60 high

     Memorial Hall
     104 by 60, & 50 to 60 high

---

[187]   [MEMORANDA.]

[Date.]	*Class of 1821.*	[Dolls.	Cts.]
	George Pratt		
	Francis C. Lowell		
	B. Tyler Reed		
Dec 1866	Charles W. Upham	150.	00
Nov. 1869	Edward Kent	150.	00
Nov. 1869	R.W. Emerson	150.	00
	↑J.L. Gardner 5000.↓²⁴		

[188] Mrs [Caroline Sturgis] Tappan   240 Beacon st

[189] "The complete incarnation of ⟨Beauty⟩Spirit, which is the definition of Beauty, demands equally that there be no point it does not inhabit, & none in which it abides."   *J*[ames]. *E*[lliot]. *Cabot.*²⁵

---

²³ The entries on pp. [183], [184], and [186] are in pencil.
²⁴ "J.L. Gardner   5000." is in pencil.
²⁵ See *JMN*, VI, 201.

[190] ↑E's Art in Φ100↓²⁶

In Elocution
Seniors.   Tuesd. & Thursday, 9. to 2.
Holden Chapel.   upper floor
Readings in Harvard Hall
⟨7½⟩Jan 13 & 14, ⟨Jan.⟩²⁷ 7½ o'clock

———

Mr Thayer notes ⟨that⟩ lessons in elocution to Seniors in Holden Chapel (upper floor) on Tuesdays & Thursdays, 9 o'c. to 2, o'c.

———

[191]²⁸ 18 March 1875   Philadelphia

Mrs ⟨S⟩Julia Hastings   1215 Sutter St   San Francisco, Cal.

F.V. Balch

[192] Mrs Russell
Mrs [Caroline Sturgis] Tappan
Mrs [S.] Mason   54 Beacon
Mrs ⟨Adams⟩Parkman   16 Primmer
Mrs [Henry] Adams, 91 Marlboro
⟨Mrs Annie L. Wister   90 Boylston st⟩
Geo. B. Chase Esq   13 Kilby St

———

Frederick Beck

———

Mr. [William Channing] Gannett   155 Boylston St.
Thursday 1, o'c
⟨Silsbee, State St⟩
Shears   Agricultural Hall

²⁶ "E's Art . . . 100" is in pencil.
²⁷ "Jan." is struck through in pencil with a diagonal line.
²⁸ The entries on pp. [191]–[194] are in pencil, except for "18 March . . . Philadelphia" on p. [191] and "Frederick Beck" and the rules that precede and follow it on p. [192]. On p. [192], "Mrs Annie . . . Boylston st" is struck through in pencil with three diagonal lines; on p. [193], "Kemble . . . Consolation" refers to Frances Anne Kemble, *A Year of Consolation*, 2 vols. (London, 1847).

[193] Garden shears
      Athenaeum
      Marsoribanks
      Ladies of Bever Hollow
Kemble Year of Consolation
          Journal
Wives & daughters
Martineau

[194] Ann Salisbury   Mt. Vernon st
———

    Miss Sara Palfrey
Grammer of Painting by Charles Blanc, ⟨of⟩ part of a larger book by
the same author in French[29]

[railroad schedule omitted]

[inside back cover] [railroad schedule omitted]

[29] See p. [74] above.

Pocket Diary 26

1875

Pocket Diary 26 is devoted primarily to recording Emerson's memoranda, addresses, and financial transactions for 1875. It also contains entries relating to the correction of materials printed in *Parnassus*. A few entries may have been made late in 1874 or early in 1876.

The notebook, bound in dark blue stamped leather, is a commercially published diary entitled "POCKET / DIARY / 1875 / PUBLISHED / FOR / THE TRADE." The covers measure 7.4 × 12.4 cm. The back cover extends into a tongue that, when the book is closed, fits into a loop on the front cover; the back cover also contains an expandable inside pocket. "DIARY" is stamped in gold on the tongue. A paper label fastened to the spine is inscribed "1875".

The white, unnumbered, gilt-edged pages measure 7.3 × 12.1 cm; pages 33–192 are faintly lined. The book consists of a front flyleaf (i, ii); a title page (page 1); a calendar for 1875 (page 3); a table of time differences relative to Boston time (page 4); interest and income rate tables (pages 5–7); a chart of foreign gold and silver values (pages 8–11); rates of postage (page 12); a table of fixed and moveable feasts and eclipses in 1875 (pages 13–14); phases of the moon and tide tables for 1875 (pages 15–26); a Chicago almanac (pages 27–32); daily appointments for 1875, three to a page (pages 33–154); pages for memoranda (pages 155–161); pages for cash accounts (pages 162–186); additional pages for memoranda (pages 187–192); and a back flyleaf (pages 193–194).

Entries by Emerson occur on forty pages. Printed matter in Pocket Diary 26 is reproduced here only in the sections on daily appointments, cash accounts, and memoranda where relevant. Otherwise, pages are designated as blank if they bear no inscription by Emerson; the presence or absence of printed matter is not specified.

Portions of a Concord-to-Boston railroad schedule are pasted onto the inside front cover. Laid in between pages 38 and 39 is a newspaper clipping of a Concord-to-Boston railroad schedule and a note, not in Emerson's hand, stating "Note enclosed by E W F says, 'See Dunvegan Sept. cash account' ". In the expandable pocket in the back cover, the following items are enclosed: an unused three-cent stamp; a canceled three-cent Canadian stamp, the back of which is inscribed "Ralph" in Emerson's hand; an unidentified newspaper clipping of the poem "The Two Angels / A Legend of the Orient" by E. Norman Gunnison; and an unidentified newspaper clipping of the poem "John Jones and I" attributed to "Charles G. Adams, in Christian Union".

[front cover verso]¹

R.W. Emerson
Concord. Masstts
1875

[i]–[48] [blank]
[49] [Thurs., Feb. 18] Philadelphia

[50] [Mon., Feb. 22] Woman's Club, 3½ P.M.

[51]–[56] [blank]
[57]² [Tues., Mar. 16] Philadelphia
    Dr [William Henry] Furness, Mrs F[urness]
                            Mrs Haven
    Horace Furness
    Frank Furness

[58] [blank]
[59] [Mon., Mar. 22] S[amuel]. G[ray]. Ward   2 Washington Sq. North
    G.C. Ward   25 W. 11th St.
    J[ohn]. H[aven] Emerson   81 Madison Av
    Mrs [Anne Charlotte Lynch] Botta   25 W. 37th St.

[60] [Tues., Mar. 23] Miss [Emma] Lazarus   36 W. 14
T[h]om[as Wren] Ward   105 E. 25⟨E⟩
    Metropolitan Museum   12⟨5⟩8 West 1⟨8⟩4th St.
[Wed., Mar. 24] Miss Ella M. Haskins aged 20 years (I suppose now)
at Maynard, Masstts temporary assistant in Boston School and at
Westfield Masstts at Normal School, and has a diploma at Boston
Her mother at No 9, East Twelfth Street, Philadelphia
    ⟨Mrs Haskins⟩
Mrs Thomas Haskins

[61] [blank]

¹ "LΦ/35" and "110/30", in erased pencil in the upper right-hand corner of p. [i], may be a stationer's marks.
² The entries on pp. [57], [59], and [60] are in pencil, except for "Miss Ella M. Haskins . . . Mrs Thomas Haskins" on p. [60].

[62]³   By the rude bridge that arched the flood
          Their flag to April's breez[e] unfurled

[63]   On this green bank by this soft flood

[64] [blank]
[65] [Wed., Apr. 7] The Sphinx is in *Stanley, 4to.*⁴

[66] [blank]
[67]⁵ [Tues., Apr. 13] Frederick K Gillette   Aurora Ohio   Sept 75
[Wed., Apr. 14] Atl[antic]. Bank-book,

———

    Whipple miniature

———

    Urbino German Store

———

    Osgood letters

———

    School Committee for Miss ⟨Emerson⟩Haskins of N.Y.

———

    Books of Mr Brooks, binder.

[68]–[69] [blank]
[70]⁶ [Thurs., Apr. 22] Wm Cummings dating from New Bedford
Mass asks for lecture before two Societies connected with New
Hampton, Institute, New Hampshire, on 30 June next

———————————

[Fri., Apr. 23] Whipple
          Clarke & Brimmer
          Mrs Tappan
          Ellen's Books

———

³ The entries on pp. [62] and [63], in pencil, are from "Concord Hymn," ll. 1–2, 9;
see *W*, IX, 158–159.
   ⁴ "The Sphinx . . . *4to.*" is in pencil.
   ⁵ The entries on p. [67] are in pencil; "Emerson", in pencil, is overwritten by
"Haskins" in ink to cancel.
   ⁶ On p. [70], "Wm Cummings . . . 30 June next" and "Osgood" are in pencil.

Mr Winsor
Mr Rogers
Osgood

[71] [blank]
[72] [Wed., Apr. 28] Overseers Meeting

[73]–[75] [blank]
[76] [Mon., May 10] Herman Grimm
    Berlin 105 Konig grise Strasse

[77][7]   Upon a rock yet un[create]
            Amid a Chaos inchoate
            An uncreated being sate
            Beneath him rock
            Above him cloud
            And the cloud was rock
            And the rock was cloud
            The rock then growing soft & warm
            The cloud began to take a form
            A form chaotic vast & vague
            Which issued in the cosmic egg
            Then the being uncreate
            Upon the egg did incubate
[78]   And thus became an incubator
            And of the egg did allegate
            And thus became an alligator
            And the incubate was potentate
            But the alligator was potentator

[79][8] [Wed., May 19] M W Wellman

            He will assimilate he will agree
            With the deep & the shallow

[7] The entry on pp. [77] and [78] is in lightly erased pencil.
[8] The entries on pp. [79] and [81] are in pencil, except for "Mrs Sargent   12,
o'clock." on p. [81].

[80] [blank]
[81] [Tues., May 25] Furness
[Wed., May 26] Mrs Sargent   12, o'clock.
     Sleep at Edith's
[Thurs., May 27] Wedding   11½

[82] [blank]
[83] [Tues., June 1] Omaha & South Western R R Bonds
                                   2000.   80

[84]–[85] [blank]
[86] [Thurs., June 10] Dr Phil. Carl. von Bergen
     777 Parker St   Roxbury[9]

[87]–[92] [blank]
[93] [Wed., June 30] New Hampton Institution   New Hampshire
at request of Wm Cummings   New Bedford   Mass

———

[Thurs., July 1] New Hampton[10]
     Mc Intire
     Mr Dyer
     Mr Ladd   Plymouth, N. Hampshir[e]
[Fri., July 2] Concord Bank. $100. due

[94] [blank]
[95][11] Mrs Beckwith   134 Fifth Avenu[e]
     autograph promised to her.
Autograph also to
     Charles Ryan   4 Union Place   Dorchester Road   Weymouth
by care of Walter Smith   24 & 38 Pemberton Sq
     Normal Art School

[96]–[100] [blank]

---

[9] "Dr Phil. . . . Roxbury" is in pencil.
[10] "New Hampton" is in pencil.
[11] The entries on p. [95] are in pencil.

[101] [Sat., July 24] Call from Mr E.S. Cox—
                    Parkersburg, W. Virginia
_____

[102]^{12} [Tues., July 27] Mr Geo Chases's Banker or Clerk
_____

Hat store
_____

⟨Mr⟩M.H. Bovee, Chicago
_____

Dr ⟨Dentalist⟩ Dentist

[103] [blank]
[104] [Wed., Aug. 4] Find the name & dates of Miss Shepherd, author of *Counterparts*. Vol I 67^{13}

[105] [blank]
[106]^{14} [Tues., Aug. 10] Revere B[an]k

Barber.

[107]–[112] [blank]
[113] [Tues., Aug. 31] Proofs sent to Osgood.

[114]–[115] [blank]
[116] [Tues., Sep. 7] Write to Miss [Mary] Withington
                    to Miss [Helen Dawes] Brown
                    to Mr Dana

[117]^{15} Parnassus
    Wordsworth's Happy Warrior 2d & last line

^{12} The entries on p. [102] are in pencil.
^{13} Elizabeth Sara Sheppard, *Counterparts; or The Cross of Love*, 3 vols. (London,
1854), is in Emerson's library.
^{14} The entries on pp. [106] and [113] are in pencil.
^{15} The entry on p. [117] is in pencil. Wordsworth's "The Character of the Happy
Warrior" appears in *Parnassus* as "The Happy Warrior."

[118]–[134] [blank]
[135]¹⁶ [Wed., Nov. 3] Rev. J.M Marsters   North Cambridge
Wants Book of Mr M on Social Reform

[136]–[137] [blank]
[138] [Sun., Nov. 14] The Night of the Meteors

[139]–[176] [blank]
[177]¹⁷ Jan 1856

⟨See Bartol for Frothingham⟩

⟨Carry Pa[r]nassus corrections to Osgood⟩

⟨Get my books from Osgood for Milton⟩

⟨Pullman Car payment⟩

Mr Thayer's Will

⟨Recovery of Ellen's check of C[hicago]. B[urlington] &
Q[uincy] $10.⟩

⟨Bank⟩

[178]¹⁸ Br
    St Patrick   17 Mar 76   evaluation

[179] Dunvegan ⟨Ba⟩Castle   Skye no 248   248
    G W. Wilson   Aberdeen

The Kilt Rock   Loch Staffin
    No 242   Skye   G.W Wilson

---

¹⁶ The entries on pp. [135] and [138] are in pencil.
¹⁷ The entries on p. [177] are in pencil. "See Bartol . . . payment" is struck through
in pencil with two diagonal lines; "Recovery of . . . Bank" is struck through in pencil with
three vertical lines and three diagonal lines.
¹⁸ The entries on pp. [178], [179], and [188] are in pencil.

[180]–[186] [blank]
[187] 1876, January.
——

Miss Margaret Forbes's manuscript Book
——

[188] Edward
    truss
——

Mr Kye's pew-rent
——

Mr Allingham's friend
——

Mr Deane
——

Mr Bean

[189] [blank]
[190] Robt Herrick, born 1591
               died 1674

[191]   New York
    Dr J. Haven Emerson   81 Madison Sq
    S[amuel]. G[ray]. Ward
    T[homas]. W[ren]. Ward   105 E. 25
——

Miss E[mma]. Lazarus

[192][19] W[illiam]. H[athaway]. F[orbes].
——

Pullman
——

Hamilton Court
——

Fuller's Worthies
——

[19] The entries on p. [192] are in pencil, except for "Lexington, . . . Porter" and the rules that precede and follow that entry.

479

Loring
____

Lowell
Fields   de Adams
_____

Lexington, 8th March, Wednesday
    Edward G. Porter
_____

[193]²⁰ ⟨Berkeley⟩
    Bailey
    fragments
    Mottoes
    ⟨Cosmic egg⟩
⟨L[ucy]. Larcom⟩
        Radcliffe
        pencils
        Dairy

[194] [railroad schedule omitted]

[inside back cover] 4th Vol[ume]
    you have 1 to 5
2 Abt[eilung]   5
4 2d Abt[eilung]²¹
____

    Varnhagen   Vol 5 p 144
    Schleiermacher
_____

        ↑Miss M. Stacy↓
    Withington   1104 L St   Washington
_____

    Monroe
_____

---

²⁰ The entries on pp. [193], [194], and the inside back cover are in pencil. For "Cosmic egg" on p. [193] see pp. [77]–[78] above; for "Varnhagen . . . Schleiermacher" on the inside back cover see Journal ST, p. [245] above.

²¹ The parts or fascicles listed here undoubtedly refer to Grimm, *Deutsches Wörterbuch* . . . , 1854–19[–], of which vols. 1–5 are in Emerson's library. See Journal LN, p. [135] above, and Pocket Diary 28, p. [258] below.

Pocket Diary 27

1876

Pocket Diary 27 is devoted to recording Emerson's memoranda for 1876. A few entries may have been made late in 1875 or early in 1877.

The notebook, bound in dark blue stamped leather, is a commercially published diary entitled "DAILY / MEMORANDUM BOOK / for / 1876 . . . ," published by Francis & Loutrel, New York. The covers measure 6.4 × 10.7 cm. The back cover extends into a flap that, when the book is closed, folds over half the front cover; the back cover also contains an expandable inside pocket. A cloth ribbon that once was sown into the back cover and that could be tied across the front cover has been cut away. A paper label fastened to the spine is inscribed "1876. x".

The white, unnumbered, gilt-edged pages measure 6.3 × 10.5 cm; pages 17–168 are lined. The book consists of a front flyleaf (i, ii); a title page (page 1); a calendar for 1876 (page 3); a table of astronomical calculations (page 4); phases of the moon and tide tables for 1876 (pages 5–16); daily appointments for 1876, three to a page (pages 17–138); pages for miscellaneous entries (pages 139–144); pages for cash accounts (pages 145–156); pages for bills payable (pages 157–168); and a back flyleaf (pages 169–170).

Entries by Emerson occur on twenty-six pages. Printed matter in Pocket Diary 27 is reproduced here only in the sections on daily appointments and bills payable where relevant. Otherwise, pages are designated as blank if they bear no inscription by Emerson; the presence or absence of printed matter is not specified.

A portion of a Concord-to-Boston railroad schedule is pasted onto the inside front cover. In the expandable pocket in the back cover is a calling card, measuring 10.1 × 5 cm, signed by Emerson.

[front cover verso][1] July 17.
[railroad schedule omitted]

[i] [railroad schedule omitted]

---

[1] "50", in pencil, in the upper left-hand corner of the front cover verso may be a stationer's mark.

[ii]–[9] [blank]
[10] leave Wash[ingto]n Tu[e]s. A.M. [June 27][2]

[11]–[34] [blank]
[35][3] [Thurs., Feb. 24?] Mr Child, Phila[delphia]

———

English Lady at Centennial

———

W.T. Harris

———

[John Greenleaf] Whittier   Snowbound

———

[Fri., Feb. 25] Bates photograph   Temple Place

A R Spofford, Lib[raria]n
Copyright
     Essays 1st [Series]
     Rep[resentative] Men
     Eng[lish] Traits
     Poems
     Carlisle's Medal

[36] [Sun., Feb. 27] The Carlyle Medal[4]
received from Alex. Macmillan   The Elms, Streatham Lane
     Upper Tooting, S.W.   Surrey, England

[37] [Wed., Mar. 1] Heart & Cross   Mrs Oliphant[5]

———————

Duties
[Thurs., Mar. 2] Return Miss Margaret Forbes the loaned manuscript.

---

[2] On p. [10], ink and pencil notations, mostly dashes and dots, have been entered in
a calendar next to June 15, 17, 21, 22, 24, and 27; their significance is unknown. "leave
Washn . . . A.M", in Emerson's hand, is next to Tuesday, June 27.
   [3] The entries on p. [35] are in pencil.
   [4] See Journal ST, p. [250] above.
   [5] "Heart . . . Oliphant" is in pencil. Margaret Wilson Oliphant, *Heart and Cross*
(New York, 1863).

Write to Mr Macmillan & acknowledge the 5 Vols. of Plato[6]
[Fri., Mar. 3] ↑Robert Woodward Barnwell's Lib[rar]y↓
    Rev. Dr. Richard Fuller, Baltimore, Md.

[38] [Sat., Mar. 4?] Memo.
Reply to Mr Joel Benton↑'s↓, (Amenia, N.Y.) invitation to stop at his
house for a day, going or coming to or from Virginia
    via Providence & Hartford, or better, *via* Albany R.R. to
Chatham Four Corners; thence to Harlem R.R.
Amenia is 88 miles north from N. York, 68, s. of Albany, & 25 n.e.
from Poughkeepsie.

[39]–[41] [blank]
[42][7] [Thurs., Mar. 16] L[idian]. E[merson]. Head framed & ↑re-
painted↓
    ⟨Edith's choice of book⟩

    Mrs Anna Hooper

    ⟨Mr Gurney.⟩

    ⟨Mr Osgood for a better colored S[ocial]. Aims⟩

[43]–[46] [blank]
[47] [Sat., Apr. 1] Recd from Atlantic B[an]k   124
                 Malcolm Forbes   112.50
                 In Atlantic B[an]k.   587.47

[48] [Mon., Apr. 3] W W Hebbard, M.D.
    23 Buckingham St   Boston
[Tues., Apr. 4] Robert Woodward Barnwell
    Rev. Dr. Richard Fuller. Baltimore, M⟨d.⟩aryland

---

[6] For Emerson's letter, see *L*, VI, 293–294.
[7] The entries on pp. [42], [47], and [48] are in pencil, except for "Rev. Dr. Richard . . . M⟨d.⟩aryland" on p. [48]. On p. [42], "Mr. Osgood . . . Aims" is struck through
in pencil with a diagonal line.

[49]⁸ [Thurs., Apr. 6] Alexander Macmillan   See *ST* p 250
[Fri., Apr. 7] Camden, New Jersey
Walt Whitman   Corner of 4th & Stevens Street
     House of George W Whitman
[Sat., Apr. 8] Samuel Bradford   227 S. 4th Street, Phila
     House   1628 Walnut St.

———

   Dr Furness   1426 Pine St.

[50]–[56] [blank]
[57]⁹ [Sun., Apr. 30] Received portrait of Rev. James Martineau
from William Schaus, Esq. New York

[58]–[61] [blank]
[62] [Mon., May 15] Gardner   Kent
                    Lathrop
                    Monroe
                    Photograph & Whipple

———

[Tues., May 16] Littell, No. 1624

———

   Warren

———

[63]–[66] [blank]
[67]¹⁰ [Tues., May 30] Heywood   Fitchburg
                      Gardner
                   ↑E.L.↓ Stanley
                      Black; & Warren;
                      ⟨Osgood W[illiam H.] Forbes⟩

[68]¹¹ [Fri., June 2] Atl[antic] B[an]k
       ⟨Southworth⟩

   ⁸ On p. [49], "Walt Whitman . . . Whitman" and "House   1628 . . . Pine St." are in pencil.
   ⁹ The entries on pp. [57] and [62] are in pencil; "Warren" and the three rules on p. [62] are in blue pencil.
   ¹⁰ On p. [67], "E.L." is in pencil and "Osgood W Forbes" is in red pencil.
   ¹¹ The entries on p. [68] are in pencil; "Mr Gardiner . . . Thursday" is canceled in red pencil.

People's National B[an]k

⟨————⟩

Guild Rowe & Dudley St

————

⟨Mr Gardiner Hubbard   25 Pemberton Sq.⟩

————

⟨Mr Gannett   Mrs Wells   ⟨2⟩1 to 4 o'c Thursday⟩

[69]–[70] [blank]
[71] [Sun., June 11] ↑Rev.↓ W.H. Channing
     Kensington   London west.
     George Buckton & daughter   ↑16 Hornton St↓[12]
[Mon., June 12] Walt Whitman   Camden, N Jersey
     Corner of 4th & Stevens St   House of Geo. W. Whitman
     cross the ferry from foot of Market St   5th st cars
[Tues., June 13] Mr Green Peyton, Proctor of University of Virginia.

[72] [Thurs., June 15] J. Haven Emerson   81 Madison Ave.
[Fri., June 16] Rev J. Lewis Diman   Angell St. Providence R.I.

[73] [blank]
[74] [Wed., June 21] New York

[75] [blank]
[76] [Wed., June 28] University of Virginia
          W[alter]. S. Perry
          Alfred P. Thom
          W[illiam]. R[obertson]. McKinney

[77][13] [Thurs., June 29] [George Frederick] Holmes   Professor of
History
     Southall   Prof. interna⟨sh⟩tional law
[Sat., July 1] Buckton

[12] "16 Hornton St" is in pencil, as is "J. Haven . . . Ave." on p. [72].
[13] The entries on p. [77] are in purple pencil, except for "Buckton". For Emerson's
visit to Virginia see Journal ST, p. [230] above.

[78]-[88] [blank]
[89] [Sat., Aug. 5] [inscription by Ellen Emerson]

[90] [Tues., Aug. 8] [inscription by Ellen Emerson]

[91]-[110] [blank]
[111] [Tues., Oct. 10] Charles Stodder[d]   Realto Building
     Devonshire St   Use the Elevator
[112]-[163] [blank]
[164] Miss Mary W. Queen   13 Temple Place   Boston

[165] My "Miscellanies" [1876,] Vol 1, p. 301
     "Nicholas present Emperor of Russia"   correct

[166] [blank]
[167] Bennett H Nash   62 Boylston st
Francis P. Nash   Hobart College   Geneva N.Y.

S. Bradford, 227 South Fourth St. Philadelphia.
↑House   1628 Walnut St.↓

Dr Furness   1426 Pine St[14]

[168][15] Munroe   106 Boylston

⟨I understand French has received $600⟩

   1076.96
    900
   176.96

[169]   Statues
Lexington (Hancock) [Thomas Ridgeway] Gould   4000
          (S. Adams) [Martin] Milmore   4000

[14] "House . . . Pine St" is in pencil.
[15] "Munroe . . . Boylston" is in pencil, as is "Statues" on p. [169]; on p. [168], "I understand . . . $600", in blue pencil, is struck through in red pencil and three diagonal lines.

Boston   (Franklin) [Horatio] Greenough   10,000
          (Webster) [Hiram] Powers   12,000
          (Everett)   [William Wetmore] Story   13,000

[170] A White Star steamer from New York, the "Britannic" on her last run from Queenstown, made the passage in seven days, sixteen hours 36 minutes the quickest run on record toward New York. *Daily Advertiser*   7 August, 1876

[inside back cover] [blank]

Pocket Diary 28

1877

Pocket Diary 28 is devoted to recording Emerson's memoranda for 1877. A few entries may have been made late in 1876 or early in 1878.

The notebook, bound in black stamped leather, is a commercially published diary entitled "THE / STANDARD / DIARY / 1877", published by Nichols & Hall, Boston. The covers measure 7.5 × 12.5 cm. The back cover extends into a tongue that, when the book is closed, fits into a loop on the front cover; the back cover also contains an expandable inside pocket. "THE / STANDARD / DIARY" is stamped in gold on the tongue. A paper label fastened to the spine is inscribed "1877."

The white, unnumbered pages, whose edges are marbled, measure 7.2 × 12.2 cm; pages 33–256 are faintly lined. The book consists of a front flyleaf (i, ii); a title page (page 1); a calendar for 1877 (page 3); a table of time differences relative to Boston time (page 4); a table of weights and measures (page 5); interest and income rate tables (pages 6–8); a chart of foreign gold and silver values (pages 9–11); a metric conversion table (page 12); rates of postage (page 13); eclipses in 1877 (page 14); phases of the moon and tide tables for 1877 (pages 15–26); a Chicago almanac (pages 27–32); daily appointments for 1877, two to a page (pages 33–215); pages for memoranda (pages 216–225); pages for cash accounts (pages 226–250); additional pages for memoranda (pages 251–256); and a back flyleaf (pages 257–258).

Entries by Emerson occur on sixty-four pages. Printed matter in Pocket Diary 28 is reproduced here only where relevant. Otherwise, pages are designated as blank if they bear no inscription by Emerson; the presence or absence of printed matter is not specified.

Portions of Fitchburg Railroad and Lowell Railroad schedules are pasted onto the inside front cover. In the expandable pocket in the back cover the following items are enclosed: a blank calling card, measuring 8.8 × 5.5 cm, and an unused three-cent stamp.

[front cover verso]   Fitchburg Railroad
                       Lowell Railroad

[i]   R.W. Emerson
                                                 Concord, Masstts

[railroad schedule omitted]

[ii]–[32] [blank]
[33] [Mon., Jan. 1] Con[cord]. Library.   Ripley's Library
     Landor's Works
     DeQuincy's
     Coleridge
     Longfellow's Poems of Places

[34] [Wed., Jan. 3] Memory of dreams *GL* 358[–359], 305[–307], 65

     Dahabeeyah of ⟨Miss⟩Amelia B. Edwards' "Thousand miles up the Nile"   [Hatem] Ti's biography[1]

[35] Memory
———

     Demonology
———

     Leasts & Mosts
———

     Boston
———

     Art
———

     Webster
———

     Father Taylor
———

     Everett
———

     Yarmouth

———
[1] "Dahabeeyah . . . biography" is in pencil. Amelia Ann Blanford Edwards, *A Thousand Miles up the Nile* . . . (London, 1877). For "Memory of dreams" see also Pocket Diary 24, p. [99] above.

489

_____

Perpetual Forces.

_____

Virginia Discourse[2]
⟨Tufts⟩
Education
France
Landor ⎫
Carl⟨is⟩yle ⎭ in the Dial

[36] [blank]
[37] [Wed., Jan. 10] Lectures, I[ndex] M[ajor] 49,
Try MSS of "Art"
             "Education"
             "Demonology"
             "Boston"[3]
Lars & Lemurs, *IL* 168,

[38][4] Dues

_____

        E[llen]. T. E[merson].'s notes for Mr Walcott

_____

George Stewart   of Belford's Monthly   *Toronto*

_____

Send home ⟨to⟩Miss F. Forbes's papers.   ↑Sent.↓

_____

        Collect & return the College Papers

_____

Write to Mr   Haskins   Derry N.H
                 ___

        George W. Childs   Phila[delphia]—
        ___

Wrote to Miss   Forbes, with her letters returned.
___

---

[2] "Virginia Discourse" and the remaining entries on p. [35] are in pencil.
[3] "Try MSS . . . 'Boston' " is in pencil; " 'Demonology' " is erased.
[4] On p. [38], "Dues . . . Sent." is in pencil.

To W[illiam]. H[athaway]. F[orbes]. 'Tis better that we should print
than the other—

[39] [Sat., Jan. 13] Sen⟨d⟩t Lemuel Bradford
     Collecter   10.24   ↑sent 22 Jan.↓
↑Sent↓   ⟨Send Frank C. Brown his card from Plymouth⟩

_____

     1 Vol Historical Society   one book waiting for me[5]

[40]–[51] [blank]
[52][6] [Thurs., Feb. 8] Dr Bartlett
     Girdle

_____

W[illiam]. H[athaway]. F[orbes]. Nat[ional]. Bank of
     Commerce N.Y.

_____

     Old South

[53] [Sat., Feb. 10] Aromita
     Harp &
     Miss Loring
     Mr George Stewart Jr   Toronto?

_____

     Write to the man [William James Linton] who wants to print
Boston

_____

[54] [blank]
[55] [Wed., Feb. 14] Miss E[lizabeth]. Hoar
     W[illiam] H[athaway] F[orbes]
     Dr Bartlett
     Atlantic B[an]k
     ⟨Bicknell⟩
     Sound
     belt
     Hist[orical] Library

_____

[5] "1 Vol . . . for me" and the rules that precede and follow it are in pencil.
[6] The entries on pp. [52], [53], [55], and [57] are in pencil.

491

[56] [blank]
[57] [Mon., Feb. 19] Historical Library

———

N[ew] Y[ork] Bank

———

Dr S Bartlett

[58] [blank]
[59] [Fri., Feb. 23] Clyde Water   *VO* 269,
Is the ballad in Parnassus?

[60]–[67] [blank]
[68]⁷   *Inventions*
↑/friction/sulphur/↓ matches

[69] [Wed., Mar. 14] Hamilton Place
            Books at Fitchburg Station
⟨Letter to Mrs Dall⟩

———

Harp

———

⟨↑Return↓ Mrs Chamberlain's book⟩

———

Pay Brown for meat

———

Dowden

[70] [blank]
[71] Moulton   Hanover st

———

Bates

———

Dr J. H[aven]. E[merson]'s. check

———

Letter to T. Rice

---

⁷ The entries on pp. [68], [69], and [71] are in pencil.

492

Carry Themes & Forensics to H[arvard]. U[niversity].

Spectroscope glass

Ellen's C[hicago]. B[urlington]. & Q[uincy]. shares,

[72]–[84] [blank]
[85] [Mon., Apr. 16] Answer   Hoar's letter

[86]–[88] [blank]
[89] [Tues., Apr. 24] Atlantic [Bank] 166.45

[90]–[109] [blank]
[110]^8 Motley J[ohn]. L[othrop].   born Apr. 15. 1814
        Graduate 1831   H[arvard] C[ollege]
        Gottengen
        Rise of Dutch Repub[lic]   1856
        United Netherlands   1860–67

[111] [Thurs., June 7] Ben Jonson

Umbrella at Rogers' store

English Cyclopedia

Historical Society

Memory of Motley & Quincy

[112] [blank]
[113]^9 [Mon., June 11] Judge Hoar on Motley & Quincy

---

[8] The entries on pp. [110] and [111] are in pencil, as is "Atlantic 166.45" on p. [89]. On p. [111], "Ben Jonson . . . store" and "English . . . & Quincy" are each struck through in pencil with a vertical line. John Lothrop Motley, American historian, died May 29, 1877; among his works are *The Rise of the Dutch Republic* (New York, 1856) and *The History of the United Netherlands,* 4 vols. (New York, 1860–1868).

[9] The entries on pp. [113]–[116] are in pencil, except for "Write to . . . God.' " on p. [114]. Henry MacCormac's *The Conversation of a Soul with God: A Theodicy* (London, 1877) is in Emerson's library.

[114] [Tues., June 12] Write to Dr ↑Henry↓ MacCormac
                              Bournmouth   Ireland
his book, "Conversation of the Soul with God."

read [*Revue des*] Deux Mondes   Dix Neuvieme   15 Fevrier, '77

[115] [Thurs., June 14] Overseers
      Historical Society 11 o'c
(Quincy & Motley)
      Art Museum
      Eng. Cyclopaedia
      Umbrella
      Ben Jonson

[inscription by Ellen Emerson]   18 in high.   5½ wide base

[116] [Sat., June 16] Mr ↑W.H.↓ Channing
Care of E.W. Higginson   High st.   Brookline   Masstts

[117] [blank]
[118]¹⁰ [Thurs., June 21?] Mrs Adams
      Channing
      W[illiam] H[athaway] Forbes

[119]–[120] [blank]
[121] [Tues., June 26] Answer Hedge
[Wed., June 27] Commencement.
      Overseers, Massachusetts Hall, at 9.45
and go to the Sanders Theatre

[122] [Thurs., June 28] Φ.B.K.
      Oration, Hon. Thomas P. Bayard, of Delaware
      Poem. Edmund C. Stedman, Esq.
West Lecture Room of Boylston Hall at 10 o'c
Sanders' Theatre, 12 o'clock

---

¹⁰ The entries on p. [118] are in pencil, as is "Answer Hedge" on p. [121].

[123] [blank]
[124]¹¹ [Mon., July 2] Post office
[Tues., July 3] from J.M. Forbes, & Co   1400.36

[125] [Thurs., July 5] Afternoon

[126] [Sat., July 7] Sanborn for Stedman

[127] Boardman

———

⟨Atlantic [Bank]⟩

———

Goethe's Worterbuch

———

Little & Brown

─────────────────────────────

⟨At Joseph Bates', book of young Sampson⟩

─────────────────────────────

⟨Overseers Monday 23⟩
⟨W[illiam]. H[athaway]. Forbes⟩

Books for Library
[inscription by Ellen Emerson]   *Paid*

[128]–[133] [blank]
[134] [Sun., July 22] Annie Sawyer Douris   Andover, Mass.

[135] [blank]
[136]¹² [Thurs., July 26] ⟨Channing⟩
    Atlantic
    ⟨cooks⟩
    paper

¹¹ The entries on pp. [124]–[127] are in pencil, except for "Afternoon" on p.
[125]. On p. [127], "Atlantic", "Overseers ... 23", and "W. H. Forbes" are each
struck through in pencil with a diagonal line; "At Joseph ... Sampson" is struck through
in pencil with a vertical line and a diagonal line.
    ¹² On p. [136], "Channing ... paper" is in red pencil; "Channing" is struck
through in pencil with a diagonal line; "Carry MSS ... o clo Prov", in pencil, is struck
through in pencil with a vertical line.

[inscription by Ellen Emerson]

[Fri., July 27] ⟨Carry MSS to Osgood⟩
⟨ask send proofs to care of W[illiam] H[athaway] F[orbes]
     Woods Hole⟩

———

Tolman

———

     Train   2, o clo   Prov[idence]
[137]¹³ [Sat., July 28] 10.30 o'clock from Concord
[138] Pay
     Subscription to Lady Stanley's Tomb
     Atlantic book
     Return Goethe's Conversations
⟨G⟩For Concord Library Mr   's Oriental Religions

     "North American" ⟨paper⟩ article

———

⟨Pay Mr Wood⟩
     Johnson

     ————————————

     Adi Granth   Sikh Scriptures
     Athenaeum

———   ————————

Taine's History of English Literature

———

Morris's Story of Sigurd the Volsung, & the Fate of the Niblungs.
Roberts Brothers

———

[139] [blank]
[140]¹⁴ [Sat., Aug. 4] Library
     Lyell's writings

———

    ¹³ The entries on pp. [137] and [138] are in pencil. On p. [138], for Taine see
Journal ST, p. [187] above; William Morris, *The Story of Sigurd the Volsung and the Fall
of the Niblungs* (Boston, 1877).
    ¹⁴ The entries on p. [140] are in pencil. Alfred Russel Wallace, *Contributions to the
Theory of Natural Selection. A Series of Essays* (London and New York, 1870).

Wallace   "Contributions to the Theory of Natural Selection"
See *Unitarian Review,* July 77
    Lubbock
    Prof Gray   "Darwiniana"
        Johnson, Orientals & so^n forth
    Prof

[141] [blank]
[142]^{15} No fate, save by the victim's fault, is low,
       For God hath writ all dooms magnificent,
       So guilt not traverses his tender will.

————

       This shining moment is an edifice
       Which the omnipotent cannot rebuild.

————

       O what is Heaven but the fellowship
       Of minds that each can stand against the world
       By its own meek but incorruptible will?

————

[143] [Thurs., Aug. 9] [Robert] Chambers' Cyclopaedia of English
Literature. 3d Edition 2 Vols. [London and Edinburgh, 1876.]
    New York. R Worthington

[144]–[156] [blank]
[157] [Thurs., Sep. 6] [inscription by Ellen Emerson]

[158]–[161] [blank]
[162]^{16} [Mon., Sep. 17] Dedication of Army & Navy Monument, in
Boston, at 3 o'clock, P.M.

————

[163] [Tues., Sep. 18] [inscription by Ellen Emerson]

    [15] Of these fragments by Emerson, "No fate . . . will." is used in "Fragments on . . .
Life," II, *W,* IX, 349; "This shining . . . rebuild." is used in "Fragments on . . . Life," V,
W, IX, 350 (see *JMN,* XIV, 211). For "O what . . . will?" see Pocket Diary 25, p. [157]
above.
    [16] The entries on pp. [162], [164], and [167] are in pencil.

[164] [Fri., Sep. 21] Ask of the Insurance company to secure me insurance on my furniture to the amount of 600 dollars.

[165]–[166] [blank]
[167] [Thurs., Sep. 27] [inscription by Ellen Emerson]

Overseers
_____

Book to Atlantic B⟨k⟩ank
_____

Picture of Frenchman
_____

Rogers.   [inscription by Ellen Emerson]
_____

W[illiam]. H[athaway]. F[orbes]. for Railroad Bonds.
_____

Fitchburg
_____

[inscription by Ellen Emerson]

[168] [inscription by Ellen Emerson]

[169] [blank]
[170] [Tues., Oct. 2] Atlantic [Bank]
_____

Commonwea↑l↓th   & 15th Sept paper
_____

Ellen's Letters
[Wed., Oct. 3] Tuesday   Thomas S. Blyth of Glasgow University leaves Fifth Avenue Hotel, N.Y. of Darling   Griswold & Co next Thursday &

[171]–[173] [blank]
[174]¹⁷ [Wed., Oct. 10] frame of photograph
_____

¹⁷ The entries on p. [174] are in pencil.

498

Atlantic [Bank]

⟨Custom House &⟩

⟨Oath at Mr Hoar's office.⟩

find Mr Playfair

[175] [blank]
[176] [Sun., Oct. 14] *Missing Books*

Digby

Book of Bonaparte's man[18]

[177] [blank]
[178] [Fri., Oct. 19] [inscription by Ellen Emerson]

[179] [Sat., Oct. 20] Aubr⟨y⟩ey de Vere.
Care of Henry S. King & Co. London

Ellen's watch

Mr Playfair

Concord ⟨Aubrey⟩Library

[180][19] [Tues., Oct. 23] 135 Beacon St
[inscription by Ellen Emerson]

[181]–[187] [blank]
[188] [Wed., Nov. 7] Letters for Ellen at Forbes' office

[18] "Digby" may refer to Sir Kenelm Digby, *Private Memoirs . . . Written by Himself* (London, 1827), in Emerson's library. "Book of Bonaparte's man", in pencil, may be an allusion to some work of Étienne Geoffroy Saint-Hilaire; see Journal ST, pp. [114], [118]–[121] above.
[19] The entries on pp. [180] and [188] are in pencil.

499

Envelopes

_____

Pulmann Car

_____

St Beuve

_____

Francis E Abbot
James H Bartlett
Rev William J Potter   Grantville Mass

[189]–[190] [blank]
[191] Oct. 9, '77
Colin Rae Brown. Oakleigh Park, Whetstone. Herts. England.

Geo. W. Wright, Secy of the "Emerson Literary Association"
    4131 Paul Street, Frankfor⟨t⟩d Philadelphia, Co. Penna.

W Leighton, Jr.   Wheeling, West Virginia   2212 Chapline St.
"At the Court of King Edwin."

[192] [Thurs., Nov. 15] Arthur Gilman   11 Mason St   Cambridge
Author of the Diary
[Fri., Nov. 16] E. Dowden, Shakspear; Litera⟨ry⟩ture primer.
                              D. Appleton & Co.[20]

[193] [Sat., Nov. 17] Saint Beuve

[194] [blank]
[195][21] [Thurs., Nov. 22] Mrs Kate McDowell   39 Somerset St.

[196]–[198] [blank]
[199] [Fri., Nov. 30] Frederic G Forsyth   56 State st   Portland

[20] Arthur Gilman edited *Theatrum Majorum. The Cambridge of 1776: Wherein Is Set Forth an Account of the Town, and the Events It Witnessed: with Which Is Incorporated the Diary of Dorothy Dudley, Now First Published* . . . (Boston, 1876), in Emerson's library. Edward Dowden's *Shakspere* (London, 1877) was published in New York in 1878 in Appleton's "Literature primers" series.
[21] The entries on pp. [195], [199], and [211] are in pencil.

[200]–[210] [blank]
[211] [Mon., Dec. 24] Mr Cobb's picture of Judas in Potter's Field at
Studio Building
        Statu⟨ee⟩e of Dr Channing at Corner store

[212]–[215] [blank]
[216] George E. Tufts
In New York, his address was, Care of Dr S.F. Dickinson,
        98 Lawrence Street, Brooklyn, N.Y.

[217] Miss ↑C.↓ F↑anny↓ Forbes

F[rancis]. P[hilip]. Nash   Geneva N.Y.
Thomas Dixon   Sunderland

Alexander Ireland, Inglewood, Bowdon, Cheshire.

Hon Roden Noel   reciv↑i↓ed Dec. 28, '77——

---

[218]–[247] [blank]
[248]²² 　　　　　　Feb., '78.

        Park St ⟨&c⟩
____

        Athenaeum 3, o'c^n
____

        ⟨umbrella⟩
____

        Fitchburg Depot
____

        Atlantic [Bank]
____

        Old South
____

        W. Forbes

²² The entries on p. [248] are in pencil.

Mass. Society

[249]²³ letter to Nash
    Miss   Forbes
    Diary of 1878
    Letter to French Institute
        M. Francois A.A. Mignet.

    Elizabeth Hoar

    Mr S[amuel]. G[ray]. Ward——

---

[250]–[251] [blank]
[252] Letters due to
    Miss Fanny Forbes
    Mr Alexander
    Mr Mathew Arnold
    Aubr↑e↓y De Vere
    Thomas Appleton
    Edwd Everett Ha⟨y⟩le

Mr William H. Babcock, P.O. Box 220, Washington, D.C. Oct., '77.——

[253]²⁴   Concord Library

1843   Darwin, Descent of Man (in England) 7⟨S⟩.6d

[254] ⟨789⟩   73/45678

    Adi Granth Nanak died AD 1538
    Holy Scriptures of the Sikhs.

²³ On p. [249], "Elizabeth Hoar", "Mr S. G. Ward——", and the rules that immediately precede and follow these entries are in pencil.
   ²⁴ The entries on pp. [253] and [254] are in pencil, except for "Miss Jessie . . . York." on p. [254]. Adi Granth Nanak (1469–1538), first of the ten gurus and founder of Sikhism, compiled part of the sacred scriptures of the Sikhs.

Southern Historical Papers. Sept. '77   Richmond   Virginia

↑Boston↓ Athenaeum
     Johnson   Library

↑Miss↓ Jessie Kingsley, Hamilton, New York.

[255] Jan., '78   41.67   Pd John C.

     Diary

_____

     Cobden

_____

     Moulton

_____

     Ward   State St

_____

     William Forbes

_____

     Tolman, westcoat

     _____

Prof. Francis Philip Nash   Geneva, N.Y.

[256][25]   *Homer*
     Academy, Sept. 29, '77
     C.G. Cobet, Leiden '77

[257] [blank]
[258] Grimm   Worterbuch

     _____

     Erster Band
     Zweiter Band
     Dritter Band
     Funfter Band

[25] The entries on p. [256] are in pencil.

Thomas Dixon   Sunderland

[inside back cover] George E. Tufts—   Rawson, Nov. 1863

Lyndon, Cataraugus Co.   N. York

Pocket Diary 29

1878

Pocket Diary 29 is devoted to recording Emerson's memoranda for 1878. A few entries may have been made late in 1877 or early in 1879.

The notebook, bound in black stamped leather, is a commercially published diary entitled "EXCELSIOR / DIARY / for / 1878." The covers measure 7.7 × 12.8 cm. The back cover extends into a flap that, when the book is closed, springs forward to cover half the front cover. "DIARY" is stamped in gold on the flap. A paper label fastened to the spine is inscribed "1863.–1878. x".

The white, unnumbered pages, whose edges are marbled, measure 7.7 × 12.4 cm; pages 25–184 are faintly lined. The book consists of a front flyleaf (i, ii); a title page (page 1); a table of astronomical calculations (page 3); a calendar for 1878 (page 4); a monthly historical calendar for 1878 (pages 5–16); interest tables (page 17); gold rates for 1862–1877 (page 18); a table for calculating hourly wages paid by the week (page 19); a table of the distance of principal American cities from New York (page 20); the 1790 and 1870 censuses of states and territories (page 21); rates of postage (pages 22–23); presidents of the United States (page 24); daily appointments for 1878, three to a page (pages 25–146); pages for memoranda (pages 147–152); pages for cash accounts (pages 153–177); pages for bills receivable and payable (pages 178–183); an additional page for memoranda (page 184); and a back flyleaf (pages 185–186).

Entries by Emerson occur on fifty-four pages. Printed matter in Pocket Diary 29 is reproduced here only where relevant. Otherwise, pages are designated as blank if they bear no inscription by Emerson; the presence or absence of printed matter is not specified.

Laid in between the front cover verso and p. i are a blank calling card, measuring 9.2 × 5.2 cm, and a piece of heavy paper, measuring 11.8 × 2.2 cm, on which is inscribed in Emerson's hand "Dr. A. M. Ross, Toronto, Canada—," on one side, and "Concord, Mass." on the other. Laid in between pages 4 and 5 are two Concord-to-Boston railroad timetables clipped from a newspaper. Laid in between pages 50 and 51 is a piece of paper bearing in Ellen Emerson's hand this inscription: "Please get Eugene Sue's 'Wandering Jew'—from the Athenaeum."

[front cover verso] 54   No 3⟨3⟩22[1]
                                                           March 13, 1878—

[railroad schedule omitted]

[i]   R.W. Emerson—
                                                           Concord, Masstts

    January 10.

[ii] Tolles R.B 48 Hanover st Room thirty
↑1.31↓ Stoddard 131 Devonshire

    Nancy Col[e]sworth[y]   January

[1] [blank]
[2] In Edith's copy of "Emerson's Poems" 1876, pages 129, & 130,
to ⟨r⟩be [re]versed

    Charter st   Greenough

[3]–[25] [blank]
[26][2]   *Books for the Library*—
    Reminiscenses of Daniel Webster   By Peter Harvey
    Mr Darwin's Origin of Species

———

The Monuments of Upper Egypt
    A translation of the Itineraire de la Haute Egypte. ⟨By⟩
        Of Auguste Mariette Bey
    Translated by Alphonse Mariette   Trubner & Co   London

---

    [1] On the front cover verso, "54" and "No 3⟨3⟩22" are in pencil, as are "January
10." on p. [i] and the entries on p. [2]; "Nancy . . . January" on p. [ii] is in red pencil.
    [2] The entries on pp. [26] and [27] are in pencil, except for *"Books for . . . Peter
Harvey"* on p. [26]. Peter Harvey, *Reminiscences and Anecdotes of Daniel Webster* (Bos-
ton, 1877); Auguste Mariette-Bey, *The Monuments of Upper Egypt, a Translation [of the]
Itinéraire de la Haute Egypte,* trans. Alphonse Mariette (London, 1877); Alvin Jewett
Johnson, *Johnson's New Universal Cyclopaedia. A Scientific and Popular Treasury of Useful
Knowledge,* edition unknown.

[27] Johnson's New Universal Cyclopaedia
   A Scientific & Popular Treasury of Useful Knowledge
       Complete in four vols.

Asa Gray
Pres[iden]t Woolsey
Joseph Henry
George P Marsh   } [writers.]
Horace Greel⟨y⟩ey
O.B. Frothingham
   & others

[28] [blank]
[29]³   No fate, save by the victim's fault, is low,
         For God hath writ all dooms magnificent,
         So guilt not traverses his tender will.

         This shining ⟨h⟩moment is an edifice
         Which the Omnipotent cannot rebuild

         O what is Heaven but the fellowship
         Of minds that each can stand against the world,
         By its own meek but incorruptible will?

---

[30]⁴ [Thurs., Jan. 17?] Andrew Cushing
    19 Congre[g]ation House   Corner of Beacon & Somerset
               H B Rogers pres
[Fri., Jan. 18?] 108ⁿ Revere St   Home for Aged Women
Henry Emmons Sec   H G Denny Tre

[31] [Sat., Jan. 19?] Deacon Cushing
    Congre[g]ational Buildin[g]   Somerset St
[Sun., Jan. 20?] Nancy Colesworthy
Mrs Smith   240 Harvard st   Cambridgeport

³ For Emerson's verses on p. [29] see Pocket Diary 28, p. [142] above.
⁴ The entries on p. [30] are in pencil; on p. [31], "Deacon ... Somerset St" and
"240 ... Cambridgeport" are in red pencil, and "Nancy ... Smith" is in pencil.

[32]–[45] [blank]
[46]⁵ [Tues., Mar. 5?] ↑Leigh↓ Hunt   Whipple   Essays & Reviews

↑out;↓ Gifford Quarterly Review, Jan. 1816

List of Writings of Hazlitt & Hunt
By Alexander Ireland

⟨London Quarterly Review, Jan. 1816⟩

[47] [Fri., Mar. 8?] Thomas Dixon, Sunderland, England.

[48] [Mon., Mar. 11?] ↑Nov. 1863—↓ George E. Tufts
Rawson, N.Y.   Lyndon, Cataraugus Co.
[Tues., Mar. 12?] ↑Professor↓ Francis Philip Nash, Geneva N.Y.
Miss Jessie Kingsley; Hamilton, N.Y.
Cobden
[Wed., Mar. 13?] Thomas Dixon, Sunderland, England.
Miss Jessie Kingsley, *Hamilton, N.Y.*

[49] [Thurs., Mar. 14?] W.H. Babcock
Oct '77   PO. Box, 220, ⟨D.C.⟩ Washington, D.C.

Western Train—

[Fri., Mar. 15] library
Insurance $200⁶

[50]–[52] [blank]
[53] [Tues., Mar. 26?] Alexander Ireland
↑⟨Bowden   Cheshire⟩↓   Bowden   Cheshire
Letters of Thomas Erskine

⁵ The entries on p. [46] are in pencil. Edwin Percy Whipple's *Essays and Reviews,* 2 vols. (New York, 1848–1849), appeared in many editions; Alexander Ireland's *List of the Writings of William Hazlitt and Leigh Hunt* . . . (London, 1868) is in Emerson's library.
⁶ "Western . . . $200" is in pencil.

[54] [blank]
[55]⁷ ⟨Babcock's Poem to Howells⟩ ↑W H↓ Babcock   P.O Box
220   ↑Washington D C↓   Babcock

Athenaeum
    gloves &
⟨Pierce⟩
⟨Hovey⟩
Houghton

W.H. Forbes   book

Sleepy Hollow Cemetary

⟨Heine's Letters⟩

Bank
    ⟨meed⟩

[56]⁸ [Thurs., Apr. 4?] Bank book
                    gloves
                    spectacles

[57] [blank]
[58] [Wed., Apr. 10?] Mrs. Juliette K. Portis
    3 Oct. '77—   London, Ontario
[Thurs., Apr. 11?] Miss Jessie Kingsley, ⟨Hamilton⟩
    Hamilton, New York.   "Giot↑t↓esque & Sienese schools."
[Fri., Apr. 12?] Books

Spectacles

⁷ On p. [55], "Babcocks . . . Howells", in red pencil, is overwritten by "W H Babcock . . . Babcock" in ink to cancel; "Athenaeum" and "gloves &", in red pencil, are
overwritten by the same in pencil; "Pierce . . . meed" is in pencil; "Pierce   Hovey" is
struck through in pencil with a diagonal line; and "Heines Letters" is struck through in
pencil with three diagonal lines.
⁸ The entries on pp. [56], [58], and [60] are in pencil, except for "Mrs. Juliette . . .
schools.' " on p. [58].

W[illiam]. H[athaway]. F[orbes].
pay ⟨the⟩Cary & Co's bill for tea, $45.45
gloves

[59] [blank]
[60] [Tues., Apr. 16?] T.T. Chollar   American House
Statistical Atlas of U.S A $18.00

[61]–[63] [blank]
[64]⁹ [Sun., Apr. 28?] A.W. Stevens   308 Harvard St   Cambridge
watch
gloves   at Athenaeum
[Mon., Apr. 29?] Mr Cabot's view of paper by Miss Jessie
Kingsley   Hamilton   G[i]ottesque & Sienese schools

A W Stevens   Cambridge
Leigh Hunt   Autobiog.   S. Smiles
        Alexander Ireland   List of Hunt & Hazlitt

⟨Sufs⟩   Whipple, Essays & Reviews

London Quarterly, Jan 1860

[Leigh Hunt]   Abou Ben Adhem & the Angel   1844   1846   1857

Leigh Hunt   born 1784
        died 1859

[65]¹⁰ [Wed., May 1] Pay Boardman for demijons
Rev Mr Colliard's Hafiz
Pullman Cars

⁹ On p. [64], "A.W. Stevens   308 . . . A W Stevens   Cambridge" and "Sufs" are
in pencil. For Alexander Ireland and Edwin Percy Whipple see p. [46] above.
¹⁰ The entries on pp. [65], [67], [69], and [71] are in pencil, except for "Rev Mr
. . . W.H.F." on p. [65] and "What has become . . . reports." and "Frank S. . . . VT." on
p. [69]; on p. [69], "Committee . . . Hall" is struck through in pencil with a diagonal
line.

W[illiam]. H[athaway]. F[orbes].
Bank book
Boston bills

[66] [blank]
[67] [Thurs., May 9] 11 o'clock   Historical Society

[68] [blank]
[69] What has become of the signed papers betwe⟨n⟩en ↑Houghton↓
& Osgood & R.W.E.?

———

[Tues., May 14]   Committee of 50
    ⟨Room over the Life Office at 11 o'clock, a.m. to act on the final
reports.⟩

———————————

Harv[ar]d   Memorial Hall

Boardman   demijohns

Colli⟨ard⟩er   Hafiz, ↑88 Charles T↓
Hafiz
Pullman
Bank book
W[illiam] H[athaway] F[orbes]. & Osgood
Frank S. Weston   Windsor, VT.
⟨Academy   10⟩

[70] [blank]
[71] [Sun., May 19] Paper
    Boardman, return kegs
    Athenaeum books
    [inscription by Ellen Emerson]
[Mon., May 20?] Charles Stoddard   Rialto Build[ing]
    opposite Post Of[fice]   Devonshire st
    1 flight up & elevator

[72]–[75] [blank]
[76] [Wed., June 5] [inscription by Ellen Emerson]

511

[77]–[78] [blank]
[79][11] [Wed., June 12] Address ⟨to⟩at *"Phillips Exeter Academy"*
to "The Golden Branch."

> Sherman Hoar ⎫
> E.H. Mariett ⎬ Committee
> J.W. Babcock ⎭
>   12 June

[Thurs., June 13] ⟨Mr⟨s⟩ G.M. Richardson writes to me to choose
either the *15th,* or the *19th,* of June, to address the ⟨school⟩Academy.⟩
Mr Wm H. Gorhame invites us to spend the night of the 12 June at
his house.

[80] [Sat., June 15] Charles Morris Addison
> Letter from Mr Bancroft.

[81]–[82] [blank]
[83] [Wed., June 26] Commencement[12]

[84]–[85] [blank]
[86][13] [Wed., July 3?] Stanley's Africa
> Through the dark Continant
or the Sources of the Nile
> 2 Vols. London   1878
Nathan↑i↓el Colesworthy   ship wright
> > > lovelane
> > ship carpenter

[Fri., July 5?] 30 Pemberton Square   Austin Form

[87][14] [Sat., July 6?] Mem. William Leighton, Jr.
> Wheeling, West Virginea
> to be thanked for his gift to the Concord Library

---

[11] The entries on p. [79] are struck through in pencil with two vertical lines.
[12] "Commencement" is in pencil.
[13] On p. [86], "Stanley's Africa" is in red pencil, and the remaining entries are in pencil; "Nathaniel . . . carpenter" is struck through in pencil with two vertical lines. Sir Henry Morton Stanley, *Through the Dark Continent, or The Sources of the Nile around the Great Lakes of Equatorial Africa* . . . , 2 vols. (London, 1878).
[14] On p. [87], "Razor strap . . . Eaton" and "Roberts . . . Dichtung' " are in pencil.

⟨Razor strap⟩

———

W.E. Gill

———

⟨My Wyatt Eaton⟩

———

⟨Couture, for Boston Library⟩

———

Rev. Mr Collier

———

Telescope

———

Nancy Colsworthy
⟨Roberts⟩

[Goethe,] "Wahrheit & Dichtung"   [inscription by Ellen Emerson]

[88] [blank]
[89] [Sat., July 13?] Wm Leighton, Jr.   Wheeling   W. Virginia

———

Sands, Furber & Company.

———

Charles D. Freeman, March '78
150 Nineth⟨y⟩ Avenue, New York City

————————

[Sun., July 14?] Mrs Cabot for note of place for Nancy Colesworthy[15]

[90] [Wed., July 17] [inscription by Ellen Emerson]
[91]–[92] [blank]
[93] [Wed., July 24] [inscription by Ellen Emerson]

[94]–[97] [blank]
[98][16] [Thurs., Aug. 8] Charles Stoddard   Rialto Building
     opposite Post Office   Devonshire St
1 flight up & elevator

[15] "Mrs Cabot . . . Colesworthy" is in pencil.
[16] The entries on pp. [98] and [100] are in pencil, except for "S.H. Morse
$20.00" on p. [100].

[99] [blank]
[100] [Wed., Aug. 14] Pullman Car
                      Charles Stoddard
[inscription by Ellen Emerson]
[Thurs., Aug. 15] S.H. Morse $20.00

[101]–[105] [blank]
[106]¹⁷ [Sun., Sept. 1?] R   Rawson, Cat↑t↓araugus, Co.   N.Y.

S.H. Morse   20

[Mon., Sept. 2?] C. Stoddard Rial[t]o Building opposite
Post Office   Devonshire   1 flight up, elivater   Rea⟨to⟩lto
[Tues., Sept. 3] [inscription by Ellen Emerson]
                      Henry Lee
                      G[eorge] B[arrell] Emerson

[107]¹⁸ [Wed., Sept. 4?] ↑x↓ Bank
↑x↓   Stoddard
       W[illiam] H[athaway] Forbes
       Truss
       Tickets to Saratoga
       Nancy Colesworthy
       Athenaeum
↑x↓   Lidian's ↑dividend↓   Fitchburg R.
       Railroad Guide

[108] [blank]
[109] May 8

[110]–[113] [blank]
[114] [Wed., Sept. 25?] Strap   pd. 8.00
      W[illiam]. H[athaway]. F[orbes].
      Stanley

---

¹⁷ On p. [106], "Rawson . . . N.Y." and "Rea⟨to⟩lto" are in pencil; "S.H. Morse . . .
up, elivater" is in red pencil.
¹⁸ The entries on pp. [107], [109], [114], [115], and [117] are in pencil.

Atlantic Bank
     Mrs Smith   240 Harvard St
Corks

[115] [Sat., Sept. 28?] Dean Stanley

[116] [Tues., Oct. 1?] Dean Stanley
     Commonwealth newspaper
———Sampson, Low, & Co
     Samuel & Co   St. Louis, Mo.

[117] [Fri., Oct. 4] Meeting of Committee at 70 Water St at 11
o'clock

[118] [Wed., Oct. 9] Overseers of Harvard College meet at Water
street on Oct. 9
Shoenhof & Co. 40 Winter St

[119] [Thurs., Oct. 10?] Mrs Smith   240 Harvard st
     Cambridgeport
[Fri., Oct. 11?] Shoenhof & Moeller

[120][19] ⟨Acknowledge Houghton & Osgood's gift of Lowell's ⟨pic-
ture⟩ portrait on the 14th October⟩
———

     ⟨Wri⟨ght⟩te to Patch & Young at Bangor, Me. wish to know if
James F Coffin is known in Concord.⟩

Write to Miss Charlotte F. Bates of Cambridge
Write to Mrs C.S. Prescott, Malden
———

     Carry Grimm's Dic⟨ksh⟩tionar⟨y⟩y to Winter St.
———

[19] On p. [120], "Acknowledge Houghton . . . in Concord." is struck through in
pencil with three vertical lines; "Pay . . . Marsh." is in pencil, but the period following
"Marsh." is in ink. For Augustus Porter Chamberlain's request see Journal ST, p. [232]
above.

Pay Jordan & Marsh.

———

⟨Carry German Dic[ti]onary to Winter street.⟩ &

———

Mr [Augustus Porter] Chamberlain's request to learn what books for the Concord Library are wanting.

———

Carry Goethe to Athenaeum

[121]²⁰ [Wed., Oct. 16?] Immense super↑i↓ority of the inventions of the nineteenth century
[Thurs., Oct. 17?] Fiske A.H. Mrs   36 Commonwealth Avenue

[122]–[124] [blank]
[125] [Mon., Oct. 28] [inscription by Ellen Emerson]

[126] [Fri., Nov. 1] Return Pepys
Miss Charlott[e] Bates
B[u]y Notes of Webster, by ——— in Boston

[127] May 1878

[128]–[131] [blank]
[132] [Mon., Nov. 18] Acadamy of Arts & Sciences $10.00

[133] [blank]
[134] [Tues., Nov. 26] [inscription by Ellen Emerson]

[135]–[137] [blank]
[138] [Fri., Dec. 6?] W[illiam]. H[athaway]. Forbes.
    Athenaeum
    Mrs Colesworthy Smith   240 Harva⟨d⟩rd St.
    Pay Houghton ↑Osgood↓ & Co. for Ellen   [inscription by Ellen
        Emerson]
    Carry the New York "Nation"

²⁰ The entries on pp. [121], [126], [127], and [132] are in pencil.

[inscription by Ellen Emerson]
[Sat., Dec. 7] [inscription by Ellen Emerson]
    Pay W[illiam]. H[athaway]. F[orbes]. for
[Sun., Dec. 8?] ⟨Bicknell⟩
    ⟨Pullman Car⟩²¹

[139] [Mon., Dec. 9] Railway Guide

[140]–[142] [blank]
[143] [Sun., Dec. 22?] A[ugustus]. P[orter]. Chamberlaine
"Aristotelis Organon"   Aldi Manucii [Aldus Manutius], 1495.
The book was to be sent ⟨from Venice⟩ on the 4 October, 1878, by
Signor Ougania to his correspondent at Leipsic, who will send it
through Messrs Schoenhof, & Muller of Boston

[144]–[167] [blank]
[168] [inscription by Ellen Emerson]

[169]–[173] [blank]
[174]   ↑Library↓²²
    The Concord Library recieves annual[l]y to spend on books from
the overseers
        say $720.00
& from dog tax
        say $220.00
        ────────
        940.00

[175] [blank]
[176]²³ Athenaeum
────

    picture
        Whittier   by C.H. Brainard   127 Tremont St

²¹ "Bicknell ... Car" is struck through in pencil with a vertical line; "Railway
Guide", on p. [139], is in pencil.
²² "Library" is in pencil.
²³ The entries on pp. [176], [180], and [182]–[185] are in pencil, except for
"Sampson Low, ... 1878" on p. [185].

*Pullman Car

[inscription by Ellen Emerson]

[177]–[179] [blank]
[180] Poems of Arthur Hugh Clough   Macmillan & Co   2.00
Alice's Adventures in Wonderland. By Louis Carroll   1.50
Bret Hart[e]
Boston Directory

Star Gazing   J. Norman Lochyer   6.00

[181] [blank]
[182] Macmillan & Co.
      Mrs C S Prescott   Malden Mass

      Dr Thomas Stewardson
Write to W.S.W. Ruschenberger
      No 1932 Chestnut St   Philadelphia

Showenhof & Moeller   Grimm's Dictionary

      Directory

[183]   ⟨[BILLS PAYABLE.]⟩   Century Club
      Charles P. Daly   84 Clinton Place, N.Y.
Breakfast Saturday, Nov 2d at the Club at 10 o'clock

Ralph Waldo Carroll   Allegany   Catt. co   NY

Dr A[lexander] M[ilton] Ross   Toronto   Canada

[184] Nancy Colesworth[y]

      Gilbert Colesworth⟨e⟩y   her grandfather
      her father John C died at sea

518

[185] Mr Chamberlin   Books for Library
Sampson Low, Marston, Searle, & Rivington.
    Crown Buildings   188 Fleet St   London E.C.   Sept 10, 1878

[186] [blank]
[inside back cover] [blank]

Pocket Diary 30

1879

Pocket Diary 30 is devoted to recording Emerson's memoranda for 1879. A few entries may have been made late in 1878 or early in 1880.

The notebook, bound in black stamped leather, is a commercially published diary entitled "THE / STANDARD / DIARY / 1879 / PUBLISHED /FOR / THE TRADE." The covers measure 7.4 × 12.5 cm. The back cover extends into a tongue that, when the book is closed, fits into a loop on the front cover; the back cover also contains an expandable inside pocket. "THE / STANDARD / DIARY" is stamped in gold on the tongue. A paper label fastened to the spine is inscribed "1879. x".

The white, unnumbered, gilt-edged pages measure 7.3 × 12.2 cm; pages 33–440 are faintly lined. The book consists of a front flyleaf (i, ii); a title page (page 1); a calendar for 1879 (page 3); a table of weights and measures (page 4); a table of weights per bushel of grain (page 5); interest rates (pages 6–7); interest laws (page 8); rates of income on investments (page 9); the population of principal nations and American cities (page 10); a table of distance and time relative to New York City (page 11); a table of the value of foreign coins (pages 12–14); a metric conversion table (page 15); an account, "Business Law in Daily Use." (pages 16–17); rates of postage (page 18); a table of eclipses and fixed and moveable feasts in 1879 (page 19); a table of cycles and seasons (page 20); phases of the moon and tide tables for 1879 (pages 21–32); daily appointments for 1879, one to a page (pages 33–397); pages for memoranda (pages 398–401); pages for cash accounts (pages 402–426); pages for bills payable and receivable (pages 427–438); additional pages for memoranda (pages 439–440); and a back flyleaf (pages 441–442).

Entries by Emerson occur on forty-four pages. Printed matter in Pocket Diary 30 is reproduced here only where relevant. Otherwise, pages are designated as blank if they bear no inscription by Emerson; the presence or absence of printed matter is not specified.

Laid in between pages 32 and 33 is a piece of white paper, measuring 8.6 × 6.9 cm, bearing writing in Emerson's hand; the editors have numbered it pp. [32a]–[32b].

[front cover verso]¹ *Fitchburg Railroad*
[railroad schedule omitted]

[i]   R.W. Emerson
                                                      Concord Masstts

[railroad schedule omitted]

[ii] 18.3
     18–21

[1] [blank]
[2] Natural Wealth of California

"California" by Charles Nordhoff

Eagypt   Fortnight Review   May 1879²

---

[3]–[32] [blank]
[32ₐ] "The Defence of Guinevere & Other Poems"   [William]
Morris

[32ᵦ] Oct. 27, '77.

$$\begin{array}{r} 257.72 \\ 50.2 \\ \hline 207\ 70 \end{array}$$

961.33

[33] [Wed., Jan. 1] [inscription by Ellen Emerson]
     about 22$ each way—³

---

¹ "#3b .65", in pencil, in the upper left-hand corner of the front cover verso may
be a stationer's mark. "18.3" and "18–21" on p. [ii] are in pencil.
² The entries on p. [2] are in pencil. Charles Nordhoff, *California: for Health, Pleasure, and Residence* (New York, 1872); George Campbell, "The Situation in Egypt,"
Fortnightly Review, 149 (May 1, 1879): 787–797.
³ "*about* . . . way—" is in pencil.

[34] [Thurs., Jan. 2] Received from Salem, Mass. December 23, Letter from Mr. George I.J. Breed, to be answered.

———

[35] Robert Woodward Barnwell

John Lowell Gardner
Josiah Quincy
Athanaeum

———————————

[inscription by Ellen Emerson]

[36]–[37] [blank]
[38] [Mon., Jan. 6] [inscription by Ellen Emerson]
[39] [Tues., Jan. 7] [inscription by Ellen Emerson]
[40]–[56] [blank]
[57] [Sat., Jan. 25] [inscription by Ellen Emerson]
[58]–[62] [blank]
[63] [Fri., Jan. 31] [inscription by Ellen Emerson]

[64] ↑Hon.↓ Robert Woodward Barnwell
      Charleston, South Carolina

Cornelius Kollock, M.D.   Cheraw, South Carroliner
                              7 January, 1879
      John Lowell Gardner
      Miss Ellen W. Barnwell
      Rev. Richard Fuller

[65][4] [Sun., Feb. 2] ⟨Right⟩ Wright to thank Mrs Helen Rich, at Brasher Falls, St Law[rence], Co[unty]. New York

———

      145 Tremont St.   Chinese

———

[66]–[67] [blank]
[68] [Wed., Feb. 5] Sent letter to Miss Barnwell

———

[4] The entries on pp. [65] and [68] are in pencil, except for "Right . . . New York" on p. [65].

[69]–[85] [blank]
[86]⁵ [Sun., Feb. 23]   Answer

———

Athanae[um] Library. New vol.

———

S.G. Ward's office

———

Pullman's Palace Car

———

How many shares in Atlantic.

———

Inquire of Nancy Coleworth's condition

———

Barnwell ⟨&⟩   See Gardner.

———

⟨Sam[ue]l G Ward's office⟩

———

Answer *Sampson, Low, & Co.*

———

Call on Mrs Tappan, and Miss Lowell.

———

⟨Watch ke⟨e⟩y⟩

———

⟨Concord Bank holds how many of⟩ my shares in ↑Atlantic↓ & how
many in my box in Mr S.G. Ward office

———

Mr   name of brother

———

[87] [Mon., Feb. 24] Write to Mr
        Claims of the Bartlett Memorial
                of
                of

———

⁵ On p. [86], "Watch Ke⟨e⟩y . . . many of" is canceled in pencil; the inserted "Atlantic" and "Mr . . . brother" are in pencil.

[88]⁶ [Tues., Feb. 25] Pullman Car
    S.G. Ward's office
    Athenae[um] Lib[rary].
    Sec J[ohn] L[owell] Gardner
    Call on Mrs Tappan
    Dividend of Chicago, Ill.
    Wine

[89] [Wed., Feb. 26] *Destiny* by Mary Ferrier
————

[90]–[91] [blank]
[92] [Sat., Mar. 1] Destiny   Mary Ferrier
    ⟨Write⟩
    ⟨|| . . . || Chicago⟩

[93]–[116] [blank]
[117]⁷ [Wed., Mar. 26] Samuel Bradford
    born March 26th 1803   ⟨187⟩
————————————————

R W E born May 25 1803

[118] [blank]
[119] [Fri., Mar. 28] Théophile Gautier   Meussius

William Hurrell Mallock   Is life worth living

[120]–[121] [blank]
[122] [Mon., Mar. 31] [inscription by Ellen Emerson]

[123]⁸ [Tues., Apr. 1] [inscription by Ellen Emerson] NON

⁶ The entries on pp. [88], [89], and [92] are in pencil, except for "Dividend . . .
Ill." on p. [88]. Mary Ferrier, *Destiny; or, The Chief's Daughter*, 3 vols. (London, 1831)
and in many editions afterwards.
    ⁷ The entries on pp. [117] and [119] are in pencil. William Hurrell Mallock's *Is
Life Worth Living* was first published in London in 1881; Emerson may have known of
the work through an advance notice of its publication.
    ⁸ The entries on pp. [123], [124], and [134] are in pencil.

[124] [Wed., Apr. 2] Bank Book
⟨Osgood & Co⟩
Pullman Car
⟨"Destiny" Ferrier⟩
Dividend Chicago

[125]–[133] [blank]
[134] [Sat., Apr. 12] April 12

———

Pay W B Clarke   Frank   2 vols, 1.20

———

A string for spectacle

———

Verses for Miss Geneviev Warde

———

  H.Y. Edwards

[135] ↑May 15↓   New England Trust ↑Co.↓ comi trust,
Boston   Pullman Car   2.00

———

[136]–[154] [blank]
[155] [Sat., May 3]   30 Sept 1829   Ellen died 8 Feb 1831[9]
[inscription by Ellen Emerson]

[156]–[166] [blank]
[167] [Thurs., May 15] [inscription by Ellen Emerson]

[168]–[174] [blank]
[175] [Fri., May 23] ⟨Harvard Overseers at 70 Water Street⟩

[176]–[178] [blank]
[179] [Tues., May 27] Harvard Overseers
no 70 Water Street May 27 at 11 o'clock

———

  Carl Shoenhoff's bill

[9] "30 Sept . . . 1831" is in pencil. Emerson and Ellen Tucker were married in Concord, New Hampshire, on September 30, 1829.

D.G. Haskins

---

[180]–[191] [blank]
[192]^{10} [Mon., June 9] Bicknell

Edward P. Whipple   11 Pinkney St.

[193] [Tues., June 10] Autograph to D H Griffing
    Cutchogue, Suffolk Co. N.Y.

Henry Lee, comments on Ret— & Eng. Lit.

D.H. Griffing, Cutchogue   Suffolk Co. N Y   autograph

W.T. Washburn   59 Wall ⟨st.⟩ St.   New York

Cyrus Woodman   Cambridge

---

9 Kirkland Place

[194] [Wed., June 11] ⟨Edgar F⟨or⟩↑aw↓sett⟩
        Edgar Fawcett
          T.B. Aldrich
[inscription by Ellen Emerson]

[195] [inscription by Ellen Emerson]
[196] [Fri., June 13] Mr Cyrus Woodman
    ↑9 Kirkman Place,↓ Cambridge

[197]–[200] [blank]
[201]^{11} [Wed., June 18] Meeting for Memorial of W.L. Garrison, at
12 o'clock at 50 State Street
    G. Baty Blake   Henry P. Kidder

---

^{10} The entries on pp. [192]–[194] are in pencil.
^{11} The entries on pp. [201] and [202] are in pencil.

[202] [Thurs., June 19] 12 o'clock meet Ellen at Mr Bates's store

[203]–[221] [blank]
[222] [Wed., July 9] [inscription by Ellen Emerson]
[223]–[229] [blank]
[230] [Thurs., July 17] [inscription by Ellen Emerson]
[231]–[253] [blank]
[254]^{12} [Sun., Aug. 10] Remember to write to

[255] [Mon., Aug. 11] Picture to be framed
Pay Mr   Corner of Came↑bridge↓ St

————

    Pullman Car   2 doll.

————

    ⟨Surett⟩
Write to ⟨B⟩Ph   J. Bailey
    59 Neth⟨o⟩↑er↓wowood Road   West Kensington   London

————

↑Carry↓ Books to Osgood

————

At the corner schopp find ⟨bring home⟩ Hammer poems.

——————————————————————————————

Do not forget Mr Cyrus Woodman in Cambridge, 9 Kirkman Place

[256]–[275] [blank]
[276]^{13} [Mon., Sept. 1] ⟨Bookshop   Hafiz⟩
    ⟨Corner of School St. & Maine⟩

————

    Right to the "Index" refusal

————

    Hovey & Co. & correct their bill.

————

    ⟨Joseph Von Hammer⟩

[277]–[285] [blank]

[12] The entries on pp. [254] and [255] are in pencil.
[13] The entries on p. [276] are in pencil.

[286] [Thurs., Sept. 11] [inscription by Ellen Emerson]
[287] [inscription by Ellen Emerson]
[288] [blank]
[289]¹⁴ [Mon., Sept. 15] ⟨Pullman Car⟩

⟨↑Pay the↓ "Commonwealth"⟩

Sam. Ward's office

The Art Museum

Atlantick

---

[290]–[307] [blank]
[308]¹⁵ [Fri., Oct. 3] Dividend of Atlanktic   124

Atlantic Bank   124

[309] [Sat., Oct. 4] [inscription by Ellen Emerson]   Put 500.71 in
Atlantic [Bank]   Oct. 4, 1879

[310]–[311] [blank]
[312]¹⁶ [Tues., Oct. 7] ⟨Pay "A⟨t⟩dvertiser" and "Commonwealth"⟩
⟨Pullmen Car⟩

Sam Ward's office

Paid

Wine

---

[313]–[317] [blank]
[318] [Mon., Oct. 13] [inscription by Ellen Emerson]

---

¹⁴ The entries on p. [289] are in pencil; "Pay the 'Commonwealth' " is struck
through in pencil with two diagonal lines.
¹⁵ The entries on pp. [308] and [309] are in pencil.
¹⁶ The entries on pp. [312] and [319] are in pencil, except for "Pay . . . '80—" on
p. [319].

[319] [Tues., Oct. 14] Pay American Naturalist   4 dollars
up to Sept, '80—

———

Pay

J.L. Bates   13½ Bromfield St

[320]–[338] [blank]
[339]¹⁷ [Mon., Nov. 3] American Naturalist   4. dollars

———

J.L. Bates   13½ Bromfield
⟨MacDewell & Adams   16.2 Tremont St for lager be⟨a⟩er⟩

Saml Ward's office

———

Wine

———

Letter to Syrus Woodman   Cambridge

[340]–[346] [blank]
[347]¹⁸ [Tues., Nov. 11] William A. Eddy,
133 East 16th St. New York
        "Evolution of a New Sense,"   "Popular Science Month[l]y"

———

Pay American Natural[ist]   4 dollars

———

J.L. Bates   13½ Bromfield St

———

⟨Pay Macdowellⁿ & Adams   162 Tremont St   for Lager Beerⁿ⟩

———

[348]–[365] [blank]
[366]¹⁹ [Sun., Nov. 30] William R. Ward↑e↓

---

¹⁷ The entries on p. [339] are in pencil.
¹⁸ The entries on p. [347] are in red pencil, except for "William A. Eddy, . . .
Monthy' ". William A. Eddy, in "The Evolution of a New Sense," *The Popular Science
Monthly*, 16, no. 1 (Nov., 1879): 66–71, quotes from Emerson's lecture of February 25,
1878, at the Old South Church, Boston.
¹⁹ On p. [366], "William R. . . . string" is in red pencil; "Atlantic . . . dividend" is
in pencil.

———

Hunt's Picturies

———

O W Ho↑l↓mes

———

E⟨i⟩yeglass string

———

Atlantic Bank

———

Car, Pullman-car dividend

———

[inscription by Ellen Emerson]

[367]–[370] [blank]
[371] [Fri., Dec. 5] [inscription by Ellen Emerson]

[372]–[375] [blank]
[376] [Wed., Dec. 10] [inscription by Ellen Emerson]

[377]–[382] [blank]
[383] [Wed., Dec. 17] [inscription by Ellen Emerson]

[384]–[389] [blank]
[390] Willson Flag[20]

[391]–[398] [blank]
[399] George J. Breed, dating from Salem, Mass. Dec. 23, 1878, wrote me a noble ⟨v⟩letter which I fear, I have never replied to⟨o⟩. Perhaps I have not read until today, November 18, 1⟨7⟩879

[400]–[442] [blank]
[inside back cover] [blank]

[20] "Willson Flag" is in pencil.

Pocket Diary 31

1880

Pocket Diary 31, the last pocket diary known to have been kept by Emerson, is devoted to recording Emerson's memoranda for 1880. A few entries may have been made late in 1879; it is doubtful that any entries were made in 1881.

The notebook, bound in black stamped leather, is a commercially published diary entitled "EXCELSIOR / DIARY / for / 1880." The covers measure 8.0 × 12.6 cm. The back cover extends into a tongue that, when the book is closed, fits into a loop on the front cover; the back cover also contains an expandable inside pocket. "EXCELSIOR / DIARY" is stamped in gold on the tongue. A paper label fastened to the spine is inscribed "1880. x".

The white, unnumbered, gilt-edged pages measure 7.6 × 12.5 cm; pages 25–184 are lined. The book consists of a front flyleaf (i, ii); a title page (page 1); a table of astronomical calculations (page 3); a calendar for 1880 (page 4); phases of the moon and tide tables for 1880 (pages 5–16); interest tables (page 17); gold rates for 1862–1878 (page 18); a table for calculating hourly wages paid by the week (page 19); a table of the distance of principal American cities from New York (page 20); the 1790 and 1870 censuses of states and territories (page 21); rates of postage (pages 22–23); presidents of the United States (page 24); daily appointments for 1880, three to a page (pages 25–146); pages for memoranda (pages 147–152); pages for cash accounts (pages 153–177); pages for bills receivable and payable (pages 178–183); an additional page for memoranda (page 184); and a back flyleaf (pages 185–186).

Entries by Emerson occur on thirteen pages. Printed matter in Pocket Diary 31 is reproduced here only where relevant. Otherwise, pages are designated as blank if they bear no inscription by Emerson; the presence or absence of printed matter is not specified.

[front cover verso] [railroad schedule omitted]

[i]   R. Waldo Emerson

[ii]–[31] [blank]

[32] [Fri., Jan. 23] [inscription by Ellen Emerson]

[33]-[35] [blank]
[36] [Tues., Feb. 3] John H. Rogers
[Thurs., Feb. 5] [inscription by Ellen Emerson]

[37] [blank]
[38][1] [Mon., Feb. 9] Engagement with Dr Parker   132 Boylst[o]n St quarter to 3 P.M.
[Wed., Feb. 11] [inscription by Ellen Emerson]

[39] [Thurs., Feb. 12?] Demsye   Demsee

[40]-[41] [blank]
[42] [Sat., Feb. 21] [inscription by Ellen Emerson]

[43] [blank]
[44] [Fri., Feb. 27] [inscription by Ellen Emerson]
[45] [Mon., Mar. 1] [inscription by Ellen Emerson]
[46] [Thurs., Mar. 4?] Wiliam A. Wall

Charles A. Cutter   Librarian of the Boston Athenaeum

[Fri., Mar. 5?] Mrs Hunt of Concord
    a month's right to study in the Athenae⟨m⟩um

[47] [blank]
[48] [Wed., Mar. 10] [inscription by Ellen Emerson]

[49]-[51] [blank]
[52] [Mon., Mar. 22] [inscription by Ellen Emerson]

[53]-[56] [blank]
[57] [Tues., Apr. 6?] [inscription by Ellen Emerson]

[1] The entries on pp. [38] and [39] are in pencil.

[58] [blank]
[59] [Mon., Apr. 12] [inscription by Ellen Emerson]

[60]–[63] [blank]
[64] [Wed., Apr. 28] [inscription by Ellen Emerson]

[65]–[67] [blank]
[68] [Mon., May 10] [inscription by Ellen Emerson]

[69]–[73] [blank]
[74]² [Fri., May 28?] Per ⟨wes⟩ B. & L ⟨of⟩train ⟨7⟩from
⟨3⟩Concord at 3.20
     Bost[on] & Albany
         4.45 train to Wrookline
[Sat., May 29?] ⟨See when the⟩ Brooklin[e train] return[s]
[inscription by Ellen Emerson]

[75] [Sun., May 30] [inscription by Ellen Emerson]

[76]–[79] [blank]
[80] [Wed., June 16] [inscription by Ellen Emerson]

[81]–[90] [blank]
[91]³ [Sun., July 18?] At Bank   80 dollars for me
     D   Bicknell's Bill
[Mon., July 19] [inscription by Ellen Emerson]

[92]–[94] [blank]
[95] [Sat., July 31] [inscription by Ellen Emerson]

[96]–[100] [blank]
[101] [Tues., Aug. 17] Mr Forbes for my claim on
    and go to   [inscription by Ellen Emerson]

---

² The entries on p. [74] are in pencil. "See when the" may have been struck
through in ink by Ellen Emerson when she wrote the entry that follows "return".
³ The entries on pp. [91], [101], and [103] are in pencil.

[102] [blank]
[103] [Mon., Aug. 23] Rode to

[104]–[105] [blank]
[106] [Wed., Sept. 1] Paid Lincoln^n Taxes   4.08

[107] [blank]
[108] [Tues., Sept. 7] [inscription by Ellen Emerson]

[109]–[121] [blank]
[122] [Mon., Oct. 18?] 20   Tom. HUGHES, QC[4]

[123]–[131] [blank]
[132] [Thurs., Nov. 18] Annivers[ar]y of First church
     ann⟨e⟩iversery of at 18 ⟨of⟩teeun[?]
Dr Arthur B. Ellis

[133]–[181] [blank]
[182] [inscription by Ellen Emerson]

[183]–[185] [blank]
[186]   18 November   First Church[5]

[inside back cover] [railroad schedule omitted]

---

[4] "20   Tom. . . . QC" is in pencil.
[5] "18 . . . Church" is in pencil.

Appendixes

Textual Notes

Index

Appendix I

Journals and Notebooks in the Harvard Edition

The following table shows which of Emerson's journals and miscellaneous notebooks are printed in the Harvard University Press edition (*JMN*, I–XVI), and where they may be found, by volume and volume page numbers. Because this edition prints Emerson's manuscript page numbers of the journals and notebooks in the text, the reader should have no difficulty in locating cross-references to previously printed journals or notebooks. These are listed alphabetically, as designated by Emerson or others; the dates are supplied by Emerson, or the editors, or both. Since some passages are undated and some dates are doubtful, scholars should look at individual passages before relying on their dating.

Designation	Harvard edition
A (1833–1834)	IV, 249–387
AB (1847)	X, 3–57
AC (1858–1859)	XIV, 208–290
AZ (1849–1850)	XI, 183–278
B (1835–1836)	V, 3–268
Blotting Book I (1826–1827)	VI, 11–57
Blotting Book II (1826–1829)	VI, 58–101
Blotting Book III (1831–1832)	III, 264–329
Blotting Book IV (1830, 1831? 1833)	III, 359–375
Blotting Book IV[A] (1830, 1832–1834)	VI, 102–114
Blotting Book Psi (1830–1831, 1832)	III, 203–263
Blotting Book Y (1829–1830)	III, 163–202
Blue Book (1826)	III, 333–337
BO (1850–1851)	XI, 279–365
BO Conduct (1851)	XII, 581–599
Books Large (1870–1877)	XVI, 325–346

Designation	Harvard edition
Books Small [I] (1840?–1856?)	VIII, 442–479
Books Small [II]	VIII, 550–576
C (1837–1838)	V, 277–509
Catalogue of Books Read (1819–1824)	I, 395–399
CD (1847)	X, 58–123
Charles C. Emerson (1837)	VI, 255–286
CL (1859–1861)	XIV, 291–369
CO (1851)	XI, 366–452
Collectanea (1825–1828?)	VI, 3–10
College Theme Book (1819–1821, 1822? 1829?)	I, 161–205
Composition (1832?)	IV, 427–438
D (1838–1839)	VII, 3–262
Delta (1837–1841, 1850, 1857, 1862)	XII, 178–268
Dialling (1825? 1841? 1842)	VIII, 483–517
DL (1860–1866)	XV, 3–87
DO (1852–1854, 1856, 1858)	XIII, 3–57
E (1839–1842)	VII, 263–484
ED (1852–1853)	X, 494–568
Encyclopedia (1824–1836)	VI, 115–234
England and Paris (1847–1848)	X, 407–445
F No. 1 (1836–1840)	XII, 75–177
F No. 2 (1840–1841)	VII, 485–547
FOR (1863–1864)	XV, 313–413
France and England (1833)	IV, 395–419
G (1841)	VIII, 3–77
Genealogy (1822, 1825, 1828)	III, 349–358
GH (1847–1848)	X, 124–199
GL (1861–1862, 1863)	XV, 88–168
GO (1852–1853)	XIII, 58–128
H (1841)	VIII, 78–145
HO (1853–1854)	XIII, 207–289
HT (1864–1865?)	XV, 483–492
Index Minor (1843–1847?)	XII, 518–580
IO (1854)	XIII, 290–378
Italy (1833)	IV, 134–162
Italy and France (1833)	IV, 163–208
J (1841–1842)	VIII, 146–197

Designation	Harvard edition
JK (1843?–1847)	X, 365–404
Journal 1826 (1825, 1826, 1827? 1828)	III, 3–41
Journal 1826–1828 (1824, 1825, 1826–1828)	III, 42–112
Journal at the West (1850–1853)	XI, 510–540
K (1842)	VIII, 198–247
KL (1864–1865)	XV, 414–480
L Concord (1835, 1838)	XII, 3–32
L Literature (1835)	XII, 33–55
LM (1848)	X, 288–362
LN (1866–1868)	XVI, 3–96
London (1847–1848)	X, 208–287
Maine (1834)	IV, 388–391
Man (1836)	XII, 56–74
Margaret Fuller Ossoli (1851)	XI, 455–509
Memo St. Augustine (1827)	III, 113–118
Meredith Village (1829)	III, 159–162
N (1842)	VIII, 248–308
NO (1855)	XIII, 379–469
No. II (1825)	II, 413–420
No. XV (1824–1826)	II, 272–351
No. XVI (1824–1828?)	II, 396–412
No. XVII (1820)	I, 206–248
No. XVIII (1820–1822)	I, 249–357
No. XVIII[A] (1821?–1829)	II, 355–395
Notebook 1833 (1833–1836)	VI, 235–254
NY (1868–1870)	XVI, 97–200
O (1846–1847)	IX, 355–470
Phi (1838–1844? 1847–1851?)	XII, 269–419
Platoniana (1845–1848)	X, 468–488
Pocket Diary 1 (1820–1831)	III, 338–348
Pocket Diary 1 (1847)	X, 405–406
Pocket Diary 2 (1833)	IV, 420–426
Pocket Diary 3 (1848–1849)	X, 446–457
Pocket Diary 4 (1853)	XIII, 473–482
Pocket Diary 5 (1854)	XIII, 483–501
Pocket Diary 6 (1855)	XIII, 502–515
Pocket Diary 7 (1856)	XIV, 432–445

Designation	Harvard edition
Pocket Diary 8 (1857)	XIV, 446–455
Pocket Diary 9 (1858)	XIV, 456–464
Pocket Diary 11 (1859)	XIV, 465–473
Pocket Diary 12 (1860)	XIV, 474–482
Pocket Diary 13 (1861)	XV, 493–499
Pocket Diary 14 (1863)	XV, 500–513
Pocket Diary 15 (1864)	XV, 514–521
Pocket Diary 16 (1865)	XV, 522–538
Pocket Diary 17 (1866)	XVI, 347–355
Pocket Diary 18 (1867)	XVI, 356–369
Pocket Diary 19 (1868)	XVI, 370–379
Pocket Diary 20 (1869)	XVI, 380–391
Pocket Diary 21 (1870)	XVI, 392–402
Pocket Diary 22 (1871)	XVI, 403–420
Pocket Diary 23 (1872)	XVI, 421–444
Pocket Diary 24 (1873)	XVI, 445–456
Pocket Diary 25 (1874)	XVI, 457–471
Pocket Diary 26 (1875)	XVI, 472–480
Pocket Diary 27 (1876)	XVI, 481–487
Pocket Diary 28 (1877)	XVI, 488–504
Pocket Diary 29 (1878)	XVI, 505–519
Pocket Diary 30 (1879)	XVI, 520–530
Pocket Diary 31 (1880)	XVI, 531–534
Psi (1839–1842, 1851)	XII, 420–517
Q (1832–1833)	IV, 3–101
R (1843)	VIII, 349–441
RO (1855–1856)	XIV, 3–39
RO Mind (1835)	V, 269–276
RS (1848–1849)	XI, 3–86
Scotland and England (1833)	IV, 209–235
Sea 1833 (1833)	IV, 236–248
Sea-Notes (1847)	X, 200–207
Sermons and Journal (1828–1829)	III, 119–158
Sicily (1833)	IV, 102–133
SO (1856–1857)	XIV, 40–118
ST (1870–1877)	XVI, 201–321
T (1834–?)	VI, 317–399

Designation	Harvard edition
Trees[A:I] (1843–1847)	VIII, 518–533
Trees[A:II]	VIII, 534–549
TU (1849)	XI, 87–182
U (1843–1844)	IX, 3–92
Universe 1–7, 7[A], 8 (1820–1822)	I, 358–394
V (1844–1845)	IX, 93–181
VA (1862–1863)	XV, 234–312
VO (1857–1858)	XIV, 119–207
VS (1853–1854)	XIII, 129–206
W (1845)	IX, 182–255
Walk to the Connecticut (1823)	II, 177–186
WAR (1862–1864)	XV, 169–233
Warren Lot (1849)	X, 489–493
Wide World 1 (1820)	I, 3–32
Wide World 2 (1820–1821)	I, 33–58
Wide World 3 (1822)	I, 59–90
Wide World 4 (1822)	I, 91–113
Wide World 6 (1822)	I, 114–158
Wide World 7 (1822)	II, 3–39
Wide World 8 (1822)	II, 40–73
Wide World 9 (1822–1823)	II, 74–103
Wide World 10 (1823)	II, 104–143
Wide World 11 (1823)	II, 144–176
Wide World 12 (1823–1824)	II, 187–213
Wide World XIII (1824)	II, 214–271
WO Liberty (1854?–1857?)	XIV, 373–430
Xenien (1848, 1852)	X, 458–467
Y (1845–1846)	IX, 256–354
Z (1831? 1837–1838, 1841?)	VI, 287–316
Z[A] (1842–1843)	VIII, 309–348

Appendix II

Author and Title Entries

in Notebook Books Large

Entries in Books Large not identified in the notes are identified below. The editors have attempted to supply appropriate bibliographical data for the works listed, and have indicated through the symbol EL those volumes which are in Emerson's library. The symbol ER, followed by a library location, volume numbers, and dates of withdrawal, has been used to indicate those volumes which Emerson is known to have withdrawn from the Boston Athenaeum or the Harvard College Library. Generally, the authority for the listing of a volume below is, in order, its ownership by Emerson, its withdrawal by Emerson from a library, or its identification in previous *JMN* volumes. The notation "[edition?]" indicates the editors' uncertainty as to whether the edition cited is the one intended by Emerson, and the notation "[title?]" indicates their conjecture as to the identity of the work when Emerson entered only an author's name in a list in Books Large. Numbers in page number brackets ([   ]) show where the listed items appear in Books Large.

The appearance of a work in Books Large does not, of course, mean that Emerson read it.

Akhlak-y-Jalaly (*see Practical Philosophy of the Muhammadan People* . . .).
Allingham, William, *Poems* (London, 1850) [edition?]; EL.   [2ₐ].
The Ancient Laws and Institutes of England, ed. Benjamin Thorpe, 2 vols. (London, 1840).   [1].
Antar, *The Moallaka't; or, Seven Arabian Poems,* in *The Works of Sir William Jones,* 6 vols. (London, 1799), IV, 245–394.   [19].
Appleton Two vol[ume]s (author, work unknown).
Arago, François, *Biographies of Distinguished Scientific Men,* trans. W. H. Smyth, Baden Powell, and Robert Grant (London, 1857); ER, Boston Athenaeum, October 31, 1857–January 14, 1858.   [90].
Arnold, Matthew, *Essays in Criticism* (Boston, 1865); EL.   [90].
Arnold, Thomas, *The History of Rome* . . . , 3 vols., new ed. (London, 1871) [edition?].   [68ₐ].

King Arthur & Knights of the Round Table (*see* Malory, Sir Thomas).
Asrayh Lectures (author, work unknown).
Aurora Leigh (*see* Browning, Elizabeth Barrett).
Ballantyne, Robert Michael, *Hudson's Bay; or, Every-day Life in the Wilds of North America* . . . (Edinburgh, 1848) [edition?]. [68$_d$].
The Bhăgvăt-Gēētă, or Dialogues of Krēēshnă and Ărjŏŏn . . . , trans. Charles Wilkins (London, 1785); EL. [18], [90].
Le Bhâgavata Purâna; ou, Histoire Poétique de Krĭchna, trans. Eugène Burnouf, 3 vols. (Paris, 1840–1847); EL. [18].
Bibliotheca Indica (*see The Taittirĭya* . . .).
Blake, William, *Songs of Innocence and of Experience, Shewing the Two Contrary States of the Human Soul* (London, 1839) [edition?]; EL. [7].
Boswell, James, *The Life of Samuel Johnson* . . . (London, 1827) [edition?]; EL. [7].
Lord Brooke's Life of Sir Philip Sidney (*see* Greville, Fulke, 1st Baron Brooke).
John Brown (*see Testimonies of Capt. John Brown* . . .).
Brown, Robert, *Prodromus Florae Novae Hollandiae et Insulae Van-Diemen.* . . . Editio . . . quam ad fidem exempli prioris editionis, ab ipso auctore emendati, typis excudi curavit C. G. Nees ab Esenbeck (Norimbergae, 1827) [edition?]. [3].
Browning, Elizabeth Barrett, *Aurora Leigh* (New York, 1857); EL. [2$_a$].
Browning, Robert, *Poems,* 2 vols., new ed. (Boston, 1859) [edition?]; EL. [2$_a$].
Burckhardt, Jakob Christoph, *Die Cultur der Renaissance in Italien* (Basel, 1860) [edition?]. [15].
Cavendish, George, *The Life of Cardinal Wolsey,* new ed. (London, 1852) [edition?]. [8].
Channing, William Ellery, the younger, *Poems* (Boston, 1843) [edition?]; EL. [2$_a$].
——— *Poems,* 2nd ser. (Boston, 1847) [edition?]; EL. [2$_a$].
Chaucer, Geoffrey, *Poetical Works* . . . (London and New York, 1871) [edition?]; EL. [17].
Chesterfield's Letters (*see* Stanhope, Philip Dormer).
Chronicles of the Cid (*see* Southey, Robert).
Cinq Mars (*see* Vigny, Alfred Victor, Comte de).
Clough, Arthur Hugh, *The Bothie of Toper-na-fuosich; a Long-vacation Pastoral* (Oxford, 1848). [3].
Coleridge, Samuel Taylor, *Biographia Literaria; or, Biographical Sketches of My Literary Life and Opinions,* 2 vols. in 1 (New York, 1834); EL. [90].
——— *Specimens of the Table Talk of the Late Samuel Taylor Coleridge,* 2 vols. in 1 (New York, 1835); EL. [68$_a$].
Colloquia Mensalia: or, Dr. Martin Luther's Divine Discourses at His Table,

&c., ed. and trans. Henry Bell (London, 1652) [edition?]. [2ₐ], [3], [17], [29], [68ₐ], [91].

Darwin, Charles, *On the Origin of Species by Means of Natural Selection . . .* (London, 1859) [edition?]. [68ₐ].

Davis, Sarah Matilda Henry, *The Life and Times of Sir Philip Sidney,* 3rd ed. (Boston, 1859). [25].

Dawkins, William Boyd, *Cave Hunting, Researches on the Evidence of Caves Respecting the Early Inhabitants of Europe . . .* (London, 1874). [84].

DeVacca's De Soto Narrative (author, work unknown).

Dixon, William Hepworth, *New America,* 2 vols. (London, 1867) [edition?]. [11].

Dowden, Edward, *Shakspere* (London, 1877) [edition?]. [17], [31].

Duclos, Charles Pineau, *Mémoires Secrètes sur les Règnes de Louis XIV et de Louis XV,* 2 vols. (Paris, 1791); ER, Boston Athenaeum, (vols. 1–2) September 10–October 15, 1864. [15].

Eckermann, Johann Peter, *Conversations with Goethe in the Last Years of His Life,* trans. from the German of Eckermann by S. M. Fuller (Boston, 1839); EL. [29], [68ₐ], [91].

Emerson, George Barrell, *Forest Trees [of Massachusetts]* (n.p., 1859?). [17].

Faustina (*see* Hahn-Hahn, Ida, Countess von).

Fergusson, James, *The Illustrated Handbook of Architecture,* 2 vols. (London, 1855); ER, Boston Athenaeum, (vol. 1) December 29, 1866–February 5, 1867. [90].

Freeman, Edward Augustus, *The Ottoman Power in Europe; Its Nature, Its Growth, and Its Decline* (London, 1877). [30].

Frere, John Hookham, *The Works of John Hookham Frere in Verse and Prose . . . ,* 2 vols. (London, 1872 [1871]); ER, Boston Athenaeum, (vol. 2) June 18–25, 1872. [11].

Garbett, Edward Lacy, *Rudimentary Treatise on the Principles of Design in Architecture as Deducible from Nature and Exemplified in the Works of the Greek and Gothic Architects,* 2 parts in 1 vol. (London, 1850); ER, Boston Athenaeum, December 15, 1868–January 18, 1869, and April 6–10, 1869. [90].

Gérando, Joseph Marie de, Baron, *Self-education; or, The Means and Art of Moral Progress,* trans. E. P. Peabody (Boston, 1830) [title?]; EL. [68ₐ].

Giddings, Joshua Reed, *A History of the Rebellion: Its Authors and Causes* (New York, 1864); ER, Boston Athenaeum, July 14–20, 1864. [4].

Gilchrist, Alexander, *The Life of William Blake . . .* [With] a Descriptive Catalogue of His Paintings, Engravings, etc., by W. M. Rossetti, 2 vols. (London, 1863); ER, Boston Athenaeum, (vols. 1–2) December 11–19, 1863, and (vol. 2) April 29–May 6, 1864. [7].

Gray, Asa, *Darwiniana: Essays and Reviews Pertaining to Darwinism* (New York, 1876) [edition?]. [29], [30].

Greville, Fulke, 1st Baron Brooke, *Lord Brook's Life of Sir Philip Sidney*, ed. Sir Egerton Brydges, 2 vols. (Lee Priory, Kent, 1816); ER, Boston Athenaeum, August 3–26, 1863. [8].

Grimm, Friedrich Melchior von, *Historical & Literary Memoirs and Anecdotes, Selected from the Correspondence of Baron de Grimm and Diderot with the Duke of Saxe-Gotha . . .* , 2 vols. (London, 1814) [title?]. [3].

Hahn-Hahn, Ida, Countess von, *Faustina. A Novel . . .* From the German (New York, 1872) [edition?]. [17].

Philosophy of sin lo. Hamilton (author, work unknown).

Hazlitt, William, *Table Talk on Men and Manners . . .* , ed. William Carew Hazlitt, new ed. (London, 1871). [68$_a$], [68$_d$].

[William Carew] Hazlitt's Translation of Montaigne (*see* Montaigne, Michel Eyquem de).

Helper, Hinton Rowan, *The Impending Crisis of the South: How to Meet It*, enl. ed. (New York, 1867) [edition?]. [68$_a$].

Herbert [of Cherbury], Edward Herbert, 1st Baron, *The Life of Edward Lord Herbert, of Cherbury, Written by Himself* (London, 1826); ER, Boston Athenaeum, May 25–June 9, 1863, January 14–February 18, 1868, and August 10–October 11, 1871. [17].

Herbert, George, *The Poetical Works of George Herbert.* With a Memoir of the Author, by Robert Aris Willmot (Boston, 1866); EL. [17].

Herschel, Sir John Frederick William, *Familiar Lectures on Scientific Subjects* (London, 1866); ER, Boston Athenaeum, August 17–20, and September 3–10, 1867. [7].

Hervey, John Hervey [of Ickworth], Baron, *Memoirs on the Reign of George the Second, from His Accession to the Death of Queen Caroline . . .* , ed. John Wilson Croker, 4 vols. (London, 1848); ER, Boston Athenaeum, (vol. 1) March 16–26, (vol. 2) March 26–April 29, 1864. [3].

[Thomas] Hobbes Works (edition unknown).

Hodson, William Stephen Raikes, *Twelve Years of a Soldier's Life in India . . .* (Boston, 1864) [title?, edition?]. [68$_d$], [91].

Hogg, Thomas Jefferson, *The Life of Percy Bysshe Shelley*, 4 vols. (London, 1858). [25].

Holmes, Oliver Wendell, *The Professor at the Breakfast-Table; with the Story of Iris* (Boston, 1860) [edition?]. [68$_a$].

Huc, Évariste Régis, *A Journey through the Chinese Empire*, 2 vols. (London, 1855); EL. [91].

Huxley, Thomas H., *Lectures on the Elements of Comparative Anatomy* (London, 1864). [1].

I Promessi Sposi (*see* Manzoni, Alessandro).

Institutes of Hindu Law; or, The Ordinances of Menu, According to the Gloss of Cullúca. Comprising the Indian System of Duties, Religious and Civil.

Verbally tr[anslated]. from the original, with a preface, by Sir William Jones. A new ed[ition]. . . . by Graves Chamney Haughton (London, 1825); EL. [18].

Johnston, William, *England As It Is, Political, Social and Industrial, in the Middle of the Nineteenth Century,* 2 vols. (London, 1851) [title?]; ER, Boston Athenaeum, (vols. 1–2) August 13–23, 1852. [3].

Jones, Sir William, *The Works of Sir William Jones,* 6 vols. (London, 1799) [edition?]. [19].

King, Thomas Starr, *The White Hills; Their Legends, Landscapes, and Poetry* (Boston, 1860) [edition?]. [68$_a$], [68$_d$].

Knox, Robert, *The Races of Men: A Philosophical Enquiry into the Influence of Race over the Destinies of Nations . . . ,* 2nd ed. (London, 1862); EL. [17], [91].

Koran (edition unknown).

Landor, Walter Savage, *The Works of Walter Savage Landor . . . ,* 2 vols. (London, 1868); EL. [7], [15], [17], [29], [68$_d$], [91].

Legge, James, *The Life and Teachings of Confucius,* in *The Chinese Classics . . . ,* 5 vols. (Hong Kong and London, 1861–1872). [29].

Lewes, George Henry, *The Life and Works of Goethe,* 2 vols. (Boston, 1856); ER, Boston Athenaeum, (vol. 2) April 25–May 14, 1870. [4].

Lieber, Francis, *Reminiscences of an Intercourse with [Barthold Georg] Niebuhr (in Rome, 1822–1823)* (Philadelphia, 1835); ER, Boston Athenaeum, September 10–October 29, 1864. [4].

The Life and Letters of Barthold George Niebuhr; with Essays on His Character and Influence by [Baron] Bunsen, [Johannes] Brandis, and [Johann Wilhelm] Loebell, trans. Susanna Winkworth, 3 vols. (London, 1852); ER, Boston Athenaeum, (vols. 1–2) February 1–April 10/11, 1855, and Harvard College Library, (vol. 3) May 18, 1855. [68$_b$], [91].

The Life of General Sir William Napier . . . , ed. Henry Austin Bruce, 2 vols. (London, 1864); ER, Boston Athenaeum, (vol. 1) August 18–26, 1864, and March 15–27, 1865, and (vol. 2) August 26–September 2, 1864. [4].

Life of Lessing (*see* Stahr, Adolf Wilhelm Theodor).

Le Lotus de la Bonne Loi . . . , trans. E. Bournouf (Paris, 1852); EL. [18].

Lowell, James Russell, *The Biglow Papers,* ed. Homer Wilbur, 4th ed. (Boston, 1856); EL. [68].

Luther's table talk (*see Colloquia Mensalia . . .*).

Macpherson, James, *The Genuine Poems of Ossian,* trans. Patrick McGregor (London, 1807). [84$_a$].

Malory, Sir Thomas, *La Morte d'Arthure. The History of King Arthur and of the Knights of the Round Table . . . ,* ed. Thomas Wright, 3 vols., 2nd ed. (London, 1865–1866). [17], [90].

Manzoni, Alessandro, *I Promessi Sposi* . . . , 3 vols., 2. ed. torinese (Torino, 1827); EL. [17].

Martineau, Harriet, *Autobiography*, ed. Maria Weston Chapman, 2 vols. (Boston, 1877); EL. [17].

—— *Eastern Life, Past and Present*, 3 vols. (London, 1848); EL. [17].

Mather, Cotton, *Magnalia Christi Americana, or, The Ecclesiastical History of New England*, 2 vols. (Hartford, Connecticut, 1855). [2ₐ].

Max Müller, Friedrich, "Comparative Mythology," in *The Oxford Review*, 2 (1856): 1–87. [11].

—— *Lectures on the Science of Language*, 2 vols. (London, 1861–1864); ER, Boston Athenaeum, (vol. 1) February 26–March 5, 1862, and (vol. 2) October 11–November 19, 1867. [11].

—— *Lectures on the Science of Religion; with a Paper on Buddhist Nihilism, and a Translation of the Dhammapada or "Path of Virtue"* (New York, 1872) [title?]; ER, Boston Athenaeum, June 13–24, 1872. [90].

[Friedrich] Max Muller's Works (titles, editions unknown).

Memoirs of Samuel Pepys: Comprising His Diary from 1659–1669 . . . , ed. Richard, Lord Braybrooke, 2 vols. (London, 1825); ER, Boston Athenaeum, (vol. 1) September 11–October 25, 1854, and (vol. 2) September 25–October 14, 1854. [8], [91].

Montaigne, Michel Eyquem de, *Essays of Montaigne.* [Translated] by Charles Cotton, with Some Account of the Life of Montaigne, Notes, and a Translation of All the Letters . . . , ed. William Carew Hazlitt, 3 vols. (London, 1877). [17].

Nala and Damayanti, and Other Poems, trans. Henry Hart Milman (Oxford, 1835); EL. [15].

General Sir William Napier (*see The Life of General Sir William Napier* . . .).

Neal, Daniel, *The History of the Puritans or Protestant Non-conformists*, 4 vols. (London, 1732–1738). [60].

Niebuhr, Barthold Georg, *Lectures on the History of Rome*, ed. Leonhard Schmitz, 3 vols. (London, 1849); ER, Boston Athenaeum, (vol. 2) April 4–May 11, 1855, and Harvard College Library, (vol. 1) May 18, 1855. [1].

Niebuhr's Letters (*see The Life and Letters of Barthold George Niebuhr* . . .).

Nott, Josiah Clark, and George R. Glidden, *Types of Mankind: or, Ethnological Researches, Based upon the Ancient Monuments, Paintings, Sculptures, and Crania of Races* . . . , (London, 1854) [edition?]. [68ₐ], [68_d].

Ockley, Simon, *The Conquest of Syria, Persia and Ægypt by the Saracens*, 2 vols. (London, 1708–1718); ER, Boston Athenaeum, (vols. 1–2) September 22–December 12, 1840, and (vol. 2) October 5–25(?), 1842. [2ₐ].

Pepys's Diary (*see Memoirs of Samuel Pepys* . . .).

Pierce, Edward Lillie, *Memoir and Letters of Charles Sumner*, 4 vols. (Boston, 1877–1893). [17].

Piozzi, Hester Lynch (Salusbury) Thrale, *Anecdotes of the Late Samuel Johnson, LL.D.,* 4th ed. (London, 1786); ER, Boston Athenaeum, September 20, 1859–January 19(?), 1860. [2ₐ], [68ₐ].

Plato, *Dialogues,* trans. B[enjamin]. Jowett, 5 vols. (Oxford, 1875); EL. [29].

Plutarch, *Plutarch's Morals, Translated from the Greek by Several Hands,* corr. and rev. William W. Goodwin, 5 vols. (Boston, 1870); EL. [17], [29], [90].

Practical Philosophy of the Muhammadan People, Exhibited in Its Professed Connexion with the European, so as to Render Either an Introduction to the Other; Being a Translation of The Akhlāk-I-Jalāly, the Most Esteemed Ethical Work of Middle Asia, from the Persian of Fakir Jāny Muhammad Asāad, trans. W. F. Thompson (London, 1839). [18].

Renan, [Joseph] Ernest, *Studies of Religious History and Criticism* . . . [From] the French, trans. O. B. Frothingham (New York, 1864). [3].

Rig-veda-sanhitá. A Collection of Ancient Hindu Hymns . . . , trans. Horace Hayman Wilson, 4 vols. (London, 1850–1866); ER, Boston Athenaeum, (vols. 1–2) May 5–9, 1855, (vol. 3) August 15–October 27, 1860, and (vol. 4) July 23–28, 1866. [18].

Ritson, Joseph, *Ancient Songs and Ballads, from the Reign of King Henry the Second to the Revolution,* 2 vols. (London, 1829) [title?]; EL. [3].

Rudler, Frederick William, *Exploration of the Colorado River* (Washington, D. C., 1875) [title?]. [31].

Ruskin, John, *The Ethics of the Dust: Ten Lectures to Little Housewives on the Elements of Crystallisation* (London, 1866); ER, Boston Athenaeum, August 23–30, 1866. [7], [17].

――― *The Stones of Venice,* 3 vols. (London, 1851–1853); ER, Boston Athenaeum, November 28, 1851–January 5, 1852, and September 6–December 27, 1852. [7], [17].

Saint-Simon, Louis de Rouvroy, Duc de, *Mémoires Complèts et Authentiques* . . . , 21 vols. (Paris, 1829–1830); ER, Boston Athenaeum, (vol. 1) March 4–May 13, 1865, and October 11–November 22, 1867, and (vol. 2) November 22–December 3, 1867. [3].

Sainte-Beuve, Charles Augustin, *Portraits de Femmes,* nouv. éd. (Paris, 1852); ER, Boston Athenaeum, October 5, 1863–January 27, 1864, and December 17–19, 1864. [16].

Saussure, Horace Benedict de, *Voyages dans les Alpes* . . . , 3 éd. augm. (Paris, 1855) [edition?]. [4].

[Friedrich] S[c]hleiermacher Essay on Σιρōνεὶα (title unknown).

Selden, John, *Table-Talk,* in *The Library of the Old English Prose Writers,* vol. II (Cambridge, 1831); EL. [2ₐ], [24], [68ₐ], [91].

Self Help (*see* Gérando, Joseph Marie de).

Small, George, *A Handbook of Sanskrit Literature* . . . (London, 1866); ER, Boston Athenaeum, September 5–8, 1866. [11].

Social Condition of England (*see* Johnston, William).

Social Essays from Saturday Review (titles unknown).

Southey, Robert, *Chronicle of the Cid* . . . [From] the Spanish (Lowell, 1846); EL. [90].

Spence, Joseph, *Anecdotes, Observations, and Characters, of Books and Men* . . . , 2nd ed. (London, 1858); EL. [2_a], [68_a].

Stahr, Adolf Wilhelm Theodor, *The Life and Works of Gotthold Ephraim Lessing* . . . From the German . . . , trans. E. P. Evans (New York, 1873). [11], [17], [90], [91].

Stanhope, Philip Dormer, 4th Earl of Chesterfield, *Letters*, ed. Lord Mahon [Philip Henry Stanhope], 5 vols. (London, 1845–1853) [title?]. [3].

Swedenborg, Emanuel, *Angelic Wisdom Concerning the Divine Love and the Divine Wisdom* . . . From the Latin (Boston, New York, and Cincinnati, 1847); EL. [6].

The Taittiríya, Aitaréya, Svétásvatara, Kéna, Ísá, Katha, Prasna, Mundaka and Ma'ndukya Upanishads, trans. E. Röer (Calcutta, 1853); EL. [18].

Tennyson, Alfred Tennyson, 1st Baron, *Poetical Works*, 2 vols. in 1 (Boston, 1866) [edition?]; EL. [7].

Testimonies of Capt. John Brown, at Harper's Ferry, with His Address to the Court . . . (New York, 1860) [title?]. [68_a], [68_d].

[Henry David] Thoreau's Works (titles, editions unknown).

Timrod, Henry, *The Poems of Henry Timrod*, ed. Paul H. Hayne, new rev. ed. (New York, 1877). [29].

Trench, Richard Chenevix, *On the English Language, Past and Present*, new ed. (New York, 1860) [edition?]. [4].

———— *On the Study of Words. Lectures Addressed (Originally) to the Pupils of the Diocesan Training-School, Winchester* . . . , 16th ed. (London, 1876) [edition?]. [4].

Tyndall, John, *Sound: A Course of Eight Lectures* (London, 1867); ER, Boston Athenaeum, September 9–October 23, 1868. [6].

Upanishads (*see The Taittiríya* . . .).

Ure, Andrew, *A Dictionary of Chemistry and Minerology*, 4th ed. (New York, 1853) [edition?]. [4].

Vigny, Alfred Victor, Comte de, *Cinq-mars; ou, Une Conjuration sous Louis XIII*, 7. éd. (Paris, 1880); EL. [3].

The Vishńu Puráńa, A System of Hindu Mythology and Tradition, trans. H. H. Wilson (London, 1840); EL. [18].

Warner, Charles Dudley, *In the Levant* (Boston, 1870) [edition?]. [30].

White, Gilbert, *The Natural History and Antiquities of Selborne*, new ed. (London, 1875). [9].

Wilkinson, Sir John Gardner, *A Second Series of the Manners and the Customs of the Ancient Egyptians*, 2 vols. (London, 1841); ER, Boston Athenaeum, (vol. 1) January 16–February 20, 1868. [3].

Wilson, Sir Robert Thomas, *Private Diary of Travels, Personal Services, and Public Events, during Mission and Employment with the European Armies* . . . , ed. Herbert Randolph, 2 vols. (London, 1861) [title?]; ER, Boston Athenaeum, (vol. 1) August 19–31, 1861, and (vol. 2) August 31–September 10, 1861.   [2ₐ].

Wood, Anthony à, *Athenae Oxonienses* . . . , 2 vols. (London, 1721).   [8].

Wright's edition of Morte d'Arthure (*see* Malory, Sir Thomas).

Vedas (*see Rig-veda-sanhitá* . . .).

Textual Notes

LN

6 and   8 [carat deleted]   9 inter-[21]national | earth   12 T*alie*ssin | co*l*d   13
N*a*sh   15 jounal   17 every⟨ one⟩↑body↓ | rock-[48]work   18 chaming | cho-
rus;   21 particu-/ars   29 no ⟨conf⟩ne in | power | Destiny,   31 ⟨es-⟩ [end of line]
↑es↓tablish   34 Visited   35 time.   36 [top of semicolon blotted]   37 ["l" acci-
dentally   crossed,   then   the   crossbar   canceled.]   43   ⟨,⟩or   44   The   47
only   52   .50   56 Dela[179]ware   62 th*a*t   64 Every   66 of ⟨ecstasy⟩ | of   69
16⟨7⟩↑5↓   71 Beecher₅, Taylor₄, Bushnell₆, Chapin₇, Everett₃, Buckminster₁,
Channing₂.   72 Mountains,   73 light.   74 another   75 interest. | ? V."   77
↑but↓ the state of mind in which we see the object,₂ ⟨&⟩ not the value of the
object,₁   79 in ⟨the Athenaeum⟩   80 age.   86 &⟩ the | effect.   87 sea↑,↓ ⟨.⟩&   90
Eternity.   94 his,   95 $.500.

NY

100 : or   103 Its   105 & ⟨not⟩   108 (") Glorious   109 with↑-↓/↑out   112
Society.   113 no-/wise   114 The | an   123 lá [acute accent canceled]   124
canid↑i↓date   129 The aim of the University shd. be to aid the student in the direction in which the men of genius have helped themselves.₂ You cannot help a
Shakspeare,—he does not need it,—but you can learn from him in what direction to
apply your means in behalf of his young admirer.₁   130 in*fra*   135 office.   136
com-[120]pass;   141 s*ta*r-piece   142 & ⟨General Grant⟩ | even.   145 I⟨t⟩ask   148
*Atlan*tic   150 Prerogative,   153 Walkers' | up.   155 given,   156 re*petiti*ons |
*Ibid*em   172 T'was   173 whats'   181 less.   185 [comma fingerwiped]   187
ap⟨o⟩↑oph↓thegms   190 mag[254]nify   192 ⟨well⟩,   193 P*ai*rs

ST

205 it.   209 ⟨time⟩ &   210 explorer,   213 ⟨othese⟩ of these   214 things,   216
dreams.   218   no   223   Cowper's   227   in*trouva*ble | in*trouv*able   232
⟨9⟩nine⟨tee⟨n[?]⟩tht⟩   235   d⟨u⟩↑is↓⟨s⟩↑t↓ance."   237   Expectation   240   proba-
⟨l⟩b⟨y⟩ly   245 ↑than we,↓, | power.   252 T*wistle*ton.   253 When Alexandria was
taken₂ by a brilliant stroke of heroism₁   254 abnormal↑⟨[s?];⟩↓⟨as the few⟩ |
When   257 Poets   258 count | Phi↑l↓ip⟨ps⟩s   260 "Index,"   262 The   266
shell?"?   268 poem", Outgrown".   270 /Nar∧yena/Narayena/   271 ⟨Manufac-
turing⟩ ↑Mischievous↓ ⟨interests⟩, ↑"rings⟨,⟩"↓ [end of line] ↑in politics & in
trade;↓   276 gown,".   278 Po*e*try   285 still,"   288 tea.↓.   292 household |
pride,   295 1588.↓,   296 in.↓. | a   299 *P. 163*   303 he | one | His thoughts were
his own, & h⟩However | required.   304 he ⟨came   317 ⟨1⟩2⟨.⟩2⟨6⟩5, | Par-
nassus.   318 ↑↓Atlantic↑"↓ |The Gulistan
⟨———→⟩   ⟨←———⟩

Books Large

327 Con*cord L*ibrary   332 *Upan*ishads. | *Rena*issance.   333 May *1872*

Pocket Diaries 18–31

357 Lowell. 358 Saginaw. 375 "*Art*." 390 Lords' 417 th 458 l↑. 1↓1
497 co   501 o'c'   507 /1⟨8⟩8/108/   529 Macd⟨o⟩ell | Bear   534 Lincon

Index

This Index includes Emerson's own index material omitted from the text. His index topics, including long phrases, are listed under "Emerson, Ralph Waldo, INDEX HEADINGS AND TOPICS"; the reader should consult both the general Index and Emerson's. If Emerson did not specify a manuscript page or a date to which his index topic referred, the editors have chosen the most probable passage(s) and added "(?)" to the printed page number(s). If Emerson's own manuscript page number is an obvious error, it has been silently corrected.

References to materials included or to be included in *Lectures* are grouped under "Emerson, Ralph Waldo, LECTURES." References to drafts of unpublished poems are under "Emerson, Ralph Waldo, POEMS." Under "Emerson, Ralph Waldo, WORKS" are references to published versions of poems, to lectures and addresses included in *W* but not in *Lectures,* and to Emerson's essays and miscellaneous publications. Kinds of topics included under "Emerson, Ralph Waldo, DISCUSSIONS" in earlier volumes are now listed only in the general Index.

A., 193
Abbott, 260
Abbott, Francis E., 373, 500
Abraham, 109
Abu Bekeur, 150
Abydos, Egypt, 447
Academy of Arts and Sciences, 516
Academy of Literature and Art, 5
Acton, Mass., 52, 365
Adams family, 78, 259
Adams, 456
Adams, Mr., 467
Adams, Mrs., 494
Adams, Abby Larkin, 372
Adams, Abel, 59, 184, 301
Adams, Mrs. Abel, 279, 306, 372
Adams, Austin, 414
Adams, Mrs. Austin, 260
Adams, Charles Francis, 398
Adams, Charles G., "John Jones and I," 472
Adams, George Washington, 184
Adams, Henry, 467
Adams, Mrs. Henry, 450, 451, 456, 460, 470
Adams, John, 90, 224
Adams, John Quincy, 184, 464
Addison, Charles Morris, 512
Addison, Joseph, 144; *Cato,* 144; *Remarks on Several Parts of Italy,* 228n

Adirondack Club, 25
Adirondack Mountains, 120
Adrian, Mich., 83, 358
Aeolian harp, 62
Aeschylus, 24, 77, 453; *Agamemnon,* 93; *Prometheus Bound,* 311; *Seven Against Thebes,* 63
Agassiz, Elizabeth Cabot Cary, 35
Agassiz, Louis, 34–35, 38, 55, 58, 78, 129, 142, 161, 171, 172–173, 266, 382, 461
Agesilaus II, of Sparta, 179, 193
Aiken, John, *Select Works of the British Poets,* 255
Ainsworth, Thomas, 399
Airlie, Lady, 449
Airy, George Biddell, 213
Aitken, Mary C., 435
Akenside, Mark, *The Pleasures of Imagination,* 465
Alawic Castle, 40
Albany, N.Y., 376, 389, 411, 483
Alcott, Amos Bronson, 20, 22, 23–24, 28–29, 43, 54, 56, 66, 71, 107n, 112, 145–146, 162, 172, 188, 247, 256, 307, 462
Alcott's Club, 462
Aldrich, Mr., 75
Aldrich, C. S., 357
Aldrich, Ralph W. Emerson, 75

Christianity, 9, 26, 41, 68, 85, 91, 103, 151,
178, 262
Church, Mr.(?), 359
Church of Disciples, 398, 406
Churches, 185
Cicero, Marcus Tullius, 74, 266, 278
Cincinnati, Ohio, 350, 361
Civil War, U.S., 7, 10, 19, 25, 74, 90, 100
Claflin, Gov. 207
Clahan, John, 20, 431
Clapp, Henry, 102
Clare, John, "Address to Plenty, Winter,"
223
Clark, Mr., 260
Clark, Mrs., "The Remittance," 300; "The
Trust," 300
Clark, Alvan, 55
Clark, E. H. G., 383
Clark, Galen, 239, 407, 410, 417
Clarke, James Freeman, 22, 50–51, 317,
386(?), 402, 406
Clarke, S. G., 393
Clarke, Sarah Freeman, 22, 58, 104–105,
275, 373, 413, 438
Clarke, W. B., 525
Clarke & Brimmer, 474
Clarke Association, Boston, 199
Claudius, Emperor of Rome, 401
Clavé, Jules, "La Silviculture à L'Exposition
Universelle," 123, 124n
Clavijero, Francisco Javier, 446, 452
Clement XI, Pope, 271
Cleopatra's Needle, 128
Clerk, William, 241
Cleveland, Duke of, 288
Cleveland, Ohio, 349, 357, 358, 363
Clinton, N.Y., 376
Clough, Mr., 434
Clough, Arthur Hugh, 60n, 418, 450–451,
518; The Bothie of Toper-na-fuosich, 328,
543; Letters and Remains, 333
Clough, Mrs. Arthur, 60, 434, 438, 439
Coan, Titus Munson, "The Tree of Life,"
301
Coast Survey, U.S., 93
Coate, G. B., 422
Cobb, Mr., 501
Cobb, Mrs. Kate, 377

Cobb, M. H., 97
Cobb, Mrs. P., 440
Cobden, Richard, 503, 508
Cobet, C. G., 503
Coburn, Mrs., 361
Cockburn, Henry Thomas, 234
Code Napoleon, 74
Coe, Miss, 351
Coffin, James F., 515
Colburn, Zerah, 68
Coleridge, Samuel Taylor, 9, 21, 67, 82, 118,
272; Biographia Literaria, 345, 543;
"Christabel," 264; The Friend, 154, 229;
Literary Remains, 64, 100, 235; "Sonnet
VII," 464; Specimens of the Table Talk,
343, 543; Statesman's Manual, 261n
Colesworthy, Gilbert, 518
Colesworthy, John C., 518
Colesworthy, Nancy, 506, 507, 513, 514,
518, 523
Colesworthy, Nathaniel, 512
Collectanea Graeca Majora, see Dalzel, An-
drew
Collier, see Collyer
Collins, William, 118, 135; "Ode to Eve-
ning," 62
Collyer, Robert Laird, 59, 260, 413, 510(?),
513(?)
Collyer, Mrs. Robert Laird, 260(?)
Colonel, the, 54
Columbus, Christopher, 69, 224
Columbus, Ohio, 365
Committee of Fifty, 393, 511
Comte, Auguste, 84
Concord, Mass., 21, 51–52, 122, 166, 348,
363, 375, 381, 405, 411, 424, 430, 432,
496, 533
Concord Bank, 416, 423, 429, 430, 432,
442, 476, 523
Concord Library, 171, 201, 302n, 305, 327,
329, 334, 382, 385, 387, 416, 425, 489,
496, 499, 502, 506, 516, 517
Concord Lyceum, 262
Concord Social Circle, 98n, 176, 349, 384,
393, 425
Condor, Josiah, The Modern Traveller, 284
Confucius, 91, 110, 194
Congdon, H. B., 420

Stream! to bless. Return to Heaven as well," 240; "For deathless powers to verse belong," 251; "He lives not who can refuse me," 61; "No more I seek, the prize is found," 264; "The poet spoke his instant thought," 36; "Things oft miscalling, as the hen," 132; "This shining hour is an edifice," 185; "To embellish the moment, the part of woman," 43; "Upon a rock yet un[create]," 475, 480n

TRANSLATIONS: from *Le Bhâgavata Purâna*, 27–28, 29–33; from Crashaw, 411; from Friedrich von Müller, *Goethes Unterhaltungen*, 102; from Grimm, 282–283; from Goethe, 119, 245, 248; from *La Kalévala*, 290–291; from Michelet, 332–333; from Montesquieu, 178; from *Nouvelle Biographie Générale*, 38, 39, 133–134, 252–254; from *Revue des Deux Mondes*, 123–124; from Varnhagen von Ense, 156, 168, 173–174, 175–176, 179–183, 202, 232, 254, 308

WORKS: "Abraham Lincoln," 148, 150, 157; "Address at the Dedication of the Soldiers' Monument in Concord," 148, 150, 157; "Address at the Opening of the Concord Free Library," 337n; "American Civilization," 147; "Aristocracy," 284n; "Art," 147, 149, 150, 157, 164; "Aspects of Culture," 148, 157; "Books," 42, 147, 148, 150, 163, 164, 336n; "Boston," 159; "Boston Hymn," 92; "Carlyle [*Past and Present*]," 148, 149, 150, 157; "The Celebration of the Intellect," 148, 337n; "Character," 150, 199n; "Circles," 312n; "Civilization," 149, 164; "Clubs," 148, 149, 150, 164, 179; "The Comic," 149, 150, 157; "Concord Hymn," 474; "Considerations by the Way," 36n; "Country Life," 66, 148, 150; "Courage," 148, 164; "Culture," 337n; "Demonology," 233n; "Domestic Life," 147, 149, 150, 156, 164; "Education," 148, 150; "Eloquence," 147, 149, 150, 164; *English Traits*, 341; *Essays, Second Series*, 199; "Experience," 338n; "Farming," 149, 164; "Fragments on Nature and Life,"

497, 507; "Fragments on the Poet and the Poetic Gift," 243n; "The Fugitive Slave Law [Concord]," 184n; "Greatness," 44n, 53, 90, 110, 148, 164; "Harvard Commemoration Speech," 148, 150; "Henry D. Thoreau," 147, 150, 157; "Historical Discourse," 313; "Historic Notes of Life and Letters in New England," 20, 21, 22, 35, 136, 148; "Holiness," 312n; "Humboldt," 160–161; "Immortality," 148; "Inspiration," 24, 181n, 218n, 223n, 227n, 266n; *Letters and Social Aims*, 276, 318n; "The Man of Letters," 77n, 230n, 253; "May-Day," 46n; *May-Day and Other Pieces*, 56; "Natural History of the Intellect," 43, 96, 117, 172; "Nature in Leasts," 97; "Old Age," 148, 149, 150, 164, 174, 179, 193; *Parnassus*, 14n, 44n, 48, 105n, 108n, 109n, 118, 129, 136, 140–141, 220n, 221n, 222n, 223n, 227n, 228n, 229n, 266n, 267n, 268n, 269n, 272n, 273, 300n, 305, 310n, 311n, 312n, 313, 313n, 314, 314n, 315, 316, 316n, 317, 317n, 318, 318n, 405n, 431n, 442n, 458n, 459n, 461n, 464n, 465n, 466n, 477n; "Persian Poetry," 147, 149, 150, 157; "Plutarch," 178, 186, 187, 188, 189, 193, 216n, 217n; "Poetry and Imagination," 20, 47, 49, 107, 108, 109, 118, 127, 134, 266n, 276n, 277n, 350n; "Powers and Laws of Thought," 240n, 340n; "The Preacher," 71; "Preface" to Goodwin's *Plutarch's Morals*, 318, 396; "The President's Proclamation," 147; "Progress of Culture," 65n, 66, 148, 157; *Prose Works* (1869), 155, 164; "Quotation and Originality," 48, 67, 79, 80, 82, 157, 337n; "Resources," 148, 150; "The Scholar," 148; "Seashore," 104; "Social Aims," 148, 150, 169; "Society and Solitude," 147, 149, 150, 156, 164; *Society and Solitude*, 146–150, 150–151, 156, 163, 164, 169–170, 173, 175, 199; "Song of Nature," 61; "The Sovereignty of Ethics," 54; "Speech at Banquet in Honor of the Chinese Embassy," 99n; "Speech at the Second Annual Meeting of the Free Reli-

Macdonald, George, "The Yerl O'Watery-deck," 223
McDowell, Kate, 500
Macdowell & Adams, 529
McIntire, 476
McKeen, P. F., 98
Mackenzie, Henry, 241
McKinney, William Robertson, 485
Mackintosh, James, 133, 234, 241
McLean, Rev. J. K., 414
MacManus, Thomas, 450
Macmillan, Alexander, 309, 482, 483, 484
Macmillan & Co., 518
Macpherson, James, *Genuine Poems of Ossian,* 345, 546
McTavlane, Robert, 345
Macy, C., 350
Mad River & Lake Erie Railroad, 367
Madden, Dr., 259
Madison, James, 90
Madison, Wis., 358
Maguire, Thomas, 461
Mahabarata, The, 35, 353
Mahmoud Bedowa, 286
Maine, 278n
Maine Laws, 75
Makamat, 357
Malerne, M., 441
Mallock, William Hurrell, *Is Life Worth Living,* 524
Malone, N.Y., 361
Malory, Sir Thomas, *La Morte d'Arthure,* 331, 345, 546. *See also* Map, Walter
Malta, 103
Malta (ship), 244n
Mammoth Cave, Ky., 138
Manchester, Iowa, 363
Mandanis, 93
Mandsley, 463
Manger, Mr., 87
Mann, Horace, 60n
Mann, Mary Tyler Peabody, 61, 462
Manners, 207–208
Mansfield, Lord, 341
Mansfield, Ohio, 350
Mansfield Mountain, 120
Manutius, Aldus, *Aristotelis Organon,* 517

Manzoni, Alessandro, *I Promessi Sposi,* 227, 331, 547
Map *or* Mapes, Walter, *La Morte Darthure,* 35, 138. *See also* Malory, Sir Thomas
Marble, E., 375
March, Francis A., *The Scholar of To-Day,* 83
Marcus Aurelius Antoninus, 80, 112, 131, 162, 194, 401
Mariett, E. H., 512
Marietta, Ohio, 361, 365
Mariette-Bey, Auguste, *The Monuments of Upper Egypt,* 526
Mariposa Grove, Calif., 407
Marlborough, Mass., 388, 393
Marlborough Street, Boston, 63
Marseilles, France, 435, 437
Marsh, George Perkins, 296, 438, 507
Marshall, T. F., 314
Marsori Banks, 471
Marsters, Rev. J. M., 478
Martha, C., "L'Examen de Conscience d'un Empereur Romain," 162, 195n, 401; "Le Poète Lucrèce," 401; "Un Poète Stoicien," 401
Martial, 79, 278; *Epigrams,* 283, 338
Martineau, Harriet, 341, 471; *Autobiography,* 331, 547; *Eastern Life, Present and Past,* 85, 87, 89, 331, 547
Martineau, Rev. James, 484
Marzook Hanzar, 286, 446
Mason, Mrs. Sidney, 451, 456, 460, 470
Massachusetts, 10, 52, 72, 86, 90, 91, 186, 401
Massachusetts Historical Society, 450, 491, 492, 493, 494, 502, 511
Masson, David, *Life of John Milton,* 416
Mather, Cotton, *Magnalia Christi Americana,* 327, 547
Mathews, Elkin, 468
Mattoon, Ill., 83, 364
Maule, Mr. Justice, 61
Maximilian, Emperor of Mexico, 38
Max Müller, Friedrich, 100, 288, 306, 448; *Chips from a German Workshop,* 103; "Comparative Mythology," 329, 547; *Introduction to the Science of Religion,* 235, 295; *Lectures on the Science of Language,*